To Ken
What once was lost
Has now been found
C. Bennett
2011

Cannabis and the Soma Solution

Chris Bennett

CANNABIS AND THE SOMA SOLUTION

COPYRIGHT © 2010 CHRISBENNETT. ALL RIGHTS RESERVED.
PRESENTATION COPYRIGHT © 2010 TRINE DAY, LLC

Published by:
TrineDay LLC
PO Box 577
Walterville, OR 97489
1-800-556-2012
www.TrineDay.com
publisher@TrineDay.net

Library of Congress Control Number: 2010928292

Bennett, Chris — Author
Cannabis and the Soma Solution—1st ed.
p. cm.   (acid-free paper)
Includes bibliographical references and index.
(ISBN-13) 978-0-9841858-0-1 (ISBN-10) 0-9841858-0-1

1. Indo-Europeans — Religion. 2. Cannabis/Marijuana — History. 3. Cannabis/Marijuana — Religious aspects. 4. Cannabis /Marijuana-- Social aspects -- History. 5. Soma. 6. Haoma. I. Bennett, Chris. II. Title

FIRST EDITION
10 9 8 7 6 5 4 3 2 1

Printed in the USA
Distribution to the Trade by:
Independent Publishers Group (IPG)
814 North Franklin Street
Chicago, Illinois 60610
312.337.0747
www.ipgbook.com

PUBLISHER'S FOREWORD

God said, "Behold, I have given you every herb bearing seed, which is upon the face of all the earth, and every tree in which is the fruit of a tree yielding seed; to you it shall be for meat. And to every beast of the earth, and to every fowl of the air, and to everything that creepeth upon the earth, wherein there is life, I have given every green herb for meat": and it was so. And God saw everything that he had made, and, behold, it was very good. And the evening and the morning were the sixth day.

— Gen. 1:29-31

And he showed me a pure river of water of life, clear as crystal, proceeding out of the throne of God and of the Lamb. In the midst of the street of it, and on either side of the river, was there the tree of life, which bare twelve manner of fruits, and yielding her fruit every month; and the leaves of the tree were for the healing of the nations.

— Rev. 22:1-2

When I was growing up in the 1950s, marijuana (cannabis) was a scourge, a ne'er-do-well, the assassin of youth, the gateway drug, a thoroughly evil and nasty weed.

Then came the turbulent 1960s: what a ride! With marijuana as its main "sacrament," a counterculture was born, developing community around a joint-passing circle. Explorations of ourselves and the world led to new journeys along ancient pilgrimages of spiritual understanding.

Chris Bennett's *Cannabis and the Soma Solution* is a *tour de force*, following the trail of a hotly debated question: What was the sacred ritual drink that was written about in the *Vedas* and other early religious texts? This was a substance so revered that it became a God within the Hindu and Zoroastrian pantheons. Bennett's work covers this and much more. From archaic medical journals, venerable religious texts, colonial reports and contemporary investigations, *Cannabis and the Soma Solution* gathers a wide range of material and weaves a very coherent whole. Giving our past a new old reality.

Om Shiva Shankara Hari Hari Ganja!
Boom Somnath!
Lord of Soma, the Herb of Vitality!

Onward to the Utmost of Futures!
Peace,
Kris Millegan
Publisher
TrineDay
August 18, 2010

ACKNOWLEDGEMENTS

A very special thanks to Professor Carl Ruck and Professor Scott Littleton for taking part and offering advice in our excessive correspondence over this book and my research, and with editing advice. As well as David Malmo-Levine, Marc and Jodie Emery, Alan Piper, Jan Irvin, Dana Larsen, Daniel Quaintance, Neil Mcqueen and others who looked at early drafts of the book or helped in other ways. Thanks to John Stahl for his extensive effort in proof editing. Thank you also to *High Times* editor Steve Hager who has always shown an affinity and support for my research and introduced me to the publisher of this work, Kris Millegan, to whom I am again grateful.

TABLE OF CONTENTS

FOREWORD

Debate about the identity of the ancient enthoegenic plant known as Soma has gone on for centuries. Although the plant was once the primary sacrament of the dominant spiritual culture of Northern India, its identity became obscured. When I came to *High Times* in 1987, I first became aware of Gordon Wasson, who wrote a book asserting Soma was *Amanita Muscaria*, a mushroom. Gordon's theory had already become dogma in both the psychedelic and academic communities.

That same year I created an event in Amsterdam, "The Cannabis Cup," a celebration of all things cannabis with a harvest competition designed to identify the best strain of cannabis available in Amsterdam. About five years into that project, I suddenly realized I had a serious obligation to study the history of cannabis in ceremonies. This quest led me to meet Stephen and Ina May Gaskin, Wavy Gravy, Paul Krassner, Ken Kesey, Mountain Girl, Ken Babbs, and the rest of the Merry Pranksters. I recognized these people as masters of ceremony for the counterculture. I soon picked up a copy of the Penguin translation of the *Rig Veda*, and read the chapter on Soma. One paragraph immediately jumped out:

> "Soma is a sage and a seer inspired by poetry
> [S]he clothes the naked and heals all who are sick.
> The lame walk, the blind see."

This clearly was a reference to cannabis. I spent the next few years investigating this story, while crafting rituals for the *High Times* Cannabis Cup and World Hemp Expo Extravaganja (Whee!).

After I discovered Wasson worked for J.P. Morgan, once the richest person in America, I no longer placed much faith in the validity of Wasson's research.

While many people concede corruption plays a major role in contemporary political power structures, few believe such corruption extends to our established religious institutions. Unfortunately, the truth is the creation of organized religion was the first attempt at mass mind control, and most wars over the last two thousand years have been fomented in the name of one religion or another. Obviously, spirituality and religion are different concepts and ceremonies manifest naturally in all living things. Even people who claim not to be spiritual cannot escape the reality that everything in our universe is somehow connected.

Our modern counterculture has its roots in New Orleans because Congo Square was the only place where people of all colors and religions could gather together to hold ceremonies. When people of diverse cultural backgrounds join together to create new ceremonies, a form of cultural hybrid vigor ensues. This hybrid vigor is responsible for jazz, blues, rock'n'roll and the improvisational-based culture we know today as the counterculture.

It's no accident cannabis played an essential role in shaping this culture, for cannabis use was at the very foundation of almost every major religious institution in history. Yet almost no one knows this history because there has been a longstanding cultural war on shamanic plants and the insights and connections to spirituality that they offer. This cultural war was created to sever our spiritual connections. The best evidence we have today is the relentlessly male nature of all the religious institutions. By removing the natural male/female balance from spirituality, religions were created that manifested war, bigotry and hatred, a cultural heritage we still live with today.

The counterculture is a baby, infant spirituality that may someday blossom into a full-blown religion. When this happens, Jack Herer will probably be recognized as one of the founding saints. In fact, it was Herer who first inspired me to examine the corruption of our religious institutions. Chris Bennett, however, will someday be recognized as the most important religious scholar of our time. Just as Herer revealed the great lies behind hemp prohibition, Bennett has unveiled the great lies behind our established religions and their attempts to blot out the true history of the ceremonial use of cannabis.

The counterculture is not anything new, just a natural emanation of true spirituality. Cannabis is the sacrament of this culture and always has been. Unfortunately, we're currently trapped in a system that manufactures war to sustain economic growth. If this unfortunate dynamic is ever going to change, it will be due to the growth of the counterculture. Bennett continues to fight for our religious right to cannabis, both in the courts in Canada and in his groundbreaking research. This is one of the most important books you will ever read.

And if you go to Kumbeh Mela, the sadus will undoubtedly tell you the identity of Soma was never lost by them (and then pass a chillum to you)

Sincerely yours,
Steven Hager
June 16, 2010
Woodstock, New York

Kumbh Mela (Devanagari) is a mass Hindu pilgrimage celebrated every 4 years, the Ardh (half) Kumbh Mella is celebrated every six years at Haridwar and Prayag; the Purna (complete) Kumbh takes place every twelve years, at four places (Prayag (Allahabad), Haridwar, Ujjain, and Nashik). The Maha (great) Kumbh Mela which comes after 12 'Purna Kumbh Melas', or 144 years, is held at Allahabad.

The last Ardh Kumbh Mela was held over a period of 45 days beginning in January 2007, more than 17 million Hindu pilgrims took part in the Ardh Kumbh Mela at Prayag, and on January 15, the most auspicious day of the festival of Makar Sankranti, more than 5 million participated.

The last Maha Kumbh Mela, held in 2001, was attended by around 60 million people, making it the largest gathering anywhere in the world in recorded history.

Adapted *from Wikipaedia.*

INTRODUCTION

Generally, when discussing the role of cannabis in history, most people's minds go back to the early Sixties, or at most the reefer madness of the Jazz age in the of the 1930's. Few people realize the pivotal role that marijuana played during the foundation of ancient civilizations and still existing cultures. This Book fills part of that gap of historical knowledge, and is hoped to help better define humanity's millennia old indigenous relationship with one of our oldest plant allies.

The role of cannabis in the ancient world was manifold: a food, fibre, medicine, and as a magically empowered religious sacrament. Here the focus will be on archaic references to cannabis use as both a medicine and a sacrament, rather than as a source of food or fibre, and its use in this manner by a variety of Ancient cultures will be examined. "The history of cannabis is one of the longest chapters in the study of man's desire for intoxication" (Sarton, 1993).

Indeed, and this is a subject that this author has visited in two other books, *Green Gold the Tree of Life: Marijuana in Magic and Religion* (1995), as well as *Sex, Drugs, Violence and the Bible* (2001), along with numerous published articles on the same subject. One thing that has taken this project far beyond the scope of these previous works has been the progression of the Internet, which was totally unavailable during the writing of the first book, and still in its puberty by the time of the second. Now, the Internet has become a virtual cyber Logos, and tools such as Google Books enables a savvy research to source the indices and pages of what must the contents of tens of libraries of books at the push of a button. This advantage is not only true in regards to my own work, but is also a

clear advantage over earlier authors who have touched on some of
the subjects advanced in this considerable volume.

Shamanism, the Faith of experience, marks mankind's transition
from dreamtime into experiential-self-reflective-time, and is the
common source of all Religions, and psychoactive plants played a
pivotal role in this relationship. The very term 'shaman' itself comes
from the Siberian Tungus *'saman'* who were known for ingesting
Amanita muscaria mushroom to achieve shamanic trance (Von Bibra, 1855). Before recorded history, and to the present day, powerful
plant-entheogens[1] used for ritual and healing purposes, have played
a paramount role in shamanism world-wide. The tomb of a shaman
from the sixth millennium B.C. in Catal Huyuk contained plants with
psychedelic properties (Grof, 1984). As recorded in the *Encyclopaedia Brittannica*: "Though the idea may be strange to most modern
worshippers, drugs have played an important role in the history of
religions. The ceremonial use of wine and incense in contemporary
ritual is probably a relic of a time when the psychological effects of
these substances were designed to bring the worshipper into closer
touch with supernatural forces" (Clark, 1978)[2]. "Almost without exception the drugs and intoxicants found in nature or discovered by
primitive technology were used more or less as the nucleus of rituals
and ceremonials of a profoundly religious character..." (Vetter, 1958).

In relation, Andrew Sherratt, one of a growing number of archaeologists discussing the role of psychoactive substances in ancient cultures noted that "The deliberate seeking of psychoactive
experience is likely to be at least as old as anatomically (and be-
haviorally) modern humans: One of the characteristics of *Homo
sapiens....* Psychoactive substances can be seen as integral to the
constitution of culture. They have been fundamental to the nature
of sociality and an active element in the construction of religious
experience..." (Sherratt, 1995).

> Before man knew fire, he had grubbed for roots which, he real-
> ized through his dim perceptions, not only nourished but also
> soothed or excited him. As century moved onto century these

[1]   Entheogen is a modern word applied to a psychoactive substance used in a religious or shamanic context. The term 'Entheogen,' is a word combination from the Greek,
translated variously as "that which causes the presence of god within," or "creating the
divine within."
[2]   "Drug Cult," *Encyclopedia Britanica*, 5th edition, 1978.

bits of bark of leaf and fruit took on meaning. Some healed, some killed, some offered momentary peace or even an occasional magnificent glimpse into another realm.... So the herbalist and soothsayer came into being, and the conjurer and wizard became the leader of the tribe. (Mathison, 1958)[3]

Little known, and the basis for much of this book is the important part that cannabis had in the shamanism of the ancient world, a relationship, which according to the archaeological record alone, can be shown to stretch back 5,500 years ago. "The oldest archaeological evidence for the cultural use of hemp points to it originally having been used in a shamanic context" (Ratsch 2005).

Unfortunately, due to the deterioration of plant matter, archaeological evidence is sparse and "Pollen records are frequently unreliable, due to the difficulty in distinguishing between hemp and hop pollen" (Scott, *et al.*, 2004). Despite these difficulties in identification some remains of cannabis fibre, cannabis beverages utensils, seeds of cannabis, and burnt cannabis have been located (burnt cannabis has been carbonized and this preserves identifiable fragments of the species).

Fortunately other avenues of research regarding the ancient use of cannabis remain open, and etymological evidence regarding cannabis use in a number of cultures has been widely recognized and accepted. Indeed, the modern term *"cannabis"* comes from an ancient Proto- Indo-European root word, *"kanap"*; the *"an"* from this root is believed to have left traces in many modern terms for cannabis, such as French *"chanvre,"* German *"hanf,"* Indian *"bhang,"* Dutch *"Canvas,"* Greek *"Kannabis,"* etc.

Pointing out the widespread religious use of hemp throughout the ancient Near East, amongst the Babylonians, Assyrians, Scythians and Hebrews, as well as the early spread of its cultic use from northern Europe, to Siberian Asia, China, India, Asia minor and Southeast Asia, the famed anthropologist Weston La Barre, suggested that "cannabis was part of a religio-shamanic complex of at least Mesolithic age, in parallel with an equally old shamanic use of Soma..." (La Barre, 1980).

La Barre mentions Soma, an ancient psychoactive beverage that was the source of the Vedic religion in India, and the Mazdean religion of ancient Persia, where it was known as Haoma. This ancient

3   From a quote (Thorne, 1998).

sacrament was one of the most widely used inebriants of the ancient world. The identity of Soma-Haoma has been a long time matter of debate. La Barre, unfortunately accepted R. Gordon Wasson's identification of Soma, as the *Amanita muscaria* mushroom[4], which has remained the prevailing view since the early 1970s. As well, David Stophlet Flattery and Martin Schwartz have hypothesized that the Persian Haoma was *Peganum harmala*, or Syrian rue, and this designation has held to be equally as strong as that of Wasson's. But what if one were be able to show that these identifications were incorrect, and that the ancient Soma-Haoma, was in fact cannabis? This would mean that Hemp was the most celebrated religious sacrament in the history of humanity, and that its use would be twice as widespread as La Barre has suggested for either cannabis or Soma!

As botanist Mark Merlin noted three and a half decades ago in his short but commendable presentation on the subject:

> ...[W]hat was the famous *Soma* plant that played such an important part in the formation of the Vedic civilization? Was *Soma* really the hemp plant? There are many evidences to suggest such an identification.... [I]f it were possible to substantiate, beyond any doubt, that the plant source of *Soma* juice was *Cannabis sativa,* the diffusion of hemp into India would seem to be deeply significant. (Merlin, 1973)

Writing in the early seventies, when so little information on the matter was available in the West, Merlin lamented that "even with all the circumstantial evidence that I have collected and will list to support this identification, it would be extremely naive and in a real sense impetuous to dogmatically assert this theory" (Merlin, 1973). As for this author, let's just say I am feeling slightly more impetuous about the information collected for this considerably larger work, and I am confident the reader will fully understand why by the time they reach the closing pages of this book.

In *The Tree in Religion or Myth*, it is noted that:

> The drinking of vegetable juices, fermented or otherwise, was no doubt one of the means by which early races were accustomed to

---

4   "...[S]ince the classic work of Wasson, soma has been firmly established as the hallucinogenic mushroom *Amanita muscaria*..." (La Barre, 1980).

produce dreams and visions, and so, in their view, to get themselves possessed by or put into communication with a spirit. It
was natural, therefore, for them to assume that the spirit in question had entered into them with the drug, and was therefore present in it and in the plant from which it was derived... this... was
one of the chief factors in the origin of plant worship in general,
a main reason why plants yielding intoxicating agents, and hence
other plants, came to be regarded as containing supernatural beings. (Philpot, 1897)

Nowhere in the history of the world, has such a relationship been
more identifiable, than with that of ancient Humanity's relationship with the long lost Soma-Haoma, which was at the same time a
plant, a God and the sacrament ingested by that God's cult.

It is extremely difficult for the person who is not acquainted by
actual study with the history of religions to understand how a
plant can become deified on account of the peculiar medical or
intoxicating effects which it is supposed to possess. We may read
in the Vedic literature page after page of the virtues of the Soma
plant and the way in which it affects both gods and men, and
becomes itself an object of divine worship, but since the plant
itself is unknown, and only represented in the present day by a
substitute, we have no means of observing experimentally the
potencies which the Aryans attached to the original plant and its
juices. (Harris, 1927)

In this volume we shall show that what once was lost, has now
been found, as we explore the story of the Soma-Haoma cult from
its origins in the Indo-European use of cannabis, and how that tradition spread with them throughout the ancient world, even influ-
encing the Biblical tradition and other still existing ancient faiths,
until its eventual suppression and consequent disappearance.

Ever since the Aryans crossed the Hindu Kush into India in prehistoric times, the mystery has persisted. And ever since Sanskrit
was discovered by Europeans in the eighteenth century, an apparently insoluble riddle has lain at the heart of Vedic studies:
the identity of the mysterious, sacred psychotropic plant of the
Brahmans called soma. (La Barre, 1980)

The Vedic God Indra, who the Soma ritual was dedicated to, riding upon his elephant Airavata.

Sanctify Soma our mind, our heart, our intellect; and may thy worshippers delight in thy friendship, like cattle in fresh pasture, in thine exhilaration (produced) by the sacrificial food; for thou art mighty....

Like the winds violently shaking the trees, the draughts of Soma have lifted me up, for I have often drunk of the Soma

The praise of the pious has come to me like a lowing cow to her beloved calf, for I have often drunk of the Soma

Both heaven and earth are not equal to one half of me, for I have often drunk of the Soma

I am the sun, the greatest of the great, raised to the firmament; for I have often drunk of the Soma

— *RIG VEDA* TENTH MANDALA [excerpts]

Cannabis

Ephedra

Syrian Rue

Amanita Muscaria

1

THE SOMA-HAOMA QUESTION

*The History of the search for Soma is, properly, the history of Ve-
dic studies in general, as the Soma sacrifice was the focal point
of the Vedic religion... everything of a mystical nature within
that religion is pertinent to the identity of the plant.*
— (Doniger O'Flaherty, 1968)

The identity of the ancient Soma is undoubtedly one of the
greatest unsolved mysteries in the field of religious history.
Common in both the religious lore of ancient India and in
Persia where it was known as Haoma, the plant was considered a
God and when pressed and made into a drink the ancient worship-
per who imbibed it gained the powerful attributes of this God.

The whole Sama-Veda is devoted to this moon-plant worship;
an important part of the Avesta is occupied by Hymns to Homa.
This great reverence paid to the plant, on account of its intoxicating qualities, carries us back to a region where the vine was
unknown, and to a race to whom intoxication was so new an experience as to seem a gift of the gods. Wisdom appeared to come
from it, health, increased power of body and soul, long life, victory in battle, brilliant children. What Bacchus was to the Greeks,
the Divine Haoma, or Soma, was to the primitive Aryans. (Clarke,
1883)[1]

---

[1]   Clarke saw "the intoxicating fermented juice of the plant *Asclepias acida*" as the
identity of the Soma/Haoma, but few have since agreed with this designation (Clarke,
1883). "Since, however, soma-haoma is described as being immediately intoxicating, its
effects could not be dependent on alcohol [or fermentation]. There must have been some
narcotic substance in it" (Aalto, 1998).

As Zenaide A. Ragozin noted in his 1895 edition of VEDIC INDIA, Soma "was unquestionably the greatest and holiest offering of the ancient Indian worship":

> The Gods drink of the offered beverage; they long for it; are nourished by it and thrown into joyous intoxication... The beverage is divine, it purifies, it is a water of life, gives health and immortality, prepares the way to heaven, destroys enemies, etc.,
>
> The fierceness of the drink, its exhilarating and inspiring properties, are especially expatiated upon. The chosen few who partake it... give most vivid expressions to the state of exaltation, of intensified vitality, which raises them above the level of humanity. (Ragozin, 1895)

The origins of Soma's use goes back into the shadowy time of pre-history and to the common Aryan ancestors of the Persian Zoroastrian religion, and the Vedic religion of India[2]. It may seem strange to some readers that fair skinned Aryans are the source of both the Vedic Soma cult in India, and Avestan Haoma cult in Persia, but this is clearly the case. Fair skinned, yellow haired Indra, the celebrated Soma drinking God of the VEDAS, clearly originated as a "white man's" God.

> At the swift draught the Soma-drinker waxed in might, the Iron one with yellow beard and yellow hair. (RV.10.96)

> Fair cheeks hath Indra, Maghavan, the Victor, Lord of great host... (RV.3.30)

As I.J.S. Taraporewala explained:

> The Aryans (using the word in its narrower sense, as comprising the two peoples, the Indians and the Iranians, who called

---

2   The Aryan invasion of India is believed to have happened in two distinct and differing phases; the first came with Aryan tribes which entered India through the passes of the Hindu Kush, passing through South Afghānistān, and the valleys of the Kābul, Kurram, and Gumal rivers, finally settling in the N.W. Frontier Province and the Punjab. These tribes were nomadic groups accompanied by their wives and families; the second invasion was slightly more aggressive, coming through Gilgit and Chitral, and was carried out by men unaccompanied by women, who, therefore, needed to form alliances on a wholesale scale with the Dravidians, thus these men intermarried taking native wives. Although some indigenous Vedists dispute the Aryan invasion and origins of the Vedas, the similarity between the Yasnas and Soma/Haoma is undisputable.

themselves by that proud name) had lived together for long ages in one land, had spoken one tongue and had followed one religion. Where that ancient Motherland of the Aryans was, we have no means of determining, but it seems to have been a region far to the North, which, according to the Iranian tradition, was overwhelmed and destroyed by ice and snow. At a later period the two main stocks of these people migrated southwards, still keeping together, and after many generations of wandering, ultimately arrived in the neighbourhood of the high mountainous region which we know as the Pamir table-land today. They spread around from that region into the lower fertile and salubrious valleys of the south, west and east. The lands called by us Afghanistan and Bactria were the regions where the Aryans had long carried on their activities.

The language which these people spoke was the ancient tongue of which the language of the Vedic Hymns and that of the Gathic Chants of Zarathustra were both branches. The exceedingly close resemblance between the two has been noted by every student of Aryan philology. So close are these two languages that a mere phonetic change (or, to put it popularly, a slight mispronunciation) often suffices to translate a passage from the one into the other, keeping at the same time the sense absolutely intact. The differences are not greater than what are found between two 'dialects' of one original tongue.

The religious traditions inherited by these two great peoples, the Hindus and the Persians were, therefore, the common Aryan traditions.... *Haoma* is ... [an] Indo-Iranian Deity, being the Vedic *Soma*. In the Avesta He is not a mere personification of the Soma-plant, but a great Teacher who appeared in the very early days to lead forward our infant humanity... Some scholars believe that it was He who introduced the Haoma-(Soma-) Cult among the Aryans and thus gave His own name to the plant and its juice which formed an important item of the Indo-Iranian ritual. The Hindu and Zoroastrian rituals turn entirely upon the offering of the juice of this plant. (Taraporewala, 1926)

This common ancestry accounts for the many similarities in the Indian and Persian cosmologies and language as can be seen in the surviving religious texts the Hindu *RIG VEDA*, and the Persian, *AVESTA*, and especially to their use of the sacred plant known in India as Soma, and in Persian Haoma. As Dasturji Dr. Maneckji N. Dhalla explained of the connections between Haoma and Soma:

...[T]he resemblance between... [the Haoma] and the Soma cult is so great that they are spoken of in identical words. We shall quote a few of the more important passages to show the close parallelism between the Haoma-Soma cult. The celestial plant, it is said, was brought upon earth by birds. It is *girishta* or *girijata* and *parvata vrddhah*, say the Vedic texts, and the Avesta says it is *bareshnush paiti gairinam* and *paurvatahva viraodha*, that is, growing on mountains. It is Av. *zairi*, and Skt. *hari*, meaning green or golden. It is passed through a sieve of the hairs of the tail of the sacred bull among the Iranians and from that made of sheep wool among the Indians. The extracting process is called Av. *havana*, and Skt. *savana*. It is Av. *haomahe madho*, and Skt. *somyam madhu*, 'sweet juice of Haoma-Soma.' It is Av. *baeshaza*, and Skt. *bheshaja*, 'healing.' The plant is deified among both and then it is called Av. *hvaresh*, and Skt. *svarsh* 'celestial,' it is Av. *hukhratu*, and Skt. *Sukratu*, 'posessed of good intelligence.' It is Av. *verethraja*, and Skt. *vrtraha*, 'victorious.'[3] (Dhalla, 1936)

Unfortunately, over the millennia that have passed since these ancient texts were composed, the identity of the original Haoma\Soma was forgotten. "Whatever plant was used by the Indo-Aryans in the early centuries it is certain that it was later replace by other botanical species" (Eliade, 1978). As has been noted, the subjects of psychoactive substances in magical rituals, even in the historic period, are hard to follow, as to both Priests and shamans alike, magic revealed is secrets lost. As Rendel Harris explained, at first the use of ritual consumption of Soma was an event for the general public, but this soon changed:

Then later the club, formed by the initiates, will assert itself against the drink; the democracy of the new draught will disappear; the god-intoxicated mystics will become a caste; the Aryan in the street will no longer make nor drink the beverage: it will come under the rule, 'For the priests only' and 'By the priests only:' in the beginning it appears to have been more widely diffused and more commonly enjoyed. The religious experience becomes transferred from the many to the few; one must not over-

3   "Bhanga [hemp] is also called... *vijaya* (the victorious)" (Greirson, 1893). *Bhang* also means 'intoxicating' and both Haoma and *bhang* share epithets meaning *madini* (the intoxicating), and, as shall be discussed, Soma is even referred to under the title of '*bhang*'in the RIG VEDA.

populate the upper atmospheres! Gods there; Brahmans here: but not too many of them. (Harris, 1927)

Detailed descriptions of the plant thus likely became a form of sacred knowledge and therefore not privy to the masses administered to by the priesthood. "Apparently for some time members of the priestly clique limited the knowledge and use of *Soma* to their own esoteric activities. Thus a small influential segment of ancient Indian society controlled religion and the distribution of the Soma plant" (Merlin, 1972). "In the end it could be the case, as it appears with the soma of the ancient Vedic religion, that the priests kept it so secret that they eventually lost the knowledge themselves" (Taylor, 1985).[4] "Some scholars believe that it was an extinct variety of Indian hemp, others that it was some other long forgotten plant found only in the Himalayan foothills. It was already becoming scarce at the time of the Brahmanas, [composed 600 B.C., onwards] and the Aitareya Brahmana even suggests a substitute" (Sharma, 1985).

As Vedic scholar Wendy Doniger O'Flaherty explains, the confusion caused by this situation was further compounded as time went on:

> Not knowing what plant the poets of the RgVeda had in mind, modern scholars have often jumped to the conclusion that the hymns are vague and obscure in speaking of soma. The *Brahmanas*, dealing as they do with involved chains of substitutes, add to the confusion in almost geometric progression; the few Avestan parallels are rendered more or less useless by the overlay of purely Iranian elements; and by the time the Europeans enter the scene, with their fixed ideas and various axes to grind, the situation approaches bedlam.... there seems to have been little contact between botanists and Vedists, Indian Scholars and Europeans. (Doniger O'Flaherty, 1968)[5]

Fortunately for this author, writing in the age of the internet, access to the works of all such fields are much more easily accessible. Authorities from a variety of areas of expertise, with the inclusion of archaeology, will be cited in order to help establish the position that the original Haoma/Soma was a hemp preparation.

---

4   From a quote in (Thorne, 1998).
5   In R. Gordon Wasson's *Soma: Divine Mushroom of Immortality* (1968).

Although modern descendants of these ancient cults still perform
the rituals of their ancestors, placebo non-entheogenic sacraments
and in many cases the mildly stimulating plant Ephedra,[6] is used
as Haoma by modern Zoroastrians, and the non-intoxicating *Sarcostemma acidum,* consecrated in current Indian rites as Soma. But
ephedra and *Sarcostemma acidum,* along with other substitutions
clearly do not live up to all of the claims about the Soma/Haoma as
described in the Vedas and Avestan texts[7]. Ephedra is a branching,
dioecious shrub, which has a sharp, disgusting taste. Ephedra contains the active alkaloids pseudoephedrine and ephedrine, which
are used in a number of cold and other medicines; as well, ephedrine is the base of methamphetamine, or 'speed,' and for this it has
come under legal scrutiny in recent times.

The qualities of Soma are given in poetic detail and the ancient
composers' love and admiration for the plant can still be felt thousands of years after the texts were composed. In a spirit similar to
that of the Catholic Eucharist, Soma/Haoma, was prepared in a sacred rite and then bestowed upon the pious to give them spiritual
inspiration, wisdom, courage, health and other benefits.

The descriptions and praises of the plant left to us by antiquity
have led numerous scholars to speculate on what the botanical identity of the original plant was. Western research into the identity of

6   "The oldest date for a potentially psychoactive plant in a cultural context is from
the Neanderthal burial site at Shanidar Cave in northern Iraq where pollen of an *Ephedra*
species (E. Altissima Willk., cf. Leroi-Gourhan 1975; Solecki 1971) was dated to more than
50,000 B.C. (Solecki, 1975).... *Ephedra altissima* yields ephedrine, an alkaloid that produces sympatomimetic and amphetamine-like effects (Teuscher 1979), as well as euphoria
(Wenke 1986: 579). Therefore it may have served as an entheogen for ritualistic, spiritual
purposes, and/or a medicinal" (Merlin, 2003). [Although, as Merlin notes, there is speculation that these plant remains may have not been placed by Neanderthals, but rather put
there by burrowing rodents in the area that have been known to store flowers and seeds
in their burrows].

7   "Harry Falk [1989]... argued that the essential effect sought from *soma/haoma*
was not hallucinatory, but precisely that produced by ephedrine, namely inducing alertness and awareness. He cited as evidence the previously overlooked use of soma in the
highly esteemed night-time Atirâtra ritual as both a sleep-preventing drink for the priests
and a stimulating offering to Vrátra-fighting Indra. The alkaloid ephedrine is somewhat
milder yet more prolonged in action than adrenaline... The basic alkaloid is water-soluble
and, because of climactic conditions, its full effect could be enjoyed only in Situ, i.e., in the
mountainous borderlands between India and Greater Iran, where the ephedrine-yielding
species of ephedra (*Ephedra gerardiana, procera,* and *intermedia*) grow. This limited distribution of potent ephedra would explain the post-Vedic question put to the soma vendor,
whether his merchandise was harvested on mount Mûjavat... Interestingly, a side-effect
of ephedrine, the hindering of urination, coincides with the priestly fear to die of urine-
retention" (Taillieu,, 2002).

Soma/Haoma began in the 18th century, "but in the relatively short time that has elapsed since the investigation was initiated, over 100 species have been suggested as the source of *Soma*" (Merlin, 1972). "With the rather unusually large number of notoriously varied candidates for *Soma* and with the controversies arising from a series of misconceptions and subjectivity-centered interpretations, it is no wonder that even genuine students of the *Soma* problem become baffled and 'lost' themselves" (Swamy, 1976).

Amongst the many suggestions, besides those already mentioned, are milkweed, *Sarcostemma acidum,* mandrake, rhubarb, ginseng, opium Poppies, blue lotus, *Stropharia cubensis,* wine or liquor[8] and the still used ephedra. Most popularly and more relative to what shall be discussed here, Syrian rue, the *Amanita muscaria* mushroom and cannabis have been suggested. As the editors of the authoritative *Encyclopaedia Britannica* have recorded on the subject;

> One of the pharmacological mysteries is the nature of Zoroastrian haoma and the early Hindu soma, both sacred drinks made from plants. Their source may have been the *Amanita Muscaria* mushroom, the mind-affecting chemicals of which pass into the urine with their properties very little diminished; there are scriptural references to sacred urine drunk as the source of divine insights. Allusions to twigs and branches of haoma, however, suggest other plants, perhaps hemp. The mushroom, which does not grow in hot countries, may have been introduced to India, by Aryan invaders from the north; subsequently, other plants may have been substituted until their identity was confused and lost. (*Encyclopaedia Britannica*)[9]

References to its rich color and wonderful fragrance, the blissful state produced by Soma and the quantity and extent to which it was used also limits the number of potential candidates, as some of the botanical suggestions produce effects which could be considered far from blissful, and in some cases, if ingested in the quantities in which Soma was consumed, would have been toxic.

8   Generally discounted outright by most researchers as no fermentation process is indicated in the texts describing Soma/Haoma's preparation, although the use of alcoholic beverages infused with psychoactive plants, such as cannabis, mandrake and henbane was surprisingly widespread in the ancient world.

9   *"Pharmacological Cults'" Alcohol and Drug Consumption*

Before moving onto the reasons why the origins of the Soma/Haoma cult can be found amongst the early users of cannabis, a quick overview of the most popular candidates, *Amanita muscaria* and ephedra, is required in order to demonstrate why neither of these other substances offer a suitable answer in comparison to cannabis. The ideas that Vedic Soma was the *Amanita muscaria* mushroom as put forth by R. Gordon Wasson, and the Avestan Haoma was Syrian rue, as suggested by co-authors David Stophlet Flattery and Martin Schwartz, have become so pervasive in academic circles, in some cases seemingly accepted unquestionably as fact, that a thorough examination of the flaws in these theories is needed before moving on to a more realistic presentation. As well, an analysis of their reasons for dismissing cannabis as a candidate is also in order.

2

WHAT SOMA WAS
NOT WAS WASSON'S
MUSHROOM MANIA

Undoubtedly, currently the most popular candidate for Soma has been the *Amanita muscaria* mushroom. The Fly agaric theory was originally proposed by the banker and mycologist R. Gordon Wasson, and has been widely accepted by a number of scholars, like poet-philosopher Robert Graves, Huston Smith,[1] Clark Heinrich and anthropologist Weston La Barre.

> The careful scholarship of the dedicated amatuer mycophile R. Gordon Wasson reads like an exciting scientific, detective story. Moreover, his willingness to pursue the quest through the wide range of linguistics, archaeology, folklore, philology, ethnobotany, plant ecology, human physiology, and prehistory constitutes a object lesson to all holistic professional students of man. (La Barre, 1980)

Indeed, even one of the most in-depth anthropological studies of hemp, *Cannabis and Culture*,[2] included an essay on the role of cannabis in India, where the author concluded;

> Some scholars believe that *soma*, the mysterious plant, is cannabis... however, the idea has been strongly opposed by Wasson... Wasson's scholarly analysis of numerous verses from the *Rg Veda*

---

1   Smith initially identified Soma as cannabis, but then was so taken by Wasson's work, he switched his view to *Amanita muscaria*.
2   Vera Rubin, Ed., (1975)

and ethnohistorical and entheobotanical data advance very convincing arguments for identifying soma as the mushroom, fly-
agaric (*Amanita muscaria*). (Hasan, 1975)

Before beginning this pointed dismissal of R. Gordon Wasson's
theory of *Amanita muscaria* as the original Haoma/Soma it should
be noted that Wasson's overall contributions to the study of the role
of psychoactives in the birth of religion are more than remarkable.

My greatest criticism of Wasson's book *Soma: Divine Mushroom
of Immortality* is that for the most part it only deals with about
half the evidence; the Avestan material is only dealt with in a few
passages; and a large part of the *Vedas* are purposely left out of the
discussion!

> I exclude from consideration the latest hymns to have been writ-
> ten, the last to be included in the canon before it was closed. These
> hymns differ from the others considerably in tone and language,
> and there is reason to believe there are substitutes, which I think
> had always been occasionally used, and now almost completely
> replaced the Soma sacrifice. These hymns are mostly in Mandala
> X from 85 through 191. (Wasson, 1970)

Wasson favours the *Rig Veda* (or rather parts of it) over the *Avesta* with the acknowledgment and explanation that "Religiously and
linguistically the Avesta and RgVeda are siblings. The text of the
Rgveda is, however, much purer owing to its marvellous preservation through the ages by the disciplined human memory" (Wasson,
1970). One is left wondering who Wasson felt had preserved the
tradition of the *Avesta*! Having read translations of both texts, what
I could see was a profound similarity in both content and style.

Indeed, throughout his book, it is almost as if Wasson purposely,
or unconsciously, excluded all potential textual references that con-
flicted with his own view. Moreover, he even acknowledges that
Soma "substitutes, had always been occasionally used," as he clearly
recognized that the passages in the remaining texts from the *Vedas* which he allowed for his study (when it fit his view) indicated
a variety of the other candidates for the Soma, more so than did
his own champion, or rather *champignon*! As well, Wasson only
excludes the remaining texts when they don't support his opinion,
but when he's able to find the rare passage that he can interpret in

favour of his hypothesis, he quotes quite freely from it, and he does this numbers of times in *Soma: Divine Mushroom of Immortality.*

As Wasson conveniently states: "In the Rg Veda (excluding the latter half of the Mandala X, last to be admitted to the canon) there is no reference to the root of the Soma plant, nor its leaves, nor its blossoms, nor its seed" (Wasson, 1970). Wasson's often repeated mistake here is based solely on omission. It should be noted that only a few of the passages that are left in Wasson's exclusive study deal with the plant Soma, many deal with the beverage Soma, the God Soma, and the Moon (which was viewed as the celestial goblet of Soma from which the God's drank, and which was continually replenished by the Sun). By the exclusion of the *Rig Veda's* Tenth Mandala, which holds the most descriptive account of the plant Soma in the *Vedas*, Wasson purposely limited the passages discussed to those which fit his view. Alternatively, in the Vedic Index, MacDonell and Kieth (1958) associated the Vedic term *naicasakha* with Soma, and this indicates branches (or twigs and leaves) hanging down, which would again give indications of cannabis.[3] Vedic scholar, Dr. N. Warhadpande (who, as shall be discussed, identifies cannabis as the source of the ancient Vedic elixir) also felt Vedic descriptions indicated branches and leaves (Waradpende, 1995).

Flattery and Schwartz rightly noted that Wasson's view that the Soma was a mushroom and had no leaves, branches or roots, was due to the fact that "the soma referred to in the RgVeda and adduced by Wasson as pertaining to the mushroom is the liquid extract (soma pavamana) or the deity Soma, and hence not the soma plant at all" (Flattery & Schwartz, 1989). On one of the few occasions when Wasson deals with the Avestan literature, his textual interpretation of the passage (which he interprets as identifying the growth of a mushroom, with no stems, roots or branches) is, in the very least, original, as can be seen from a comparison with translations from the Harvard University website[4] and an Avestan website.[5]

> Increase by my word in all (your) roots
> in all (your) buds, and in all (your) protuberances!

---

3   As noted by (Merlin, 1972).
4   Which is an unbiased source, as it is not postulating any plant candidates. http://www.people.fas.harvard.edu/~witzel/Zoroastrianism.2.texts.1#_ftn59
5   http://www.avesta.org/yasna/y9to11s.htm

Grow (then) because I pray to thee on all thy stems and branches,
in all thy shoots (and tendrils) increase thou through my word!

—Y.10.5

Swell, (then,) by my word!
In all thy stalks, and all thy shoots, and in all thy sprouts.

— Wasson Y.10.5

Dieter Taillieu, an expert on Vedic and Indo-European studies states that there "seems no doubt that the haoma depicted in the Hôm Yašt is a normal, chlorophyll-bearing plant: apart from its stock color epithet 'yellow, golden, green' (Av. zairi- and zairi.gao-na-, cf. Skt. hari-) this is suggested most strongly by the mention of "stems, shoots and branches" (Av... Y. 10.5)."

> Haoma is further called 'having tender/pliant' [stem]... (Av... Y. 9.16) or 'having tasty...' [flavour] pure soma, however, is not; 'sweet', Skt. mádhu-, but 'sharp, astringent,..'. In favor of the fly-agaric theory "stalk" (Wasson, 1968) and "fibre"/"flesh.."were proposed, but this ignores the expressed necessity of pounding the [stalk]... which seems relevant only in the case of fibrous or hard plant material (twigs, roots, seed).... Reality has been sought in haoma's epithet "tall" (Av. b⊠ r⊠ zant-, Y. 10.21, Vd. 19.19;...)[6]. (Taillieu, 2002)

As Weston La Barre (who accepted Wasson's theory hook, line and sinker) attempted to explain of the differences between Soma and Haoma; "the plant that some students identify as haoma is apparently an herbaceous plant" (La Barre, 1980). Indeed, unable to find compatibility between Haoma and Soma, La Barre went on to suggest that the Haoma of the *Avesta* was a replacement for Wasson's Vedic Soma-mushroom, which he believed was used by the ancestors of both cults.

Wasson states Soma is unique amongst the Gods of the *Vedas*, "Soma was at the same time a god, a plant, and the juice of the plant. So far as we know, Soma is the only plant ever deified" (Wasson, 1970). I concur with this statement, but then it is in fact evidence in favour of cannabis as being the original plant identified as

---

6   A reference to hemp as tall appears in the Avestan creation text the Bunda-hishn, "as tall as hemp" (27.1).

Soma, and indication of this comes from India itself as a reading of the historical record shows in the following passage from *The Indian Hemp Drugs Commission Report* (1894) on "The Worship of the Hemp Plant":

> The custom of worshipping the hemp plant, although not so prevalent as that of offering hemp to Shiva and other deities of the Hindus, would nevertheless appear from the statements of the witnesses to exist to some extent in some provinces of India. The reason why this fact is not generally known may perhaps be gathered from such statements as that of Pandit Dharma Nand Joshi, who says that such worship is performed in secret. There may be another cause of the denial on the part of the large majority of Hindu witnesses of any knowledge of the existence of a custom of worshipping the hemp plant in that the educated Hindu will not admit that he worships the material object of his adoration, but the deity as represented by it. The custom of worshipping the hemp plant, though not confined to the Himalayan districts or the northern portions of India alone, where the use of the products of the hemp plant is more general among the people, is less known as we go south. Still even far south, in some of the hilly districts of the Madras Presidency and among the rural population, the hemp plant is looked upon with some sort of veneration.... There is a passage quoted from Rudrayanmal Danakand and Karmakaud in the report on the use of hemp drugs in the Baroda State, which also shows that the worship of the bhang plant is enjoined in the Shastras. It is thus stated: "The god Shiva says to Parvati—'Oh, goddess Parvati, hear the benefits derived from bhang. The worship of bhang raises one to my position." In *Bhabishya Puran* it is stated that "on the 13th moon of Chaitra (March and April) one who wishes to see the number of his sons and grandsons increased must worship Kama (Cupid) in the hemp plant, etc."[7]

Conceivably, the elements of plant deification in these independent small districts could be indications of a more ancient surviving

---

[7]   These traditions did not survive throughout India. "Mr. J. H. Merriman (witness No. 28, Madras) says: 'I know of no custom of worshipping the hemp plant, but believe it is held in a certain sort of veneration by some classes.' Mr. J. Sturrock, the Collector of Coimbatore (witness No. 2, Madras), says: 'In some few localities there is a tradition of sanctity attached to the plant, but no regular worship.' The Chairman of the Conjeveram Municipal Board, Mr. E. Subramana Iyer (witness No. 143, Madras) says: 'There is no plant to be worshipped here, but it is generally used as sacrifices to some of the minor Hindu deities.'" (Indian Hemp Drugs Commission, 1894).

tradition. Anthropologists often look to the folklore and customs of the common folk for evidence of the survival of more ancient traditions. Thus, in regard to Soma being the only plant ever deified in the Old World, either Wasson is wrong in his statement: for if cannabis is not the Soma, then in the area he is writing about we have evidence of another plant being worshipped; or he is wrong about the identification of the Fly agaric, and we have more evidence in favour of cannabis being the Soma through its continued deification in the surviving traditions of the common folk who would have been less influenced by the eventual Vedic reforms which led to the plant's disappearance than their more cosmopolitan counterparts.

Possibly aware of some of these connections, Wasson himself discounted the cannabis Soma theory with an arrogant sounding comment that comes off as something written during the British Raj!

> In 1921 an Indian advanced the notion that Soma, after all, was nothing but bhang, the Indian name for marijuana, *Cannabis sativa*, hemp, hashish. He conveniently ignored the fact that the Rg Veda placed Soma only on the high mountains, where hemp grows everywhere; and that the virtue of Soma lay in the stalks, whereas it is the resin of the unripened pistillate buds of hashish that transport one into the beyond; or, much weaker, the leaves, which are never mentioned in the Rg Veda. (Wasson, 1970)

Without digressing too far, as we will be returning to the subject in detail later, it should be noted that Wasson goes to great lengths to properly reference other authors and researchers, but when he comes to this topic, he disrespectfully drops all sense of propriety and refers to an indigenous researcher on the subject, as simply "an Indian" disregarding his learned input! Little wonder that Wasson's theory has accumulated no visible support amongst Vedists in India.

The "Indian" was Braja Lal Mukherjee's and as an indigenous researcher he could read the actual *Vedas* in the language they were written; Mukherjee was the first amongst a number of Vedic researchers who suggested *bhang* (hemp) as a candidate for Soma. Mukherjee's 1921 article "The Soma Plant" was published in *The Journal of the Royal Asiatic Society of Great Britain & Ireland*. It should also be noted that, as shall be discussed later, this interpretation has been suggested by more than one "Indian": Joges Candra

Ray (1939), Chandra Chakraberty (1944; 1952; 1963; 1967), Vikramasimha (1967), Indian botanist B. G. L. Swamy (1976), Ramachandran and Irāman Mativānan (1991), Dr. N.R. Warhadpande (1995),
Indra Deva and Shrirama (1999) have all identified the Vedic Soma
with *bhang* (Hemp). I know of no indigenous Vedic scholars who
have agreed with Wasson's hypothesis. (Wasson later revealed his
own long held prejudices against cannabis, through his requests
that it not be considered an 'entheogen' when the term was being
coined.)

In reference to Wasson's comment that it is only the buds of cannabis which contain the resin, and the power lay in the stalks, Indian botanist B. G. L. Swamy, a proponent of the cannabis theory,
noted:

> It is true that the maximum quantity of the narcotic is collected
> from the resinous secretions on the female inflorescence. The
> leaves, however, rarely exude the resin but yet do contain narcotic
> substances. As attested by Watt [(1889)], in plants inhabiting the
> montane habitat the bark spontaneously ruptures and the nar-
> cotic resin exudes.... it is not correct to say that it [the narcotic
> principle] is endemic only in the pistillate buds. The Vedic texts
> refer to this part as *amsu*. Certainly it does not mean specifically
> a leaf. The word merely imports the meaning of 'a part' (cf *amsa*).
> Contextually it may refer to a part of the stem, leaf, stalk and
> leaves. In other words any part of a body, shoot in this case, is an
> *amsu*. (Swamy, 1976)

References to stalks of the plant being crushed for the Soma,
from the vague description give in the *Vedas*, could just as easily refer to the long stalk-like bud covered branches of cannabis as
any other plant. *A Glossary of Colloquial Anglo-Indian Words and
Phrases* refers to "bhang, the dried leaves and small stalks of hemp"
(Crooke, 1903). Moreover a mushroom stalk makes up little of the
mushroom, probably just a few inches at most when dried. As well,
a mushroom only has one small stalk per plant, and as Mahdihassan notes "Wasson... has not correctly worded the problem. What
calls for question is not only stalks but a *thousand boughs* per plant.
Abiding by what the Rgveda actually states *soma* would be an assembly of a 'thousand boughs.'" (Mahdihassan, 1986).

...soma/haoma is prepared from stems or stalks, which most probably should be regarded as fibrous... while the fleshy stems of *A. muscaria* contain only very small amounts of the pharmacologically active compounds, which are concentrated in the mushroom cap (these are the only parts of the mushroom used in northern Siberia. (Nyberg, 1995)

The lack of active compounds in the stalk of the Fly agaric is interesting when compared to Wasson's earlier comments which discounted cannabis as a candidate, reasoning that its active ingredients were in the leaves and flowers, not the stalks (Wasson, 1970). In the case of the proposed Fly agaric, most of the mushroom is made up by the cap and Wasson is able to offer little in the way of indication of the caps of the *Amanita muscaria* when trying to milk the *Vedas* for evidence.

One would think the phenomenal looking Cap of the Fly agaric, which takes up most of the mushroom itself, would be a subject that would receive at least as much reverence as the stalk, if not more, if the *Amanita muscaria* were indeed the Soma. But in this respect, Wasson was only able to find a few Vedic references (RV.9.27.3; 9.68.4; 9.69.8; 9.71.4; 9.93.3) and devoted less than a page to the subject. Many of the passages cited by Wasson in this regard are made in reference to the God Soma as the "Head and Chief" being infused into the Soma, and have nothing to do with the physical preparation of the ancient sacrament. Clearly in Sanskrit, as in English, "Head" has a variety of applications, and when the Vedic passages that make reference to "Head" are looked at in the context of the verses in which they appear, it is an obvious stretch to interpret any as making reference to a bright red spotted mushroom cap. Notably, none of the references to "Head" cited by Wasson appear alongside the many references to the preperation of the stalks of Soma in the *Vedas*, which is where someone would expect them to appear if they were in fact part of the Soma beverage. [8]

---

[8]   Wasson's translations in comparison with (Griffith, 1896) shows there is little in way of evidence indicating the bright red white spotted cap of the *Amanita muscaria* in the few scant passages he could muster up to make his case.

This Bull, heavens head, Soma, when pressed, is escorted by masterly men into the vessels, he the all-knowing

— Wasson RV.9.27.03

In reference to cannabis, Wasson noted the "fact that the Rg Veda placed Soma only on the high mountains, where hemp grows everywhere" (Wasson, 1970). For this same reason Wasson discounted a variety of Soma candidates. "What a useless business it is for us to go chasing in the valleys after rhubarb, honey, hashish,

---

The men conduct him, Soma, Steer, Omniscient, and the Head of Heaven, Effused into the vats of wood.

— Griffith RV.9.27.03

This passage uses 'head' in the context of 'chief.'

While Soma enters the contact with fingers of the officiants, he protects his head.

— Wasson RV.9.68.4

The stalk is mixed with grain: he comes led by the men together with the sisters, and preserves the Head.

— Griffith RV.68.4

If this were a reference to a mushroom head as Soma, it would be in regards to being pulverized with the stalks, not preserved; this is likely a reference to preparing the soma in the proper way to make sure it was active and not inert. The complete verse indicates an analogy of the mixing and preparation as a birth process, as discussed later in Chapter 6.

For you are, O Soma juices,... the heads of heaven, carried erect, creators of vital force.

— Wasson RV.9.69.8

Ye, Soma, are my Fathers, lifted up on high as heads of heaven and makers of the strength of life

— Griffith RV. 69.8

The height factor rules a mushroom out in this reference, thus Wasson didn't include it in his citing.

On Soma's head the cows with full udder mix the best milk in streams.

— Wasson 9.71.4

They pour out meath around the Master of the house, Celestial Strengthener of the mountain that gives might;
In whom, through his great powers, oblation-eating cows in their uplifted udder mix their choicest milk.

— Griffith RV.9.71.4

Here Griffith translates the same phrase as meaning 'Master of the House,' as in 'Head' of the House.

The Udder of the cow is swollen; the wise juice is imbued with its streams. In the vessels the cows mix with their milk the murdhan [head]

— Wasson 9.93.3

Yea, swollen is the udder of the milch-cow: thither in streams goes very sapient Indu. The kine make ready, as with new-washed treasures, the Head and Chief with milk within the vessels.

— Griffith RV.93.3

wild afghan grapes; in hot arid countries after species of Ephedra, Sarcostemma, Periploca!" (Wasson, 1970)

First off, it is difficult to understand how Wasson ever came to the conclusion that the Fly agaric mushroom is purely a Mountain species. This author has witnessed first-hand wild Fly agarics growing in coastal sand dunes and valley forests. In regards to cannabis, Wasson's view is based on the situation contemporary with his own time, after thousands of years of cannabis cultivation, not at the composition of the *Vedas*. Indeed cannabis spread "everywhere" quickly but numbers of sources have seen the Hindu Kush Mountains and Tien Shan Mountains as possible places of Hemp's origin, both of which have also been suggested as the Aryan's secondary homeland. The Hindu Kush Mountains are particularly associated with the origins of *Cannabis indica*, which is the species of hemp indicated by the Vedic description, particularly in the Tenth Mandala, as we shall discuss later in Chapter 4. The Hindu Kush Mountains, suspected homeland of the Soma, are still renowned for the quality ganja they have produced for millennia, eventually spreading to the rest of the Himalayas, as cannabis now grows wild throughout the area.

> Geographical references in the Rg Veda also indicate that the Soma plant eventually diffused to locations along the banks of the Saravati and Arjikiya rivers. The fertile alluvial soils adjacent to these other rivers that have their headwaters in the Himalayas ..' are exactly the situations of the wild growth of *Bhanga* (hemp)."[9] (Merlin, 1972)

As Witzel has also noted of Soma's association with water sources, " the hymn RV 10.75 has the following stream: The Su_omå 'the one having good Soma' .... the modern Sohån/Suwan..." (Witzel, 1999). The widespread distribution of Haoma is referred to in the Avestan tradition as well.

> Thus the life-giving birds launched there
> carried you out in various directions:
> to Ishkata Upairi.saêna,
> to Staêra Starô.sâra,
> to Kusrâdha Kusrô.patâdha,

---

9   Merlin quotes (Chopra and Chopra, 1939).

to Pavrâna along the path of the birds,
to the two *White-color Mountains.[10]

— Y.10.11

Moreover, Wasson ignores comments from the Avestan literature that indicates widespread growth of the plant early on:

I praise all the haomas,
even when on the heights of the mountains,
even when in the depths of the streams,
even those in the narrow passes of ravines.

— Y.10.17

As Dieter Taillieu has commented "haoma and soma are accord-
ed fragrance (Av. hubaoiδi-, Y. 10.4, cf. Skt. surabhintara-) and a
mountainous location; the additional reference to river valleys in
Y.10.17 is probably... way of saying 'all haomas, wherever they may
be'" (Taillieu, 2002). Taillieu makes a good point in reference to the
fragrance of Haoma, something attested to in a variety of passages
in both the Vedic and Avestan literature, and which could hardly
designate a mushroom:

O king Soma, O Soma which the priest carefully prepares. High with power that is real, its flowing blends together, together blend the fragrances of the fragrant,
purifying you by the formula, O wild god. Flow, O elixir, for Indra
all around

— RV.9.113

I praise the earths, where, O Haoma, you grow,
fragrant, fleetly-moving.

— Y.10.4

Y.10.4 also has the added description of "fleetly moving," a description likely identifying a plant that is blown around in the wind,
which again would hardly describe a mushroom. To explain incon-
sistencies with his theory Wasson put forth that the RV.10.85 gave
indications of a substitute; "One thinks one drinks Soma because
a plant is crushed. The Soma the Brahmans know – that no one

---

10   Mountains in Central Asia and modern Afghanistan.

drinks." Because of this Wasson decided to disallow all following passages from the 10th Mandala regarding the identity of Soma in the *Vedas*.

Conceivably the RV.10.85 reference could have been an ancient differentiation between the more common *Cannabis sativa* and the more potent *Cannabis indica* which grew on the sides of mountains.[11] Another possibility is that this is a reference to sinsimllia, and perhaps one of the secrets of the Soma cult was holding back the males from pollinating the females?

> Watt[12] felt that by... [1000-800 BCE] the sexual dimorphism of cannabis was already evident to its cultivators, as well as the superiority of *bhanga* (mistakenly assigned as female) for cordage, and *bhang* (mistaken as male) for medical and mystical application. It was also likely about this time that the preparation of *ganja* (labeled *sinsemilla* in contemporary North America) was developed by isolating female cannabis plants to prevent fertilization, and increase resin production. (Russo, 2005)

Alternatively, the reference to the "Soma the Brahmans know" may have had to do with the belief of the Brahmans that their preparation of the Soma was magically imbued with powers through the rites of preparation only known to the elite priest class. And still again, perhaps more than one plant was involved in the Soma, Haoma (and this is a subject we will return to again) but even that scenario does not by necessity include the *Amanita muscaria* Mushroom.

Wasson's logic is similarly askew when he tries to pass off Vedic verses referring to the 'Moon' as the 'Mainstay of the Sky,' as references to the *Amanita muscaria* (RV.9.2.5; 9.72.7; 9.74.2; 9.86.35; 9.86.46; 9.87.2; 9.89.6; 9.108.16; 9.109.6). In the symbolism of the *Vedas*, the Moon was the celestial vessel of Soma, which was continually drunk by the gods and replenished by the Sun. This is a clear example of Wasson turning to Vedic references regarding

---

11   As a Sensi-Seeds advertisement reads for the Hindu-Kush strain of cannabis; "This pure Indica seed-strain comes directly from the massive mountain range for which it is named. The Hindu Kush is the western spur of the Himalayas, covering half of Afghanistan and straddling the borders of Pakistan and India, reaching almost to China. This desolate and beautiful region forms an important trade-route between the Middle East, central Asia and the Far East and the ancient cannabis traditions of the surrounding cultures have met and merged here over centuries."

12   (Watt, 1889).

Soma that are clearly not a reference to a plant, to make his case. It was for such twisting of the scriptural meaning that Wasson's work has been highly criticized by other researchers.

Likewise for references to the "Single Eye" (RV.1.87.5; 9.9.4; 9.10.8; 9.10.9; 9.97.46), which Wasson ludicrously compares with a photo of a newly forming *Amanita* rising from the ground, but which actually make reference to the psychological state caused by the sacred beverage. Just as the God Soma entered the beverage Soma, so too did Soma enter the devoted imbiber, enabling devotee and God to see with a "Single Eye." Moreover, this identification is almost identical to Zoroastrian references to the use of Haoma preperations for opening the "eye of the soul" which are discussed in Chapter 15. I suppose it is this particular type of out-of-context twisting of the Vedic texts for interpretation of symbolic imagery indicating the different stages of the life span of the *Amanita muscaria* which irks me most about Wasson and other proponents of the Fly agaric-Soma theory.

Also questioned by many scholars are the Vedic references that have been interpreted by the Wasson camp as identifying the color of the Soma as "red." The Vedic term for 'red' 'aruna' is only applied to Soma when he is referred to as a bull, "the bull is 'red'" (Wasson, 1970). The color generally applied to Soma in the *Vedas* is "hari" and is generally interpreted as refering to colors ranging anywhere from golden to yellow and even green; "there are numerous non-Soma hymns in the texts where hari means only one shade, that is greenish or greenish-yellow" (Swamy, 1976). Wasson tries to work this Vedic term for shades of green and yellow in his favour with the comment that:

> *Hari* is not only a color word: the intensity of the color is also expressed by it. It is dazzling, brilliant, lustrous resplendent, flaming.... The mythological horses of the sun-god were *hari*: in this context the word is usually rendered by 'bay' or 'chestnut', but one doubts whether any mundane color such as 'bay' would describe the steeds of the sun. They are flaming and full of brio. (Wasson, 1970)

Thus we can see to what lengths Wasson will go to make his point, unable to find a Vedic translation that suits his view he re-

sorts to a novel interpretation of a text that has nothing to do with
Soma! Wasson tries to disregard the accepted interpretation in a
footnote with the comment that: "Occasionally in later times *hari*
came to include 'green' among its meanings, but this usage seems
not to be Rg Vedic, except possibly in the late hymns that we exclude from consideration" (Wasson, 1970).

As shall be discussed later, English translations of the *Rig Veda*
list the color of Soma as golden, purple[13] and green.[14] Likewise with
English translations of the *Yasnas*, where the color of Haoma is ref-
ered to green and gold throughout the texts,[15] all of which suit quite
well the colors of ripe hemp.

> The Vedic description for the color of Soma include the word
> *hari*, which may be interpreted as meaning 'green or greenish
> yellow.'[16] At Indore in Madra Pradesh the male (or more cor-
> rectly the female) form of the hemp plant is called hari. In addi-
> tion MacDonell and Keith[17] also designated *babbru* (brown) and
> *aruna* (ruddy) as possible color of the Soma plant. These color
> interpretations also could fit the hemp plant. (Merlin, 1972)

The pivotal point of Wasson's identification of the Fly agaric
as Soma were Vedic references that Wasson viewed as referring
to the practice of drinking a priest's urine after he had consumed
Soma, Wasson's so-called "second form." To Wasson this indicated
the use of the Fly agaric, for its hallucinogenic effects would still
be present and accounts of Siberian Shamans record the ritual ingestion of such mushroom-infused urine up until modern times.
This view of alleged Vedic urine drinking has been shared by a variety of other researchers. The following excerpt is typical of those
quoted by Wasson in this respect, and this particular passage was
considered crucial by him regarding references to psychoactive
urine in the *Vedas*:

13   The color of ripe Cannabis Indica.
14   Splitting, but unsplit, you, O stones… enjoying the Soma, flowing green (with
Soma), they made heaven and earth resound with their clamour.

> They speak, they received into their mouth the sweet (Soma juice)…chewing the
> branch of the purple tree, the voracious bulls have bellowed.
> —Rig Veda 10.8.4

15   Haoma's epitheta include "the Golden-Green One" (zairi-, Sanskrit hari-).
16   Merlin cites (Ray, 1939).
17   (MacDonell & Kieth, 1958).

Butter and milk are drawn from animated cloud; thence *Amrta* is
produced, centre of sacrifice.
Hini the Most Bounteous Ones, ever united, love; him as our
Friend the Men who make all swell rain down.[18]
— *Rig Veda* 9.74.4

Wasson's translation of the same verse:

Soma, storm cloud imbued with life, is milked of ghee, milk. Na-
vel of the Way, Immortal Principle, he sprang into life in the far
distance. Acting in concert, those charged with the Office, richly
gifted, do full honour to Soma. The swollen men piss the flowing
[Soma].

It should be noted in regard to the different translations of the
same verse, that in order to accept Wasson's theory on the Soma,
you also have to accept his novel translations of the Vedic texts! In
this particular passage, which he felt offered compelling evidence
of his case, he even had to add the term 'Soma' to the end of it himself to make the point he wanted to express. Wasson stated that;
"If the final clause of this verse bears the meaning that I suggest for
it, then it alone suffices to prove my case" (Wasson, 1970). Wasson
clearly makes an enormous intellectual stretch when he interprets
the reference to 'rain' as a reference to Soma infused 'piss.'

For the sake of discussion, R.V.9.74.4 if interpreted and translated in Wasson's favour, could also be a symbolic magical gesture
aimed at bestowing the Soma plant with the rains which helped it to
grow and which was believed to have been divinely sent, i.e., when
they drank the Soma, through imitative magic the Gods drank with
them in Heaven, and when they passed it back out again, so did the
Gods as well, resulting in the rains from heaven, causing the Soma
to grow.[19] Rain, was a crucial element for the authors of the *Vedas*,
as ancient people started settling down they found that the two
elements of nature that were crucial for cultivation were the rain
and the sun. This is still true in India today where beliefs about the
coming of the Monsoons are ripe with religious fertility symbol-

18   *Rig Veda*, tr. by Ralph T.H. Griffith, [1896], at sacred-texts.com
19   A comparable magical relationship still occurs in India's Jagganath festival
where a priest and priestess ritually imbibe a cannabis preparation before having sex to
ensure the monsoon rains, and this ritual inebriation was likely done in honour of Indra, a
god intimately connected with the Soma sacrifice, see Chapter 18.

ism. Thus for the Soma farming people the rain-god Indra gained in prominence and became the king of the gods. Often rain was accompanied by storms, which personified became the Maruts, the followers of Indra. As Stausberg has also noted:

> ...one effect of Indra's inordinate consumption of soma on his bladder, which he needs to empty, thereby releasing thundering streams of fertilizing liquid all over the world in the form of rain... Rigveda 8.4.9-10 (to Indra)...'*drink the soma according to wish! Pissing it down day after day*'".... In the Vendidad, a... Avestan text on ritual cleansing, we are told that one of the places where the earth is most happy is where people and animals urinate the most and where it is cultivated, which shows there is a link between urine and fertility.... Vedividad 3.6 'Where... of this earth is it happiest? Then Ahura mazda said: *wherever animals, small and large, piss the most*.' (Stausberg, 2004)

In reference to 9.74.4 Wasson pointed to the work of Renou, a French scholar who spent a lifetime immersed in the *Vedas*, stating that Renou "discerned that the 'swollen' men had full bladders and that they were urinating Soma. But to give meaning to the sentence he introduced the gods of rain, the Maruts" (Wasson, 1970). Renou's interpretation is similar to the one both Stausberg and I myself have suggested; Wasson agreed with the first part of Renou's interpretation, but not the second. Wasson argued that Gods are not referred to, but rather "men" are, whom Wasson identifies as the Soma Priests, bringing his interpretation "swollen men piss the flowing [Soma]" although as noted he had to add 'Soma" to the sentence to establish his point!

> Let us pause for a moment and dwell on a rather odd figure of speech. The blessings of the fertilizing rain are likened to a shower of urine. The storm-clouds fecundate the earth with their urine. Vedic scholars have lived so long with their recalcitrant text, and so close to it, that they remark no longer on an analogy that calls for explanation. Urine is normally something to cast away and turn from, second in this respect only to excrement. In the Vedic poets the values are reversed and urine is an ennobling metaphor to describe the rain. The values are reversed, I suggest, because the poets in Vedic India were thinking of urine as the carrier of the Divine inebriant, the bearer of *amrta*. This would explain the

role that urine – human and bovine – has played through the centuries as the medico-religious disinfectant of the Indo-Iranian world, the Holy Water of the East.[20] (Wasson, 1970)

In reference to Wasson's interpretation of *Rig Veda* 9.74.4 Flattery and Schwartz contended that "even interpreting this literally (and supposing the 'men' to refer to priests, which is not at all certain), there is still nothing to suggest the drinking of such urine... [N]one of the data presented by Wasson on the subject of urine drinking has any relevance for soma" (1989).[21] Another important point in this regard is made by one early reviewer of Wasson's book:

> Where Wasson errs is in supposing that the Vedic soma was drunk in the same way [as the Siberian urine]. To justify such a thesis he is forced to suppose that Vedic priests impersonated their gods: that when the text says, "I offer soma to you, Indra; drink of the good soma," someone was offering amanita juice to a priest.
>
> Actually, there is no shred of evidence for priestly impersonations in the Rigveda. Where priests do act in *persona dei* (as they do in some forms of Hinduism and Buddhism) the procedure is clearly revealed by the language of the ritual and litany. Wasson finds one out of the 35,000 lines of the Rigveda that seems to say the priests are micturating diluted soma. I interpret the line [RV.9.86.2][22]...to mean that bearers of the soma pots are pouring the fluid down into the filter-covered trough. One cannot hang the explanation of a major cult on a single image, which may be metaphorical, taken out of context. (Ingalls, 1971)[23]

Wasson explained that Hindu references occur in the text of the *Mahabharata*, when the god Indra, disguised as an outcaste, gives

20   "In some rites soma was given to a bull–Soma is also a sacred bull in the texts–and the bull's urine is consumed, a rite similar to the practice today where both cow's urine and feces are still partaken of in certain ceremonies of purification" (Rice,1978).

21   As quoted by (Riedlinger, 1993)

22   Wasson stated that the priest acting as Indra in RV.9.85.5 drinks Soma (Indra certainly does, the priest acting as him is a Wassonism) then connects it with a passage 8 full verses later from RV.9.86.2 ("Thy inebriating drinks, swift, are released ahead, like teams running in divers directions, like the milch cow with her milk towards her calf, go to Indra, thunder-bolt carrier"), Wasson follows this with a series of out of sequence verses which he interprets as indicating Indra pissed Soma back out again for consumption. When read in sequence and context, Indra drinks Soma, the scene changes and then the priests are preparing Soma, streaming it through woollen filters.

23   Curiously, Ingalls accepted that Wasson had correctly identified Soma as *Amanita muscaria*, but disputed the urine connection. (Ingalls,1971).

the hero Uttanka, amrta (ambrosia), to drink in the form of urine, an interpretation I am willing to accept. But it should be noted that this reference does not appear in the *Vedas*, and by Wasson's own acknowledgment, it occurs, much, much later than the dates in question:

> In the... *Mahabharata*... there occurs one episode – an isolated episode of unknown lineage – that bears with startling clarity on our *Second Form* [i.e. Fly agaric enriched urine]. It was introduced into the text perhaps a thousand years after the fly-agaric had ceased to be used in the Soma sacrifice, and perhaps the editor did not know its meaning... (Wasson, 1970)

Rather than relating the psychedelic effects of Fly agaric enriched piss, the *Mahabharata* story may indicate that Indra was so holy, even his piss was sacred. Alternatively, urine-drinking has a number of applications in Eastern medicine and is thought to be beneficial, which could also just as easily explain this account. Also, as Prof. Scott Littleton has noted, bull urine was "also used as a form of 'holy water' to purify persons and objects, especially those that have been in contact with death" (Littleton, 2008).[24] Zoroastrian priests use unconsecrated cattle urine, *gomez*, as a disinfectant, and consecrated and properly aged Bull's urine, *Nirang*, for internal use.

Certain Indian Tantric sects and the Aghori ascetics of Benares have also been known to ritually consume urine. "Although these examples from India and Iran show that the drinking of urine for its alleged therapeutic and spiritual effects is far from rare in traditional beliefs and practices, there is no reason to connect them with the fly-agaric mushroom" (Rudgley, 1993). Moreover, there is no reason to connect this with the Soma rite, although there may be reason to discount such an association.

The Sacred Laws of the Aryas,[25] records that "the sacrificial cup (*kamasa*) is declared to be pure on account of its contact with the Soma juice."[26] This purity was ruined by contact with urine, "at all soma-sacrifices (the cups must be) cleaned with water only... If

24   Personal Correspondence.
25   Circa 450 B.C., but likely based on and influenced by earlier Vedic material.
26   *Prasna* 1, *Adhyaya* 4, *Kandika* 7: 4, As translated in (Buhler, 1882). In reference to the "cups and vessels" used in the sacrifice, *The Laws of the Aryas* is explicit; "The Veda (declares), "They do not become impure through Soma." *Prasna* 1, *Adhyaya* 5, *Kandika* 8: 50-51, As quoted in (Buhler, 1882)

these same (cups are defiled) by urine, ordure, blood, semen and the like (they must be) thrown away."[27] A situation that would be hard to reconcile with Wasson's concept of divine Soma enriched piss.

Another problem concerning the identity of the *A. muscaria* with Soma, is the rarity of a seasonal mushroom in comparison with the abundance of Soma in the original home of the Aryans as described in the *Vedas*. As Harri Nyberg has noted "the mushroom must have been rare in any proposed Indo-Iranian homelands. In contrast, when the use of *soma/haoma* began, the Aryans seem to have been inhabiting a region where the to-date unidentified plant was abundant" (Nyberg, 1995).

Interestingly, before his death in 1986, R. Gordon Wasson referred to the fallacy of David Flattery's identification of Haoma as the *Peganum harmala* as Soma on the basis that ingestion of the "plant does not lead to a blissful state." In response to this statement, R. Gordon Wasson had it pointed out to him by interviewer Robert Forte, that "the Amanita does not lead to a blissful state either." Wasson, with a slightly dumbfounded explanation replied, "Well, I know. That troubles me too. I cannot explain it, but there must be some explanation. No white man enjoys a blissful experience that I know of from the Amanita. Now there are occasions" [As quoted in (Forte, Ed. 1997)]. Wasson goes on to weakly describe an occasion when a Japanese associate received a state which as an outside observer he perceived as being "blissful."

Unfortunately, Soma use was not recorded amongst the Japanese of the ancient world, so the comparison is somewhat weak. Alternatively, such blissful states have long been attributed to another candidate for the sacred drink, cannabis hemp, which has been acknowledged for the feeling of "bliss" it instils in its users the world over and has been celebrated for such in some of humanity's earliest written records. On this particular note I challenge anybody to produce as much as one half of the literature referring to the blissful state produced by any of the other plant candidates for Soma, as I could for hemp (especially in Persian and Indian literature)[28] – an impossible task. Indeed researcher Dr. Raphael Mechoulam discoverer of both THC and the Brain's cannabis receptor, dubbed the indigenous molecule that attaches to the receptor (the human

27   *Prasna* 1, *Adhyaya* 6, *Kandika* 13: 31-31, As translated in (Buhler, 1882)
28   See, *Green Gold the Tree of Life: Marijuana in Magic and Religion* (Bennett, et al., 1995)

body's natural THC) anandamide, from "*ananda*," the Sanskrit word for 'bliss.'[29]

Although Wasson's sensational claims helped to ferment new and inspired research into the origins of the Haoma/Soma, many have seen his contributions to the matter as a muddling factor. "The [Soma] question has been confused by the enthusiastic advocacy of R. Gordon Wasson for the implausible view that soma was prepared from mushrooms" (Sherratt, 1995). I have chosen only a few of Wasson's own key passages to show the error of his hypothesis, but let it be known similar inaccuracies can be found throughout *Soma: Divine Mushroom of Immortality*. As the Indian botanist B. G. L. Swamy rightly held, the "view that the Rg-vedic Soma plant is an Agaric is negated by the interpretation of the Rg-vedic text itself.... There is no evidence whatsoever in the Rg-veda to point out... that it [Soma] was leafless or that it was a mushroom" (Swamy, 1976). As Harri Nyberg notes Wasson's work has rightly been criticized "on the grounds that some of the translations he used were misleading and that he seemed to arbitrarily connect Rgvedic phrases and verses which do not properly belong together" (Nyberg, 1995).[30]

Indeed, after a thorough review of Wasson's material it is hard to understand how it has been so willingly accepted by so many almost four decades after it was first proposed. The mushroom theory of Soma is not worth the manure that mushrooms grow in. But at the same time, Wasson's book reinvigorated 20th century study into the origins of the Soma more than any other publication before or since.

Despite a lifetime of effort Wasson failed to prove his case for the Fly agaric being the Soma. Even Vedist Wendy Doniger O'Flaherty, who contributed a chapter to Wasson's *Soma: Divine Mushroom of Immortality*, failed to agree with his identification of the Fly agaric as Soma, the best support she could muster being; "Wasson's novel solution of this old question revivifies a body of speculation" (Doniger O'Flaherty, 1968). After Wasson's death Doniger revealed that Wasson never did convince her of the identification of Soma with the *Amanita muscaria* (Doniger, 1990). Wasson's Soma theory may have been the downfall of his otherwise notable research into psycho-active plants and the origins of religion.

---

29   THC and CBD were first isolated by Roger Adams, University of Illionois in the 1930s and '40s.
30   Nyberg cites (Brough, 1971).

In this respect it should be noted that R. Gordon Wasson hypothesized that the genesis of religion could be found in humanity's relationship to the hallucinogens. For this, and his lifelong research into entheogenic history, Jonathon Ott compared Wasson to Charles Darwin. For Darwin's hypothesis of natural selection helped to document the reality of Evolution, in the same way "Wasson's theory suggested a natural mechanism to explain the historical *fact* that strikingly similar religious concepts arose independently in diverse parts of the... globe in protohistory, having certain pangaen motifs relating to ecstatic communion with the entheogens, the use of which has likewise been shown to be common virtually to all cultures studied... of the *Axis Mundi* or 'World Tree' ('Tree of Life,' 'Tree of the Knowledge of Good and Evil,' etc.) with its sacred fruit... of communion with sacrament... of the souls separability from the body... of the Otherworld..." (Ott 1995) Ott further contends that just as the fundamentalists are being overwhelmed by the gaining world acceptance of Evolution over the belief in Biblical Creationism, so too as data accumulates will the world come to see the Wasson theory of the origins of religion vastly more believable than the theologies put forth by any of the modern day followers of today's orthodox religions.

Other researchers have been less kind in their assessment of Wasson's role in the study of entheogens. Author Jan Irvin, who has studied humanity's historical relationship with psychoactive mushrooms extensively, suggests Wasson may have been influenced by the works of a much earlier writer, and failed to give him his due credit:

> A comparison of the effects of Soma with those of the *Amanita muscaria* and cannabis was first proposed in the book *Scatalogic [sic] Rites of All Nations* by John G. Bourke, 1891. The author dedicated more than 30 pages (pgs. 65-99) to the study of the ritualistic use of mushrooms, including the Siberian *Amanita muscaria* urine drinking custom, and Mexican mushroom practices. This is probably where Wasson first learned of the ritualistic use of mushrooms, urine consumption, and Soma. On page 98 is a letter to Bourke by a Dr. J. W. Kingsley:
>
> "I remember being shown this fungus by an Englishman who was returning [...] from Siberia. He fully confirmed all that I had heard on the subject, having seen the orgy [mushroom rituals]

himself. ... Nothing religious in this, you may say; but look at the question a little closer and you will see that these 'intoxicants,' [...] were at first looked upon as media able to raise the mere man up to a level with his gods, and enable him to communicate with them, as was certainly the case with the 'soma' of the Hindu ecstatics and the hashich [sic] I have seen used by some tribes of Arabs."

Most scholars claim that Wasson was the progenitor of these ideas, but this is not wholly accurate. It appears that Wasson may have 'borrowed' several key ideas from Bourke's research and expanded upon them throughout his career, subsequently creating the field of ethnomycology. Thereafter it appears that Bourke was relegated mostly to rare catalogue and bibliographical entries published by Wasson and a few other scholars of his ilk. However, Bourke is not to be found, as one should expect for the extent of his studies on the subject, in the main body of text in most of the books published on the subject for the last half century. (Irvin, 2009)

Bourke, in fact, put forth one of the better pieces of evidence for the ancient Vedic use of the mushroom, noting this ironically through accounts of strong prohibitions of mushrooms in the early Indian period, something Wasson surprisingly failed to adequately address. Bourke was referring to references in *The Sacred Laws of the Âryas* (450 BC) and *The Laws of Manu* (a.k.a. *The Book of Manu*) thought to have been composed sometime around 200 B.C., although both texts likely contained much older material and influences.

The *Laws of Manu* record that a Brahmin should "avoid honey and meat and mushrooms coming from the ground" (Manu 6:14). *The Sacred Laws of the Aryas* declares "Yama has declared such (food to be) impure; (to eat it is as sinful) as to partake of cow's flesh. ... For eating garlic, onions, mushrooms, turnips, ..."[31] Bourke cites earlier researches in reference to this: "The ancient Hindus held the fungus in such detestation that Yama, a legislator, supposed now to be the judge of departed spirits, declares : 'Those who eat mushrooms, whether springing from the ground or growing on a tree, fully equal in guilt to the slayers of Brahmins and the most despicable of all deadly sinners." — (*Asiatic Researches*, Calcutta, 1795, vol. iv. P. 311).[32]

---

31   (*Vasitha* 15.13), As translated in (Buhler, 1882).
32   As quoted in (Bourke, 1891)

As Bourke noted, Jean Antoine Dubois, refers to the same subject. "The Brahmins," he says, "have also retrenched from their vegetable food, which is the great fund of their subsistence, all roots which form a head or bulb in the ground, such as onions, and all those that assume the same shape above ground, like mushrooms and some others...."

> Are we to suppose that they had discovered something unwholesome in the one species and proscribed the other on account of its fetid smell... all the information ever obtained from those among whom I have consulted on the reasons for their abstinence from them being that it is customary to avoid such articles, together with all those that have had the germ of the living principle. This is what is called in India, *to eat becomingly*. Such as use the prohibited articles cannot boast of their bodies being pure, according to the estimate of the Brahmans. I am aware that, amongst these also, some secret infractions of the rule have occurred; but the secrecy with which it is violated proves that it is generally observed; and it may be fairly assumed that the great body of the Brahmans rigidly abstain from all sorts of animal food, as well as from whatever has had the principle of vitality. " – (Abbe Dubois, *People of India*, London, 1817, p.117.)[33]

In reference to this, Bourke reasonably suggested that "This inhibition, under such dire penalties, can have but one meaning. In primitive times the people of India must have been so addicted to this debauchery induced by potions into the composition of which entered poisonous fungi... and the effects of such debauchery must have been found so debasing and pernicious, that the priest-rulers were compelled to employ the same maledictions which Moses proved the efficacy in withdrawing the children of Israel from the worship of idols" (Bourke, 1891).

Interestingly, *The Laws of Manu* contains references regarding the prohibition of Soma to certain castes of Vedic society so one would think Wasson would have made more of the connection regarding the prohibition of mushrooms. However, Wasson felt that that it was "impossible to say whether this prohibition was related to a sacred use of the Fly agaric; probably not" (Wasson, 1970). Moreover, this was Wasson's sole reference to *The Laws of*

---

33   Ibid.

Manu, an ancient text that is pivotal in understanding the eventual prohibitions surrounding the original Soma and its later substitution with a non-psychoactive placebo, and which is more fully discussed in Chapter 18.

Others have suggested that this prohibition of mushrooms has nothing to do with intoxication, but rather the development of vegetarianism in India. "Brahmins never ate this food, supposedly because it tastes and is prepared like meat. It is the writer's opinion that the smell of mushrooms, and their association with decay, may account for them being considered impure. They have been viewed with distrust since the time of Manu" (Robson, 1980).

Another factor that would stand against the prohibition of the mushroom having to do with potential intoxicating effects and its subsequent use in the Vedic Soma beverage is that the references in *The Sacred Laws of the Aryas*, come from the supposed authorship of Yama. Yama is central in the history of both the Indian Soma and the Persian Haoma, where he is known as Yima, and this combined recognition indicates his primordial involvement in the original Aryan rites surrounding the sacred beverage that led to the later tradition in both India and Persia. In the Persian tradition, Yima's father was the first to press Haoma, and Yima himself is credited with spreading the cultic use of Haoma. In the Indian accounts, a funeral hymn from the *Atharva Veda* records that "For Yama Soma juice flows clear, to Yama oblation is paid" (A.V.18.2) and the *Rig Veda* commands "To Yama pour the Soma" (R.V. 10.14.13). "Every competent scholar recognizes a close affinity between the Iranian Yima and the Hindu Yama, between the *soma*-cult and the *haoma*-cult..." (Hopkins, 2007). Any future hope of resurrecting the Soma mushroom theory that would make reference to these Vedic era prohibitions of the mushroom, needs to address the fact that they are said to come through Yama, the traditional ancestor of the Soma-Haoma cult.[34]

---

34   In this respect, it should be noted that in this statement, there is the problem created of accepting that a pre-Vedic era figure like Yama, authored a text at the end of the Vedic period, such as the *The Sacred Laws of the Aryas*, which is thought to have been composed around 450 B.C.. This situation, however, may be reconciled with the above statement, if one accepts the general view that *The Sacred Laws of the Aryas* is believed to have been adapted from much older material, and it would seem likely that there were traditions based on Yama that had been passed down from earlier generations. Still, it is not impossible that later Vedic authors, like their Avestan and Biblical counterparts, were not above attributing newer documents, to older cultural figures in order to endow them

No Hope for Harmaline

Just as the identification of the Fly agaric mushroom as Soma has been widely accepted, the Harmaline containing plant Syrian rue has come to be identified with the Persian Haoma, and this is largely due to the exhaustive work of David Stophlet Flattery and Martin Schwartz in their admirable book *Haoma and Harmaline* (1989). Noting that the modern plant used in the Haoma ritual Ephedra had none of the psychoactive properties alluded to in the Avestan texts, Flat-

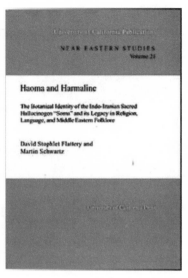

tery and Schwartz put forth the suggestion that the original brew also held the Harmaline containing plant Syrian rue.

Syrian rue was actually the first candidate suggested for Haoma by a western historian, in this case by Sir William Jones in 1798.[35] Flattery and Schwartz have done a commendable job with the research they have put together in an attempt to resurrect this theory. In their view the "Vedic descriptions of soma are so general that they cannot be used to prove or disprove [Wasson's] or any other hypothesis" (Flattery Schwartz, 1989). The co-authors believed that "any probative evidence for the botanical identification of sauma[36] must have its basis outside of this text" (Flattery Schwartz, 1989).

Taking up much of their research with material excluded from Wasson's study, Flattery and Schwartz focus their own investigation on the *Avesta* and other ancient Iranian literature, which indeed shares a common "Proto-Indo-Iranian" ancestry with the *Rig Veda*. Flattery and Schwartz saw the Avesta as a more reliable doc-

with more respect and authority. If this is the case, then the prohibition of mushrooms in the Vedic religion, may have indeed occurred close to the time surrounding the disappearance and prohibition of the original Soma-Plant. But even this does not connect the two, as the whole closing Vedic period was wrought with a variety of prohibitions (see Chapter 18) including the prohibition of both meat and alcohol. The references to the prohibition of mushrooms in both *The Sacred Laws of the Aryas* and *The Laws of Manu*, occur in association with meat, rather than with Soma or "spirituous liquor," which themselves appear together in accounts from both ancient text. Thus, it would seem clear that, mushrooms were forbidden based on a dietary code, rather than for their speculated potential intoxicating effects, as with Soma and "spirituous liquor."

35   As noted by (Sherratt, 1995).
36   Flattery and Schwartz have chosen to use "sauma" instead of the standard "Haoma."

ument as they felt there was "a scholarly consensus that in general the *Avesta* is the more conservative text, that is, it more faithfully reflects archaic reality than does the RgVeda, which is prone to extensive poetic elaboration" (Flattery & Schwartz, 1989).[37] In this regard it is the view of this author that the texts of both cultures have to be taken into account if the true identity of the original Soma/Haoma is to be deduced.

The duo convincingly identified the Persian references to Haoma (which he translates as *sauma*) and *bhang* (also *mang*, which is the later Pahlavi form of the word) as identifying the same entheogenic preparation. But they both saw the Persian term *bhang\mang* (identified as cannabis by numerous other researchers, and still in use in this context in both Persia and India to this day) as having a more general meaning such as narcotic or intoxicant, and particularly for Flattery's purposes as identifying Syrian rue, but here the co-authors disagree, as Schwartz saw the term as more likely identifying Henbane or Datura, an etymological view that is more further explored and challenged in its context in Chapter 15.

Although Syrian rue can in fact become hallucinogenic by itself, it's use is accompanied by nausea. In *Tihkal*, Alexander and Ann Shulgin report the following accounts of the ingestion of Syrian rue, seeds and extract; and the nausea sounds extreme even when following dietary precautions, a fact that would be hard to reconcile with the pleasant effects of Haoma and Soma as described in the Vedic and Avestan literature:

(with 2 g *Peganum harmala* seeds, ground, in capsules) "No effects."

(with 5 g *Peganum harmala* seeds, ground, in capsules) "At about 1:45 tinnitus was obvious. At 2:00 precise movements were problematical and nystagmus was noticeable. Mild nausea and diarrhea, …. sensitive to light and sound… Hallucinations were intense, but only with the eyes closed. They consisted, initially, of a wide variety of geometrical patterns in dark colors, getting more intense as time went on. They disappeared when the eyes were opened… loose bowels and nausea were pretty constant through the… the trip."

(with 7 g *Peganum harmala* seeds, ground, in capsules) "Very sick for 24 hours."

37   As quoted by (Riedlinger, 1993)

(with 20 g *Peganum harmala* seeds, as extract) "This is equivalent, probably, to a gram or so of the harmala alkaloids. This was ground up material extracted with hot dilute lemon juice. Within a half hour, I found myself both trippy and sleepy. Then I became quite disorientated, nauseous, and with an accelerated heart beat. I had the strong sensation of moving backwards, drifting, with faint visuals under my eyelids. Restraining the vomiting urge was an ongoing problem. I could have gone out of body quite easily, except that I was completely anchored by the nausea. After about three hours, I knew that it had peaked, and I went to sleep and experienced intense and strange dreams. The entire experience was a conflict between tripping and being sick." (Shulgin & Shulgin, 1997)

As David Flattery himself noted: "The effects actually experienced from a preparation of harmel were well known in Middle Eastern lore: as reported in early Islamic materia medica they are chiefly vomiting, sleep, intoxication, and an inclination toward coitus" (Flattery & Schwartz, 1989). Beyond indications of aphrodisiacal qualities, none of these effects are referred to in either the Avestan or Vedic literature. Moreover, in the Avestan accounts, Haoma is used in nocturnal rituals, where participants are wide awake, dancing and singing.

Because of its unpleasant effects, few modern psychonauts partake of Syrian rue as a hallucinogen by itself, but rather use Harmala in conjunction with other plants to increase the psychoactive effects contained in them. This brings us to some important points of criticism from entheobotanist Jonathan Ott.

Jonathan Ott, cited a number of problems with *Haoma and Harmaline*, such as Flattery's failure to provide first hand evidence of *Peganum harmala's* entheogenic capabilities, and little historical evidence. Instead, Flattery bases his speculations on comparisons between the effects of the Near Eastern Syrian rue, and the ethnographic literature on the South American visionary vine, *Banisteriopsis caapi*, more popularly known as *ayahuasca*, but in both cases, the plants only become what is considered entheogenically active when mixed with other DMT containing plants such as as *Mimosa hostilis*, *Diplopterys cabrerana*, and *Psychotria viridis*. (Without a MAOI, the body quickly metabolizes orally-administered DMT, and it therefore has no hallucinogenic effect).[38] "The

---

38   MAOIs can also increase the visual effects of psilocybin mushrooms and certain

reader of the Flattery/Schwartz book finishes with an empty feeling… where is evidence, from the authors' own experimentation…,
that *Peganum harmala* is even an entheogenic plant? Why must
the authors base their arguments on alleged correspondence with
ayahuasca, an unrelated potion from another continent,[39] which…
owes its entheogenic effects primarily to additives containing di-
methyltryptamine and other entheogenic compounds, and not
harmel-type alkaloids" (Ott 1993).

Even in smaller doses strict dietary observances must be met
when using MAOIs. For psychoactive purposes, fasting is often a
prerequisite for cultures that consume Ayahuasca, but none of this
is indicated in the Avestan or Vedic texts, in fact just the opposite.
For the add-mixture to Syrian rue in their hypothesized Persian
counterpart of the Ayahuasca, Flattery and Schwartz instead of
suggesting a potential DMT containing plant, speculate that the
current plant used for Haoma, Ephedra, was used. Ephedra is the
source of the medicines ephedrine and pseudoephedrine as well
as the harmful street drug, methamphetamine. This again would
seem to produce a state of being far from the blissful experience as
described in the *Vedas* and Avestan literature.

Flattery and Schwartz concluded that it was "therefore neither
likely that Ephedra was a substitute for sauma nor that it was sauma itself" (Flattery & Schwartz, 1989). Instead the coauthors suggested that the ephedrine and psuedoephedrine only achieved the
effects needed through their combination with Harmel. Flattery
considered Harmel to be the real *Haoma*, with Ephedra only being
the secondary ingredient in the mixture, directed at keeping the
devotee awake during the experience, a use ephedra, as a powerful
stimulant, would be well suited for.

Although the suggestion that Haoma may have been a mixture
of more than one plant does pan out to have historical accuracy -
as shall be discussed later, the idea that one of the ingredients was
Syrian rue does not. Harmala is clearly far too toxic, and the effects
of deliriousness, nausea, diarrhea, sensitivity to light and sound can
in no way be reconciled with the pleasant and blissful effects of

---

other psychedelics. Moreover, this author owns a shop that specializes in enthoegenic
plants, and has sold kilos of both B.caapi and Harmaline to numerous customers, none of
whom have used them independently of other plants.

39   A view also noted by Harri Nyberg in The Problem of the Aryans and the Soma: the
botanical evidence (Nyberg, 1995)

Soma and Haoma as described in the ancient hymns dedicated to the plant.

In "The Problem of the Aryans and the Soma: the botanical evidence," Harri Nyberg noted other aspects of *"Peganum harmala* which do not fit very well with the general picture of soma/haoma..."

> 1) if the use of *P. harmala* were an ancient Indo-Iranian custom, the areas where the plant commonly occurs seem to disagree with the proposed original or secondary homeland of the Indo-Aryans... 2) *P. harmala* is fairly common in India, and it is odd that knowledge of the original soma/haoma should have been lost there[40]...3) the harmaline alkaloid is the highest in the ripe seeds of *Peganum harmala* (2-7%), but there is no textual connection (Rgvedic or Avesta) between *soma/haoma* and plant seeds. Instead, it is repeatedly stated in the Rgveda that stems are identical to soma... 4) the alkaloids of *P. harmala* have a sedative, not stimulating effect. Therefore, in my opinion, the evidence of Flattery is inconclusive and *P. harmala* cannot be identified with the original *soma/haoma*. (Nyberg, 1995)

Still, despite the assertion that the *Peganum harmala* was Haoma and *bhang*, I liked Flattery and Schwartz's book immensely; it put together a great deal of information regarding the connections between Haoma and *bhang/mang* in the Persian literature that I otherwise was unfamiliar with at the time when I first read it, and for that I am greatly in debt to them. It is a considerably more worthy academic study on the subject than that of Wasson's.

---

40   This author will have to address an identical issue regarding the designation of cannabis as Soma.

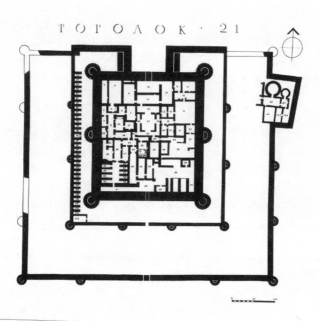

ТОГОЛОК · 21

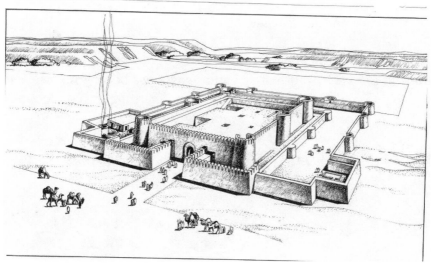

Reconstruction (by V. Antov) of a 4000 year old "Soma" Temple, discovered in the Bactria Margiana region by the Russian archaeologist Victor Sarianidi, who reported finds of cannabis, ephedra and poppy at the site, all of which were still growing in the region, alongside the implements used in the making of Soma. (Sarainidi, 2003).

— 3 —

SEEDS OF THE SOMA-HAOMA CULT; ANCIENT EUROPE

Harri Nyberg in his dismissal of Syrian rue, *Amanita muscaria* and other candidates for Soma-Haoma makes some very important points. First, the Soma plant was not indigenous to India, but brought by the Indo-European invaders; thus it is important that the candidate plant be found in the "original or secondary homeland of the Indo-Aryans," as well as fitting Vedic descriptions (Nyberg, 1995). Cannabis as we shall see, answers to both of these requirements.

With rich and eloquent language Wasson explained of the Aryans' Exodus into the Northwest of what is now Afghanistan and the valley of the Indus. "They were a warrior people, fighting with horse-drawn chariots; a grain growing people... a people whose language was Indo European, the Vedic tongue, the parent of classical Sanskrit, a collateral ancestor of our European language" (Wasson, 1970). What Wasson failed to mention was that 'they were a hemp growing, smoking and drinking people,' and as the archaeological evidence and pollen analysis show they had been doing so for millennia prior to the date in question.

Just as the Aryans brought Soma with them to India, the general consensus is that cannabis came to India through them as well. "By ca. 3000 BP, *Cannabis* had most likely migrated west and south over the Himalayas and into India, probably coming with nomads and traders over the trade routes that crossed the region" (Clarke & Fleming, 1998).

As shall be explained, the Indo-European use of the hemp went beyond that of just a fibre source, and the inhalation of cannabis fumes and consumption of cannabis laced drinks already had a long established ritual tradition amongst the Indo-Europeans by the time of the composition of the Vedic and Avestan texts.

The ancestors of the Indo-Europeans, are known as the Proto-Indo-Europeans and were located in Eastern Ukraine and Southern Russia, and, in relation, it is important to note that it is there we can find the oldest evidence of the use of cannabis for ritual purpose. The people of the pre-historic Eurasian plains have had an indigenous relationship with cannabis stretching back thousands of years before recorded history, as has been documented by both archaeological evidence and pollen analysis from ancient cultural sites.[1] Interestingly, this relationship is thought to have originated long before the development of agriculture, when cannabis was still a wild uncultivated plant. The late Harvard University Professor of Ethnobotany, Richard Evans Schultes speculated about early man's discovery of cannabis:

> Early man experimented with all plant materials that he could chew and could not have avoided discovering the properties of cannabis (marijuana), for in his quest for seeds and oil, he certainly ate the sticky tops of the plant. Upon eating hemp, the euphoric, ecstatic and hallucinatory aspects may have introduced man to the other-worldly plane from which emerged religious beliefs, perhaps even the concept of deity. The plant became accepted as a special gift of the gods, a sacred medium for communion with the spiritual world and as such it has remained in some cultures to the present. (Schultes, 1973)

As Europe has the oldest archaeological evidence of the use of cannabis for psychoactive purposes, it seems an appropriate place to begin our study. As explained by Israeli researcher Lumír Onder Hanuš, in his discussion of humanity's ancient relationship with cannabis and the development of the (endo)cannabinoid system in

---

1   Many have quoted the claim by Jan Kabelik, that "Cannabis was found by our archaeologists to have existed in central Europe in the Bylony Culture (7,000 years ago)" (Kabelik, 1955). But it is difficult to understand what Kebelik based this assumption upon, as in 1955 little data was available on the subject. Although more current pollen analysis indicates that Europeans may have been using hemp, much, much, earlier than previously believed.

both plant and man, the time span for European man's relationship with cannabis is considerably vast:

> Recent discoveries from Southern Moravia in the Czech Republic provide circumstantial evidence of the oldest use of hemp. The inhabitants of the two most famous eastern Gravettian settlements, the upper paleolithic sites of Pavlov and DolnıVstonice some 29,000 to 22,000 years ago were expert weavers. The Czech archeologist Klım unearthed clay fragments bearing a series of impressions from a zone that was radiocarbon dated to between 26,980 and 24,870 years ago.[2]
>
> According to Adovasio, the impressions were almost certainly created from fabrics woven of fibers from wild plants, such as nettle or wild hemp, that were preserved by accident.
>
> "Because the impressions of the Pavlov and Vestonice fibers are not of the highest resolution, it is presently only possible to specify which plants they may represent. In this case, it seems that nettle or, more remotely, wild hemp are possible choices whose presence in the area is attested to by pollen. If we had better impressions, it might be possible to specify with greater precision which of these two plant sources or some other plant source might be represented."[3]
>
> It is tempting to assume that this site may have produced the world's oldest archeological evidence of Cannabis use. (Hanuš, 2008)

Hanuš' time frame fits in well with Elizabeth Wayland Barber's, who is considered the foremost authority on ancient textiles and weaving, and believe that hemp was used "since 25,000 B.C. at least" (Barber, 1999). In relation to the time period suggested, it is interesting to note that other scientists (again like Hanu top researchers in the field of the study of cannibinoids), have postulated that plant based cannibinoids ingested by ancient Man, may have been responsible for pre-historic man's "Great Leap Forward."

---

2   Hanuš cites, Soffer O, Adovasio JM, Hyland DC, Klım B, Svoboda J., "Perishable technologies and the genesis of the Eastern Gravettian," *Anthropologie* 1998;36:43–68; Adovasio JM, Soffer O, Hyland DC, Klım B, Svoboda J. "*Textil, košıkrstvıá sıt v mladém paleolitu Moravy,*" (Textiles, Basketry, and Nets in Upper Paleolithic Moravia.) *Archeol Rozhledy* 1999;51:58–94; Adovasio JM,SofferO, HylandDC, Illingsworth JS, KlımB, Svoboda, J., "Perishable industries from DolnıVstonice I: New insights into the nature and origin of the Gravettian," *Archaeol Ethnol Anthropol Eurasia*, 2001;2:48–65; Soffer O, Adovasio JM, Hyland DC. "Perishable technologies and invisible people: Nets, baskets, and "venus" wear ca. 26,000 B.P." In: Purdy BA, editor. *Enduring records: The environmental and cultural heritage of wetlands*. Oxford, Oxbow Books; 2001. pp. 233–245.

3   Adovasio JM. personal private communication to L. Hanuš (December 15, 2006).

The study of cannabis has led to all sorts of new medical and scientific discoveries through investigations into the psychoactive and medicinal properties of the plant, found in plant ligands, that resemble the indigenous (endo)cannibinoids in the human body. The reason cannabis makes us high is that certain molecules in cannabis resins are able to mimic similar shaped molecules in the human body, and attach themselves to receptors in man's brain and body. How these similarities between cannibinoids found in hemp and those in man developed is a subject of much current speculation, and theories about some sort of coevoletionary development have become the topic of current scientific thought. Doctors John McPartland and Geoffery Guy, in their fascinating paper, "The Evolution of Cannabis and Coevolution with the Cannabis Receptor – A Hypothesis," postulate that a plant ligand, such as the cannibinoids of the hemp plant, "may exert sufficient selection pressure to maintain the gene for a receptor in an animal. If the plant ligand improves the fitness of the receptor by serving as a 'proto-medicine' or a performance-enhancing substance, the ligand-receptor association could be evolutionarily conserved" (McPartland & Guy, 2004).

> In a hunter-gatherer society, the ability of phytocannabinoids to improve smell, night vision, discern edge and enhance perception of colour would improve evolutionary fitness of our species. Evolutionary fitness essentially mirrors reproductive success, and phytocannabinoids enhance the sensation of touch and the sense of rhythm, two sensual responses that may lead to increased replication rates.
>
> Some authors have proposed that cannabis was the catalyst that synergised the emergence of syntactic language in Neolithic humans (McKenna, 1992).[4] Language, in turn, probably caused

---

4   Terence McKenna suggested that "No plant has been a continuous part of the human family longer than the hemp plant" (McKenna, 1992). As McKenna explained, at a very early stage cannabis "came to the attention of hunter-gatherers as a source of cordage for weaving and rope making. But unlike other cordage plants... cannabis is also psychoactive... the English vocabulary that refers to spoken discourse is often the same as that used to describe cordage-making and weaving. One weaves a story, or unravels an incident, or spins a yarn. We follow the thread of a story and stitch together an excuse. Lies are made from whole cloth, reality is an endless golden braid. Does this shared vocabulary reflect an ancient connection between the intoxicating hemp plant and the intellectual process that lay behind the art of weaving and storytelling? I suggest that such may well be the case" (McKenna, 1992).

what anthropologists call 'the great leap forward' in human behaviour, when humans suddenly crafted better tools out of new
materials (e.g. fishhooks from bone, spear handles from wood,
rope from hemp), developed art (e.g. painting, pottery, musical
instruments), began using boats, and evolved intricate social
(and religious) organizations. This rather abrupt transformation
occurred about 50,000 years ago... this recent burst of human
evolution has been described as epigenetic (beyond our genes)
– could it be due to the effect of plant ligands [i.e. plant based
cannibinoids]? (McPartland & Guy, 2004)

Archaeological evidence indicating ancient man's use of hemp
30,000 years ago fits within the time period for Man's evolutionary 'Great Leap Forward.' Considering that the location of the cannibinoid receptors are the greatest in the "cerebral cortex, stria-
tum, basal ganglia, cerebellum and thalamus... humans ingesting
phytocannibinoids"[5] could have had a considerable evolutionary
edge over non-cannabis using homo-sapiens.

It can be reasonably suggested that soon after agriculture started, if not at its very inception, the cultivation of cannabis began to
spread widely, carrying its name and its cult with it.[6] In his study
on the botanical history of cannabis and man's relationship with
the plant, Dr. Mark Merlin put forth that "perhaps hemp was one
of the original cultivated plants... [of] the progenitors of civilization" (Merlin, 1973). Merlin was not alone in this train of thought.
In his *The Dragons of Eden: Speculations on the Evolution of Human
Intelligence*, the late Carl Sagan[7] also speculated that early man may
have begun the agricultural age by first planting hemp. Sagan used
the pygmies from southwest Africa to demonstrate his hypothesis;
the pygmies had been basically hunters and gatherers until they be-

---

5   (McPartland & Guy, 2004).
6   The ultimate origins of cultivated and wild cannabis are hard to identify. Authorities on the history of botany and cultivation of plants point to two candidates for the
original seat of cultivation of cannabis and its botanical origins as a species, although they
may not be identical (Merlin, 1978). These regions are Northern China and Central Asia,
in the vicinity of Turkmenistan and Iran, as both of these regions have given evidence of
cannabis going back to Neolithic times, but whether ancient man took the plant from east
to West or visa versa, is at this point unknown. Feral populations of the plant may also be
an indication of botanical origin, and both these areas have feral cannabis going back far
back into prehistoric times.
7   After Sagan's death, Dr. Lester Grinspoon, author of *Marijuana Reconsidered*, revealed that his good friend Carl Sagan had been a copious user of cannabis during life.

gan planting hemp which they used for religious purposes (Sagan 1977).[8] More recently Entheobotanist Christian Ratsch explained:

> No other plant has been with humans as long as hemp. It is most certainly one of humanity's oldest cultural objects. Wherever it was known, it was considered a functional, healing, inebriating, and aphrodisiac plant. Through the centuries, myths have arisen about this mysterious plant and its divine powers. Entire generations have revered it as sacred.... The power of hemp has been praised in hymns and prayers. (Ratsch 1997)

It has been said that agriculture led to culture and perhaps in our cultivation of cannabis, the plant has in some way cultivated humanity? Archaeological evidence from 3,500 BC gives clear proof that European man was using cannabis as an incense and inebriant very early on.

> Hemp seeds, which could be identified as those of *Cannabis sativa*, were recovered in the Neolithic band ceramic... layers of Eisenbergin Thuringia, Germany... The layers were dated to around 5500 b.c.e. Hemp seeds have also been found in the excavations of other, somewhat more recent Neolithic layers, such as those in... Switzerland,... Austria,... and... Romania... These finds date from a period of peaceful, horticultural, pre-Indo-European cultures who venerated the Great Goddess[9]. The linear band ceramics that lend their name to this Stone Age cultural epoch are decorated with graphics representing the archetypi-

8   The Pygmies say "We have smoked hemp since the beginning of time... There are great fields of hemp in the kingdom of the dead... God gave hemp to the pygmies. Hemp keeps us healthy and happy" (Hallet & Pelle, 1975). The "beginning of time" to the Pygmies, likely means; since the pygmies' conception of time. A common effect noticed by novice users of cannabis is a differentiation in the usual experience of time; i.e., "It seemed like an hour but it was only a minute," or visa versa. Noticing a difference in the experience of linear time may well have played a role in the conception and formulation of the idea of time itself. (Likewise, a deeper awareness of seasonal time may have developed alongside agriculture and the necessity of keeping track of the growing season). Interestingly, both Father Time and the Grim Reaper hold a scythe, an ancient tool used for harvesting cannabis and whose imagery and name go back to the Scythian cult of the Dead, who used hemp for ritual ecstasy. In the ancient world, such an effect on the experience of time contributed immensely to marijuana's reputation for containing magical properties.

9   Pioneering cannabis researcher Sara Benetowa (aka, Sula Benet) believed that the origins of the ancient "cannabis cult" in the Near East could also be tied to the cult of the Great Goddess. "Taking into account the matriarchal element of Semitic culture, one is led to believe that Asia Minor was the original point of expansion for both the society based on the matriarchal circle, and the mass use of hashish" (Benetowa,1936).

cal motifs and patterns of hallucinatory or psychedelic themes...
(Ratsch, 2005)[10]

The late archaeologist Andrew Sherratt of the Ashmolean Museum, University of Oxford, pointed to the use of cannabis incenses at a gravesite of a group known as the Proto-Indo-Europeans, the Kurgans, who occupied what is now Romania 5,000 years ago. The discovery of a smoking-cup which contained remnants of charred hemp seeds at the site documents that 3,500 years before Christ humanity had already been using cannabis for religious purposes for millennia. This "clay vessel with carbonized seeds" provides the "earliest evidence for the burning of cannabis" (Anthony, 2008). From remnants of the charred hemp seeds we can see that the combustible (and psychoactive) parts of the plant – namely flowers and leaves – had been consumed and the carbonized hard shell like residue of the seeds left behind. This find fits in well with what we know about the area from which originated the linguistic roots of the term 'cannabis,' as well as the spread of cannabis around the ancient world. In *Incense and Poison Ordeals in the Ancient Orient*, Alan Godbey felt that in such immolation of psychoactive plants, we may find the Genesis of the concept of "divine plants":

> As to the antiquity and genesis of such practices, it is to be recognized...that they began when the primeval savage discovered that the smoke of his cavern fire sometimes produced queer physiological effects. First reverencing these moods of his fire, he was not long in discovering that they were manifested only when certain weeds or sticks were included in his stock of fuel. After finding out which ones were responsible, he took to praying to these kind gods for more beautiful visions of the unseen world, or for more fervid inspiration... So one group of "animate and divine plants," ... results from the most primitive empiricism, because of purely objective or concrete experiences... (Godbey, 1930)

The authors of *The Encyclopedia of Indo-European Culture* note that "Hemp has not only been recovered from sites in Romania but also from a Yamma burial at Gurbanesti (Maldova) where traces were found in a 'censer' (a shallow footed bowl believed to have been used in the burning of some aromatic substance). It has been

10   Ratsch's citings omitted.

found in a similar context from an early bronze age burial in the north Caucasus.... Ceramics were more elaborate than those of the Yamma culture and included, especially in female burials, low footed vessels interpreted as 'censers,' presumed to be used in rituals involving some narcotic substance such as hemp" (Mallory, et al., 1997). "It seems, therefore, that the practice of burning cannabis as a narcotic is a tradition which goes back in this area some five or six thousand years and was the focus of the social and religious rituals of the pastoral peoples of central Eurasia in prehistoric and early historic times" (Sherratt, 1995). "These 'censers' often highly decorated with 'sunburst' motifs, are widespread across the steppe region in the third millennium b.c. (extending at least from the Dnieper to the Yenisei) and may be part of a ritual complex. The censers also diffuse westward at this time in Romania, Hungary and further along the Danube" (Mallory, et al., 1997). In relation to burning psychoactive herbs in censers, Godbey noted:

> The immediate point is that a large portion of humanity has not yet hit upon the idea of a pipe, and when the powers of incense are desired, men resort to the primitive chimneyless hole or hut with the proper material to throw upon the fire. The Turkoman nomad smokes more economically by putting coals at the bottom of a tiny pit, dropping down some tobacco, and then taking a few sniffs at the top of the hole. But midway between such method and the pipe is the portable bowl or saucer for coals, upon which the proper fumigant can be sprinkled. (Godbey, 1930)

The *Oxford Illustrated History of Prehistoric Europe* reports that: "In France the ceramic repertoire included highly decorated small burners, with a very widespread distribution; it has been suggested that these may have been used for burning some aromatic or narcotic substance—again probably as the accompaniment to ritual and ceremony"[11] (Cunliffe, 2001).

> This pattern, surviving on the Steppes, [of burning cannabis in braziers] may be a model for temperate Europe before the introduction of alcoholic drinks. The archaeological record for Western Europe contains other examples of artefacts which find

---

11   "There are also reports of hemp fibers from objects recovered at Adaouste in the South of France (2000 BC)" (Sneader, 2005).

their most logical explanation as burners for narcotics, usually concealed under descriptions such as "incense cups"... A series of small vessels which appear as accessories in rich burials in the early Bronze Age of southern England (mid-second millennium BC)... are a prime candidate[12].... the realization is gradually dawning on archaeologists that such practices, widespread in the ethnographic record, are inherently likely to have existed in prehistoric times.... it seems entirely probable that in their practices and associated mythology the societies of aboriginal Europe were 'smoking cultures.' (Sherratt, 1995)

Sherratt suggested that the cannabis burning braziers eventually went to the wayside, and were replaced by a beverage, although he believes that cannabis use continued through this cultural shift. The "disappearance of ceramic braziers in northern and western

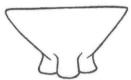

Fig. 3.1: "Pottery polypod bowls from eastern central Europe, probably used for burning hemp" (Rudgley, 1993).

Europe" was followed "by the appearance... of prominent forms of pottery drinking vessels. Corded-ware beakers and early bell-beakers are ornamented with impressions of twisted cord: if these are hemp fibres, then the decoration may indicate that their contents were connected with cannabis" (Sherratt, 1995). A view shared by other researchers: "As cannabis can also be infused, i.e., served as

---

12   "An earlier and more widespread set of examples of small braziers, dating to the earlier fourth millennium, pre-dates the appearance of highly decorated drinking vessels. These are... typical of the megalith-building cultures of southern and western France, and often found in association of megalith tombs. Their widespread occurrence and distinctly decorated appearance, as well as evidence of burning, make them comparable with the cannabis-braziers described above; and it is likely they were used in the ritual inhalation of some other narcotic, perhaps in the context of mortuary ritual and communication with the ancestors. It is significant that they are culturally associated with engravings inside megalith tombs... which have recently been discussed as possible examples of entoptic images produced under the influence of hallucinogens... Small pottery burners, typically decorated with animal protomes, are known from the earliest farming societies in the Balkans and suggest a long-standing interest in the symbolism of flame, smoke and perhaps, the burning of sweet-smelling or pharmacologically active substances..." (Sherratt, 1995).

a component in a drink, it has also been suggested that the spread of cord-(hemp?) decorated pottery from the steppe westward may also have been part of this same complex" (Mallory, et al., 1997).

> The corded decoration may hint that its contents contained more than the weak alcohol obtainable from forest honey and wild fruits, for if cannabis was smoked on the steppes it could have been infused by neighbouring drinking cultures. (Cunliffe, 2001)

The clay vessels with the cord impressions[13] are believed to be remnants of the Sredni Stog culture that flourished from about 4500 – 3500 BC in Eastern Europe. Sherratt suggested that the Sredni Stog used cannabis to make a "socially approved intoxicant," celebrating its significance "by imprinting it on their pottery" (Sherratt, 1987, 1997).[14] Ian Spencer Hornsey, Royal Society of Chemistry, in his *A History of Beer and Brewing*, expands on Sherratt's theory about the cord impressioned pottery:

> The joys of the native hemp plant (*Cannabis sativa*), which was ostensibly grown for its fibres had... been discovered by... ancient inhabitants of the Pontic steppe, the ...Sredeni Stog culture, who almost certainly incorporated it into a highly-intoxicating drink (part of the process, apparently, involved heating hemp leaves in butter)... this explains the reason for the ubiquitous thread-like cording, found on the first generation of Bell-beaker... Cord ornamation originated on the steppes in the Sredeni Stog and Pit-Grave cultures. (Hornsey, 2003)

Sherratt's educated speculation was that the steppe people were so taken with their cannabis infused beverages, and braziers that they indicated its importance by making impressions of the plant on the clay vessels which contained them. Further evidence of cannabis surviving in clay fragments have also been found in the vi-

---

13   "[C]ord decorations remained typical of northern Bronze Age pottery well into the second millennium BC. Hemp was probably ousted as a fibre, by wool, and as an intoxicant by better brews of alcohol, perhaps beer. It survived on the steppes, of course, and was passed on via Persians, to the Arabs" (Sherratt, 1997).

14   Sherratt noted that cord decoration of clay vessels was also being utilized in eastern Asia from considerably early Neolithic times (China's Sheng-wen horizon and Japan's Jomon: both terms identifying 'corded ware'). Importantly, the Sheng-wen horizon has been clearly associated with the early use of hemp, and awareness of the plant's narcotic properties has been documented (Hornsey, 2003).

cinity from the same time period, so this is a very realistic bit of speculation: "...clay shard showing impressions of what are thought to be *Cannabis* seeds from around 3000 BC were discovered during excavations at a Linearbandkeramik culture site north of the Black Sea" (Sneader, 2005). Sherratt believes that the cord impressions were a method of symbolizing the contents of the container on the container itself, and he compares this to the similar way Late Bronze Age Cypriot opium jugs were manufactured in the shape of poppy capsules.[15] In both cases, the vessels overtly advertised their contents. Hornsey was deeply taken by this train of thought: "I like these ideas immensely, and feel that the drink that the AOC beakers contained had a tremendous ritual and prestige value" (Hornsey, 2003). It should be noted that the "Corded Ware" culture has always been considered important in locating evidence of Indo-European origins.

Fig 3.2: Opium poppy capsule, and Poppy shaped vessel, Egypt Eighteenth Dynasty (Rudgley,1993).

The Sredeni Stog culture, are considered by many scholars to be the proto-Indo-Europeans, i.e the ancestors of Indo-Europeans culture. As Sherratt explains, "The Bronze Age kurgan cultures, have been plausibly associated with the first speakers of Indo-Iranian languages" (Sherratt, 1995). Moreover, their descendants extended "widely across the Eurasian steppes and affected a wide arc of cultures from Siberia to Northern India" (Sherratt, 1995). As we shall discuss in the following chapters, these nomadic groups had a profound role in spreading cannabis throughout the ancient

Fig 3.3: Corded-Ware Beaker.

world, thus many modern cannabis terms have an Indo-European origin. This is believed to have left traces in many modern terms for cannabis.

All the Indo-European languages have dialectically equivalent terms for hemp: Anglo-Saxon *henep*,... Middle English *hemp*,

---

15   The first to make this suggestion was Robert Merillees in 1962, and the idea was "since confirmed by chromatographic analysis of their residues" (Sherratt, 1995).

Danish and Middle Low German *hennep,* Icalandic *hampr,* Swedish *hampa,* German *hanf,* Polish *konop,* Bohemeian *konope,* Old
Bulgarian and Russian *konoplya,* Lithuanian *canapés,* Lettish *ke-
nepa,* Irish *canaib,* Persian *qinnab,* Greek *kannabis,* Latin *cannabis,* French *chanvre,* and Sanskrit *cana.* An earlier anthropologist,
Berthold Laufer, believed that the Indo-Eoropean term for hemp
was a loan word from ancient Finno-Ugrian and Turkic stocks
of north central Eurasia; but "Scythian," by some etymologists
(doubtless influenced by a earlier mention in Herodotus), has also
been the proposed donor of the term in several Indo-European
languages independently. However, since the appropriate linguistic rules for sound-change appear to have been followed, the word
would seem very old in Indo-European, rather than multiply borrowed. Again if as the anthropologist Sula Benet proposes, the
cannabis terms are borrowed from a Semitic language, then there
is the problem of a seemingly pan-Indo-European term diffused
from ancient northern Eurasia. And cannabis, of course grows
wild in north central Eurasia, whence the Indo-Europeans came.
That the terms are manifest dialectic equivalents would constitute the solidest possible evidence for the antiquity of the word,
since the undivided Neolithic Indo-Europeans began to migrate
(spreading prehistorically all the way from Ireland to Ceylon) and
to break up dialectically in the early Bronze Age. (La Barre, 1980)

As noted by La Barre, it has been suggested that the very name of
cannabis itself came into the Indo-European language from the ancient Finno-Ugric language family, comprising Finnish, Estonian,
Hungarian and related languages. Words such as *kanapish* for *cannabis* occur in Finno-Ugrian languages. (Source of Rus. *konoplja,*
Pers. *kanab,* Lith. *kanapes*). Some scholars believe that the original
homeland of the Sredeni Stog, Ukraine, is also the source of the
Finno-Ugric language. The Finnish academic Kalevi Wiik believes
that the earliest Finno-Ugric speakers and their languages originated in the territory of modern Ukraine (the so-called "Ukrainian
refuge") during the last glacial period when the whole of northern
Europe was covered with ice.

Considering that cannabis is thought to have been spread around
much of the ancient world by the later descendants of the Sredeni
Stog, the Scythians, whose mobility was due to their early use of the
horse, it is also of interest to note that besides their use of cannabis,
the Scythians may have also inherited their horsemanship from the

Sredeni Stog, and this also may be related to their use of cannabis. As Mark Merlin, Professor of Botany at the University of Hawai'i has noted:

> The crucial relationship between horse and human rider origi-
> nated in the Sredni Stog culture which flourished in the Ukraine
> 6,000 years ago... The origin of horse riding was the first signifi-
> cant innovation in human land transport predating the invention
> of the wheel, and hemp fibers may have played an important role
> in this crucial invention of horse riding. (Merlin, 2003)

In the *Discover* article "First to Ride," (the appropriately named) William Speed Weed, interviews archaeologist Sandra Olsen, who also makes reference to the utilization of hemp in the domestica-tion of the horse, a pivotal and evolutionary step for ancient man:

> "Prior to horseback riding, most people carried all their cargo on
> their shoulders, or they were restricted to using boats along rivers
> and coastlines," says Olsen, an archaeologist at the Carnegie Mu-
> seum of Natural History in Pittsburgh. "Horses were swift of foot,
> could easily support one or two human passengers, carry heavy
> loads, and survive on very poor quality vegetation or fodder. They
> were our first form of rapid transit."
> "They probably had a simple bridle made of hide or hemp," she
> says, "drawing a little schematic of a rope looped around the front
> teeth of a horse's skull. They might also have had lassos, whips,
> tethers, and hobbles of the same material." (Weed, 2002)

This early use of the horse is the probable reason that the an-cient cannabis cult spread throughout ancient Europe in this early time period. Concievably, with the spread of cannabis came a reli-gious cosmology often based around the plant itself. Ethnobotanist Christian Ratsch has contributed greatly to the study of cannabis in the ancient word, as this multilingual scholar has brought in-formation and references from a variety of non-English European sources to the likes of linguistically challenged solely English speak-ing researchers such as this author. Referring to German authori-ties, Ratsch states that in ancient Germanic culture cannabis was used in honour of the Goddess Freya as both a ritual inebriant and an aphrodisiac and that the harvesting of the plant was connected

with an erotic high festival.[16] "Hemp, sacred to her, was used to promote desire, fertility and health in humans" (Ratsch, 2001). It was
believed that Freya lived as a fertile force in the plant's feminine
flowers and by ingesting them one became influenced by this divine
force"[17] (Ratsch 2001, 2005). This view is supported by the archaeological discovery of cannabis in a pre-historic German tomb.[18]

> Remnants of hemp dating from prehistoric times were discov-
> ered in 1896 in northern Europe when the German archaeolo-
> gist, Hermann Busse opened a tomb containing a funerary urn
> at Wilmersdorf (Brandenburg). The vessel in question contained
> sand in which were mixed remnants of plants. It dated from the
> 5th century BC. The botanist, Ludwig Wittmaack (1839-1929),
> was able to find among this plant debris fragments of the seed and
> pericarp of *Cannabis sativa L.* At the session of the Berlin Soci-
> ety for Anthropology, Ethnology and Prehistory on May 15, 1897,
> Busse presented a report on his discovery and drew the conclu-
> sion that hemp had already been known in northern Europe in
> prehistoric times… one must agree with C. Hartwich that hemp

16   Ripe cannabis can have an intoxicating effect, "…the fresh plant also possesses
an extremely potent, unpleasant, often intoxicating scent, and it is known that dizziness,
headache and even a kind of drunkenness frequently results if a person spends too much
time in a blooming hemp field" (Martius, 1855/1996).
17   Ratsch also writes that the Teutonic Goddess Ostara's spring worship involved a
meal of a sacred hare, washed down with hemp beers, followed by a public orgy! According to many researchers, the modern holiday Easter takes its name from this Germanic
Goddess. As Ratsch laments "How wonderful it would be to celebrate an old Germanic
Easter! A festival of erotic inebriation, a festival of joy, of nature, of hemp,… Into the arms
of the Love Goddess with hemp!" (Ratsch, 2001)
18   The use of cannabis by the cult of Freya, may have spanned more than a thousand years, as indicated by later archaeological finds. "The richest archaeological material
from Viking times in Norway is the Oseberg find. Two women were buried in a mound in
the county of Vestfold around the year 850 in a splendid ship with ample equipment. The
find includes a small piece of hempen material, the use of which has not been determined,
but even more interesting is the fact that four seeds of *Cannabis sativa* were also found.
One of these seeds was discovered in a small leather pouch. The well respected archaeologist, Anne Stine Ingstad…, is… among many historians who believe the younger of
the two buried women – usually called the Oseberg Queen – was a priestess of the great
Norse goddess Freya…. Ingstad sees the presence of the Cannabis seed in the (talismanic)
pouch as an indication of possible ritual use of cannabis as an intoxicant in pre-Christian
Scandinavia… It is… reasonable to suppose a cultural connection to Cannabis seeds that
were placed in tombs in central Europe more than a thousand years previously. Worth noting in connection with the Oseberg find is the lack of ropes and textiles made from hemp.
This is one reason for suggesting a ritual use for the Cannabis seeds. The women in the
Oseberg ship had clothes made from flax, wool, silk and nettle, but not from hemp. The
ropes were made from lime fibres in spite of the better quality of hemp rope" (Vindheim,
2002).

was already employed in northern Europe at the same time that it was by the Chinese and the Scythians for food and pleasure. (Reininger, 1941)

Celtic use of cannabis has also been identified through pollen analysis of a bowl from a rich woman's grave of the late Hallstatt Period at Niedererlbach, Bavaria (Rosch, 2005).[19] The authors of *The Encyclopedia of Indo-European Culture* likewise note that "hemp has... been discovered in an iron age contexts in western Europe, e.g. a Hallstatt burial, presumably Celtic, at Hochdorf in Germany" (Mallory et al., 1997). Other Celtic evidence of cannabis is evidenced by "reports of hemp fibres from objects recovered at... St. Andrews in Scotland (800 BC)" (Sneader, 2005). In relation to this study, it is interesting to note that in *Ploughing the Clouds*, Peter Lamborn Wilson has suggested a Celtic Soma, but in this case he has been taken in by the work of R. Gordon Wasson, and unconvincingly tries to identify the use of the *Amanita muscaria* in Western Europe.

Cannabis may also have been a sacred plant of the Druids. According to ancient literature the most prized plant of the Gallic Druids was known under the name verbena, and this has generally been interpreted as the plant, *vervain*. But due to the fact *vervain* fills little of the ancient attributes of the magical *verbena*, its identity has been called into question. Christian Ratsch comments that "An Old High German Gloss" stated that "vervain, which is called *hanaf*" (*hanaf* being German for *Hemp*). "The Gauls thus used the Germanic word for hemp to refer to the magical "vervain" of the Druids. There is archaeological and ethno-historical evidence for a Gallic-Celtic use of hemp as a fumigant"[20] (Ratsch, 2001).

As the authors of the exhaustive *Encyclopedia of Indo-European Culture* have noted, "There are... at least three chronological horizons to which the spread of hemp might be ascribed: the early distribution of hemp across Europe; during the Neolithic c5000 b.c. or earlier[21]; a later spread of hemp for presumably narcotic purposes

---

19   Rosch, Manfred, "Pollen analysis of the contents of excavated vessels—direct archaeobotanical evidence of beverages" in the journal, *Vegetation History and Archaeobotany,* Volume 14, Number 3 / August, 2005

20   Ratsch quotes Jean Markale, author of *Die Druiden: Gesellschaft und Gotter der Kelten*, in realtion to Druidic use of cannabis incense, who noted that "With great likelihood, it can be assumed the Druids... availed themselves of it" (Markale, 1989).

21   As noted at the start of the chapter, this may have been as early as 29,000 BC.

around 3000 b.c.; a still later spread, or, at least, re-emergence of hemp in the context of textiles during the first millennium b.c...." (Mallory, et al., 1997). Indeed, it can clearly be shown that the use of cannabis in Europe for magical or religious properties goes much further back than recorded history and it was obviously an integral part of pre-historic and pre-Christian European culture.

What is most interesting is that there are growing indications that the corded-ware beaker culture of Europe, as the use of its cannabis beverage grew in popularity and spread into parts of Asia, later developed into the Soma Cult of the Hindu Vedic literature and the Haoma cult of the Persian *Avesta*. Both these Cults have their origin in an earlier Indo-European tradition.

> ...[T]he Aryans had an oblation... called Soma, which was drunk by the participants and fed to the gods. They had large wooden vats near-by in which they brewed Soma, a sap beaten out of a plant (probably cannabis) gathered in the mountains. They filtered the brewed sap through a woolen cloth and mixed it with honey, milk, curds and barley... This mix was put in jars, from which they ladled the meath (mead) into the fire or into beakers bowls and cups. Beakers are frequently mentioned, and a significant feature of megalithic burials along the Atlantic coast of Europe and in the Balkans, was beakers. (Copeland, 2007)

It is widely believed that a sort of mini-ice age, or "global-cooling" around 2000 B.C. resulted in a southward migration of the Indo-Europeans (Hsü, 1998). Interestingly, the Avestan texts have left an indication of this, in the story of Yima, whose father was the first to press the sacred Haoma, while Yima was said to have initiated the rite amongst his people. In the *Vendidad* account of the Aryan 'deluge' the god Ahura Mazda came to Yima, whom he had given a golden plough to cultivate the land, and warns him of the coming cold threat:

> "O splendid Yima, towards the sacred Aryan land will rush evil as a severe fatal winter; evil will rush as thick snow flakes falling in increased depth. From the three directions will wild and ferocious animals attack, arriving from the most dreadful sites."
>
> "Before this winter, any snow that fell would melt and convey the water away. Now the snow will not melt (but form the Polar

ice cap). In this place, O Yima the corporeal world will be damaged. Before in this seed land the grass was so soft the footprint of even a small animal could be observed. Now, there will be no footprints discernible at all (on the packed sheets of hard ice that will form)." (*Vendidad*, Fargard 2)

The respected Vedic scholar Lokmanya Tilak studied both the *Vedas* and the *Vendidad* in trying to understand the origins of the Aryan ancestors of his culture. Based on his knowledge of astronomy and the descriptions of certain star constellations that the Aryans saw, described in the *Vedas*, Tilak concluded that the ancient home was in the North Pole, which may be a little too far north, but still close enough to the realms of Russia and the areas we are dealing with. Tilak, felt the Vendidad account above contained the most ancient history of mankind, since it properly explained the origins and reasons for the migrations of the Aryans.

Thus, both historical and mythical accounts more or less agree and horse riding, cannabis consuming Europeans, due to the threat of ice and snow, began their southward migration, and in so doing carried the seeds of the longest established spiritual tradition in the history of humanity, the drinking of Soma-Haoma. Interestingly, it has been suggested that the names Soma-haoma themselves may have originated from this region and were connected with the term for cannabis. The "root as the Avestan *haoma* and Indic soma...[is] *konoplja*, [Rus.] 'cannabis hemp'" (Woods, et al., 2006).

Images of the Vedic God Soma, here personified as the moon travelling through the night sky.

— 4 —

SOMA: A CANNABIS CONCOCTION

Maintaining a theory that fits in well with the view of this author, Andrew Sherratt suggested that the Indo-European Soma cult developed out of the proto-Indo-European culture which was known to have burned cannabis and other plants in braziers.[1] Sherratt suggests that the cannabis burning proto-Indo-Europeans came into contact with wine consuming cultures that were already present in the mid-East, and one of the results of the cultural exchange was the development of the Haoma/Soma beverages. "Chewing, sniffing or smoking thus seems to have been the original modes of ingestion; the use of liquid media for consuming psychoactive substances in many areas of the world can be argued to reflect practices originally associated with alcoholic drinks"[2] (Sherratt, 1995).

> The Genesis of the [Soma/Haoma] tradition… would thus have taken place in the context of an interaction between oasis communities – probably familiar with alcohol, since wine has been prepared in Western Iran since the fourth millennia – and steppe and desert tribes which were part of the expanding pastoralist complex…. The ritual plant products traditionally consumed on the steppes in braziers would now have been prepared as a euphoriant or inebriant drink – including the substance later known as haoma…. It was from this area, at some time during the second millennium, that Aryan speaking groups infiltrated into northern India, to assimilate the Dravidian-speaking populations of the collapsed Indus civilization, and introducing the religious

[1]   A practice which started at the latest around 3,500 BC.
[2]   "…[T]he finding of the fire-water, even in a moderate percentage of alcohol, was as momentous as the finding of fire itself." (Harris, 1927)

ideas described in the Rig Veda. It seems likely, therefore, that the drink described as soma involved the infusion of various plant products known earlier on the steppes, and there is no single answer to the *soma* question." (Sherratt, 1995)

Likely due to European cultural prejudice against the use of cannabis in India, the idea of a hemp preparation was originally rejected outright by Western Historians researching the identity of the Soma in the 19th century, such as Regel (1884). Regardless of this initial rejection this suggestion re-emerged a few years later with George W. Brown`s *Researches in Oriental History*:

> What was the Haoma or Homa, the production of the moon-plant, growing in those regions of Asia too far north for the successful growing of the grape, and yet yielding such intoxicating properties? It is known in the medical books as *Apocynum Cannabinum*, and belongs to the Indian Hemp family, *Cannabis Indica* being an official preparation from it. It is now known in India as *bhang*, and is popularly known with us as *hashish*, the stimulating and intoxicating effects of which are well known to physicians. The extract from its young and tender top has a fragrant odour, and a warm bitterish and acrid taste.[3]
>
> The adoration paid to the prepared juice of this plant, and its use on sacrificial occasions, and the drinking of it... can best be appreciated by members of the medical profession who have personally experienced its exhilarating effects on some fellow student, who was elevated by his own estimation, on a high pedestal and was capable of taking in all that has been, is, and may be in the material universe.
>
> ....Haoma ...an intoxicating beverage, prepared from the green stalks of the moon-plant... *Cannabis Indica*, or Indian hemp... was tasted by the priests on sacrificial occasions, whilst hymns were sung in its praise. Its action was that of hashish. It produced intoxication and stimulation of the senses, which were taken for inspiration. (Brown, 1890)

An 1895 edition of *Folklore* (Jacobs, et al., 1895) contains an article "Argument that the Soma plant was bhang (a preparation of hemp)" which I was unfortunately unable to track down. Edward Albert Gait refers to "hemp (Soma) in Vedic times" (Gait, 1902),

---

3   Ironically, this book, the earliest I could find identifying cannabis as Soma, was 420 pages long.

but it is unclear what he based this assertion on. In 1921 an article by Braja Lal Mukherjee, "The Soma Plant," appeared in the *Journal of the Royal Asiatic Society* (which was a response to an earlier paper on the identity of Soma) also put forth a theory presenting cannabis, "*bhang*," as a serious candidate for the Soma.[4]

Mukherjee based much of his assertion on references in the *Satapatha Brahmana* that refer to a plant "*usana*" from which Soma is made, claiming this *usana* was a name of cannabis. As Mukherjee explained, the "u" in *usana* was a prefix carryover from the Kiratas, with whom Soma originated, and when the "u" is dropped you return to one of the original Sanskrit names for cannabis '*sana*.' "The English word hemp, Greek kanna and Latin canna-(bis) are the same as Sana" (Ray, 1948). "The name Sana is derived from Sana, the true hemp. It is the same word as Gk. Kanna from which the Latin name of the plant, *Cannabis sativa* is derived" (Chatterjee, 1943). As Muller and Oldenberg noted of the term *sana* in their *Vedic Hymns*:

> The occurrence of the word *sana* is of importance as showing how early a time the Aryans of India were acquainted with the uses and name of hemp. Our word hemp, the A.S. haenep, the old Norse hanp-r, are all borrowed from Latin cannabis, which like other borrowed words, has undergone the regular changes required by Grimm's law in Low-German, and also in High-German, hanaf. The Slavonic nations seem to have borrowed their word for hemp (Lith.kannape) from the Goths, the Celtic nations (Irish cannib) from the Romans... The Latin cannabis is borrowed from the Greek, and the Greeks... most likely adopted the word from the Aryan Thracians and the Scythians. *KavvaBis* [sic, *kannabis*] being a foreign word, it would be useless to attempt an explanation of the final element bis, which is added to *sana*, the Sanskrit word for hemp[5]... Certain it is that the main element in the name of hemp was the same among the settlers in

---

4   See Appendix A.

5   More current views consider the term 'bis' as designating, 2, in regards to the two sexes of cannabis. This likely came about through the use of *kanna, sana*, to identify other fiber plants, and to distinguish cannabis from them. "The history of the word *kavvaBis* [kannabis] must be kept distinct from that of the Greek *kavva* or *kava* [i.e *kanna, kana*], reed... This word *kava* may be the same as the Sanskrit *sana*, only with the difference, that it has retained as common property by Greeks and Indians before they separated, and was applied differently later by the one and the other" (Muller & Oldenberg, 1892, 2001).

Northern India, and among the Thracians and Scythians through whom the Greeks first became acquainted with hemp. (Muller & Oldenberg, 1892, 2001)

The *Satapatha Brahmana*, which records the name '*usana*' as the main component of the Soma beverage, is thought to have been composed during the first half of the 1st millennium B.C., belonging to the Brahamic period of Vedic Sanskrit. The group of texts to which it belongs, the Brahmanas are generally described as occupying an intermediate position, in chronology, character, language, and mythology, between the Vedic hymns, and the Indian epic poems and *Puranas*. The *Satapatha Brahmana* is a very important text, containing accounts of Creation, the Deluge of Manu (Great Flood), as well as, in great detail, the preparation of altars, ceremonial objects, ritual recitations, and the Soma libation, along with the symbolic attributes of every aspect of the rituals. Verses 3.4.3.13 and 4.2.5.15 of the Madyhyandina recension of the *Satapatha Brahmana* refer to the plant called "*usana*" which can clearly be identified as cannabis, and from which Soma is made.

> Soma is a God, since Soma (the moon) is in the sky. 'Soma, forsooth, was Vrita; his body is the same as the mountains and rocks: thereon grows the plant Usana,'—so said Svetateketu Auddalaki 'they fetch it hither and press it; and by means of the consecration and the Upasads, by the Tanunaptra and the strengthening they make it into Soma.' And in like manner does he now make it into Soma by means of consecration and the Upasads, by the Tanunaptra and the strengthening.[6]
>
> — *Satapatha Brahmana*, 3.4.3.13

> Thereupon he proceeds with (the offering of) the cakes of the Soma feast. Now Soma is a god, for Soma was in the heaven;--Soma forsooth, was Vritra; the mountain and stones are his body: thereon grows that plant called Usana, said Svetateketu Auddalaki; that they bring hither and press....'. when he proceeds with (the offering of) Soma feast cakes, he puts sap into it: thus it becomes Soma for him.
>
> They all belong to Indra; for Indra is the deity of the sacrifice: that is why they all belong to Indra.
>
> — *Satapatha Brahmana*, 4.2.5.15-17

---

6   Translated from the Sanskrit by Julius Eggeling (1885)

These references in the *Satapatha Brahmana* to *usana*, are the clearest textual identification of the plant from which Soma was originally made in the whole of Sanskrit literature. That more notice has not been paid to this clear identification of Soma with cannabis, other than a few passing references, is evidence of the over enthusiasm of researchers, such as Wasson, for their different candidates, rather than for the facts at hand.

As the *Satapatha Brahmana* refers to Indra as the deity of the Soma sacrifice, in relation to the word 'usana' and 'sana' for cannabis, it is important to note *The Calcutta Journal of Medicine* recorded "The Sanskrit name of Cannabis Sativa is Indrasana" (Sircar, 1906). Likely the name Indrasana came about through these references in the *Satapatha Brahmana* and this name as a designation for cannabis has been widely acknowledged. "The hemp plant in Sanskrit is referred to as bhang and Indrasana. In the east, it had been known as a fibre plant from pre-historic times" (Roy & Rizvi, 1986). "Ganja or Indian hemp (*Cannabis sativa*)... is generally taken in the form of *bhanga* (also called *Indrasana* or *Vijaya*), a drink made from its flowers" (Shukla, 1994). "Indrasana a favourite drink of Indra (the king of gods)" (Fernandez, 1894). In *Pharmacographia Indica* we read:

> Indrasana, 'Indra's hemp.' is described in the Atharvaveda as a protector, and it is supplicated to protect all animals and properties. The gods are said to have three times created this herb (oshadhi). Indra has given it a thousand eyes, and conferred on it the property of driving away all disease and killing all monsters; it is praised as the best of remedies, and is worn as a precious talisman... (Dymock, et al., 1893)

Thus Indrasana has medicinal, spiritual and fibrous properties. Interestingly, as we shall discuss later, all these same attributes are applied to Soma. Likely due to such connections regarding hemp, Indra and "soma, the favorite drink of the God Indra, which was offered to the mortal so that they might find happiness," C. Stefanis, C.Ballas and D. Madianou concurred that the sacred elixir "contained cannabis" (Stefanis, et al., 1975; 1977).

As well, Murkherjee noted the use of the terms similar to "Soma" in the names for cannabis in the languages of the Tibetans, "somarasta": and the Tanguts, "dschoma." A connection that has been noted by a variety of other sources; "[T]he Tibetan word for Cannabis and its drug products is So.Ma.Ra.Dza. This appears to be a direct borrowing from the Sanskrit soma-raja (Eng.: 'King soma,' 'Royal soma'). The term soma-raja is glossed as 'king soma, the moon'[7] in Monier-Williams' Sanskrit dictionary although the *Rig Veda*, in its hymns of praise to the drug, refers to it frequently as 'King soma' (8.48.8, 8.79.8 etc.)" (Crowley, 1996). As Helsinki researcher Pentti Aalto has also noted: "...[I]n Tibetan the hemp is, according to the lexica, *so ma, so ma raja* or *zla ba* (=Moon, since in India Soma as a god was identified with the Moon)... [and] other synomonous names,... root shoot of the moon... 'the king (?) of the Moon'" (Aalto, 1998). *The Rangjung Yeshe Tibetan-English Dharma Dictionary* (2003) lists the following cannabis and other potentially related words under '*so ma*':

> *so ma* – genuine, naturalness, no bias in its naturalness... new, climbing plant whose juice was offered to the gods and Hindus worshipped for intoxicating qualities, fresh, freshness [JV]
> *so ma* – hemp; freshness; fresh, freshness Syn naturalness, [present awareness], brand new.
> *so ma ra tsa'i ngan thag* – hashish [JV]
> *so ma ra rtsa* – hemp [JV]
> *so ma ra tsha* – hemp, marijuana, flax, jute [IW]
> *so ma ra dza* – flax cannabis sativa l. [JV]
> *so ma rwa dza* – datura stramonium l. [JV] [likely included through the sense of its intoxicating properties]
> *so mang[8] skyes* – Indra [IW]
> *so mang bu* – Indra [IW]

Mukherjee also notes that Soma's "habitat is Mujavan." 'The name is important in the light of the search for good Soma, for example on the Mūjavant mountain, which appears in Mbh, with popular etymology, as Muñjavant" (Witzel, 1999). The RgVeda de-

---

7   As Chakraberty notes in the *Vedas*, Soma refers to the "Soma drink (Av. Haoma), Soma plant and Soma as the moon, though entirely separate" (Chakraberty, 1944). Thus Soma is both a god and a plant, but the moon also was considered the celestial vessel of Soma from which the gods drank from in the heavens, its waning replenished by the same sun which caused the plant Soma to grow, thus connecting the symbolism of all three, plant, moon and god.
8   It would be a stretch to suggest a connection, but it is curious that '*mang*' was a later Pahvali translation of the Avestan '*bhang*,' meaning cannabis.

scribes Soma explicitly as *parvatiivrdh* or 'mountain grown.' It uses the term Soma *Maujavata*, 'the Soma from Mujavat.'

> The best Soma, maujavata-, is supposed to come from the mūjavant mountain, "having mūja/Mūja (people)." This can be compared to Avestan, Muža... the present name Munjân, an area north of the Hindukush, perhaps even the modern Turkish name Muz Tagh Ata 'Ice Mountain-Father' for the mountain range dividing Tajikistan and China (Hsinkiang). (Witzel, 1999)

The Hindu-Kush Mountains identified as being near the source of the "best Soma" are also thought to be the homeland of the resinous *Cannabis indica*.

Another point made by Mukherjee is that "Soma is called Amsu (a ray) or that which is full of rays or soft hairs" and in relation it is interesting to note that the glandular hairs which cover ripe cannabis, take their name *Trichomes*, from the Greek meaning "growth of hair."

Besides the above points, Mukherjee, who was of Indian descent, noted the long Hindu history regarding the sanctity of the cannabis beverage *bhang*, its similar preparation to Soma, its use in the worship of Shiva[9] and also in that of his counterpart Durga, where it still appears in the Soma sacrifice.[10]

As well this early 20th century Indian scholar also noted the comparative medical qualities of both *bhang* and Soma (an issue regarding Soma, which Wasson notably failed to identify with the Fly agaric). Finally, like numerous later researchers Mukherjee noted the obvious parallels between ancient descriptions of the preparation of the Soma and the traditional preparation of *bhang*. As we shall show, numerous other researchers have reached this same conclusion about the identification of Soma with cannabis for similar reasons.

Curiously, Wendy Doniger O'Flaherty (whose contribution to Wasson's *Soma: Divine Mushroom of Immortality*, was the best part of that book), felt that Mukherjee's theory on cannabis and Soma was a "strange argument, combining linguistic reasoning with the purest twaddle" (Doniger-O'Flaherty, 1968).[11] One is

---

9   The connections between Indra and Soma, and Shiva and *bhang* (hemp) are quite profound – See Chapter 18.
10   . In relation to the Soma cakes, made from the sana [hemp] (*Satapatha Brahmana* 4.2.5.15-17), as will be noted later, these are similar to the *bhang* balls, little round desserts prepared with the cannabis beverage bhang.
11   Doniger O'Flaherty provided an excellent resource for the different plant candi-

left wondering what exactly Doniger O'Flaherty thought Wasson based his theory on? (Out of respect for Wasson's contributions to the study of psychoactive substances and religion, this author will refrain from the obvious retorts, and instead, with clearer scholarship, put Wasson's Soma-Amanita theory to rest once and for all).

In 1939 Joges Candra Ray developed more on Mukherje's work noting that Soma is actually called *bhang* in the *Rig Veda* (IX: 61:13)[12] and from ancient descriptions that the Soma sacrifice "was a feast and the drink added hilarity; bhang has been used on similar occasions" (Ray, 1939). "The method of preparation of Soma and Bhang is the same, and the effects of the drink on the consumer remarkably agree" (Ray, 1939). Ray also pointed out that both Soma and *bhang* were annual plants, "coming up at the beginning of the rainy season" (Ray, 1939).[13] As Ray expressed:

---

dates for Soma and did in all fairness, identify a number of sources that indicated cannabis as a candidate. "In 1922 Wilhelm Hauer published a work that lent a kind of peripheral support to the *bhang* theory, [Wilhelm, 1922] for he referred to the Soma cult as the most highly developed form of the use of narcotics to induce ecstasy, calling particular attention to the late Vedic hymn (X 136) that describes a long haired sage who drinks poison with Rudra. Hauer believed that Soma was the most important toxic means of inducing ecstasy, but not the only such means, and he suggested that the Vedic references might be traces of primitive ecstatic hallucination caused by certain plants"(Doniger O'Flaherty, 1968). Hauer hints that these original hallucinogens may have been smoked with the closing comment that "every time we light up a good cigar we experience a faint reflection of the splendour of the rapture of the primeval ecstatic" (Hauer, 1922). A view that fits well with that of Sherratt, who suggested that plants which had been burnt on the Steppes, later became the ingredients of the Soma (Sherratt, 1995).

Interestingly, Hauer mentions Rudra, a Vedic god who shares many features with Indra the Lord of Soma and Shiva the Lord of *Bhang* (Hemp), the latter whose devotees have continued the spiritual tradition of smoking and drinking cannabis preparations into the modern age (see Chapter 18). Both Shiva and Rudra are viewed as the same personality in a number of Hindu traditions. In the *Rig Veda*, Rudra plays a lower role of one of the intermediate level gods (*antariksha devata*) and he is celebrated in only a few hymns. Rudra is described as fierce, armed with bow and arrows, endowed with strong arms, lustrous body and indicating his Aryan roots, flowing golden hair. Rudra is not purely benefic like other Rig Vedic gods, but he is not totally malevolent either. Double natured Rudra punishes and at the same time rescues his devotees from trouble. By the time that the Ramayana was written (400BC), the name *Rudra* is taken as a synonym for Shiva and the two names are used interchangeably. In the Puranas, he becomes one of the Trinity and is the destroyer. He is the Lord of the universe, the cosmic dancer, the Supreme yogi and master of all yogis.

12   It is hard to find an English translation that refers to hemp in this passage, most choose the original meaning of the word as "break," but the context is clearly in the context of the preparation of the Haoma, and the term appears as an epithet of Soma. This etymological relationship is discussed more fully in Chapter 15

13   As quoted in (Merlin, 1972).

The effects of Soma drink are exactly the same as those of Bhang. Soma used to be drunk between eating of food[14] (IX.51.3).It is nourishing when taken with milk and food[15] (IX.52.1) It is exhilarating (VIII.48), exciting (II.41.40) and intoxicating (IX.68.3; 69.3). It stimulates the voice and impels the flow of words (IX.95.2: 101.6). It awakens eager thought (V.47.3), and excites poetic imagination[16] (IX.67.13). It induces sleep (IX.69.3), and desire for women[17] (IV.67.10-12). It bestows fertility (IX.60.4: 74.5). It cures diseases (VIII.48.5) and was believe to prolong life (VIII.48.5). None but the strong can tolerate it (IX.53.3; 81.1)... It was drunk before military engagement[18] (IX.61.13; 85.12) and after victory (IX.101.1), for which Indra's favour was prayed for.[19] (Ray, 1939)[20]

In regards to the claims Soma "cures diseases," as well as references recording that Soma heals "the blind and the lame" (RV.10.25.11) it should be noted that, although not the intent of this study to document, cannabis has been used up until modern times for the treat-

---

14   One of the medical effects of cannabis is increased appetite, i.e.,the "munchies."
15   If seeded cannabis buds were used, it would in fact be "nourishing" as hemp seeds are one of the most complete sources of the important omega oils, and for this reason they have become a popular Health food in the 21st century.
16   Comparatively: "The Hindu poet of Shiva, the Great Spirit that living in bhang passes into the drinker, sings of bhang as the clearer of ignorance, the giver of knowledge... To the meaner man, still under the glamour of matter or maya, bhang taken religiously is kindly thwarting the wiles of his foes and giving the drinker wealth and promptness of mind"(Campbell, IHDC, 1894).
17   In *Sex Life in Ancient India*, Chandra Chakraberty refers to "Soma.... Cannabis sativa... a nervine aphrodisiac" (Chakraberty, 1963). In *The Encyclopaedia of Erotic Wisdom*, which contains a number of entries regarding different preparations and utilizations of hemp, Rufus C. Camphausen notes that, "It is well known among the users of hashish and marijuana that THC, the main active ingredient of cannabis, is--among other things–a strong aphrodisiac, a fact even recognized by the *Encyclopaedia Britannica*" (Camphausen 1991). Likewise, in his extensive book on aphrodisiacs, *Plants of Love* Christian Ratsch writes "No matter which culture, no matter what time: hemp has been repeatedly deemed the aphrodisiac" (Ratsch 1997).
18   Cannabis has been used by Zulu Warriors for similar reason, as well the legendary Assassins, Viet Cong and cannabis is still used by Indian ascetic wrestling groups. As the Indian Hemp Drugs Commission noted at the close of the 19th century: "Another great spirit time during which bhang plays an important part is the time of war... Its power of driving panic... has gained for bhang the name of Vijaya, the unbeaten. So a drink of bhang drives from the fighting Hindu the haunting spirits of fear and weariness. So the beleaguered Rajput, when nothing is left but to die... drinks the sacramental bhang and rushing on the enemy completes his *juhar* or self-sacrifice. It is this quality of panic-scaring that makes bhang, the Vijaya or Victorious, specially dear to Mahadev in his character of Tripur, .the slayer of the demon Tripurasur.... Shiva [as]... Tripuresvar [is] fond of bhang leaves" (Campbell, 1894).
19   From a quote in (Merlin, 1972).
20   As quoted in (Merlin, 1972).

ment of numerous diseases. The Modern medical marijuana pioneer, Dr. Todd Mikuriya recorded over 250 indications for the use
of cannabis (2005). A review of modern medical literatures identifies an established effect from cannabis in the treatment of nausea,
vomiting, premenstrual syndrome, unintentional weight loss, lack of
appetite, glaucoma, movement disorders, neorogenic pain, Crohn's
disease and other bowel disorders, asthma, epilepsy, skin diseases,
autism, multiple sclerosis, skin tumours, and a variety of other ailments (Mikuriya, M.D. 1973, Grinspoon, M.D. & Bakalar 1993). Further, the role of cannabis as a medicine dating back to most ancient
times, including in India, has been well documented (Russo, 2005,
2007; Mikuriya, 1973, Abel 1983) and the plant has a long held and
widespread history as a folk medicine as well.[21] There are numerous
books by various physicians on the medicinal use of cannabis, and

---

21   " In Argentina cannabis is considered a real panacea for tetanus, melancholia,
colic, gastralgia, swelling of the liver, gonorrhoea, sterility, impotency, abortion, tuberculosis of the lungs and asthma. In Argentina even the root-bark has been collected in spring,
and employed as a febrifuge, tonic, for treatment of dysentery and gastralgia, either pulverized or in form of decoctions. The root when ground and applied to burns is said to
relieve pain. Oil from the seeds has been frequently used even in treatment of cancer; we
have also come across this application in European folk medicine. Also in Argentina, in folk
medicine, hemp shoots extracted with butter (*Extr. Cannabis ind. pingue*) are supposed to
have a powerful hashish effect, it is believed already, in an amount of 0.1 g; it is employed
as a remedy in the Basedow disease. The ethereal extract is less active, and in Argentina it
is administered for headache, neuralgia, gout, rheumatism, chorea, melancholia, hysteria,
delirium, gastralgia and anorexia. The aqueous macerated product has no narcotic effect
at all, and is employed for treatment of tuberculosis of the lungs and as a hypnotic for children and to relieve spastic constipation. An infusion of the leaves is considered to possess
a diuretic and a diaphoretic effect. In Europe we also come across many of these uses. Thus
Graemer (cit. Dinand) recommends the following for treatment of gastralgia: 0.75 g Extr.
Cannabis ind., 10 g ether; 10 drops daily on sugar. For rheumatism a decoction of leaves
(15-20 g/0.5 1) is taken internally, and externally poultices prepared of seeds and packings
of shreds or tow are used. In Brazil hemp is considered to be a sedative, hypnotic and an-
tiasthmatic remedy. A pronounced antibiotic effect has been observed in South America,
where fresh leaves after being ground are used as a poultice for furuncles, and in folk medicine in Europe for treatment of erysipelas (Dinand). Even seed pulp is applied in such cases,
but as there are no antibiotics in the seeds we must assume that there is another therapeutic factor involved. In the popular treatment of headache, the plant is preserved in vinegar
together with juniper, and the extract is used in form of compresses. Githens and also Watt
& Breyer-Brandwijk report on the utilization of cannabis (dagga) in South Africa. There it
is smoked because of its narcotic action, but it is also used medicinally. Next to the effect
upon the central nervous system we find a considerable use as an antibiotic. For example,
the Xosa tribe employs it for treatment of inflammation of the feet. In Southern Rhodesia it
is a remedy for anthrax, sepsis, dysentery, malaria and for tropical quinine-malarial haemo-
globinuria. The Suto tribe fumigates the parturient woman to relieve pain. These analgetic,
sedative and antibiotic properties of cannabis in internal and external application are well
known to African tribes." (Kableik, 1955)

in recent years, a number of national and international groups have been successfully lobbying for unfettered access to cannabis for patients who wish to use it in treatment of their illness or chronic pain. In relation to this, it is important to note for this study, that in *The Classical Doctrine of Indian Medicine: Its Origins and Its Greek Parallels*, Jean Filliozat saw "...the identification of the soma plant with the Indian hemp extremely probable" (Filliozat, 1964).

Joges Candra Ray (1939) also mentions that Soma was believed to "prolong life," and other researchers have commented on this and a connection to cannabis as well. In the article "Beliefs about Aging and Longevity in Ancient China," Alain Corcos notes: "The sacred intoxicating drink, named haoma by the Iranians and Soma by the Aryans in India was believed to cure disease and to confer immortality. Hemp was an active ingredient of both drinks" (Corcos, 1981). Interestingly, the *Anandakanda* (Root of Bliss) a considerable text of 6900 verses on tantric alchemy and yoga, which is thought to have originated around the 12th or 13th century AD, has similar references to cannabis and these are believed to have been based on the descriptions of Soma.

> [T]he Anandakanda describes rejuvenation treatment based on cannabis. This involves treatment over a long period in a specially constructed hut (kut.i). This procedure is strongly reminiscent of a similar rejuvenation procedure described in the earliest Sanskrit medical literature, one that requires not cannabis but the unknown plant Soma. And that procedure itself echoes a rite of ritual rebirth that dates from the mid-first millennium BC. (Wujastyk, 2001)

Similarly, Vaíngasena's *Compendium of the Essence of Medicine*, an eleventh-century Bengali medicinal text, prescribes cannabis as a medicine to enhance longevity (Wujastyk, 2001). Likewise, the *The Mahanirvana Tantra* (XI,105–108) records that those who consume bhang "are to be likened to immortals on earth."

In this respect, ancient wisdom and modern science may also concur and further aid us in the identification of cannabis with Soma. In a recent news story "Expert Testifies Cannabis Helps Slow Aging," Dr. Robert Melamede, a University of Colorado at Colorado Springs biology professor, and former head of the UCCS Biology Department stated that:

"You can look at the harm caused by free radicals as biological friction or biological rust and the endocannabinoid[22] system minimizes the impact of that and directly acts as an antioxidant[23] as well as modifying the biochemistry in a way that minimizes the impacts," said Melamede outside court Thursday, likening endocannabinoids to humans like oil is to cars. He said if you don't have lubrication in your car, your car breaks. In the human body, the damage comes in the form of age-related diseases.

"I'm saying what science has now shown is that marijuana and cannabinoids are effective anti-aging agents which means that they are effective in minimizing the onset and the severity of age-related illnesses which include cognitive dysfunction things like Alzheimers,[24] cardiovascular disease, be it heart attacks, strokes, or clogged arteries," he said. (Newham, 2008)

---

22   Endocannabinoids are indigenous cannibinoid like substances in the human body. Cannibinoids found in cannabis are able to mimic the similar endocannibinoids in the human body.

23   US Patent 6630507 - *Cannabinoids as antioxidants and neuroprotectants.* Abstract - Cannabinoids have been found to have antioxidant properties, unrelated to NMDA receptor antagonism. This new found property makes cannabinoids useful in the treatment and prophylaxis of wide variety of oxidation associated diseases, such as ischemic, age-related, inflammatory and autoimmune diseases. The cannabinoids are found to have particular application as neuroprotectants, for example in limiting neurological damage following ischemic insults, such as stroke and trauma, or in the treatment of neurodegenerative diseases, such as Alzheimer's disease, Parkinson's disease and HIV dementia. Nonpsychoactive cannabinoids, such as cannabidoil, are particularly advantageous to use because they avoid toxicity that is encountered with psychoactive cannabinoids at high doses useful in the method of the present invention. A particular disclosed class of cannabinoids useful as neuroprotective antioxidants is formula (I) wherein the R group is independently selected from the group consisting of H, CH3, and COCH3. ##STR1##.

24   "Scientists are suggesting that cannabis can offer some benefit for Alzheimer's sufferers," The scientists from Israel and Spain say cannabis-based treatments could improve memory loss in Alzheimer's sufferers.

The revelation was made this week at a symposium of cannabis experts hosted by the Royal Pharmaceutical Society of Great Britain (RPSGB) where the scientists said that a compound present in cannabis significantly slows memory problems caused by the disease.

Ten years ago the RPSGB launched its protocols to demonstrate the therapeutic effectiveness of cannabis which led to Government-funded trials in Britain to explore the benefits for patients with multiple sclerosis and in the treatment of severe pain....

Experts are calling for clinical trials into the potential benefits of the non-psychoactive components of cannabis and they too stress that such treatments are not the same as recreational cannabis use.

Professor Tony Moffat, chairman of the Symposium says progress has been made in the last ten years but more research is needed as there is considerable interest in the medical benefits of cannabis and related compounds for a range of conditions including arthritis, multiple sclerosis and neurological pain.

Alzheimer's disease is the commonest form of dementia, which affects an estimated 24.3 million people worldwide. (The medical news, March 11, 2008) http://www.news-medical.net/news/2008/03/11/36068.aspx

As another recent news story recorded of cannabis' potential rejuvenating qualities:

Marijuana may live up to be "the elixir of life" for brain cells

A study by University of Saskatchewan researchers suggests beneficial aspects of smoking marijuana at least among rats, who appear to have sprouted new brain cells and besides benefiting from reduced depression and anxiety. The study's results appearing in the 'Journal of Clinical Investigation'[25] have actually given a fillip to the traditional and mythological view that associates the addictive weed in some ways with immortality.

The Canadian researchers led by Xia Zhang, suggested that the illicit substance marijuana actually may promote new brain cells in region of the brain called the hippocampus that is associated with memory. They concluded that marijuana was possibly "the only illicit drug whose capacity to produce increased neurons is positively correlated with its (anti-anxiety) and anti-depressant-like effects."

For the study, the researchers injected laboratory rats two times everyday for 10 days with HU210, a synthetic cannabinoid chemical (obtained from marijuana) and evaluated them against a normal group. The rats that underwent the HU210 injections developed new nerve cells in the brain's hippocampus dentate gyrus region of the brain that facilitates memory development. The injections also appeared to counter depression and anxiety, but could not be held as 100 percent akin to smoking marijuana, which the researchers felt would require additional studies.

Zhang suggested that the study did indicate that marijuana could have its medical uses particularly "for the treatment of anxiety and depression." But these results are unlikely to buy the favor with the US administration or the possibility of legalization on medical grounds. In fact only recently [May 2001] the US Supreme Court ruled against marijuana growth or possession for medical reasons.

Unlike most addictive drugs that are known to inhibit the development of new neurons, causing loss of memory and impairing learning on chronic use, it appears that marijuana or ganja may actually be the mythological "elixir of eternal life" that Indian gods churned from the oceans. A sharp contrast from ordinary addictive

---

25   "Cannabinoids promote embryonic and adult hippocampus neurogenesis and produce anxiolytic- and antidepressant-like effects," (*Journal of Clinical Investigation*, Volume 115, Issue 11, November 1, 2005)

substances, the researchers suggested that marijuana's neurogenetic properties may actually be unique given that the rats showed some correlation between their cannabinoid treatments, the increased nerve genesis and their altered stress or anxiety levels.

Marijuana that has traditionally been used by many cultures over centuries "for medical and recreational purpose," as the researchers suggest appears to be able to modulate pain, nausea, vomiting, epilepsy, stroke, cerebral trauma and variety of other disorders both for humans and animals alike. But it maybe several more studies before the mysterious benefits of marijuana that currently stand shrouded in tradition and mythology, become accepted by the modern scientific world. (Ravi, Chopra, *Earthtimes*, Oct. 15, 2005)[26]

In reference to this, it is worth noting that the Fulla Nayak, who may have been the world's oldest woman, was a copious cannabis smoker, and attributed her great age to her use of the herb:

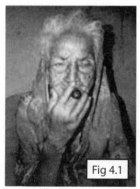

"I'm 120 but my joints are OK" – A *great-great* granny reveals how she has lived to be 120[27] ... by smoking *cannibis* every day.

Fulla Nayak believed to be the world's oldest woman puffs "ganja" cigars and drinks strong palm wine in her cow-dung hut in India.

She lives with her 92-year-old daughter and grandson, 72, by the Indian Ocean.

Fig 4.1

The Sun (UK) Oct.21st, 2006,

Interestingly, a more recent researcher has independently made the connection between Fulla's belief that cannabis use extended her life, and the Vedic claims about Soma:

Fulla Nayak died in November 2006, at the ripe old age of 120. Before her death, she was the oldest woman in the world... A great number of people want to know the secret to Fulla's good health in old age, and she herself attributes it to her use of mari-

---

26   http://www.earthtimes.org/articles/show/4241.html
27   Fulla Nayak herself claimed to be 125, but her photo identity card issued by the government in 1995 lists her age as 120 years Wikipedia names the world's oldest woman as Jeanne Clement, died in 1997 at age 122. "Fulla is certain it is the pot that made her reach a Guinness World Record breaking age, and her grandson, Narayan, said he wanted to write to the Guinness World Record authorities and get his grandmothers name in its deserved spot" (Kane, 2009).

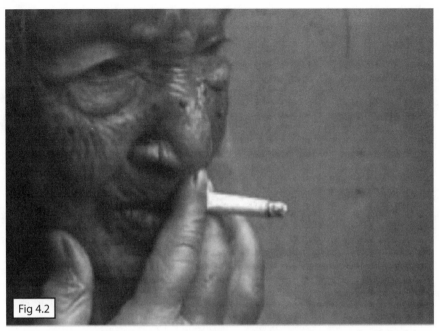

Fig 4.2

juana. In India, cannabis seeds are something of a sacred symbol, and use of the plant is entrenched in daily life.

Fulla Nayak enjoyed a long and healthy life, and she certainly didn't sacrifice any of life's little delights. She smoked marijuana and cigars and drank strong palm wine, a life-style that is frowned upon by Western conservatives. But perhaps her permanent state of relaxation and joy allowed this intriguing woman to remain in perfect health for well over a century.

Cultivating marijuana seeds is common in the community, and Fulla Nayak used leaves to make tea and joints....

India has a long and varied history of marijuana use, and it has a strong connection with cannabis seeds. Marijuana's use in religious ceremonies and practices dates back to 1500 BC, and is an integral part of religious rites.

Marijuana seeds have long been known to grow in abundance in various parts of India in the wild, and it has been recorded in the sacred texts of the Hindus, the Rig Veda, where a description of a drink called Soma can be found. It is believed that Soma was in fact a marijuana drink. (Kane, 2009)

With all the connections between cannabis and Soma apparent in Indian literature, it is not all that surprising to find that the view that Soma was cannabis has been held by a variety of Indian authors, most prominently by Chandra Chakraberty who has made this association clear in a number of different books; "Soma was... made of the flowering tops and resins of Cannabis sativa which is an aphrodisiac and stimulant, and a nourishing food..." (Chakraberty, 1952); "Soma.... Cannabis sativa... a nervine aphrodisiac" (Chakraberty, 1963; 1967); "Of all the plants Soma (Cannabis indica) is the king (X, 97,19)" (Chakraberty, 1944); "...[I]t is safe to conclude that Soma is Cannabis sativa" (Chakraberty, 1944).

Indeed, Chakraberety, Ray (1939) and Mukherjee (1921) are far from alone amongst Indian researchers regarding the identity of Soma with hemp; "...the plant now known as Bhanga in India (Indian hemp)... was used as H(a)oma or Soma" (Shrirama, 1999); "Soma (a kind of hemp)" (Ramachandran and Mativānan, 1991); "Soma was a national drink. This was a green herb which was brought from the mountain and pounded ceremoniously with stones. It was mixed with milk and honey and drunk. Probably this was a type of hemp (Bhang...) which is still drunk by some people in India" (Vikramasimha, 1967).

In 1976, the Indian botanist B. G. L. Swamy, whom we have cited in this study already, put forth cannabis as a candidate for Soma in a well thought out, but little recognized, article "The Rg Vedic Soma Plant," in the *Indian Journal of History of Science*. Swamy built on the presentations of Mukherjee (1921) and Ray (1939) noting that the Vedic descriptions of the plant indicated leaves, stalks and branches; that Soma was green, *hari*; that cannabis grows wild in areas associated with the Aryan ancestors of the Vedic authors such as the "Caspian sea, in Siberia, in the desert of Kirghiz. It is also referred to as wild in Central and Southern Russia and to the south of the Caucasus... it is almost wild in Persia and it appears to be quite wild on the Western Himalayas and Kashmir" (Swamy, 1976); that Soma was pulverized, filtered and consumed immediately as with the Indian beverage *bhang*, noting that it must "be borne in mind that there were three pressings in a day and that the juice once expressed was useless for a second offering":

> Therefore, the brief interval between pressing and consuming is too short a period for fermentation to set in, even should the juice be mixed with milk, curd, etc.... It was essential not only to soak them [the branches] in water but also pound the pieces

with stones in order to express the juice.... The dry twigs of Soma
(Cannabis) were soaked in water; crushed in flowing water; the
last washing was filtered and used almost immediately... (Swamy,1976)

Based on such clearly thought out evidence B. G. L. Swamy
rightly felt that: "The summation of evidence leads to the irresist-
ible conclusion that the Rg-vedic Soma was prepared from *Cannabis sativus*" (Swamy, 1976).

In *The RgVedic Soma*, the indigenous Vedic scholar Dr. N.R.
Warhadpande, who identified cannabis as the ancient sacred drink,
suggests that based on the Vedic meaning of the words involved
in the descriptions given in the 9th and 10th Mandalas of the *Rig
Veda*, the Soma plant was an indigenous Indian plant with roots,
branches, leaves, and resin on the leaves and flowers (Waradpende,
1995). Unfortunately, despite extensive efforts, I was unable to lo-
cate a copy of Warhadpande's book[28] and I am limited to comments
from reviewers, who noted: "To reinforce his [Warhadpande's] argument he... juxtaposes the sketch of a hemp plant to that of Ran-
guze's sketch of Soma from 'Vedic India' bringing out the close similarity. It is the paradigm which has changed throughout the Vedic
times" (Roy, 1999).

> ... Warhadpande has highlighted with great ingenuity three inter-
> esting issues, namely, 1) repudiation of the mushroom and urine
> theory of Richard Wasson, 2) identification of Soma as hemp-
> plant, and its three products, hemp-juice (vamsu), marijuana and
> hashish (charas), and 3) interpretation of the Rgvedic mantras
> referring to Soma....
> Warhadpande ingeniously agitates that the Soma plant was
> an indigenous Indian plant with roots, branches, leaves, resin
> on the leaves and flowers on the basis of the hymns RV* 10.85,3;
> 9,86,46; 9.5,1; 9.25,2; 9.38,2; 9.67; 9.61,13; 9,70,1 and so on, He
> demonstrates that 'all these verses can be interpreted as refer-
> ring to both the Soma plant and the Moon' and the adjectives
> referring to them can be interpreted accordingly. The descriptive

28   After scanning the globe's bookstores via the internet, and then doing a world
library search, the only copy I could find in existence was at the University of Oxford, making it somewhat difficult to obtain from my Canadian residence and I only know about its
contents through very positive reviews contained in a two Journals of Indian study: *Sri
Venkateswara University, Oriental Journal*, Volume XXXVIII: 1995; and *Man in India* (1999),
reviewer, Roy, K.

characteristics of the Soma plant and the physio-psychological effects caused on consumption of the Soma can be compared with the contemporary knowledge about the intoxicating drugs hemp, marijuana and hashish. The leaf (patra) of the hemp plant is called bhanga (Hindi biarig), the flower (puspamanjari) ganja and the resin (niryasa) charas. Because of its medicinal qualities it is also called vijaya, jaja and matulai and because of intoxicating qualities it is called bhanga, madini and ganja. He concludes that Soma was nothing but bhang, 'hemp' and it was consumed by the Vedic Aryans in three ways, as a hemp-juice (soma-rasa) by drinking, the flowers of hemp known as marijuana by smoking and the resin on leaves known as hashish by smoking. (*Sri Venkateswara University, Oriental Journal,* Volume XXXVIII, 1995)

Dr. Warhadpande believes that by the time of the Indian commentator Sayana (died 1387) the identification of the Soma was lost, explaining that if Sayana had known that Soma was hemp, he would not have been puzzled by the description of Soma as samiddha, i.e., kindled and as being 'blown' or 'puffed,' now it is common practice to smoke *bhanga* as well as drink it,[29] (Warhadpande, 1995). Warhadpande feels much of the confusion is due to the fact that many Vedic terms remain obscure regarding their derivation and denotation for want of adequate knowledge of the contemporary Vedic society. Patanjali, the grammarian of second century B.C. recorded that even during his time some of the Vedic words were considered to be obscure. Sayana's interpretations of Vedic terms are also doubted by later Western as well as Indian scholars. Besides the language factor, Warhadpande feels that the loss of the knowledge of Soma's identity was through the decline of the Vedic ritual, the Yajna, which came about under the influence and development of Buddhism, see Chapter 18. Sacrifices continued in the Vedic mode, but this was far different from the Yajna being in common practice (Warhadpande, 1995).

In the *The Indus Script and the Rg-Veda*, Egbert Richter-Ushanas falls short of stating that Soma is cannabis (or any other candidate) but does record that "The Soma can be compared to cannabis that

---

29   Warhadpande is likely referring to the *Aitareya Brahmanam,* 3:15-16, "When the king Soma has arrived, then they produce fire by friction. Agni being the animal of the gods, this rite of producing Agni (and throwing him into another fire) is equivalent to the slaughter of an ox or a cow." Like the smoke produced from this offering, "The oblation (of Agni in the Ahavaniya fire) of him who has this knowledge goes up to the gods; and does not become infected by the contagion with a wicked man." As translated in (Haug, 1863).

is produced from the resin of a plant too. Like cannabis the Soma may have been used for making mats and rope. This may be another reason for representing it by a net"[30] (Richter-Ushanas, 1997). (Undoubtedly this net motif fits as a symbol for cannabis far better than any of the other known candidates).

Respected religious scholar Alain Danielou (1907-1994) the first Westerner to be fully initiated into the cult of Shiva, at first rejected the hemp/Soma theory, but came to accept it in 1960,[31] and held this hypothesis up until his death.

> This ancient sacred drink was likely to resemble a drink what today is called bhang, made from the crushed leaves of Indian Hemp. Every Shivaite has to consume bhang at least once a year. The drink, which intensifies perceptivity, induces visions and above all leads to extreme mental concentration. It is widely used by Yogis. Details concerning its preparation are to be found as early as the Vedic period. The description of the way soma was prepared and its immediate use without fermentation, can only apply to bhang and is identical to the method employed today. (Danielou 1992)

A view shared by other religious scholars as well "The drink prepared from the plant... was made with great ceremony in the course of the sacrifice, when the herb was pressed between stones, mixed with milk, strained, and drunk on the same day.... The effects of soma... are rather like those attributed to such drugs as hashish. Soma may well have been hemp, which grows wild in parts of India, Central Asia and South Russia, and from which modern Indians produce a narcotic drink called 'bhang'" (Basham 1961). "...[I]t is quite likely soma is the same thing as bhang, a drug commonly used in modern India, especially among saddhus and sannyassis" (Paz, 1991).

The instantaneous preparation of Soma, as with *bhang*, is the main reason why many scholars have discounted alcoholic preparations. As Jean Filliozat noted the effects of the Soma "are immediate when it is prepared is prepared extemporaneously by pressing with the addition of water. The alcoholic fermentation required a long interval between preparation and consumption.... This will bring it very near *bhang*..." (Filliozat, 1964).

---

30   Mahadevan suggests that the net represents a filter for the purification of the Soma (Mahadevan, 1994), but this is a hypothesis, and the suggestion of others that it is representative of Soma's fibrous properties seems a much more likely reason.
31   *Le Polytheisme Hinduo* (Danielou, 1960).

A look at the ancient references themselves does indeed seem reminiscent of the pressing of hemp leaves and flowers in the preparation of the beverage *bhang*:

> O king Soma, O Soma which the priest carefully prepares.
> High with power that is real,
> Its flowing blends together,
> together blend the fragrances of the fragrant,
> purifying you by the formula, O wild god.
> Flow, O elixir, for Indra all around!
>
> There where the priest, O purified Soma,
> Speaking the language of poets,
> Is exalted by Soma, holding in his hand the stone,
> Creating ecstasy for himself through Soma.
> Flow, O elixir, for Indra all around!
>
> — *Rig Veda* 9. 113

Even the stones used for crushing the Soma, were invoked as a deity, the clacking of their work likened to speaking. Note the references to the rocks pressing the Soma as being turned green in the process and also the reference to Soma as "the purple tree" in what seems to be a clear description of the color of ripened *Cannabis indica*:

> Let these (stones) speak.... Ye solid, quick moving stones, you utter the noise of praise... full of the Soma juice.
>
> They roar like a hundred, like a thousand men; they cry aloud with green-tinted faces; obtaining the sacrifice, the pious stones... partake of the sacrificial food...
>
> They speak, they received into their mouth the sweet (Soma juice)...chewing the branch of the purple tree, the voracious bulls have bellowed.
>
> Splitting, but unsplit, you, O stones... enjoying the Soma, flowing green (with Soma), they made heaven and earth resound with their clamour.
>
> The stones proclaim it with their clamour at the issue of the Soma-juice,... like cultivators sowing the seed, they devouring the Soma, mix it, and do not hurt it.

....Proclaim the praise of (the stone), which has effused (the So-
ma-juice); let the honoured stones revolve.

— Rig Veda 10.94

In relation to the smashing of the stones above, it is interesting
to note that a Vedic reference that uses *Bhang* directly as an epithet
of Soma (IX.61.13) has been interpreted as indicating the term in
its original connotation of "smashing, breaking through" (Flattery &
Schwartz, 1989). "...[I]n the Rig Veda IX 61,13 bhanga is used when
speaking of Soma, though the translators seem to render it by 'breaker',
originating from the verb *bhanj-*, *bhanakti* 'to break'" (Aalto, 1998).

Others have interpreted this slightly differently. "In the Rigveda
(IX.61.13) (bhanga) is an epithet of Soma, presumably in the sense
of 'intoxicating' which then came to designate hemp" (MacDonell
& Kieth, 1958).[32] The idea would be a comparison of the English
term "smashed" for drunk. Although most current English translations seem to prefer to interpret the *bhang* reference in question in
the context of 'smashing or breaking', rather than 'intoxicating', but
this may well be due to the prejudices of the translators.

From the available translations, it seems likely '*Bhang*' came as
an epithet for 'Soma' through the noise made in the preparation
method of the sacred beverage as described in both the Yasnas and
the *Vedas*. The epithet *Bhang* apparently stuck, and as cannabis
was Soma, combined with the obsessive secretiveness of the Soma
priests, this led to later confusion. According to both the *Yasnas*[33]
and the *Vedas*, (RV.10.94) preparers of the sacred drink would bang
the 'Haoma' plant with rocks, and indeed the etymology fits in well
with this view; Proto-IE: *bhong*, Meaning: to break, to beat; Old Indian: *bhanakti*, pf. *babhánja* 'to break, shatter'; *bhangá-* m. 'breaking, splitting, a break or breach'[34]; all of which clearly describe the

---

32   As quoted in (Merlin, 1972)
33   Y.10.2
        Also, the foremost (part of) your mortar
        I approach praising with speech,
        O you of good guiding thought,
        (that) which receives (your) twigs.
        Also, the uppermost (part of) your mortar
        I approach praising with speech,
        O you of good guiding thought,
        (that) in which (the haoma) is pounded
        with the strength of a man/hero.
34   http://starling.rinet.ru/cgi-bin/etymology.cgi?single=1&basename=/data/ie/
piet&text_number=2072&root=config

actions of the preparation of both Haoma and Soma. In fact, English 'bang' comes from the same Indo-European root-word):

The suggestion that the term Bhang[35] came to be used for Soma, through the method of preparation is further probable when the etymology of Soma itself is examined. The linguistic root of the word *haoma*, *hu-*, and of *soma*, *su-*, suggests 'press' or 'pound'[36] (Taillieu, 2002).

It should also be noted the Soma and cannabis share other epithets as well. "Bhanga is… called… *vijaya* (the victorious)"[37] comparable to *vrtraha*, 'victorious' an epithet of Soma in (RV.1.91.23) and "Bhanga is… called… *madini* (the intoxicating)"[38] comparable to the Avestan term *madahya* (intoxicant) (Y.48.10) which is used as an epithet for the Haoma drink.

Vedic references to Soma's fibrous qualities are pointed to by one of the more vocal proponents of the hemp Soma theory, the knowledgeable ceative director of *High Times*, Steve Hager; "The restless Soma – you try to grab him but he breaks away and overpowers everything. He is a sage and seer inspired by poetry. He covers the naked and heals all who are sick. The blind man sees; the lame man steps forth."[39] A description that certainly does hold connotations of medicinal, fibrous, and psychoactive properties. Another Vedic verse on Soma has been referred to by earlier researchers in reference to the fibrous qualities of cannabis: "In the *Sukla Yajurveda* (IV.10), *mekhala*, the girdle, is described as 'tying the knot of Soma.'[40] Is this an implication that the Soma plant had the same fibrous qualities as the hemp plant?" (Merlin, 1972). "In the *Avesta* it was Haoma for whom Ahuramazda first brought

---

35   Alternatively, Barber sees the term *bhang*, coming into play as a reversal of the Indo-European word for cannabis, 'kan(n)aB.'"This must have to do with the fact, well documented in ethnographical data… that two of the most common ways of gaining access to the spirit world are by taking hallucinogenic drugs… and by doing things in reverse…" (Barber, 1991).

36   "The Sanskrit *soma*; akin to *sunoti*, he presses," *The American Heritage Dictionary of the English Language*: Fourth Edition (2000). The word is derived from an Indo-Iranian root *sav-* (Sanskrit *sav-*) 'to press,' i.e. *sav-ma-* is the drink prepared by pressing the stalks of a plant. The root is probably Proto-Indo-European (*sewh*), and also appears in *son* (from *suhnu-*, 'pressed out' i.e. 'newly born').

37   (Grierson, 1893),

38   (Grierson, 1893)

39   In a 1999 interview Hager got the respected Ayreuvedic Doctor Deepak Chopra, to acknowledge that from what we can see of Vedic descriptions, "It is possible soma was a cannabis like substance."

40   (Ray, 1939)

the 'sacred girdle, star-begemmed, woven by the two Spirits'[41]" (Taraporewala, 1926). Also, the following verse has indications of rope in relation to Haoma: "May not Haoma bind you like he bound the villain" (Y.11.7). In *A History of Indian Literature*, the authors write that:

> At the consecration of the Soma-sacrifice the sacrifice ties round his girdle a belt made of hemp and reed-grass with the words "You are the power of Angiras [ancient fire and magic priests] soft like wool; lend me power!" Then he binds a knot in his underclothing and says "you are the knot of soma." (Winternitz & Srinivasa, 1996)

The *Satapatha Bramana*, which we discussed earlier for its reference to cannabis (usana) as the plant used for Soma, also refers to the Brahminical thread, in this case called "the Zone," in a description given of a complicated ceremony. Interestingly, the *Satapatha Bramana* specifically identifies hemp (*sana*) as the fibre to be used (and it also seems to indicate some sort of symbolic connection with feminine power of the Universe):

> He then girds himself with the Zone. For once upon a time when the Angiras were consecrated, they were seized with weakness, for they had prepared no other food but fast-milk. They then perceived this [source of] strength [viz., the Zone], and this [source of] strength they put in [or round] the middle of their body as a [means of attaining] completion: and thereby they attained completion. And so does he now put that [source of] strength in the middle of his body, and thereby attain completion. It is made of hemp. Hempen it is in order to be soft. Now when Pragapati, having become an embryo, sprung forth from that sacrifice, that which was nearest to him, the Amnion, became hempen threads; hence they smell putrid. And that which was the outer membrane [and placenta] became the garment of the consecrated. Now the Amnion lies under the outer membrane, and hence that [Zone] is worn under the garment. And in like manner as Pragapati, having become an embryo, sprung forth from that sacrifice, so does he become an embryo and spring forth from that sacrifice.
>
> — *Satapatha Bramana*

---

41   Y.9.26

Haoma

A little research into the Iranian counterpart of the Soma, the Haoma, offers a variety of interesting insights. As noted, Ephedra is the current plant source used in modern preparations of Haoma, but many scholars, including Zoroastrian sources, have seen this as substitute. Dr. Jehan Bagli, a Zoroastrian priest sees the Haoma as "one of the most controversial and debated rituals that forms the central sacrament of the yasna... The *Haoma* plant has a checkered history associated with it. Although the original identity of the plant has [been] obliterated through the antiquity, the plant is generally [now] regarded as one of *ephedra* species. It is clearly evident from the Haoma yasht that the consecration of Haoma is a pre-Zarathushtrian ritual" (Bagli, 2005). As Zoroastrian scholar Dr. Daryoush Jahanian has noted of the current Haoma, and the history of the plant in his essay on "Medicine in Avest and Ancient Iran":

> Haoma (Ephedra Vulgaris, Soma in Hindu Rig Veda) - This plant is indigenous to the Iranian plateau and its scientific name is *EphedraVulgaris*. Haoma contains large doses of Ephedrine, which is effective in the treatment of cardiovascular and respiratory diseases. It is a small plant with yellow flowers. Conceivably due to various therapeutic effects, it was consecrated and entered the rituals of the pre-Zoroastrian faith, and a Yasht was composed and devoted to it. But Haoma was not used only in herbal medicine and soon another effect was recognized. A juice made of Haoma (prahum), was intoxicant and caused drunkenness. Some authors maintain that Ephedra Vulgaris and the intoxicant Haoma are two different plants. (Daryoush, 2005)

In reference to this last statement Daryoush refers to the work of another Zoroastrian scholar, Dr. Ali Jafarey's essay "Haoma, its Original and Later Identity," which, as we will discuss shortly, identifies the original Haoma as *bhang* (cannabis) (Jafarey, 2000). The physical attributes of Haoma give clear indications of cannabis as described in the *Avesta*:

> Haoma is golden-green (*Yasna* 9.16 et al)
> Haoma is tall (*Yasna* 10.21, *Vendidad* 19.19)
> Haoma has roots, stems and branches (*Yasna* 10.5)

Haoma has a pliant stem, asu[42] (*Yasna* 9.16)

Haoma is fragrant (*Yasna* 10.4)

Haoma grows on the mountains, 'swiftly spreading,' 'apart on many paths' (*Yasna* 9.26, 10.3-4 et al) 'to the gorges and abysses' (*Yasna* 10-11) and 'on the ranges' (*Yasna* 10.12)

Haoma can be pressed (*Yasna* 9.1, 9.2)

All of which can be applied to cannabis. The effects of drinking Haoma are:

Haoma has healing properties[43] (*Yasna* 9.16-17, 9.19, Y.10.7, 10.8, 10.9)

Haoma has aphrodisiacal qualities[44] (*Yasna* 9.13-15, 9.22)

Haoma increases strength[45] (*Yasna* 9.17, 9.22, 9.27)

Haoma stimulates alertness and awareness[46] (*Yasna* 9.17, 9.22, 10.13)

---

42   The term asu is only used in conjunction with a description of *Haoma*, and does not have an established translation. Generally translated as stalk, but others see "twigs" (Taillieu,2002) "golden-colored with pliable twigs" (Y.9.16)

43   Y.10.7 "the healing of healing Haoma" Y.10.9; "O Haoma, give me (those) of the remedies, by which you are the best (disease-) smasher through remedies!" As discussed earlier, such medical qualities, also associated with Soma, make a strong case for cannabis as a candidate for the ancient Vedic and Avestan sacraments.

44   In *Sex Life in Ancient India*, Chandra Chakraberty describes "Soma…. Cannabis sativa… a nervine aphrodisiac" (Chakraberty, 1963); Cannabis is a cross culturally renowned aphrodisiac and was used in Tantric rites as a sexual stimulant (Bennett & McQueen, 2001; Ratsch 1997; Camphausen 1991).

45   The 11th century Indian text the *Rajanighantu* of Narahari Pandita refers to cannabis as "balyatva (strength-giving)" (Grierson, 1893).

46   The *Rajanighantu* relates cannabis has "*medhakaritva* (inspiring of mental power)" (Greierson, 1893). Similar claims about cannabis are detailed in a recent Globe and Mail news story, 'Thursday, November 20, 2008, "*A toke a day keeps memory loss at bay: Small doses of marijuana improve the function of aging brains, scientists find.*"

"We are not trying to make anyone high," said Gary Wenk, professor of psychology and neuroscience at Ohio State University. "We are trying to tease out the positive aspects of this plant."

The benefit was found in a synthetic compound identical to tetrahydrocannabinol, or THC, the psychoactive substance in marijuana, which researchers say activated areas of aged brains in rats affected by memory loss, and stimulated the formation of new brain cells.

Prof. Wenk, who presented the research in Washington, yesterday at the annual meeting of the Society for Neuroscience, was motivated to look into the effects of marijuana on aging brains after repeatedly noticing the drug mentioned on the blogs of patients with MS who use it to curb pain. Memory impairment is connected to such chronic brain inflammation.

"There was discussion of smoking a little pot to reduce inflammation, which makes their disease less painful," Prof. Wenk said.

Pot is popular among older sufferers, because conventional anti-inflammatory medications are not effective in older brains.

Haoma can be consumed without negative side effects[47] (*Yasna* 10.8)
Haoma is 'most nutritious for the soul'[48] (*Yasna* 9.16)
Haoma bestows spiritual wisdom (*Yasna* 9.22)

All these attributes, as we have shown in this discussion on Soma/Haoma already in relation to the Vedic literature, can be applied to cannabis. Indeed, Haoma is the premier way, if not only way of gaining spiritual wisdom in the Avestan literature. Y.9.22: "On those who in their homes, sit asking about the holy texts, Haoma bestows insight and wisdom."[49] Comparatively, the *Indian Hemp Drugs Commission*, recorded: "The students of the scriptures at Benares are given bhang before they sit to study. At Benares, Ujjain, and other holy places yogis, bairagis and sanyasis take deep draughts of bhang that they may Centre their thoughts on the Eternal" (IHDC, 1894). Thus, not surprisingly the effects of Haoma were held in deep contrast with those of alcohol:

"Millions of people have used this plant for thousands of years," Prof. Wenk said. "There is a lot of evidence that there are some interesting things going on in the brains of these people."

So, while testing with rats, researchers used a THC-like drug, called WIN-55212-2, to activate receptors in the brain's endocannabinoid system - usually stimulated by smoking marijuana - which involves memory, appetite, mood and pain response.

After three weeks, the rats were given a memory test where they were placed in a small swimming pool to determine how well they used visual cues to find a platform hidden under the surface of the water.

The treated rats were given enough of the drug to boost brain cells, though not enough to get high, and did better in the swimming-pool test than the control - strait-laced rats without THC - in learning and remembering how to find the hidden platform.

"Old rats are not very good at that task," said Yannick Marchalant, co-author of the study and assistant professor of psychology at Ohio State. "When we gave them the drug, it made them a little better at that task."

They also experienced reduced inflammation and growth of new brain cells.

The researchers hope their findings could lead to the development of a drug to stave off memory loss in people with a history of degenerative disease in their families.

"The model could be used for anyone at risk," Prof. Marchalant said. "Perhaps 20 years before the usual onset of the decline in memory." (Sokolov & Wingrove, 2008)

47   Cannabis has thousands of years of recorded use, and no deaths.
48   The Indian hemp drugs Commission reported "The soul in whom the spirit of bhang finds a home glides into the ocean of Being freed from the weary round of matter-blinded self" (Campbell,1894).
49   Likewise in the *Vedas*, Soma "has given increase (to our understanding); it has increased the intelligence" (RV.10.25.10).

For all other intoxications
are accompanied by Wrath with the bloody club,
but the intoxication of Haoma
is accompanied by Order (and) bliss.
The intoxication of Haoma quickens
the man who would honor
Haoma like a young son.
Haoma enters these bodies to heal them.[50]

— Y.10.8

Dasturji Dr. Maneckji N. Dhalla, writing in the 1930s also noted many of the above descriptions and in addition commented:

Haoma is the sovereign lord of all plants among both the Indians and the Iranians. Physically it is the plant that grows on the highest summits ... The birds carried it from there in all directions... The nourishing earth is its mother where it grows in vales and dales, spreading sweet perfume all around. (10:4, 17) It is of golden hue... and the celestial drink prepared from its branches is most invigorating and profitable for the soul of man. (9:16)... The pounding of the Haoma juice for sacrifice is tantamount to the destruction of the demons by thousands. (10:6) Misery vanishes and happiness and health enter the house in which Haoma is prepared. (10:7) The exhilarating drink gives inspiration and enlightenment to his supplicant and makes the beggar's mind as exalted as that of the rich. (10:13). (Dhalla, 1938)

Comparatively the *Indian Hemp Drugs Commission* wrote; "Bhang is the Joy-giver, the Sky-flier, the Heavenly-guide, the Poor Man's Heaven, the Soother of Grief....The mere sight of bhang, cleanses from as much sin as a thousand horse-sacrifices or a thousand pilgrimage" (Campbell, 1894).

As will be discussed in Chapter 14 the Persian religion and its use of Haoma went through a variety of reforms and changes from the influence of the prophet Zoroaster (also known as Zarathustra), who is generally believed to have lived about the 6th century BC, although dates centuries prior to that have been suggested. Zoroaster's influence was so great over Mazdaism, that the religion later became known as Zoroastrianism.

50   As discussed in Chapter 14 Some Zoroastrian scholars see this as a reference to Haoma, after reforms which saw the intoxicating qualities removed, and the current placebo sacrament in place.

From the 7th-6th centuries BC one of the centers of the Zoroastrian religion was Azerbaijan. "The hemp plant has been cultivated in Azerbaijan from prehistoric times" (Alakbarov, 2001). As well, I.A. Huseynov, in the Russian language publication *History of Azerbaijan*, suggests that Haoma was prepared from a base of cannabis (Huseynov, 1958).[51]

Avestan scholar Dr. Ali A. Jafarey[52], who has been writing about the Zoroastrian religion for over forty years sees Haoma as "very possibly 'marijuana' or 'hashish' (Cannabis Sativa)" (Jafarey, 2000). Jafarey states that Wasson's sugestion of a "mushroom seems to be farfetched" and the commonly used modern ingredient for the Haoma ceremony, Ephedra, is "void of all the qualities described in the *Avesta* and the *Vedas*, is definitely a late substitute. The author, a teetotaller, has drunk large glassfuls of hûm [Haoma] juice in Yazd without feeling any side effects. Ephedra supplies 'ephedrine' medically used to treat low blood pressure. Ephedrine is decongestant. It does not push a person 'high' but it does make one feel 'hyper'!" (Jafarey 2000)[53] As Jafarey concludes of the original identity of the Haoma:

> The description of the plant that it was greenish in color (*zairi/hari*), grew on mountains well north of the Indus Valley and was traded by outsiders, had a special ritual to prepare, was an instant intoxicant prepared from pounding and extracting its juice, and that the Saka tribes of eastern Central Asia are called "haumavarka" (haoma-gatherers) by Achaemenians; all point, in my opinion, to what is now known as Indian hemp (cannabis sativa).
>
> ...the ceremony resembles... the present practice of solemnly pounding... extracting and straining its juice, and mixing it with water, milk, poppy seeds, and almonds by sufîs, faqirs, pirs, sadhus, and other Muslim and Hindu mystics of certain orders and circles in Iran, Afghanistan, Pakistan, and India, particularly those connected with shrines and holy places. It still has a halo around it!.... The drink, an instant psychoactive mixture, is greenish in

---

51   As noted in (Alakbarov, 2001)

52   Dr. Ali Akbar Jafarey, was born in Kerman, Iran. He received his schooling up to the university level in Karachi. He has a doctorate in Persian Language and Literature, and has self-studied thirteen living and ancient languages, and also studied linguistics, anthropology, Indo-Iranian literature, history, geology and research methods... In 1991, Dr. Jafarey, with seven other co-founders, established the Zarathushtrian Assembly in Los Angeles. www.zoroastrian.org .

53   Jafarey cannot be considered biased in his assertions, as he is no fan of cannabis believing it "has proven quite devastative."

color. It is called "dûgh-e vahdat" (unity milk) by Iranian mystics and "thâdal" (cooling, refreshing) by Sindhi sufis. One description says its addicts "never die," a far echo of "dûraosha" for haoma. (Jafarey, 2000)

Jafarey makes an interesting point in reference to the "Saka tribes" of Central Asia, a group more popularly know as the Scythians, and who were referred to in the writings of Herodotus (440 BC) in reference to their use of burning cannabis to achieve ecstasy. Indeed, as shall be discussed Chapter 7, numerous cannabis related artefacts, and even cannabis itself has been discovered by modern archaeologists at a number of Scythian burial sites! In relation it is interesting to note that in the *RgVedic Soma*, Warhadpande suggests that Vedic references also indicated the burning an inhalation of Soma smoke, and the Vedic scholar sees this as an indication of cannabis (Warhadpande, 1995). The idea that Haoma and Soma could be burnt and inhaled has been the long standing view of a number of scholars, as Allen Godbey noted close to 80 years ago in "Incense and Poison Ordeals in the Ancient Orient":

Among the Iranic peoples this haoma seems to have been bhang, or Indian hemp, for Herodotus (iv. 75) tells us that the Iranic Scythians... burned Indian hemp in their religious exercises, until bystanders were intoxicated with their fumes. In India the soma was the juice of a certain milkweed in some districts, but others insist that the bruised green leaves of hemp provide the orthodox soma. (Godbey, 1930)

Preparation

In the *Vedas*, "soma was... an intoxicating liquid, pounded or pressed out of the plant using special pressing stones (RV IX.11.5-6;IX.109.17-18), filtered through wool, and presumably mixed with other ingredients" (Bedrosian, 2006). The plant was soaked in water in large tubs and then beaten and pressed into milk, a process directed at releasing the THC rich trichomes from the plant matter.[54] Then this preparation was placed into large pots which had a

---

54   This is similar to the modern method of making water hash, popularized in the last decade, where cannabis is mixed with water and ice, then stirred vigorously releasing

hole in the bottom covered with a wool filter, and the final preparation was recovered in a vessel placed below. As described in Joseph Chandra Ray's 1939 essay "The Soma Plant":

> The shoots bearing leaves (X.82.3) were first cleaned and next moistened with, or steeped in, water when the stalks would swell (IX.31.4). The mass was then crushed and ground between a pair of stones (IX.67.19) or in a mortar and pestle (1.28.1). The ground paste was next mixed with water in a jar and the mixture poured from one jar into another causing sound (IX.72.3). Then it was strained over sheep's wool (IX.69.9). Thus prepared it was 'pure' drink. Often it was mixed with milk or *dadhi* (IX.71.8), sometimes with honey and barley meal (IX.68.4). (Ray, 1939)[55] [As quoted in (Merlin, 1972)]

the frozen trichomes from the plant matter, the vegetation floats and the trichomes sink; the water is then poured through a screen filter which is big enough for the trichomes to get through, but stops the vegetable matter from passing into it. If this is the method of the ancient Soma, they would be dealing with a very potent form of extract.

55   A slightly more detailed description of Soma preparation based on the Vedic references has been put together by Mel Copeland:

"Collect Soma stalks from the mountains (Book 3, XLVIII.2); Grind stalks of Soma between broad-based grinding stones (Book 1, Hymn XXVIII.1). Press the Soma with water with the stones (Book 9, Hymn XXX.5); Strain the sap with water through a woolen filter (Book 1, Hymn CXXXV.6), (Book 8, Hymn II.2); Mix the Soma juice with milk (Book 8, Hymn II.2); Soma in the jar is mingled with the milk (Book 9, Hymn LXXII); blended with milk and curds he flows on through the long wool (Book 9, Hymn CIII); the Soma flows tawny to the straining-cloth (Book 9, III.9) [into the beakers]; [from the beakers] Pour the sap into a large wooden vat; and settles in the wood (Book 9, Hymn VII.6); when through the filter poured, clothed with milk (Book 9, Hymn VIII.5); Swelling, as 'twere, to heights of heaven, the stream of the creative juice falls lightly on the cleansing sieve (Book 9, Hymn XVI.7); the swelling wave… flows into the sieve… hastens to the pitchers, poured upon the sieve (Book 9, Hymn XVII.3,4); blend in the midst with milk and curd (Book 8, Hymn II.9); ..And pour the sweet milk in the meath..blend the libation with the curds (Book 9, Hymn XI 5,6; Book 4, Hymn XXIV); cook with milk..(Book 9, Hymn XLVI.4); mix the milk with honey of the bee (Book 8.IV.8); Soma mixed with butter (Book 10, Hymn XXIX.6); Let the Soma ferment for three days? (Book 3, Hymn XXVIII);.. poured upon the filtering-cloth, the men conduct him..effused into the vats of wood (Book 9, Hymn XXVII.2,3), (Book 9, Hymn XXVIII.1,4), (Book 9, Hymn XXX 1,4); the living Somas being cleansed..turned to the vat (Book 9, Hymn XXIII.4); pour into the Soma the milk, prepare the cake and mix the Soma-draught (Book 8, Hymn II.11); serve three beakers of Soma to Indra (Book 1, XXXII.3), three beakers filled to the brim (Book 8, II.8). When sacrificing the Steed, bring forth a goat, followed by the Steed, following him are sages and singers. The wise Priest sits to complete the sacrifice (Book 5, XI.2). Sing, and the priest dances (like Indra) around the fire-altar. The sages form a ring, looking and singing to the Ram [Indra] (Book 8, Hymn LXXXVI.12);The color of the Soma mixture is brown (Book 8.IV.14) pressed from yellow stalks (Book 8, IX.19)." (Copeland, 2007)

The Vedic descriptions of Soma preparation are almost identical to that of *bhang* recipes in India, to this day, albeit on a somewhat scaled-down version.

> Some practices of soma preparation are sill used today to prepare *bhang*. First the *soma* was washed... then ground between pressing stones and filtered through a cloth sieve... it was then combined with cow's milk... In addition *soma* was invoked directly and in one hymn, the god Indra was asked to join the drinkers... All of these elements are steps in bhang preparation.
>   ...Before *bhang* is distributed, an invocation must be made, generally by pouring a small quantity over the grinding stone, in a style resembling *vijaya abhishika*. These invocations resemble the Vedic invocation associated with *soma*. It is often, but not necessarily addressed to Shiva.... (Morningstar, 1985)

The center of *bhang*[56] use is Varanasi, the land of Shiva, where *bhang* is prepared on its famous ghats. Anywhere on the ghats, one can find large numbers of men engaged in the process of preparing *bhang*. The preparation of *bhang* has not changed much since ancient times, a 'mortar and a pestle,'[57] is used to grind the buds and leaves of cannabis into a powder, which is then moistened and worked into a green paste. To this mixture milk, ghee, and spices are added. Then, as with Soma, this mixture is pressed through a cloth and the strained liquid is then served to devotees.

> ...when prepared for consumption the fragments of the plant are ground to a paste, and of this an emulsion is made which after being filtered through a cloth, may be consumed in that form, or flavoured with sugar spices, cardamons, melon seeds or milk." (Watt, 1908)[58]

---

56   *Bhang* has been used throughout India for millennia, and is particularly associated with the Holidays of Holi and Baisakhi, although consumption is by no means limited to these dates. *Bhang* has been taken in tribute to a number of deities, such as Indra, Krishna and Kali, but the use of *bhang* is particularly associated with the cult of Shiva, and numbers of depictions of the god preparing his sacred beverage have been produced over the centuries.

57   "Golden-green eyed" *Haoma* was the first to offer up *haoma*, with a "star-adorned, spirit-fashioned mortar" (*Yasht* 10.90). Mortars and pestles are also clearly referrerd to in relation to medieval Indian cannabis lore as well: "The epic poem of Alha and Rudal, of uncertain date, but undoubtedly based on very old materials (the heroes lived in the twelfth century A.D.), contains numerous references to ganja as a drink of warriors. For instance, the commencement of the canto dealing with Alha's marriage, describes the pestle and mortar with which the ganja was prepared." (Grierson, 1893)

58   As quoted in (Merlin, 1972)

Other accounts record that "the leaves are pounded and mixed with water to form a thick paste called 'panga'" (Watt, 1908).[59] This could either be mixed with water or milk and served, or alternatively mixed with spices and ghee then pressed into '*bhang* balls' known as 'golees' (see image) for storage or sale in the market place. James Wheeler noted of the "Homa, consisting chiefly of ghee," that "when the presentation of the homa was over, the remaining portion of the medicinal herbs was reduced to powder and formed into balls" (Wheeler, 1867).

Fig 4.3: *Bhang* shop. Fig 4.4: *Bhang* balls. Fig 4.5: Mortar and pestle for preparing *bhang*.

Fig 4.6: Parvati serving *bhang* to Shiva after straining it through a cloth.

Dan Quaintance of the Church of Cognizance, a modern group which uses cannabis as the Haoma, believes the drink was originally made with water alone and not milk, an idea many would dispute due to THC needing oils to be properly released, but as Dan points out, with smashed seeded buds this is not an issue, as the oil of the seeds of the cannabis would be enough to extract the THC. Quaintance, who is very knowledgeable on the history of Haoma believes this accounts for Avestan references that indicate Haoma was nourishing (*Yasna* 9.4, 10.20) as the hemp seed itself is also highly nutritious[60] (Quaintance, 2008). "The Avesta points to

---

60   Hemp seeds contain all the essential amino acids and essential fatty acids necessary for human life, as well as a rare protein known as globule edistins that are very similar to the globulin found in human blood plasma. Because of this, hemp seed has been touted by some as "Nature's perfect food for humanity." Four short years after the Marijuana Tax Act passed in the US, a researcher writing for a 1941 edition of *Science* lamented the loss of access to the hemp seed's rare and important globule edistins; "Passage of the Marijuana Law of 1937 has placed restrictions upon trade in hempseed that, in effect, amount to prohibition.... It seems clear that the long and important career of the protein is coming to a close in the United States." Still, research continued elsewhere, and in 1955 the Czechoslovakian Tubercular Nutrition Study concluded that hemp seed was the "only food that can successfully treat the consumptive disease tuberculosis, in which the nutritive processes

a food value in Yasna 10:20; it comes right out with 'yield thou us food'" (Quaintance, 2006). Later 6th century BC references show cannabis seed was held in high regard by the Persians by its name *Sahdanag – Royal Grain*; or *King's Grain*,[61] (Low, 1925). Currently, these qualities of hemp seed are going through a renaissance, a variety of hemp seed milk and health food products have become commercially available in Canada and other countries.

Considering the praise given to cattle and the many references to milk mixed with Haoma in both the Vedic and Avestan literature, I find this suggestion unlikely (although attractive to the vegan minded, I am sure). It seems from what we can know about the Soma and Haoma, that it was likely a cannabis infused milk beverage analogous to the still used Indian hemp drink *bhang*.

---

are impaired and the body wastes away" (Robinson 1996). Hemp seeds contain the most balanced and richest natural single source of essential oils for human consumption. The E.F.A.'s not only help to restore wasting bodies, but also improve damaged immune systems, so it is not so surprising that modern researchers have studied them in relationship to the modern immune attacking AIDS virus (Eidlman, M.D., Hamilton, ED.D, Ph.D 1992).

61   See "A History of the Royal Grain" (Bennett, 1999) for more on the historical role of cannabis as a food source.

Contemporary cannabis chillum smokers in Nepal and India.

Zoroastrian priests with tightly bound Barsom.

— 5 —

THE BUNDLES OF HAOMA?

I t is has been suggested that the barsom, bundle of twigs, collected for the fire offering[1] was originally a bundle of Haoma stalks.
The barsom or sacred bundle of twigs (or "slender wands"), is a
ritual implement which has played an important part in the Persian
religious practices since prehistoric times. Like the Haoma, much
about the original identity and use of the barsom has become lost
in time. In ceremonies, where it serves purely as a symbolic representation, a variety of different plants have been used as barsom,
even brass rods. "In many passages of the Avesta, Niyayeshes and
Yashts, it is always associated with the Haoma... ceremonies (Ha-
omayo gava baresmana). So, as the Haoma ceremony is very ancient, it follows that the barsom ceremony also is as ancient as that
(Modi, 1922).

An etymological clue to the function of barsom, that appears to
have eluded authorities to date, lies in the Albanian word *bar*,
which means 'grass' and 'herb, 'as well as 'medicine', 'remedy', or
'drug'.[2] This calls to mind the fact that Arabic hashish means simply

---

1   Zoroastrian Fire Litany - "May there be hope to that person who truly shall sacrifice to you with fuel in his hand, with the Baresman in his hand.... Then if that one brings
to the fire either fuel rightly brought, or Baresma rightly spread, or the plant Hadhanaepa-
ta, to him thereupon, in fulfillment of his wish, the Fire of Ahura Mazda, propitiated, unof-
fended, gives a blessing."
2   "Prof. Dr. Ilo Stefanllari, *Albanian-English. English-Albanian Dictionary*, Hippo-
crene Books, 1996. There may be a connection with the Arabic term bars for a psychoactive confection of honey and spices mixed with various psychoactive ingredients such
as cannabis, opium and datura used for therapeutic purposes in Iraq from at least the
twelfth century and latterly throughout the Islamic world as a recreational drug. On bars
see: Solaz del espíritu en el hachís y el vino y otros textos Árabes sobre drogas, introduc-
ción traducción y notas de Indalecio Lozano, Universidad de Granada, 1998" (Piper, 1994).

'grass' a fact duplicated in modern epithets for cannabis such as herb,' 'weed' and 'grass.' In fact *bar-* is a prefix in a great many Albanian plant names, including many medicinal herbs. The identification of *bar* as grass, herb, or medicine is important for two reasons. Firstly because Albanian is an IE language that is relatively close to its ancient roots, traced directly to the ancient Illyrian or Thracian inhabitants of the Balkans less mediated than other modern IE languages due to the relative isolation of the Albanian peoples. Secondly because it may identify barsom as a entheogenic plant like Haoma with which it is so closely associated. Tailleu suggests that barsom may simply be IE bar- (= grass, etc) with the suffix -man/-men common to ritual objects, thus 'sacred grass.'[3] (Piper, 2004)

The German Iranist, Geo Widengren (1965) suggested an identification of the Haoma with the Barsom, and a similar view was put forth by Flattery and Schwartz (1989), who suggested that Avestan references to "Baresma rightly spread" (Zoroastrian Fire Litany), identified the seed, heads, roots and other debris left over from the pounding of the Haoma with a mortar and pestle, which were strewn about as a consequence. In Flattery and Schwartz's opinion, the remaining husks and plant matter would have been remnants of Syrian rue, but their view would hold true in the case of a cannabis candidate as well.

The late Iranist Mary Boyce noted the term not only identifies stalks, but also refers to leafy matter: "Barsom - name of both strew of herbage and bundle of consecrated twigs" (Boyce, 1982)."The word barsom is the Middle Persian form of the Avestan barsman, which is derived from the root *barz*, Sanskrit *bráh* to grow high" (Kanga, 2007). Interestingly, one of the adjectives used to describe Haoma is "Tall" (Yasna 10.21, Vendidad 19.19), and the Bundahishn, contains the statement "as tall as hemp" (27.1), in a descriptive reference to the height of another plant. The association with Haoma is further exemplified through the references to the Haoma "cut for the bundles bound by women" in the following verse:

Praise to Haoma, Mazda-made. Good is Haoma, Mazda-made. All the plants of Haoma praise I, on the heights of lofty mountains, in the gorges of the valleys, in the clefts (of sundered hillsides) *cut for the bundles bound by women*. From the silver cup I pour Thee to the golden chalice over. Let me not thy (sacred) liquor spill to earth, of precious cost.

Yasna 10.17

3   See Dieter Tailleu, Baresman, Acta, *Orientalia Belgica* X (1995-96 [1997]),

Possibly this was a method of ritual collection and storage of the Haoma for off-season use, as the verse also indicates none of the Haoma should be wasted at "Precious cost." (Comparably at times in the modern world cannabis has been worth more than gold, and quality seeds more than diamonds). Considering the copious use of Soma/Haoma that is suggested by the ancient texts, storage and transportation would have been of great concern. "A close reading of the original texts gives the impression that the quantity of *Soma* plant required for three pressings should be quite heavy during the Rg-vedic times. Even the *Soma* of the Brahmins was transported in carts" (Swamy, 1976).

> For a time the plant was procured from long distances and trans-ported in carts to the place of the sacrifice, where the article was bought by the performer of the sacrifice. (This episode soon found codification as an integral part of the Soma rite in subse-quent times). Progressive migration of the Vedists in the plains caused practical difficulties in obtaining the required plant...
> (Swamy,1976)

Clearly such a valuable commodity would have been carefully prepared for storage. Archaeologist and art scholar Trudy Kawami has noted that "the so-called 'barsom bundles carried by some fig-ures in Achaemenid reliefs are usually thought to be a reference to this plant offering...of Haoma" (Kawami, 2002). Mazdean priests often went on pilgrimages to preach the faith and they took with them the "usual implements for rituals" which included: "milk-bowl,... strainer, standard mortar, *haoma* cups, and *baresman* twigs (V 14.8)" (Jafarey, 2000). A reference which further indicates that the Barsom, was originally a reference to 'bundles of Haoma,' prepared for storage, travel and later ritual use.

Zoroastrian priest Dr. Jehan Bagli notes that another verse "Yasna XXV appears to associate *Barsam* with the twigs of Haoma plant" (Bagli, 2005).

> ...[W]e worship this Haoma, this flesh and branch, and these Zaothras for the good waters, having the Haoma with them... and we worship the two, the stone mortar and the iron mortar; and we worship this plant for the Baresman... and these wood-billets with the perfume (even) thine, the Fire's, O Ahura Mazda's

son! and we worship all good objects which are Mazda-made, and
which contain (and are) the seed of Righteousness.

Y.25.1-3

Like the mystery of the Haoma, the identity of the original barsom has been lost in time, and over the centuries a variety of other
plants have been used as a substitute for the real barsom, such as
Myrtle, Laurel, Tamarisk, Willow, Juniper and others.

> The baresman [sic] twigs were twigs of the haoma plant or the
> pomegranate [substitute] used in certain ceremonies. They are
> first laid out and then tied up in bundles... [Today] brass or silver
> wires are used in place of twigs. (Kanga, 2007)

Currently, the *barsom* serves no immediate practical purpose. At
Zoroastrian ritual it represents plant creation, accompanying the
other symbolic tokens that represent other facets of creation "While
the baresman bundle is now an item only used in rituals, old references to the baresman indicate more extensive uses .... [but] [d]es-
pite making frequent reference to the baresman, the existing Avesta
texts do not explicitly explain the baresman's significance. However,
many books of the Avesta have been destroyed and these books
could very well have provided more information." (Eduljee, 2007).

There are certain indications that like the Haoma beverage, the
barsom likely had some sort of entheogenic effect. According to
Kotwal and Boyd, authors of *A Persian Offering*, the barsom is an
"ancient Indo-Iranian emblem of seeking the Holy," and it "estab-
lishes a connecting link between this getig [material] world and
the menog [spiritual] realm. The barsom is, as it were, the conduit
through which the archetypal principles and powers manifest their
presence and receive the offerings" (Kotwal & Boyd, 1991). In this
sense it is like a prototypical 'magic wand.' "According to the Niran-
gistan, the barsom ceremony existed in the time of Zoroaster, whose
contemporary, Jamasp, is said to have celebrated it in a particular
way" (Modi, 1922). Interestingly, Modi mentions the tradition of
Jamasp, one of the figures initiated by Zoroaster, and surviving Persian texts record Zoroaster performing a number of initiations with
mang (hemp), as will be discussed in Chapter 15, In the *Jamasp Namag*, this hero receives the gift of knowledge by means of a flower

given to him by Zoroaster. "He gave the flower to Jamasp, the best of men and he was taught, by means of visions, about all events present, past and future." As Boyce explains "Jamasp by inhaling certain perfumes, attained all knowledge" (Boyce, 1982).

Indeed, when one looks at what can be known about the barsom from ancient Avestan references it certainly does seem that it was

Fig 5.1: Barsom stand, used for drying Haoma? Fig 5.2: Zoroastrian priests with tightly bound Barsom.

Haoma, "cut for the bundles bound by women" (Y.10.17), laid out before the fire "Baresma rightly spread" (Zoroastrian Fire Litany), or dried by the fire on the ritual barsom stand. Possibly in order to make the transportation of the Haoma more compact and to preserve the sticky resin of cannabis for travel, the leaves and buds were bound and tied to the branch for preservation much like the later method used for cannabis in Asia known as Thai sticks. Thus the Haoma was ritually prepared for storage and future sacrifice through the long winter months.

In reference to the name "Haumavarka," generally translated as "Haoma-Gatherers" which was used in reference the cannabis using Iranian Scythians who will be discussed in Chapter 7, Rüdiger Schmitt, made some comments that fit in well with this view, noting that "Karl Hoffmann...[1976] compared *–varga-* with Av. *varj*, Ved. *varj*, *vrnákti* 'to turn (over, away), to lay (around something),' especially with Ved. *vrnktá-barhis-* [counterpart of the Avestan barsom] 'having laid the sacrificial grass around (the fire).' He thus interpreted and translated the entire compound as 'laying *hauma*-plants (instead of the usual grass) around (the fire)'"(Schmitt, 2000). In this reference it is hard not to see the identification of the nomadic Scythians as the gatherers of Haoma, who ritually collected and dried the plant as in the scenario suggested above. Indeed, the growing and harvest of such a sacred plant along with the bringing down to the village of the Haoma from the mountains and fields to the central fire area for drying, were likely as much a part of the Haoma "ritual" as the "pounding" with "mortar and pestle" was in the preparation of the sacred beverage.

6

THE ARCHAEOLOGCAL EVIDENCE

R ecent archaeological evidence has emerged from Russian excavations in the Kara Kum desert of Turkmenistan which gives the cannabis-Soma theory an element of legitimacy that the other candidates (save for the still used ephedra) cannot top. This site is known as The Bactria-Margiana Archaeological Complex (or BMAC, also known as the Oxus civilization). An area regarded by some sources, as the original home of cultivated cannabis.[1]

Fig 6.1: BMAC Temple site.
Fig 6.2: BMAC reconstruction by V. Antonov (Sarainidi, 2003).

In modern times Margiana is known as Merv and in relation to the Aryan origins of the Soma cult it should also be noted that this has been suggested as their secondary homeland. "The lands called by us Afghanistan and Bactria were the regions where the Aryans had long carried on their activities" (Taraporewala, 1926). Mount Meru has been identified with the "existing town of Merv... in modern Russian Turkestan... situated in the depression of the Hindu Kush range which stretches from the Caspian to the Pamirs...." (Bolton, et al., 2000). "In... Hindu literature... Meru, is the most

1   The 19th century naturalist V. Hehn, suggested that cannabis, among a number of other plants, may have originated in or close to this same area. Cannabis "...originally came from Bactria and Sogdiana, the regions of the Aral and Caspian Seas, where it is said to grow luxuriantly in a wild state to this day...From the Pontus and Thrace this excellent material for rope was exported to the Greeks" (Hehn,1885). Hehn calls Pontus "the fatherland of poisons and antidotes."

sacred mountain of the Aryans and their possible place of origin..."
(Frawley, 2000).

> As the origins of the Aryan race has not yet be determined might
> not the tradition which identifies it with the Oasis of Merv... be
> true?... In the Avesta the plant known by the Sanskrit name Soma
> grew on the slopes of Mount Meru and when pressed, gave froth
> a sacred intoxicating juice, which was *mixed with milk* to form
> the nectar of the Gods... (Bolton, et al., 2000)

Further, it is also widely believed that the Indo-European languages came from this same region, disseminating from a locus
"somewhere in the vicinity of ancient Bactria..." (Nichols, 1997).
As this has been indicated as the homeland of cultivated cannabis,
the Aryans, the Indo-European Language and even the Soma cult,
it is satisfying to see archaeological evidence would be found in
this area, which tied it all together. Although the discovery of this
Soma temple in the homeland is ripe with historical implications,
for the most part few people outside the fields of study it encompasses have yet become aware of it. This may in part be due to the
lack of funding for archaeological expeditions in the bureaucratic
chaos that is the post Soviet Union. In order to finance the Margi-
ana-Bactria expedition, the Russian archaeologist, Victor Sarianidi,
had to seek financing from the Greek Government. Sarianidi's very
important book on the subject, *Margiana and Protozoroastrianism*
(1998), was published in Greece as well, but is now out of print with
no plans for republishing. Suffice to say, it was extremely difficult
to acquire. As Victor Sarianidi explains of what must be one of the
highlights of his life's work:

> [F]or the first time in the world archeological practice, monu-
> mental temples were found in which intoxicating beverage of the
> soma-haoma type were prepared for cult ceremonies.... The ex-
> cavations documentally proved that poppy, cannabis and ephe-
> dra were used for making the soma-haoma drinks, and thickets of
> these plants were found in excess in the vicinity of the excavated
> temples of Margiana. (Sarianidi, 2003)

Soviet archaeologists uncovered a large shrine, about the size of
a football field dating from 2,000 BC and consisting of two parts,

one of which was obviously for public access, but the other, as researcher Richard Rudgley describes "hidden from the gaze of the multitude, an inner sanctum of the priesthood" Sarianidi found three cermic bowls in this hidden room, and later analysis of the vessels by Professor Meyer-Melikyan identified traces of both cannabis and Ephedra. "Clearly both these psychoactive substances had been used in conjunction in the making of hallucinogenic drinks" (Rudgley, 1998).

> In the adjoining room of the same inner sanctum were found ten ceramic pot-stands which appear to have been used in conjunction with strainers designed to separate the juices from the twigs, stems and leaves of the plants. In another room at the other end of the shrine a basin containing remains of a considerable quantity of cannabis was discovered, as well as a number of pottery stands and strainers that have also been associated with making psychoactive beverages. (Rudgley, 1998)

Evidence of Fire worship, a key element of the Mazdean (later Zoroastrian) religion, alongside the remnants of utensils for making a sacred beverage that contained cannabis and other ingredients caused archaeologist Andrew Sherratt to question; "Was the interest in fire derived from the older, steppe custom of burning psychoactive substances, at a time when these substances were becoming beverages?" (Sherratt, 1995). Another possibility is that the fires aided in the drying process of the Haoma, and the harvesters came here from the hills and mountains to deliver the harvested Haoma to be dried and prepared in bundles, 'barsom' for later use. In this scenario, from the massive site of the temple, the concept would be that it served as a storage place and depot for the cultic use of Haoma for a very widespread area.

Remnants from vessels recovered at the site and involved in the preparation of the sacred drink have impressions from cannabis seeds left in the gypsum that settled over the millennia and the remants of ephedra, poppy[2] and mostly cannabis in the white sedi-

---

2   Of the poppy Sarianidi notes that "linguists repeatedly noted that poppy is not listed among the stimulators in the Avesta and that this plant is poor in alkaloids. But probably in the Avesta they had mentioned only the strongly effective plants and for this reason had neglected mentioning the poppy. Another possible explanation is that the high demand for intoxicants made people use any kind of hallucinogenic plants including poppy in making the ritual drink" (Sarianidi,1998).

ment stuck to the sides of ancient pots and pitchers. Russian archeologist Victor Sariandidi believes this proves these plants "were used for making the soma – haoma drinks..." (Sariandidi 2003). British anthropologist and author Richard Rudgley suggests that this "identification of haoma has an archaeological background which neither the fly-agaric nor Syrian rue can match, unless such evidence comes to light[3]" (Rudgley, 1998).

The Cult of the White Room

The BMAC temples, "like others built slightly later at nearby oasis forts, consists of a roofless courtyard (room 221) surrounded on all four sides by long skinny rooms" (Barber, 1999):

> Close to this complex, excavators always find a small room entirely plastered with white gypsum and fitted with three or more vessels set into a wall bench, also plastered white (Room 137). Inside the White room vessels at early Gonur, Russian scientists found residues identifiable as Ephedra and hemp, while at nearby Togolok 21..., the white room residues deposited a few centuries later proved to contain ehedra and poppy... (Barber, 1999)

Victor Sarianidi's *Margiana and Protozoroastrianism* (1998), which details the finds of the Margiana temple sites, includes an "analysis of floral remains" in an appendix piece by N. R Meyer-Melikyan and N.A. Avetov, discussing the evidence of cannabis and other plants, found at the site. The scientists analyzed a "ceramic vessel... which had apparently served for many years to preserve an especially valuable substance which had once had a medicinal/ritual purpose":

> The bottom of the vase had multiple layers of gypsum, lime and clay mixed with sand. Each layer of the mixture differed in composition, causing the layers to varying color and density and to separate easily from the other layers. The substance measures as much as 3 cm thickness, while each layer is from 1 mm to 7 mm

---

3   Rudgley also felt that due to the variety of plants found in the Bactria complex, identifying a single source of Haoma/Soma might be impossible. "Despite the considerable efforts made to discover the botanical identity of soma, it may be that this is one mystery that will never be satisfactorily solved" (Rudgley, 1998).

thick. The remains of material that was once kept in the vase were very well preserved between the layers.

To determine its purpose, the vase was dismantled into separate layers and each of the layers was carefully studied under a magnifying glass. Separating the layers revealed some very well preserved fruits, seeds, stems and other parts of plants that were all isolated and scanned by an electron microscope. In addition, a pollen analysis of each separate layer was performed by special means. The analysis of pollen and spores is based on the fact that the membrane of spores and pollen contains a highly resistant biopolymer, the sporopollenin... it almost never changes over long periods of geological time. Moreover, plants produce pollen and spores in large amounts; and they have quite clear morphological indicators which allow their classification into a certain family, genus or species.

Pollen disperses for long distances from the plant that produces it, and settles practically everywhere. But it is very unlikely that the pollen grains found in the vase under study settled there accidentally, since the vase was kept in a closed room. One can ignore the small probability of an accidental occurrence and can assume that all the pollen in the vase was either produced by those plants that had been put in the vase or that it had been carried there on those plants... The majority of the pollen grains are assumed to have been produced by the plants which the vase held, while small amounts of other kinds of pollen grains are assumed to have been carried to the vase from other plants which grew in the area where the preserved material had been growing.

The contents of the vase consisted of seven layers (C1-C7) and the following plant remains were isolated:

C1 (surface) – a large amount of hemp fruit, separate hemp flowers, fragments of Ephedra stems, pollen grains of hemp in large quantity, pollen grains representative of Chenopodiaceae, Poaceae, Polygonaceae, Artemisa. The composition of the floral remains in this layer confirms that for a certain period of time, the vase preserved substances received from hemp fruit as well as young Ephedra stems prior to their reproduction period proved by the absence of Ephedra pollen in the layer. The sporopollen analysis shows that all the plants were probably local.

C2 – many fruits and pollen grains of hemp, Ephedra stems, pollen grains of Chenopodiaceae, Poaceae, Polygonaceae, Artemisa and some plants from the Northern areas or from the high mountains... [bringing to mind the original Mountain home of

Haoma!]. The floral remains confirm that during the time period corresponding to this layer, the vase contained substances of a mixture of hemp fruit and Ephedra stems probably with an addition of other material that was carried down from the mountains or from the northern areas.

C3 – Ephedra stems, single pollen grains of Compositae, Poaceae, Chenopodiaceae and Artemisa. Probably, at the time that this layer was formed, the vase contained substances made only of the stems of local Ephedra.

C4 – the same composition as the one in the period of time of the C3 layer.

C5 – a few Ephedra remains, no pollen.

C6 – remains of Ephedra stem and a few pollen grains of poppy.

C7– a lot of hemp fruit in a good state of preservation; some seeds even have embryos. Pollen grains of Poaceae, Chenopodiaceae and Artemisa

The substance that was kept in the vase at this point of time probably consisted only of hemp fruit.

Thus, the substances that were kept in the vase at different periods of time were made of various plant combinations but always included hemp, Ephedra and less often poppy, all plants that are known to be used in the extraction of narcotics....

Based on these data, the analysis confirms that the given ceramic vessel was used for keeping various narcotics that had a wide sphere of application. For many ages, different amounts of narcotics have been used for treatment of disease as pain reducing agents and for temporarily increasing the capacity for work. The find of such a vessel speaks for the high level of knowledge in the preparation of narcotics and also speaks for their ritual use during rites and ceremonies of that time. (Meyer-Melikyan & Avetov, 1998)

Seeds of Dissent

Contradicting Meyer-Melikyan & Avetov's analysis of the seed imprints found in a number of the pots used to make the sacred beverage, Prof. Bakels has suggested that the seed imprints in question are too small and the wrong shape to have been cannabis seeds

The impressions caused by seeds are not of hemp. They are too small, for instance, do not have the right shape nor the right type of surface pattern... My interpretation is that the vessels were filled with not yet dehusked broomcorn millet. (Bakels 2003)

A photographic comparison with the impressions of cannabis seeds from the Margiana site provided by Sarianidi, with a picture of cannabis seeds, prepared by Haoma researcher Daniel Quaintance, clearly contradicts Bakels claim about the shape of the impression not fitting the shape of cannabis seeds. This picture clearly shows the "the similarity of the findings and the Hemp seed" (Quaintance, 2008). Bakels comments about the size of the seeds are likewise mistaken. As Daniel Quaintance has noted there are a number of problems with Bakels assertions:

> Researchers that discount Hemp as a viable candidate for Haoma should become more familiar with the seeds of Hemp as there are varieties with very small seeds and then there are effects of nature that can produce a crop of smaller than normal seeds at full maturity. Also without seeds remaining in the samples one does not know if the seeds had reached maturity and if not they would be very small. (Quaintance, 2008)

As noted by cannabis botany expert Robert Connell Clarke (1981), cannabis seeds occur in sizes ranging from 2mm to 6mm in length and 2mm to 4 mm in maximum diameter. "Mature Cannabis seeds vary widely in size, shape, color and seed – coat pattern. Colors range from light gray to black, and from buff to dark brown" (Clarke H. 1998). That ancient world seeds from the area were generally of the smaller size is clearly indicated by seeds collected from the Scythian burial site in Pazyryk, which fit well within the range of those identified by Meyer-Melikyan & Avetov. A comparison that was also noted by Dr. Ethan Russo:

> Bakels examined residual seed impressions in gypsum and suggested these as too small to be cannabis, rather suggesting broomcorn millet as having been present. The original description of a higher layer, however, referred to cannabis flowers and seeds... Additionally, examination of contemporary feral cannabis seeds from Kashmir... indicates that these average 2.2 mm in length... while broomcorn millet, Panicum miliaceum, seems to average 2.8 mm in diameter" [making them too large for the seeds in question]. (Russo, 2007)

As well, similar small cannabis seeds fitting within this range, have been found at a Chinese site where evidence of an ancient trade connection with BMAC has also been noted, as will be discussed in Chapter 9.

Fig 6.3: Showing wide size variations, "Modern 'Novosadska' hemp, Pazyryk Iron Age and British medieval Cannabis seeds" (Clarke & Fleming, 1998). Fig 6.4: Fruits of Cannabis sativa. Scale bar = 1.0 mm." (Jiang, et al., 2007), from a Chinese site that shows evidence of BMAC contact.

Finally, modern cannabis breeders, in search of early flowering strains, have bred varieties of *indica* with its older uncultivated predecessor *ruderalis*, developing, one would consider, a strain of cannabis possibly similar to that of those in question from Margiana, as cultivation of the plant then was much closer to its origins

Cannabis (Hemp) Seeds

Fig 6.5: Comparison of cannabis seeds with impressions in white gypsum recovered from BMAC prepared by Dan Quaintance. Fig 6.6: BMAC basin which contained white gypsum with seed impressions (Sarianidi, 2003).

than now. The seeds of this strain of cannabis, popularly known as "Mighty Mite" are of the smallest and darkest variety to be found, being of a solid color, almost black and about 2mm in length. Thus it can clearly be seen that Meyer-Melikyan & Avetov's original analysis of the seed imprints at Margiana, were likely correct, as the impressions fit well within the range of size and shape of cannabis seeds, particularly in association to the indigenous cannabis of the area and time period in question.

Unfortunately, there is debate about the identification of cannibinoids that were provided to Sarianidi by Meyer-Melikyan, N.R. and N.A. Avetov[4], in the fossilized sediment from the pots used for making the sacred beverage which were found at the site. Bakels analysis of the sediments, as with the seed impressions noted above, turned up negative.

> The white substance shows on the section several layers, as has been described by the authors mentioned above. Some of these are very thin, with a thickness of more or less 1 mm, others are thicker, but the thickness of the whole does not exceed 1.5 cm. N.R. Meyer-Melikyan and N.A Avetov succeeded in separating the layers and could describe different contents for each of them. I did not succeed in separating layers with significantly different aspects. It might be that I did not obtain quite the same material as what was published, or a different part of the deposit in the vessels. (Bakels, 2003)

But, as noted by Sarianidi, Bakels' examination of the material took place after several years of exposure in the open air and elements, which could well have caused the decomposition of the cannabis remains in the gypsum from inside the ancient clay vessels. There is a clear possibility that as with the seed impressions, which we have shown were clearly cannabis, Bakels is once again mistaken. For alternatively, as Mark Merlin, who revisited the subject of the identity of Soma more than thirty years after originally writing about it in light of Sarianidi's finds, has pointed out:

> According to Miller (2003)[5], photographs of the *Ephedra, Cannabis*, and *Papaver*, and archaeological specimens presented in the Togolok-21 report by Meyer-Melikyan (1990), appear to be consistent with the respective species; however, the determination of the *Papaver* species needs further study to confirm that it is *P. somniferum*. (Merlin, 2008)

---

4   Meyer-Melikyan, N.R. and N.A. Avetov. 1998. Analysis of Floral remains in the Ceramic Vsselsfrom the Gonur Temenos. In: (Sarianidi, 1998), Appendix I
5   Miller, N. 2003. University of Pennsylvania. Personal Communication with Merlin. [1/2/03].

More recently, Prof. Carl Ruck, who has researched the identification of Soma for more than three decades, and who wrote books with R. Gordon Wasson, has acknowledged that "The actual ingredients [of Soma] probably differed over the long history of the religion's continual existence, but archaeological evidence can document cannabis used in a ritual haoma ceremony as early as 2000 BCE at the sanctuary at Gunur in eastern Turkmenistan" (Ruck, 2009).

Based upon the massive size of the archaeological site, the Russian team believes that the temple served as a major depot for the entheogenic drink and that devotees travelled from a wide area to imbibe of it there. If, as the evidence indicates, this site was one of the earliest remnants of the Soma cult, then here with this cannabis cult we can find the very ancient roots of many modern existing religions.

As Rudgley explains "the discovery in the shrines of the remains of opium, cannabis and Ephedra in ritual vessels that are dated between 2000-1000 BC show that soma in its Iranian form haoma may be considered as a composite psychoactive substance comprising of cannabis and Ephedra in one instance and opium and Ephedra in another" (Rudgley, 1998). In BMAC we see the meeting place of the cultigens from a variety of cultures. "Cannabis consumption constituting an intrinsic part of Eastern European mysticism, whilst opium was consumed in Western Europe and the Mediteranean regions (where the plant actually originated) and fermented alcohol in the fertile crescent" (Scott, et al., 2003).

This archaeological evidence goes a long way to answering the riddle of the ancient Soma-Haoma; it accounts for the current use of one of the main candidates, ephedra, as it was a part of the original ingredients. The use of ephedra in modern Haoma preparations has been such a matter of controversy for researchers that it has been difficult not to identify the Avestan plant with the plant actually used by the descendants of the authors of the Avestan Literature, as numbers of researchers have done, no matter how many facts argued against this identification; and indeed with the evidence of cannabis, ephedra and poppies at the Margiana site, that relationship is now explained.

According to Mary Boyce a major authority on Zoroastrianism, *Homa* was "prepared from milk, the leaves of one plant and the juice obtained from pounding the stems of another. The pounded plant was

Fig 6.7-1, White room reconstructions, used for fixing hallucinogenic drinks, according to Sarianidi there were 3 storage vessels containing a residue of Ephedra and hemp. Fig 6.7-2, Ceramic ritual vessel. Fig 6.7-3, Vessel with cannabis seed impressions. Fig 6.7-6 & 10, Strainer for making Haoma. Fig 6.7-7, Bone drinking tubes, which when analyzed bared "the remains that contain threecolpus pollen grains of poppy... Remains of poppy seeds are also found on... [a] pestle..." (Meyer-Melikyan, 1998). Images from (Sarianidi, 2003).

called 'soma' in Sanskrit in the Vedic scriptures and in Avestan 'homa' a name which is widely agreed to mean simply 'that which is pressed.' The identity of the original plant used by the proto-Indo-Iranians is uncertain, but it may well have been a species of ephedra as is the 'hom' used by Zoroastrians today" (Boyce, 2001). Note here Boyce's statement that the homa sacrament was a mixture of one plant and another. Unfortunately Boyce's personal prejudice against cannabis has caused her to never consider it as the other plant in question.

Sarianidi's archaeological finds in Margiana helps answer this riddle. The addition of the mildly stimulating plant ephedra to such a preparation, likely accounts for the reputation of Soma to keep one awake, and was probably done in the same spirit as medieval Sufis, who would eat hashish and drink lots of strong stimulating coffee, a beverage that was a Sufi creation, then stay up all night praying and playing religious music. It also accounts for the survival of Ephedra in the modern Haoma sacrifice.

It should also be noted that in their speculations of Syrian rue as the Haoma, Flattery and Schwartz also put forth that the Syrian rue was mixed with Ephedra in the sacred preparation for this same reason (Flattery & Schwartz, 1989), so we must give them some credit for being half right.

Elizabeth Wayland Barber, was so taken with the work of Flattery and Schwartz, that despite being aware of and acknowledging the findings of cannabis at BMAC, she was still attached to the duos identification of Harmaline as the psychoactive property of Haoma. Regardless of that her comments in regard to the use of two plants in the preparation of the sacred beverage offers some good insights, particularly if one inserts cannabis in place of harmala in this context, which as we pointed out before, is largely excluded due to the nausea associated with it, nausea which Barber also notes (but the *Vedas* and *Avesta* do not):

> Prior to a performance of the ... ritual of Yasna, it seems, a priest sat by himself in a specially equipped and consecrated space and pounding two types of twigs in a mortar with water. After squeezing the juice through a strainer into a sacred cup, the priest carried this drink through the temple to a second priest, who drank it while reciting certain liturgical texts. Evidence suggests that the drink always consisted of at least two different plants, but that the hallucinogen itself constituted one of them only if it was deemed

necessary to visit the spirit world. Otherwise the preparer substituted an innocuous ingredient... One can understand the reluctance to use the drug more than needed, after reading about
the violent stomach cramps, vomiting, diarrhoea, and such that
harmine and harmaline cause.

... Ephedra was added to harmel specifically to keep the person
awake during the experience—and in fact that of all the pharmacologically active plants known from Iran, Ephedra is by far the
most suited for this purpose. Apparently the priests had learned
to balance harmel and Ephedra carefully as the ingredients of
soma/haoma for trips to the spirit world.[6] (Barber, 1999)

It seems very probable that both Soma and Haoma were always prepared with a variety of plants, with cannabis being one of the premier constituents, and this mixture became Haoma/Soma through
the ritual of preparation. This is in agreement with the *Satapatha
Brahmana* , 3.4.3.13, where it explains the plant *usana* (cannabis) is
pressed and then made "into Soma by means of consecration." Such
a description left Soma wide open to a variety of substitutions.

In RV X.89.5 we read: Soma is all shrubs and trees. This agrees
with his name vanaspati and virudham pati, king of trees and
plants.... Residues of Ephedra, poppy, and cannabis have been
found recently in vessels and mortars in the Zoroastrian temples
in Bactria, but this does not mean that the Soma-plant was identical with one of these plants. It seems more likely that these are
only herbs, with which the Soma was flavoured. (Richter-Ushanas, 1997)

There are even indications of this possibility indicated in both
the Vedic and Avestan literature, which seem to refer to different
types of Haoma and Soma.

And on those mountains
you grow in many varieties,
as the milky, golden-colored haoma.

---

6   "When 'tripping out' wasn't necessary, something else—usually an extract of
pomegranate wood—took the place of harmel in the sacred daily ritual, according to the
evidence. Ephedra, however, a gentler drug than harmel, could always remain in the brew.
When the India folk, who had already substituted something for harmel upon moving to
northern India, moved yet further south, out of the habitat of even Ephedra they substituted an inert "epehedra look-alike" for the second ingredient as well" (Barber, 1999).

Your remedies have been mixed
by the creative magic of Good Thought.

Y.10.12

I praise all the Haomas,
even when on the heights of the mountains,
even when in the depths of the streams,
even those in the narrow passes of ravines,
in the clutches of women.

Y.10.17

We sacrifice to tall, golden Haoma.
We sacrifice to ruddy Haoma, furtherer of living beings.
We sacrifice to death-averting Haoma.
We sacrifice to all the Haomas.

Y.10.21

Of all the many Plants whose King is, Soma,
Plants of hundred forms,
Thou art the Plant most excellent,
prompt to the wish, sweet to the heart.
O all ye various Herbs whose King is Soma,
that o'erspread the earth,
Urged onward by Brhaspati, combine your virtue in this Plant.

RV.10.97

With its references to "Twins," "Pair" and "Parents," in the preparation of the Soma and birth like description of the prepared beverage in RV.9.93, it could be inferred that through the bringing together of the two plants Soma was "born":

The drops of Soma juice like cows who yield their milk have flowed forth, rich in meath, unto the Shining One... He bellows with a roar around the highest twigs: the Tawny One is sweetened as he breaks them up. Then passing through the sieve into the ample room, the God throws off the dregs according to his wish. The gladdening drink that measured out the meeting *Twins* fills full with milk the Eternal Ever-waxing *Pair*... Wandering through, the *Parents*, strengthening the floods, the Sage makes his place swell with his own native might. The stalk is mixed with grain: he comes led by the men together with the sisters, and preserves the Head. With energetic intellect the Sage is *born*, deposited as germ

of Law, far from the Twins. They being young at first showed visibly distinct the Creature that is half-concealed and half-exposed.
RV.9.93[7]

As well, the later use of opium poppies in the Bactria Temples
indicate other plants may have later been used as a substitution for
cannabis, possibly in times of shortage, or even in addition to it,
and this may in fact be the source of much of the confusion on this
issue. Indications of a variety of plants being used may be found in
the later *Atharvaveda*, written centuries after the original *Vedas*, in
reference to a number of plants including cannabis, being governed
by the god Soma; "We tell of the five kingdoms of herbs headed by
Soma: may it and the Kusha grass, and *bhanga* and barley, and the
herb Saha release us from anxiety." This fits in well with the view
of the late British archaeologist Andrew Sherratt "It seems likely...
that the drink described as *soma* involved the infusion of various
plant products known earlier on the steppes, and there is no single
answer to the *soma* question." (Sherratt, 1995).

In the 2007 BBC program *Story of India*, host Michael Woods
visted Victor Sarianidi at BMAC, and the Russian archaeologist
was still of the strong opinion that the identification of cannabis,
ephedra and poppy still stood. But, as it stands, until the results of
N.R. Meyer-Melikyan, and N.A. Avetov (1998), and further confirmation of Miller, can be tested against the work of Bakels and
associates by independent parties, or further test material is found,
the identification of the sacred beverage which was prepared in this
4000 yearr old temple sites, remains a mystery.

Interestingly, Sarianidi, still working hard at archaeology in the
area, reported another find in 2006, of an even older but related
5,000 year-old temple, again dedicated to the production of the Sacred Haoma!

In the previous years of excavations the shrine Togoluk-21 excavated first among those identified with the process of cooking
and the rituals praising the sacred potion was completely uncovered in the old delta of the Murghab River. However, the shrine
Togolok-21 is dated to the mid-second millennium BC, and it has
not been known so far whether the shrines of such kind existed
earlier, i.e. at the late 3rd early 2nd millennia BC? Now, we have

---

7   (Griffith, 1896)

found the answer to the question of great scientific significance which has been rousing our curiosity for many years!

....Another cult construction used for the similar purposes was excavated in the southeastern part of Gonur, near the royal necropolis. The fact that the temple is located outside the enclosing wall of the palace-temple ensemble can indicate its early construction, circa the late 3rd millennium BC.... The most striking thing is a number of the vessels coated inside with gypsum and dug into the ground testifying that local people prepared Soma/Haoma too....

We had excavated the vessels of such kind before. An extant sample was uncovered in Togoluk-1. The sculptural elements of the cult vessels serve as the illustrations to myths and legends popular among the people of Margush....

The figurines found this spring absolutely identify those known before. We have no doubts on their similarity to the vessels of such kind. It is accepted, the Soma/Haoma cult trace back to the period of the Indo-European unity. Discovery of two shrines in Gonur North dated back to the 3rd-2nd millennia BC clearly attest to that the rituals related to the Soma/Haoma cult were quite popular among the indigenous tribes among which the oldest religion Zoroastrianism emerged. (Sarianidi, 2006)

Hopefully, this new find, complete with the 5000 year-old gypsum covered pots for preparing Soma/Haoma, will provide more ancient material for analysis and the claims of Sarianidi, Meyer-Melikyan, and Avetov (1998) can be reproduced.

In "The problem of Aryans and the Soma: Textual-linguistic and archeological evidence," Asko Parpola, explains of the Soma enigma in light of Sarianidi's work in Margiana and makes some statements that coincide with the words of Sherratt, and also serve as a good transition point for our next Chapter, on the Scythian Huamavarga (Haoma-Gatherers):

The botanical identity of the *Soma* plant has been debated for a long time but most specialists nowadays opt for Ephedra... In Margiana, Sarianidi has discovered vessels which chemical analysis has shown contain organic remains of Ephedra... the ritualistic vessels also contained remains of poppy and cannabis... These finds are of the greatest interest, as they may provide the earliest available evidence of the *Soma* cult... Suffice it is to say that if the Margiana Temples date back to the BMAC[8] period (c. 1900-1700 B.C.) and if the vessels contain remains of Ephedra, we may assume that the... [people] of Margiana did in fact press the *Soma*.... the Soma cult was... [likely] introduced to both Bactria and Margiana by the conquerors of the [inhabitants of Margiana and Bactria], who belonged to the same group as the Rgvedic Aryans. In that case the use of Soma might have started... [with] the Andronovo culture, [2300-900 BCE] and this could have taken place in the Ferghanna or Zerravasham mountains, the area of the later Saka Haumavarga... or in fact anywhere in the vast Andronovo territory, including the Tian Shan on the border of China where "Ephedra... has been recognized for many centuries as a medicine."[9] (Parpola, 1995)

The term 'Andronovo culture' is a blanket name for a collection of similar Bronze Age tribes that flourished ca. 2300–1000 BCE in western Siberia from the southern Urals, to the Yensie River and the west Asiatic steppe. The term applies to communities that were largely nomadic pastoralists as well as those settled in small villages, especially in Central Asia. The Andronovo culture is strongly associated with the Indo-Iranians and is often credited with the invention of the spoke-wheeled chariot around 2000 BCE. Archaeological data from Bactria and Margiana shows that Andronovo tribes penetrated into Bactria and the Margianian oases. The Andronovo cultures are generally considered to be the ancestors of the Scythian Haomavarga, discussed in the next Chapter, and it is through this group, as we shall show, that the Haoma cult became surprisingly widespread....

8   BMAC- Bactria, Margiana, Archaeological Complex. There are a number of so far neglected words in Indo-Iranian without Indo-European etymologies; some of these are believed to come from Iranian/BMAC substrate language(s), such as the local words for the newly introduced domesticated camel. Interestingly the following terms for cannabis are listed amongst the most likely BMAC words; *'kana/k'ana,*'"hemp,"*'bhang,*'"hemp."
9   (Flattery & Schwartz, 1989).

7

THE SCYTHIAN
"HAOMA-GATHERERS"

One of the most fascinating, yet barbaric pre-common era cannabis using societies can be found in a group of no-madic tribes now known collectively as the Scythian (as the Greeks referred to them) or Sakas (as the Persians knew them). For some centuries (7th century B.C., to the 1st century B.C.) the Scythians played a very prominent role in the Ancient World. The Scythians were expert horsemen, and considered one of the earliest peoples to master the art of riding, and use horse-driven covered wagons. Their Eastern European origins, mastery of the horse and their well known cultic use of cannabis clearly identify them as the descendants of the Sredeni Stog culture described in Chapter 3. With this common ancestry it is not surprising to find many of the same cultural beliefs amongst the Scythians as those of the Indo-European Soma/Haoma cult. The Scythians early high mobility is probably why many scholars credit them with the spread of canna-bis knowledge throughout the ancient world and it is likely "that as they spilled across much of Europe and Asia, they were the ones to introduce the natives to the ritual use of the plant" (Benet, 1975). Indeed, the Scythian people are said to have traveled and settled extensively throughout the Mediterranean, Central Asia, India, Russia and Europe.

Scythian Culture came into the ancient world came through three major phases of migration. First, the 'proto-Scythian'or 'Tim-ber Grave Culture' originating from the Urul Mountains of Western Russia (which divides Europe and Asia), began a westward expan-sion around 1800 B.C. This was followed around 1100 B.C. when another Scythian migration through the Pontic Steppes took place, and these nomads incorporated indigenous agricultural communities into their fold, leading to their classification as "Agricultural Scythians." "Then, ca. 600-550 B.C.E., a third wave migrated westward out of southern Siberia. These late-comers, who eventually pushed west along the north coast of the Black sea as far as Bulgaria and who invaded Iran as well, bore several ethnic labels... among them were the Massag-etae (southeast of the Aral sea), the Saka (northeastern Iran, Western Afghanistan), the Thyssagetae (the central Urals), and... the 'Sauromatae.'" (Littleton & Malcor, 1994-2000).

Throughout much of this period the Scythian tribes were believed to have maintained well-used trade routes that connected their many distant settlements. Though no-madic, the Sythians had a single patriarchal sovereign (whose powers were transmitted to his son at death), and the different tribal chieftains all paid him tribute. This leader had an entourage of wealthy nobles who acted as his courtiers.[1] From the accounts of Herodo-tus there were three major groups in Scythian cul-ture, the aforementioned nobles, who were known as 'Royal Scythians,' nomadic 'Warrior Scythians,' who ensured the continued rule of the king and nobles, and 'Agricultural Scythians,' "most likely compro-mising conquered, 'Scythianized,' indigenous peo-ple" (Littleton & Malcor, 1994: 2000).

The Scythians' horses, like their riders, were dressed in beautiful ornate armor. Undoubtedley the fierce look of these invading nomads must have had a formidable effect on the people of the lands they traveled through, many of whom would have never seen a horse before.

A number of astonishing victories in battle brought Scyth-ians a great deal of fame, and much of Western Persia fell under the rule of Scythian chieftains. It has been recorded that they invaded Syria

Fig. 7.1: Scythian Suit of Armor. Fig. 7.2: Horse Headgear.

1   Interestingly the Scythian model has been suggested as the proto-type for the later tales of Arthur and his Court of Knights, see From *Scythia to Camelot* (Littleton & Malcor, 1994: 2000).

and Judea around 625 B.C., and even reached the borders of Egypt where peace terms were reached with them by the not surprisingly intimidated ruling Pharoah of that time.

The act of war was one in which the Scythian men as well as women, are said to have participated. The ancient historian Diordorus commented that Scythian women *"fight like the men and are nowise inferior to them in bravery."* Greek sources recorded that Scythian women. (who are also known to have been tattooed like their mates) had to kill three enemies in battle before marrying, and that a mastectomy of the right breast was performed on female infants, in order that their pectoral muscle wouldn't weaken and they would be able to brandish a sword better! It was also said that when the Scythians saw for the first time the fierce warrior women, the Amazons, they were determined to have children by them. Herodotus wrote that young Scythian men were eventually successful in their hopes of this seduction and the Amazonian women learned their language, although they were somewhat reluctant to give up their occasional raiding campaigns with their fierce warrior sisters.[2] Alternatively, Prof. Littleton explains "Re the Amazon myth, a much simpler explanation is that they were in fact the wives of the Scythian warriors, who often fought alongside their husbands. This so freaked out the patriarchal Greeks that they came up with an elaborate myth to explain it" (Littleton, 2008).

Some scholars have pointed to the similarities between these Caucasian nomadic warriors of the Russian steppes and North American Indians, noting the similar tepee like tents used by both, the collecting of the scalps of their enemies, nomadic, similar medicine men and shamans, tribal art and motifs, etc..

The Scythians had no written language and much of what is known about them has been derived from the many precious and exquisitely crafted artifacts found in frozen tombs in Russia, Kazakhstan and the Eurasian plains. A variety of precious items, weapons, jewelry, clothing, etc., meant to follow the deceased into the afterlife, and well preserved from their stay in the frozen tombs, can be viewed in Russian museums:

> ...each burial throughout the entire area contained a cast bronze caldron of the distinctive Scythian shape. These caldrons varying

---

2   Herodotus; *The Histories* (Penguin Classics,1954)

size from quite small examples to others weighing as much as 75 pounds; an overwhelming majority have a solid base, shaped like a trunctuayted cone, around which the fire was heaped. The upper section is a semispherical bowl provided ...with handles (shaped like animals) fixed to the rim opposite each other....at Pazyryk, small caldrons filled with stones and hempseeds were found standing beneath leather or felt tentlets with three or six supports.[3]

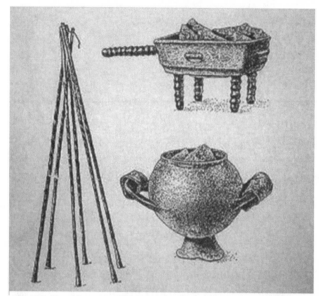

The poles associated with the caldron and stand would be set up like a tepee with the cauldron in its center which held heated stone and cannabis thrown on the stones, causing vapour to pour forth; the structure was covered with a blanket so that the participants could inhale the trapped vapours from

Fig 7.3: Tent frame and bronze vessels with stones and cannabis seeds found in a series of burial mounds at Pazyryk in the Altai Mountains of Siberia dating to the fifth century B.C.

within the small enclosure. At a Paryzyk tomb a beautifully made leather blanket decorated with winged lion griffins that were pouncing upon elks was included in the burial for this purpose. As Andrew Sherratt notes, for the Scythians, this was a very ancient custom by this time, "the practice of burning cannabis as a narcotic is a tradition which goes back in this area [Romania and the Caucasus] some five or six thousand years and was the focus of social and religious rituals of the pastoral people of central Eurasia in pre-historic and early historic times" (Sherratt, 1995). "In 1712 the famous German geographer Engelbert Kampfer (1651-1716) identified the plants that the Scythians used for their purifications as hashish. And in 1802 a Polish Count, Jan Potocki (1761-1815), identified the Scythian seers with 'les Schamanes de la Siberie.'" (Bremmer, 2002)

3   The Scythians: *Encyclopaedia Britannica*

...[T]he ecstasies and trances produced by intoxication among the adepts of Bachus, and the delirium of the Corbybantes when they celebrated the Great Goddess of Phrygia and Asia Minor, had their equivalent in those provoked by Indian hemp in the vapor baths in which Scythians indulged. (Charriere, 1979)

The Russian anthropologist V.A. Kisel comments that the "fact that censers are numerous indicates that they were a collective property of a clan or tribe" (Kisel, 2007):

Even vessels from elite burials such as Pazyryk II, Tolsty, Mys V mound 2, Kosh-Pei-1 mound 2 ... can be viewed, not as the deceased person's property, but as a ritual instrument ensuring his/her transition to the other world... As analyses have shown, certain censers were used for a long time, and were sometimes repaired. (Kisel, 2007)

Cannabis was an integral part of the Scythian cult of the dead wherein homage was paid to the memory of their departed leaders. In a famous passage written in about 450 B.C., Herodotus describes the funeral rites that took place when a king died among the Scythians. After burial, he recorded, the Scythians would purify themselves by setting up small tepee-like structures covered by rugs which they would enter to inhale the fumes of hemp seeds (and the resinous flower calyxes surrounding the seeds) thrown onto red-hot stones.

The burial completed, the Scyths cleanse themselves in the following manner. They soap their heads and wash their hair, and then to cleanse their bodies they do as follows: they set up three sticks leaning together which they cover with woolen felts, and in the circular shelter created as best they can they put stones heated in a fire into a vessel set within a shelter... In Scythia they grow hemp...And then the Scyths take some of its seeds, creep under the felt and scatter the seeds over the hot stones, which gives off greater clouds of steam than in any Greek steam bath. The Scyths delighted by the steam, are loudly exultant. (Herodotus)[4]

It is most likely the seeds described by Herodotus, were seeded buds, and the charred carbonized seeds found by archaeologists,

4   From a quote in (Rudenko, 1970)

what was left over from the burnt buds.[5] From the evidence discussed in Chapter 3 this was already a very old method of cannabis
inhalation by this time.

In the Paryzyk tombs Rudenko also found some metal censors
designed for inhaling smoke which did not appear to be connected with any religious rite. As Rudenko noted "smoking hemp, like
smoking hashish, took place without a doubt not just as a ceremony
of purification after burial but in ordinary life; hashish was used
as a narcotic. Not without reason Hesychius of Alexanandria in
his Lexikon... calls hemp 'the Scythian smoking which has such
strength that it brings out in a sweat anyone who experiences it.
They burn hemp seeds'" (Rudenko, 1970). From the accounts of
Herodotus and Hesychius it seems likely that the Scythians introduced their method of intoxication to a variety of different cultures
throughout the ancient world.

Rudenko points to both recreational and ceremonial use of cannabis amongst the Scythians. Others have commented more on the
ritualistic implications of the hemp-rite, such as the German researcher Geo Widengren who noted that "this purification had no
mundane meaning, rather it corresponds to a shamanistic ritual, by
which the shaman escorts the dead soul to the underworld. In fact
the shaman is not mentioned in Herodot's [sic] description, but all
the crucial details recur otherwise in the Scythian purification: cult
of the dead, use of hemp, 'baths' and howling together constitute a
complex ritual whose aim is ecstasy" (Widengren, 1965).

It should also be noted that it "is possible that purification
rites practiced by Asian nomads included simple forms, which
did not require the use of special paraphernalia. Judging by the
ethnographic evidence, fumigation was sometimes performed by
means of smouldering bunches of plants held by the participants
or put on the ground, on a stone, or on the burial construction"
(Kisel, 2007). It has also been suggested "the slabs of stone in the
form of rams discovered in Siberia and central Asia... were possibly portable altars used to burn hemp seeds [i.e. seeded buds]"
(Ginzburg,2004).

Herodotus noted a similar ritual amongst the Massagetae, a tribe
that has been connected with the Scythians:

5   19th century observers noted that the Ossetes of the Caucus, an Indo-European
people, believed to be direct descendants of the hemp inhaling Scythians of Herodotus'
day, were still practicing this method of self-intoxication close to 2,500 years later.

...[T]rees... they have found... bear fruit of a peculiar kind. Gathering in groups they sit in a circle around a fire and they cast this fruit into the flames. As it burns, it sends out smoke, the smell of which makes them drunk, just as wine does the Greeks. The more fruit they cast into the flames, the more drunk they get, until they jump up and start singing and dancing.[6] (Herodotus)

As the editors of *On the War for Greek Freedom* have noted "This 'fruit' is of course cannabis or marijuana, still cultivated in the part of the world where Herodotus locates the Massagetae" (Shirley & Romm, 1982).

Referring to the Scythians under their alternate name of the 'Sakas,' Guive Mirfendereski notes "etymologically, many have concluded that the name Massagetae meant 'Great Saka'... Massagetae, the reasoning goes, referred to Saga/Saka and 'ma' meant 'big' or 'great' so the whole name meant 'Great Saka'...." (Mirfendereski, 2005). This was a conclusion that Mirfendereski rejected, noting that Scythians of eastern Central Asia are called '*haumavarka*' (Haoma-gatherers)[7]; "I believe the key to the meaning of 'Massagetae' then ought to be in the possibility of it being a Greek rendition of Homavarka - in which 'homa' appears in the form of the first syllable 'ma'[8] and Saka is represented in 'sagetae' or 'saketae.' Herodotus's Massagetae therefore was a direct translation of 'Homa Saka'" (Mirfendereski, 2005). Like Mirfendereski, who believes the title Haomavarga came to the Scythians through their use of hemp, archaeologist Bruno Jacobs has likewise suggested that the name was derived from the Scythian practice of laying cannabis on hot stones to release its intoxicating vapours (Jacobs, 1982). A view further strengthened by the archeological finds of cannabis present at a 4000 year old Temple site in BMAC that was devoted to the preparation of the Haoma discussed in Chapter 6, and finds of cannabis at Scythian sites.

Noted Hemp scholar Sula Benet commented that the "Scythians apparently did not use hemp for manufactures such as weaving and

6   As translated in *On the War for Greek Freedom* (Shirley & Romm, 2002)
7   The Iranist Rüdiger Schmitt put forth a variety of other potential etymologies for the Haomavarka, see Appendix B.
8   Due to a similar view, some have come to see an etymological connection between the Chinese term for cannabis 'ma,' and the ancient cannabis drink 'hao-ma,' a conclusion strengthened by recent finds of ancient cannabis using Caucasian mummies in China – see Chapter 9

rope-making," which has now been shown to be untrue, as a variety of hemp garments have been recovered from Scythian sites. Regardless, Benet noted that Scythian use of hemp for incense was copious, "despite the plentiful quantity of wild hemp, the Scythians cultivated the plant to increase the amount available for their use. Apparently their need for it was great indeed" (Benet, 1975).

Herodotus' ancient records of the Scythian hemp rites were thought to be mythical, until they were verified in 1929, with the discovery of a Scythian tomb in Pazyryk, western Altai, by Professor S.I. Rudenko. In a trench that was 160 feet square and 20 feet deep, Rudenko and his crew found the embalmed remains of a Scythian man and a bronze cauldron of charred cannabis seeds. The man was obviously a chief or some other high ranking individual, as his tomb was accompanied by the skeletons of a number of horses that were sacrificed in order to accompany him into the afterlife.

Attesting to the vigor of these people, the man, who was about 60 years of age at the time of his death, was very powerfully built, and he did not succumb to natural causes, but rather most likely died in the midst of battle. The right parietal bone was perforated by two oval shaped holes caused by a pick like instrument that probably caused his death, probably in a battle with an enemy, as after he was killed he had been scalped in the Scythian fashion. For

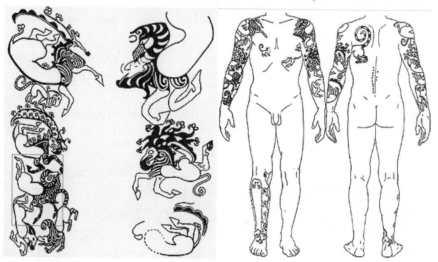

Fig 7.4 & 7.5: Illustrations of Scythian tattoos found on a mummy at the Paryzyk site, "Fantastic theme from the tattooing of the man in the Pazyryk burial. It suggests some hallucination caused by drugs" (Charriere, 1979).

his burial, a false scalp was laid over the skull and sewn back on
with horsehair, probably by the man's relatives after the body was
recovered. A false beard had also been tied on to the man's shaven
chin. In life, elaborate tattooed designs had been made on his chest,
back, arms and legs.

In *Scythian Art: Crafts of the Early Eurasian Nomads*, Georges
Charriere saw a profound influence from cannabis in the psychedelic like designs incorporated into the tattoos of a Scythian mummy from Paryzyk:

>...[T]he bodies of the dead... were adorned with extremely com-
>plicated tattooings, which motifs are fantastic ones, all derived
>from animal forms. One specialist has written that they are 'so liv-
>ing, so full of energy in their conception and execution, that they
>easily take their place among the finest in Scythian art.' Antlers
>gradually take on the appearance of huge outbursts of blossom,
>and the tails of animals depicted describe circumvolutions or fold
>themselves elegantly under the legs of the protagonists, to end in
>equally flowery or leafy appendages. It is rare to find designs that
>give such impression of rabid almost frenetic movement, with the
>bodies interlaced, twisted, coiled, dislocated, in such unexpected
>postures that they sometimes lose all similarity to life. It is a fan-
>tasy of forms and color, in which the variations on a given theme
>do not come from simple observation of nature. Hashish is as
>evocative as this — even more so than all other modifiers of the
>mind, at least the natural ones known in the world of antiquity:
>it opens to the artist the gates of a magical paradise in which jos-
>tling and unstable forms offer themselves to his exalted sensitiv-
>ity, his intelligence, and his taste. It is lucky for us that a painter
>and poet like Theophile Gautier should have experimented with
>hemp, for every image in his account can be illustrated by the
>strange bestiary and the treasures of the Eurasian nomads. He
>wrote: "I saw quite clearly in my chest the hashish I had eaten,
>in the form of an emerald from which there darted millions of
>little sparks. My eyelashes grew longer and longer, curling like
>gold threads around small ivory wheels which were turning of
>their own accord with dazzling speed. Round about me precious
>stones of every hue were trickling and crashing down, and con-
>tinually renewed floral designs, which I could best compare with
>the play of patterns of a kaleidoscope. I still saw my companions

now and then, but changed in shape, half-men, half-plants, with pensive airs like an ibis, standing on one foot like an ostrich, beating wings, such strange ones that, in my corner, I writhed with laughter." (Charriere, 1979)

As Rudenko describes the hemp burning implements:

In each vessel besides the stones, as already mentioned above, there was a small quantity of seeds of hemp (Cannabis sativa L. of the variety C. ruderalis Janisch.). Burning hot stones had been placed in the censer and part of the hemp seeds had been charred. Furthermore the handle of the cauldron censer had been bound round with birch bark, evidently because the heat of the stones was such that its handle had become too hot to hold in the bare hands.

...in barrow 2, two smoking sets were found: vessels containing stones that had been in the fire and hemp seeds; above them were shelters supported on six rods, in one case covered with a leather hanging and in the other case probably with a felt hanging, large pieces of which were found in the southwest corner of the tomb. Finally, there was a [leather] flask containing hemp seeds fixed to one of the legs of a hexapod stand. Consequently we have the full set of articles for carrying out the purification ritual, about which Herodotus wrote in such detail in his description of the Black Sea Scyths. There had been sets for smoking hemp in all the Pazyryk barrows; the sticks for the stand survived in each barrow although the censers and cloth covers had all been stolen except in barrow 2. Hemp smoking was practiced evidently not only for purification, but in ordinary life by both men and women.

The habit of purifying by fire after burials (fumigation)... among the Scyths was evidently widely practiced by tribes over an area that included High Altai. (Rudenko, 1970)

As noted earlier, the burnt seeds discovered by Rudenko and his crew were the remnants of the seeded buds that the ancient Scythians threw on the hot coals. Besides seeds, hemp shirts were also found. A later find in 1972 at Ordzhonikidze in the southern Ukraine was reported on by *Time* magazine:

For the first time in more than half a century, diggers uncovered an unlooted royal tomb of the fabled Scythian tribesmen who roamed and ruled great areas of the Russian heartland more than 2,000 years ago. The Scythians left behind no written record when they finally vanished from the steppes in the 2nd century B.C., victims of intermarriage and conquest.

But there was no end of legends about their ferocity in battle and their great troves of gold. The Greek historian Herodotus devoted more than half a volume to them. Still, it was not until the 19th century, when archaeologists began serious studies of the puzzling remains found scattered from the borders of China to the banks of the Dniester, that scholars would admit there might be more than a shard of truth to the old Scythian tales.

Now, the discovery of the royal tomb, which contains the skeletons of a prince, a princess and an infant-as well as other recent digs in the U.S.S.R. - gives the old stories the ring of historical fact. Herodotus tells, for instance, how the Scythians beheaded their fallen enemies and brought the skulls back to camp to use as wine goblets. Archaeologist Renate Rolle, a young West German woman and the first Western scientist allowed to participate in a Soviet dig since 1920, reports that there is new evidence of Scythian ferociousness. Lances and bows and arrows found in graves along with female skeletons and ornaments suggest that the Scythian women fought beside their men. Thus Herodotus may well have been correct when he said that bloodthirsty Scythian Amazons had to kill a man in battle before they were allowed to marry.

Ancient bronze vessels found in Scythian graves in the Altai mountins near China and Mongolia, still contain remnants of the nomads' favourite hemp seeds. They were also highly successful herdsmen and farmers who traded their grain to indulge their taste for expensive jewellery, such as a magnificent gold pectoral ornament recovered from the new-found grave in the Ukraine. Crafted by Greek goldsmiths, who probably lived among the Scythians along the Black Sea, the chestpiece contains no fewer than 44 exquisitely carved animals. Among them; such fantasy creatures as the griffin, which has the head, wings and forelegs of an eagle and the body of a lion.

Like the Egyptian pharaohs, Scythian rulers believed in taking their worldly goods with them. Their graves contain not only necklaces, rings and the small golden plaques that they fastened onto their garments, but also household implements, horses and even the remains of faithful servants. (*Time* magazine, 1972)

It is known that massive sacrifices took place with the death of Scythian Kings, as the physical evidence collected by archaeologists can attest to. For 40 days after the death of a king, the mourners would travel the country conducting the dead body of the king through the lands he had ruled in life. After this the body was taken to a tomb for burial, where the massive sacrifice of not only horses, took place, but that of humans as well. The King's wives, cupbearers, principal servants, etc. were destined to join him, willingly or not, in the afterworld.

> Similar slaughters in some districts of central India, where religions equally costly in human life have been practiced, show how the use of the local hemp made the victims undergo the sacrifice voluntarily. There after the wife had chosen the day for the holocaust, a particularly strong dose increased her courage against any shrinking: in an ecstasy she would go to the altar of her own accord. One may therefore wonder if it was not the same with the sacrifices forming part of the great Scythian funerals. For neither Herodotus nor the excavations suggest that there was ever, even in the last moments of life, any violent natural defensive reaction on the part of the men and women who had to follow their lord and masters into the tomb.
>
> The anesthetic properties of hemp might also be the explanation of the relative ease with which the Scythians in the funeral procession were able to undergo the physical torments that were considered obligatory and seemly. During the last century it was the same at the Indian festivals of the ferocious goddess Kali: not only did an impressive number of drugged fanatics throw themselves under the feet of the sacred elephants and under the cutting wheels of the chariots of the gods, but others, from devotion, mutilated themselves horribly: religion and the drug combined to produce such apparent derangement. (Charriere, 1979)

Herodotus attributed some other rather bizarre and barbaric customs to the ancient Scythians; such as holding a party for one of their elders, whom they think is about to die from natural causes, and then sacrificing them along with a general sacrifice of cattle; "then they boil the flesh and eat it. This they consider the best kind of Death."[9] (Grock that!) It was a Scythian custom for every man to drink the blood of the first man he killed, and they scalped their enemies and used the skin as a sort of handkerchief, even going so far as to sew a number of scalps together in order to make a cloak. They would use the skin off the right hand of their enemies, nails and all in order to make a sort of case for their quiver of arrows.

9   Herodotus; *The Histories* (Penguin Classics,1954)

And to top off this savagery they drank from goblets made of the skulls of their enemies, both of foreign and their own kinsmen, as already noted.

Herodotus recorded that "the only Gods the Scythians worship are Hestia (their chief deity), Zeus, and Earth (whom they believe to be the wife of Zeus, and as deities of secondary importance, Apollo, Celestial Aphrodite, Heracles, and Ares. These are recognized by the entire nation; the Royal Scythians also offer sacrifice to Poseidon."[10] Interestingly the Scythian Goddess chose as her weapon, the Scythe, a tool used in the harvesting of cannabis and named after the culture from which it is thought to have originated, the Scythians.

> The only deity shown in Scythian art was the Great goddess whom the Greeks called Artemis, or Hestia or Gaea (The Earth)...Scythians were governed by priestess-queens, usually buried alone in richly furnished Kurgans (queen graves)...The moon-sickle used in mythical castrations of god was a Scythian weapon. A long handled form therefore came to be called a scythe, and was assigned to the Grim Reaper, who was originally Rhea Kronia in the guise of Mother Time, or Death - the Earth who devoured her own children. Scythian women apparently used such weapons in battle as well as religious ceremonies and agriculture. (Walker, 1986)

Walker's comments regarding the use of the scythe and agriculture, can be particularly applied to the Scythians favorite and most versatile crop, cannabis hemp, as the long handled scythe with its curved blade is particularly designed for harvesting hemp, enabling the harvester to cut the hemp along the soil line thus preserving its long fibrous stalks. In relation to the Scythian Goddess, it is interesting to note that along with the cannabis burning braziers found Pazyryk, two extraordinary rugs were also found in the frozen Scythian tomb. One rug had a border frieze with a repeated composition of a horseman approaching the Great Goddess Tabiti-Hestia, the patroness of fire and beasts, who holds the 'Tree of Life' in one hand and raises the other hand in welcome. Professors Schultes and Hoffman refer to this carpet in a chapter on cannabis (Schultes & Hoffman, 1979). Interestingly, as shall be discussed,

10   .Herodotus; *The Histories* (Penguin Classics,1954)

the symbolic imagery on this rug, repeated elsewhere in Scythian artifacts, has been connected with the Haoma/Soma ritual. "Like the Aryans... who composed the Rig Veda, the Scythians may have been grinding the plant and throwing it into their mead and possibly trading it to the Aryans to the south of them in the Indus Valley" (Copeland, 2007).

The Scythian Soma

Fig 7.6: Carpet Frieze depicting a horseman approaching the great Goddess who holds the Tree of Life in one hand. "Perhaps this is a potentially early source for the Grail legends" (Bennett, et al., 1995).

In the essay, "Remarks on the Scythian, Sarmatian and Meotian Beliefs," Russian researcher Sergei V. Rjabchikov (2004), refers to similar imagery occurring on a variety of Scythian relics and connects it with the Haoma ritual of the Persians (Rjabchikov, 2004).

> ..... This goddess is well known as the Scythian main sun goddess Tabiti (associated with the Greek goddess Hestia). The Scythian goddess Tabiti 'Heating' is related to the Indo-Aryan god Agni 'Fire' (Afanasiev 1868: 24; Raevsky 1994: 204-205).... Let us consider this drawing. The World Tree is on the left. A goddess sits on the throne and holds a pot.... this image is repeated in other analogous images..... The chief character is the sun goddess Tabiti

(Ma, Aga/Yaga, Rada). She is holding a vessel.... According to the Rig-Veda (II.36.1), the god Indra is appealed to drink the soma liquor from the hotar's bowl, moreover, he has the first right to it. Old Indian soma and hotar mean 'elixir' and 'sacrificial fire' respectively. On the other hand, according to the Rig-Veda (I.1.1, I.76.2), the god Agni corresponds to the hotar. The soma liquor is produced with the enkindled flame (Rig-Veda IV.25.1)... Indra received the pressed soma liquor from Agni (Rig-Veda III.22.1). Indra is the lord of the soma; Agni brings him this juice (Rig-Veda I.76.3). The soma always helps Indra (Rig-Veda I.4.1, I.32.3, I.52.3, II.11.11, II.16.2, II.17.1)..... Therefore it is safe to say that the god Targitai (= Indra) took the rhyton/vessel (= the hotar's bowl) with the soma liquor from the goddess Tabiti (= Agni)[11],..."

....I shall try to realise this information. According to the Rig-Veda (II.36.1), the god *Indra* is appealed to drink the *soma* liquor from the *hotar's* bowl, moreover, he has the first right to it. Old Indian *soma* and *hotar* mean 'elixir' and 'sacrificial fire' respectively. On the other hand, according to the Rig-Veda (I.1.1, I.76.2), the god *Agni* corresponds to the *hotar*. The *soma* liquor is produced with the enkindled flame (Rig-Veda IV.25.1); furthermore, the longing *Indra* received the pressed *soma* liquor from *Agni* (Rig-Veda III.22.1). *Indra* is the lord of the soma; *Agni* brings him this juice (Rig-Veda I.76.3). The *soma* always helps *Indra* (Rig-Veda I.4.1, I.32.3, I.52.3, II.11.11, II.16.2, II.17.1). (Rjabchikov, 2004)

Rjabchikov states that the Scythian/Sarmatian god *Tara* (Targitai) in Fig 10 corresponds to the Indo-Aryan god *Indra*. Rjabchikov refers to "the fragment of a net is depicted on his clothes," which he interprets as a fertility symbol but in the context of what we now know, it is more likely a symbol of the Haoma/Soma beverage. "Like cannabis the Soma may have been used for making mats and rope. This may be another reason for representing it by a net" (Richter-Ushanas, 1997). Mahadevan suggests that the net represents a filter for the purification of the Soma (Mahadevan, 1994), but this is a hypothesis, and the suggestion of others, with which

---

11   In reference to the change of goddess to god in the above scenario, as well as cannabis originally burned in braziers becoming an addition to a beverage, it is interesting to note that archaeologist Andrew Sherratt states of the ancient cannabis burners of Easter Europe, the Sredni Stog culture discussed in Chapter 1, the ancestors of the Scythians, that "They passed on their knowledge and their cultigens, [*Cannabis sativa*] to their neighbours, the Eastern wing of the Globular Amphora culture, who incorporated it into the complex of male associated paraphernalia inspired by the southern alcoholic tradition" (Sherratt, 1997).

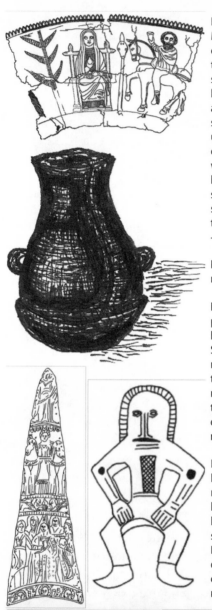

Fig 7.7: "depicted on the golden plate of a Meotian (Sindian) rhyton which was discovered at the village Merdzhany (near Anapa, the Krasnodar region, Russia).... Let us consider this drawing. The World Tree is on the left. A goddess sits on the throne and holds a pot. A horse's skull hangs at a pole [a horse sacrifice was associated with the Haoma ritual]. A rider holds a rhyton [horn cup]" (Rjabchikov, 2004). In relation a bone cup (Fig 8) was discovered in a Paryzyk tomb, image below, which botanist Robert C. Clarke describes as "8 inches tall, crafted from neatly sewn plates of steamed and bent horn – contained ceremonial drink *includes cannabis, -light, -portable, unbreakable" (Clarke, 1998).

Fig 7.8: Leather and bone cup, contained cannabis beverage (illustration by author).

Fig 7.9: The bottom panel of this image depicts devotees and the Scythian Goddess holding vessels, from a representation on the Scythian or Meotian golden ornament of a female head-gear of the 4th century B.C. from the Karagodeuashkh barrow (the Krasnodar region, Russia), Rjabchikov also brings attention to the 'net' pattern in the base of the outfit in the center panel, which he sees as a representation of the "Targitai (= Indra)."

Fig 7.11: A Scythian devotee drinking from a horn cup before the throne of the Goddess; note the net design on the male figures left leg (interestingly this picture was not noted by Rjabchikov, so it is another independent source for his hypothesis on these images). Fig 7.12: Scythian tapestry image of women drinking from horn cups and burning incense at an altar. Fig 7.13: Gold image of two men sharing a horn cup.

this author agrees with, is that the net motif is representative of Soma's fibrous properties.

In association with the scenario put forth by Rjabchikov, combined with the documented use of cannabis by both the Scythians and Irananian Haoma imbibers, it is interesting to note again that the Scythians of eastern Central Asia,, "are called '*haumavarka*' (haoma-gatherers) by Achaemenians," (Mirfendereski, 2005). This connection has caused more than a few scholars to view the Scythians as a Nomadic branch of the original Aryan race that prepared the sacred Haoma/Soma beverage.[12]

This brings to mind vessels discovered by Rudenko that contained what the Russian archeologist described as "undoubtedly filled with fluid, probably a milk drink, kousmiss and possibly milky vodka," these were discovered in the same tomb that held a "leather flask containing hemp" (Fig 14) (Rudenko, 1970). Flasks are generally used for storing liquid, but Rudenko is unclear as to the form of the hemp in the flask. Unfortunately there is also no reference to any analysis of the milky residue found in the accompanying vessels, so we can only speculate that it was the remnants of a cannabis based beverage based on the single analysis that Clarke refers to above. Cups comparable to those in the depiction of the Goddess discussed and that referred to by Clarke (which contained residues of cannabis) have been found in a number of Scythian sites and tombs, indicating their ritual importance.

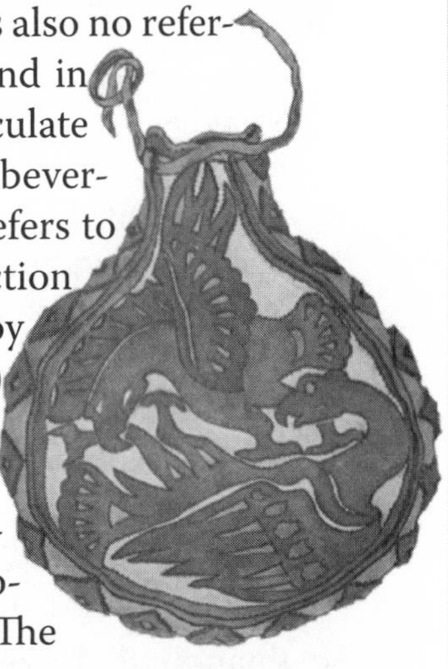

As well, the Scythians may have been practicing the Old World tradition of mixing aromatic plants such as cannabis, with wine. "...[The mixing bowl... had,... among the Scythians, ceremonial and funerary functions... [T]he nomads authorized to take part in royal libations were those who had

Fig 7.14: Leather flask that contained cannabis (Rudenko, 1970).

12   A number of scholars classify the Scythian language as a member of the Eastern Iranian languages, and the Scythians as a branch of the ancient Iranian peoples (Szemerényi, 1980; Grousset, 1999; Mallory, 1989). As with the Iranian language, the Scythian language and its sub dialects were all part of the Indo-European class of languages. J.P. Mallory in his conclusion to Sarianidi's *Margiana and ProtoZoroastrianism* states that the nucleus of Indo-Iranian linguistic developments formed in the steppes and, through some form of symbiosis in Bactria-Margiana, pushed southward to form the ancient languages of Iran and India (Mallory, 1998). "There are strong grounds for believing that their [Scythian] culture is associated with the Indo-Aryan culture" (Mirfendereski, 2006).

scalped enemies and could produce the heads as evidence. Then,...
the heroes poured themselves great drafts... and drank them at one
go—Russian fashion... Impressive receptacles were therefore needed for mixing water with a strong, full bodied wine that was usually
flavoured with resin and aromatic plants" (Charrier, 1979). As shall
be seen in following chapters, such wines, infused with cannabis or
cannabis resin, were known by a variety of ancient cultures, such as
the closely related Iranian group, the Zoroastrians.

If the assumption that the Scythians were drinking cannabis infused preparations is right it would offer an explanation to the inclusion of ritual cups and vessels in Scythian tombs as described by
V.A. Kisel in "Herodotus's Scythian Logos and Ritual Vessels of the
Early Nomads." Kisel makes some interesting connections between
the braziers the Scythians used and later drinking cups, that are
comparable to the analogies Sherratt pointed to in Chapter 3 in
regards to the development of the corded ware vessels as indicating
the cannabis that had been burnt as a fumigant in earlier times:

> Some censers are small. Therefore, rather than being receptacles for
> heated stones, they served a different purpose. Possibly they were
> used for burning crushed dry plants or for ritual drinks. This is
> quite likely since the function of vessels changed with time or simi-
> lar specimens may have been functionally different. (Kisel, 2007)

Kisel points to a Scythian legend of a fiery golden cup which fell
from the sky and that would burst into flames when approached
unless the recipient was the future king, who in the myth is the
progenerator of Scythian culture and the direct ancestor of Scythian royalty. All this is very reminiscent of the Grail legend, and the
Scythian myth, recorded by Herodotus, is very comparable to that
of the Arthurian myth of the "sword in the stone"[13]. The Legend
has it that a son of Zeus[14], a certain Targaitaus, wedded a daughter of the river Borsythenes. This marriage produced three sons,

---

13   In relation, Prof. Scott Littleton, who beyond his expertise in Indo-European
studies, has extensively researched the Grail myth refers to "the Scythian custom of em-
bedding a sword in a pile of brush atop an altar in honor of the War God. And according
to Ammianus Marcellinus, the ancient Alans [a related culture] used to embed swords in
the earth and dedicate them to the same deity... I think all this relates to the Arthurian
sword-in-the-stone episode" (Littleton, 2008). See *From Scythia to Camelot* (Littleton &
Malcor, 1994/2000)

14   The Scythian's deities can be identified in both Vedic and Greek mythologies
and indicate that both developed from an identical earlier mythology.

the youngest of which was Colaxias. The legend has it that during their reign there fell from the sky a golden plough, a golden battle axe, and most importantly in Kisel's view a golden cup. The two older brothers tried to pick up these miraculous gifts but as each of them tried the gold burst into flames. But when the younger brother tried to pick up the prizes, the fire went out and he was able to carry the golden implements home victorious. The elder brothers recognized this as a sign from heaven and gave over the whole kingdom to Colaxais.[15] Mythologicaly, this myth identified the origins of the Scythian caste sytem; Colaxais was the ancestor of the "Royal Scythians," one brother the forefather of the "Warrior Scythians" and the other the "Agricutrual Scythians."

In a related myth, Hercules, after losing his horses, is travelling on foot, and on these travels he is seduced by a serpent woman, whom he agrees to sleep with in exchange for his stolen horses. After returning the horses the snake woman thanked Hercules for the three sons that their encounter had produced and asked the ancient hero how she should decided which of the children should be permitted to live in the homeland of his mother. Hercules told her that she shall know the one who is to remain by his being able to

---

15   Littleton notes these mythologies may have had an influence in the Far East as well, following the Scythians on their extended travels "The Targitaos myth, as reported by Herodotus, has some interesting parallels. First, his three sons seem to reflect what the late George Dumézil called the three primary Indo-European 'functions,' that is, sovereignty, physical force, and fertility (cf. the three 'twice-born' Indian castes: the Brahmans, the Kshatriyas, and the Vaishiyas). Second, the idea of three sacred objects descending from Heaven and becoming talismans of sovereignty can be found in Japanese mythology. In the Kojiki and Nihon Shoki, the oldest Japanese religious texts (712 and 720 C.E., respectively), the objects are a mirror, a sword, and a fertility jewel, or magatama, replicas of which are given to each Japanese emperor at his enthronement. This parallel is not fortuitious, and reinforces my contention that there was a North Iranian (Alanic?) impact on late prehistoric Japan, ca. 370 C.E., that is, at the time the 'horseriders' (Kiba Minzoku) invaded (from Korea) and found the imperial dynasty" (Littleton, 2008). One can only speculate that the Shinto religion's continued ritual use, since ancient times, of hemp fibres for priestly garments and other items, is somehow also related to this cultural connection. Prof. Littleton, who has written books and articles on ancient Asian culture and Shintoism, notes, "hemp, especially hempen ropes, have indeed played--and still play--an important part in Shinto rituals":

Indeed, the vestments worn by kanushi, or Shinto priests, are partially woven from hemp fibres, and in some out of the way places, like Sado Island and parts of the Tohoku (northern Honshu), hemp seeds are still burned (shades of Pazyryk and Herodotus!)--and the smoke inhaled--by Yamabushi and other shamans as offerings to the kami, or gods. But most Japanese today don't make the connection between sacred hemp objects like ropes, etc. in shrines and traditional priestly garments and cannabis, and it's ingestion/inhalation is as illegal in Japan as it is here. (Littleton, 2009)

draw Hercules' bow and put on his girdle, which had a golden goblet attached. The youngest son, Scythes, accomplished this, and it was this Scythes, son of Hercules, who became father of the line of Scythian kings."[16] Having related the legend, Herodotus adds: "And from the circumstance of the goblet which hung from the belt, the Scythians to this day wear goblets on their girdles."[17] A warrior had to kill some enemies and show personal heroism to be awarded with such a cup, and only the most respected men were allowed to wear one with gold appliqué. (These goblets were in some periods also made from a human skull recovered from the body of a dead enemy, reminiscent of the skull cups used by Shiva and his devotee saddhus to drink *bhang* from.)

Kisel states that in looking "for analogues to the legendary cup, one should pay special attention to vessels with segment shaped handles. These vessels raise many questions that are yet unresolved" (Kisel, 2007). [images below] Kisel felt that the segmented handles, and shapes of these vessels, were inspired by the braziers used for burning cannabis, and that their imitative shape indicated a fiery beverage that was related to what was being burnt in the braziers. "These silver gilt vessels decorated with relief representations occupied a central place in Scythian funerary assemblages" (Kisel, 2007). In relation, as noted earlier, Andrew Sherratt has suggested "The ritual plant products traditionally consumed on the steppes in braziers [circa 3,500 BC, or earlier] would now have been prepared as a euphoriant or inebriant drink – including the substance later known as haoma" (Sherratt, 1995).

> All these facts suggest that vessels with segment shaped handles were the key element of the Scythian cult and were used in the most sacred rites that were tabooed for the profane. Unlike censers, they may have been only symbolically related to fire and were used as receptacles for sacral 'fiery' liquids, such as those used in many traditions. It appears possible that the Scythians indeed associated such vessels with the legendary cup that had fallen from the sky.
>
> ...In a separate publication, I have attempted to demonstrate that the "fiery" drink was indeed drunk by the Scythians (Kisel, 2002[18]). Also, broken-off handles on clay vessels made in the

16   Herodotus; *The Histories* (Penguin Classics,1954)
17   (Hdt. IV. 10, trans. by G. Rawlinson).
18   Unfortunately this paper has not been translated into English

Scythian animal style and found at Ziviyeh, Iran, indicate that such cups were already used at the early stages of Scythian history. The similarity between censers, cauldrons, dippers, and bowls with segment-shaped handles is not restricted to their globular shape. They were evidently united by the same idea: connection with fire. Their common "divine prototype" – the heavenly bowl – was endowed with a magical ability to catch fire, and the same capacity was probably attributed to all these vessels…. The image of a blazing cup was apparently related to Indian mythology and Zoroastrism; Zoroastrian texts mention ritual vessels with fire burning inside them. (Kisel,2007)

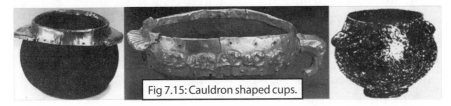
Fig 7.15: Cauldron shaped cups.

Another factor in the conception of the Scythian 'fiery cups' may have involved the mythology of Haoma/Soma. As noted, the Celestial Soma, was produced by the Sun, acted out by Agni in the Vedic tradition and the Goddesss Tabiti in the Scythian,[19] and poured out into the Celestial bowl, the moon. As such the earthly Soma represented the life giving fire of the sun in liquid form.

Kisel concluded that despite having a common mythological heritage, the ritual life of European and Asian Scythians held some differences, notably involving their purification rites and objects of adoration. "European Scythians did not practice the vapour bath described in the Scythian logos, and their principal sacral vessel was a round bowl or a dipper, which often had segment-shaped handles. Asian nomads commonly practiced purification with hemp-vapor, and their most sacral vessels were a cauldron, a dipper, and a censer, most of which are vessels used by large groups of people, possibly clan members…" (Kisel, 2007). Making his connections all the clearer, Kisel also noted it was likely "that saucers, like most nomadic stone altars, served as press stones for expressing Soma-Haoma, because in

Fig 7.16: Scythian caldron used for burning cannabis.

---

19   (Rjabichiov, 2004).

this case, too, both plants and fire could have been used" (Kisel, 2007).[20]

Obvious similarities between a ritual Soma vessel from BMAC

Fig 7.17

(Fig 17) and a later Scythian Cauldron (Fig 18) can be seen by the animals which decorate the rims of both objects, as well as noted, a horn cup has been recovered from a Scythian site that still held remains of a cannabis drink. It seems clear there was good reason that the the

Fig 7.18

Scythians, of eastern Central Asia,, are called 'Hauma-varka' (Haoma-Gatherers).

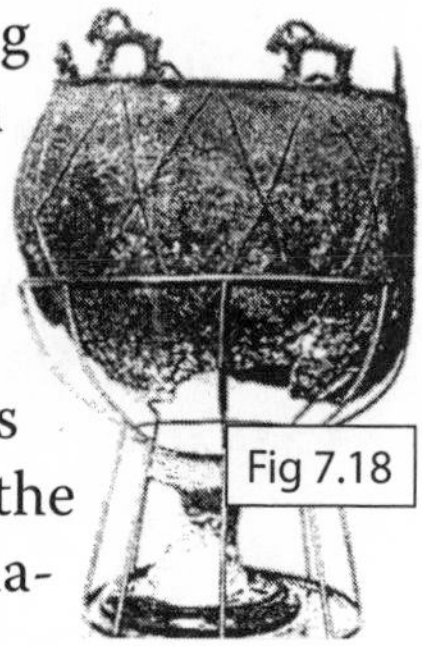

On the topic of Margiana, it is interesting to note that Prof. Victor Sarianidi states that it has been a longstanding theory with some historians that the "nomadic Scythians/Saka from ancient times had made attempts to settle on the fertile lands of Margiana. This assumption is now fully supported by such archeological facts as for example, the sites of the Andronovo tribes located next to settlements within the limits of Margiana" (Sarianidi, 1998). The 'Andronovo culture' referred to is a kind of blanket term for a group of Bronze Age cultures, from which the Scythians descended, and which flourished ca. 2300–1000 BCE in a broad area from western Siberia and the west Asiatic steppe. It is probably better termed an archaeological complex or archaeological horizon.[21]

Sarianidi continues pointing to the Scythians other name of, "'Saka-Haomovarga' or in other words 'Saka who prepare haoma.' according to Helanik they lived in the environs of Margiana.... The ancient Persian scribes knew... the distant and mythical Saka... prepared haoma...." (Sarianidi, 1978).

---

20   In relation to this suggestion it is relevant to note that during excavations at Pokrovka, Kazakhstan, in 1993, Jeannine Davis-Kimball's expedition found an odd bronze container with large (~25mm) perforations in the bottom (Davis-Kimball, 2002). One can only speculate that this item served the function of a Haoma strainer, as with the similar perforated pot discovered amongst the Haoma making implements of Margiana. At first puzzled by the object, Davis-Kimball later speculated that it was a colander for scooping large pieces of meat based on functionally similar items she saw in Mongolia, but this, of course, as with our hypothesis, is only a suggestion (Davis-Kimball, 2002).

21   The name derives from the village of Andronovo where in 1914, several graves were discovered, in the typical Scythian burial style with skeletons in crouched positions, buried with richly decorated pottery.

It is extremely important to add that in the temples of Margiana... especially in the tremenos of Gonur, [particularly associated with large finds of cannabis evidence] typical Andronovo vessels (or their fragments) were found in the rooms associated with the preparation of the soma-haoma type beverages... the presence of these articles in all three temples confirms the conclusion that the predecessors of Scythian-Sakas, that is the Andronovo tribes, were familiar with the ritual drink as early as the second millennium B.C.

... Herodotus witnesses that Scythians used to make fire in their tents and threw hemp on the scorching stones and then "the Scythians screamed loudly in the pleasure of inhaling it.". The same custom was practiced by the Altai Scythians (the Pasyryk tombs). This means that Scythians used narcotics that were traditional for those Andronovo tribes that had close contacts with the Margiana tribes which apparently could have borrowed this custom from them. (Sarianidi, 1978)

Besides the obvious associations shared between the Scythian fiery cups and the Soma/Haoma beverages of their Indo-European relatives, there is strong evidence that this 'sacred cup' motif was even more widespread. In *From Scythia to Camelot* Prof. C. Scott Littleton, who has been a considerable source of advice for this project, and co-author Linda Malcor have argued "that the core of the Arthurian and Holy Grail legends derives originally from a region known in antiquity as Scythia, that is, the western portion of the great 'sea of grass' that stretches from the Altai Montains to the Hungarian Plain" (Littleton & Malcor, 1994: 2000).

Littleton and Malcor convincingly demonstrate that central Asian myths of swords, horseback riding knights and magical chalices likely accompanied Scythian groups such as the Alans and Sarmatians who worked as Roman mercenaries and settled in Western Europe in the first few centuries AD. Amongst the stories known as the 'Nart Sagas,' or 'Knight Sagas' of the Scythians can be found parallels of many Arthurian legends, such as the 'sword in the stone,' which may be based on the Alan practice of impaling a sword into the burial mound of deceased kings. Particularly interesting are references to the "cup of the Narts" which like the Grail, was said to hold magical properties, such as elevating itself to the lips of a hero "without flaw" (Littleton & Malcor, 1994: 2000). One can only speculate that the longing of these displaced Scythians, cut off from the quality cannabis which once made the intoxicating beverage that filled the fiery cups in their homeland, led to the mythology of the long lost Grail and the quest for its rediscovery.

The Scythian Queen

With the strong elements of Goddess worship in the Scythian culture, it is not surprising to find a matriarchal hierarchy as well, and we know from surviving artefacts that Scythian women took powerful leadership roles in the tribe. As well "Both men and women probably smoked [hemp], since we found two sets of apparatus for smoking with the burial of a man and a woman" (Rudenko, 1970). Indeed later finds of cannabis seeds at the site of a "Scythian Queen" provide evidence of this.

In 1993, a female Scythian mummy was discovered. The *China Daily* reported of the find "The mummy was buried alongside six horses in full harness, dishes, a mirror, a brush, and even a small pot of cannabis to help her travel into the afterlife."[22] A 1995 episode of the *National Geographic Explorer*, "The Frozen Siberian Tombs," profiled a dig centered around a recently discovered Kurgan, and the program televised such things as an over 2,000 year old hemp shirt, woven as fine as silk; A beautifully embroidered and decorated bag, used for holding cannabis; And an exotic Persian rug, testifying to wide ancient trade routes. This find was in the Altai Mountains of Siberia, an area where the borders of Russia, China, Mongolia and Kazakhstan converge. The *New York Times* story on the find reported; `

> ...[S]he was elegantly laid out in a white silk blouse, red skirt and white stockings. She had been buried in a hollowed tree trunk alongside horse harnesses, a mirror, dishes and a small container of cannabis, which archaeologists believe was smoked for pleasure and used in pagan rituals. ....That, and the intricate tattoos on her left arm, led the archaeologists who found her to conclude that she was a Scythian princess and a priestess. (Stanley, 1994)

Cannabis was not only used by the Scythians for relaxation and ceremonies for the dead. These ancient nomads had a class of

---

22   *China Daily*, June 6th, 1994, as quoted in (Clarke, 1998).

Shaman-magicians, the *Enaries*, ancient transvestites, who uttered prophecies in high pitched voices while twisting fibers in their fingers a technique which they held was taught to them by Aphrodite. This at first sounds, bizarre, but in actuality, homosexuality was a very common trait in shamans of tribal peoples, worldwide, who believed that these people, who had characteristics of both sexes, were somehow also living in both worlds, and could travel between the two. It has been recorded that the Scythians believed that the feminine characteristics of the shamans were punishment from the Great goddess for desecrating her shrine at Ashkelon. The messages "channeled" by these ancient diviners was taken as authoritative advice by the chieftains and the tribe. In this sense, the Shamans acted as the conscience or mind of the whole group.

That the hemp smoke had somewhat mellowed Scythian culture can be seen from the comments made by the ancient Greek historians, Ephorus (4th century B.C.) who stated that the Scythians "excel all men in justice," followed by the comments of Strabo (1st century B.C.): "we regard the Scythians as the most just of men and the least prone to mischief, as also far more frugal and independent of others than we are."[23]

With the important role of cannabis in Scythian culture, it is not surprising to find that, although rare, influences of the plant's motif can be found in surviving artifacts. The gold pectoral chest piece from the tomb of a Scythian King in Tovsta Mogyla, is one of the most beautiful pieces of surviving Scythian art; the details and craftsmanship have been discussed by numerous scholars. Curiously, none have commented on the stylized cannabis leaves which are woven throughout the design.

Steppes art is known for the way it mixes together aspects of animals to come up with new mythological creatures, such as the griffins attacking a horse in the details of the necklace pictured in Fig.19. They utilized plant characteristics in a similar way, morphing different aspects together, thus the following image, although not as immediately recognizable as cannabis in the necklace depicted, is indicated

Fig 7.19

---

23   as quoted in *The Druids*, Stuart Piggott (Thames and Hudson, 1975).

Fig 7.20: Elaborate Gold chest plate and detail. Stylized cannabis leaves were incorporated into a pattern on this chestplate of a Scythian king which includes detailed depictions of both real and imaginary beasts.

by the pistilate-like tendrils coming from a magical flower in the following image of Scythian embroidery on silk.

...[I]n Scythian art... there is such a debauch of forms and colors, such a quantity of singular fantasies verging on madness and revealing so clearly the use of hemp, that it is hard to believe that its use was exceptional and confined to the function of tranquilizer during the funerals. The saddlebags found... at Pazyryk carry fantastic scenes of fighting between griffins and ibex, whose bodies, instead of being modeled by the classic play of light shade, are expressed simply in appliqués with vivid colors quite unrelated to the natural tints of animal pelts:

Fig 7.21: Cannabis like Pistils coming out of a imaginary flower. Fig 7.22 Cannabis pistils

greens, yellows, and reds are dominant, and one is reminded of
the pictures... of that colorist of genius and eventual madness,
Van Gogh.... Besides superimposition of objects and motifs and
the transformations of things and creatures (particularly at their
extremities), all of which are phenomena and process that recur
in Scythian art, the takers of hashish undergoes other visual and
psychic illusions. He becomes inclined to imagine himself as a
superman, or as a god gifted with immortality and with extraordinary physical capabilities that enable him, for instance, to fly
in an atmosphere made to his measure. His hallucinations then
become peopled with Pegasus and other horses, with griffins,
or winged mammals. These fantastic aggregates—which belong
within the context in which modern hashish users live... are such
that necessarily each ethnic group makes them its own, in spite of
their common features. (Charrier, 1979)

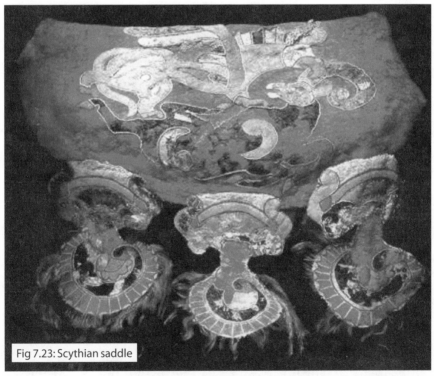

Fig 7.23: Scythian saddle

   As shall be discussed in the next few chapters, the influence of
the Scythians, aka the 'Haoma-Varga' and their cultic use of cannabis can be seen in a wide variety of cultures, such as Greece, Rome,
Mesopotamia, China, and, what may be surprising to many, even
amongst the Hebrews:

Since the history of cannabis has been tied to the history of the Scythians, it is of interest to establish their appearance in the Near East. Again, the Old Testament provides information testifying to their greater antiquity than has been previously assumed. The Scythians participated in both trade and wars alongside the ancient Semites for at least one millennium before Herodotus encountered them in the fifth century B.C.. The reason for confusion and the relative obscurity of the role played by the Scythians in world history is explained by the fact that they were known to the Greeks as Scythians but to the Semites as Ashkenaz. Identification of the Scythian-Ashkenaz as a single people is convincingly made by Ellis H. Minns (1965) in his definitive work on Scythians and Greeks. The earliest reference to the Ashkenaz people appears in the Bible in Genesis 10:3, where Ashkenaz, their progenitor, is named the son of Gomer, the great-grandson of Noah. (Benet, 1975)

The Nomadic Scythians travelled extensively, bringing their cultural influence and their holy plant cannabis everywhere they went. "In short, by the time Herodotus visited them on north Pontic coast, ca. 450 B.C.E., and did what many anthropologists consider to have been the first true ethnography (i.e., Book IV), the Scythians proper were at the western end of an ethnic continuum that included the Sarmatians (or 'Sauromatians') east of the Volga, and then the Saka, Massagetae, Alans, etc. and stretched eastward to the Altai and beyond" (Littleton, 2008).

In Asia, we know that a Scythian-related culture settled in China, as early as 1800 BC, and likely traveled as far as Japan and Korea. The influence of the Scythians has been noted throughout pre-Christian Europe and evidence of cannabis use at Celtic and Druidic site is often related to their influence. As well Greek and Roman culture contain many references to the Scythians, and the Greeks even adopted deities from Scythian related tribes. The Scythians penetrated into Northern India, where they were known by their Persian name, Sakas, invading Punjab and Kashmir in 85 BC and maintaining control of some areas of central India, into the 5th century AD. In this case we can again see the mellowing effects of cannabis on Scythian culture, as the Scyths are said to have converted to Buddhism and a later King, Kanishka the 1st, turned over the administration of his kingdom to a group of Mahayana Buddhist monks led by one of the sect's most influential philosophers Nagarjuna. Indeed, the connection between Buddhism and the Scythians is so great, that for more than a century researchers have been noting that the "Buddha himself is said by some have been a Scythian" (Hunter, 1884).

If one can see the Scythians as the descendants of the Eastern European, horseback riding, cannabis burning and drinking, Sredeni Stog Culture, then we are looking at a cultic use of cannabis amongst the Scythians that had continued for three millennia by the time Herodotus encountered them. In relation it is interesting to note that in his intriguing essay Cannabis, Radical Agriculture, and Epistomology of Plant Pathology, John McEno, speculates that it was from such a group that the cultivation of cannabis may have originated, and leaves us with some comments that set us up well for the next Chapter:

> Setting our clocks back 10,000 years we find cannabis being domesticated somewhere in Central Asia. Domesticated by whom? Our other ancient crops are linked with classic civilizations: the Incas the Aztecs with potatoes, amaranth and maize; Egyptians with wheat, Chinese with rice... perhaps cannabis is associated with a lost civilization, a Shangri-La or Shambala of central Asia. Alternatively Cannabis could have been domesticated by globe-trotting nomads and not an established civilization. This scenario is supported by its simultaneous appearance in several locations (central China, northwest India, Persia).
>
> No one knows exactly where Cannabis originated.... I suggest a Cannabis home in the southern Altai or Tien Shan Mountains.[24] These hills border the central Asian steppes, the great Neolithic 'nomad belt' stretching from the Black Sea to Mongolia. A tribe of migrants, the Scythians, emerged from this region at the dawn of history. They ranged east and west across the steppes, from China to Europe. Scythian Johnny Hempseeds probably carried cannabis seeds to China. Along the Yellow River 6,500 years ago, Chinese began cultivating the plant, using hemp fiber for rope, fishing nets, and clothing. Chinese ate the seeds as a grain or ground them into oil. They medicated themselves with the plant's resinous leaves and flowers... when they invented a written language, the ideogram for Cannabis was among the first invented. (McEno, 1998)

---

24   This is near the Scythian burial site at Paryzyk discussed earlier.

端拱宾心圖

元君端拱坐玄都
三疊胎仙舞八佾
役化絕陽天地合

痴人猶待問菩薩
頂中常放白毫光
妖至彼岸又焉用法
未到彼岸不能無法

無心於事
無事於心
超出萬幻

而與吉會
宾心至趣
宅神枩为
遺照於外

A Taoist alchemist mediatates, allowing his spirit to ascend into other spheres. He sits upon a bed of what a re clearly hemp leaves. Hemp has always been a part of Chineses culture: shamans, alchemists, physicians, and folk healers have long used it as a medicine and as an elixir of life. (from *Secret of the Golden Flower*, ca third century C.E.)

–Christian Ratsch, *Marijuana Medicine*, 2001

8

Hu-ma, Cannabis in China

T hought by some botanists to be the original home of un-domesticated cannabis,[1] in Asia Hemp use dates back far into the Stone Age, with hemp fibre imprints found in pottery shards in Taiwan, just off the coast of mainland China, that were over 10,000 years old. Alongside these shards were found long rod-shaped tools, similar to those used in mainland China in later times to decord hemp. As well, indicating its use and popularity throughout the intervening millennia, the famous terracotta warriors were equipped with hemp-soled shoes before their long sojourn into *Terra-firma*. As such it is not surprising the Chinese were amongst the first people to discover both the medicinal and magical properties of the plant with a history of use in these cases, along with its use as a food, fibre, and oil source for lighting and paints, going back thousands of years. "According to a Neolithic Chinese legend, the gods gave humans one plant to fulfill all needs. The plant was *Cannabis sativa*.... This assertion is not so far-fetched; *Cannabis* assuredly ranks among the world's most remarkable plants" (Pooja, 2005).

> ...it is generally accepted that *Cannabis sativa L.* was first cultivated in China around 4500 BC when its seed served as a grain crop.[2] Soon after its decaying stems became the source for making

---

1   Others point to Central Asia, in the vicinity of Turkmenistan and Iran.
2   In China hemp seed was celebrated as one of the seven main grains, and was popularly used up until the sixth century AD in a variety of oriental recipes (Abel 1980). Some centuries later, in the fourteenth century AD, hemp started to become an important Chinese medicine and a large section of the famous Chinese pharmacopoeia text, the *Pen T'sao Kang Mu*. The text's compiler Li Shih Chen referred to works from previous authors dating back centuries before his own time in his discussion of hemp seed as both a food and medicine. According to the ancient author, the Chinese had hybridized hemp

hemp fibre for making clothes, ropes, and fishing nets. However, reports of early hemp use in China are open to question either because of inadequate fiber remains or because they relate to impressions on pottery and other objects... Such cord impressions have been found on material from 4000 to 3000 BC unearthed in Taiwan and also similarly dated pots found in Henan Province, eastern China, at an archeological site of the Yang Shao culture, the first civilization to manufacture pottery. (Sneader, 2005)

Archaeologist Andrew Sherratt saw a similar indication of cannabis use indicated in the cord impressed pottery of ancient China, as that of Europe from the same period discussed in Chapter 3, stating "that the early use of cord-impressed pottery in China the so called Sheng-wen horizon - was associated with an early use of hemp and an appreciation (explicit in the early historical records) of its narcotic properties" (Sherratt, 1997). In relation to this comparison, it is interesting to note (and as will be discussed later in this Chapter) recent discoveries in China document contact with Indo-European culture began considerably earlier than previously believed. Thus it has been suggested that "Cannabis, or marijuana, probably originating north of South Siberia, was a key trade item and part of the religio-shamanic complex in the Mesolithic period spreading from Romania to China prior to the end of the Stone Age" (Sinclair, 2007).

As Professor of Botany Hui-Lin Li, an expert on the history of cannabis in China notes, "The evidence... suggests that the medicinal use of the hemp plant was widely known to the Neolithic (Stone Age) peoples of north-eastern Asia and shamanism was especially widespread in this northern area and also in China, and cannabis played an important part in its ritual" (Li, 1975). Likewise, expert on Chinese history, Joseph Needham has also noted, "...the hallucinogenic properties of hemp were common knowledge in Chinese medical and Taoist circles for two millennia or more" (Needham, 1974).

The Chinese glyph for hemp, *Ma*, 麻 is usually described as a depiction of two harvested hemp plants hanging to dry in a shed.

---

to such an extent that it grew as large as garden peas and was reputed to have been of the highest quality. The ancient text recommended hemp seed for everything from urinary problems, blood flow, palsy, increasing the amount of mother's milk for suckling infants, the growth of muscle fiber, both dysentery and constipation and a variety of other applications (Jones 1995).

Generally this has been regarded as representing the use of cannabis for fibre, but contrarily, like most cultures, the Chinese retted their fibre hemp in fields or in ponds, soaking the stiff stalks of the of the plant in order to break down the cellulose and allow the long fibres of the stalk to break free more easily.[3] However,

Fig 8.1: Ma-'Hemp'

when psychoactive effects are the goal, hanging to dry is the more common cross-cultural method used with cannabis. Professor Hui-Lin Li, in his extensively researched essay "The Origin and Use of Cannabis in Eastern Asia: Their Linguistic-Cultural Implications," notes a double meaning for *ma* (hemp); the first, "numerous or chaotic... derived from the nature of the plant's fibres. The second connotation was one of numbness or senselessness, apparently derived from the properties of the fruits and leaves which were used as infusions for medicinal purposes[4]" (Li, 1975). This double connotation has been noted by other scholars; in her essay "Religious and Medicinal Uses of Cannabis in China, India and Tibet," Mia Touw notes;

> There may... be some etymological evidence to support the idea that the Central Asians were the first to learn about the biodynamic potentialities of cannabis. Of the various Chinese words for hemp, *ta-ma* (great hemp), *huo-ma, huang-ma, ban-ma* (Chinese hemp), it was *hu-ma*, or fiery hemp (as the meaning has been construed by some etymologists), which also meant Scythian hemp (Stuart1911)[5] and this latter kind was held to be especially potent. (Touw, 1981)[6]

In relation to this it is relevant to note that *Ma*, Hemp, 麻 appears in two characters which also indicate the preparation of cannabis for intoxication. The first comes from the Chinese symbol for 'Rub,' *Mo,* 摩 comprised of the symbols for 'hand' and 'hemp.' This could conceivably be derived from the ancient technique of crumbling cannabis into a powder by rubbing the dried leaves and flow-

3   For a description of the Hemp harvest in China, with beautiful illustrations, see *Science and Civilization in China* (Needham, et al., 1954).
4   This is similar to the way the Indian bhang is said to have been developed out of a word meaning "break, broken," that later developed into an association with intoxication, in the same way "smashed" can mean "drunk" in English.
5   Stuart, G.A., *Chinese Marteria Medica Vegetable Kingdom* (1911).
6   The ancient Chinese also identified the medicinal and psychoactive qualities of the resinous seed bracts, which they called ma-fen.

ers together between the palms, which has been seen as a common method of preparation in China (Starks, 1990). Li also notes *"mo, grind (combining *ma* with stone)"* (Li, 1975), Which also brings to mind the another age old technique of breaking down cannabis with stones, as in the preparation of Haoma/Soma. The linguistic root of the word *haoma*, *hu-*, and of *soma*, *su-*, suggests 'press' or 'pound' (Taillieu, 2002).

Although from what can be gathered from the ancient references we are dealing with whole dried cannabis preparations instead of rubbed hashish, it is also worth mentioning that a traditional method of collecting cannabis resin is to rub the palms of the hand together over the flowering sticky buds of cannabis, and then scrape the resin off of the palms of the hand, a technique popular in both Nepal[7] and Chinese Turkestan. The suggestion that *hu ma* originally grew in Turkistan, a site known for the production of hashish up until modern times, has been attributed to the Taoist adept T'ao Hun Kin (AD 451 - 536). In relation, modern archeological evidence for the use of "hemp for textiles, ropes, fish lines, and threads" have been found at Neolithic sites in the area dating back 5,000 years (Merlin, 1972). T'ao Hun Kin was "a drug hunter and alchemist, and immortality fiend"[8] and this would explain his interest in cannabis, for as we shall soon show the trinity of Taoism, drugs, and the search for immortality, has had a long shared history of combination.

The earliest reference to the use of marijuana as a medicine, however, is traditionally believed to have occurred sometime around 2,800 BCE (although this date may be considerably contentious[9]), in the medical compendium, the *Pen Ts'ao* of the legendary Chinese Emperor Shen-Nung. The *Pen Ts'ao* has it that by the time of its composition cannabis was already quite widespread, "hemp grows along rivers and valleys at T'ai-shan, but it is now common everywhere." As Emperor, Shen-Nung was concerned that the priests were unable to effectively treat the maladies of his subjects by per-

---

7   "In the Mustang region of Nepal, mummified human remains of probable Mongolian ancestry have been dated 2200–2500 years BP in association with cannabis, probably transported from elsewhere... but with insufficient detail to ascertain its use" (Russo, et al., 2008).

8   (Laufer, 1919).

9   Although it is widely believed to have originated around 2800 BC, no original copies of the text have survived. The oldest copy of the *Pen Ts'ao* dates to about 100 AD, and was compiled by an anonymous author who claimed to have incorporated the more ancient material into his own medical compendium.

forming magical rites, and decided to find alternative remedies for the sick. Despite being emperor, Shen-Nung was apparently also an expert farmer, and had a thorough knowledge of plants. With this in mind, undoubtedly taken alongside a knowledge of indigenous folk remedies, Shen-Nung decided to explore the curative powers of plants, using himself as the test subject. History turns to myth here, as ancient compilers state that Shen-Nung was aided in his studies by having the superman like power of being able to see through his abdominal wall and into his stomach, enabling the Emperor to observe the effects of the plants he experimented with on his digestive system! In relation to such testing by imperial methods it is interesting to note that the *Pen Ts'ao* also mentions ma-pho, a term that means a sudden change of mood, such as intoxication.

In the Chinese cosmology, the universe is composed of two elements, the Yang, representing the strong, active, positive masculine force and Yin, the weak, passive and negative female influence. In the individual, when these forces are in balance, the body is healthy, but too much of one or not enough of another and the result is disease. In the case of the application of marijuana to such an ailment, this was difficult as it had both male and female plants, and contained both yin and yang. Shen-Nung determined that it was the female plant that contained the most potent medicine, being a very high source of yin, and prescribed *chu-ma* (female hemp, as opposed to *ma*, hemp) for the treatment of absentmindedness, constipation, malaria, beriberi, rheumatism and menstrual problems. The "Father of Chinese Medicine," Shen-Nung, was so thoroughly impressed with the beneficial effects of *chu-ma*, he deemed it one of the Superior Elixirs of Immortality.[10] Hemp's association with immortality in China, was apparently quite widespread. In *Myths of China and Japan*, MacKenzie refers to a "Rip Van Winkle story that two men who wandered among the mountains met two pretty girls. They were entertained by them and fed on a concoction prepared from hemp. Seven generations went past while they enjoyed the company of the girls" (MacKenzie, 1923).

---

10   The acquisition of Immortality and or long life, is associated with both the Soma and Haoma; as well Indian references to cannabis for this use can be found in the Tantric text, the Mahanirvana Tantra (XI,105–108): "Intoxicating drink (containing bhang) is consumed in order to liberate oneself, and that those who do so, in dominating their mental faculties and following the law of Shiva (yoga) - are to be likened to immortals on earth."[as quoted in (Hanuš, 2008)].

The hemp (old Persian and Sanskrit bangha) was cultivated at a remote period in China and Iran. A drug prepared from the seed is supposed to prolong life and inspire those who partake of it to prophecy
after seeing visions and dreaming dreams. (MacKenzie, 1923)

From the time of Shen-Nung onward, Chinese physicians con-
t i n u e d   to prescribe marijuana, and as they became more familiar with the effects of the plant, new discoveries
were made about its properties, such as that made
in 200 AD, by the early and well-known Chinese
surgeon, Hua T'o. Almost 2,000 years ago Hua
T'o is reputed to have performed such complicated operations as "organ grafts, resec-
tioning of intestines, laparotomies (incisions into the loin), and thoracotomies
(incisions into the chest)" (Abel 1980).
Moreover, these dangerous and complicated surgeries were rendered painless

Fig 8.2: Emperor Shen Nung, by author.   by an anesthetic prepared from cannabis
resin and wine known as *ma-yo*. An excerpt from his biography
gives us a descriptive account of how this ancient medical sage utilized cannabis in these procedures;

> ... if the malady resided in the parts on which the needle [acu-
> puncture], cautery, or medicinal liquids were incapable of acting,
> for example, in the bones, in the stomach or in the intestine, he
> administered a preparation of hemp [*ma-yo*] and, in the course
> of several minutes, an insensibility developed as if one had been
> plunged into drunkenness or deprived of life. Then, according to
> the case, he performed the opening, the incision or amputation
> and relieved the cause of the malady; then he apposed the tissues
> by sutures and applied liniments. After a certain number of days
> the patient finds he has recovered without having experienced
> the slightest pain during the operation.[11]

Throughout the ancient world, medicine held all sorts of magical connotations in people's minds; thus not surprisingly, "The
Chinese pharmacopeia Rh-Ya, compiled in the 15th century B.C.
contains the earliest reference to *Cannabis* for shamanistic purposes" (Langenheim, 2003).[12] Ancient Chinese Shamans showed

11   As quoted in (Walton 1938)
12   Beyond medicinal use, recreational use can also be inferred; "...hemp euphoria

their awareness of cannabis medical powers symbolically, by carving serpents into a stalk of hemp and using it as a magic wand for healing ceremonies. In reference to shamanism it is important to note that China's ancient use of cannabis flowers and leaves was not limited to medicine, "...in ancient China...medicine had its origin in magic. Medicine men were practicing magicians" (Li, 1978). Emperor Shen-Nung stated that beyond medical use, cannabis: "If taken over a long term, it makes on communicate with spirits and lightens one's body."[13] In relation to this it is interesting to note that the use of the glyph for Hemp, *Ma* in combinations with other characters appears in glyphs with supernatural connotations, as with *Mo* devil 麻 [14] and this gives clear indications of the awareness of cannabis' use in Chinese sorcery, which, as we discuss shortly, cannabis had a long history of use in. "In these early periods, use of cannabis as an hallucinogen was undoubtedly associated with Chinese shamanism" (Schultes and Hoffman, 1992).

Around 200 BCE a variety of new aromatic plants and resins appeared in the Chinese marketplace, accompanied by a new kind of incense burner, known as the *boshanlu* (po-shan-lu) 'magic mountain' brazier, and these braziers have been specifically associated with cannabis use. Not surprisingly this method became quite popular for some centuries and cannabis "occurs in various... prescriptions for gaining visionary powers" (Needham, 1974). Referring to the mythological origins of such braziers, Frederick Dannaway has suggested that the "curious episode on Daoist liturgy of the 'stealing' of an incense burner has similarities to the ritual 'stealing' of soma" (Dannaway, 2009).

The Boshanlu incense burners were sculpted in the form of mountain peaks rising over waves, depicting the abode of the Immortals. These were essential items in the rooms of the

Fig 8.3: Boshanlu incense burners

was sought after at least by the Chou period (c. 1000-221 B.C.), when it was used for 'the enjoyment of life'" (Merlin, 1972).

13   As quoted in (Li, 1978). A late edition of the Pen Ts'ao adds this note: "To take much makes people see demons and throw themselves about like maniacs. But if one takes it over a long period of time one can communicate with the spirits, gain insight, and one's body becomes light" (Needham, 1974).

14   (Li, 1975)

scholars of the time. As the incense burned, the smoke rose through the perforations in the lid like an enchanted fragrant mist engulfing miniaturized mountain peaks. Focusing on his inner eye, a scholar could then imagine that he traveled in spirit to the Magic Mountain to walk with the immortals[15]. Indicating the long term popularity of this technique a 4th century text records "For those who begin practicing the Tao it is not necessary to go into the mountains.... Some with purifying incense and sprinkling and sweeping are also able to call down the immortals. The followers of Lady Wei... and the Hsu... are of this kind."[16]

Analysis of ashes from these burners verified the use of a variety of fragrant plants, some of which held medicinal properties or 'magical' qualities that enabled communication with spirits. For spirit communication "The 'incense' burned was a hallucinogenic 'sacred herb'- what we know as marijuana... the intoxicating smoke of the burning incense would waft upward from the canyon-like openings between the mountains and create the illusion of this mythical landscape."[17] "For these psychedelic experiences in ancient Taoism a closed room would have been necessary, and precisely the 'Pure Chamber' of the oldest Taoist rites..." (Needham, 1974). Expert on Chinese history, Joseph Needham, also reports that Taoists mystics were alleged to add "hallucinogenic smokes to their in-

---

15   A Tibetan Folktale from Sichuan Province, *The Story of the Three Genjias*, indicates the belief that cannabis could aid in such astral ascents was quite widespread throughout Asia. In the story, a carpenter is given the unwanted task of building a mansion in heaven for his deceased master. Not in a position to say 'No" to the task, the carpenter requests that they hold a Twig Burning Ceremony in the hemp field behind his house to send him off. "Then I'll be able to ascend to heaven to build the mansion for the old chief." The crafty carpenter plays on the beliefs of the time, and digs a tunnel to escape through at the site of the fire ceremony just prior to his scheduled ascension. The people follow his request, burn a fire in the hemp field and command the carpenter to sling his tool-kit over his shoulder and stand in the middle, for the lighting of the fire. As the fire begins to burn they watch the smoke rise, "carrying him up to heaven." Unknown to his farewell party, as the fire burns and the smoke rises, the carpenter, obscured from view, escapes through the tunnel, returning safely sometime later after a mock sojourn to Heaven to build the mansion (Minford, 1983). See also Hakim Bey's description of the T'ang Dynasty tale 'The Blue Bridge' for more Oriental Hempen inspired allegorical folklore (Bey, et al. 2004).

16   As quoted in (Needham, 1974)

17   From "In Search of Immortality," http://www.arthist.umn.edu/classes/AH8720/Spring2001/reading3.html, originally published in *Searching for Immortality*, in the exhibition catalog of Weisbrod Chinese Art Ltd., Sept. 19, 2000, pp. 10-11 (http://www.weisbrodchineseart.com). The plant we term *Cannabis* was mentioned in ancient Chinese herbals - Bretschneider, E., M.D. *Botanicon Sinicum* (as Article III in *Journal of the North-China Branch of the Royal Asiatic Society*, 1881, New Series, Vol. XVI, Part I, Shanghai, 1882), pp. 31-32.

cense burners... The addition of hemp (*ta-ma, huo-ma, Cannabis sativa = indica*) to the contents of incense-burners is clearly stated in one Taoist collection, *Wu Shang Pi Yao (Essentials of the Matchless Books)*, which must place it before +570..." (Needham, 1974).

This shamanic relationship with cannabis obviously lasted some centuries amongst Taoists and this is not surprising as "...the Taoist technique of ecstasy is shamanic in origin and structure" (Eliade, 1984). The magical use of cannabis was not limited to smoking. In the Chen Kao, "Yang Hsi describes... his own experience using the Chhu Shen Wan (Pill of Commencing Immortals) which contains much hemp" (Needham, 1974). A Taoist priest writing in the fifth century B.C. about seeded buds of cannabis noted that "magician-technicians (*shu chia*) say that if one consumes them with ginseng it will give one preternatural knowledge of events in the future." [18] "...[O]ne could add a fine +6th-century example from a *Wu Tsang Ching (Manual of the Five Viscera)*... 'If you wish to command demonic apparitions to present themselves you should constantly eat the inflorescences of the hemp plant'" (Needham, 1976).

As Needham explains, cannabis was one of the establishing factors of Taoist Philosophy:

> The chain of events which led to the establishment of Mao Shan... as the first major permanent centre of Taoist practice began in +349 or slightly earlier with visitations by immortals to a young man named Yang His... in a series of visions, there appeared to Yang a veritable pantheon of celestial functionaries, including the lady Wei... and the... Mao [Brothers]... In the course of these interviews, aided almost certainly by cannabis, Yang took down in writing a number of sacred texts which the immortals assured him were current in their own supernal realm as well as oral elucidations and answers to Yang's queries about various aspects of the unseen world. He treasured and disseminated these scriptures as the basis for a new Taoist faith more elevated than the 'vulgar' sects of his time. (Needham, 1976)

Hakim Bey also notes that in "the early Taoist tradition of the Mao Shan, or 'Supreme Clarity' school, a great many shamanic 'survivals' can be traced, among them the intriguing fact that the Mao Shan revelations were supposed to have taken place under the

---

18   As quoted in (Needham, 1974)

influence of a 'hemp laced incense'" (Bey, et al, 2004). "The teachings of the Tao emphasize that one must forget his own conciousness in order to attain the goals of the Tao. It is precisely this state which can be attained with Cannabis, (Emboden, 1982).[19]

> Moreover, Taoism has the honor of being the only religion (as far as I know) to personify Cannabis as a deity. In the T'ang period there existed a cult of Ma Ku, or 'Miss Hemp.' It was centered at Mt T'ien T'ai, at a place called the precipice of Miss hemp; a statue of her stood there in Sung times…. Ma Ku was depicted as a beautiful maiden of the Taoist 'grotto fairy' type, but with a bird's claws instead of feet…. In T'ang poetry she is often associated with important motifs, connected to Mao Shan meditation techniques, constellated around the imagery of time distortion. (Bey, et al, 2004)

Ma Ku, literally, 'Hemp Lady,'[20] was a Taoist 'Immortal,' who had strong connections with the 'elixir of life,' bringing back to mind that cannabis was deemed one of the Superior Elixirs of Immortality by Shen Nung millennia prior to this and it would seemed to have enjoyed this reputation in the intervening centuries. "…Taoist dreamed of ascending to heaven after so many years of asceticism and by taking an elixir of life concocted from various rare herbs" (Suzuki, 1961).

> Something might… be gained by pursuing the mythological connection with the hemp Damsel, Ma Ku, goddess of the slopes of Thai Shan, where the plant was supposed to be gathered on the seventh day of the seventh month, a day of séance[21] and banquets in Taoist communities. (Needham, 1974)

In relation, the Taoist philosopher Wang Yuan (146-168 CE), was said to have invited Ma Ku to a feast on the cannabis gathering day of the "seventh day of the seventh month" where "The servings were piled up on gold platters and in jade cups without limit. There were rare delicacies, many of them made from flowers and fruits, and their fragrance permeated the air inside and out." Wang served the guests a strong liquor from "the celestial kitchens," and warned that it was "unfit for drinking by ordinary people." According to the ancient account, even after diluting the liquor with water, everyone became intoxicated and desired

19   From a quote in (Ratsch, 2001)
20   (Kohn, 1993)
21   Bringing back to mind, cannabis' long association as an aid in contacting spirits in China.

more.[22] It is believed by some sources that the elixir referred to was a special wine made from cannabis.[23] A Chinese poem about Ma ku by Ts'ao T'ang clearly brings to mind the beauty of budding cannabis:

> Blue Lad transmits the word, requiring them to come back:
> His report tells that Miss Hemp's 'jade stamens' have opened.
> The watchet [Blue-grey] Sea has turned to dust –
> All other affairs may be disregarded:
> They mount dragon and crane and come to observe the flowers.[24]

The 'Blue Lad' is a Taoist deity, and the poem describes him summoning all the fairies and immortals to witness the blossoming of Ma Ku's flowers. "Apparently the T'ang literati argued about the identity of this 'jade stamen-and-pistil' flower suggesting that the truth was understood only by a few, who knew how to cultivate hemp flowers till (according to one description) they sported 'whiskers like threads of ice, with golden grain sewn on top'" (Bey, et al., 2004).[25] Conceivably, this could indicate that the Taoist gardeners new the secret of separating the male from female cannabis plants, to produce resinous seedless cannabis known as *sinsemillia*, a cultivation technique generally assumed to have been developed much later.

Considering that Shen-Nung's references in the *Pen Ts'ao* are thought to have originated around 2,800 BCE, and that as late as the tenth century CE references to cannabis' ability to enable one to 'communicate with spirits'[26] were still being noted, in China, we are discussing the shamanic and cultural use of a plant that stretches over 3,500 years. A beautiful quatrain from the classic 'Greater Lord of the Long Life,' believed to be written around 300 BC, gives a clear impression of cannabis' importance to the mystics of ancient China:

---

22   See (Campany, 2002)

23   Such is the view of a surviving Taoist sect, 'The Way of Infinite Harmony,' who worships Ma Ku as the Goddess of Hemp. During the 'Cultural Revolution' the sect all but disappeared, but since religious reforms in China have now eased up the sect is currently gaining in popularity, gathering new devotees from around the world. According to Wikipedia other sects have seen a mushroom at the core of the elixir prepared by Ma Ku.

24   As quoted in (Bey, et al., 2004).

25   It should be noted that some might question Hakim Bey, a sort of post modern trickster, as a legitimate historical source.

26   Li (1978) refers to the 10th century writings of T'ang Sheng-wei in reference to this.

First a yin then a yang
No one knows what I do
Jade buds of holy hemp
For the one who lives apart[27]

The Chinese love affair with cannabis eventually soured, as Mia Touw explained; "During the Han Dynasty shamanism steadily declined, becoming disreputable as well, and with it, no doubt, the practice of using cannabis as an hallucinogen" (Touw, 1981). Others have seen this decline through the rise of the more 'morality' based philosophy of Confucianism. Alternatively Hui-Lin Li concluded "The discontinuation of use of cannabis can perhaps simply be referred to its unsuitability to the Chinese temperament and traditions" (Li, 1975).[28] Although it should be noted that Li's statement fails to take into account the popularity of the plant amongst Chinese shaman and Taoist adepts for over three millennia prior.

Mark Merlin offers another possible reason for Chinese culture's eventual disdain for what was once considered a "delight giver," suggesting that "the use of hemp for intoxicating purposes by the barbarians of the west of north China probably explains much of the prejudice against the plant in ancient China. Any habits of the war-like barbarians who continually and viciously harassed the more sedentary Chinese civilization were frowned upon emphatically" (Merlin, 1972). Recent discoveries in China, discussed in the next Chapter, may add considerable weight to Merlin's speculations of more than thirty years ago.

---

27   As quoted in *Road To Heaven: Encounters with Chinese Hermits* (Porter, 1993)
28   In relation Norman Taylor noted on the subject of the eventual Chinese cultural disdain for cannabis, that "to be a little happy is suspect, and to be very happy is quite sinful. Hence they were soon calling the resinous female plant the 'Liberator of Sin'" (Taylor, 1966).

9

CHINA'S HAOMAVARGA

An archeological find in Xinjiang, China, that included both remnants of cannabis and a mummified Caucasian body have not only radically altered what we know about the history of cannabis, but also have forever changed long standing beliefs about the movements and communications of whole cultures in the ancient world.

In Xinjang, China, archaeologists found a sack of marijuana leaves buried alongside the mummified remains of a middle age man, as well as a mortar and pestle that was used for grinding the plant matter, bringing to mind the mortar and pestle of the Haoma priests. Additional finds of bundles of Ephedra at similar sites of mummified Caucasian remains in the orient have caused more than a few researchers to view this discovery as evidence of the Bactria Margiana Haoma cult extending into China, a hypothesis we shall further explore shortly. China's *The People's Daily* reported the following of the find in a December 25th, 2006:

> Chinese scientists have carefully stripped a 2,800-year-old mummy, only to find the corpse underneath the delicate attire of a possible shaman priest had decayed and broken at the neck and arms.
>
> But research work on the mummy would continue, said Dr. Li Xiao, head of the heritage bureau in Turpan, of northwest China's Xinjiang Uygur Autonomous Region.
>
> "We didn't expect the mummy to be so badly decayed, but technically, it won't prevent us from confirming his status and further research on the history of shamanism in northwest China," said Li, a noted historian. The Caucasian-looking mummy

was unearthed from a cluster of ancient tombs in Turpan in 2003 and research has been going on since.

Scientists stripped the mummy last week hoping to better preserve it and find out more about the clothing, culture and life of the time the shaman lived, Li said.

The mummy had seemed perfectly intact in his heavy outfit: a leather coat, a knitted mantle as well as hat and boots, said Jia Yingyi, a researcher with the regional museum of Xinjiang

"His clothing was largely brown: a brown-and-red mantle with triangular webbing and pants of the same color and with wavy patterns," he said.

Archaeologists found a sack of marijuana leaves buried alongside the mummy.

He also wore huge earrings of copper and gold, and a turquoise necklace, and held a copper laced stick in his right hand and a bronze axe in the left. His hands were crossed in front of his chest.

"From his outfit and the marijuana leaves, we assume he was a shaman," said Li. "He must have been between 40 and 50 years old when he died."

...The man was the best preserved and most decoratively-dressed of 600 mummies excavated in 2003 from a cluster of 2,000 tombs in Turpan. A dozen of the mummies are believed to have been shamans.

Archaeologists assume the tombs, which date from the Bronze Age to the Tang Dynasty (618 - 907), belonged to several big clans.

The tombs also produced a wide variety of stone implements, bronzeware, colored chinaware pieces and knitwear.

Fig 9.1: Body of Shaman found with 2 pounds of cultivated cannabis.

Shamanism used to be common in many parts of north China and shamans, who were believed to be able to communicate with the gods and conjure up the dead, enjoyed a high status.

According to Dr. Jiang Hong'en, when the cannabis was unearthed in 2003, "it was still green, as if it had just been plucked, and completely intact." Dr. Jiang said the Kunming Botanical Institute confirmed the bud was 2,500 years old.

In the 2006 *Journal of Ethnopharmacology* article "A new insight into *Cannabis sativa* (*Cannabaceae*) utilization from 2500 year-old Yanghai Tombs, Xinjiang, China" the authors discuss this

rare well preserved archeological find consisting of 789 grams of dried cannabis and conclude that "Based on the shamanistic background of the deceased man and ancient customs, it is assumed that the Cannabis was utilized for ritual/medicinal purposes" (Jiang et al. 2006).

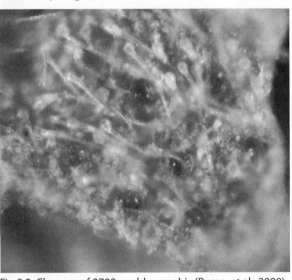

Fig 9.2: Close up of 2700 yr old cannabis (Russo, et al., 2008).

Fig 9.3: (A), Bag that contained 2 pounds of cannabis. (B). wooden bowl used for grinding cannabis (with perforated holes from continual grinding with pestle). (C), 2700 yr old cannabis (Jiang, et al., 2006).

Prior to this find, the main finds of ancient cannabis had come from Eurasia, and the majority of these were carbonized or decayed due to climate and storage conditions. The remains from the Turpan Basin's Yanghai Tombs were extremely well preserved due to the overtly dry climate of the area, and leaves, buds and seeds, including glandular trichomes were preserved in three dimensions, free of distortion, surviving intact for 2700 years. "These remains of hemp are the oldest examples of Cannabis thus far reported in which macroscopic/microscopic structures can be demonstrated in such great detail. These materials provide us with significant information on ancient civilization... and about the utilization of hemp" (Jiang et al. 2006).

> ....All the Cannabis remains could be used for psychoactive purposes, which would suggest that the deceased man knew of the narcotic value of Cannabis. Moreover, based on the analysis of all the funerary objects... the owner was considered to be a shaman.
> ...Due to its apparently prolonged use as a pestle, the inner surface of the wooden bowl containing Cannabis had become smooth, and one side became perforated... The Cannabis was presumably pulverized with a mortar before being consumed for psychoactive purposes. Thus, we assume that the deceased was more concerned with the intoxicant and/or medicinal value of the Cannabis remains.
> ....The deceased... may have been mainly concerned with the ritual of communication between the human and the spirit world. The gift of Cannabis may have been to enable him to continue his profession in the afterlife. A shaman who knew the utility of herbal medicine also played the role of physician in ancient times..... The new discovery of hemp in the Yanghai Tombs, Turpan, China provides evidence... [that] hemp was used for medicinal and religious rituals in NW China... (Jiang et al. 2006)

Dr. Ethan Russo, arguably the leading authority on the history of cannabis medicines, has also written about this and similar finds noting that the mummified remains were not those of the Oriental people generally assumed as the indigenous inhabitants of the area, but were rather of Caucasian descent;

> ... A large amount of cannabis radiocarbon dated to 2500 years ago was found in the tomb of a Caucasoid male, dressed as a shaman.... This site and contents resemble those of other 'mummies' of the Tarim Basin associated with hemp artefacts. These nomads may have been speakers of Tocharian, an Indo-European language, and, as the Yuezhi-Kushan people may have provided

cultural linkage and possible passage of cannabis knowledge to and from China and India. (Russo, 2007)

Indeed, the shaman's hat was actually covered with cowry shells believed to have come to the site via the Indian Ocean. Other finds from the area include Bronze objects associated with the Russian Steppe Scythians and items indicating a BMAC influence, and these demonstrate that a vast trade network was at play centuries earlier than previously thought.

In a more recent news story "Researchers find oldest-ever stash of marijuana," Russo is quoted in in regards to this amazing find, noting that other evidence of cannabis use from the area also exists:

> The substance has been found in two of the 500 Gushi[1] tombs excavated so far in northwestern China, indicating that cannabis was either restricted for use by a few individuals or was administered as a medicine to others through shamans, Russo said.... "It certainly does indicate that cannabis has been used by man for a variety of purposes for thousands of years."... The region of China where the tomb is located, Xinjiang, is considered an original source of many cannabis strains worldwide. (*The Canadian Press*, 11/27/08)

This story was followed by a CNN report, "Ancient cannabis stash unearthed in China," as news of the controversial find spread around the world:

> "It had evidence of the chemical attributes of cannabis used as a drug," said Dr. Ethan Russo, an author of a study published in the *Journal of Experimental Botany*. "It could have been for pain control. It could have been for other medicinal properties. It could have been used as an aid to divination."
>
> They don't think it was used to make hemp clothing or rope, as some other early cultures did. Genetic analysis of the plant suggests it was cultivated rather than gathered from the wild.
>
> This find is not the first or the oldest example of ancient people using cannabis, but it may be the best studied.
>
> "There may have been older finds of cannabis, but not with this level of scientific investigation attached to them," Russo said. (CNN, 11/12/2008)

---

1   This is the first time I've seen the term 'Gushi' used in reference to this ancient culture.

In the *Journal of Experimental Botany*, report, "Phytochemical and genetic analyses of ancient cannabis from Central Asia," Russo and his co-researchers go into more detail on the find, noting that the most likely conclusion was that these people "cultivated cannabis for pharmaceutical, psychoactive or divinatory purposes."

> In examining the botanical evidence from this 'old and cold' site with its unique degree of preservation, the cannabis consisted of a processed (pounded) sample whose seed size, colour, and morphology... suggest that it was cultivated rather than merely gathered from wild plants. The considerable amount of cannabis present (789 g) without any large stalks or branches would logically imply a pooled collection rather than one from a single plant. Importantly, no obvious male cannabis plant parts (e.g. staminate flowers, not infrequently observed in Indian herbal cannabis, or bhang (Russo, 2007) were evident, implying their exclusion or possible removal by human intervention, as these are pharmacologically less psychoactive. ....It would appear, therefore, that humans selected the material from plants on the basis of their higher than average THC content.
>
> ....The excellent preservation of the cannabis from this tomb allowed an unprecedented level of modern botanical investigation through biochemistry and genetics to conclude that the plant was cultivated for psychoactive purposes. While cultivation of hemp for fibre has been documented in Eastern China from a much earlier date..., the current findings represent the most compelling physical evidence to date for the use of cannabis for its medicinal or mystical attributes. (Russo, et al., 2008)

A second find of cannabis in the area has gone somewhat less reported. *The Journal of Ethnopharmacology* paper, "The discovery of *Capparis spinosa* L. (*Capparidaceae*) in the Yanghai Tombs (2800 years b.p.), NW China, and its medicinal implications," focuses instead on the plant, *Capparis spinosa* L. (caper) which has both medical and food stuff qualities, and treats the evidence of cannabis as only a secondary subject. As the authors reported of a jar containing cannabis found in the tomb of this other Shaman:

> There were two kinds of plant remains in that jar: the upper part consisted of several clumps of seeds from *Capparis spinosa* L....
> while the lower part contained fruits, leaves and shoots of *Can-*

nabis sativa L. (Fig. 5(H) and (I)). The well-preserved samples gave us an opportunity to study them in detail.....

Below the seeds of caper and in the same jar are fruits, leaves, and shoots of *Cannabis sativa*. Plant remains of *Cannabis sativa* do not appear to have been used for food/oil or as seeds for mass cultivation. If so, only the fruits would be preserved. Thus, in the jar which contains the fruits of common millet (*Panicum miliaceum L.*), only the seeds were left and there were no shoots or leaves mixed in with them. So the ancient Yanghai people appear to have been careful to prepare the food stuff properly in order to show their respect for the dead. Moreover, the mixture of shoots, leaves and fruits of *Cannabis sativa* unearthed in... the Yanghai Tombs seems to have been known by the ancient indigenous Yanghai people for its religious/medicinal value... Since *Cannabis sativa* and *Capparis spinosa* are found together, the seeds of caper do not appear to have been used as a food/condiment or as seeds for mass cultivation. The significance of the combination of the two plants may lie in their medicinal value. To date, both hemp and caper are still important Uigur medicines in Turpan... As caper is now an important medicinal herb with countless uses..., the ancient Yanghai people may already have been aware of its medicinal value. The plants which had special value were accredited supernatural status and paid more attention to in prehistoric times. The therapeutic properties of caper could have been discovered in ancient times.

.... However, did the ancient Yanghai people use the plant parts of *Cannabis sativa* and *Capparis spinosa* separately or mixed together? And how did they use these two plants? Further study will be necessary to answer these questions. (Jiang, et al., 2007)

Unfortunately, as shall be discussed shortly, the Chinese Government is very sensitive about these finds of Caucasian mummies,

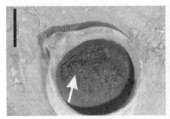 

Fig 9.4: "Small shoots, leaves and fruits of *Cannabis sativa* stored in the lower part of the jar. Scale bar = 5.0 cm (arrow: some clumps of caper seed adhering to the mixture of *Cannabis sativa*). Fig 9.5: Fruits of *Cannabis sativa*. Scale bar = 1.0 mm."(Jiang, et al., 2007). It should be noted that the size of the seeds from this site fit well within those found by Sarianidi at BMAC, see Chapter 6.

as they alter accepted Chinese history in a number of very radical
ways. As a result, archaeologists are restricted for the most part
from further exploration in the area, except for those few that have
managed to navigate through the Gordian Knot of government red
tape involved in getting a permit for access.

The Caucasian mummies found in the Tarim Basin have been
dated at least as far back as 1800 B.C. and ranging to around 200
B.C., when it is believed they succumbed to Chinese conquests of
the area. Over 300 such mummies have been recovered and examined, although it is expected many more exist. Not surprisingly
there "has been the proliferation of popular articles, books, and
television documentaries devoted to the discovery of prehistoric
Bronze Age 'Caucasoid' or 'Europoid' populations in the western
Chinese Xinjiang Uyghur Autonomous Region" (Hemphill & Mallory, 2004):

> Where it has been possible to identify a phenotypic pattern,
> the majority of these individuals are identified as possessing a
> stronger resemblance to a 'Western' pattern (e.g.,fair hair, high-
> bridged noses, heavy beard) rather than the phenotypic pattern
> common to the Han of China... Not surprisingly, such identifi-
> cations led many to ask... 'Who were the[se] corpses from the
> Tarim Basin? Where did they come from? And how did they get
> there?' (Hemphill & Mallory, 2004)

The discovery of an ancient Caucasian culture living in what has
long been considered the heartland of the Han people has raised a
number of questions regarding what has become the accepted history of China. The Chinese have generally considered their culture
as developing on its own,[2] and not receiving any influence from
"Western Culture" until about the mid second century BC. The
mummies, who were skilled horsemen, had chariots, expert weavers and used bronze, all much earlier than the traditional Chinese
dates for the oriental "invention" of such items, and the mummies,
along with linguistic evidence of an Indo-European origin of certain Chinese words to be discussed shortly, are now indicating that
such technology came to the Orient via these mummies and other
Indo-European avenues.

2   Via 'Peking Man,' many Chinese see the oriental Race as evolving independently
as well!

As it happens, quite a few words attested in Old Chinese have turned out to have Indo-European etymologies. For example, a whole cluster of words to do with wheels, wheel spokes, axles, and chariots—all objects first invented in west-central Eurasia — has proved to be Indo-European in origin. (Barber, 1999)

As well, Indigenous populations of Western China, who show clear indications of European genetics in their appearance, have long considered themselves as a separate people from the Han Chinese. As a result, China, which has been known to have problems with other provinces seeking autonomy, does have realistic concerns about increasing calls a for independence in their Western provinces, as some of the people in the region have seen these finds as evidence of their culturally separate background from the Han Chinese.

Such concerns have vastly limited the amount of research the Chinese government has allowed into these areas or the mummies that have been recovered from the sites. In the late 1990s when the documentary *Mysterious Mummies of China* (1998) was being filmed, the film crew, being led by Victor Mair[3] and including a number of other well-known researchers, were only allowed to travel to the area accompanied by Chinese officials. Further, Mair and company found themselves taken to a site that had obviously been tampered with, containing a headless corpse. The feeling of the documentary filmmakers, was that the Chinese government had tampered with the site, and "planted a headless body here, to avoid the risk of unearthing a European-type face."

Complicating things further, what has been exhumed for study is kept in poor conditions, due to lack of funding, and some of the most important archeological finds of human remains, are now disintegrating before they can be adequately examined and studied in order to understand their historical implications and importance.

Interestingly, ancient Chinese documents dating back to about the 5th century make reference to these people, and until this find they were generally regarded as being the fantastical tales of the ancient Chinese, analogous to the Greek references to centaurs and Cyclops. Victor Mair, an expert on the ancient Chinese, says that the ancient oriental texts referred to people in the Western regions

3   Victor Mair can be credited with first noticing the Western appearance of the Mummies during a visit to a Chinese Museum.

who "had red hair, bluish-green eyes... long noses. And they looked like monkeys, hairy all over" (Mair, 1998).[4]

As noted in the 2004 article "Horse-Mounted Invaders From the Russo-Kazakh Steppe or Agricultural Colonists From Western Central Asia? A Craniometric Investigation of the Bronze Age Settlement of Xinjiang" by Brian E. Hemphill and J.P. Mallory, there have been two main strands of thought about the identity of this Caucasian cannabis cult in China, which may both hold some accuracy through overlapping with each other. The two hypotheses which are currently debated by archeologists regarding the origins of the Bronze Age populations of the Tarim Basin are: the Steppe hypothesis, and the Bactrian oasis hypothesis, areas of which we have already discussed in this study. Although other theories about the mummies' origins do exist.....

Real Mummies Wear Plaid

The Xinjang mummies were dressed in what has been described as a 'Celtic tartan' style of clothing. "A detailed examination of a textile fragment by Good (1995) yielded evidence of the same decorative technique as that found in Scottish tartans which, in turn, exhibited similarities to tartans found at Hallstatt in Austria dated to the late second millennium B.C." (Hemphill & Mallory, 2004). In *A Meeting of Civilizations: The Mystery of China's Celtic Mummies,*[5] Clifford Coonan reports "The discovery of European corpses thousands of miles away suggests a hitherto unknown connection between East and West in the Bronze Age.... DNA testing confirms that... hundreds of... mummies found in Xinjiang's Tarim Basin are of European origin" (Coonan, 2006).

> Best preserved of all the corpses is Yingpan Man, known as the Handsome Man, a 2,000-year-old Caucasian mummy discovered in 1995. He had a gold foil death mask - a Greek tradition - covering his blond, bearded face, and wore elaborate golden embroidered red and maroon wool garments with images of fighting Greeks or Romans. The *hemp* mask is painted with a soft smile and the thin moustache of a dandy. Currently on display at a museum in Tokyo, the handsome Yingpan man was two metres tall

4   *Mysterious Mummies of China.*
5   (*Independent*, UK, 28 August 2006)

(six feet six inches), and pushing 30 when he died. (Coonan, 2006) [Emphasis added]

Commenting on the seeming Celtic connection with China that these mummies indicate, Coonan writes:

Fig 9.6: Yingpan Man wearing a hemp "death-mask."

The similarities to the traditional Bronze Age Celts are uncanny, and analysis has shown that the weave of the cloth is the same as that of those found on the bodies of salt miners in Austria from 1300 BC.... The burial sites of Cherchen Man[6] and his fellow people were marked with stone structures that look like dolmens from Britain, ringed by round-faced, Celtic figures, or standing stones. Among their icons were figures reminiscent of the sheela-na-gigs, wild females who flaunted their bodies and can still be found in mediaeval churches in Britain. A female mummy wears a long, conical hat which has to be a witch or a wizard's hat. Or a Druid's, perhaps? The wooden combs they used to fan their tresses are familiar to students of ancient Celtic art.... These mummies... suggest... that the Celts penetrated well into central Asia, nearly making it as far as Tibet. (Coonan, 2006)

A Celtic origin for the Tarim mummies is more than a bit of a stretch in the minds of most scholars researching the finds. A more likely explanation is that both groups represented divergent geographical ends of the same cultural complex through which the Scythians traveled and migrated through, and indeed a Scythian connection to both the Celtic culture and Tarim mummies has been suggested by more than a few researchers. "The finest examples of Celtic art are directly derived from contact with the Scythians"[7]

6   The name given to one of the mummies found in the region.
7   Referring to Celtic jewellery found dug up near Lake Lucerne in France, Edward Bacon refers to Celtic ornaments "in which every motif... 'sprouts' into another motif and so on—a dream like sequence which is related to the art of the steppes, usually called 'Scythian.' The modern word psychedelic might well be applied to it, since the art form in either case immediately or remotely derive from the drug takers fantasies" (Bacon, 1971). Other scholars suggest that the discovery of cannabis seeds in an archeological dig of a twenty five hundred year old tomb in Germany, along with similar finds [See chapter 3] give further indication of the nomadic Scythians penetration into Europe.

(Frazier, 1991). A fact that would also account for the finds of cannabis at a variety of Celtic sites as discussed in Chapter 3.

Victor Mair, in his article "Prehistoric Caucasoid corpses of the
Tarim Basin" suggested that the textiles worn and associated with
the Xinjiang remains were "highly diagnostic, perhaps still more
so than DNA analysis, for identifying the origins and affiliations
of the Tarim Basin Bronze Age people" (Mair, 1995). The textile
and clothing recovered from the sites includes an array of items
such as fur-lined and fur-trimmed coats, long stockings, pants,
pointed hats and other items "that Mair (1995, 1998), Mallory and
Mair (2000), and Barber (1999) claim are indicative of a close relationship with Indo-European-speaking pastoralist nomads from
the Russian steppe" (Hemphill & Mallory, 2004). Textile expert
Elizabeth Wayland Barber, considered the world expert on ancient
textiles, after examining the tartan-style cloth, claimed it could be
traced back to Anatolia, the Caucasus and the steppe area north of
the Black Sea. This same area was the home of the ancient cannabis using Sredeni Stog identified in Chapter 3. A connection to the
Tarim Basin mummies with these people is further evident by the
early use of the horse by the Tarim Basin culture, a means by which
that they were able to migrate to the area so far from their original
homeland, and colonize it, almost three millennia ago.

Cherchen Man, who like Yingpan man stood an intimidating 6
foot 6, was in his mid-50s when laid to rest 3 millennia ago. A leather saddle and horse skull and hoof were placed in the grave with
him, and he was wearing the world's oldest pair of pants, a clothing
innovation associated with the Scythians, and likely developed for
their efficiency when riding horses (those damned plaid kilts were
always blowing up in the wind!). This find is believed to support the
growing belief of archeologists that the spread of Indo-European
genes, culture, and language from their origins in Eastern Europe
6,000 years ago, are likely linked with the spread of horse riding and
the revolutionary technology of horse-drawn vehicles.

Again like the Scythians, who were known to slaughter the
wives, concubines, and slaves of dead Royalty at their elaborate funeral rites, the indications from Cherchen Man's tomb are that the
two women and the baby that were found with him, were likely
sacrificed in order to accompany this imposing figure, probably a
chieftain, into the afterlife.

In relation to the pointed hats and remains of cannabis, it is interesting to note that Guive Mirfendereski, in his article, "Homavarka: Potheads of Ancient Iran,"[8] states of the Scythians, also known as 'Sakas'; "We know from Darius' inscriptions that Saka Tigraxauda were so-called because they bore a tall pointed hood.. The representations of their fallen king Skuxa at Bisotun, national delegate at Apadana's eastern stairway and throne bearers at Naqsh-e Rostam all were shown with a tall pointed hood as if the headgear was a part of everyday attire" (Mirfendereski, 2005). Herodotus also noted

> The Sacae, or Scyths, were clad in trousers, and had on their heads tall stiff caps rising to a point. They bore the bow of their country and the dagger; besides which they carried the battle-axe, or sagaris (fokos in Hungarian - Villaman-). They were in truth Amyrgian (Western) Scythians, but the Persians called them Sacae, since that is the name which they gave to all Scythians. (Herodotus VII. 64)

Mysterious Mummies of China reported of a female specimen dating from the third century B.C.: "One of the most important discoveries is a fully clothed woman wearing a conical hat. Symbolic of a high priestess of the nomads, [Scythians] it would one day become the hallmark of witches in Europe." In relation, a Scythian

Fig 9.7: Assyrian image of Scythian prisoner, wearing pointed hat.

influence on European witchcraft has been realistically suggested (Ginzburg, 1991), and the use of cannabis, and other narcotic plants in European witchcraft has also long been identified (Bennett, et al., 1995, Bennett & McQueen, 2001; Thompson, 1927, 2003: etc.). Interestingly, as we shall discuss shortly, the nomads of this area may have had their ancient counterpart to the orgiastic rites of the later witches as well.

Another connecting factor between these mummies and the Scythians is the use of cannabis by both cultures. As noted in the Chapter 7, the eastern most branch of the Scythians, living in the Tien Shan Mountains are called *Haumavarka* (Haoma-Gatherers). Thus, the idea that these people were preparing a beverage from cannabis seems completely plausible. It should be noted that if "this cannabis were smoked or inhaled, no mechanism for so doing has been excavated in the area.... Numerous questions remain. Current data do not permit it to be ascertained how the cannabis from the tomb was administered" (Russo, et al., 2008).

This brings in a connection with the Bactria Margiana Archeological Complex (BMAC), temple site that was devoted to the preparation of the sacred Aryan drink the Haoma. As noted the cannabis seeds from this site seem to be of a smaller size variety and fit within the range of those found at the BMAC (as were seeds recovered from a Scythian burial site in Pazyryk[9]). In relation to the BMAC it should also be noted that many mummies were found that had bundles of Ephedra with them, and these include even the earliest of the mummies found in the Tarim Basin (1,800 B.C.).[10]

Ephedra does not grow on the Russian steppes, but was cultivated in the region of the Margiana Temple. This would indicate that the Tarim Basin was a meeting point for the Russian Steppe Scythian and their eastern Central Asian cousins the 'Haoma-Gatherers' and that the latter acted as a conduit of goods and culture from the BMAC civilization.

As discussed in Chapter 6 evidence has emerged in BMAC that indicate that more than one plant was involved in the preparation of Haoma, and both cannabis and Ephedra have been identified (and

---

9   See, image "Modern 'Novosadska' hemp, Pazyryk Iron Age and British medieval Cannabis seeds." (Clarke & Fleming, 1998).
10   Alternatively, Russo suggests, "If used orally, perhaps it was combined in some fashion with Capparis spinosa L., as these plants were found together in a nearby but later tomb at Yanghai" (Russo, et al., 2008).

in some cases poppies were also possibly used). This combination accounts for the use of Ephedra in the surviving tradition of the Haoma sacrifice, and the variety of effects attributed to the Haoma. A situation is also indicated by scriptural references which indicate a variety of Haomas (Y.10.12; Y10.17; Y10.21). This combination is important to note in relations to the finds of both Ephedra bundles with Tarim mummies and the bag of cannabis with a Shaman holding a mortar, pestle, axe, and a leather bound wand - likely a "a flogging instrument," certainly bring to mind the items attributed to the Haoma priest as described by Dr. Ali Jafarey:

> His usual implements for rituals were *ashtra* (whip), milk-bowl, *paitidâna* (mouth-veil), *khrafastraghna* (for killing noxious animals), *sraosho-charana* (flogging instrument), strainer, standard mortar, haoma cups, and baresman twigs. (V 14.8) One may take a careful note of the absence of some of the implements used in modern rituals and vice versa, and how the Avestan priest went armed to punish the faulty and kill the noxious. (Jafarey, 2000)

Jafarey, here referring to some items that would have appeared likely after the time of Zoroaster, such as the 'mouth veil,' but the mortar and pestle, flogging instrument, axe, bag of cannabis-Haoma, clearly indicate the apparatus included in the Xinjiang burial of a 'shaman,' were those of the 'Haoma priest.' Not surprisingly, a number of researchers have seen a connection with the Haoma Cult of the Bactria Margiana Archeological Complex (BMAC), with the Tarim Basin culture. As Elizabeth Wayland Barber explains in her book on the subject, *The Mummies of Urumchi*:

> ...[W]e know that early oasis hoppers were experimenting with hashish and opium... New cross-cultural archaeological data shows that the oasis settlers set up major ties to the south as they worked their way eastward. Thus the cult of the White room [BMAC] had ready avenues for a rapid southward spread across the Iranian plateau. (Barber, 1999)

This connection of course brings us to the Bactrian oasis hypothesis for the Tarim Basin mummies. "Proponents of this model assert that settlement of this region of western China came not from nomadic pastoralists of the steppe, but from sedentary, agriculturally based populations of the... Bactrian-Margiana archaeological complex (BMAC)" (Hemphill & Mallory, 2004). The suggestion here is that the archaeological evidence indicates that the initial colonizers of the Tarim Basin were agriculturalists from the BMAC region, rather than nomadic pastoralists from the Russian steppe. The evidence for this theory "not only includes irrigation systems, evidence of western cultigens such as wheat, and bones of sheep and goats, but also evidence of carefully bundled bags containing *Ephedra sp.* found accompanying many Bronze Age Xinjiang burials" (Hemphill & Mallory, 2004):

> Use of ephedra is well-known in... [BMAC] and Sarianidi... found evidence of specialized areas known as "white rooms" where it is believed a ritual drink, known as *haoma* in Iranian and *soma* in India, was consumed... Ephedra does not grow on the Russo-Kazakh steppe, nor is it associated with either Afanasievo or Andronovo cultures. (Hemphill & Mallory, 2004)

In relation to this Chinese connection with the pre-Zoroastrian cult of magi that prepared the sacred Haoma at the BMAC site, it is interesting to note the etymological sleuthing of Victor Mair, who has shown that the old Chinese word *m ag*, derives from the Persian *magus*, also source of English *magic*. The Chinese term *m ag* identified powerful individuals in the Chinese court, who Mair states, "were primarily responsible for divination, astrology, prayer, and healing with medicines,"[11] all traits of the Persian Magi.

Elizabeth Wayland Barber believes that the Bronze Age settlement of the Tarim Basin was a two-step process which saw an initial immigration from the oases of Bactria and Margiana, as indicated by finds at southeastern sites, and this first incursion was followed by a second wave of immigration soon after 1200 B.C. of Andronovo populations, ancestors of the Scythians, previously located to the northwest, and participants in this 2nd wave of immigration may be associated with the remains found at northern Tarim Basin sites. Barber contends that evidence for these two waves of immigration are indicated by dramatic differences in textile manufacture, and also textual evidence dating from the first centuries A.D. which shows that the southern Tarim oases population spoke Ira-

---

11   As quoted in (Barber, 1999).

nian languages (such as Saka and Sogdian), while those inhabiting the northern oases spoke Tocharian.

Scott Littleton, a Professor of Anthropology and an expert in Indo-European culture, believes the Tarim mummies are the remnants of the "nomadic cousins of the Tocharians [Tocharian-speaking inhabitants of the Tarim Basin, making them the easternmost speakers of an Indo-European language in antiquity] with western roots and/or North Iranian forerunners of the Saka, [Scythians] et al... Like most Central Asian nomads, modern as well as ancient, they almost certainly ingested cannabis and other drugs in the course of shamanic rituals (cf. the Saka at Pazyryk and elsewhere)" (Littleton, 2008),[12] a view supported by the discovery of Tocharian language documents in the Tarim Basin. The Tocharian language shares no definable characteristics with Indo-Iranian dialect, other than loan words.

> Within the phylogeny of the Indo-European languages, Tocharian languages are either placed with the "western..". languages of Europe[13]... or are regarded as languages that split from the rest of the Indo-European languages at such an early date that they lack many of the isoglosses found between other Indo-European languages... Mallory and Mair (2000...) suggested that the separation of Tocharian speakers from other Indo-European-speaking communities may have occurred as early as the fourth millennium B.C., and they identified the Afanasievo culture (ca. 3500-2500 B.C.), a primarily pastoralist culture found in the Altai and Minusinsk regions of the Eurasian steppe, as a possible source for a Tocharian presence in the Tarim Basin)... Wall paintings of Tocharian speakers depict these individuals as possessing red or blonde hair, long noses, blue or green eyes, and wearing broadswords inserted in scabbards hanging from their waists... (Hemphill & Mallory, 2004)

Commonalities between the Tocharian languages and various other Indo-European language families from Western Europe (as with Celtic, Germanic, Balto-Slavic, even Italic or Greek) have been suggested. But the only consensus on the matter is that Tocharian

---

12   Personal correspondence.
13   The similarities between Tocharian and western Indo- European languages such as Celtic and Italian are believed to come from a collective retention of proto-Indo-European archaicisms.

was already far enough removed, at an early date, from the other eastern Indo-European proto-languages (Proto-Balto-Slavic and Proto-Indo-Iranian), not to share some of the common changes in the later languages that developed out of them.

As the use of the horse was so instrumental in the colonization of the Tarim Basin at such an early date (1800 BC), along with ritual imagery associated with Eastern Europe, and the cultic use of hemp which originated in that same area, and finally the older form of Indo-European language of the Tocharian dialect, it is hard not to see these people, like the Scythians, with whom they traded, as the distant relatives of the cannabis burning and consuming corded ware culture of Eastern Europe. In fact the Tocharian languages are a major geographic exception to the usual pattern of Indo-European branches, being the only one that spread directly east from the theoretical Indo-European starting point in the Pontic steppe, ie, an area extending through Romania and Ukraine, the homeland of the horse domesticating, cannabis burning and drinking corded ware culture the proto-Indo-European Sredeni Stog!

The similarity of language with Western European dialects, such as Celtic and German, like the use of cannabis in these regions, and the similar textiles, can be explained by a distant but common European ancestry with the Sredeni Stog in their homeland of Romania to Ukraine. The suggestion is that both cultures split off from the Sredeni Stog culture around the same time, and the early Indo-European dialect did not go through the same changes as later groups who left later, and which are more identifiable. Most of their common ancestors migrated west, becoming the Celts and Germanic people. The people represented by these Chinese mummies went east, through the Russian Steppes, to the Tarim Basin. A recent CNN story "Ancient cannabis stash unearthed in China," concluded that these people "were a Caucasian race with light hair and blue eyes who likely migrated thousands of years ago from the steppes of Russia to what is now China. A nomadic people, they were accomplished horsemen and archers" (CNN, 11/12/2008). In relation, it should also be noted that the original researchers of the Cannabis find at the Yanghai shaman's tomb, suggested a European–Siberian origin for the plant material (Jiang et al,. 2006).

It has been suggested that the separation of Tocharian speakers from other Indo-European-speaking communities may have occurred as early as the fourth millennium B.C., which would account for the anomalies involved in placing Tocharian on the traditional Indo-European language family tree.

As it turns out, evidence of a now-extinct Indo-European people who lived in central Asia has long existed, although until the discovery of these mummies they have not generally been regarded as being in China and exerting their influence until the first few centuries A.D. and not to the earlier periods associated with the Tarim Basin mummies. This group was known by their language name, Tocharians, but more accurately can be seen as the *"Arsi,"* which is cognate with Sanskrit *arya* and Old Persian *ariya*, meaning *"Aryan."* Tocharian, which as noted has similarities to the Celtic and Germanic branches of the Indo-European tree, is recorded in manuscripts dated between the sixth and eighth centuries A.D., and solid evidence for its existence can be found as far back as the third century. These people apparently acted as Buddhist emissaries to the Chinese regions, and the traces of their presence can still be seen in the European features of the Western Chinese.

Some researchers believe that Tocharian was also the language of the Great Yuezhi to whom references occur in Chinese texts as early as the fifth century B.C., and who were a major source of jade for the Chinese. The Great Yuezhi were an aggressive Caucasian tribal culture to the raids of which the Chinese Han culture often fell victim and they are also thought to have chased out the Saka-Haumavarga from their location in the Tien Shan mountains around 300 B.C.. This fits well within the time frame of the Tarim Basin mummies, and we can expect at the very least all such groups had forms of contact, a trading relationship, and could conceivably have shared a common tongue for trading purposes.

The Tocharians are vividly depicted with European features (long noses, blue or green eyes set in narrow faces, red or blond hair parted neatly in the middle, and tall bodies), in 4th-5th century wall paintings at Kizil and Kumtura near the Tien Shan Mountains and north of the Tarim Basin. Likewise the Yuezhi of the first century B.C. also are depicted in striking painted statues discovered in Khalchayan ancient Bactria, which depict them with the same European features of long noses, thin faces, blond hair, pink skin, and bright blue eyes. Historically we know that during the second century B.C. the Greater Yuezhi moved from northwest China

Fig 9.8: Ancient Chinese jade piece, showing marked Scythian artistic influence, Fig 9.9.

founded the mighty Kushan empire and adopted Buddhism as the national religion. The latter, in turn, extended its power back into the Tarim Basin and with it spread Buddhism, which eventually reached China.

The latest genetic research indicates that the Tarim Basin mummies were far from being the pure Aryan race that they were thought to be and were a mixed race indeed. The earliest mummies, who were dressed in primitive woollen weaves, unlike the intricate Scythian-like patterns found on later finds, show a genetic history most closely associated with the eastern Asian populations. But during the period in which clothing styles and technological patterns radically changed, the evidence indicates, so did the genetics of the people, and as a trade of goods and knowledge developed between cultures, so did an exchange of DNA through cross-marriage.

> After 1200 B.C., this population experienced significant gene flow from highland populations of the Pamirs and Ferghana Valley. These highland populations may include those who later became known as the Saka and who may have served as 'middlemen' facilitating contacts between East (Tarim Basin, China) and West (Bactria, [BMAC], Uzbekistan) along what later became known as the Great Silk Road. (Hemphill & Mallory, 2004)

Indeed, indicating their profound role at this ancient cross roads between cultures, the later Tarim Basin mummies show a genetic heritage indicating ancestors from all over Eurasia, Western Europe, Siberia, The Mid East, Mongolia, Tibet and even India! An ancient melting pot at the center of the world that was likely the birthplace of Haoma.

That the Scythians played a major part in this cultural exchange is provided by maternal genetic analysis of Saka period male and female skeletal remains from a double inhumation kurgan located at the Beral site in Kazakhstan. Research on the pair determined that the two were most likely not blood relatives and were a husband and wife. The HV1 mitochondrial sequence of the male was similar to that most frequently found in European populations. Contrarily, the HV1 sequence of his female partner indicated a greater likelihood of Asian ancestry. The study's findings were in line with the view that mixings between Scythians and other populations occurred and were buttressed by the discovery of several objects with a definitive Chinese inspiration in the tomb (Clisson, et al., 2002).

Evidence from around the area of the Tarim Basin, to be discussed shortly, indicates that these ancient Tocharians worshipped from the Mountains. With their distant and exotic pastoral home, places of exotic Mountain worship and use of cannabis-Haoma, it is difficult not once again to wonder if this as of yet unidentified culture in the Tarim Basin brings us closer to the secondary home of the Aryan ancestors of the Soma cult, and the mountains on which the Haoma/Soma grew. With this in mind, and the Chinese geographical location, one is drawn to make some analogies between this scenario and that of the Chinese, who viewed cannabis, as did the Aryans, the "death-averting haoma" (Y.9.19-20), as an Elixir of Immortality, grown in the mysterious mountain abode of the Immortals!

According to H.H. Dubs, in *The Beginings of Alchemy*, the idea of an elixir of immortality came into China via the myths about the Indo-Iranian Soma and Haoma plants. Dubs believed knowledge of the plant came from the Iranian culture area into China around the 4th century B.C. or possibly even earlier (Dubs, 1947). Many researchers dismissed this claim outright, as at the time there was little in the way of evidence pointing to such early contact between the Han Chinese and Indo-European influences. However, the discovery of the Tarim Basin Mummies proves that such early avenues of contact did in fact exist, and moreover, dates back centuries prior than the date in question. Dubs' view was followed later by Pierre Huard and Ming Wong, who, in regard to Taoist references to immortality elixirs, also noted that "Traces of Indo-European immortality potions can be seen here: The Iranian Haoma... and the Indo-Aryan Soma... For centuries Taoists and alchemists were to seek the elixir of life in plants[14] and pills[15]..." (Huard & Wong,

14 "Shen Nung classified chu-ma [cannabis] as one of the Superior Elixirs of Immortality" (Robinson,1995).

15 Such as the 'Pill of Commencing Immortals' which contained "much hemp"

1959: 1968). "…[T]he elixir-of-life concept came to China by way of the ancient Vedic soma tradition of the divine plant of immortality" (Philosophers, 1972). In the article "Beliefs about Aging and Longevity in Ancient China," Alain Corcos refers to some of these earlier researches, adding that Haoma and Soma, like certain Chinese immortality elixirs, contained hemp:

> The idea of imbibing plant potions to gain immortality did not originate with the Chinese. Apparently, the idea came from the Aryan tradition (Huard and Wong 1959). The sacred intoxicating drink, named Haoma by the Iranians and Soma by the Aryans in India was believed to cure disease and to confer immortality. Hemp was an active ingredient of both drinks. The Aryan belief in a miracle drug conferring immortality and curing diseases reached China in the fourth century B.C. (Dubs,1947), giving rise to the idea that there was a place where longevity could readily be achieved.[16] (Corcos, 1981)

The connection between cannabis, Haoma, the Chinese Hu-Ma, the mountain home of the Immortals, and the mountainous origins of the Haoma Cult becomes even clearer when one looks at evidence that points to the nearby "the heavenly mountain of Tien Shan, the paradise of the Taoist immortals"[17] and land of the Haumavarga, as the homeland of all these elements at play. Elizabeth Wayland Barber, when referring to evidence of Tocharian words in the Chinese language, pointed out evidence of this influence in the naming of certain mountain ranges, including the Tien Shan! "The names of both the Qilian and Kunlun Mountains evidently came from a Tokharian word for "holy, heavenly" (… *klyon*, …*klyomo*—probably cognate with the Latin *caelum* ["sky, heaven"], from which we get the English *cel-estial*)" (Barber, 1999). According to Barber, these terms were in use for sometime starting around the mid-first millennium. As Elizabeth Wayland Barber specifically notes of the Tien Shan Mountains, "Still today the mountain range

(Needham, 1974).

16   As Frederick Dannaway has rightly commented: "The primordial relationship of a death defying plant of immortality evolved into a concept of an elixir alchemy which persisted from prehistoric metallurgical guilds into quite modern times" (Dannaway, 2009). From China, many of these themes made it into Arabic alchemy and from there to European alchemists; cannabis can be seen to have followed this same trail (Bennett, et al., 1995).

17   (Houk, 2002)

rimming the north side of the Tarim Basin is called the Celestial or Heavenly Mountains (since that is what Chinese Tien Shanand Uyghur Tangri Tagh mean), and the Southern Mountain rim is called the Kunlun" (Barber, 1999).

The Tien Shan mountains are located in a remote section of north western China, situated at the intersection of the national boundaries for China, Kyrgyzstan, and Kazakhstan. Even in modern times much of the Tien Shan mountain range remains unexplored and unmapped.

Interestingly Russo and his co-researchers, have suggested that the Shaman, whom we have discussed in relation to the over 2 pounds of well preserved cannabis with which he was buried with, may have been from this same location. "His burial as a disarticulated skeleton, as opposed to a mummified body as more frequently was found, suggested that he probably died in the highlands of the Tian Shan ('Heavenly Mountains,' or Ta¨ngri Tagh in Uighur) and his bones were later interred at Yanghai" (Russo, et al., 2008).

The ancient Chinese held that Taoist immortals made their homes in the highest peaks in places such as Tien Shan. In the Taoist tradition the Goddess of the West is believed to guard the peach trees of immortality in the Tien Shan Mountains ('Celestial Mountains'). "The Tien Shan were regarded not just as the mountain home of the gods, like Olympus or Sinai, but actually as a deity themselves, venerated as the most sacred mountains in China since the third millennium BC" (Shackley, 2001).

In "The Problem of the Aryans and the Soma: Textual-linguistic and Archaeological Evidence," Asko Parpola suggests that the use of "Soma might have started… in the Ferghana or Zeravshan mountains, the area of the later Saka Hauamavarga… or in fact anywhere in the vast Andronovo territory, including the Tian Shan mountains on the borders of China…" (Parpola, 1995). Interestingly Parpola continues with a quote from Flattery and Schwartz pointing out that also in this area "Ephedra… has been recognized for many centuries as a medicine" (Flattery and Schwartz, 1989). And indeed species of ephedra are also native to this region, and are still harvested and exported as *ma-huang* or 'yellow hemp,' which is used in traditional Chinese medicine.

As noted in Chapter 7, John McEno saw this same spot as the possible homeland of cannabis and the original cultivators a Scythian like people living in this area:

...I suggest a Cannabis home in the southern Altai or Tien Shan Mountains. These hills border the central Asian steppes, the great Neolithic 'nomad belt' stretching from the Black Sea to Mongolia. A tribe of migrants, the Scythians, emerged from this region at the dawn of history. They ranged east and west across the steppes, from China to Europe. (McEno, 1998)

This same are has been put forth by Nikolaï Ivanovich Vavilov who is considered by many to be the best expert on cannabis' origins:

There are very few indigenous crops in Central Asia but they do exist. Hemp appears to be the most important one among the field crops. Wild *Cannabis sativa* var. *Spontanea* Vav. Is a very common plant in Northern Tien Shan, especially on Northern facing slopes and valleys, but also north of this range. (Vavilov, et al., 1992)

This area is also very close to the Paryzyk tomb discussed in Chapter 7 for its evidence of Scythian cannabis use. Petroglyphs attributed to the Sythian-Saka, Huamavarga have been found in the Tien Shan, and their implications are quite profound. Up until modern times, this area has still been well known for its quality cannabis crop, a product of export into India and other regions.

Although Cannabis (both wild and cultivated) grows abundantly in Hindustan, there is very little production of charas. Until recent years most of the latter came from Central Asia (Chinese Turkestan), and the principal market was at Yarkand.
   There the charas grown on the northern spurs of the Chung-Kyr mountains and bought in Khotan, Zanju, Kugiar and Kargha-lik was collected. Kashgar was the main depot for the crops bought at Yangi-hissar and Rabat Kupriuk and grown on the last shoulders of the Pamir and the southern slopes of the *Tianshan (Tien Shan) mountains....* [emphasis added]
   Exportation... used to take place... by the old "Silk Road." (Bouquet, 1950)

For the filming of *The Mysterious Mummies of China* a group of researchers, led by Victor Mair were taken to the location of a impressive mountain site place of worship of the Huamavarga culture of the nearby Tien Shan Mountains, where a huge rock wall is full of petroglyphs testifying to the ecstatic practices of these people. Looking down at the lush valley from the mountain location, Jeannine Davis-Kimball described "magnificent grasslands that are so immense, it boggles the mind. And they go very high. One could not possibly take advantage of this territory without having had a horse. There's no doubt that horseback riding had a great impact upon the expansion and occupation of the territory in this region." The excitement of the research team upon reaching their mountainside destination was very apparent:

> VICTOR MAIR: Oh, God! Amazing! Look at that!
> JEANNINE DAVIS-KIMBALL: Oh, look at those!
> NARRATOR: A colossal rock face, covered with elaborate engravings.
> VICTOR MAIR: This mountain is the perfect setting for a reproductive fertility rite ceremony. There's a lot of grass here. It's very lush. And the mountain itself is so grand that it's natural that people would want to come here and have ceremonies.
> JEANNINE DAVIS-KIMBALL: [pointing to details in the imagery of the petroglyphs] I see females performing a very ritual dance, and some of them even falling into ecstasy during the dance time, and the copulation between the male and the female are prominent in these scenes.
> NARRATOR: These 3,000-year-old dancing women with their narrow waists and stylized gestures are nearly identical to figures found in Bulgaria and in the Ukraine, dated to about 1,000 years earlier. There too, the dancers celebrate fertility and reproduction. These figures have large noses, long faces, and round eyes. The nomads are thought to have Iranian origins. Here, their Western roots are literally carved in stone.

Dr. Jeannine Davis-Kimball was so enraptured with the site, which with its view of a valley with lush vegetation really does have a Shangri-La like look to it, that she traveled to the Kangjiashimenzi petroglyph site at the Tien Shan Mountains in Xinjiang, China twice, in August of 1991 and again in May and June of 1997. Davis-Kimball feels these anthropomorphic rock carvings are unique in style and content. The costume elements depicted link Xinjiang with the whole of Central Asia. "Because of the immense quantity of petroglyphs in Eurasia featuring primarily zoomorphisms, the low relief anthropomorphic tableau located in the Tien Shan

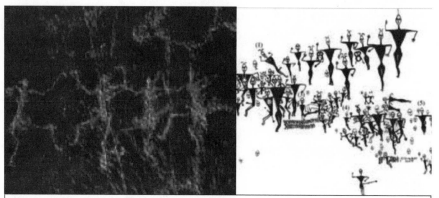

Fig 9.10: Eastern Europe petroglyphs. Right, Fig 9.11: Tien Shan petroglyphs, showing similar dancing figures. The state of arousal apparent in the lowest of the figures offers clear indications of the erotic nature of the festival, as does the prostrate and fainting figures indicate the ecstatic nature of the rites involved.

Fig 9.12: Close up of Tien Shan petroglyphs showing European features (round eyes, long noses). From (Barber, 1999). Fig 9.13: Image of dancing woman, ram and brazier from Scythian bracelet. Fig 9.14: Scythian Gold plaque, with dancing women drinking from horn cup.

Mountains at the site of Kangjiashimenzi, 75 kilometers southwest of the Hutubei county center stands out. Here the low relief images are finely executed and clearly depict a somber fertility ritual" (Davis-Kimball, 1998).

Other imagery makes it clear these people were aware of the "magical" properties of their flora and fauna, as these reproductions of Tien Shan petroglyphs of an ancient Shamans 'Tripping' in the Tien Shan amply illustrates, Fig 15.

Fig 9.15: Psychedelic Tien Shan petroglyphs.

The orgiastic rites of the Vedic religion are clear in the surviving iconography of India, and many have long noted the fertility cult origins of the Soma cult. Likewise, the Persian prophet Zoroaster rallied against the nocturnal erotic activities of the Haoma cult, purging the Iranian religion of these elements as we shall see in Chapter 14. Likewise the Nomadic herding culture who lived in the higher reaches of the fertile Tien Shan mountains associated with the Tarim Basin pastoralists, via trade and intermarriage, are reputed to have performed erotic fertility rights at a Mountain location, and this area has been clearly associated with the origins of both cannabis and Soma. Moreover, the petroglyphs attest to the same sort of erotic and ecstatic activity that one would expect to find with that associated with the early days of the Soma/Haoma cult. Further imagery at the site of this cannabis consuming fertility cult has now been compared to that found in Ukraine, where as we discussed in Chapter 3, the oldest known evidence of a cannabis brazier exists, and home of the corded ware believed to have been a trademark container for a cannabis beverage that has been suggested as the prototypical Soma (Sherratt, 1995).

Thus it would seem that it was here, a meeting place of cultures, that the Haoma/Soma cult may have first originated under the name hu-ma. Cannabis has its own Indo-European name *kanna*, and this is derived from the proto-Indo-European language, Finno-Ugric, *kannap*. As we shall show, the name Haoma, may have been developed from a Chinese term. Like the Haoma beverage which contained both Ephedra and cannabis, allied forms of the Chinese term "huang-ma" can be applied to both plants. As we have noted, there are Chinese words indicating an Indo-European origin, it would not be surprising if the "linguistic may... have been two-way... European words for silk... are related to the oldest reconstructable Chinese words for silk, *s'e(g)-" (Barber, 1999). "It is interesting that the Chinese character hu, which refers to barbarians or foreigners of the West, can be connected to the character for hemp (*hu-ma*) to indicate western or foreign hemp and the potent female hemp plant"[18] (Merlin, 1972).

In relation, we should note the comments of Mia Touw, referred to earlier, that "it was *hu-ma*, or fiery hemp (as the mean-

---

18   "The character (hu) is also used in the phrase (hu meng tin tao), which means to have extraordinary dreams. Is his an indication of hallucinogenic visions or dreams induced by ingesting hemp?" (Merlin, 1972).

ing has been construed by
some etymologists), which
also meant Scythian hemp"
(Stuart1911)[19] and this latter
kind was held to be especially potent" (Touw, 1981).

Leaving little room for
doubt on the matter, a connection between the Chi-
nese name for cannabis, *Hu-
Ma*, and that of the cannabis

Fig 9.16: Ephedra, *Ma-Huang*, photo (Yamasaki).

containing beverage Haoma, has also be given by etymological research:

> The two medicinal plants, Cannabis and Ephedra, are give very al-
> lied names in Chinese; Cannabis = *Huang-Ma* and Ephedra=*Ma
> Huang*. These names are mirror images of each other and as such
> next to being identical. The similarity of these names assumes that
> Ephedra, Ma-Huang, was discovered later than Hemp, Huang-
> Ma, and that Ephedra was given the name of Hemp itself[20]. This
> is so because at that early stage Ephedra had no name of its own
> so that the designation of Hemp was transferred onto Ephedra....
> (Mandihassan, 1982)[21]

It should be noted that along with the finds of hemp already discussed, bundles of ephedra twigs were found with some of the bodies of the mummies discovered in the Tarim Basin.

Mandihassan notes that in later times cannabis became known
under the more generally used name of *Ho-Ma*. Writing sometime

---

19   Stuart, G.A., *Chinese Marteria Medica Vegetable Kingdom* (1911)
20   Interestingly, Ephedra is also mentioned in the writings of Emperor Shen Nung:
"An oral tradition in China dating back to approximately 2800 s.c., which is associated with
the legendary first Chinese emperor and herbalist or shaman, Shen Nong (or Shen Nung),
refers to the medicinal use of the dried stems of *Ma Huang* to cure multiple ailments, such
as the common cold, coughs, asthma, headaches, and hay fever. *Ephedra* ('mahuang')
pollen has been recovered from the Banpo sites (dated to ca. 4800 to 4300 B.C.) of the
Neolithic Yangshao culture in east Xi'an, in the Shaanxi Province of China (Manhong and
Jianzhong 1990)" (Merlin, 2003). Comparatively, evidence of hemp use comes from the
Yangshao culture of China dates back to about 4500 BC, so the use of both plants goes
back considerably far in Chinese history.
21   For more on Mahdihassan's etymological theory, see his confusingly titled 1986
article: "Ephedra as Soma Meaning Hemp Fibres with Soma Later Misidentified with the
Hemp Plant Itself."

prior to the discovery of the archeological find of remnants from both cannabis and ephedra at the Haoma temple in Margiana, and recognizing the modern use of ephedra in Haoma preparations, Mandihassan concludes;

> Aryan ascetics must have... come into contact with those of China with the results that the Chinese name, Ho-ma, for Ephedra, as also its energizing properties, were communicated to their Aryan compatriots. As a result, Ho-Ma, as Hao-Ma is found in Avesta while Ho-ma became So-Ma in Sanskrit; it is known that 'H' mutates into 'S.' This in brief is the etymology of the names Homa and Soma. It is natural to expect that the plant would be known first... and later the name of the plant Soma would be transferred on to the juice which is also called Soma. [22] (Mandihassan 1982)

Mandihassan was very close, but contrarily, the later Margiana find "shows that Homa's preparation was a temple activity, along with extracting of juices from poppy, hemp and ephedra. It is clear that the whole consumable was called "*hom*" and that the word did not correspond to the name of a specific ingredient. Among the effects of the ephedra itself was to speed up the metabolism and raise the blood pressure"[23] (Mirfendereski, 2005).

The combined etymological connection through cognate pronunciations combined with the shared characteristics of the subjects "*Ho-Ma*" and "*Homa*." along with archaeological and historical information make a strong case that these could be loan words from one culture to another.[24] In this regard Prof. Littleton also notes "the strong probability that at least some, if not all of the folks who settled

---

22   Michael Strickmann in *Homa in East Asia* renders the Chinese characters representing Sanskrit *homa*, as *hu ma* noting the earliest occurrence of this being approximately around the Eighth century BCE (Strickman, 1983). The rendering of the Sanskrit *Soma*, using the same phonetic *ma* character, also occurs in Eitel's Dictionary which explained the term as 'the flower that exhilarates the mind,' (Eitel, 1888).

23   As George Thompson notes, in his essay "Soma and Ecstasy in the Rgveda," the surviving Zoroastrian religion (more commonly known as 'Parsi') refer to the ephedra they have been using in their rituals for many centuries, as '*um*,' '*oman*,' '*hum*,' '*huma*,' or '*hom*,' etc., in Iranian languages (from '*haoma*'), or in Indic '*som*' or '*soma*' or '*somalatA*,' etc. (from '*soma*') (Thompson, 2003).

24   "In passing it may be worth mentioning that the Tibetan word for Cannabis and its drug products is *So.Ma.Ra.Dza*. This appears to be a direct borrowing from the Sanskrit *soma-raja* (Eng.: 'King soma,' 'Royal soma'). The term soma-raja is glossed as 'king soma, the moon' in Monier-Williams' Sanskrit dictionary although the *Rig Veda*, in its hymns of praise to the drug, refers to it frequently as 'King soma'" (Crowley, 1996).

in Xinjiang and left us their mummified remains were North Iranians and passed cannabis to their Han neighbors, who didn't get there until ca. 1000 B.C., along with the label *"ma"* (which may well connect with Soma and Haoma), seems highly probable" (Littleton, 2008).

Seen as in favor of an Indo-European origin of the term 'Haoma' is that it has been put forth that the root words, *hu-*, of *haoma* and of *soma, su-*, suggests 'press' or 'pound',[25] (Taillieu, 2002). However, Kieth's rejection of the I.E. connection with this root may speak in favour of a Chinese origin: "Soma is derived from the root su, and means merely pressed-out drink, and there is no parallel word in the other Indo-European languages" (Kieth, 1925). Mahdihassan's explanation to this was taking the word to the "Chinese which then gives it the meaningful name *haoma* in Avesta and Soma in Sanskrit" (Madihassan, 1986).

But still others have suggested that the "root as the Avestan *haoma* and Indic *soma* …[is] *konoplja*, 'cannabis hemp'" (Woods, et al., 2006) just the sort of early form of a name for 'cannabis' which one might expect to find in an early Indo-European language such as Tocharian.

Interestingly, the Caucasian Tarim mummies span over a time period of around 1800 years. In later tombs, there are both Caucasian and Oriental mummies, showing that a strong cultural exchange and even inter marriage took place. Around the 8th century BC Chinese jade carvings began to be produced that demonstrated a very strong influence of the artistic style associated with the Scythians, such as animals locked in battle (See Fig. 9.8 & 9.9).

For a time, at least, it appears as if the Chinese and Aryan inhabitants of the Tarim Basin, lived in peace and shared an enriching cultural exchange that included the use of cannabis. Who brought the beneficial plant to the other at this time, as both cultures were utilizing hemp for so long by that period, like the linguistic origins of Haoma, remains an open question. As well, the finds of both Ephedra (1800 B.C.) and cannabis (700 B.C.) at these Chinese sites, occurs much later than those of these substances at BMAC, so the suggestion that the BMAC culture adopted their use of cannabis

---

25   "The Sanskrit *soma*; akin to *sunoti*, he presses,"The American Heritage® Dictionary of the English Language: Fourth Edition (2000). The word is derived from an Indo-Iranian root *sav- (Sanskrit sav-) "to press," i.e. *sav-ma- is the drink prepared by pressing the stalks of a plant. The root is probably Proto-Indo-European (*sewh-), and also appears in *son* (from *suhnu-, "pressed out" i.e. "newly born").

from people in this area, at this point, is purely conjecture, based on interesting linguistical speculations and later evidence at best. Until the Chinese government allows more access to what mummies have been found, and moreover new expeditions into these sites themselves, by properly funded and trained archeologists and other researchers who are allowed to pursue the study of the evidence unhindered by the concerns of Governmental bureaucracy, the real questions on these matters will remain unanswered.

The Tarim Basin seems to have disappeared around 200 BC, after close to 2000 years of continual habitation. Possibly, as some researchers suggest they evolved into the culture that were known in China as the Tocharians, and who lived comfortably with the Chinese for the first few centuries A.D., and as time went on through continual cross-marriage they became genetically assimilated into the genetics of Western China as the Uyghur people and other regions that display signs of a partially European heritage.

Indicating a potential continuing influence of cannabis through Tocharian Buddhists, it is interesting to note that in *Chinese Magical Medicine*, Michel Strickmann records that "in an anonymous Chinese Tantric Buddhist text of the eighth century… the officiant is instructed to burn henbane seeds in a Homa fire… together with hemp seed… [and other plants] accompanied by the recitation of the appropriate spell. Thereupon the 840,000 devils and demons of falling frenzy… and so on will all cry out in distress and run away" (Strickmann, 2002).

It has also been suggested that later Tocharians acted as a conduit for the introduction of the Gnostic religion of the Manicheans into China, and here again we find evidence of the continued use of cannabis during China's middle ages. Chinese records record the establishment's concerns about the nocturnal activities at Manichean[26] 'Incense-Houses,' which were eventually banned, and like

Fig 9.17: Image of 'Tocharian' Buddhist missionary (circa 900-1000 AD). Fig 9.18: Tocharian emissaries baring offerings to a Buddhist temple (900 AD), showing marked Western features, red hair and blue eyes.

---

26   A Gnostic sect that worshipped Jesus right alongside Zoroaster, Buddha, and the religions founder, Mani.

the Manicheans themselves, seemed to have completely vanished by around the 12th century BC. In medieval China, the "general opinion of their religion was that it involved drug-induced ecstasy, for their leaders had titles like 'spirit-king' and 'spirit-father and 'spirit-mother,' but the common folk deliberately mispronounced the word for 'spirit' (*mo*) as '*ma*,' meaning '*Cannabis sativa*' (as if 'Pater' were changed phonetically to 'pothead')" (Ruck et al. 2001).

With aspects of their beliefs driven underground, any survivors intermarried with Han Chinese. Despite considerable intervening generations, Tocharian genetic traits are still recognizable in the people inhabiting Western Chinese Provinces.

Another view holds that these Chinese Indo-European were forced out by some of the less accepting groups of Han Chinese culture, who saw them as a polluting foreign force. "...in China... steppe influences were constantly resisted as alien in Chinese culture" (Sherratt 1995). Possibly in this cultural conflict we may find the source of Oriental China's disillusionment with cannabis through its association with the Scythian culture who used it. With the find of mummified European remains and cannabis in China, along with the indigenous use of cannabis in Chinese shamanic and medical practices, ancient China, like much of the ancient world, was occupied by cannabis using people, and, as with other cultures, this use influenced Chinese thought and culture in countless profound ways, the still extant philosophy of Taoism but one of which fruits that comes to mind.

One of the most interesting things about the Tarim Basin discoveries is that they indicate that this culture was involved with a considerably widespread trade network, and this has forever changed concepts of the connectivity of cultures in the ancient world. In the laying of the foundation for the Great Silk Road, this ancient culture shaped the very future of human civilization.

The Tarim Basin Mummies prove that the European penetration of China did not begin with the opening of the transcontinental Silk Road trade route that the history books usually place in the mid second century B.C., but rather more than a millennium earlier at the turn of the Neolithic and Bronze Ages. Accumulating evidence from other regions seems to be pushing that date back even further.

Archaeological excavations at the site of Sapalli tepe, located in the North Bactrian oasis of southern Uzbekistan, during the

1960s and 1970s yielded the earliest evidence of silk outside of China and raised the possibility that contacts between East and West along the Great Silk Road may be far older than previously thought... No longer were contacts dated to 13th century A.D., nor to the second century B.C., nor even to the 10th century B.C. Rather, the presence of silk at Sapalli tepe raised the possibility that contacts along the Great Silk Road may have occurred near the end of the third and the beginning of the second millennia B.C. ...Yet, as provocative as this discovery was, few scholars outside the former Soviet Union knew of these discoveries. (Hemphill & Mallory, 2004)

It was through the establishment of this vast trade network reaching from the Russian Steppes, China, Bactria, Margiana, into Mesopotamia, Persia, the 'Holy Land', Greece, Rome, Egypt, and India, that hemp came into the ancient world, and although to many it came with linguistic cognates of its earlier Indo-European name of Kanna, and not Haoma, it often came bearing aspects of its earlier mythology connecting it to the sacred beverage. Indeed, the ancient trade caravans not only acted as a conduit for an exchange of human genetics and rare goods, but also for stories and mythologies that were often adopted to suit the different deities of the areas along this ancient trade route, that in reality was as much an a cross continental high-way of Cannabis Culture as a Silk Road.

These Assyrian clay tablets from around 650 BC. (now located in the British Museum of London) are believed to be the earliest written prescription for Medical cannabis still known to be in existence.

10

A Scent Pleasing to the Gods: Mesopotamia

Mesopotamia is largely regarded as the birthplace of civilized culture, and from the most ancient recorded times cannabis was used both medicinally and as a sacrament - oils and incenses were prepared from the plant because its "aroma was pleasing to the Gods" (Meissner 1925). In *Fragrance: The Story of Perfume from Cleopatra to Chanel*, Edwin Morris wrote that "Marijuana (*Cannabis sativa*) may have been the first incense in the ancient Near East" (Morris, 1984). The pioneering cannabis researcher Sula Benet saw such a primordial relationship with cannabis in this region she believed that "the ritual use of hemp as well as the name, cannabis originated in the Ancient Near East" (Benet 1975). Regardless of its origins, it's clear from early times cannabis played an important role as a fiber, medicine, and ritual sacrament in the ancient near East from very early times on. "*Cannabis*, which figures prominently in healing in China and India, also would have been a major element of barter along the early trade routes leading into and out of Assyria" (Emboden, 1995). "Cannabis might have been traded from the Steppes to Mesopotamia. Greek *kannabis* and Proto-Germanic *hanipiz* seem related to the Summerian *kunibu*" (Anthony, 2008).

What are thought to be the earliest Mesopotamian references to cannabis are found on inscriptions from the Sumerian period, and come to us under a variety of names, and not all researchers agree on their designations as cannabis. Although most sources concur that around 3000 B.C., the Sumerians were likely the first to develop a practical form of writing, now known as Cuneiform, there is by no means a consensus on many of the translations of the Sumerian words used in the ancient texts. Historians agree on many general aspects, such as the Sumerian clay tablets designate the world's oldest medical documents, but the details of these texts, such as which plants were referred to by what names, are still open to interpretation, and a matter of etymological debate. The following list includes the suggested names for cannabis in Sumerian and Assyrian, with their likely English translations:

> Sumerian, *Azalla*; Assyrian, *azalluu*; English, cannabis
> Sumerian: *Saminiissati*; Assyrian, *a-zal-lu-u*; English, "drug for grief"
> Sumerian: *Ganzigunnu*; Assyrian, *a-zal-lu-u*; English, hemp (from Persian [cognate to ganja]) *gan-zi-gun-nu* has also been translated as 'the drug that takes away the mind'
> Sumerian: *Gurgurru*; Assyrian, *a-zal-lu-u*; English, hashish, "The drug that takes away the pain, but also robs the user of his soul"[1]
> Sumerian: *Harmuum*; Assyrian, *gur-[gu-ru]* ; English, fodder
> Sumerian: *Hargad*; Assyrian, *gur-[gu-ru]* ; English, Resembles Hebrew, *herem*, "net"
> Sumerian: *Azalla ut-lis*; Assyrian, *sâmu*; English, cannabis

Reginald Campbell Thompson, who spent over 50 years deciphering cuneiform Assyrian medical texts, summarized his reasoning regarding these translations in *A Dictionary of Assyrian Chemistry and Geology*:

> *Sami nissati* 'a drug for sorrow,' coupled with the property of spinning and making a cable, makes 'hemp,' Cannabis, the Indian *bhang, binj*, certain, which is further borne out by the Persian *gargarinj*, Cannabis sativa, L. (the −nj is a frequent termination). *GAN.ZI.GUN.NU* is one of the most interesting words in cuneiform; we have already seen that *GAN.ZI.SAR* is *kanasu*, a narcotic

---

1   In regards to this translation it should be noted that many of the Sumerian medical texts consisted of magical spells, or incantations, to drive away the evil demons that were thought to be the cause of illness. A belief that penetrated into Biblical times, where even in the early Christian period we see the followers of Jesus casting out demons with Holy Oil. Thus other interpretations of this word have been offered such as "The drug that takes away the pain, as well as the evil spirit afflicting the victim"; "The medicine that takes away the pain as well as drives away the evil demons" - http://www.reefermadness-museum.org/history/Aasyria.htm

'like mandragora,' presumably opium; *GUN.NU* is the equivalent of some form of *burrumu*, originally apparently 'to twist, weave' as well as 'to be two-coloured.' Consequently the word = *GAN.ZI* +"weave," i.e. the weaving narcotic, and there is great philological similarity between this and the Hindustani *ganjha* (cannabis). (Thompson, 1936)[2]

The indications of medicinal, intoxicating, and fibrous qualities associated with some of the plant names in question has had more than a few researchers regard them as indicating Hemp.

Cannabis sativa, Indian hemp, is the *azallû* of the Assyrians according to M.R.C. Thompson; its virtue is in combating "depression of the spirits," anxiety, sorrows, which accords well with its action; its name reconciles with the Syriac verbal root which signifies to spin or weave, a term which also accords with the usage that one makes with hemp in the rope industry. (Contenau, 1940)[3]

These early Mesopotamian names do not have any etymological indications of an Indo-European origin, and if they are indeed references to cannabis, this combined with their identification of going back as far as the third millennia, may mark an original indigenous cultic and medicinal use of cannabis, possibly separate in origin than that of the traditions we have been discussing, or alternatively, vastly removed by periods of time even greater than what we have been dealing with in this study, which from what we have learned so far, is a very realistic possibility.

As in China and India, the medicinal properties of the plant were well known in ancient Mesopotamia as noted in the groundbreaking paper by medicinal cannabis expert Dr. Ethan Russo, "Clinical Cannabis in Ancient Mesopotamia: A Historical Survey with Supporting Scientific Evidence" (2005) which analyzes these ancient remedies alongside modern knowledge of cannabis' medical uses. Russo gives a number of ancient medicinal Mesopotamian preparations that likely included cannabis, as the recipes included the above names. These remedies parallel many of the medical applications of cannabis historically, as well as those being 'rediscovered'

---

2   As quoted in (Russo, 2005)
3   Ibid.

in our modern day and were used in the treatment of diseases of the chest and lungs, stomach problems, diseases of the ears, urinary problems, Kidney stones, skin lesions, lice, neuralgia, epilepsy, bruises, and swollen joints as well as a variety of other maladies (Russo, 2005).

> An important indication for cannabis, even in ancient times, concerned its ability to modulate mood. One passage of Ebeling (Ebeling, 1915)(203,I,59) was translated (Thompson, 1949) (p. 221), "*Depression of spirits*, eat and drink alone without a meal," and another: (Ebeling, 1915)(203, r.IV, 35) was translated (Thompson, 1949)(p. 221), "for SA-ZI-GA (i.e. impotence), and 'that he have not depression of spirits.'"Another attestation derives from (Köcher, 1963)(161,iii,35), is transliterated and translated (Oppenheim et al., 1968)(p.524), ":*a-zal-la-a* KI.MIN (= KU): SAG.PA.KIL NU Tuk-*si* if he eats *a*.-plant he will have no sorrows." (Russo, 2005)

In texts attributed to the period of the Assyrian king Assurbanipal (c.650 B.C.) there were recipes for hashish incense which "are generally regarded as copies of much older texts" and this archaeological evidence "serves to project the origins of hashish back to the earliest beginnings of history" (Walton 1972). Russo believes the ancient Mesopotamians "pounded and strained" cannabis to make "hashish":

> A large portion of ancient medicine was devoted to treatment of "poisons," but whether these were actual toxic disorders, psychosomatic or represent illness sustained as a perceived result of witchcraft is most unclear. One example is of particular interest, as it seems to be the earliest documentation of the process of producing *hashish* and exposing a patient to its smoke as part of a compound prescription...
> If "poison" in all a man's members "touches" [him], shoot of caper, shoot of acacia, shoot of *Conium maculatum*, shoot of *Vitex*, shoot of tamarisk, seed of tamarisk, seed of laurel, seed of *Arnoglosson*, root of fennel, root of licorice, *Oenanthe*, kelp (?), *LAL-plant*, seed of *Eruca*, *Cannabis* [a.zal.la], root of male mandrake, sixteen drugs thou shalt dry, pound, strain (and) fumigate [him] (there-with) over the fire. (Russo, 2005)

Apparently cannabis was used not only as an incense, but in topical lotions as well, and not only for medicinal purposes such as skin conditions and dressing wounds, but also for spiritual purposes. As Russo noted; "cannabis was used with the plant El in petroleum to anoint swelling... [and] was also employed as a simple poultice" (Russo 2005). More interestingly, records of topical ointments used in the treatment of "Hand of Ghost" an ancient malady now thought to be epilepsy, included cannabis as a key ingredient and indeed cannabis is known to be effective in the treartment of epilepsy. A prescription for the disease was "Cannabis, styrax, oak, Ricinus, Oenanthe, linseed, kelp (?), myrrh, wax of honey, lidrusa-plant, sweet oil, together thou shalt mix, anoint him therewith with oil."[4]

The following passage regarding the topical application of cannabis is very interesting when compared alongside the use of the cannabis infused "Holy Oil" for similar purposes amongst ancient Hebrew figures, as will be discussed in Chapter 16. "An Assyrian medical tablet from the Louvre collection (AO 7760)(Labat, 1950) (3,10,16) was transliterated as follows... 'ana min sammastabbariru sama-zal-la samtar-mus.'[5] Translating the French [EBR], we obtain, 'So that god of man and man should be in good rapport: - with hellebore, cannabis and lupine you will rub him'" (Russo 2005).

Cannabis was clearly an important ritual implement from early on in Mesopotamia. Professor George Hackman referred to 4000 yearr old inscriptions indicating cannabis in *Temple Documents of the Third Dynasty of Ur From Umma*. The inscription in Fig 1 is described as a "Memoranda of three regular offerings of hemp" (Hackman, 1937). Unfortunately it is unclear as to which of the Sumerian terms is being translated as hemp.

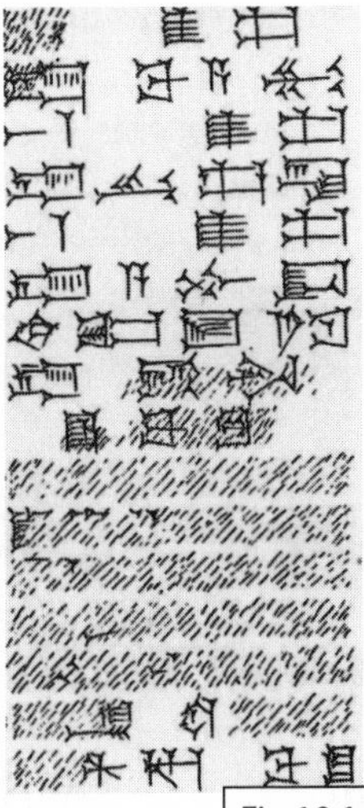

Like the evidence indicating the fibrous qualities of the Soma/Haoma, ritual use of cannabis fiber in ancient Mesopotamia has also been noted: "'hu-sab A.ZAL-LA' to be knotted on a white thread and hung on the neck."[6] Also in relation to Soma it is relevant that the Sumerian also

Fig 10.1

---

4   As quoted in (Russo, 2005).

5   The term 'sam,' means 'plant.'

6   As quoted in (Russo, 2005).

likely prepared beverages from cannabis as well. "Cannabis was cited as a drink for unknown purposes (Thompson, 1949)(p. 221) (Thompson, 1923)(41,2,7). Similarly, (Oppenheim et al., 1968) (p.524) noted a potion of cannabis, 'A.ZAL.LA *isattima*' in (K. 13418)(97,2,4)(Thompson, 1923)" (Russo, 2005).

The frieze depicted in Fig 2, found outside of Al Ubaid, was described in *Ur of the Chaldees*, by author Sir Leonard Woolley, as depicting the preparation of a sacred drink. Interestingly others have seen this same passage as indicative of the Sumerian use of Soma:

> Men seated on stools milking cattle. On the other side of the byre two men, shaven and wearing the fleece petticoat which in later times seems to survive as the official dress of priests and priest-kings,are putting milk through a strainer into a vessel set on the ground, while two others are collecting the strained liquid in great store jars.
>
> It is a typical scene of pastoral life, but the costume of the actors make it likely that it is something more than this. There were in later days at least sacred farms attached to the temples and here we may have the priests preparing the milk of the Mother-Goddess Nin-Kharsag which was the nourishment of kings. That the very domestic-looking picture of milking had a religious bearing is made more likely by the fact that in the same frieze there was introduced between the figures of the walking cattle a small panel of a curiously incongruous character: it shows a bearded bull rampant in hilly country, on whose back is perched a lion-headed eagle apparently attacking him and tearing at his rump; this is certainly an illustration of some mythological legend and its presence here cannot but affect our view of the frieze as a whole. (Wooley, 1929)

Fig 10.2: Preparing the Soma? at a Ur temple, Image (Wooley, 1929).

The Lion headed eagle attacking the rump of a bull [not shown here] certainly brings to mind imagery associated with the Haoma drinking and burning Scythians."Is it too much to hazard the suggestion that the frieze may represent the preparation of Soma?" (Bolton, et al. 2000). Considering later evidence under the designa-

A Scent Pleasing to the Gods: Mesopotamia   207

tion of 'Qunubu,' which we shall discuss, this association becomes much more likely.

As noted the above potential references to cannabis concern the term *Azalla* and other Sumerian names, and their designation as hemp has been matter of debate, having both its adherents and detractors.

> ...In a review, Farber (Farber, 1981) pointed out that there is no unequivocal proof of cannabis being the identity of *azallu*. Other dictionaries have conservatively labeled it as "a medicinal plant" (Black, George & Postgate, 2000; Oppenheim et al., 1968), but, as we have seen, many of the great Assyriologists of the age accepted Thompson's assignation, and it is certain that no other known plant in nature aside from cannabis remotely conforms to Thompson's description of its attributes. We have a plant that was considered psychoactive, was used in fabric, was administered as a fumigant, insecticide, orally, cutaneously, and as an enema. It was pounded and strained as hashish, and its seed, stem, leaf and flower were all utilized. An alternative identification beyond cannabis strains credulity. (Russo, 2005)

In the second quarter of the first millennium b.c., the "word *qunnabu* (*qunapy, qunubu, qunbu*) begins to turn up as for a source of oil[7], fiber and medicine" (Barber 1989). There is a more general acceptance of the identification of *qunubu* as cannabis amongst researchers than with *azallu* (Reiner, 1995). In our own time, numerous scholars have come to acknowledge *qunubu* as an early reference to cannabis.[8] "It is said that the Assyrians used hemp as incense in the seventh and eighth century before Christ and called it 'Qunubu'" (Schultes & Hoffman 1979).

> ...[T]he Assyrians knew of hemp... and ... called it "Qunubu".. a term apparently borrowed from an old East-Iranian word "Konaba," the same as the Scythian name Kánnabis (cannabis), which later designation the plant bears at the present day, and as the word "Kanabas" which is derived from the primitive Germanic word "Hanapaz." These words are evidently identical with the

---

7   Hemp seed oil is an extremely healthy food oil, as well as skin oil. Because of hemp's high seed yield, and the seed's high oil content, it has been used throughout the millennia in paints, varnishes, and as a lighting fuel.

8   (Meissner 1932-33,Benetowa 1936, Frisk 1960-72, Benet 1975, Abel 1982, Bennett et al. 1995, etc.).

Greek term konabos, i.e. noise, and would seem to originate from the noisy fashion in which the hemp smokers expressed their feelings.[9] This furnishes us with the means of interpreting some statements of the ancient Herodotus (486-406 B.C.) He mentions that the Scythians of the Caspian and Aral Seas cultivated a plant whose seeds on combustion produced an intoxicating vapour... (Lewin,1931)

Demonstrating a connection with earlier terms for cannabis such as *azalla*, many of the medicinal applications of the latter came to be designated under this new name. In *Science and Secrets of Early Medicine*, Jurgen Thorwald records: "Quunabu – such was the Assyrian name for Indian hemp. This is basically the same word as it was later known by cannabis (Cannabis India), and hemp is cognate with it ... it was often employed in Mesopotamia to relieve the pain of bronchitis, bladder trouble, rheumatism, and as a remedy for insomnia" (Thorwald, 1963).

Referring to the difficulties in deciphering plant identification from the vague and long forgotten names found in the ancient texts, respected Assyriologist Erica Reiner reveals an interesting connection with the ancient world Goddess and "*qunnabu*," that few other Assyriologists have noted:

Sometimes the etymology of the name is transparent, While 'sunflower' (u.UTU *sammi samas*) probably describes any heliotrope, that is a flower that always looks at the sun: 'the flower of Samas that faces the setting sun,' other names composed with the name of a god or goddess are more suggestive. We do not know to what botanical species for example the herb called 'Ninurta's aromatic' (Summerian *sim. Ninurta*, equated in Akkadian with *nikiptu*) refers, both varieties of which, masculine and feminine, are mentioned in recipes; however, the name of the herb called Sim.Ishara'armoatic of the Goddess Ishtar,' which is equated with the Akkadian *qunnabu*, 'cannabis,' may indeed conjure up an aphrodisiac through the association with Ishara, goddess of love, and also calls to mind the plant called ki.na Istar. (Reiner, 1995)

As we shall see later, this is a valuable piece of information when trying to understand the ritual practices and beliefs of ancient Mesopotamia, especially regarding the considerably widespread wor-

---

9   This is a rather doubtful etymology in the view of this researcher.

ship of Goddesses such as Ishtar, Ishara, Ninurta. Curiously few Assyriologists discuss the qunubu references in the ancient cuneiform tablets, and when they do, it is usually just in a passing reference, such as Reiner's citation above. Until serious research is done explaining such passages in the context of the ancient documents in which they originally appear, their full implications will not be understood.

> ...[T]he multifaceted goddess Ishara. She does not appear to be a native Mesopotamian deity, but was worshipped by many people throughout the ancient Near East, which has led to a confusing array of attributions – she is known as a great goddess to the Hurrians, the wife of Dagon among the West Semites, and to the Akkadians she was a goddess of love with close affinities to Istar, whose sacred plant cannabis (qunnabu) was known as the aromatic of Ishara... from her widespread worship she is also known as the queen of the inhabited world. (White, 2008)

This association was likely widespread and considerably ancient, as the continuous worship of the Goddess, under a variety of evolving and related names, and images, can be traced back far into the Stone Age. "The worship... of the 'Syrian Goddess,' be she Astarte, or known by whatever other name... was full of... rites, in which the effects on the mind could only have been produced by narcotic stimulants" (Brown, 1868). William Emboden Jr. has also pointed to the use of cannabis amongst the cult of another popular Near Eastern Goddess, Ashera, whom we will have reason to discuss in Chapter 16 in relation to her association with Hebraic cannabis use and its later prohibition:

> There is a classic Greek term, cannabeizen, which means to smoke Cannabis. Cannabeizen frequently took the form of inhaling vapors from an incense burner in which these resins were mixed with other resins, such as myrrh, balsam, frankincense, and perfumes; this is the manner of the shamanistic Ashera priestesses of pre-reformation Jerusalem, who anointed their skins with the mixture as well as burned it. (Emboden 1972)[10]

Fig 10.3: Ivory Canaanite image of the Goddess Asherah in the form of the 'Tree of Life, flanked by goats jumping at buds of vegetation.

---

10   I am unclear as to Emboden's source for this claim.

Fig 10.4: Assyrian images (13th-10th century BCE) of Tree of Life images with similar Goats. Fig 10.5: Canaanite fertility Goddess holding long stalked plants with multi speared cannabis like leaves.

Sula Benet believed that it may have been here amongst the Near Eastern worshippers of the goddess that the cultic use of cannabis may have originated: "Taking into account the matriarchal element of Semitic culture, one is led to believe that Asia Minor was the original point of expansion for both the society based on the matriarchal circle and the mass use of hashish" (Benetowa,[Benet], 1936). In relation to cannabis as an aromatic of the Goddess, it is interesting to note that *qunnabu* was "an ingredient in a perfume recipe and as a female personal name and 'hypocoristic,' or term of endearment!" (Russo, 2007)

In *The Cults of Uruk and Babylon*, Marc Linssen notes another cultic use of cannabis, "some of the known aromatics, such as ... *qunnabu*... are mentioned in the... Kettledrum ritual text TU 44, IV, 5ff.... In the list of ingredients for this rite 10 shekel *qunnabu*-aromatics" (Linssen, 2004). From the ancient inscription, it would seem this was a guarded secret of the Priests involved:

Fig 10.6: Interestingly Ishtar was often depicted as a bundle of reeds, known as the 'knot of Ishtar.' With the Goddess' association with cannabis, one can only speculate that this may make reference to the fibrous qualities of her favored aromatic plant, in a similar way that a depiction of a 'net,' symbolized the Soma plant. Fig 10.7: Noting that the "venation is... like that of cannabis, as is the leaf morphology," William Emboden Jr. suggested that the beaten gold leaves in the center of this elaborate priestess headdress from dynastic Ur, "strongly suggest cannabis" (Emboden, 1995).

You will make a libation of first quality beer, wine and milk. With censer and torch you will consecrate (the kettledrum). You will lead the Kettledrum before the gods... The ritual procedure you perform, only the novice may see (it); an outsider, someone who is not responsible for the rites may not see (it) (because if this happens) his days will be short. The one who is competent may show (the tablet only) to one who is (also) competent; he who is not competent may not see (it). Taboo of Anu, Enlil and Ea, the great gods. [11]

---

11   From a translation in (Linssen, 2004)

Recipes for cannabis, qunubu, incense, regarded as copies of much older versions, were found in the cuneiform library of the legendary Assyrian king Assurbanipal (b. 685 – ca. 627 BC, reigned 669 – ca. 631 BC). Cannabis was not only sifted for incense like modern hashish, but the active properties were also extracted into oils. "Translating 'Letters and Contracts, no.162' (Keiser, 1921), *qu-un-na-pu* is noted among a list of spices (Scheil, 1921)(p. 13), and would be translated from French (EBR), '(qunnapu): oil of hemp; hashish'" (Russo, 2005).

An ancient Babylonian inscription reads: "The glorious gods smell the incense, noble food of heaven; pure wine, which no hand has touched do they enjoy." According to MacKenzie, in Babylonian religious rites, "inspiration was derived by burning incense, which, if we follow evidence obtained elsewhere, induced a prophetic trance. The gods were also invoked by incense" (Mackenzie, 1915). A view that was shared by even earlier researchers:

> The Chaldean Magus [Mesopotamian holy men of the Chaldean kingdom, circa 400-500 BC] used artificial means, intoxicating drugs for instance, in order to attain to [a] state of excitement acts of purification and mysterious rituals increased the power of the incantations Among these mysterious rituals must be counted the use of enchanted potions which undoubtedly contained drugs that were medically effective. (Lenormant 1874)

Records from the time of Assurbanipal's father Esarhaddon (reigned 681 – 669 BC) give clear evidence of the importance of such substances in Mesopotamia, as cannabis, '*qunubu*' is listed as one of the main ingredients of the paramount 'Sacred Rites.'

In a letter written in 680 bc to the mother of the Assyrian king, Esarhaddon, reference is made to *qu-nu-bu*. In response to Esarhaddon's mother's question as to "What is used in the sacred rites," a high priest named Neralsharrani responded that "the main items... for the rites are fine oil, water, honey, odorous plants (and) hemp [*qunubu*]."[12]

The periods of Esarhaddon and Assurbanipal bring us to the subject of some interesting depictions engraved in stone during the reigns of these ancient kings, which have been discussed in relation to their potential connection with cannabis (Bennett, et al., 1995;

---

12   From a translation in (Waterman 1930).

Bennett & McQueen, 2001), as well as Soma (Lenormant, et al., 1881). "It would indeed be extraordinary if a substance, the use of which was to have a considerable effect on the social and politico-religious development of the peoples of Asia acquainted with it, had not left many traces in the monuments left behind by thinkers of those days" (Bouquet, 1950).

Green Gold the Tree of Life: Marijuana in Magic and Religion used Fig 8 for the depiction in the upper level where "king Esarhaddon stands before an elaborate incense chamber with smoking... censer pictured in cut-away in the lower portion of the chamber; the upper chamber is tent-like with an opening" (Bennett et al. 1995). Concievably, the tent was used to hold the smoke of cannabis incense, which the king would inhale by placing his head inside of it; a common means of marijuana inhalation in the ancient world, and an act of worship. In relation to this practice which like the word qunubu, is indicative of a Scythian influence, Brotteaux referring to ancient Assyrian use of cannabis, noted that "They called it '*Quounoubo*' and employed it in the manner of the Scythians" (Brotteaux, 1934).[13]

The Basalt Stela of King Essarhaddon.

Interestingly also on this Basalt Stela of Essarhaddon (Fig 8) we find directly behind the ancient king a recurring symbol for the Tree of Life in the form of an elaborate looking plant directly behind the ancient monarch, to which we will return again.

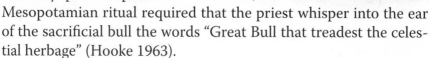

Behind the tree we find the "Bull of Creation," while below are the early tools of ancient agriculture, perhaps indicating an intimate connection between the three symbols. Possibly in relation to the bull's association with the holy plant depicted on the stele,

Fig. 10.8

Mesopotamian ritual required that the priest whisper into the ear of the sacrificial bull the words "Great Bull that treadest the celestial herbage" (Hooke 1963).

---

13   As quoted in (Russo, 2005).

In this imagery, one is reminded of the Biblical account of the Babylonian king Nebuchadnezzar eating *"grass as doth an oxen"* for seven years, in order to humble himself (Daniel 4:32).

In a 1903 essay, "Indications of the Hachish-Vice in the Old Testament," Dr. Creighton put forth the idea that the tale of Nebuchadnezzar eating grass gave indication of cannabis use. He stated that "in the case of Daniel's apologue of Nebuchadnezzar's fall, it arises from the eating of 'grass', the Semitic word having both a generic and a colloquial meaning (hachish), as well as from the introduction of the subjective perceptions of hachish intoxication as gigantic or grotesque objects" (Creighton 1903).

Likely influenced by identical origins, Zoroastrian mythology recounts how the ailing Bull of Creation was eased of its pain with cannabis by the God of Light Ahura-Mazda (Hinnels 1973). The imagery of the plough in the Essarhaddon stela also fits in with this line of thought, as King Yima who was believed to have instituted the Haoma ritual, was given a 'golden plough.' The plough is also clearly associated with the partaker of Soma in the Vedic tradition as well; "The Plough is attended by strong males, provided with a useful share and with a handle (to be held) by the drinker of Soma."[14]

Fig. 10.9: Engravings from the time of Essarhaddon's son Assurbanipal, who as noted is another ancient Assyrian king associated with cannabis, also depict the sacred tree shown in the basalt of his father, King Esarhaddon (figure 3). In 1951, Professor Widengren postulated that every temple had a holy grove, or garden with a Tree of Life that was taken care of by the king, who functioned as a 'master-gardener.' By watering and caring for the Tree of Life, the king gained power over life.

---

14   Vasitha 2:34, As quoted in (Buhler, 1882).

In *Sex, Drugs, Violence and the Bible*, we discussed these images at great length, citing a wide variety of references in relation to them, noting that:

> ...[T]he symbol behind king Esarhaddon, which also appears in numerous other depictions, has "in modern literature on the subject...[,been] often described as the tree of life...but unfortunately no texts are known which describe in more detail the contents of these pictures. (Ringgren, 1973)
>
> Likewise, not one single item from all of the existing ancient pictorial inscriptions has ever been suggested as an illustration of the ancient *qunubu*, which by all accounts played a very important role in both life and worship in the ancient Near East, particularly in the Sacred Rites, which likely are what the aforementioned inscriptions represent. This study proposes that the unidentified symbol of the sacred plant, and the undepicted plant for the word qunubu, are in fact a word and picture that describe the same thing - Cannabis, which was grown and revered as the Tree of Life in the ancient Near East.
>
> The reason that this connection has not been noted before may be due to the fact that in the Ancient Near East matters involving religious and technical methods were considered closely guarded secrets. Professor H.W.F. Saggs noted that texts dealing with such matters ended with instructions such as; "Let the initiate show the initiate; the non-initiate shall not see it. It belongs to the tabooed things of the great gods."[15] Such holy knowledge was either only passed along verbally and not committed to writing, or "were written in a manner which was deliberately obscure..." (Saggs 1969). The image of the Tree of Life and its divine association with the king, as well as the use of cannabis as an holy incense and entheogen both fall into such a category. (Bennett & McQueen, 2001)

This connection is made more notable by the pine cone like buds, reminiscent of cannabis flowers, held by the Shaman like winged figures, and which seem to be a means of transferring the divine properties of the plant to the image of the king, likely denoting an anointing right analogous to that practiced by the later Hebrews in the installation of both priests and kings (Chapter 16). As well it should be pointed out that the leaves of the plant appear in 7 seg-

---

15   As quoted in (Saggs 1969).

ments, as with cannabis, although in this case, stylized, possibly in order to hide their identification from the uninitiated.

In the 19th century George Rawlinson noted of the pine cone-like buds from the Assyria Tree of Life, that it is "as though it were the medium of communication between the protector and protected, the instrument by means of which grace and power passed from the genius to the mortal which he had under his care" (Rawlinson, 1881). As Rawlinson's contemporary Francois Lenormant noted, "Often ... it is held under the king's nose, that he may breathe it" (Lenormant, et al., 1881). A scribe of the Assyrian king Assurbanipal recorded in 650 BC: "We were dead dogs, but our lord the king gave us life by placing the herb of life beneath our noses" (Ringgren, 1973).

When one reads the full passage regarding the qunnabu reference in the Sacred Rites in relation to the stella with Esarhaddon, the incense tent, Tree of Life, and the sacred ox, their connection is even more cemented, as is the imagery of the woven basket depicted in the other images of the Tree of Life:

> To the queen mother, my 'lord': your servant, Nergal-šarrani. Good health to the queen mother, my 'lord.' May Nabû and Marduk bless the queen mother, my 'lord,' May Tašmetu, whom you revere, take your hands. May you see 1,000 years of kingship for Esarhaddon.
>
> As for what the queen mother, my Lord, wrote to me, saying: "What is going into the ritual?"
>
> These are its constituents: sweet-scented oil, wax, sweet-scented fragrance, myrrh, cannabis [ŠEM.ŠEŠ ŠEM.qu-nu-bu], and sadīdu-aromatic. [I will] perform it [for a]ll [the ... th]at the queen mother com[manded].
>
> [On the xth] day, they will perform the whole-offerings: one ox, two white sheep, and a duck.
>
> Damqaya, the maid-servant of the queen mother, will not be able to participate in the ritual. (Accordingly,) whomever the queen mother, my 'lord,' designates should open the basket and perform the ritual.

So here we see cannabis, in association with both the sacred ox, or sacrificial "Great Bull that treadest the celestial herbage"[16] in the stella from Esarhaddon, as well as a reference to the "basket" from the other depictions of the Tree of Life, making it clear a connection exists to the images of the sacred tree and cannabis.

16   (Hooke 1963).

Fig. 10.10: Assyrian image of priest approaching the Sacred Tree with poppies[?] in hand. Fig. 10.11: older seal with man and goat standing by sacred tree with enlarged cannabis like leaf.

In relation to the role of the "queen mother" in the Sacred Rite, and also references to the use of cannabis, the "aromatic of Ishara," in the cult of the goddess as discussed earlier, it is relevant also to note the earlier association of the Goddess with the imagery and mythology of the Tree of Life.[17]

> Like the tree of life, the tree of knowledge was... a symbol associated with the Goddess in earlier mythology.... Groves of sacred trees were an integral part of the old religion. So were rites designed to induce in worshippers a consciousness receptive to the revelation of divine or mystical truths-rites in which women officiated as priestesses of the Goddess. (Eisler 1987)

The Feminist scholar Buffie Johnson noted that not only is the "Mother Goddess, strongly connected with the Tree of Life, [she] is in a sense the tree itself. At the same time she is outside the tree, vivifying it to bud and flower" (Johnson 1981). Thus a Babylonian Prayer to the goddess Ishtar proclaimed;

> *Who dost make the green herb to spring up, mistress of mankind!*
> *Who has created everything, who dost guide aright all creatures!*
> *Mother Ishtar, whose powers no god can approach!*[18]

---

17   A topic more thoroughly examined in *Sex, Drugs, Violence and the Bible* (Bennett & McQueen, 2001).
18   Quoted in (Walker 1983).

As we pointed to a similar connection with the Goddess and cannabis amongst the Scythians, it should also be noted that the stylization of the sacred tree, with the seven speared leaves and association with pine cone like fruits, differs in many respects from earlier images (Fig 12) and seems to have developed after the Assyrians established contact with the Scythians, and around the same time the Indo-European influenced term '*Qunnabu*' came into use. This new stylization of the 'sacred tree' (Fig 13) may have developed out of a composite of Scythian imagery.

Fig. 10.12

Fig. 10.13

Sergei Rjabchikov, refers to the stylized image of two trees (Fig 14) that were "presented on a wall of a Scythian crypt from the village Ozernoe, the Crimea, Ukraine" (Rjabchikov, 2001). Rjabchikov believed the "figures of both trees represent respectively the Tree of Life and the Tree of Knowledge or vice versa known in the Bible (Genesis 2: 8), in the Egyptian and Babylonian mythologies" (Rjabchikov, 2001). Interestingly, when this glyph is combined with that of another symbol from the motif of a Scythian gold plate which covered a vessel, we are able to arrive at a symbol that becomes considerably close to those of the Assyrian 'Tree of Life.'[19]

Fig 10.14

19   Elsewhere Rjabchikov gives indications of Scythian elements of Vedic mythology relating to Soma: "the name of the god *Goitosir* [a phallic god, bottom left] is written down together with the sign of the sun [circle]. Another sign of the sun is recorded near the sign of an arrow/a bow (it is a solar symbol). Signs read *tada*, cf. Old Indian *tada* 'mountain; beating' (these sign may be read as *data*, too, cf. Old Indian *data* 'cleansed; given'). Two signs *so* 'the sun' which surround sign *(a)ya* 'the vitality' mean 'the sun – the vitality.' The word reads *para*, cf. Old Indian *para* 'highest; supreme; guardian; keeper'; the word reads *soma*, cf. Old Indian *soma* 'elixir.' The zigzag inserted in the sign of the sun is a symbol of the sky (thunder) god (9). Apparently, the information obtained here correlates with the

Fig 10.15

The image of the God, in a winged vehicle directly above the tree in Fig 9 image gives clear indications of the divine association between the two, as with Avestan and Vedic descriptions of the God Haoma whose spirit was present in the plant Haoma. In a related Babylonian image, a disembodied eye, [Fig 15] again indicative of psychoactive properties, is used in place of the God.

> ...[I]t is part of the essential characteristics of the tree of life that an intoxicating liquor might be extracted from its fruit, a beverage of immortality; the book of the Sabeans or Mandaites[20] also associate with the tree Setarvan, the 'fragrant vine,' Sam-Gufno, above which floats 'the Supreme Life' after the same fashion that the emblematic image of the divinity hovers over the plant of life, in the monumental representations of Babylonia and Assyria. (Lenormant, et al., 1881)

The Man in the Fish costume in the above image is believed to be a priest of Oannes, a Babylonian deity developed out of the earlier Summerian God known variously as the 'crafty' god, Ea, Enki, Dagon,[21] who is discussed at great length in, *Sex, Drugs, Violence and the Bible*[22] for his association with the Crafty Serpent in the

Indo-Arian mythology" (Rjabchikov, 2004).

20   A Gnostic sect which has been associated with cannabis (Bennett, et al., 1995; Bennett & McQueen, 2001).

21   "In earlier Sumerian times, Oannes had been known as both, *Ea*, "God of the House of Water," and *En-ki* "the Lord (*en*) of the goddess Earth (*ki*)" (Campbell, 1962). A connection noted by numerous researchers, such as renowned ancient Near East and Biblical scholars , Helmer Rinngren (1973), Joseph Campbell (1962,1964) and John Gray (1969)" (Bennett& McQueen, 2001).

22   (Bennett & McQueen, 2001) www.forbiddenfruitpublishing.com

Eden myth. A number of researchers have seen an identification of this God with Vishnu "...[C]learly Vishnu is connected to Enki, Dagon and Oannes..." (Twyman & Metzger, 2005). The view regarding the identity of Vishnu with Oannes has been held by different religious scholars for more than a century.[23] In the *Vedas*, Vishnu is the younger brother and Soma drinking companion of Indra,[24] (RV.6.69). Under the name Ea, in his temple 'the house of Apsu' in Eridu "there was a notable tree, *kiskanu*, whose branches were used in ritual sprinklings.... The incantation priest was the representative of Ea" (Ringgren 1973). The ancient texts record that the roots of the *kiskanu* reached into the abyss (apsu) and branches stretched to the heavens. Like Soma, the *kiskanu* tree held both sacramental and medicinal qualities. "The *kiskanu*-plant, according to tradition, grew in Eridu when the gods were nearer to mankind than in after days, and it was they who originally plucked it for medicinal use... and performed with it certain ceremonies..." (Thompson, 1903).

> ...[T]he Sumerian name of the tree, *kiskanu*... serves as our connection between the Tree of Life and cannabis. The *kiskanu* tree "was the central point of various rites. A holy grove in the temple is...mentioned" (Ringgren 1973). The second part of the name of this notable tree, *kis-kanu* has phonetic similarities with the early names for cannabis, through the linguistic root an, "which is found in various cannabis related words" (Abel 1980); such as the ancient Sanskrit name for hemp *kana*, or *kene*, Persian *canna*, and of course the original Assyro-Babylonia name for hemp *kan-*

---

23   "At the turn of the 19th century, the Orientalist Thomas Maurice concluded that 'the Chaldean *Oannes* , the Phoenician and Philistine *Dagon*, and the *Pisces* of the Syrian and Egyptian Zodiac, were the same deity with the Indian *Vishnu*'(Maurice 1798) 'In the temple of *Rama*, in India, there is a representation of *Vishnu* which answers perfectly to that of *Dagon*.' (Doane 1882)" (Bennett & McQueen, 2001).

24   RV.6.69.2-7 "Ye who inspire all hymns, Indra and Vishnu, ye vessels who contain the Soma juices, May hymns of praise that now are sung address you, the lauds that are recited by the singers. Lords of joy-giving draughts, Indra and Vishnu, come, giving gifts of treasure, to the Soma. With brilliant rays of hymns let chanted praises, repeated with the lauds, adorn and deck you. May your foe-conquering horses bring you hither, Indra and Vishu, sharers of the banquet. Of all our hymns accept the invocations, list to my prayers, and hear the songs I sing you. This your deed, Indra-Vishnu, must be lauded: widely ye strode in the wild joy of Soma. Ye made the firmament of larger compass, and made the regions broad for our existence. Strengthened with sacred offerings, IndraVishnu, first eaters, served with worship and oblation, Fed with the holy oil, vouchsafe us riches ye are the lake, the vat that holds the Soma. Drink of this meath, O Indra, thou, and Vishnu; drink ye your fill of Soma, Wonder-Workers. The sweet exhilarating juice hath reached you. Hear ye my prayers, give ear unto my calling."

nab, (later becoming *qunubu*). (Benetowa 1936). (Bennett & Mc-Queen, 2001)

Apparently it was quite prevalent as the ancient texts refer to the "*kiskanu*, which 'grows like a forest' or 'grove'" (Thompson, 1903). Referring to an incantation text regarding the *kiskanu* R. Campbell Thompson described:

> This document... indicated to the magician, who was about to treat his afflicted patient, that a certain kind of plant or tree, the original which... grew in Eridu, and... contained magical qualities; and acting on this information the magician was directed to make use of a potion of the kiskanu plant or tree on behalf of the said patient. The text actually states the gods themselves made use of this plant to work a miracle of healing, and the implication is that the *kiskanu* plant was on this occasion of great benefit, it may again be made to perform the healing of a sufferer... provided that suitable words of power were recited... and appropriate ceremonies were performed, before the plant itself was used as a remedy. (Thompson, 1903)

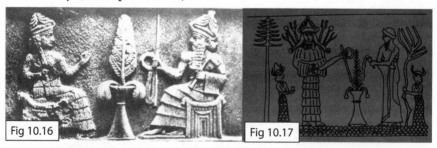

Fig 10.16   Fig 10.17

Referring to the Fig 16 image of the Ur moon god Nannar seated before the sacred tree, across from the Goddess, Sir Wallis Budge noted:

> He holds in his outstretched hand a reed or rod, a loop of cord, and a circular object made of cord or reeds, which are tied round with a cord. What this object is unknown. In his left hand the god holds a digging tool.... the two clusters of fruit which hang over the sides of the vase may be intended to represent clusters of dates, but I cannot think they have anything to do with the tree (?). It seems to me that it represents some grain-producing plant, perhaps wheat, which... supplied both gods and men with food. It is clearly a plant closely associated with and sacred to the god. (Budge, 1925)

Budge came very close, but unfortunately seemed unaware of the profound role of cannabis in the ancient world. With the associations of a fibre plant which also produces a food for both "gods and men" alongside what we now know of the use of cannabis in the sacred rites of the time, a stronger case for the hemp plant can be made than any sort of other grain producing plant.

The German researcher Immanuel Low referred to a sixth century Persian name for a preparation of cannabis seed, *Sahdanag* – Royal Grain; or King's Grain, which demonstrates the high regard the ancient Persians held for the nutritious oil rich seeds that came from the same plant which provided them with their means of inspired religious revelation. *Sahdanag* was generally prepared in the form of a heart shaped cookie, possibly indicating that the ancient Persians recognized the seed's close relationship with health and vitality (Low, 1925; reprinted 1967).

Thus like Soma/Haoma the Mesopotamian 'Tree of Life' is not only a spiritual and healing plant, but also likely a source of fibre. Also of interest in Fig 15 is the woven net like pattern incorporated into the tree, likely indicating fibrous qualities, which may be related to the woven baskets the Shaman or priest in the images are shown carrying, in order to collect the fruits of the sacred tree. As noted earlier, a similar 'net' pattern was used as a symbol for Soma.

> The woven basket Oannes and his priests always carry for collecting the fruit of the sacred tree (Fig 19) are likely made from fiber of the Tree itself... Later depictions show the basket being used to collect the pine-cone like buds of hemp from the image of the sacred tree by bird-masked shamans who as winged angels, indicate the power of the sacred fruit to take its partaker between worlds. Identical to the different uses attributed to the sacred *qunubu*, these ancient images of the *tree of life* associate it not only with leaves and buds similar to hemp but also connect it with the production of anointing oil, incense and fiber. Associations which would seem to tie both image and plant name together. (Bennett & McQueen, 2001)

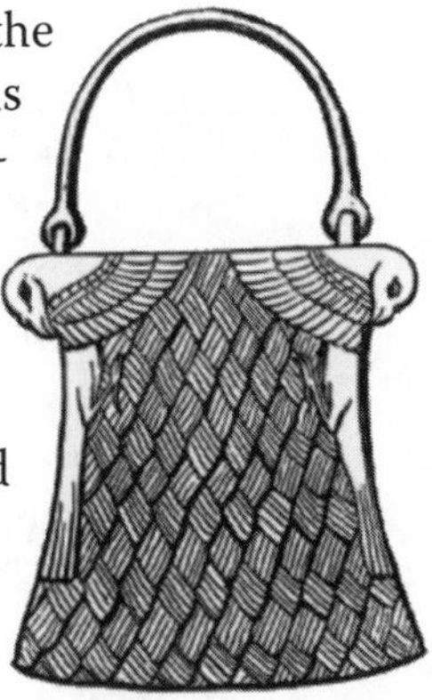

Fig 10.18 The woven baskets.

The bird headed genii which surround the sacred tree have been suggested as representing the Garuda, who brought and spread the

Fig 10.19 Bird masked Shaman collecting the pine-cone like buds of the sacred tree in woven baskets.

Haoma from its original Mountain abode (Lenormant, et al., 1881). The motif of birds dwelling near the summit of a mountain from which the sacred Soma was said to have originated, protecting and distributing the Soma, is shared by both Iranian and Indian accounts, so can be seen as part of their even earlier shared common ancestry.

> ...[O]n the Assyrian bas-reliefs the sacred plant is guarded by winged genii, with the heads of eagles... There is a singular analogy between these symbolic beings and the... Garudas of the Aryan in India, genii, half men and half eagles... in the Indian myths... it is the Garuda who recover the ambrosia,... or sacred juice of Soma, with which the libations were made... giving it back to the celestial gods... [the Garuda] is made its keeper. His office, therefore, as well as the eagle-headed genii of the Assyrian monuments, besides the plant of life, is similar to the duty ascribed in *Genesis* to the kerubim which Yahveh placed at the garden of "Eden, after the driving forth of the first human pair, to defend the entrance, "and to keep the way of the tree of life." (Lenormant, et al., 1881)

Lenormant referring to the "Soma plant of the Aryans of India and the Haoma of the Iranians...the celestial drink of immortality," noted that "the sacred plant assumes a conventional decorative aspect which corresponds exactly with no type in nature... it is precisely this wholly conventional figure, borrowed by the Persians from Assyro-Babylonian art, which represents Haoma on the gems, cylinders or cones of Persian workmanship, engraved during the period of Achaemenidae" (Lenormant, et al., 1881).

Such an adoption of the figure, most frequently used to represent the sacred tree of the Chaldeans and Assyrians, on the part of the Persians, to signify Haoma, though bearing no resemblance whatever to the genuine plant, proves that they recognized a certain analogy in the conception of the two emblems. In fact, adaptions of this nature were made with great discrimination by the Persians... The adoption of the Chaldeo-Assyrian tree, to represent Haoma, therefore shows decisively that it was possible to trace some kinship between these symbols... (Lenormant, et al., 1881)

Fig 10.20 : Drinking Haoma collected from the tree of Life?

Moreover, figure 20 is clearly associated with the images of the Sacred Tree, the Garuda-Bird like winged Shaman and the buds collected in the woven baskets, depict the consumption of a sacred beverage, indicating that the Assyrians practiced a Soma like ritual. Considering cannabis' profound role in Assyria, its association with the Sacred Rites depicted, it is hard not to see the Assyrian Tree of Life as an Assyrian Soma-Haoma, which in all these cases would have been prepared from the medicinal, nutritious and fibrous hemp plant.

Seshat holding rope to the heavens, cannabis stalk, with cannabis leaf above?

SHEMSHEMET:
A LADDER TO THE
HEAVENS – EGYPT

U p until recent times, many Egyptologists, failed to acknowledge much of a role for cannabis in ancient Egypt beyond
that of a source of fiber for ropes,[1] but recent research
identifying a plant in the Egyptian texts with fibrous and medicinal
properties, as well as edible seeds, under the name *shemshemet*,
or *sm-sm-t*, are now generally regarded as identifying cannabis. In
ancient Egypt the healing herb *shemshemet* was believed to have
been a creation of the Sun God Ra.[2] Besides this linguistic source,
pollen analysis of ancient soil layers and deep tissue samples from
Egyptian mummies, have indicated that in Egypt, like much of the
rest of the ancient world, cannabis held an important role.

In fact from about around 3000 BC onward there is evidence of
cannabis pollen in Egypt. According to the *Codex of Ancient Egyptian Plant Remains*, (1997) pollen has been identified at Egyptian
sites dating from the Predynastic period (c.3500-3100 BCE); the
12th Dynasty (c.1991-1786 BCE) includes not only pollen, but also
a hemp "fibre (ball)"; from the 19th Dynasty (c.1293-1185 BCE)
found on the Mummy of Ramses II; and the Ptolemaic period (323-
30 BCE) (Vartavan & Asensi, 1997).

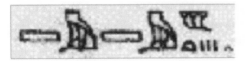

Fig 11.1: *Shemshemet.*

---

1   Some have even questioned this use: "Historically, the ancient Egyptians used
flax (Linum) and cotton (Gossypium) for spinning and weaving and there is no mention of
Cannabis use for any purpose" (Clarke & Fleming, 1998).
2   (Graindorge, 1992).

Shemshemet

> There is general agreement with the view of Dawson (1934a) that
> *shemshemet* means cannabis, and the identification was strongly
> supported by the use of hempen rope making. As a drug, it has
> remained in active use since pharaonic times. It... was adminis-
> tered by mouth, rectum, vagina, bandaged the skin, applied to
> the eyes, and by fumigation. However, these applications provide
> no clear evidence of awareness of the effects of cannabis on the
> central nervous system. (Nunn, 2002)

Although most modern Egyptologists acknowledge a role for cannabis as a source of fiber and as a medicine, few see a role for hemp
as a ritual intoxicant, and many researchers claim that the Egyptians
were unaware of these properties. As noted in *The Mummy Congress*:

> Under the reign of the pharaohs, Egyptian traders had bartered
> avidly for seeds of *Cannabis sativa*. Their Asian neighbors prized
> the plant for its hempen fibers, and the Egyptians seem to have
> taken a similar interest. They retted the stems and twisted the
> fibers into sturdy ropes and ground the plant to make a sooth-
> ing eyewash, a treatment they recorded in the medical papyri.
> But the Egyptians made little mention of the other parts of *C.
> sativa*—the flowering tops and leaves that yielded marijuana or
> the dark resin that produces hashish. (Pringle, 2001)

Prof. Jan Kabelik noted of shemsemet; "From the Egyptian medical papyruses, information has been gained about a plant from
which cordage could be made, and it was probably cannabis which
was referred to":

> But no records could be found on its narcotic action. The prepa-
> rations made from it (in all probability from the cannabis shoots)
> were applied externally-namely, exclusively as antiseptics - and
> then perhaps even as analgetics, in the same way as in Hellenic
> medicine. Cannabis extracts have been employed for irrigation
> in diseases of the anus, and in form of compresses the drug has
> been applied to sore toenails. In Rhamses' papyrus, washing sore
> eyes with extracts from cannabis and also from some other plant
> is recommended. The papyrus of Berlin recommends fumigation
> with cannabis in some undefined disease. (Kabelik, 1955)

Indeed, one would be hard pressed to identify narcotic use of hemp under the name shemshemet, but then as we shall see, with the Egyptians, as with other cultures, ritual knowledge was secret knowledge, and thus evidence of such use likely lays in veiled references. Realistically, even medical applications were imbued with magical and religious connotations. "…[M]ost physicians in Egypt were priests… elements of religion and magic were closely intertwined with drug use, incantations routinely being uttered prior to administration in order to confer the healing property upon it" (Spencer, 2000). Like the temple gardens of the Assyrians, where the 'tree of life' was reputed to grow, the Egyptians also likely cultivated shemshemet and other sacred plants:

> Considering the Egyptians' highly developed pharmacopeia they must have had 'physics gardens,' most likely in connection with a temple, for it was among the priests that knowledge of the medicinal properties of plants was concentrated. (Manniche, 1989)

Egyptian medical texts that include references to cannabis include the *Ramesseum III Papyrus* (1700 BC), *Eber's Papyrus* (1600 BC), the *Berlin Papyrus* (1300 BC), the *Chester Beatty VI Papyrus* (1300 BC). Possibly due to the sticky and adhesive quality of honey a number of Egyptian topical medical preparations required it as an admixture to cannabis based medicines. According to the ancient papyri such topical cannabis preparations were used to treat inflammations of the vagina, and to treat ingrown toe and finger nails (Ghalioungui 1963). Egyptian medical applications of cannabis show an astute knowledge of the efficacy of herbal remedies, and virtually all of their remedies containing it utilize it in a way in which cannabis has been known to be medically effective (Russo, 2006/2007).

> If the hieroglyph "smsm.t" in the ancient medical papyri of Egypt indicates cannabis, it was used as an incense, as an oral medication for "mothers and children," (in childbirth?)[3], in enemas, in eye medications, and as an ointment in bandages. This may be its first mention in world literature as an eye medication. (Mathre, 1997)

---

3   "In ancient Egypt, Cannabis… was used in incense and oral medications for 'mothers and children' (probably for the prevention of haemorrhage in childbirth)…" (Ellis, et al., 1987).

The reference to eye medicine identified by Mathre, occurs in the *Ramesseum III Papyrus* (1700 BC), and is thought to occur in a prescription for the treatment of glaucoma, and has been translated as, Ein Heilmittel für die Augen:"A treatment for the eyes: celery; shemshemet [cannabis] is ground and left in the dew overnight. Both eyes of the patient are to be washed with it in the morning."

Although the existing copy of the *Eber's Papyrus* is dated at about 1600 BC, making it the oldest known complete medical textbook, many scholars believe that it is copied from an even older text dating approximately 3100 BC. The *Eber's Papyrus* refers to "A cure for the uterus to cool: Hanf wird in Honig zerstoßen und in die Vagina gefüllt.Hemp [shemshemet] is crushed in honey and stuffed into the vagina. Dies verursacht eine Kontraktion des Uterus."This causes a contraction of the uterus."[4] The *Ebers Papyrus* also refers to a topical application of cannabis for ingrown toe or finger nails and mixed with carob for use in an enema or combined with other remedies and used as a poultice. The *Berlin Papyrus* (1300 BC) records a topical treatment for swelling: "A remedy to treat inflammation: "Blätter (oder Blüten?) des Hanfs und reines Öl.Leaves of hemp and pure oil. Gebrauch es als Salbe." Use it as an ointment."

In the second millennium BC hemp fiber was used for ropes, but the term shemshemet occurs as early as in the Pyramid Texts, written down a thousand years prior to that, again in connection with rope making. "Pieces of hemp have been identified at the tomb of Amenhopis IV (Ahkenaten) at el-Armana" (Manniche, 1989). As with the ritual use of fibers associated with Haoma/Soma and the Assyrian Tree of Life, it is interesting to note that here in Egypt, shemshemet was considered a sacred fiber and was referred to in the context as a means of bridging the gap between heaven and earth.

A Rope Ladder to the Heavens

In the pyramid text of Unas, which seems to concern the king's ascension into the heavens through the northern passageway of his pyramid, hemp ropes seem to be the means for climbing into the starry sky. In the ancient inscription, the devotee is command-

---

4   "Women stooping due to a disease of the uterus were said to stand up straight again after having inhaled the smoke of burning cannabis" (Kabelik, 1955).

ed to say the following words in praise of Unas a celestial Bull, who is the guide of the dead to the heavens:

> This Unas is the bull of double brilliance in the midst of his Eye. Safe is the mouth of Unas through the fiery breath, the head of Unas through the horns of the lord of the South. Unas leads the god... Unas has twisted the SmSm.t-plant into ropes. Unas has united (zmA) the heavens...[5]

Or as Budge translates it: "He raises up the cords (fibres?) of the shemshemet plant, he unites the heavens" (Budge, 1911). A similar indication regarding hemp ropes may be found in the mythology of the Goddess Seshat, who appears to be holding a rope and a stalk in the below depiction. More interesting is the image that appears above the head of the ancient Goddess.

A number of different researchers have noted the similarity between a cannabis leaf and the symbol attached to the head of the Goddess Seshat in Egyptian images. (See image page 224.) Seshat was the Egyptian Goddess of temple architecture and mistress of scribes, presiding over the "House of Life," also known as the "House of Books." This temple was a sort of library and school of knowledge, and served as a store place of texts regarding tradition and rituals. Since very early Egyptian times, Seshat's main function was to assist the king in "stretching the cord" for the layout of temples and royal buildings, and in this one is reminded of the Ur depictions discussed in Chapter 10.

Author and researcher H. Peter Aleff has put forth an intriguing theory that this symbol is associated with the use of hemp cords. "It was... consistent with the ancient Egyptian visual canon that the artists who portrayed Seshat the rope-stretching goddess of measuring and geometry would have labeled her with pictures of her principal tools, or with easily recognizable symbols for these. Indeed, they combined evocations of these tools ingeniously in her emblem":

> Many Egyptologists have long speculated about the emblem which Seshat wore as her head dress. Sir Alan Gardiner described it in his still category-leading "Egyptian Grammar" as a "conventionalized flower (?) surmounted by horns." His question mark after "flower" reflects the fact that there is no likely flower which

---

5   From a translation in (Faulkner, 1969).

resembles this design. Others have called it a "star surmounted by a bow," but stars in the ancient Egyptian convention had five points, not seven like the one in Seshat's emblem. This number was so important that it caused king Tuthmosis III (1479 to 1425 BCE) to give her the name Sefkhet-Abwy, or "She of the seven points."

There is no need for such groping speculations because the various elements in Seshat's emblem simply depict the tools of her geometer's trade in the hieroglyphic manner.

Her seven-pointed "flower" or "star" is an accurate image of a hemp leaf. This leaf is made up of seven pointed leaf parts that are arranged in the same pattern as the most prominent sign in Seshat's emblem. Hemp is, and has long been, an excellent material for making ropes with the low-stretch quality required for measuring cords, particularly when these are greased to reduce variations in their moisture content which would influence elongation.

The characteristic leaf of the plant used in making these ropes was thus a logical choice for the emblem designer who wanted an easily recognized reference to Seshat's job. This leaf is so unique that its picture allows no confusion with other items.... the hemp leaf in Seshat's emblem is unmistakable evidence that the ancient Egyptian rope- stretchers used hemp for their measuring cords, and that Seshat cannot deny her now illegal patronage and ownership of this psycho-active plant.

Add to this flagrant evidence that in Coffin Texts Spell 10, "Seshat opens the door of heaven for you" (7), and the case against her is solid enough to get her busted if she still plied her trade today. (Aleff, 1982/2008).

Both the references in the account of Unas the Bull, and that of Seshat may symbolically indicate hemp as a means of reaching the heavens. In relation it is interesting to note that Catherine Graindorge mentions cannabis in a funerary offering: "some Theban tombs mention an offering of... plants to the deceased... [including] smsmt [shemsemet, cannabis]... According to the tomb of Neferhotep... the smsmt-plant was created by Re" (Graindorge, 1992). Unfortunately it is unclear as to what the nature of this offering was (fiber?, food?, incense?, Beverage?), but apparently it occurred during "certain activities concerned with private funerary worship," where "the priests of the ka, or the family of the Theban deceased, make libations and fumigations in the chapel of the tombs" (Graindorge, 1992). A situation which certainly brings to mind the Scythian Funerary rites and fumigations with burning hemp referred to earlier.

Evidence of Hemp Entheogenic Use in Ancient Egypt

Not all Egyptologists agree with the view that the ancient Egyptians were unaware of hemp's potentially potent narcotic effects, a property of the plant highly esteemed by many of the cultures with whom the Egyptians traded. As Rosalie David, Keeper of Egyptology, for the Manchester Museum, has noted, the Egyptians are known to have used a variety of psychoactive substances:

> The lotus was a very powerful narcotic which was used in ancient Egypt and presumably, was widespread in this use, because we see many scenes of individuals holding a cup and dropping a lotus flower into the cup which contained wine, and this would be a way of releasing the narcotic.
> The ancient Egyptians certainly used drugs. As well as lotus they had mandrake and cannabis, and there is a strong suggestion the also used opium.... [these] elements were certainly in use. (David, 1996)

Considering that the Egyptians traded with cultures that used cannabis for its intoxicating properties, it is hard to accept that these considerably advanced herbalists, who had clear knowledge of cannabis' medical effects, somehow failed to recognize the provocative state which could be produced from burning or ingesting the plant, a quality highly prized by their trading partners.

In this author's view there are a number of indications of the use of cannabis for entheogenic use that can be inferred from the accumulated knowledge of ancient Egyptian lore. Possible sources for this sort of use of cannabis include the Kyphi incense and perfume, the drink Nepenthe, the 'Sacred Shrub' and the Maat Plant.

Kyphi, the Scent 'Welcome to the Gods'

Some sources have suggested that cannabis was an ingredient in the ancient incense and perfume of the Pharaohs, known as kyphi. Kyphi was used as an offering to the Gods. As the sun set, Egyptian worshippers would burn this fragrant mind altering preparation to the Sun God RA (who created canna-

Fig 11.2: Offering Incense.

bis) praying for his return the following morning. Indicating the medical qualities of it's ingredients, Kyphi was applied on the skin to heal wounds. It was also considered to be a potent relaxant and an aphrodisiac. Unlike the ointments of the Assyrians, the Kyphi was a rather solid and wax like concoction. A cone of kyphi was placed on the top of the head, and as the hot Egyptian Sun and body temperature of the devotee warmed it, the potent ingredients of the preparation would slowly melt and drip down off the head and onto the body.

Researchers have suggested more than 50 natural ingredients for making the Kyphi, the most popular probably being: Aloeswood, Benzoin, Cannabis Resin, Cardamom Seeds, Cassia, Cedar, Cinnamon, Copal, Frankincense, Galangal Root, Ginger, Honey, Juniper, Lemongrass, Mastic, Mint, Myrrh, Orris, Pistachio, Raisins, Red Wine, Rose Petals, Saffron, Sandalwood, Storax Balsam. Archeologist Joel Zias, who has found evidence of the use of psychoactive substances at sites of ancient Near Eastern cultures, notes that "the Egyptians wrote a lot about medicine however the formula is always a bit of this a bit of that etc., therefore one can never know the exact method of replicating it. Hash was very common as was opium" (Zias, 2005).[6]

Writing in 1920, the Occultist Oliver Bland, after naming many of the suggested ingredients of the Kyphi and demonstrating some knowledge of its preparation, put forth the following unverified, but interesting, etymological suggestion:

> The clue to the secret of the ancient incense lies not in what we have been able to recover from the papayri, but in the word itself. Kyphi is recognizable to-day in "keef," the popular name for the smokeable variety of the herb Cannabis Indica or Indian Hemp.

---

6   Personal correspondence.

> Cannabis Indica is none other than our friend hashish.... It is not
> after all, a far cry from the mysteries of Osiris, in Egypt.... Osiris...
> "died" annually, and mimicry of the symbolic event was the basis of
> all ritual. In the mysteries the initiate "died," too: but the death was
> no mere formula, but an actually induced state of stupor or deep
> trance brought about by the fumes of *keef.* (Bland, 1920)

More recently, a European news story reported on the efforts
of a well known perfume company to recreate the Ancient Kyphi:
Ananova, Monday, 7th October, 2002, "Scientists recreate the perfume of the pharaohs."

> Scientists in France say they have recreated the perfume of the
> pharaohs which they believe was used by the ancient Egyptians
> to boost their love-lives.
>
> But as the ingredients of Kyphi perfume, said to be an aphro-
> disiac which helps wearers relax, include cannabis it cannot be
> commercially produced.
>
> Experts from L'Oreal and C2RMF, the Centre for Research and
> Restoration of French Museums, succeeded in recreating the leg-
> endary Kyphi perfume.
>
> French researcher Sandrine Videault, who for years had at-
> tempted to recreate the aroma, was finally able to do so with the
> help of Greek historiographer Plutarch.
>
> The Greek writer had written that Kyphi had the power "to
> send someone to sleep, to help them have sweet dreams, to relax
> them, to drive away the worries of the day and to bring peace."
>
> The numerous ingredients include pistachios, mint, cinna-
> mon, incense, juniper and myrrh.
>
> Videault says all previous attempts to use traces of the per-
> fume found in Egyptian museums had failed because not enough
> was provided for analysis.
>
> The expert says the recreation of the aroma is a long process
> because there are many different recipes for it: "In some samples
> only ten ingredients are used, in others up to 50," she said.
>
> According to written documents, the perfume, which came in
> block form and unlike modern-day scents was not alcohol based,
> was worn by ancient Egyptians in their hair and in intimate places
> to boost their sex lives.
>
> But Videault said: "Kyphi will never be sold because some of
> the ingredients are illegal substances. In any case the smell is
> probably much too pungent for the modern world."

The Nepenthe

In relation to the above references to hemp in funerary rituals, it is interesting to note the nepenthe, a drug which the Egyptians were said to have used to ease the grieving of mourners for the dead. The *Odyssey* of Homer (9th-8th century BC) describes the Nepenthes which came to the Greeks from Egyptian Thebes:

> Then Helen, daughter of Zeus... cast a drug into the wine whereof they drank, a drug to lull all pain and anger, and bring forget-fullness of every sorrow. Whoso should drink a draught thereof, when it is mingled in the bowl, on that day he would let no tear fall down his cheeks, not though his mother and his father died, not though men slew his brother or dear son with the sword be-fore his face, and his own eyes beheld it. Medicines of such virtue and so helpful had the daughter of Zeus, which Polydamna, the wife of Thon, had given her, a woman of Egypt, where earth the grain-giver yields herbs in greatest plenty, many that are healing in the cup, and many baneful. There each man is a leech skilled beyond all human kind...

The historian Diodorus Siculus, who lived in the 1st century B.C., noted that still in his time, more than 7 centuries after the composition of Homer's *Iliad*, "people say that the Egyptian women make use of the powder (of this plant, *scil.* the nepenthes) and they say from ancient times only those women who lived in the 'Town-of-Zeus' [i.e. Thebes, which was also known as Diospolis] had found medicines which cure wrath and grief" (1, 97, 1-9; Eus. *PE* 10, 8, 9-12; cf. also Ps.Iustinus, *Cohort. ad gent.* 26e).[7]

"It is generally assumed that the drug, which Helen is supposed to have learned in Egypt, was opium,[8] but the effects as described in

---

7   .[as quoted in (Arata, 2004)]

8   Opium is excluded by its obviousness. Opium would have been referred to quite clearly if it were the nepenthe as the poppy was very well known to the ancient Greeks, and is depicted throughout Grecian art and clearly associated with a variety of Greek Deities and mythical figures. "In Classical Greece, the opium poppy was a multi-purpose plant that had secular and sacred uses, including mundane medicinal and food applications ... Ancient Greeks associated fertility and abundance with the opium poppy, and therefore with the goddess Demeter. This deity in particular was connected with the opium poppy... she was frequently depicted with stemmed grains of barley or wheat and opium poppy capsules in her hands or headdresses... The divine twin brothers, Hypnos and Thanatos, representing sleep and death, were also often showed with poppies in their crowns or their hands, manifesting the Greek awareness that sleep induced by opium brought rest and oblivion, but an overdose might be fatal..... The opium poppy, both

the poem are much more like Cannabis, which was also widely employed in Egypt and throughout the Near East" (Ruck, et al., 2007). Numerous researchers have seen nepenthe as a cannabis concoction. An idea first put forth by the French Pharmacist Joseph Virey (1775—1846) who suggested in 1813 that hasheesh was Homer's nepenthe (*Bulletin de Pharmacie*). Many others have since concurred: "The opinions entertained by the learned, on the nature of the Nepenthe of the ancients have been various. By Th. Zwinger, and... by Sprengel, in his history of botany, it is supposed to be opium... But the best authorities, with whom our author coincides, are of opinion that the Nepenthe was derived from the Cannabis sativa of Linnaeus" (Christen, 1822); "the famous nepenthe of the ancients is said to have been prepared by decocting the hemp leaves" (Watt, 1853); "nepenthe which may reasonably be surmised was bhang from the far east" (Benjamin, 1880). As the authors of *The Manners and Customs of the Ancient Egyptians* also concluded: "Nepenthes... Perhaps the Bust or Hasheesh, a preparation of the *Cannabis sativa*" (Wilkinson & Birch, 1878). See also (Walton, 1938; Burton, 1894; Lewin, 1931; Singer and Underwood, 1962; Oursler, 1968; Wills, 1998). It is clearly the Nepenthe that Prof Richard Evans Schultes and Prof. Albert Hofmann are referring to when they wrote in a chapter on cannabis "In ancient Thebes the plant was made into a drink with opium like effects" (Schultes & Hofmann, 1979).

In *A Glossary of Colloquial Anglo-Indian Words and Phrases*, Yule and Crooke note an interesting connection between a Coptic (Greek-Egyptian) term and the nepenthe; "Bhang is usually derived from Skt. Bhanga, 'breaking,' but [Sir Richard] Burton derives both it and the Ar. Banj from the old Coptic Nibanj, 'meaning a preparation of hemp; and here it is easy to recognize the Homeric Nepenthe'[9]" (Yule, et al., 1903/1996). As Abram Smythe Palmer also notes in *Folk-etymology*: "Nepenthe, the drug which Helen brought from Egypt, is without doubt the Coptic *nibendj*, which is the plural of *bendj*, or *benj*, hemp, '*bang*,' used as an intoxicant" (Palmer, 1882). When one returns to the contemporary Avestan term for cannabis, b'aŋ'ha, the similarity in this context, ne- b'aŋ'ha, brings us to an even closer to the cognate pronunciation 'nepenthe.'

in plant and in capsule form, appears on various coins of the ancient Greek and Roman periods, at least in some cases, testament to the use of the poppy as a symbol of various divinities" (Merlin, 2003).

9   *Arabian Nights*

One can also note a similarity to the Indian term *"panga,"* which refers to a paste made from pounded cannabis leaves mixed with water (Watt, 1908). (It should be noted that by the time the pyramids were built, there had already been large cities in India's Mohenjoda-ran-Harappan in India, [geographically close to Mesopotamia and Scythian southwest Asia], for some centuries). The Hebrew term *"pannag,"* which Dr. Raphael Mechoulam believes identifies a preparation of cannabis (Mechoulam, et al., 1991) is also similiar. Interestingly, as nepenthe was a powder it is notable that both of these terms are believed to identify prepared forms of cannabis as well.

As the Nepenthe was infused in wine, it is important to note that ancient Amphorae, clay wine vessels from an Egyptian site, from the time period in question, revealed evidence of cannabis. In the 2004 paper, "Pollen analysis of the contents of excavated vessels—direct archaeobotanical evidence of beverages, Manfred Rosch refers to vessels collected from a site in ˇSaruma/Al-Kom Al-Ahmar in Middle Egypt on the Nile:

> At this place the Institute of Egyptology of the University of Tubingen is excavating a graveyard which was used from the 6th Dynasty until the Roman period... Here some wine amphorae were excavated, from the bottom of which we obtained samples of organic material for pollen analytical investigations.... The useful plants, *Cerealia* and *Humulus/Cannabis* were present. (Rosch, 2004)

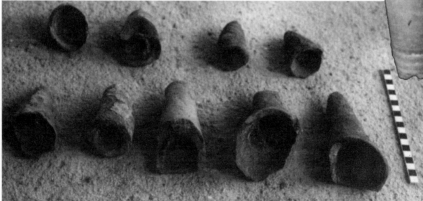

Fig 11.3: Coptic wine amphora from ˇSaruma. Scale size 70 cm.. Broken bottoms of Coptic amphorae from ˇSaruma, showing black organic residues inside containing pollen. Scale size 20 cm. (Photos: B. Huber).

The Sacred Shrub

Undoubtedly, as with many of the cultures we have already dealt with, in Egypt sacred knowledge was secret knowledge. Clearly, the possibility that knowledge of the psychoactive properties of cannabis was a secret of the temples and priesthood cannot be easily discounted. In an earlier work, *Green Gold the Tree of Life: Marijuana in Magic and Religion* (Bennett, et al., 1995), this idea was examined in reference to a "sacred shrub" said to enable the speech of the "star gods":

The ancient Egyptians believed that humans held the potential for becoming godlike. They maintained that a sacred plant was a major part of that transhumanization. It is written in the *Harris Papyrus* 501, dated 311 BCE: "...and a like measure of the divine shrubs to prompt the speech of the star gods."[10]

> The Ancient Egyptian prototype - nothing less than the quest and prescription for the release of humanity's nascent divinity, in turn enabling the rejoining of a world and an already functional community of highly advanced beings who welcome the newcomers to joyous puissance.
>
> The principle agent of this transformation was "the divine food" which, like what some super royal jelly could do for bees, would stimulate metamorphic neurosecretory organs in the human central nervous system and enable a super biological process to take place to mature a higher body that can transcend at death and is capable of furnishing a sensorium to perceive and function in a world freer than the transient three-dimensional one in which we are currently confined. This was the ageless promise that Ancient Egypt held forth most explicitly. And this is the essence of any religion worthy of the name that is to be more than a mere excuse for the seizure of power and control. (Muses, 1989)

Another papyrus, No. 10,477, sheet 30, in the *Egyptian Book Of The Dead*, states the speech of the star gods, was prompted by the Divine Shrub, adding:

> I am Yesterday and Tomorrow, and have the power to regenerate myself... The hitherto closed door is thrust open and the radiance in my heart hath made it enduring. I can walk in my new immortal body and go to the domain of the starry gods. Now I can speak

---

10   Translated by E.A. Wallis Budge (1910).

in accents to which they listen, and my language is that of the star
Sirius. (Muses, 1989)

Unfortunately, Muses chose khat, which is compared to coffee
in its effects, for his identity of the Egyptian's sacred shrub, which
as a mild stimulant would hardly fit the descriptions of inspiration
suggested. The use of cannabis for similar purposes by surrounding
cultures would seem to make it a much more likely candidate.

The Maat Plant

Another possible source of Egyptian use of cannabis may be
indicated in inscriptions regarding the Maat plant, depicted
in the lower parts of the following stele being tended by devotees
and eyed by a waiting harvester with the traditional Scythian hemp
harvesting tool the Scythe in hand. Generally this stele has been interpreted as identifying the activities of the dead in the after-world,
but often such myths were acted out by devotees on the material
plane, so indications of some sort of sacred rite involving earthly
offerings of the Maat plant cannot be easily dismissed.

> The Egyptians associated the Maat plant with Osiris, as we see
> here from the scenes and texts which are here reproduced from
> the alabaster coffin of Seti I.... In the middle register we see the
> wicked tied to the jackal headed standards... In the register below
> we see figures of men engaged in tending a plant... and one figure
> has a scythe, which indicates he was the reaper of the plant. In
> the register above we some men carrying on their heads a loaf,
> and others a feather, symbolic of Maat, the goddess of Truth. The
> former group of beings (Second Register) are the blessed whose
> 'Kau (i.e. dispositions) have been washed clean,' and who have
> been chosen by Osiris to live with him in the house of 'holy souls.'
> The latter group of beings (Third Register) are the 'labourers in
> the wheat field of the Tuat' (i.e. Other World), and the plants they
> tended and reaped are said to be 'the members of Osiris.' The
> plant was Osiris, and Osiris was the plant, and the blessed in eat-
> ing 'the bread of everlastingness' which was made from the grain
> of the plant ate Osiris. But Osiris was Maat, i.e. Truth, therefore
> in eating the bread they ate Truth. In eating his body they became
> one with him and therefore eternal... (Budge, 1925)

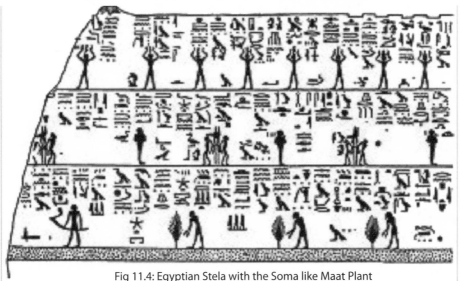

Fig 11.4: Egyptian Stela with the Soma like Maat Plant

Curiously, Budge interpreted the plant image in the lower part of the Egyptian stele, along with similar depiction in Mesopotamian art (Chapter 10, Fig 16) as a "colossal ear of wheat." More likely it represents some other plant, one that was harvested with the Scythian tool the Scythe, one which held divine properties and an association with immortality as well as rites for the dead. In relation to this depiction and the suggestion that the Maat plant was prepared into some sort of sacramental loaf, the body of the lord Osiris, it is important to note that in Persia cannabis was also known by the name *Sahdanag* – Royal Grain; or King's Grain, and was prepared in a number of confections (Low, 1926).

In the account of the Maat plant and its association with the dead, one is again reminded of the role of cannabis in Scythian funerary rites, as does the Eucharistic elements involving it invoke the mythology of the Soma and Haoma, the original Eucharistic sacrament. It should also be noted that Maat's symbol was a green feather, and this symbolism has also been used to identify the Soma. "In RV X.89.5 the Soma is called simivat. In the context it should be translated as feathered, literally it means 'like simi or sami.' The pinnate leaves of the sami... look like a feather.... The feather in relation to the Soma-Plant is mentioned in RV IV.27.4" (Richter-Ushanas, 1997). As Homer Smith noted in *Man and his Gods*:

Those who lived by the laws of Maat took a sacramental drink, comparable to the Hindus' Soma or its Persian counterpart Haoma, which conferred ritual purity.... Egyptian scribes writing in the third millenium B.C. wrote: "My inward parts have been washed in the liquor of Maat." (Smith, 1952)

Egyptian Soma?

Interestingly, the idea that there may be indications of the penetration of the Soma cult into Egypt has been proposed. In an article by Dr. D.V.S. Reddy, "The History of medicine in India," published in a 1936 edition of *The Journal of Oriental Research*, Dr. Reddy refers to ancient references to a figure known as Somaka, sometimes depicted as a demon, but Reddy regards this figure as a mortal individual, later demonized, who apparently stole the sacred plant knowledge contained in the *Vedas*. "Ancient Vedic tradition and the Puranic story agree about the stealing of the *Vedas* by a Non-Aryan called Somaka probably a follower of the cult of the Soma Juice..." (Reddi, 1936). Dr. Reddy suggested "that the knowledge or Vedas stolen by Somaka found a way into ancient Egypt or Assyria and were preserved there as Papyri and tablets respectively" (Reddi, 1936).

Others have suggested a connection between the Indian Shiva, Lord of *Bhang* and the Egyptian Ra, creator of the plant *shemshemet*. As H. Heras has put forth in *The Anu in India and in Egypt*:

> ...Anus were of the five RV tribes... [but the] Anu, an Aryan tribe, bears a name which appears to be of non-Aryan origin.... Aryans assimilated the dogmas of the Dravidians which resulted in a complete amalgamation between Aryan and Dravidian religions.... Monotheism of the Dravidians generally taken up.... Name of God in the Proto-Dravidian was *An* (= the Lord). Those Aryans who accepted this dogma were called Anus. Aryans later on accepted the god of the other neighboring tribe of the Dravidians called Sivas, namely Siva. Siva was the same *An*.... Anu in Egypt: *Ra* (= Sun-god) and *An* seem to have the same meaning and consequently refer to the same person. Among proto-Indians *An* was identified with the Sun, named *El*.... The worshippers of *An* in India and the *Anu* of Egypt belonged to the proto-Davidian race.... (Heras, 1943)

In relation to what we have learned from the Tarim Mummies in Chapter 9, it is important to note that less speculative avenues of a cultural exchange do exist. Indicating that Egypt was a depot of the ancient Silk Road, is the "recent discovery of a strand of silk in the hair of an Egyptian mummy, which a combination of infrared and chemical analysis strongly suggests came from China. If correct this means that Chinese silk reached the eastern Mediterranean around 1000 B.C., centuries before the traditional date" (Allsen, 1997).

Other research has opened up the possibility that ancient trade routes were not only older, but considerably wider than has been traditionally thought. The results from tests on hairs of Egyptian mummies dating back as far as 1000 B.C. showed positive results for not only copious use of cannabis, but, opening up a hot bed of controversy, evidence interpreted as indicating the use of New World plants Coca and Tobacco as well!

Drug Testing Mummies

Research by German scientist, Dr Svetla Balabanova in the early 1990's has continued to baffle Egyptologists, and call into question whole areas of science, archeology, chemistry and botany, as well as current drug testing techniques. In 1992 researchers in Munich, who were using the latest scientific techniques on mummified remains in order to understand more about the lives of ancient Egyptians, decided to test for evidence of ancient drug use. In this quest they turned to respected toxicologist Dr Svelta Balabanova, who had developed groundbreaking methods for the detection of drugs in hair and sweat.

In order to make sure that the tests on the mummies were beyond reproach, Balabanova used the supposedly reliable and standard hair shaft test. Drugs and other substances consumed by humans make their way into the hair protein, where they stay for months, even after death. To ensure there is no contamination hair samples are washed in alcohol and the washing solution itself is then tested. If the testing solution is clear, but the hair tests positive, then the drug must be inside the hair shaft, which means the person consumed the substance during their lifetime. The hair shaft test is considered proof positive against contamination before or after death. As British toxicologist Dr. John Henry has noted: "The hair shaft test is accepted. If you know that you've taken your hair sample from this individual and the hair shaft is known to contain a drug, then it is proof positive that the person has taken that drug. So it is accepted in law. It's put people into prison" (Henry, 1996).[11]

As a toxicologist and endocrinologist at the Institute of Forensic Medicine, in Ulm Germany, Balabanova, who also worked closely with the German Police, was more than familiar with postmortem techniques. Samples from the mummies were taken by Balabanova, pulverized and dissolved into a solution. As with the still standard drug testing technique, she used antibodies to detect the presence of drugs and other properties. As a backup the samples were also put through the GCMS machine which can accurately identify substances by determining their molecular weight. The unexpected results of both tests, which Balabanova in disbelief ordered to be redone a number of times, have embroiled the German researcher in a hot bed of controversy for over a decade.

Although Balabanova was not particularly surprised at the evidence of THC, the active chemical of the Old World plant cannabis, results indicating new world plants such as Coca, and Tobacco sent the researcher reeling. "The first positive results, of course, were a shock for me. I had not expected to find nicotine and cocaine but that's what happened. I was absolutely sure it must be a mistake" (Balabanova, 1996).[12] After repeating the tests and later publishing the results, Balabanova found herself in a hotbed of controversy that has followed her career ever since.

> This is the first study which shows the presence of cocaine, hashish and nicotine in Egyptian mummies, dating back to about 1000 BC. This means that these three organic substances are capable of surviving in hair, soft tissue and bones for ca. 3000 years under favorable conditions. However, it cannot be determined at present whether the concentrations measured represent the original amount of these drugs during life or immediately after death, or what kind of decomposition might have taken place in the past 3000 years. (Balabanova et al. 1992)[13]

Not surprisingly academic criticisms poured in from all quarters. As Balabanova described, "I got a pile of letters that were almost threatening, insulting letters saying it was nonsense, that I

---

11   *The Cocaine Mummies*
12   Ibid
13   As quoted in (Clarke & Fleming, 1998).

was fantasizing, that it was impossible, because it was proven that before Columbus these plants were not found anywhere in the world outside of the Americas" (Balabanova, 1996).[14]

> The presence of cannabinoids in the tissues of Egyptian mummies brings up the possibility that Cannabis was used recreationally/religiously or medicinally by the early Egyptians. However, most of the controversy centers around the reports of cocaine and nicotine contents in these Egyptian mummies predating Columbus' "discovery" of the New World. The plant genera Erythroxylum (the sole source of cocaine) and Nicotiana (the sole source of nicotine) are both considered to have only a New World distribution prior to European contact during the 15th century, much later than the dates (ca. 3000 BP) of the mummies analyzed by Balabanova et al. (1992). These results are so unusual that they cast some doubt over the cannabinoid findings as well. (Clarke & Fleming, 1998)

Representing the view of the vast majority of Historians, Prof. John Bains an Egyptologist with Oxford University, commented on the speculations that were growing around the findings of Balabanova. "The idea that the Egyptians were traveling to America is, overall, absurd. I don't know of anyone who is professionally employed as an Egyptologist, anthropologist or archaeologist who seriously believes in any of these possibilities, and I also don't know anyone who spends time doing research into these areas because they're perceived to be areas without any real meaning for the subjects" (Bains, 1996).[15]

Although, like the taboo subject of drugs in the ancient world, a minority of researchers such as Prof. Alice Kehoe, of Marquette University seem more open to the possibility of pre-Columbian transatlantic trade. "I think there is good evidence that there was both trans-Atlantic and trans-Pacific travel before Columbus. When we try to talk about trans-oceanic contact, people that are standard archeologists get very... skittish, and they want to change the subject... They seem to feel that it's some kind of contagious disease they don't want to touch, or it will bring disaster to them" (Kehoe, 1996).[16] It should be noted that prior to the discovery of

14   *The Cocaine Mummies*
15   Ibid.
16   Ibid.

a Norse settlement in Newfoundland in 1965, the theories about Viking voyages to America were likewise dismissed as fantastical nonsense.

As the makers of the sensational TVF documentary *The Cocaine Mummies* commented "If the cocaine found in mummies could not be explained by contamination or fake mummies or by Egyptian plants containing it, there appeared to be only one remaining possibility... An international drug trade whose links extended all the way to the Americas."

At the center of an unexpected controversy that threatened her professional reputation, Balabanova combed the historical record to see if any other researchers had ever recorded similar results. She was encouraged to find potential corroboration in a story about a scientific team trying to salvage the badly deteriorating body of Ramses II in 1976. The bandages with which Ramses II was wrapped with needed replacing and botanists were given pieces of the fabric to analyze what they were made from in order to replace them. One researcher, Dr. Michelle Scott found some plant fragments in her piece, and on closer analysis she detected the tiny crystals and filaments which were the unmistakable indications of a plant that should clearly not have been there.

> I prepared the slides, put them under the microscope and what did I see? Tobacco. I said to myself, that's just not possible - I must be dreaming. The Egyptians didn't have tobacco. It was brought from South America at the time of Christopher Columbus. I looked again, and I tried to get a better view and I thought, well, it's only a first analysis. I worked feverishly and I forgot to have lunch that day. But I kept getting the same result. (Scott, 1996)[17]

Placing herself in a storm of controversy identical to that in which Balabanova would find herself in, Dr. Michelle Scott found little support for her findings. Most researchers saw the tobacco find as a clear case of contamination. Indeed, the explanation of Prof. Nasri Iskander, Chief Currator of the Cairo Museum seems more than plausible: "According to my knowledge and experience, most of the archeologists and scientists, who worked on these fields, smoked pipes. And I myself have been smoking pipes for more than 25 years. Then maybe a piece of the tobacco dropped by

---

17   Ibid.

haphazard or just anyway and to tell this is right or wrong we have to be more careful" (Iskander, 1996).[18]

As the controversy around Balabanova's results continued to brew, the original researchers who requested that she test the mummies distanced themselves from her. As Dr Alfred Grimm, Curator, The Egyptian Museum, Munich, from where the mummies came commented "It's not absolutely proven and I think it's not absolutely scientifically correct" (Grimm, 1996).[19] After trying to gain access to the mummies, the makers of *The Cocaine Mummies* concluded that "it seemed that the museum wanted nothing more to do with the research they politely pointed out was far from respectable."

As a result of the controversy, even researchers from other Museums were barred from further examination of the mummies, such as Rosalie David, the Keeper of Egyptology, Manchester Museum. David, who was completely skeptical of the results turned in by Balabanova, unable to acquire test material from the same subject matter as Balabanova, due to the reluctance of her Munich colleagues, decided to test different mummies and was herself astounded when the test material came in: "We've received results back from the tests on our mummy tissue samples and two of the samples and the one hair sample both have evidence of nicotine in them. I'm really very surprised at this" (David, 1996).[20]

Results that were more than welcome by Balabanova "The results of the tests on the Manchester mummies have made me very happy after all these years of being accused of false results and contaminated results, so I was delighted to hear nicotine had been found in these mummies, and very, very happy to have this enormous confirmation of my work" (Balabanva, 1996).

In the 1994 paper, "Presence of drugs in different tissues of an Egyptian mummy," Franz Parsche and Andreas Nerlich came to almost identical biochemical conclusions as Balabanova through deep tissue, bone and internal examination of a mummy that was dated at approximately 950 B.C.. Using the techniques of gas chromatography/mass spectrometry, these researchers reported that "significant amounts of various drugs were detected in internal or-

---

18   Ibid.

19   Ibid.

20   Ibid. David's tests turned up evidence of nicotine, but not cocaine and, no mention is made of THC either way, and it is unclear if she tested for that.

gans (lung, liver, stomach, intestines) as well as in hair, bone, skin/ muscle and tendon. These analyses revealed a significant deposition of tetrahydrocannabinol (THC), nicotine (and its metabolite cotinine) and cocaine in the tissue from the mummy....." (Parsche and Nerlich, 1994).

> The major finding was that the drugs (and some of their metabolites) could clearly be identified in the tissue samples analyzed, indicating that these substances are stable over an unexpectedly long period of time... we observed that significant amounts of various drugs were present in several different tissues. Although the absolute values of the drug concentrations may show considerable interbatch variation in particular when tested by the immunoassay system, the intrabatch analysis, as in this study, reflects correct relative proportions. Thus, our analysis of the concentrations of various drugs in different mummy tissues sheds some light on historic therapeutic measures... the evidence for the nicotine metabolite cotinine, which was... found in the present material, argues in favour of an intravital consumption of nicotine (with subsequent metabolization) rather than simply a contamination by nicotine post mortem. Furthermore, these findings are well in accordance with previous observations on bone samples from other Egyptian mummies... The observation of significant concentrations of tetrahydrocannabinol which represents the psychoactive substance of drugs as in hashish in the lungs with values above those of the other internal organs, argue for a preferential incorporation of this substance by inhalation. This is in accordance with the reports by medical papyri indicating smoking ceremonies, e.g. with hashish.[21] The accumulation of THC in skin/muscle tissue may be due to contamination during the postmortal embalming procedure. The way of cocaine and nicotine consumption which has remained unclear until now may have been uncovered by the analysis of this "case": Since these drug concentrations were found to be highest in the stomach and the intestine, this observation points to an oral ingestion of these substances. (Parsche and Nerlich, 1994)

Parsche and Nerlich findings of strong concentrations of THC in the lungs of the Mummy fit well with the view that the popular Egyptian perfume and incense, *kyphi*, contained cannabis. Like-

21   The authors cite Grapow H (1958) *Medizin der Alten A-gypter IV/I*. Akademie Verlag, Berlin, pp 151-152

wise, the "accumulation of THC in skin/muscle tissue" which the authors suspect was "due to contamination during the postmortal embalming procedure," ties in with the idea that cannabis was used in Egyptian funerary rites, as discussed earlier.

In relation to the finds of nicotine Parsche and Nerlich pointed ou that contemporary "analyses on the nicotine content of various vegetables yielded significant amounts of nicotine in some plants other than the tobacco plant, like aubergines, tomatoes and others"

> Furthermore, it has recently been shown that in Southern Africa a nicotine containing plant (Nicotiana Africana) occurs, which may have been accessible to ancient Egyptians. Thus, the use of these substances as therapeutic drugs may have had a firm place in the old Egyptian medicals' repertoire. (Parsche and Nerlich, 1994)

Sandy Knapp, of the herbarium at the Natural History Museum feels that the test results only identify the family from which tobacco comes, and not the specific plant, pointing to other members of the tobacco family, which existed in ancient Egypt, such as henbane, mandrake or belladonna. "I think that they [Balabanova, Parsche, etc.] had a certain amount of evidence, and they took the evidence one step farther than the evidence really allowed them. Sometimes you can only go so far down the road towards telling what something is, and then you come against a wall and you can't go any farther, otherwise you start to make something up" (Knapp, 1996).[22]

> I think it is very unlikely that tobacco has an alternative history, because, I think we would've heard about it. There'd be some use of it present in either literature, temple carvings, somewhere there would've been evidence to point and say 'Ah, that's tobacco,' but there's nothing. (Knapp, 1996)[23]

Balabanova herself entertained the idea of a lost species of tobacco, possibly even some extinct species of plant. The suggestion that a plant could have been harvested into extinction is more than plausible, and we have the contemporary example of the Egyptian Blue Lotus, prized by the ancient Egyptians for its narcotic properties, which was nearly harvested into extinction due to it's popular-

---

22   Ibid.
23   Ibid.

ity. As has been noted "many medical plants have become extinct through overuse. For example, the demand for *silphium*, a plant prized for its medicinal and contraceptive properties, was so great in ancient Greece that it was extinct by the third or fourth century AD" (Peters, et al., 2005).

But even with the suggestion of an alternative source of nicotine, Balabanova was still puzzled by the high concentrations of the substance found in Egyptian mummies, as much as 35 times that of the typical smoker of today. Such levels would have been potentially lethal, had tobacco been consumed in such quantities in life.

Balabanova felt these high doses of nicotine in Egyptian bodies could be explained if the nicotine containing substance as well as being consumed in life, had also been used in the mummification process. High levels of nicotine in tobacco can kill bacteria, and it is more than conceivable that some lost plant, or even other members of the tobacco family such as those suggested by Dr. Knapp and others could well have been part of the secrets of embalming that Egyptian priests kept so closely guarded for over 3000 years of practice.

As well, in regards to the evidence of nicotine, the possibility of contamination from early pipe smoking archeologists can still not be ruled out completely. The authors of *The Biomarkers Guide* refer to tests conducted by exposing a nicotine free femur from the Bronze-age to environmental exposure to tobacco smoke for a period of six weeks, analyzing the bones before and after washing. "Surprisingly, the unwashed sample contained 11.6 ng nicotine per gram of bone, while the washed sample contained 35.5 ng/g... [The researchers] attributed this increase to tobacco smoke deposits being rinsed from the surface into the bone's interior during the washing step, thus concentrating the nicotine" (Peters, et al., 2005).

It would be nice if one could end with just the open question of a nicotine containing plant, but as Dr. Svelta Balobanova, still holding her results as accurate lamented: "The cocaine of course remains an open question. It's a mystery – it's completely unclear how cocaine could get into Africa. On the other hand, we know there were trade relationships long before Columbus, and it's conceivable that the coca plant had been imported into Egypt even then" (Balabanova, 1996). A situation even this broad minded student of ancient history would have a hard time accepting.

A much more likely suggestion for the evidence of cocaine was noted by the authors of *The Biomarkers Guide*, "Tropane alkaloids that are structurally related to cocaine are present in henbane, mandrake, and nightshade and may have been altered during the mummification process into a cocaine like compound" (Peters, et al., 2005). As Heather Pringle notes in *The Mummy Congress*:

> ...[I]n the absence of any other compelling explanation, it now seems likely that Balobanova's findings were thrown off by conditions that few other hair testers have to contend with. When Egyptian embalmers smoothed handfuls of spices, oils and plant resins on the flesh of the dead, they anointed the body and its tresses with a complex chemical cocktail that mummy experts have yet to describe, much less fully understand. Conventional hair tests were never designed to deal with such concoctions, nor were they intended to deal with an immense, almost unfathomable span of time. Over centuries and millennia of entombment, compounds in these concoctions could have easily broken down, yielding substances that could easily pass for cocaine today. (Pringle, 2001)

But unfortunately confounding the situation even further and reasonably calling into question all previous results, research from Balabanova and Parsche, published elsewhere, identified these same three substances, THC, cocaine, and nicotine in pre-Columbian mummies which dated from about 115 A.D. to 1500 A.D. (Balabanova, Parsche, Pirsig, 1992: 1993). In this case, evidence of traditionally South American plants such as tobacco and coca was to be expected, but THC, indicating the traditionally Old World plant source of cannabis, opens up the whole can of worms, that the just discussed evidence of Coca and Tobacco in ancient Egypt did. Having researched the subject extensively, I can say there is nothing reliable in the way of archaeological or historical evidence I have seen that supports the position that cannabis was available in ancient Peru. Possibly these tests turned up evidence of endocannabinoids naturally produced in the human body and these were mistaken for plant cannabinoids due to the deteorization process.

With such controversial findings through supposedly state-of-the-art methods, it is hard not to share the view of Egyptologist John Baines, "it struck me that these days there must be a lot of drug convictions of people for possessing substances they had not in fact had."[24] Indeed, it would be surprising if some savvy lawyer did not at some point raise these very issues in a court of law.

Despite these mixed results, from the accounts of *shemshemet* recorded in the ancient papyri, we can be sure that the Egyptians used cannabis both medicinally and as a fibre. Accounts of Kyphi, Nepenthe and the Maat plant indicate that as with their ancient world neighbours, the Egyptians also likely used cannabis as a ritual intoxicant, along with other plants. Hopefully with continued archaeology and scientific investigations in the area the ultimate role of cannabis and other entheogens in ancient Egypt will one day be more fully uncovered from the desert sands.

---

24   As quoted in (Pringle, 2001)

12

KANNABIS IN GREECE

The myths and philosophy of ancient Greece have influenced Western Society and Sciences in many profound ways. Considering the metropolitan nature of Greece, it would is hard to believe that they too, would not have come under the spell of a magical plant that was so clearly popular in the ancient world and surrounding cultures. Especially considering that Egyptian, Persian, and Scythian influences on Greek culture are well documented. Medical references in Greek literature are definite and clear, magical references however, require pulling back the veil to reveal the ancient secrets of the Greek inner sanctum.....

Clearly Greek knowledge of the plant went far beyond its use as a fibre. As Michael Lahanas records in his well researched essay "Examples of Ancient Greek Medical Knowledge": "The ancient Greeks used cannabis as a remedy to treat inflammation, earache, and edema (swelling of a body part due to collection of fluids)" (Lahanas, 2006).[1]

> Other medical uses of cannabis are attested though: its root is believed to treat inflammations and melt corns[2] (Diosc. 3, 149; cf. *Eup.* 1, Luigi Arata 4554), and it is one of the ingredients of a medicine used against tumors[3] of various types (Aet. 15, 7; Orib.

---

1   http://www.mlahanas.de/Greeks/Med.htm
2   Cannabis was still one of the main ingredients in corn plasters prior to prohibition.
3   Researchers from the Dept. of Biochemistry and Molecular Biology, School of Biology, Complutense University, Spain, in a study of the use of cannabis-based ointment on skin tumours reported that: "Local administration induced a considerable growth inhibition of malignant tumours generated by inoculation of epidermal tumour cells into nude mice. Cannabinoid-treated tumours showed an increased number of apoptotic cells... These results support a new therapeutic approach [cannabis-based ointment] for the

Syn. 3, 29). In veterinary medicine, it seems to have been used in cataplasms against inflammations (*Hippiatr. Berol.* 10, 11, *Hippiatr. Paris.* 154, 219) or as a cathartic of wounds (*Hippiatr. Paris.* 216), especially of the rachis (*Geop.* 16, 15; *Hippiatr. Cantabrig.* 17, 3) or even against taenias (*Hippiatr. Cantabrig.* 70; it is interesting to observe that a portion of cannabis is said to be useful against taenias in human beings by Archigenes fr. 17) or for injuries (*Hippiatr. Paris.* 270).[4] (Arata, 2004)

Clearly cannabis had a place in the Greek Pharmacopeia, thus it would be curious that a plant with combined medical and psychoactive applications would escape the more magically minded members of the society. As Christian Ratsch has noted: "It is... possible that hemp as 'Scythian fire'... was used as an incense in the cult of Asclepius, the god of healing" (Ratsch, 2005). As Professor of Classical Mythology Carl Ruck and co-authors have so eloquently noted:

treatment of skin tumours:"

"Tumours require an adequate supply of oxygen and nutrients to grow more than a few millimetres. For that purpose they produce proangiogenic factors that promote the formation of new blood vessels... important differences were observed when vessel morphology was examined: while control carcinomas showed a network of dilated vessels, cannabinoid-treated tumours displayed a pattern of blood vessels characterized predominantly by narrow capillaries. Morphometric analyses confirmed that cannabinoid treatment induced a statistically significant decrease in blood vessel size, as determined by the total area occupied by vessels, the area per vessel, and the vessel larger diameter length." (*The American Society for Clinical Investigation*, "Inhibition of skin tumour growth and angiogenesis in vivo by activation of cannabinoid receptors," 2003).

Also: "Active Component Of Marijuana Has Anti-cancer Effects, Study Suggests, *Science Daily* (Apr. 1, 2009) — Guillermo Velasco and colleagues, at Complutense University, Spain, have provided evidence that suggests that cannabinoids such as the main active component of marijuana (THC) have anticancer effects on human brain cancer cells.

In the study, THC was found to induce the death of various human brain cancer cell lines and primary cultured human brain cancer cells by a process known as autophagy.

Consistent with the in vitro data, administration of THC to mice with human tumors decreased tumor growth and induced the tumor cells to undergo autophagy. As analysis of tumors from two patients with recurrent glioblastoma multiforme (a highly aggressive brain tumor) receiving intracranial THC administration showed signs of autophagy, the authors suggest that cannabinoid administration may provide a new approach to targeting human cancers."

"Cannabis extract makes brain tumors shrink, halts growth of blood vessels." http://www.medicalnewstoday.com/articles/12088.php and http://cancerres.aacrjournals.org/cgi/c ... 64/16/5617

4   "Aet. 11, 33 (quoting from Galen); Orib. Eup. 4, 107. It is extremely possible that the receipt quoted by the author of *De remediis parabilibus* 14, 548, 11-14, in which cannabis is used against urinary problems, has to be referring instead to gonorrhoea" (Arata, 2004).

It is generally assumed that the Greeks of the Classical Age were unaware of Cannabis until Herodotus, and then were not particularly interested in it. It is, however, hard to imagine how a plant that was so widely employed amongst their trading partners and the neighboring peoples for its valuable fibers as well for its medical applications and intoxicating fumes could have remained outside their own cultural traditions. The Scythians, in fact, were employed as mercenaries to supply the police force of Athens in the Classical Age, and hence they lived as alien residents within the city... It is impossible to assume that these foreigners did not bring their native customs and deities with them. (Ruck, et al., 2007)

In relation, Luigi Arata of the University of Genoa, in his essay "Nepenthes and Cannabis in Ancient Greece" notes; "Given the connection made in medical tradition between the effects of cannabis and wine[5] and taking into consideration that cannabis was used as a stupefacient by Scythians, as we have seen in Herodotus, we must suspect that ancient Greeks knew that cannabis could have neurological effects because they observed it. In fact, cannabis was firstly burnt or toasted and then reduced to powder in almost all medical receipts" (Arata, 2004).

Among the confounding factors in the search for Greek cannabis references, as we shall show, is that there are a plethora of names that may have been used to identify the plant. The first Greek botanist Theophrastus (4th century BCE) likely knew the plant as *dendromalache* or 'tree-mallow' and he gave an accurate account of its effect,[6] but a Greek version of the name 'cannabis' was also used and a variety of other names have been suggested. There was also a desire for secrecy amongst the cults that would have used it for ritual purposes, as magic revealed is magic lost.

The view that "there is no evidence that cannabis was used by ancient Greeks for commercial, ritual, or euphoric purposes,"[7] has clearly been the prevailing one amongst Greek scholars. The reasoning being "Since mention of its psychotropic properties is so

---

5   "What is most interesting for our purposes is that fact that, as Galen states, cannabis is *kephalalgès* (literally 'painful for the head,')....This is what is implied by the anonymous author of *De alimentis* 31:'[among] things that hit the head [there are] ... the fruit of cannabis ... and red, dry wine: and all perfumed wines attack head and nerves'...." (Arata, 2004).
6   (Ruck, e. al., 2007; Emboden, 1972),
7   (Stefanis, et al., 1975).

sparse, either the Greeks must not have valued it or used it very little for that purpose" (Touw, 1981). Alternatively, in his *The Chemical Muse: Drug Use and the Roots of Western Civilization*, D.C.A.
Hillman suggests that cannabis and other psychoactives played an
important role in ancient Greece, and explains another possible
reason why there is so little written on the subject:

> Recreational drugs had a significant impact on ancient society,
> but they are still—and probably always will be — the ugly duck-
> ling of Classical studies. Drugs are an academic hot potato. Few
> Classicists ever choose to study this scandalous topic, and far
> fewer will ever choose to admit the prevalence of drugs in ancient
> society. (Hillman 2008)[8]

As Hillman has also noted, the main obscuring factor in regard
to the role of entheogens in the Classic world has been the intervening 1,700 years of institutionalized Christianity, where from the
suppression of pagan and Gnostic sects that used such psychoactive sacraments up until the dawn of the Dark Ages, was followed
through with a global suppression of Shamanism and shamanic
plants globally, most notably, much later, in the 'New world.'[9] These
originally religious prejudices, with the passage of time, became
cultural prejudices and then later academic prejudices. Fortunately
a new, more "enlightened" age of Greek studies is upon us, and as
Hillman, Prof. Ruck, and other scholars are starting to demonstrate
that there are clear indications the Greeks were fascinated by the
magical properties of their botanicals, and there is evidence that

---

8   Hillman tells the story of his PhD. dissertation examination, "The choice was
simple. Take out the chapter on the ancient world's recreational drug use, and any references to narcotics in the rest of the dissertation, or fail the exam. I had seen the evidence
for myself, and I knew my conclusions were sound. But… the committee just didn't like
the implications of a drug-friendly Western society… the head of the department, had re-
futed my conclusion that the Romans and Greeks used recreational drugs with the seemingly non-academic response, 'They just wouldn't do such a thing'" (Hillman, 2008).
9   One can only speculate that the tale by Aesop (550 BC) of *The Swallow And The
Other Birds*, has underlying tones of a Greek cultural distaste for the use of cannabis:
     It happened that a Countryman was sowing some hemp seeds in a field where a Swal-
low and some other birds were hopping about picking up their food. "Beware of that
man," quoth the Swallow. "Why, what is he doing?' said the others. 'That is hemp seed he
is sowing; be careful to pick up every one of the seeds, or else you will repent it." The birds
paid no heed to the Swallow's words, and by and by the hemp grew up and was made into
cord, and of the cords nets were made, and many a bird that had despised the Swallow's
advice was caught in nets made out of that very hemp. "What did I tell you?" said the Swallow. "Destroy The Seed Of Evil, Or It Will Grow Up To Your Ruin" (Aesop, 550, B.C.).

cannabis and other substances played a prominent role in such applications. "The Classical world was thoroughly convinced that mind-altering drugs were an avenue to spiritual realms that were typically inaccessible to mortals, and that people who were completely intoxicated were closer to the gods that the rest of us; their madness was a sign of their proximity to the divine" (Hillman, 2008).

Shamanistic ecstasy is described as 'one in which the spirit leaves the physical body' and cannabis was utilized to induce this state on the Thracian plains almost 3,000 years ago. Although closely related to Scythian tribes, the Thracians are included in this Chapter, as the Thracians deeply influenced Greek culture in a number of ways. A fact demonstrated by the Thracian origin of two figures prominent in Greek mythology; the god of intoxication, Dionysus and the shaman-prophet, Orpheus, the founder of Mysteries. A red haired, fair skinned people, the Thracians were a well-organized group of horseman and hunters who held "a belief in the soul and a hereafter comparable to the Christian heaven...Their shamans, known as Kapnobatai, used hemp smoke to induce visions and oracular trances" (Emboden 1972). Such a technique of ecstasy amongst a group that held so much of an influence over the Greek Magical Philosophies could hardly have gone unnoticed.

> There is a classic Greek term, *cannabeizein*, which means to smoke cannabis. *Cannabeizein* frequently took the form of inhaling vapors from an incense burner in which these resins were mixed with other resins, such as myrrh, balsam, frankincense, and perfumes. (Emboden, 1972)[10]

As Ratsch notes: "Another word from the period is *methyskesthai*, 'to become inebriated through drug use'; Herodotus used this word to describe the inebriation that the inhabitants of an island in Araxes... produced by smoke" (Ratsch, 2005). The Araxes River travels through areas frequented by the Scythians, Thracians and other related tribes.

Andrei Oisteanu, a researcher at the Romanian Academy of at the Institute for History of Religions, also wrote about hallucinogenic, psychotropic plants amongst the Thracians and other groups,

---

10   Unfortunately, Emboden failed to list any ancient Greek textual use of the term 'cannabeizein.'

noting the ritual fumigations with cannabis, which he viewed as the magic cure from the Thracian High-God Zalmoxis, a cure able to heal the soul, and used in the quest for immortality (Oisteanu 1997). Elements that certainly bring to mind those attributed to Soma-Haoma.

Fig 12.1: Ritual Orphic Bowl. Fig 12.2: Orpheus, with lyre, soothing both real and imaginary beasts.

The *Kapnobatai*, or "Smoke-walkers,"[11] burned cannabis believing that the living entity within the plant reassembled itself inside their bodies to give divine revelations. The 1925 book, *Psyche: The Cult of Souls and the Belief in Immortality Among the Greeks*, Erwin Rohde states that "The Thracians knew hemp. It was thus with a sort of hashish that they intoxicated themselves... The Thracians... may very well have used intoxication through hashish-fumes as a means of exciting themselves to their ecstatic religious dances.—The Ancients were quite familiar with the practice of inhaling aromatic smoke to produce religious hallucinations" (Rohde, 1925). Sophocles (496-406), used "the word *Cannabis*, apparently to add ethnic detail for his *Thamyras* tragedy, which tells the tale of the Thracian shaman-singer who contested the Muses ..." (Ruck, et al. 2007).

---

11   Prof. Carl Ruck notes as variations of such names, a 'smoke-walker,' a *kapnobates*, a 'smoke-diviner,' a *kapnomantis*, a 'smoke-seer,' a *kapnoauges* . The "*kapnobatae* were Thracian shamans who accessed their trance through the medium of an inspiring smoke and there can be little doubt that this was Cannabis and that the other terms designate similar phenomena" (Ruck e. al., 2007).

According to a Greek dictionary in Roman times, the *Antiatticista*, which recorded words acceptable to use by those who wanted to write correct Greek, Sophocles mentioned the word *kannabis* in his tragedy Thamyras... This drama about the defeat of the Thracian singer Thamyras in a singing match against the Muses contains references to ecstatic dancing... but unfortunately we can hardly be certain about a single scene, except that apparently Thamyras broke his lyre after his defeat... As... the dictionary explicitly mentions that the word *kannabis* occurred in Herodotus and Sophocles, the latter's debt to Herodotean ethnography is considerable and the *Antiatticista* would hardly select *kannabis* as a routine reference for clothing, the conclusion seems reasonable that Sophocles somehow connected the Thracian Thamyras with an ecstatic use of cannabis. It fits in with this conclusion that Posidonius mentions Thracian 'smoke-walkers' (kapnobatai) and that Pomponius Mela reports the use of certain seeds by the Thracians which results in a *similis ebriatati hilarities*... (Bremmer, 2002)

Likewise, noted theologian Mircea Eliade also commented on elements of shamanism in the Thracian cult of Dionysus, and referred to their use of cannabis:[12]

Prophecy in Thrace was connected with the cult of 'Dionysus,' a certain tribe, that of the Bessi, managed the oracle of 'Dionysus,' the temple was on a high mountain, and the prophetess predicted the future in 'ecstasy,' like the Pythia at Delphi.

Ecstatic experiences strengthened the conviction that the soul is not only autonomous but that it is capable of *unio mystica* with the divinity. The separation of soul from body, determined by ecstasy, revealed...the fundamental duality of man... [and] the possibility of a purely, spiritual post-experience.... Ecstasy could... be brought on by certain dried herbs... (Eliade,1982)

In a foot note to dried herbs, Eliade referred to the use of hemp among the Thracians, stating that the Kapnobatai were "dancers and 'shamans' who used the smoke of hemp to bring ecstatic trances" (Eliade, 1982).

---

12   Surprising, considering Eliade's disdain for what he referred to as drugs and narcotics, calling their use "a vulgar substitute for pure "trance.""Just before his death, Eliade evaded an interview by one of his students on the subject of 'sacred substances and the history of religion,' confessing 'I don't know anything about them' and noting 'I don't like these plants.'" (Ott 1995).

More recently, Renaissance man Dale Pendell wrote; "Dionysus's home was usually assumed to be Thrace... whose shamans
used hemp smoke to induce visions and oracular trances. Hemp
probably came to Thrace through Central Asia and the Caucasus.
A...similar route may have been followed by the grapevine...It is...
possible that...Dionysus carried not only the vine but ganja as well"
(Pendell 1995). The Encyclopedic Jonathon Ott states that Dionysus is "erroneously regarded to be the god only of alcoholic inebriation owing to a misunderstanding of the natures of Greek Wines,
potent infusions of numerous Psychoactive plants, in which the alcohol served as a preservative, rather than as inebriating principle,
and which often required dilution to be drunk safely"[13] (Ott,1995).
"Dionysus actually possessed his followers, and Euripides' Greek
audience clearly equated this act with the use of mind-altering
drugs" (Hillman, 2008).[14]

Such infusions, believed to contain hemp, under the names
"*thalassaegle*,"[15] "*potammaugis*" and "*gelotophyllis*" were recorded by Democritus (c.a. 460 b.c.) (Walton, 1938). "Democritus's famous recipe for a hemp wine is suitable for internal use:
Macerate 1 teaspoon of myrrh... and a handful of hemp flowers in 1 litre of retsina or dry Greek white wine... strain before
drinking."(Ratsch, 2005) "The *gelotophllis* of Pliny... a plant
drunk in wine among the Bactrians, which produced immoderate laughter, may very well be identical with hemp, which still
grows wild in the country around the Caspian and Aral Seas"
(Houtsma, et al., 1936/1993). Pliny (23-79 a.d.) quotes the following description from Democritus:

13   That Dionysion 'wine' required dilution is interesting, as, like Jesus, the Greek
God changed water into wine, an act probably accomplished by slight of hand and a hidden vile containing a potent psychoactive extract.
14   "Plutarch, in Table Talk, a sort of mock philosophical dialogue, discussed how
Jewish sacraments of the pre-Christian era reflected the union of the religious practices
surrounding the god of Abraham with the public worship of Dionysus, the god of intoxication and ecstasy. According to Plutarch both gods were associated with the same
delirium=inducing plants, both used similar religious symbols and sacred implements,
both used music in the same manner during worship, and the priests of the Jews wore
garments very similar to those used in the worship of Dionysus. Plutarch even claimed
there was a direct linguistic connection between the Hebrew word for the Sabbath and
the Greek word Sabi, which was used to denote the crazed, intoxicated followers of Dionysus" (Hillman, 2008).
15   "The plant was also known as *thalassaigle* or 'sea-shine,' which the standard
Liddell-Scott-Jones *Greek Lexicon* glosses quite simply as 'bhang' or *Cannabis sativa*" (Ruck
2007).

Taken in drink it produces delirium, which presents to the fancy visions of a most extraordinary nature. The theangelis, he says, grows upon Mount Libanus in Syria, upon the chain of mountains called Dicte in Crete, and at Babylon and Susa in Persia. An infusion of it imparts powers of divination to the Magi. The geolotophyllis, is a plant found in Bactriana [i.e. BMAC][16], and on the banks of the Borysthenes. Taken internally with myrhh and wine all sorts of visionary forms present themselves, excite the most immoderate laughter.[17]

Fig 12.3

Fig 3: This 4th century BC Scythian Rhyton with the head of Dinysus on its tip offers physical evidence that the cannabis consuming Scythians, like their close relatives the Thracians, also included Dionysus in their pantheon. As the March, 2009 eBay description of this priceless antiquity (which held a starting bid of $10,500,000.00) described this: "Scythian, Greek gold Rhyton... depicting Greek God Dionysus is one of the rarest privately owned treasures in the world! Half of the Rhyton is made from pure gold with most beautiful ornaments at both ends. The other half is a silver alloy in the form of magnificent botanic stem that becomes a head of Greek God Dionysus. The cultural aspect of this artefact cannot be measured. This is an international rarity that transcends borders and continents. Rhyton is in very good condition considering it is 2400 years old!"[18]

---

16   The site of Soma temple described in Chapter 2. In relation it is interesting to note the speculations of Patrick McGovern in his *Ancient Wine*, regarding the finds of cannabis, ephedra and poppies at the Haoma Temple site in Margiana. McGovern pondered on the possibility of a wine based concoction for the sacred Haoma, "An alcoholic beverage like wine would be the best vehicle for dissolving the other substances, besides carrying its own symbolic import and creating additional mind-altering effects" (McGovern, 2003).

17   Pliny, natural history, as quoted by (Walton, 1938). Walton notes "Bostock and Riley, in translating these passages, consider that those references may be to hemp or hashish. Urquhart, some years before, also made this comment" (Walton, 1938).

18   The Rhyton is published on the cover and inside on pg. 15 of 2007 Tamoikins

In Chapter 15 we discuss the use of wine infused with potent cannabis extracts by Persian Zoroastrian figues, a group the Iranian Scythians were closely related to and whom they traded with. As the Scythians not only burnt cannabis but prepared it into the Haoma beverage, it is interesting that 19th century ancient world scholar François Lenormant referred to "the god Soma or Haoma, prototype of the Greek Dionysus" (Lenormant, et al., 1881). A connection that has been noted by other researchers:

> ...[W]e know that the vine is his [Dionysus] accredited symbol, and it is suspected that this is itself a substitute for an original ivy-plant, which may be not very remote from the Aryan Soma... Dionysos is a deified vine, or at least the juice of a divine plant.
>
> ....The great Aryan sacrament is older than the discovery of the vine. The first Bacchae in Greek lands were ivy-chewers[19] or ivy-drinkers, in association with a fermented honey-drink, which we also find employed in the consecration of the Soma. For Graeco-Roman peoples, the Soma-plant is replaced by the vine... We do not, however, doubt that for the Indo-Germanic peoples, the original medicine which makes man immortal is the juice of the Soma-plant.
>
> .... Since we find the ivy divinised in Greece as Bacchos-Dionysos (for Dionysos was an ivy-god before he was a vine-god), we may infer that the Soma of the Vedas, which is also the Haoma of the Zend-Avesta, is the same thing as the Nectar of the Greek gods. Nectar, also, is a drink which confers and sustains immortal life. We shall probably be safe in our philology, if we explain the first syllable of nec-tar as meaning death (cf. the Greek... *nekus*) and the second syllable as connected with the Greek... *teiro*, to wear away, to destroy; the Nectar or Soma is the death-destroyer; its religious use is, then, inevitable: it is in Keats' language;
> 'An endless fountain of immortal drink,
> Pouring unto us from the heaven's brink.'

Nor need we be surprised if it should turn out that this immortal drink flowed upward at the first before it flowed down. It was brewed down here before it was given from up there. The eagle

---

Museum Exhibition Catalogue. At the 2008 Ukrainian Gold Exhibition the Rhyton was chosen as main symbol exclusively decorating the cover page of Tamoikins Museum Catalogue

19   "....[D]oes not Plutarch tell us in his Roman Questions of the women-worshippers who chewed the 'ivy-god'?" (Harris, 1927).

of Zeus carried it heavenward, as in Greek legend, before he brought it earth- ward as in Vedic thought. The main point to be remembered is that, for all our race, the drink means immortality; it makes us like the blessed gods. The discovery of this intoxicant is, therefore, an epoch. (Harris, 1927)

The connections between Soma Dionysus were returned to by J. Wohlberg in the article "Haoma-Soma in the world of ancient Greece.." Wohlberg felt that:

> While Iranian and Indian peoples preserved their original worship in their final settlements, Indo-European tribes, including the Thracians, the Phrygians, and the Greeks, after settling in Europe and Asia Minor, abandoned their ancestral worship of Soma (Sabazios) and substituted the Semitic (alcoholic) Dionysos. However, they retained traces of the original Soma worship in Dionysiac rituals. This modified Dionysiac worship spread throughout the Western world. Evidence of the worship of (nonalcoholic) Haoma-Soma in Iran and India... can be found in Greece and its neighboring lands. (Wohlberg, 1990)[20]

Wohlberg used Six formal criteria to establish the identify of Soma with Dionysos (Sabazios): "(1) both cults had the same aim (to cause ecstatic behaviour); (2) both cults required the attainment of the same spiritual state (purity); (3) both cults had an idiosyncratic myth in common; (4) both cults showed the identical word root in the name of the worshipped god; (5) both cults had identical zoological and botanical associations with their god; and (6) the alcoholic god (Dionysos) was depicted as having the same physical effects on human beings as that of the ancient non-alcoholic god (Soma)" (Wohlberg, 1990).

As the Indian God Shiva's relationship with *bhang* is thought to be a later development of Indra's relationship with Soma (See Chapter 18), it is interesting to note that it was recorded during the time of Alexander, that when the cult of Dionysus traveled to India, the Greek god was "assimilated with the god Shiva, with whom he shares many iconographic similarities, to the extent that they may have been originally the same deity, and both involved with the hemp sacrament" (Ruck, et al., 2007). Ruck and his co-authors are

---

20   Wohlberg accepted Wasson's designation of the *Amanita muscaria* as the original Haoma-Soma (Wohlberg, 1990)

not alone in their view regarding Dionysus' potential connection to cannabis, as the Arabic author Nawal Nasrallah, has likewise noted in regards to the god of wine that: "It is also significant that another offering to Dionysus was Indian hemp (qinnab Hindi)" (Nasrallah, 2007).[21] As the 19th century Indian author Bholanauth Chunder noted of the Roman version of Shiva's in relation to Dionysus, under his Roman epithet of Bachus:

> Shiva, with his matted locks, besmeared body, and half-closed eyes, well personifies the man who drinks a glass too much. The toper-god may be thought to represent the Indian Bacchus. His phallic emblem is undoubtedly from the Romans, whose ladies used to wear it round their necks as a charm against sterility. The Brahmins, fully appreciating the advantage of idolatry over the idealism of the first Buddhists, must have introduced it from abroad. (Chunder, 1869)[22]

Orientalist scholar Alain Danielou, the first Westerner initiated into the cult of Shiva, also points to the similarities between

21   Nawal Nasrallah, makes this comment in Annals of the Caliphs' Kitchens, a translation of a medieval Arabic cookbook that has a variety of recipes containing cannabis. this connection is made in regards to pinecones, under the Arabic name dadhi, which also has the more esoteric meaning of (the ingredient) a "'mystery' plant described as having… aromatic qualities, used to enhance date wine…. This additive is sometimes described as having narcotic properties that intensify the intoxicating effects of wine on its drinkers" (Nasrallah, 2007). (In Chapter 19, the Arabic use of such 'drugged' wines containing cannabis are discussed in more depth). Nasrallah explains that medieval references to dadhi are "brief, vague and even contradictory…. It is referred to as… a seed, a leaf, a cluster like a bunch of grapes, and a cone". Nasrallah believed that descriptions point to the female hop plant, on which a cluster of hop cones grow. (Hops is known in Arabic as hashishat al-dinar, a name that Nasrallah states indicates its closeness to cannabis). Dionysus is often depicted with a pinecone on the end of a staff or rod, and thus Nasrallah goes on to explain that "Dadhi is also pinecones with their seeds and pine resin" noting that in "Greek mythology, the pine was one of the offering to Dionysus," and it is in a footnote to this that the above reference regarding Dionysus receiving offerings of cannabis occurs. Unfortunately, it is not clear as to how Nasrallah came to this conclusion. Although, he never draws a clear connection between the unidentified dadhi and the pine cone like buds of resinous cannabis, Nasrallah does go onto connect dadhi with the Vedic Soma, noting that "associating pine resin with the moon god and immortality… can be traced further back to the ancient Soma drink in Indian mythology" (Nasrallah, 2007). Nasrallah continues further with this discussion, stating that "in Hindi dadhi is tatkan… which can be easily read as dad-kan… 'tree of life'" (Nasrallah, 2007). These comments are particularly interesting when considered in the context of the discussion of the "pine cones" in the Assyrian "Tree of Life" images looked at in Chapter 10, along with their suggested association with Soma/Haoma..

22   Chunder, ofcourse writing this before the discovery of the Pashupati seal, (2000 BC?) which is believed to depict a 3-faced Shiva with erect phallus, see Chapter 18..

Dionysus and the Indian god of hemp, Shiva, suggesting the two have their origin in the same figure; "Greek texts speak of Dionysus' mission to India, and Indian texts of the expansion of Shivaism to the West...Innumerable similarities in mythological accounts and icongraphic survivals leave no doubt as to the original unity of Shivaism and the wide extent of its influence" (Danielou 1992). As noted by Namita Gokhale:

> There have been suggestions of a degree of lateral influence by the Dionysic cults of the ecstatic ritual aspects of Shiva worship in the Indian subcontinent. The Greeks who came to India around 300 BC found commonalities with their own god Zagreus-Dionysus. The Indo-Aryan god did share some attributes in common... Dionysus was, like Shiva, a priapic god, characteristically symbolized by an erect phallus. The vine leaf was sacred to him, as the leaf of the belva was sacred to Lord Shiva. Shiva's ganas corresponded with the satyrs of the Orphic Mystery cults. Like Shiva, Dionysus had a temperament which could concede of excess, and like Shiva, he was associated with hills and mountains. Greek myth and literature both record the Indian sojourns of these gods, and among others, Megasthanes has written about the travels to India of essentially Greek Gods such as Dionysus... (Gokhale, 2001)

Dionysus and Shiva share the totem animals snake, lion, and bull as well as strong elements of phallic (lingam) worship. Likewise, Shiva's blue skin and holy markings have similarities among the Thracians, as demonstrated by ancient references to their tattooed shaman, and surviving artefacts depicting blue gods. There is clear evidence that the mutual use of cannabis may have been another meeting point of the two Gods. "Since the wine of Dionysus is a mediation between the god's wild herbal ancestors and the civilized phenomenon of his cultivated and manufactured manifestation in the product fermented from the juice of the grape, it is most probable that this was the way in which the Greeks incorporated hemp into their pharmacopoeia" (Ruck, 2007).

> Greek people knew about its fumes, obviously, and about its effects. The fact that almost nobody directly described abuse of this stupefacient was perhaps due to its rarity (cannabis was not a

Greek product, it seems) or its unusual utilization. Yet, it is not at all strange if we bear in mind the silence of our sources about the drugs that were used by the Maenads in Bacchic mysteries and by the initiates in Orphic mysteries. We know that those people who found their way of happiness celebrating those rites tried to come into communion with gods through orgies and narcotics. Sex and drugs were thus the media through which men and women became gods or, better, similar to gods.... Who knows? Perhaps, nepenthes or cannabis were the drugs that were used in those rites, and this would be the reason why we know so little of them and about how they were used. (Arata, 2004)

The mythology has it that Dionysus appeared in the Grecian provincial town of Thebes, after extensive travels through Central Asia and the even more mysterious India. The effeminately dressed, long haired youth, angered city officials by proclaiming himself a god, but even more by introducing strange rites and initiating others with the sacraments he brought back from the East. Horrified by rumors of frenzied orgies taking place among Dionysus followers, the Maenads, the dour king, Pentheus, had the youth sent to prison. Shortly after a messenger from distant snow peaked mountains [the land of the Scythians?] approached Pentheus, and bade him to reconsider his decision:

O King, receive this Spirit, who'er he be,
To Thebes in glory. Greatness manifold
Is all about him; and the tale told
That this is he who first to man did give
The grief-assuaging vine. Oh, let him live;
For if he die, then Love herself is slain,
And nothing joyous in the world again![23]

Dionysus was not imprisoned long before a magical incantation was heard from behind the jail walls; "Kindle flame of blazing lightning - Burn, burn, the house of Pentheus to the ground!" Within an instant lightning pierced the jail-house, destroying it with a thundering explosion. Dionysus casually walked out unhurt, and invited the now curious Pentheus, to view for himself the secret rituals performed in the mountain woods. After dawning women's clothes so that he could view the rites undetected amongst the all

23   Euripdes' *The Bacchae*, translated byMurray, Allen & Unwin (1946)

female worshippers, Pentheus was led by Dionysus, who assumed the form of a Bull. They came upon a clearing in the woods where Dionysus's devotees were singing and dancing ecstatically. Interrupted, in the midst of their frenzied ritual, the Maenads, now including the king's own mother, set upon Pentheus and tore the unrecognized politician into pieces.

> Clearly this myth is closely connected with religious experience, in fact with ritual. it provides a charter and sanction for an ecstatic cult. That the ecstatic religious experience described... was a reality in Greece... [is] no doubt. It was interpreted as possession by Dionysus, or as 'madness.' Plato attributed such 'madness.'to poets... inspired by the Muses, and to the priestess possessed by Apollon when she prophesized in trance. (Kane 1987)

As Dale Pendell poetically commented "The true living Dionysus is hiding in the hemp plant not the wine bottle....we can spot the god's young companions by their flutes and drums, by their dancing and the tie-dyed colors. We can watch the re-enactment of the ancient tragedy as we lock them away in our prisons" (Pendell 1995).

Fig 12.4: Perhaps it was a jade bud of holy hemp originally depicted on the end of Dionysus's magical rod, rather than the pine cone usually described?

The musician prophet Orpheus was considered to be the hero-incarnation of Dionysus. Also "Significantly, Orpheus was supposedly a Thracian priest of Apollo..." (Ruck, et al., 2007). Grecian relics show Orpheus surrounded by Thracian followers. The "Dionysiac religion, like Orphism, was of northern Thracian provenance, and was fraught with orgiastic-mystic elements, on which Orphism fastened, adopting its emotionalism, its doctrine of Enthousiamos, and of possession by the deity, rejecting its wild frenzy, and transforming its savage ritual into a sacramental religion" (Angus,1975).

The Lyre playing poet-hero, Orpheus, was said to have descended to the underworld, in search of his wife, Eurydice, who ended up there after being bitten by the proverbial 'snake in the grass.' Although he failed to save his beloved, Orpheus returned from his sojourn in Hades with the secrets on which he based his system of initiation.

From the 6th century BC onward, Orpheus, was known as the 'founder of initiation' and credited with instituting the famous Eleussian mysteries. "Orphism was steeped in sacramentalism, which flooded the later Mysteries and flowed into Christianity. Salvation was by sacrament, by initiatory rites, and by an esoteric doctrine.... Orphism was the most potent solvent ever introduced into Greek religious life" (Angus,1975). Unlike the placebo-sacraments of later Christianity, the Orphic references to the ecstatic state of Enthusiamos (from where we get the word enthusiasm), was obviously produced by a powerful entheogen. Such ecstatic rites leave little wonder why Orphism competed with Christianity for popularity with the masses through the first few centuries AD.

Orphics believed in reincarnation, teaching release from 'the sorrowful wheel' of life through ascetic contemplation and astral-projection type journeys, i.e.-shamanistic ecstasy. Ward Rutheford commented, "[H]istory provides several examples of...ritualized shamanistic initiation. Typical is the case of Orphism...derived from the...musician-prophet Orpheus. He was almost certainly a Kapnobatai...who induced trance by smoking possibly hemp" (Rutherford 1993).

> 'Smoke' was apparently an element in the Mystery initiation of the Orphics. Most explicitly in Euripides' Hippolytus tragedy, Theseus in accusing his son of perfidy, saying, "You who have Orpheus for your lord: go on, get ecstatic, owing your allegiance to the smokes in their many scriptures." There were indeed numerous holy scriptures amongst the Orphics,[24] but 'smoke' in the context of ecstasy certainly does not mean that they were unsubstantial or worthless... (Ruck, et al., 2007)

Referring to Orphic worship, researcher Frederick Dannaway suggests that pagan elements of Greco-Roman worship were considerably "infused with psychoactive smoke rituals... due to the heavily 'shamanic' component... [of] much of their mystery traditions... The Orphic hymns contain a highly systematic array of fumigations containing some highly pungent, psychoactive substances that would synergize to be more potent in combination..." (Dannaway, 2009). We can be sure through the Thracian origins of Orpheus, that his cult would have included cannabis in such preparations.

Orpheus arose under the joint signs of Dionysus and Apollo, whose cult has also been connected with the use of psychoactive

24   Plato, Republic 364e.

substances, including cannabis. "Tacitus, for example, visited the oracle of Apollo at Claros about AD 100 and described how the entranced priest listened to his decision-seeking petitioners; he then '... swallows a draught of water from a mysterious spring – though ignorant generally of writing and of meters – delivers his response in set verse'"[25] (Jaynes, 1976). Apollo's priestess at Delphi, however, was reported to inhale certain inspiring fumes, rather than drink a magical potion:

> Dr. Charles Winick, director of the Narcotics program for the American Health Association, suggests... Apollo may have been the first celebrity to use cannabis... as witness the exhilaration of his priestess at Delphi. (Oursler 1968)

In *The Greek Myths*, scholar and poet Robert Graves wrote that in Delphi through to Classical times "the Pythoness had an attendant priest who induced her trance by burning barley grains, hemp, and laurel over an oil lamp in an enclosed space, and then interpreted what she said... but it is likely that the hemp, laurel and barley were once laid on the hot ashes of the charcoal mound, which is a simpler and more effective way of producing narcotic fumes" (Graves 1955).

The visionary priestess of Greece's oldest oracle, Delphi, was known as the Pythia, in reference to the serpent power believed to speak through her. She was chosen from amongst peasant women to prophesize at the Temple of Apollo and was consulted on all matters of national importance until its closure in the fourth century a.d. by the prohibitions of the Christian Emperor Theodosius (who left the sacred site to be later destroyed by rampaging Christian monks).

Figured monuments show the Pythia in a calm, serene, concentrated state, sitting at a stool, breathing in fumes that rose from an open fissure in the floor that were believed to produce a *"pneuma enthusiastikon"* or an *"ecstatic exhalation."* As Mircea Eliade commented "By what means she attained this second state remains a mystery:"

> The laurel leaves that she chewed, fumigations with laurel, the water from the spring Cassotis that she drank, have no intoxicat-

25   Tacitus, Annals, as quoted in (Jaynes, 1976)

ing properties and do not explain the trance. According to tradition, her oracular tripod was placed over a cleft (chasma) in the ground from which vapors with supernatural virtues arose. Excavations, however, have brought to light neither a fissure in the ground nor the cavern into which the Pythia descended... the fact is we know nothing about it. (Eliade 1978)

With the disassociated trance-like state produced from the vapors and Thracian influence on the Delphic Oracle, it can be conjectured that the Pythia likely put forth her revelations from behind a veil of cannabis smoke, that arose from brazier beneath the floor, and this idea has been suggested by a variety of different sources (Oursler, 1968, Littleton, 1986). "Delphi is heavily linked with psychoactive substances... and *Cannabis*/Scythian and Indo-European *Soma* associations..." (Dannaway, 2009). Professor C. Scott Littleton[26] explored this possibility in a 1986 essay "The Pneuma Enthusiastikon: On the Possibility of Hallucinogenic 'Vapors' at Delphi and Dodona":

> To be sure, Cannabis was neither a generally recognized component of the ancient Greek pharmacopoeia nor widely noted in classical antiquity for its hallucinogenic effects ... However, the plant has been cultivated in Greece for millennia... and would have been readily available. Moreover, its hallucinogenic potential was almost certainly appreciated in at least a few esoteric circles... and, as Delphi was perhaps the most important single religious establishment in Greece, it is highly probable that some members of its priesthood were privy to the knowledge that *Cannabis sativa* can alter one's state of consciousness - especially in light of the inherently shamanic character of what went on there.... I suggest that the practice of inhaling hemp smoke managed to diffuse from the steppe cultures to Greece - or at least to the Delphic Hosioi and their counterparts at Dodona and perhaps elsewhere - at some point well before the middle of the first millennium B.C.. (Littleton, 1986)

Littleton noted that "It should be emphasized that the foregoing is still highly conjectural, and will remain so until the residue in the

---

26   Former Professor of Anthropology as well as former Chairperson of the Department of Anthropology at Occidental College in Los Angeles, California. Currently enjoying Emeritus status.

omphalosst is chemically analyzed. Several chemist colleagues (via personal communications) have indicated that such an analysis might be possible if a sample of that residue were subjected to state-of-the-art spectrometry, even after 23 centuries..." (Littleton, 1986). Unfortunately, as Littleton later lamented "the Greek authorities wouldn't let me take a scraping" (Littleton, 2008).[27]

The mystery in regards to the Pythia's vapors, however, may have been brought to light by recent archaeological and geological research, and the possibility of cannabis, at least partially, put to rest. More current geological research by De Boer, et al. (2001), strongly suggests that a 'fragrant' natural hallucinogenic gas, ethylene, did issue from some newly discovered fissures beneath the Temple of

Fig. 12.5: The Pythia, Priestess of Delphi, seated upon a tripod, and inhaling sacred fumes from a fissure in the floor. (John Maler Collier, 1850 – 1934)

Apollo (not available at the time Eliade wrote his comments above) and has led Littleton to question the hypothesis he put forth in 1986, when the consensus among geologists was that there were no naturally occurring fumes at Delphi. However, Littleton still regards the "possibility that cannabis fumes may have been mixed with the naturally occurring ethylene so as to augment the hallucinogenic impact on the Pythia. This is reinforced by the fact that cannabis was well-known in ancient times, from Western Siberia (e.g., Pazyryk) to Western Europe; indeed, its use as a psychotropic drug may well date from Proto-Indo-European times, ca. 3500-4000 B.C.E." (Littleton, 2008).

Although this new evidence regarding ethylene is interesting and may denote the use of subterranean emissions as an entheogen, as Dr. Littleton noted, it does not necessarily preclude a role

27   (C. Scott Littleton, personal communication, 2008).

for the shamanic use of cannabis in ancient Greece, even amongst the Pythia. Indeed, substantiating evidence showing the use of cannabis in Grecian Oracles can be found in the fascinating book *The Mystery of the Oracles*, by Phillip Vandenberg, who in discussing the archaeologist Sotirios Dakaris finds in the excavation of the 4th-3rd-century "Nekyomanteion" (a place for consulting the dead) on the River Acheron (one of the most famous entrances to the netherworld) notes: "The black lumps of hashish that Dakaris discovered by the sackful leave no doubt that clients of the oracle were drugged into an *incubatio*, a kind of temple sleep, so they could experience the dreams and revelations that they should while close to the dead and the divine forces. Temple sleep was customary among the Babylonians, Egyptians and Greeks..." (Vandenberg, 1982). As the 19th century author John Porter Brown noted of such rites:

> The peculiar pleasures affecting especially the nerves, and produced by narcotics... belong apparently to modern times — that is to say, that it is only in modern times that we find them in general use. Amongst the ancients there is very little doubt of their existence, but they were the secrets of the priests, or of the initiated. We read, for instance, of certain temples in Cyprus or in Syria, to which the votaries thronged from all parts of the world, in expectation of having their wishes gratified. Those wishes generally were in such cases interviews with some beloved object, or visions of future happiness. The votary was bathed, dressed in splendid robes, given some peculiar food, after which he inhaled a delicious odour, and was then laid on a couch strewn with flowers. Upon this he probably went to sleep; but in all events such an intoxication of the mind was produced that the next morning he rose satisfied that in the night all his desires had been realised. (Brown, 1868)

Unfortunately, little can be found on Vandenberg's alleged find of Greek Hashish. James Wiseman in his review of Dakaris' work omits any reference to hashish;[28] likewise for the on-line web-site of the Hellenic Ministry of Culture's page for this archaeological site, which makes no reference to these sacks of hashish. Such censoring leaves one to believe that here again we may find academic prejudice acting as superstitious flaming cherubim, blocking the way to historical fact. If reports of this find are indeed correct, then here

28   "Rethinking the Halls of Hades," in *Archaeology*, vol. 51, no. 3, May/June, 1998.

in a Grecian temple we have our oldest examples of hashish. As entheobotanist Christian Ratsch has noted of Dakaris' alleged find: "It is entirely possible that the temple sleepers at Acheron were administered a hemp preparation so that their dreams would be especially vivid" (Ratsch, 2005). Vandenberg still referred to Dakaris' find of ancient Greek hashish in the 2007 edition of *Mysteries of the Oracles*, so one might conclude that this claim holds, and has simply been ignored (Vandenberg, 2007).

The riddle-like oracles given at Delphi were deciphered by a priesthood that, in times of corruption, interpreted them to suit their own agendas. Pythagoras (d. c. 497 B.C.), the Greek philosopher and mathematician, reformed this priesthood through purifying rituals, and despite angry protests from the male priests, he went against tradition and initiated the female Pythia, Theocla. Interestingly, *The Book of Lists*,[29] has Pythagoras first on a list of marijuana users, and Iamblichus referred to 'libations and sacrifices with fumigations, and incense,' being performed by his initiates (Guthrie 1987).

As Dannaway has noted, "psychoactive, i.e., magical, *Thymiamata* (that which is burnt as incense) of exotic ingredients are used by Pythagoras ('who could prophesize with frankincense')" (Dannaway, 2009). Commenting on the word *frankincense*, which means *pure-incense* aromatherapy expert Susanne Fischer-Rizzi noted that; "We once called all herbs burnt as incense 'frankincense'" (Fischer-Rizzi 1990). That ancient incense blends sold at considerable cost as "frankincense" could have contained the highly aromatic and "magically" effective cannabis seems likely. Today the word *frankincense* has come to specify the gum resin from the North African tree *Boswellia* and Fischer-Rizzi points out that this modern source also contains psychoactive properties, comparable in some ways to those of cannabis, and that its use in modern churches helps to instill a chemically induced feeling of religious awe.[30]

The suggestion that Pythagoras received inspiration from cannabis was first put forth by the 19th century author and hashish experimenter, Fitz Hugh Ludlow, who suggested elements like Pythagoras

---

29   (Wallechinsky, et al., 1978) - Unfortunately, the compilers cite no source for this inclusion.

30   "In the last few years, scientists have grown interested in frankincense. They were intrigued by reports that inhaling certain fragrances became addictive for some people, such as altar boys. Some members of the Academy of science in Leipzig, Germany, found in 1981 that when frankincense is burned, another chemical is produced, trahydro-cannabinole. This psychoactive substance expands the subconscious" (Fischer-Rizzi 1990).

hearing his name called out in the gurgling of a stream along with taking on the identity of deities and other events, indicate, as in Ludlow's own experience with the drug, intoxication with hemp (See Appendix C): "It would be no hard task to prove... that the initiation to the Pythagorean mysteries, and the progressive instructions which preceded it... consisted in the employment... of hasheesh" (Ludlow, 1856). Pythagoras based his system around the hemp using Thracian Orphic teachings, and he himself can clearly be described as a shaman—as Pythagoras allegedly had the ability to leave his body while in trance.

Pythagoras traveled throughout the ancient world and studied under the Babylonian Magi, a group renowned for their plant-magic. "Pythagoras and Democritus journey to Egypt, Ethiopia, Arabia, and Persia, visiting sects of drug-using wise men, known as Magi; the very same religious group that visited Jesus according to the Gospels; and wrote extensively about the potent psychotropic substances with which they experimented" (Hillman, 2008). Porphyry recorded that the Greek philosopher personally met the Persian shaman "Zaratus [Zoroaster] by whom he was purified from the pollutions of his past life" (Guthrie 1987). Scholars have long noted Zoroaster's use of cannabis to achieve ecstasy, and the mythology around the Persian Psychopomp shows that he initiated others into its use; see Chapter 15.

Also of interest is that Pythagoras considered Abaris, a Scythian shaman who came to learn from him, so experienced that he didn't compel him to wade through the complicated introductory period involved with his teachings but contrarily considered him fit to be an immediate listener to his doctrines, and instructed him in the shortest possible way. As discussed in Chapter 7, the Scythians were renowned for using cannabis for ritual purposes. Pythagoras's teachings were surrounded in secrecy and his quick acceptance of the Scythian shaman Abaris may indicate that the mutual use of cannabis constituted a meeting point of some kind.

Another potential foreign conduit for Greek cannabis use may come from the cult of Cybelle. Originally a Phrygrian and Hittite Goddess, Cybelle's worship is believed to go back to Neolithic times in Anatolia, where she likely originated as a deification of Mother Earth. Her Roman equivalent was 'Magna Mater,' or 'Great Mother.'[31] Cybelle's cult was popularized around the 5th century

---

31   Walter Burkeert who treats *Meter* among "foreign gods" in *Greek Religion* described the evolution of the cult as follows: "The cult of the Great Mother, *Meter*, presents a complex picture insofar as indigenous, Minoan-Mycenean tradition is here intertwined

BC in Greece, where she was associated with the later cult of Dionysus, whom she was said to have both initiated and cured of Hera's madness. Cybelle later became a life-death-rebirth deity through the connection with her son/consort Attis.

Cybelle's original Phrygian priests, known as *Gallus*, or *Galli*, assumed women's clothing after a sacrificial castration, the gender transfer being a form of worship of the Goddess by identification. "We know that the Phrygian tribes… during the 1st millennium BCE were weavers of hemp[32] (and possibly imbibers of intoxicating hemp preparations)" (Merlin, 1973). References to some *Galli* being awakened to this form of worship, after ingesting a certain kind of "herb growing along the banks of the Maeander River" (Conner 1993), as well as acknowledged use of mysterious sacraments amongst the cult, indicate clearly that they were practicing the common trait of mystery religions of the time—ingestion of entheogenic sacraments. Referring to the visionary dream which was said to awaken the *Gallus* to their new identification with the Goddess, Randy P. Conner commented; "It is possible to see the… drinking or eating of special substances as a fated occurrence that triggered the awareness of one's destiny. Such experiences were said to cause an individual to experience *sophrene*, to 'recover one's senses'" Conner 1993).

Recent finds have established that Cybelle was worshipped among the Thracian tribes (Camphausen 1991), who as discussed were well-known for using cannabis to attain mystic states, especially amongst their own transvestite shamans. Interestingly, certain male functionaries of Cybelle and Attis' cult were known as *cannophori*, which has usually been translated as *"reed-bearers,"* but linguistically, with "canno," this may have implications of "cannabis-bearers" instead. Archaeological evidence shows the Phrygian culture from which the religion arose used hemp (Abel 1980). Similar cannabis using transvestite worshippers of the Goddess, known as *Enarees*, could be found amongst the Scythians, who were closely related to the Thracians, referred to above, and who possibly picked the cultic practice up from contact with the Galli, or alternatively carried it on from an even earlier identical source.[33]

---

with a cult taken over directly from the Phrygian kingdom of Asia Minor" (Burkeert, 1985).
32   Merlin quotes Godwin's, 'Ancient Cultivation of Hemp'; "…excavations…at the Turkish site of Gordon… produced hempen fabrics… of the late 8th century B.C., from gravemounds in the Phrygian kingdom" (Godwin, 1967).
33   Included in this grouping is the Canaanite male cult prostitutes of Ashera, the

One can only speculate that these instances are representative of the same ancient widespread tradition, with varying local names.

A number of sources have suggested that Homer's *Odyssey* (9th-8th century BC) contains references to cannabis under the name "Nepenthe," which as discussed in Chapter 11 was said to have come to the Greeks via the Egyptians.[34] In the Grecian account nepenthe was infused in wine to soothe the survivors of the siege of Troy. "Jove-born Helen... Employ'd into the wine which they drank, a drug infused, antidote to the pains, Of grief and anger, a most potent charm for ills of every name" (Homer, 1992, edition). The preparation clearly had a lasting popularity as Diodorus Siculus (1st century B.C.) still reports it in use in the same area, more than 700 years later:

> The ancient Greek historian Diodorus Siculus states that the Egyptians laid much stress on the plant called 'nepenthe,' which Homer's 'Iliad' says was used by Helen of Troy. The plant was given was given to her by a woman from Egyptian Thebes. Women of Thebes were celebrated for possessing a secret whereby they could dispel anger or melancholy. The secret is supposed to be the intoxicating values of hemp. (Oursler, 1968)

As discussed in Chapter 11 this view has been shared by a variety of scholars: "There has been much speculation as to the identity of the substance; some have suggested that it may have been cannabis (Singer and Underwood, 1962; Burton, 1894 edn [a]; Walton, 1938)" (Wills, 1998). Some sources have suggested opium for Nepenthe, but as the effects of the poppy were widely known in ancient Greece, this seems unlikely.

> ...[T]he guests do not become sedated or start to hallucinate... so presumably the nepenthe was given to promote relaxation and discourse rather than heavy intoxication... It has also been suggested that Greek warriors may have taken nepenthe as a courage-boosting intoxicant before charging into combat (Cooper, 1995). Others have speculated that the 'wine of the condemned' cited by the Greek writer Amos about 700 BC as a method of reducing pain of a slow death was also cannabis (Walker, 1985).

quedeshim, who were also cannabis-bearers, through their use of hemp for ritual weavings, as well as anointing their bodies with it and burning it as an incense.
34   According to Homer, the drug came via an Egyptian, 'For Egypt teems with drugs.'

In reality it is impossible to determine substances such as these from the vague descriptions given. (Wills, 1998)[35]

Wills notes speculation that the Greeks may have used nepenthe "before charging into combat," a use that has been applied cross-culturally with cannabis as well (Zulus, Hashishins, Hindu Warriors, etc.). It should also be noted that the use of Soma-Haoma by warriors is often referred to in the ancient texts as well. In relation "leaves of cannabis" have been found in an underwater archaeological excavation of a Carthaginian warship from 241 BC which are on display in Sicily,[36] and researchers have associated it with this same purpose.

Dr. Phillip Seff reported that aboard the find of an ancient Carthaginian vessel "There was so much of this plant material that a bagful was easily obtained, more than enough for laboratory analysis. The results confirmed that the material was most probably *Cannabis sativa*..." (Seff, 1986).

> What can one conclude from abundant supplies of marijuana aboard a fighting ship? In the quantities that were found, it seems to have been a regular ration. Since most of the plant material was stems, which provide mild doses of the drug, it may have been used as a medication to reduce fatigue. Or the soldiers may have been encouraged to use the marijuana to become euphoric, to reach what is today known as a 'high' to intensify their courage and fearlessness. The soldiers may have chewed on the stems and infused the weed into a tea. (Seff, 1996)

Daniel Morneau also notes, "That the Punic sailors drank wine on board came as no surprise, and the presence of amphorae with the resinous lining associated with wine-carrying proves it. But the totally, unexpected discovery of a bundle of cannabis sticks indicates the sailors indulged in a mild form of marijuana tea as well" (Morneau, 1986). The *Times* (UK) reported of the find:

> The Marsala Punic Ship was uncovered in Marsala harbour by a dredger in 1969, and restored by a team of underwater archaeologists from the British School... They concluded that the warship had been sunk stern-first after being rammed by the Romans.

---

35   Wills's references omitted.
36   Rossella Giglio, *The Regional Archaeological Museum Baglio Anselmi of Marsala* (Sicily)

The crew had apparently abandoned ship, taking their weapons with them, but left evidence of their diet including deer, goat, horse, ox, pig and sheep as well as olives, nuts and fruit.

There were also traces of cannabis, which the crew may have chewed as a stimulant before going into battle or simply to keep awake. (Owen, 2004)[37]

That the material was mostly cannabis stalks, also opens up the possibility that the hemp in question was used for making Soma-Haoma, the use of which, as we have shown, was considerably widespread in the ancient world. Or alternatively it may have been infused into wine which was an equally widespread technique of cannabis ingestion.

Another mythical Grecian reference might be found in the story of Jason and the Argonauts. May Sinclair suggests that the Argonauts learned magical formulas from the Scythians "that included the use of cannabis and a wolf's bane mixture that caused a person to feel their bodies had fur or feathers" (Sinclair, 2007). Others have suggested a profoundly negative role for hemp, amongst the Spartan nobility, "King Kleomenes 1 of Sparta went mad... and committed suicide. Most Greeks... attributed it to his heavy drinking... others have argued... that he may have indulged in cannabis having learnt the habit from the Scythians" (Knox, et al., 1979).

Showing the controversy about potential Greek cannabis references is still alive and well, Prof. Carl Ruck and co-authors have suggested yet another ancient reference to its potential use, here under the guise of "The sacred plant called *thymbra*";

> ...The *thymbra* is so named as the 'smoke-plant,' derived from the verb *typhein*, 'to make smoke.' The act of sacrifice in Greek is the same root in the verb thyein or literally 'to make smoke,' cognate with 'fume' and 'funeral' in English, since the sacrifice involved the burning of the inedible portions of the slaughtered animal, converting them into incense or smoke as transmuted spiritual food for the celestial deities.... The plant is identified as savory, *Satureia Thymbra*, but its etymology from *thyein* suggests that it is sacred or a surrogate for something psychoactive. Its occurrence as an epithet of Apollo Thymbraeus and its association with satyrs or with Saturn in its botanic nomenclature would similarly indicate that it was in some way entheogenic. Related words are

---

37   Other sources have stated cannabis may have been used to motivate the rowers.

typhos for a 'delusional fever', *typhomania* for 'delirium', and *ty-phoön* for 'to be crazy'. In English, we have the disease called ty-phoid fever. And indeed it does appear to have been a 'visionary' herb....The phrase *thymbrophagon blepein* or 'to see like someone who has eaten *thymbra*' would seem to suggest that it affected the eyesight.... Its name... as the 'smoke-plant' and its inducing of the visionary clouds of smoke suggest that it is probably a slang term for the most notorious and well documented smoke that goes by the official name of Cannabis. It was no doubt a common ingredient in the *thymiama* or 'incense' burnt in *thymiateria* or 'censers'. And wine called *thymbrites oinos* could be flavored with it as well.... In all probability, the Greeks encountered the 'weed' in terms of their own long-established social norms, as an ingre-dient in the incense for the thymateria and in the variable doctor-ing of wine with other intoxicating substances. There was, in fact, a wine called *kapnias oinos* or 'smoky wine'. (Ruck, et al., 2008)

The glory of ancient Greece, was one of the heights of the an-cient world; its ideals have influenced the political development of our Western culture at least as much as Christianity has religion, if not more. Clearly, despite the lack of recognition of past scholars, cannabis was a part of the Greek social fabric, both as a medicine and as a magical plant that operated as a gateway between worlds.

The unstigmatized use of drugs was just one aspect of the ideal society the Athenians strove to achieve. For these Greeks, a free state allowed its citizens to make their own decisions, especially when it came to what they chose to do with their own bodies. Democracy and individual liberty went hand in hand, the free-dom to consume alcohol or drugs was no less or more important to Athens than the right to speak one's mind or to vote in the assembly... [F]reedom-loving Athenians,... unlike their Spartan counterparts, considered their individual liberties the foundation of a good society. (Hillman, 2008)

Claudius Galen

Pedanius Dioscorides

Pliny the Elder

During the Roman era, widely known historical figures such as Claudius Galen (130-200 AD), Pedanius Dioscorides (90 A.D.) and Pliny the Elder (23-79 AD) all made reference to cannabis in their writings.

13

A DRUG FOR HILARITY: ROME

L ike the Greeks, the Romans were surrounded by cannabis using cultures, and up until Christian times they also shared a similar polytheistic religion that was open to the adoption of a variety of foreign deities, such as Cybelle, Dionysus, under the name Bachus, Egyptian Isis,[1] and Persian Mithras. One can safely assume that the worship of these foreign deities included the consumption of a variety of psychoactive substances, including hemp, as had been the practice in their respective homelands. Again, as with the Greeks, Roman medicinal references are more known and established. There would have also been the same clear desire to keep the secrets of the mysteries of such cults veiled from the profane.

> Marijuana was a common drug, possibly imported by Roman merchants from the Scythians or even India. In fact, cannabis was so popular that the ancient world used it in not only human medicine but also animal husbandry[2] ...As a drug, marijuana was successful in treating a number of morbid conditions, and escaped any ire one might expect on the part of ancient medical authors or Classical historians. Many potent psychotropic substances were considered to be potentially poisonous, but cannabis was never vilified; the ancient world clearly trusted the drug as much as they did any other safe medication. (Hillman, 2008)

1   "That the expression 'elixir of immortality,' belongs to the Pagan mysteries may be seen from the account which Diodorus Siculus gives of the Cult of Isis; he tells us that Isis was the discoverer of the medicine of immortality... by means of which she restored to life her son Horus, and made him to partake of immortality. But this does not tell us whether Isis discovered a solid or a liquid drug." (Harris, 1927)

2   Up until the time of prohibition, cannabis had continued to be used as a veterinary medicine, for colic, bloat, and other maladies.

The ancient physician Claudius Galen (130-200 AD) wrote of a cannabis seed dessert that was popular with the Romans which was reputed to promote "hilarity"; "some people eat it toasted together with other teasers. What I call "teasers" is what is eaten for pleasure of drinking during the meal" (Galen).[3] "If consumed in large amounts," Galen wrote "affects the head by sending to it a warm and toxic vapour."[4] "It is possible Galen misinterpreted what he saw... Like Herodotus, he also may have described the parts of the plant used as 'seeds' through ignorance, when resinous material from the whole plant may have been used [i.e. seeded buds]" (Wills, 1998). Ephippus (4th century B.C.) a writer of comedies, also included cannabis on a list of delicacies (Brunner 1977).

Around 100, Dioscorides, a surgeon in the Roman Legions under the Emperor Nero, identified the herb "kannabis" and recorded numerous medicinal uses. "The physician, pharmacologist and botanist Pedanius Dioscorides (90 A.D.) described cannabis in the *Materia Medica*. He described Kannabis emeros (Cannabis . . . 'when it is green is good for the pains of the ears') and Kannabis agria ('The root being sodden, and so laid on hath ye force to assuage inflammations and to dissolve Oedemata, and to disperse ye obdurate matter about ye joints')" (Hanu , 2008).

The Roman historian Pliny (23-79 AD) recorded cannabis seed oil's use in the extraction of "worms from the ears, or any insect which may have entered them." (Pliny likely refers to the common earache, which was believed to have been caused by burrowing parasitic worms.) "Pliny... described additional indications for hemp: 'The root boiled in water eases cramped joints, gout too, and similar violent pain; it is applied raw to burns'" (Weiner, 2002). The ancient historian may have also identified recreational use of hemp as well. "Pliny delights in vivid descriptions of these powerful mind-altering drugs and the many diverse reasons for which they were used" (Hillman, 2008).

> ...in the 1st century, Pliny the Elder wrote in his Natural History... The gelotophyllis grows in Bactria and along the Borysthenes. 'If this be taken in myrrh and wine all kinds of phantoms beset the mind, causing laughter which persists until the kernels of pine-nuts are taken with pepper and honey in palm

3   As quoted in (Arata, 2004)
4   Galen, *De Facultatibus Alimentorum*

wine.' In subsequent notes… the translators identify gelotophyllis as 'Indian hemp, Cannabis sativa.' The Borysthenes River of
Pliny's narrative is identified as the Dnieper, probably in the present day Ukraine, which was part of the empire and territory of
the cannabis-using Scythian tribes…. The reference to Bactria is
key, as actual physical remnants of cannabis flowers and seeds,
along with opium poppies and ephedra, dating to the late third or
early second millennium B.C. have been excavated in Margiana
(in present-day Turkmenistan), one component of what has been
labeled the Bactria-Margiana Archaeological Complex (BMAC).
Excavation has yielded artifacts supporting usage of these plants
ritually as haoma-soma hallucinogens. (Russo, 2007)

Evidence of the Soma-Haoma cult brings us to the topic of potential Haoma use amongst Roman warriors, who were known to have
worshipped the originally Indo-European God, Mithras. Mithras
became popular in Rome in the late 1st century A.D., particularly
amongst Roman legionnaires.

In the Rig Veda (IX.108.16), Mitra is "pleased by soma." In the
Avesta, haoma is offered to Mithra (Yasht X.6). Mithra's weapon
is the mace or thunderbolt (vazra), similar to Indra's bolt (vajra)…
Ethnobotanists see several features of the soma cult in this god's
attributes…. His secret cult, which had strong astrological/al-
chemical/eschatological components, involved a sacred meal and
meetings in caves and/or subterranean chambers…. According
to Pliny the Elder, in 66 A.D., when the Armenian king Trdat I
travelled to Rome to receive coronation from the emperor Nero,
he may have initiated Nero into certain "Magian" (?Mithraic)
rites, involving a secret sacrament.[5] (Bedrosian, 2006)

Interestingly, as we shall discuss in Chapter 17, Mithra shared a
variety of mythological motifs with the Christian God Jesus. These
similarities were so profound that when the Roman Empire chose
Christianity as the State religion, outlawing all other cults, the newly formed Roman Catholic Church fathers tried to deny claims that
they had borrowed elements of the Mithraic mythology (which
long predated their own) and attributed them to their own god, by
claiming that the Devil, with evil foresight, had seen the coming of
Christ and decided to pre-empt the arrival of the Holy Child and

---

5   Pliny the Elder, *Natural History, a Selection*, J. F. Healy trans. (New York, 1991)

placed the motifs on the pagan God before his arrival! These adoptions included the Virgin Birth, Christmas, and, most notably, the Eucharistic ceremony, which was clearly based on the ancient Haoma ritual. Although as we shall see in the next Chapter, by the time Haoma ritual was appropriated by the cult of Mithras, it may have already gone through radical changes regarding the plants used.

We shall return to Rome later, as it was under the rule of this ancient Empire, and through their adoption of the originally Jewish cult of Christianity, that so much knowledge of the past, science, history, art, and also the entheogenic sacraments, came to be lost to history. This rape of history came through the encroaching, all consuming reforms of the Catholic Church, which beckoned the coming of the millennia long night of the Dark Ages.

ZOROASTER, PSYCHO-POMP OR PARTY-POOPER?

T housands of years ago Iran was the source for the great Persian Empire which for some centuries held dominion over much of the ancient world. Iran is located slightly to the northeast of the ancient kingdoms of Sumeria, Babylonia, and Assyria. This area was the home of Mazdaism, which was a combination of the beliefs of the Assyria-Babylonian religions and the Aryan invaders who brought down their pre-Vedic faith from the Hindu-Kush Mountains to Persia, while their brothers went South and invaded India. As noted in the opening chapters, the common ancestry of the Vedic and Avestan texts accounts for the many similarities in the Hindu and Zoroastrian cosmologies and language, particularly notable in the Hindu hymns, the *Rig Veda*, and the Persian *Yashts* (or *Yasnas*) and *Gathas*. The affinities between two is most apparent in the many references to a sacred plant known in India as Soma, and in Persian as Haoma. As discussed, in both cultures this plant was considered a god, and when pressed and made into a drink, the ancient worshipper who imbibed it gained the powerful attributes of this god.

The communicants of the Mazdean religion later became known as the Zoroastrians, after going through a variety of radical changes under the religious reformer and prophet Zoroaster, also known as Zarathustra Spitma. "There has been and continues to be, much debate about the homeland of the prophet Zoroaster, but he is usually placed in Seistan or Bactria – Margiana [the site of the Soma temple at BMAC discussed in Chapter 6]... the date of Zarathustra is even more controversial: while some scholars defend the traditional date of the Zarathustrian clergy, placing him in the 6th century B.C., many date him to c. 1000 B.C., some as early as the 15th century B.C." (Parpola, 1995). Adding to this confusion, some scholars have even suggested that the character of Zoroaster and the tales of his exploits is the composite account of a number of different ancient Iranian shamans and the name 'Zoroaster' a title of office, rather than the name of an individual.

Mazdaim was initially a polytheistic nature-based fertility cult, and Zoroaster, a reformer somewhat like Moses, took the religion not quite to Monotheism, but rather a Dualism, very similar to the ongoing war between the forces of Heaven and Hell, later adopted by Christianity. Zoroaster taught that all of history is the story of the war between good and evil, epitomized by the god of light, Ahura Mazda, and the God of Darkness, Ahriman. Unlike many of the dualistic religions that grew out of it, Zoroastrianism never taught that evil was contained in matter, so all of creation was considered Holy, with humanity as its sacred guardian. The devil, known as Ahriman, was only capable of destructive acts and was seen as a parasite acting on creation in the form of falsehood, death, disease, evil words, thoughts, and deeds. Raising crops and cattle and a large family were considered Holy acts by these ancient people, and beyond common evils such as stealing or murder, to pollute the land, water or sky, or treat livestock cruelly, were considered grave sins.

Zoroastrian mythology has it that the prophet Zoroaster was conceived after his body came down to earth through heavenly rain, which brought forth plants that were consumed by cows belonging to the people selected to become his parents. The cows gave milk which was pressed with Haoma and drank by the prophet's parents, who later conceived him while making love for the first time (Y.9.13).

As an adult, the Yasna has it, that the God Haoma appeared before Zoroaster "at the time of pressing" in the form of a "beautiful man" (this is the only anthropomorphic reference), who prompts him to gather and press Haoma plants.

> At the proper time, at the Haoma-pressing Hour,
> Haoma went up to Zarathustra,
> who was purifying the fire and chanting the *Gathas*.
> Zarathustra asked him:

Who are you,
the most beautiful I have ever seen
in the entire bony existence,
with your sunny immortal life?

Y.9.1

Thus he answered me,
the Orderly death-averting Haoma:
I am, O Zarathustra,
the Orderly death-averting Haoma.
Ask me hither, Spitamid,
press me forth to drink.
Praise me for strength,
like the future Revitalizers too will praise me.

Y.9.2

In light of this auspicious introduction it is curious to note that since the 19th century the view has been that Zoroaster condemned the offering up of Haoma. The view that Zoroaster rallied against the Haoma cult is based on the following two verses and a thorough analysis of them, and the discussion they have engendered amongst religious scholars, offers some very interesting insights into the matter:

When, O Mazda, will the nobles understand the message? When will thou smite the filthiness of this intoxicant, through which the Karapans evilly deceive, and the wicked lords of the lands with purpose fell?

Y.48.10

The 'glutton' and the 'poets' deposit their guiding thoughts here in this cord work
Their 'miracle-works', by daily pouring when they are ready to be help for the one possessed by the Lie
And when the cow has been mistreated to (the point of) being killed (by him) who 'purifies' the haoma by burning'

Y. 32:14

Dr. Jafarey, who as discussed believes the original Haoma written of in the Yashts was a cannabis-based preparation which Zoroaster prohibited, wrote of these verses: "Zarathushtra condemns '*Dûrao-*

sha' (Yasna 32.14). This word is definitely an epithet of Haoma alone and of no other object in the Avesta.[1] Paradoxically, Zarathushtra is shown by the composer/narrator of the Hom Yasht to be praising it by using this very word *'Dûraosha.'* How could he have a double standard?!?! The word literally means "far-from-death" and also 'far-from-intellect.' In another Gathic stanza, Y.48.10 Zarathushtra calls it *'mûthrem mada…,'* literally 'intoxicating urine' (Y.48:10)" (Jafarey , 2000).

> Two terms, *mada* (intoxicant)[2] and *duraosha* (death repeller), used for the *haoma* drink in the Younger Avesta, are found in a manner that shows complete rejection of the substance and as well as the cult connected to it. Haoma stands condemned in the Gathas (32:14;48.10). (Jafarey, 2000)

This view has prevailed with a number of scholars as well as historians of the Zoroastrian faith. Daryoush Jahanian notes that "The text of the Gathas clearly indicates that in the rituals of the pre-Zoroastrian faith it [Haoma] was consumed by the princes (Kavis) and priests (Karapans), and caused them to behave irrationally.[3] Zarathushtra has derided and condemned the Haoma ritual by mentioning its epithets as invincible (!), and wisdom wasting (Dura Osham) (Y32.14) and intoxicant (Madahya) (Y48.10)" (Daryoush, 2005). This has been a longstanding view "It is therefore the haoma cult that Zarathustra is fighting, and it is for that reason totally correct that we find a severe breakdown against Yima in the same Gatha. Yima, who is indeed… the mythical founder of haoma"[4] (Nyberg,1938).

This has been a difficult issue for many orthodox Zoroastrians to reconcile with their current religious practice, as a form of the Ha-

---

1   In Yasna 42.5 the term duraosha appears in a positive context as an epithet of Haoma: "We revere Haoma from whom death flies."
2   Y.10.8 records that, "the intoxication of Haoma is accompanied by Order (and) bliss."
3   "The Gathic texts, particularly the Gathas and the Haptanghaiti, show that there was no profession as priesthood under any name during the Gathic [Zoroastrian] period. In fact, Zarathushtra overthrew the professional priests who had plagued the society. Zarathushtra himself was chosen as the *'Ahu'* (Leading Lord), *'Ratu,'* (Righteous Guide). He was the Divine *Mâñthran* (Thought-provoker). Later others were chosen as *'ratus'* of house, settlement, district, and land, strictly according to their qualifications. Those engaged in teaching, preaching, and spreading the Message were *'mâñthrans'''* (Jafarey, 2000).
4   "Vivahvant, Yimas father, was the first person to press it [Haoma] for the physical world" (Widengren, 1965). Yima later spread the use of Haoma to the wider Aryan community.

oma ritual has continued down to the present day. Jafarey's claims that the pre-Zoroastrian version of the Haoma contained cannabis, has caused Jafarey to be viewed as a very controversial figure amongst fellow members of his faith.[5]

The issue of Zoroaster's alleged condemnation of Haoma, in addition to other verses where Zoroaster sings the praises of Haoma, such as those below, have indeed been a cause of considerable confusion:

> Thus said Zarathustra:
> Homage to Haoma! Good (is) Haoma,
> well set up (is) Haoma, set up straight,
> good, healing according to the established rules,
> of good shape, giving good invigoration,
> an obstruction-smasher,
> golden-colored with pliable twigs,
> the best when they drink (him)
> and the best flight-maker for the breath-soul.
>
> Y.9.16

> I call down, O golden one, your intoxication
> and your might and your obstruction-smashing power,
> your talent, your healing,
> your furthering, your increasing,

---

5   Ervad Jal Birdy, President of the North American Mobeds Council and the Vice-President of the Traditional Mazdayasni Zoroastrian Anjuman, saw Jafarey's "Haoma, Its Original and Later Identity" as an attack on both the Zoroastrian faith and its rituals:

Mr. Jafarey tells us that Zarathushtra strongly condemned Haom and its ritual in the Gathas because He considered Haom to be a strong intoxicant, which led the ruling class to oppress and mistreat their subjects in their fits of drunkenness. He also tells us that Zarathushtra never performed this ceremony, which was really only concocted by priests for their own benefit. These statements have hurt and distressed many devout Zarathushtis and have made them speak out against Mr. Jafarey, or anyone else, making such misleading statements at their community gatherings.

Continuing with the deceit, having pronounced Haom as the substance that Zarathushtra condemns in the Gathas as an intoxicant, Mr. Jafarey now finds himself in a tight corner. He knows fully well that the Haom that is used in our rituals today is not strong enough to really intoxicate anyone (Mr. Jafarey has apparently himself drunk glassfuls without any side effects). So he proceeds to invent through his research" another substance, like "Bhang" - a much stronger intoxicant, which he incidentally also calls "Haom" and asserts that it was this substance that was really used in pre-Gathic times by the priests and which was condemned by Zarathushtra. It almost seems like Mr. Jafarey was present there, in a previous incarnation perhaps, to be able to make such wild statements. If this is not causing deliberate confusion and deception among the devotees, I don't know what is. (Birdy, 2000)

your strength in the whole body,
your all-adorned wisdom.
(I call) down (all) that so that I may go forth
among the living beings commanding at will,
overcoming hostilities, conquering the Lie!

Y.9.17

Zaehner noted in *Dawn and Twilight of Zoroastrianism* "It seems contrary to the evidence of the history of religion that a cult which has been fervently denounced by the founder of a religion should have been adopted... by that founder's earliest disciples" (Zaehner, 1961). As Zoroastrian scholar Mary Boyce also noted:

> In this case the assumption of fervent denunciation was based on a Gathic verse Y.48.10: 'When, O'Mazda... wilt thou smite the filth (*muthra-*) of this intoxicant (*mada-*), with which out of enmity, the pagan priests... deceive...' The term *mada-* is, however of wide application, and can be used of anything which exhilarates the spirits; and in view of the honored place enjoyed by haoma in Zoroastrianism it seems that the mada condemned here by the prophet must be something else perhaps a dehibilitating drug such as opium or hemp,[6] which enslaves those who take it in chains of addiction. The words he uses are very strong (for *muthra* literally means either excrement or urine),[7] and evidently expressed the harshest condemnation. The only other piece of positive evidence adduced from the *Gathas* for the prophet's condemnation of the *haoma* cult comes from an obscure verse Y.32.14, where amid a puzzling account of evil-doing the term *duraosa* occurs. This is a word of disputed meaning, which is known only as an epithet of *haoma*; but since translations of the Gathic passages in which it occurs differ widely, no sound deductions can be drawn from its implications there. As for negative

---

6   Both now shown to have been ingredients in Haoma, through Sarianidi!
7   Wasson saw the verse in question as a reference to Haoma as Fly agaric enriched urine, but as Boyce notes in relation to Wasson's view "if the *mada* of Y.48.10 is not *haoma*..." the Wassons claim is "irrelevant to it" (Boyce, 1982). Likewise Flattery and Schwarz put forth "the passage ... has nothing remotely to do with sauma [Haoma]" (Flattery & Schwartz, 1989). Alternatively, if we accept the passage as noting Zoroaster's condemnation of the Haoma as "intoxicating urine," this still would be a hard case to make for the Fly agaric, as the many references to Haoma in the Avestan literature clearly refer to a tall green plant, with aromatic properties, branches etc. Thus the references would be on par with the now common derogatory term referring to someone who has drunk to much alcohol, as "pissed" i.e., Y.48.10 would be seen as a denunciation of the sacred Haoma as vile intoxicating dirty "piss" not literal piss drunk for intoxication.

evidence, there is the fact there is no explicit reference to *haoma* in the *Gathas*. Considering the character of these hymns, this is a weak argument to rely on. (Boyce, 1982)

Mircea Eliade explained that "[r]ecent research has shown that the *haoma* ritual... was not condemned by Mazdaism [Zoroastrianism], not even in the Gathas... It seems... that Zarathustra primarily opposed the excess of orgiastic rites, which involved countless blood sacrifices and immoderate absorption of *haoma*" (Eliade, 1978). "The violent hallucinations it [Haoma] engendered were probably intensified by the sight of blood" (Messadié & Romano, 1996). It has been suggested that Zoroaster "made modifications... in the rituals..." (Boyce, 1990). Modifying her earlier view, Boyce explained:

> It seems very possible that Zoroaster... did this because he regarded *haoma* as potentially dangerous in its potency to people (cf. his probable denunciation of it, as *mada-*, in Y. 48.10). An extract from it was drunk by warriors to stimulate their battle lust, and (on Vedic evidence) it was prominent in the cult of warlike Indra, to Zoroaster a *daêva* [demon]... If then he restricted its use in his own act of worship to yielding a libation to the Waters,[8] it must be supposed that, as his religion spread, priestly converts in ever increasing numbers were reluctant to abandon the old rite, believed to give the celebrant an increase in awareness and power, and so this came to be reinstated as a preliminary to the one he had established. (Boyce, 1990)

This brings us to some very interesting points; first it should be noted that Boyce had varied opinions on Y.48.10, in the above reference she seems more willing to accept the reference of *mada* "intoxicating urine"[9] but earlier she saw it as a possible reference to "a dehibilitating drug such as opium or hemp" both of which have

---

8   The suggestion is that Zoroaster did not drink the Haoma, just poured it out as an offering to the waters. "(We make known) to the good waters, these libations containing haoma and milk and pomegranate, set up in Orderly fashion. (We make known) to the good waters, both the haoma water and the stone mortar, and the iron pestle" (Y.24.2). This may also indicate that originally the Haoma was an offering to the Avestan river goddess "Harahvati"/Sanskrit "*Sarasvati*," later known as *Aredvi Surâ Anâhitâ*.

9   It should be mentioned that in the dualistic world of Zoroastrianism there are both good and bad names for things. This is particularly true of urine, as urine clearly played a role in Zoroastrian purification rituals, but the Iranian term for urine in Y.48.10 depicts a dirty 'devilish' urine.

been identified at the site of a pre-Zoroastrian Haoma Temple in
BMAC. In relation to this it is interesting to return to the work of
Dr. Ali Jafarey who believed that "the pre-Gathic Haoma was most
probably '*bhang*' and that the post-Gathic priests, wanting to retain
their pre-Gathic rituals, substituted it with 'Ephedra,' the present
plant used in the Haoma ritual. I repeat, the present Haoma twigs
used is not the original pre-Gathic plant. It is a substitute and de-
void of the harms the original had" (Jafarey , 2000). A look at the
other verse which has been identified as evidence of Zoroaster's
prohibition of the cannabis in the Haoma offers evidence that col-
laborates with Jafarey's controversial solution to the debate:

> The 'glutton' and the 'poets' deposit their guiding thoughts here
> in this cord work.
>   Their 'miracle-works,' by daily pouring when they are ready to
> be help for the one possessed by the Lie.
>
> And when the cow has been mistreated to (the point of) being
> killed (by him) who 'purifies' the haoma by burning.
>
> Yasna 32:14

Some have seen this reference as a condemnation of cattle sacrifice, but as this continued unfettered throughout the period, and
even Zoroaster took part in such rites, this must not have been too
much of a concern for the Persian reformer. Obviously there was
more than this at issue in the Y.32.14 reference.

> In the prevailing religious tradition, Zarathustra probably found
> that the practice of sacrificing cattle, combined with the con-
> sumption of haoma (intoxicating drinks), led to orgiastic excess.
> Zarathustra In his reforms, did not, as some scholars would have
> it, abolish all animal sacrifice but simply the orgiastic and intoxi-
> cating rites that accompanied it. The haoma sacrifice, too, [after
> Zoroaster's reforms] was to be thought of as a symbolic offering.
> It may have [originally] consisted of unfermented drink or an in-
> toxicating beverage or a plant. (Hoiberg, et al., 2000)

Henrik Nyberg saw the Y.32.14 as evidence of a new cult in
which the "haoma... 'is brought to flames,'" instead of consumed
as a consecrated beverage, and this new cult vied for power with

Zoroaster,[10] (Nyberg, 1938). Similarly, the respected religious scholar R.C. Zaehner, saw the reference in Y.32.14 as not condemning cattle sacrifice, but likewise "a sacrament involving the immolation of the Haoma plant" (Zaehner, 1961). Zaehner notes that the sacrifice of the Bull was not at issue for the Persian reformer, as in Y.29.7 Zoroaster himself refers to the "sacred formula of the oblation of fat," indicating a ritual involving the fat of an animal which had been immolated.

> What Zoroaster actually condemns is not the Haoma ritual as such but some peculiar combination in which the plant appears to have been burnt.... He did not object to the haoma rite as such, but to the daeva-worshippers method of performing it. (Zaehner, 1961)

This view has been shared by other sources as well, "Zoroaster... condemns certain barbarian heretics who 'burn' the Haoma rather than drink it" (Bey, 2004). In *Incense and Poison Ordeals in the Ancient Orient* Allen Godbey expands on this theme, giving even clearer indications as to what was being burnt:

> Zarathustra... was protesting without avail against the ancient Aryan intoxicant haoma or soma. The Sanskrit literature makes this religious narcotic all but omnipotent, and invokes it as a god, a great warrior conquering all enemies of man, a cure for every ill. Among the Iranic peoples this haoma seems to have been bhang, or Indian hemp, for Herodotus (iv. 75) tells us that the

10   As Henrik Nyberg explained of Zoroaster's feud with the Haoma cult in *Irans forntida religioner*:
A new cult broke in to the congregation; it is preached by a man named Grehma – the name may simply mean 'eater of the sacrifice' – and is already accepted by a band that is searching to procure supernatural power through it. The Karapans and the Kavis are roped in to the movement and make themselves spokespeople of the new doctrine, they tempt people to defect from 'the good deed,' in other words from the traditional ecstatic practices of the tribe, and Grehma and his guardians turn against Zarathustra, being the leading man of the old tribal religion, in order to eliminate him. The character of the new cult is completely clear. It consists likewise of ecstatic practices, but of those, by which animals are slaughtered and haoma – 'Todabwender,' *duraosa*, is the regular epithet for haoma in early Avesta - 'is brought to flames.' (Nyberg, 1938)
Although it should be noted that Nyberg also thought that the sacrifice of the animal was a core issue for Zoroaster: "The train of thought in the surprising turn from verse 14 appears to me to be such: it is about the ritual slaughter and consumption of a sacrosanct, divine animal, that, through it's divine nature, should stimulate the intoxicating potion in the human body, let it burn up in the divine fire and therefore facilitate ecstasy" (Nyberg, 1938).

Iranic Scythians... burned Indian hemp in their religious exercises, until bystanders were intoxicated with their fumes. In India the soma was the juice of a certain milkweed in some districts, but others insist that the bruised green leaves of hemp provide the orthodox soma.[11] (Godbey, 1930)

So it was the burning of Haoma that was at issue, which if it were cannabis, as has been suggested by literary, archeological and other historical evidence, would make much more sense. Likewise Gérald Messadié and Marc Romano in reference to "sacrifices and the ritual consumption of haoma" have noted that as this was the long-standing practice to which Zoroaster would have been exposed to from the early stages of his life onwards. "In his youth Zoroaster may have participated in the ecstatic hemp ceremonies of Scythian shamans" (Messadie & Romano, 1996). In a rejection of these cultic activities the "Zoroastrian cult banned the use of intoxicants and haoma (soma), probably the old Persian name for hashish" (Bowles, 1977).

The Scythians, as discussed in Chapter 7, burned cannabis and inhaled its fumes as well as prepared the Haoma beverage from it. From the descriptions of their religious practices it is clear they were practicing the older pre-Zoroastrian form of Persian polytheistic nature worship. As Victor Sarianidi notes: "In the Avesta one finds numerous references to the fact the settled Zoroastrians had constant contacts with the nomadic Scythians who are mentioned under the name of Saka in the ancient Persian inscriptions.... The Scythian element played an important role in Zoroastrianism and... it... emerged in direct contact with the Scythian environment"[12] (Sarianidi, 1998).

---

11   As noted earlier in Chapter 4, the Vedic scholar Dr. N.R. Warhadpande points out that references to soma as samiddha, i.e., kindled and as being 'blown' or 'puffed' puzzled the Indian historian Sayana (died 1387), in his own quest to understand the identity of Soma, and if Sayana had known that Soma was hemp, suggests Warhadpande, he would not have been confounded by the description of it being smoked as now it is common practice to smoke *bhanga* as well as drink it (Warhadpande, 1995).

12   Sarianidi refers to the fluctuating relationship between the Scythians and their Iranian kin, "...in the second millennium B.C., in Margiana the relations between the settled steppe cultures were characterized by peaceful and neighbourly manners, but the situation could have changed in the Scythian period, that is in the middle of the first millennium B.C. That was the time of hostility which can be explained in different ways. From the point of view of archaeology, this change was mainly caused by the fact that due to the natural change of the ancient delta of the Murgab River, people in Margiana also moved far to the southwest. The complete absence of any Scythian traces on the new

It seems clear that it was this older practice of burning Haoma, as had been done by the Scythians and their ancestors for millennia, which the "new" Zoroastrian religion was rallying against, rather than a new competing cult that was burning Haoma, as Nyberg (1938) suggested in footnote 314.[13] Godbey's comments about the Scythian's burning hemp/Haoma in relation to those of Zaehner's and Y.32.14 give clear indications that this was the core issue for Zoroaster's reforms.[14] Further identification of cannabis is given in Y.32.14 reference to its fibrous qualities "The 'glutton' and the 'poets' deposit their guiding thoughts here in this cord work."

Thus Zoroaster's reforms are on par with those of the earlier Hebrew reformer Moses, who similarly rallied against the influences of the polytheistic Canaanite fertility cult in the Golden Calf incident.[15] Gone from Zoroastrian worship were the Old Gods and orgiastic rites, all future Haoma sacrifice would come via the pla-

---

Margiana lands can be explained by the fact that they did not follow the tribes of farmers but stayed behind on their old lands. The territorial separation could have gradually led to the end of the former neighborly contacts and finally to hostilities. As a result, the Scythians arranged raids on the farming oases aiming to steal their cattle. This situation could have found its reflection in the Avesta. But one should bear in mind that most likely this was the fight between two branches of Iranian tribes: nomad Scythians and settled tribes…" (Sarianidi, 1998).

13   In this relation it should be noted that Widengren identified the same cultic group, referred to by Nyberg as a new element, as represnaive of older cultic practices through their association with Yima, an ancestral figure associated with Haoma, who was demonized in Zoroaster's reforms: "In one Gatha, Zarathustra launches a sharp attack on the ancestral king and sapient Yima, because it was he, who gave them pieces of beef to eat. This Yima is… a great hero of the male society and he performed as a sort of carnival king at the annual festival, which was celebrated by his loyal young warriors. As Zarathustra turned against Yima's slaughtering of the bull, he rejected the rites of the male society. The same is the case, when he strictly opposes the holy, long-standing patrimonial potion of intoxication, that 'keeps death at bay,' duraosa, haoma, the counterpart of the Indian soma potion. Grehma is mentioned as a representative of this cult that is disapproved of with horror by Zarathustra (assuming that an individual person is really meant with this word, otherwise this name refers to a group or a class)" (Widengren, 1965).

14   A contributing factor may have been that Zoroaster, as a fire worshipper, would have also been upset by the making of smoke, which was viewed as an impure element in the sacrificial fire. This was one of the reasons for continued animal sacrifice, the fat could be burned with almost unperceivable smoke.

15   Indeed, there are a number of profound similarities between Zoroaster and Moses; both received revelations from a plant-god, Moses the Burning Bush, Zoroaster – Haoma; both had to flee a their homelands after taking up their missions; both led violent reforms against paganistic fertility cults; both are credited with usurping Polythiesm with Monotheism (with Zoroastrian, a sort of dualism); both used cannabis for shamanic purposes; both restricted cannabis use to an elite class.

cebo sacrament void of its former entheogenic effects, and offered ritualistically to Zoroaster's one supreme God, Ahura Mazda:[16]

> Let them go away from here,
> old gods and deceptive females![17]
> ...here in this home, in which Ahura Mazdâ is sacrificed to,
> which (is that) of Haoma, conveyor of/through Order.
>
> Y.10.1

In this transference Indra a revered deity of the old pantheon, and the former celebrated recipient of Soma offerings, becomes in Zoroastrianism the leader of "false gods" (which refers to virtually all gods other than Ahura Mazda, Zoroaster's supreme deity). "Indra was undoubtedly associated with *Haoma*... in this religion against which Zarathustra rebelled – Indra is invoked by the Mitanni Aryans in 1380 B.C.[18] – but he was dethroned and made a demon by Zarathustra" (Parpola, 1995). In the *Vendidad*, Indra is identified as one of the six chief demons; thus, in the eyes of Zoroaster and his new faith, Indra is the opponent of order, truth, and righteousness.

> From what has been stated, it clearly emerges that the appearance of Zarathustra in the ancient Arian milieu, that is widely similar to the Vedic-Indian, brought with it a complete upheaval. Zarathustra arises as a representative of a new religion contrary to the ancient Aryan religion. Not only that he condemned bloody sacrifices and haoma intoxication, but rather with him we seek the ancient names of deities in vain. They were replaced by spiritual entities, the so called *Amesa Spentas*, the 'holy immortals.' After the

---

16   In later times, the rite was transferred to Mithra, a popular Mazdian deity that re-emerged after the time of Zoroaster.

17   Likely a reference to the cult prostitution of the older Iranian religion. According to Jafarey, in the pre-Zoroastrian religion women were "reduced to serve the male priests and pilgrims as temple prostitutes, remnants of which one finds in the so-called 'Devadasis' of southern India" (Jafarey, 2000). The prominent role the cult priestess/prostitutes played is likely indicated by the following verse (Y.10.15): "I relinquish the aperture of the woman, the villainess, whose dirt has not been removed, who thinks she is deceiving the priest and Haoma, she who (herself, however,) deceived goes to perdition, she who sits down devouring the draonah which belongs to Haoma. (Haoma) does not give her priests as sons, nor indeed any good sons."

18   The Treaty of Mitanni c. 1,380 B.C. invokes gods important to the Persian ancestors of the Zoroastrians: Mitra and Varuna, Indra and the two Nasatyas. In the Greek cosmology this translated into the Fire/Sun god, Mitra (Helios / Apollo), the Sky-god, Varuna (Uranus) and Thunder-god, Indra (Zeus).

> results of the latest research, it can certainly no longer be doubted
> that the *Amesa Spentas* represent a spiritualising reinterpretation
> of the gods of the Indo-Iranian society. (Widengren, 1965)

Although some figures from the earlier pantheon remained on as the *Amesa Spentas*, many more of the other long-standing Aryan deities, such as Indra the original Lord of Soma, were transformed into demons through the words of Zoroaster and the cult which formed around his teachings.

The difficulty of many Zoroastrians in accepting the evidence of the reality of Zoroaster's reforms of the Haoma ritual, in light of its continued use, is on par with that of Christians who have a hard time reconciling the conflicting texts of the Old and New Testament, with the wrathful, jealous Jehovah of the Old, and the forgiving father of the New. In the case of the Bible, it is clearly due to the texts being composed by different authors, from different times, with different religious beliefs and practices. As Dr. Ali Jafarey explains, "The same holds true about the Avesta, 'the Sacred Books of the Zoroastrians'" (Jafarey, 2000).

Like many ancient myths and religious texts, it is likely that the accounts in the *Avesta* were passed down as an oral tradition, a reason for them being in verse, long before they were written down, which likely first took place "during the Achaemenian period (550-330 BCE) when the Iranians learned how to read and write" (Jafarey, 2000).

In 321 BCE the collection suffered a disaster from Alexander's invasion of Iran, which put an end to the Achaemenian Empire, and devastated the royal treasuries in which the *Avesta* was reportedly kept. During the Parthian period (250 B.C.-224 A.D.), an effort began to collect what remained in scattered records and the memories of the priest class. This considerable task was completed and the collection was collated, augmented, and canonized centuries later during the reign of the Sassanian King Chosroes I in about 560 A.D.. There was a Pahlavi translation and commentary created for every Avestan text and it was these Pahlavi renderings which the later priests counted on for expounding the religion. As the original language of *Avesta* became less and less utilized, it eventually became a mystical divine dialect that was not only unknown to the common people, but even the Sassanian and post-Sassanian priests.

The collapse of the theocratic Sassanian Empire in 651 CE left the Zoroastrian church without its dominating royal support, and the whole system, including the Avestan and Pahlavi scriptures, began to fall apart. Nevertheless much of the collection survived as late as the 10th century CE, a period during which many of the Pahlavi scriptures were written—also revised to suit the times—in a rather salvage operation. It is estimated that between one-third to one-fourth of the entire collection has been salvaged. The extant Avesta, mostly religious, has been *re-shaped*, somewhat casually, sometimes after the 10th century, to make a little more than six books. (Jafarey, 2000)

Jafarey suggests that the *Gathas*, the texts attributed directly to Zoroaster "miraculously suffered no loss. We have the entire divine message of Zarathushtra—fresh and inspiring—in the very words of the Teacher, *a feature none of the ancient religions can boast of...* The... *Gathas...* [are] the only doctrinal documents and... the remaining parts of the extant Avesta and Pahlavi writings... have their ethical, historical, geographical, and anthropological values. They are, nevertheless, of significant help in better understanding the Staota Yesnya from philological and sometimes philosophical points of view. And they a part and parcel of the rich Iranian Heritage" (Jafarey, 2000).

The... post-Gathic period, clearly shows that Zarathushtra... [the author] of the Gathas, did not recite any "Yasna Liturgy" to perform the *haoma* ceremony. He only sang his Gathas, the only liturgy, before a fire-altar. It also shows the way the traditional priests brought in their age-old haoma cult into the Good Religion. This time it was not *'bhang'* or another strong intoxicant but a very mild substitute, *ephedra*. The Yasht mentions this mildness: 'Indeed all other intoxicants (*maidhyâongho*) are accompanied by wrath of the bloody standard but the intoxicant (*madho*) of Haoma has the right calm following it. Its intoxication gives lightness.' It is acknowledged as an intoxicating drink and is compared with other intoxicants. The substitute "Ephedra" was soothing, indeed. Haoma was re-introduced to continue to be 'central to the [expanded] Yasna liturgy'! (Jafarey, 2000)

As Jafarey tried to explain to his detractors "No one is <<attacking the ritual use of Haoma.>> It has already been attacked and well attacked. Zarathushtra was/is the first, foremost, and best to attack the ritual and/or any other use of the *haoma dûraosha*, the wisdom wasting drink" (Jafarey, 2000).

> It is true that haoma was an integral part of the Daevayasna rituals. It is true that since the composition of the Later Avesta, particularly the Haoma Yasht (Yasna 9-11), *haoma* (the substitute) has been <<central to the Yasna liturgy.>> It is true that in the Gathas, the original Haoma, *bhang* or any other instant intoxicant, stands rejected and condemned. It is equally true that the Sublime Songs, with their simple and sublime rituals, cannot accommodate the elaborate Haoma ceremony in any form. (Jafarey, 2000)

Dr. Jehan Bagli[19] sees the Haoma sacrifice as "one of the most controversial and debated" rituals of the Zoroastrian religion.

> The *Haoma* plant has a checkered history associated with it. Although the original identity of the plant has obliterated through the antiquity, the plant is generally regarded as one of *ephedra* species. It is clearly evident from the *Haoma* yasht that the consecration of *Haoma* is a pre-Zarathushtrian ritual. However history has evolved it as a central sacrament in the Zarathushtrian traditional ritual. The twigs of *haoma* plant are ceremonially consecrated for use in the preparation of *parahaoma*. It is the enactment of straining of the crushed *haoma* and the pomegranate twigs with consecrated water that constitutes the ritual of *parahaoma*. The symbolism of the pounding and filtering of the juice through the recital of four *Ahunavar* is explained as the birth of the four apostles: Zarathusht and his followers to be Hushedar, Husheder-mah, and Soshyos bringing the Good Daena to the humanity. (Bagli, 2005)

Thus, we can see that certain members of the Zoroastrian religion acknowledge that the Haoma was at one time a psychoactive sacrament, but was later replaced with the current placebo, void of the entheogenic properties of its former counterpart. As Prof. Victor Sarianidi explained:

> The linguists long ago noticed that in the ancient parts of the *Avesta* it is said that in the beginning the Prophet rejected this

---

19   Bagli has testified on behalf of the Zoroastrian religion as an expert witness in a US court in a case against a group, the Church of Cognizance, that was using cannabis as the Haoma, see Chapter 20.

narcotic beverage but then it was included in his religious doctrine as one of its main cults. Some authors qualify this fact as a
"restoration of the 'pre-Zoroastrian' ritual"... Indeed, judging by
the Margiana temples, this ritual beverage played almost the primary role in the religious ideas of Iranian paganism and if the
Prophet had denied its role, he would have risked losing his followers. It seems that this was the compelling reason that made
Zoroaster change his first decision and include this beverage as
one of the main ritual ceremonies of his doctrine.

    ...Zoroaster was the product of the pagan community that was
represented by that part of Iranian paganism which is best studied on the basis of the... material of Margiana and Bactria...The
temples of Margiana and Bactria substantiate that the main cults
that were practiced in this area were: (1) fire worship, (2) the libation of hallucinogenic drinks of the soma-haoma type, (3) and
probably, the worship of water. In other words, the same cults
that later became the main elements of the origin of Zoroastrianism. (Sarianidi, 1998)

As the German researcher Geo Widengren explained, in his *Die
Religionen Irans*, of this contradictory situation regarding Haoma's
combined sanctity and disdain in the Zoroastrian religion:

It is significant for the syncretism of the post-Zarathustrian period that the haoma cult, fervently disputed by Zarathustra, recovered a central position in the cultic life. In those Yasna appears
a section dedicated to haoma, which is referred to as *Hom-Yast*
and encompasses Y. 9-11: 12; here it certainly does not concern a
standard literary composition.

    When Zarathustra 'fixed' the fire and recited the Gathas, as
it is told in Y. 9:1, haoma came to Zarathustra. A dialogue un-
folded between the two. Zarathustra initially asks for the name of
the arrival. Haoma reveals itself and advises Zarathustra to collect, press and bless it. The prophet then asks which people have
pressed it and which blessing will be bestowed upon them. The
poem is presented as such that over its course, Zarathustra himself becomes the narrator:

  Then answered me yon
  The righteous, the obstructing of death haoma:
  Vivahvant was the first human
  To press me for the physical world

This blessing is bestowed upon him
He received this gift of grace:

That to him was born a son
King Yima, the rich of herds
The one with richest beliefs among those born
The one with the sunniest eyes among people

To our astonishment, Yima [who was credited with spreading the use of Haoma] is also mentioned here, whose governance is then portrayed in exuberant words – the Yima, of whom Zarathustra could not express himself harshly enough.[20]

However it gets worse: In Y. 11:4-7 commandments are given about the shares of the sacrifice, that show as clearly as conceivable, that the drinking of haoma is still linked to bloody sacrifices, which Zarathustra had just so harshly criticized. We can see here how not only the divine figures but also the cult of the pre-Zarathustrian era was allowed access to Zarathustra's religion. The resistance however was obviously strong and lead to different compromises – also within the domain of the cult. Indeed haoma, as it appears, was completely accepted – still today it is found in the Mazdayasnian congregations. Haoma though disappeared in the form of an intoxicating potion and was replaced by a harmless and probably no more flavoursome as stimulating blend of plant juice, water and milk, *parahom*. In all likelihood however, the congregation lead an incessant fight against the bloody sacrifices, which resulted in the outright victory of the view and practice of Zarathustra; for the sacrifices cannot be found in today's congregation.

Through its report of the conversation between Zarathustra and Haoma, the Hom-Yast obviously has the intention to motivate the introduction of the haoma potion in to the Zoroastrian cult. Is it plausible that this compromise, this 'denatured' haoma, goes back to the personal initiative of Zarathustra? That would not be inconceivable. However, peculiarly in this case it would be so that the Hom-Yast portrays Zarathustra only as fixing the

---

20   "From the outset, Yima, as an Indo-Iranian figure, does not belong to Zoroastrianism, but also not to the national traditions inherited from Zarathustra. Rather on the contrary: in Y.32: 8, Zarathustra expresses a very derogatory opinion about Yima, because he persuaded people to eat beef. Otherwise, it is said that Vivahvant, Yima's father, was the first to press haoma in order to have Yima as a son (Y. 9: 3-5). The haoma cult is therefore linked with Yima's name, as is the slaughtering of the cow, and one was inclined to see in Yima the representative of a cult that appeared particularly disagreeable to Zoroastrianism and to implicate him in the Mithra worship frowned upon by the eldest Zoroastrianism" (Widengren,1965). [Translated by Jake Czerpak]

fire and Gathas as chanting. Does this happen therefore because the tradition in contrast was alive, so that the founder contented himself with both of these rites at worship? Then one had particular difficulties in defending haoma. Zarathustra left behind only stark words about haoma in the Gathas. If he would have taken on a more positive stance later on, what would have possibly been easier than introducing him as a worshipper of haoma? This however did not happen. (Widengren, 1965)

Widengren came very close, as he acknowledged Zoroaster's own use of hemp, but the collected research also indicates that cannabis was part of the original Haoma sacrament.[21] Clearly Zoroaster instilled prohibitions against the plant's use in the Iranian cult and then later a placebo version of the originally entheogenic potion appeared in Zoroastrian ritual use. But, as shall be discussed in the next Chapter, there are a number of references in Zoroastrian literature that clearly indicate Zoroaster continued to use cannabis himself for shamanic purposes, as well as in the initiations of his select chosen few. As Eliade noted, "Zoroastrian reform was directed against wild ecstasy but the younger Avestan priests, reintroduced the use of *bang, mang* and hom..." (Eliade, 1987).

> Haoma curses the eater:
> May you have no offspring and be followed by bad fame,
> who keep me for yourself when pressed,
> as (if I were) a thief whose head is forfeit.
> For my head is not forfeit,
> mine, the Orderly death-averting Haoma.
>
> Y.11.3

---

21   This view, however, was not shared by Henrik Nyberg, who believed that Haoma was an alcoholic beverage (unlikely) and its reintroduction in later Zoroastrian times, resulted in the disappearance of cannabis, see Appendix D.

15

BHANGA; ZOROASTER'S GOOD NARCOTIC

In these times of ecological disaster and potential global war, it is hard not to get caught up in the Apocalyptic visions of Judgment Day popularized in the modern day Christian Mythos. Interestingly the concept of the 'end of the world' and a 'Judgment Day' aren't ones that originated in the Bible, but come from the ancient Persian cosmology. In fact many other so-called Christian beliefs such as Heaven and Hell, a coming Savior, the Devil, all have their origins in the ancient Persian tradition. Even more interesting is that the ancient Persian shamans who had the visions in which these concepts originally occurred were stoned out of their gourds on psychedelic doses of cannabis when they had them.... In fact the Persian Magi were so adept at the use of magical plants that they have been referred to as "the great drug peddlers of the ancient world."[1]

Part of the reason for the confusion regarding Zoroaster's relationship with Haoma has to do with the fact that another plant name begins to take precedent in the Magi literature at the time of Zoroaster's prohibitions, *banga*, a term that is still in use to this day in both Persia and India (*bhang*), and is generally used to describe cannabis and its products, although this has not always been the case. As with the identification of Haoma and Soma, there is indeed controversy surrounding the identity of the plant designated by *banga*, and its Pahlavi counterpart *mang*. As Gnoli explains of the situation in *Encylopedia Iranica*:

> BANG (Middle and New Persian; in Book Pahlavi also *mang*, Arabicized *banj*), a kind of narcotic plant. In older Arabic and Persian sources *banj* is applied to three different plants: hemp

---

1   (Allegro 1980).

(*Cannabis sativa* or *indica*), henbane (*Hyoseyamus niger*, etc.), and jimsonweed (*Datura stramonium*). The effects of these three narcotic plants vary something which may explain the widely differing descriptions of *bang* in the Middle Persian texts. In modern Persian *bang* is hashish.

In the Middle Persian texts *bang* (*mang*) is described sometimes as a lethal and sometimes as a hallucinogenic drug. Thus, when Ahriman attacked the creation, Ohrmazd gave the primordial bull a "medicinal" *mang* (*mang bēšaz*) to lessen its injury. The bull immediately became feeble and sick and passed away (*Bundahišn* , tr. chap. 4.20). However, bang was also an ingredient of the "illuminating drink" (*rōšngar xwarišn*) that allowed Wištāsp to see the "great *xwarrah*" and the "great mystery." This *mang ī wištāspān* (Pahlavi Vd. 15.14; *Ardā Wirāz-nāmag* 2.15) was mixed with *hōm* (*Dēnkard* 7.4.85) or wine (*Pahlavi Rivayat* 47.27). It was an integral part of the ecstatic practice aimed at opening the "eye of the soul" (*gyān čašm*; Gnoli, pp. 414ff., 435ff.) and was therefore drunk by Ardā Wirāz (*Ardā Wirāz-nāmag* 1.20, 2.9, 15, 16) before his journey into the other world (Gignoux, p. 152 n. 4; cf. Vahman, p. 14 n. 9). (Gnoli, 1979)[2]

The *Bhang, Mang* Debate

As Gnoli's comments indicate, there is considerable confusion regarding *bhang* and *mang*, regarding both its use and identity. In 1938 the renowned Swedish Orientalist and historian of religion, Henrik Samuel Nyberg wrote the following regarding the role of *bhanga* in the Zoroastrian religion, which he identified with cannabis, as had a number of other historians:

Now hemp (bangha, banha) really appears in the Avesta. In the Gathas it is not found, but in the Fravasi-yast, that contains long

2   Bibliography : H. W. Bailey, "Ambages Indo-iranicae," AION-L 1, 1959, pp. 113-46. W. Belardi, *The Pahlavi Book of the Righteous Viraz*, Rome, 1979. Ph. Gignoux, *Le livre d'Ardā Vīrāz*, Paris, 1984. G. Gnoli, "Ašavan," in *Iranica*, ed. G. Gnoli, Naples, 1979, pp. 387-452. W. B. Henning, *Zoroaster, Politician or Witch-doctor?*, London, 1951 . H. S. Nyberg, *Die Religionen des alten Iran*, Germ. tr. H. H. Schaeder, Leipzig, 1938, pp. 177f., 290f., 341f. Idem, *A Manual of Pahlavi II*, Wiesbaden, 1974, p. 125. F. Vahman, *Ardā Wirāz Nāmag*, London and Malmö, 1986. G. Widengren, "Stand und Aufgaben der iranischen Religionsgeschichte," *Numen* 2, 1955, pp. 47-132. Idem, *Die Religionen Irans*, Stuttgart, 1965, pp. 70ff. Idem, "Révélation et prédication dans les Gāthās," in *Iranica*, ed. G. Gnoli, Naples, 1979, pp. 339-64. Idem, *Göttingische Gelehrte Anzeigen* 231, 1/2, 1979, pp. 56ff. (review of B. Schlerath, ed., *Zarathustra*, Darmstadt, 1970, with reference to K. Rudolph, "Zarathuštra-Priester und Prophet," ibid., pp. 270-313, reprinted from *Numen* 8, 1961, pp. 81-116).

lists of the members of the Zoroastrian ancient congregations, a man emerges with the meaningful name Pouru-bangha 'possessing much hemp.' (Nyberg, 1938)

As shall be discussed, Nyberg went on to describe the use of cannabis by a variety of Zoroastrian heroes, as well as detailing the later rejection of the ritual use of cannabis by the Parsi, as indicated in the surviving Zoroastrian documents. Considering that cannabis is known both in Indian and Persia under the name *bhang*, *banj*, *bang*, and various related names, and this interpretation of the Avestan texts seems clear upon a first reading, as time went on, the matter has become considerably confused. Finnish researcher Peenti Aalto has summarized some of the international debate and controversy regarding the Zoroastrian references to bhanga and its later Pahlavi counterpart *mang*:

In the opinion of Henning[3]... the derivative of Indian hemp called *bang* became known in Iran only in the eleventh century of our era as a result of the Muslim conquest and its name is also a loan from India. There had, however, been an indigenous word *bang* 'henbane,' while the Avestan word *banha* is very unlikely to be connected with Pahlavi *mang* and Persian *bang*. Mayrhofer[4]... states that the relationship between these Indian and Iranian words cannot be considered settled. The confusion is increased by the German word *Bangenkraut* (=*Cicuta virosa* 'cowbane' or *Conium maculatum* 'hemlock'?), a poisonous plant with an etymologically obscure name. Interestingly enough, in the Rig Veda IX 61,13 *bhanga* is used when speaking of Soma, though the translators seem to render it by "breaker," originating from the verb *bhanj-*, *bhanakto* 'to break.' In the Bundahisn *mang* ~ *bang* is a lethal poison: IV 20... (God wanted to save the Cow from the painful death which the Evil Spirit was preparing for her) 'before he (the Evil Spirit) came to the Cow, Ohrmazd, gave medical (Anklerasia translated "healing") *mang*, to the Cow to consume... (and) she passed away.'
    Even McKenzie,[5]... *bang* and... *mang*, translates both as 'henbane.' Lewin[6]... explains *ganja* as the blossoms of the unfertilized female *Cannabis Indica*, *bhang* the pulverized leaves of resinous female plant, *majun* sweets from hemp with opium or datura,

---

3   *Zoroaster, Politician or Witch-doctor* (Oxford, 1951).
4   *Kurzgefasstes etymologisches Wortenbuch des Altindischen* (1956-1980).
5   *Concise Pahlavi Dictionary* (London, 1971)
6   *Phantastica* (Berlin, 1927)

etc. Munkacsi[7]... connects *bhanga*... with FU Mordvinian *pango*, [mushroom] etc. Setala repeated this in 1914...

Nyberg[8] explained (Mannual II) *banjak* 'hemp' and a *mang* 'a narcotic.' *Banga* was not mentioned in the oldest part of the *Avesta*, but in the *Frawasi Yast* (13, 124) a personal name occurs, *Pourubhanga*, 'possessing much hemp ~ henbane.' In the Yast 19,20 it is stated that Ahura Mazdais 'without dreams and without hemp': *a-hwafna abi a banha*, or, according to Henning [1951]... 'not subject to sleep, not liable to perish'... In the Videvdat 16,14 *banha* is mentioned as a demoniac plant since it was used to provoke abortion. Mayrhofer [1956-1980] seems to leave it undecided whether bangha is derived from cannabis through a metathesis or not... In any case, Vasmer[9]... derives Russ. *pen'ka* 'Cannabis' from *bangha*. (Aalto, 1998)

In relation to the Russian term for cannabis, *pen'ka*, and the Mordvinian *pango* (mushroom), it should be noted that even R. Gordon Wasson took part in this etymological cunundrum, coming into it through the etymology of the Ostyak term "*panx*" meaning "mushroom, Fly agaric":

In the name *panx* of this narcotic we recognize the Old Persian word *banha-*, whose meaning, according to Bartholomae... is the following '1. Name of a plant (and its juice) which was also used for producing abortions; 2. Name of a narcotic made from that plant and also a designation of the state of narcosis produced thereby.' Other instances of the word are: Sanskrit: *bhanga-*, ... meaning 'hemp; a narcotic prepared from hemp seeds'; modern Persian: *bang*, 'hyoscyamus'; Afghan: *bang*, 'hemp'.. From all this we conclude that the... word *panx*, ...[originally meant] 'intoxicating,' 'narcotic,' and that the knowledge of this cultural product... comes from the Aryans... (Wasson, 1970)

Wasson was far from alone in this view, as Mircea Eliade also noted in reference to the term *bangha*:

The importance of the intoxication sought from hemp is further confirmed by the extremely wide dissemination of the Iranian term through Central Asia. In a number of Ugrian languages the

---

7   *KSz: Keleti Szemle*
8   *A Manual of Pahlavi I-II* (Wiesbaden 1964, 1974)
9   *Kritches und Antikritches zur neureen slavischen Etymologie*, Rocznik Slawistcyzny, VI.

Iranian word for hemp, *bangha*, has come to designate both the pre-eminently shamanic mushroom, *Agaricus muscarius*... and intoxication; compare, for example, the Vogul pankh, "mushroom" (*Agaricus muscarius*), Mordvinian *panga*, *pango*, and Cheremis *pongo*, "mushroom." The hymns to the divinities refer to ecstasy induced by intoxication by mushrooms. These facts prove that by the magico-religous value of intoxication for achieving ecstasy is of Iranian origin. Added to the other Iranian influences on Central Asia,... *bangha* illustrates the high degree of religious prestige attained by Iran. It is possible that, among the Ugrians, the technique of shamanic intoxicationis of Iranian origin. (Eliade, 1964)

Fortunately, as Wasson makes no claims that the term *bhanga* originally meant mushroom, and seems to accept Eliade's explanation that it was later adopted and applied to the mushroom, we need not go into details regarding any alleged original connection to the term with the mushroom, as we were forced to do with the Soma/Haoma references. Interestingly though, this adoption of the term *bhanga* for the hallucinogenic mushroom, does make a case for how the name could also have come to be applied and adopted to henbane and other plants as well, as shall be explained shortly.

So now we are dealing with at least 4 different potential botanical candidates for these terms as well, henbane, datura, mushrooms and cannabis... But wait, there is more, added to this is Flattery's suggestion of Syrian rue as *mang*, which he also identified with Haoma, as discussed (Chapter 2). A very confusing situation indeed! We will now try to unravel some of the linguistics and opinions at hand in regard to this.

In many ways, just as the work of R. Gordon Wasson have become a confounding factor in the research of Soma, the work of David Stophet Flattery and Martin Schwartz have become the confusing factor in the discussion around the Zoroastrian references to *mang* and *bhang*. We discussed Flattery and Schwartz's *Haoma and Harmaline* (1989) in Chapter 2, and noted their work connecting the Haoma tradition with Avestan and Pahlavi references to *bhang* and *mang*. Due to the popularity and acceptance of the linguistics put forth in *Haoma and Harmaline* we now need to return to their work again.

In *Haoma and Harmaline*, Flattery suggests that both the Haoma, and *bhang*, in the Zoroastrian references, can be identified with the harmaline producing plant Syrian rue, *Peganum harmala*.

Although it seems likely that Syrian rue, or Harmaline as this duo prefers to have it called, was an additive to incense braziers and other concoctions in the ancient world, the identification of it with *bhang* is wholly hypothetical and unsubstantiated by any historical reference what so ever (as is the duos designation of Harmaline as the Soma/Homa). As noted in Chapter 2 harmaline has very unpleasant side effects when used in amounts large enough to produce hallucinogenic states, As David Flattery himself noted: "The effects actually experienced from a preparation of harmel were well known in Middle Eastern lore: as reported in early Islamic materia medica they are chiefly vomiting, sleep, intoxication, and an inclination toward coitus" (Flattery & Schwartz, 1989). Beyond the effect of a deep sleep, none of these other indications are referred to in either the Avestan or Pahlavian accounts of *bhanga/mang*.

These days Harmala is seldom used as an intoxicant on its own and Syrian rue is usually used in conjunction with other psychedelic substances in order to become active. Harmaline is amongst a few plants that work as MAOIs (Monoamine oxidase inhibitors). MAOIs are particularly used in modern times as a powerful source of anti-depression drugs, but due to potentially lethal dietary interactions, they are generally used as a last resort after other medications have been tried and failed.

As discussed in Chapter 2, Flattery was unable to provide evidence for the role of Syrian rue as an entheogen, and instead pointed to the role of another MAOI in the entheobotanical literature of South America, where the MAOI containing Ayahuasca vine *Banisteriopsis caapi* is mixed with DMT containing plants such as as *Mimosa hostilis*, *Diplopterys cabrerana*, and *Psychotria viridis*. (Without a MAOI, the body quickly metabolizes orally-administered DMT, and it therefore has no hallucinogenic effect). For this reason Haoma and Harmaline was highly criticized by the extremely knowledgeable Jonathan Ott (1993), for not offering evidence of personal experience with Syrian rue, or adequate evidentiary material.

It should also be noted that even in smaller doses strict dietary observances must be met when using MAOI's such as harmaline. Fasting is often a prerequisite for cultures that consume Ayahuasca. Both wine and Cheese in this regard can become quite probalmatic, and ancient references, that shall be discussed, report that the *mang* was drank with wine in both the accounts of Vishtaspa and Ardu Viraf. Moreover, Viraf is described as consuming the *mang* with 3 glasses of wine and a large meal! No mention was made of omitting cheese, so considering the role of cheese amongst the cattle loving Zoroastrians, we can only assume it was included in the feast as well. This combination could have had drastic and potentially lethal results if Syrian rue were taken in the amounts suggested by Flattery.

The Magi would have been very experienced herbalists by this point, and considering the level of their culture we can safely assume that they would have been at least as familiar with the effective use of their plants, as are the tribesman of South America were in the aformentioned use of Ayahahusca, which is genrally consumed with all sorts of dietary taboos directed at lessening the effects of nausea and diareha associated with its use. Niether the nausea associated with high does of Syrian rue, nor the dietary precautions needed to ensure its safe use is indicated in the *Avesta* or Pahvali references to *mang, bhang* or Haoma.

In respect to this, even Flattery's own co-author Martin Schwartz disputed Flattery's identification of *mang* and *bhang* with Syrian rue. In Schwartz's view *mang\bhang* likely had a more generic meaning, "psychotropic substance," but alternatively, one "which could give specific senses 'henbane, datura.'" (Flattery & Schwartz 1989). Schwartz also suggested that the term *mang*, had indications of deception; "It may be assumed that Iranian inherited two homophonous words, **manga* –'deceit, trickery' and **manga...** 'magic potion, hallucinogen'" (Flattery & Schwartz 1989).

As we shall see the more logical and general view is that '*banga*,' '*banha*' and '*mang*,' all with "an" in them, follow in league with other terms for cannabis in languages which originated from Indo-European dialects; English, *cannabis*; French, *chanvre*; German *hanf*; Indian *sana* and *bhang*, Avestic *baṇha* etc..

Beyond the etymological argument, the suggestions of Henbane and Datura, as *mang*, I would argue, are far too toxic to have been the plant ingested in such quantities in the ancient texts. This is especially true of the Avestan and Vedic descriptions of Haoma and Soma which depict a drink that was joyful, healing and taken quite liberally.

The dose-response curve for the combination of alkaloids in Datura is very steep, so people who consume the plant can easily take a potentially fatal overdose, thus its use as a lethal poison. In recent times there have been media stories of adolescents and young adults dying or becoming seriously ill from intentionally ingesting datura for recreational purposes Even when taken in non-toxic amounts, the effects can last for up to 2 days and include such symptoms as intense thirst, headaches, nausea, fever, high blood pressure, dry mucous membranes, difficulty swallowing and speaking, blurred vision, sensitivity to light, confusion, agitation, combative behaviour, and vivid visual and auditory hallucinations.

The toxicity of the plant is even more of an issue with Henbane, the name of which has been said to literally mean "murder-death."[10] In "Henbane - The Insane Seed that Breedeth Madness," Rowan explains that henbane "has a similar effect on the body to that of belladonna which also contains hyoscyamine, although the higher proportion of this alkaloid in henbane produces less of an excitory effect. It also has generally sedative effects on the central nervous system. The results of overdose include dry mouth, dilation of the pupils, restlessness, then hallucinations and delirium leading to coma and ultimately death" (Rowan, 1998). Hardly pleasant! Moreover, henbane would be potentially deadly if taken in the amounts described in both the Avestan and Pahlavian *bhang/mang* and Haoma references. It was for this reason that Iranist Mary Boyce disagreed with Henning's assertion about henbane as *mang*, as it would have killed Ardu Wiraz who drank three cups of *mang* mixed with wine or Haoma in the Pahlavi texts (Boyce, 1982). Henbane is so potentially toxic when taken internally that later European witches developed flying ointments applied topically for shamanic purposes, to avoid the risk of taking it orally.

The Iranist and linguist Walter Bruno Henning in his virulent rejection of H.S. Nyberg's view, put forward that the Avestic *baŋha* and the Middle Persian *mang* did not mean "hemp," and that they instead referred to "henbane." Henning's view was that New Persian bang did not acquire the meaning "hemp" before the 12th century (Henning, 1951). And of the role of cannabis in the Avestan literature? "There is nothing here to show that Zoroaster so much as knew of the existence of hemp" (Henning, 1951). Further, Hen-

10   "Originally henbane was called hen-bell 'death-bell.' Once the meaning *hen- 'murder, death' had been forgotten an association of hen- with the bird hen arose... and the second element was replaced with the word –bane. The resulting compound is... 'death-murder or death-death'" (Liberman & Mitchell, 2008).

ning asserted that it "is very far from certain that the Avestan word banha is connected at all with Pahlavi, *mang*, Persian *bang*" (Henning, 1951). There is little support for this view, as Gnoli points out in regards to this term:

> The word must be etymologically related to Avestan *banha/ bangha* (AirWb., col. 925, in compounds: *abaṇha, Pouru, baṇha, vībaṇha*, see AirWb., cols. 87, 901, 1447) and further to OInd. (Atharvavedic) *bhanga*. This etymological connection was challenged by Henning (pp. 33f.), but unconvincingly (see Widengren, 1955, pp. 66ff.; Boyce, *Zoroastrianism* I, pp. 231 n. 11, 280 with n. 14; Belardi, p. 117). (Gnoli, 1979)

Gnoli refers to the respected German Iranist, Geo Widengren, who disagreed with Henning on a number of points, and agreed with the earlier identification of *bhanga/mang* with hemp, as put forth earlier by Nyberg in 1938.

> The... usage of *bang* (alternatively *mang*) obviously proceeds the Avestan terminology. Indeed it is disputed that *bangha > bang* (*mang*) means (Indian) hemp but this objection is not well-founded in any respect. In actual fact, it can be maintained that the same name, in Iran as well as in Central Asia, can describe various intoxicating substances, where it has spread. It is important to note that in Central Asia the magic-religious meaning of intoxication with ecstatic intentions is after all of Iranian origin. (Widengren, 1965)

The main reasons for Henning's rejection of *bang, banha, mang*, as hemp, has less to do with linguistics and much more to do with Henning's view that cannabis was not toxic enough!

> To come now to the Pahlavi literature, we read in the Bundahahishn that Ahura Mazda gave a dose of *mang* to the Primordial Bull to kill him painlessly, so he should escape the slow death that Ahriman had planned for him. Then there is the story of Arda Viraf... selected as messenger to heaven hell to discover the fate of the soul after death. To speed him on the long and dangerous journey he is to be given a drink of wine mixed with *mang*. At first he refuses the poisonous cup; for he does not wish to die. His seven sisters, whose support he is, implore him to persist in

his refusal; for they know that *mang* is a deadly poison. But it is hoped that God will not accept his sacrifice and will allow his soul to return to the Living. So in the end he allows himself to be persuaded, makes his last will and testament, and performs the last rites as a dying man would do: he drinks the poison and is dead for seven days and nights, then comes to, miraculously, and tells his anxiously waiting friends what he has seen.

In this story I find no trace of any ecstatic practice. The point is that *mang* was a deadly poison: Arda Viraf returned to life in spite of having taken a poison that ordinarily brought certain death; that he survived was a miracle. The view is confirmed by the story in the Bundahishn: The primordial Bull died after swallowing *mang*; he did not gambol and frisk about in ecstasy. Zoroaster would have been ill-advised, had he tried to make a habit of taking *mang*; after the first attempt he would have been no longer in a position to compose any Gaths. Incidentally, the two Pahlavi passages show clear enough that *mang*, whatever it was, was not hemp ; for even a large overdose of the worst derivative of hemp does not kill. (Henning, 1951).

In reference to the non-toxicity of cannabis, and Nyberg's assertion that Zoroaster used the plant, Henning states that in order to understand "how deeply this suggestion must shock those who call themselves Zoroastrians, one has to understand the effects which habitual indulging in hemp produces on the human organism" (Henning, 1951). In reference to this Henning refers to a Dr. Schlimmer, a 19th century Austrian physician, who described how he spent three days attempting to awaken a man "drugged with Indian hemp oil":

In spite of these terrible effects, I have never heard a strictly mortal case; but the repulsive habit of taking the oil of the tops of Indian hemp and various electuaries made from it, in order to secure a moral calmness which lets one envisage all vicissitudes and miseries of human life in an agreeable light, induces in habitual takers a state of remarkable dullness and indolence, which makes them renounce all human decency and delicacy. (Shlimmer, 1874) [11]

After ruling out cannabis due to its non-toxicity, Henning goes on to state that the intoxicating properties of cannabis were un-

---

11   As quoted in (Henning, 1951)

known at the time of Zoroaster and the Iranian term '*bang*' actually means 'henbane' in the Avesta accounts.

> In Persian books *bang* never means anything but 'henbane', at least until the twelfth century... This meaning, of course, is appropriate also to Pahlavi word *mang*, which as we have seen was a deadly poison. (Henning, 1951)

Referring to the early Iranian term which is the basis for '*mang*', *banha*, Henning stated that it "is mentioned in the Avesta with disapproval throughout. The use of *banha*, as a drug employed in producing miscarriage, is prohibited" (Henning, 1951). Here Henning is referring to Vendidad, 15.14, where '*Banga*' appears on a list with some other herbs for inducing abortion:

> And the damsel goes to the old woman and applies to her for one of her drugs, that she may procure her miscarriage; and the old woman brings her some Banga, or Shalta, or Ghnana, or Fraspata or some other drug that produces miscarriage... (*Vendidad*, 15.14)[12]

This reference occurs in conjunction with three other plants, the identity of which are unknown, and it seems the '*banga*' in this passage, was used in conjunction with these. The *Vendidad* gives no clear indication that the *banga* is the poisonous abortive ancient itself, but rather it may have been used with an abortive ancient to help with the abortion, as in this context cannabis would fit, as it conceivably could have been used as a uterine sedative. Cannabis has been used as an aid in childbirth in ancient times, and as a uterine sedative in up to near modern times.[13]

Interestingly, according to some sources the Pahlavi version of this text refers more specifically to the "*mang ī wištāspān* (Pahlavi Vd. 15.14),"[14] 'wištāspān' being a reference to Vishtaspa, who, as shall be discussed shortly, became Zoroaster's first powerful convert after drinking '*mang*'. Alternatively, Darmester, whose translation is used above elsewhere in reference to this same verse, here translating from the Avestan, refers to the "Bang of Zoroaster, Vendidad XV, 14" (Darmesteter, 1883). So clearly even here, where the act of abortion is condemned, it is this particular use that is condemned, not cannabis itself.

12   (Darmesteterr, 1883)
13   I put together a museum collection of cannabis medical bottles and saw first-hand a label for a 'Uterine Sedative' that contained cannabis.
14   http://www.iranica.com/newsite/ - 'Bang'

In noting this reference, Henning omits many other accounts of the term, such as the Den Yasht, 16.14-15, account which refers to it as 'Zoroaster's good narcotic." As De Jong explains, "hemp (Av *ba gha-* Phl. *mang*), which although not spoken of favorably in the Vendidad, is consumed of by some of the holiest men of the Zoroastrian tradition (Vistaspa and Arda Wiraz) and can therefore not have been wholly evil" (De Jong, 1997). Henning's comments below, which clearly detail his prejudices against cannabis, also lead us into some interesting points about the *mang* use by the Zoroastrian figures just mentioned:

> It is well-known that in Persia hemp, with all its derivatives, *bang*, *cars*, or *hasis*, has a particularly bad reputation. A man who is addicted to them is held in universal contempt. I need scarcely remind readers of the story of the Hasisyyin, the Assassins of the twelfth and thirteenth centuries, one becomes inclined to reject Nyberg's suggestion without further consideration. (Henning, 1951)

Interestingly, Henning mentions the assassins, who also are reputed to have used strong preparations of cannabis to induce devotees into a death-like stupor in which they received phantastical visions of the afterlife as did the aforementioned Arda Viraf and other figures after drinking *mang*! In relation it is interesting to point out that it has long been suggested that the "hymns of Zoroaster,... particularly the Haoma Yasht,...might supply a source... of the hasheesh... of the Assassins..." (Carus, 1918). In the cases of both the Assassins' use of hashish and the Zoroastrian's of *mang*, the safety of the psychonauts who took it is attested to. Indeed shortly we will discuss the use of *mang* by a variety of Zoroastrian figures, including the prophet and his good wife, and there are no references to any sort of lethal or toxic effects, as suggested by Henning.

Not surprisingly, a variety of other Iranists disagreed with Henning's designation of *mang*, *bhang* as a "deadly narcotic" or "henbane" (Widengren, 1955; Belardi,1979, Boyce, 1982). As Mary Boyce noted of the *Bundalishin* account referred to by Henning in which Ahura Mazda administered *mang* to the first created ox to ease its pain after it had been put in the throws of death by the evil Ahriman:

> It has been argued that this *mang* was not a sleep inducing narcotic, but a deadly poison [referring to (Henning, 1951)]; but

apart from the contrary Pahlavi occurrences of the word [where it is used safely by devotees]... this interpretation appears impossible on theological grounds. Death is an evil that belongs to Ahriman and it is he who brings it upon the creatures of Ohrmazd. (Boyce, 1982)

According to Harri Nyberg the verse in question refers more specifically to "'Medical *mang*' (*mang besaz*)...Bundahisin 4:20" (Nyberg,1995), which like its counterpart in the Avestan texts *anklerasia* 'healing', would hardly be a good term for a deadly poison. Not surprisingly, many scholars have clearly seen the Bundalishin account as indicating cannabis. In *Persian Mythology* John Hinnels, translates *mang* as cannabis in the Zoroastrian creation myth account where (G Bd. 4.20) Ahura-Mazda (God) gave the first created ox "cannabis [*mang*] to ease her discomforts in the throes of death."[15] Likewise the authors of *The Cambridge History of Iran* record of the reference in this same verse as "*bang*, identified with *mang* (hemp) [used for] inducing unconsciousness" (Fisher, et al., 1993).

Most preposterous of Henning claims is the statement that: "The derivatives of Indian hemp known as *bang*, *hasis* and so on, were not known in Iran anywhere before the eleventh century of our era at the earliest. Aquaintance with Indian hemp is ultimately due to the Muslim conquest of India in the first years of that century" (Henning, 1951).

> The Persian word *bang*, in so far as it means 'Indian hemp', is a loan-word from the Indian term *bhanga*. In Persian – unfortunately – the loan-word collided with an indigenous word *bang* which also designated a plant, namely, 'henbane'. (Henning, 1951)

After going through Henning's sources, it seems he was only able to find references supporting his view as far back as the Islamic period; the rest of his claim is based on his mistaken assumption that *mang/bang* was a potentially toxic substance. Henbane's designations as "*bang*" is clearly the later, and not original situation. Prof. Franz Rosenthal, who was a well known expert in medieval and ancient Middle Eastern cultures and languages, explained: "As is well known, *banj*, in its pre-Islamic history, represented, in fact, 'hemp'" (Rosenthal, 1971). In later times, "Among the Persians the

---

15   (Hinnels, 1973)

Indian name in the form *bang* became the general term for narcotic and was given to the henbane" (Houtsma, et al., 1936/1993). Thus the Persian term for cannabis was later borrowed and applied to henbane, but this happened, in the opinion of Rosenthal and others, after the conquest of Islam.

> ... But in the usage of [*banj* in] Muslim times, it was commonly the scientific word for "henbane" .... Physicians and scientists appear to have been by and large consistent in their usage of *banj* for henbane. Ali b. Rabban at-Tabari in the middle of the ninth century, speaks of three kinds of *banj*.... The three kinds seem to be characteristic of *banj* in the meaning of henbane. (Rosenthal 1971)

Rosenthal's comment on the "three kinds of *banj*" as "characteristic of *banj* in the meaning of henbane," which Dymock (1881), also noted, helps us to identify how the miss-designation of *banj* as henbane came to take place after the rise of Islam.

Diosocrides' *Materia Medica*, Contains a description of henbane (*hyoscycamus*) identifying three kinds, white, black and brown, and all the later Persian descriptions of *banj*, are merely copies of Dioscorides' description, with the older Persian term *bang* mistakenly applied to it. Any interpretation taking the designation of *banj* as henbane, beyond the early Islamic period is purely unfounded speculation. As is explained of the situation in *E.J. Brill's First Encyclopaedia of Islam*, 1913-1936:

> *BANDJ*, A Persian word, originally from the Sanskrit, meaning a narcotic drug, more exactly the henbane (*hyoscycamus*). The meaning of the Sanskrit *bhanga* is really "hemp" (*Cannabis sativa* L.), i.e. the variety which grows in southern climes which contains in the tip of its leaves an intoxicating resinous substance (Arabic hashish), whence the Zend *banha* "drunkenness." In Persian the loan word *bang*... was applied to the henbane and Hunain b. Ishak in his Arabic translation of the *Materia Medica* of Dioscurides (c. ...850) equated it with the Greek... [*hyoscycamus~*henbane] With this meaning the word *bandj* is found in the early Persian medical writers who as a rule write in Arabic... and in more modern Persian medicine... (Xth century) while it appears to be unknown in the old Arabic poetry as al-Biruni in his pharmacology in the article *Bandj* (MS. In the Brussa library) gives no quotations from

the poets, and he would not have omitted to do so. The early physicians of western Islam... also identified *bandj* with henbane... which however Ahamad al-Ghafiki (a Spanish Moorish physician of the (XIIth century) in his pharmacology considers wrong.... In modern times the word *bandj* (in the popular dialect of Egypt *bing*) is used for every kind of narcotic and the verb *bannadja*, 'to narcotize,' infinitive *tabnidj*, "narcosis" etc. derived from it. (Houtsma, et al., 1936/1993)

Thus, an early Islamic period misidentification of henbane, as *bang*, occurred in a popular translation of Diosorides' *Materia Medica*, and this mistake was copied and passed on by later Islamic, and then Western authors. From the above references, it even appears some contemporary sources acknowledged some sort of mistake had been made, as the Moorish physician al-Ghafiki, considered this identification wrong, and earlier poets made no reference to this term. A similar situation happened with Dioscorides' description of hemp:

... All Arab and Persian authors have simply reproduced what Dioscurides says and give hemp, especially the seed, the Greek Syriac loan-name *kinnab* or the arabicized Persian name *shah-danadj* "royal-seed."[16] Not till the... (VIIIth) century was Ibn al Baitar... the first physician to describe the intoxicating effects of *cannabis indica*... which grew in Egypt and there known as *al-hashisha* (the herb). The mendicant dervishes... were particularly given to the use of this drug.... The use of narcotic drugs by dervishes and fakirs was widely disseminated[17]... (Houtsma, et al., 1936/1993)

Although some of the Islamic sources are in agreement with Henning regarding the late introduction of cannabis into the mid-East, like the designation of *banj* as henbane, there was dispute about this as well. Even Henning was forced to acknowledge there

16   Apparently under this name *shad-danaj*, Royal grain, also King's grain "the literary sources seem not to say anything about their use" (Aalto, 1998). It was this word, which only occurs in the Bundashisn XVI:19, on a list of seed and nut oils, as the correct word for hemp in the Pahlavi language. I would argue that it is likely the only word for the nutritious hemp seed, but not the only word for cannabis. Significantly, the seed is referred to as of 'royal' lineage... a clear indication that it may have been a product of the Avestan king of plants, Haoma.
17   As discussed in Chapter 19, the dervish use of cannabis was a remnant of the earlier Zoroastrian tradition of *bangha*.

was confusion on the matter in the early Islamic period. As the authors of *E.J. Brill's First Encyclopaedia of Islam*, 1913-1936, explain of the situation:

> ...according to a Persian authority, the use of hashish was introduced into eastern Persia in the... (XII) century by an Ismaili Shaik Haidar,[18] while another authority says that the use of the intoxicating drugs was already known in pre-Muhammadan times under Khusraw Parwez, [ruled 590-623 A.D.] having been brought from India to Persia and the Irak and even the Yaman. This is really much more probable, as the intoxicating effect of a preparation of hemp was apparently well known in India in ancient time. (Houtsma, et al., 1936/1993)

The 19th century botanist William Dymock also referred to the Persian tradition regarding the introduction of cannabis during the reign of the Sassanian king, Khusraw, but held the view that the use of cannabis in the area was much more ancient:"According to tradition, the use of hemp as an intoxicant was first made known in Persia by Birarslan, an Indian pilgrim, in the reign of Khusru [sic] the First... but... its injurious properties appear to have been known long before that date" (Dymock, 1893).

Khusraw Parwez was a Sassanian King who ruled from 590-628 A.D. "Mazdean tradition... condemns him as an unjust tyrant, responsible for the decline of the religion and the empire" (Yar-Shater, 1983). Thus even in the end period of the Zoroastrian empire, it seems likely that the ancient use of cannabis had continued, and that this was recognized by certain Islamic sources. Thus we are not alone in the opinion that the use of cannabis for its psychoactive purposes in the Arabic world, was a carryover from an older Persian tradition. "Hemp... as an intoxicant... was passed on via Persians, to the Arabs" (Sherratt, 1997).

It should be noted that even during periods of the Zoroastrian use of cannabis, this was not at all a common practice and was far from widespread. Unlike the use of the pre-Zoroastrian Haoma, and its de-natured counterpart after Zoroaster's reforms, which were open to much of the community, the use of *bang/mang* in the Zoroastrian period was strictly prohibited from anyone but the most elite members of that society. The secrecy surrounding

18   See Chapter 19 for more on the Persian Shiek Haidar.

the use of *bang/mang* is likely largely responsible for much of the confusion surrounding the terms *mang* and *bang*. In "Quests and Visionary Journeys in Sassanian Iran," Shaul Shaked notes that the use of *mang* (which he saw as hemp) for visionary quests, "was not a way open to all":

> It was confined to select individuals, who would have regarded themselves as representative of the community, and who would then reveal to the others what they had been privileged to witness. Even for those people this was not a trivial experience that could be undertaken casually or easily repeated. Such journeys were rare occasions, surrounded by grave risks. The danger lay in the very fact that this was the path trodden by the dead, and would have to be brought back to life. Certain encounters along the way may put the power of endurance of the traveler to the test. (Shaked, et al., 1999)

Clearly, such limited and secretive use as this, would have created a situation where few were even aware of the closely guarded secret of the source of Iranian revelation. The secretiveness with which *bang/mang* would have been used throughout the Zoroastrian period was likely further compounded through initial Muslim prohibitions against intoxicants. Further confusion may have arisen to *bhanga's* identity may have occurred in times of shortage, and through its association with other plants used in its stead (as with Soma/Haoma) the term *bhanga* came to be applied to a variety of intoxicating plants.

Undoubtedly, Datura and henbane were, and still are, sometimes added by unscrupulous venders to preparations of *bhang*, to increase the effects of weaker concoctions when good cannabis is not available, and this may have generated confusion at some point. In later Persian times the "*fedayeen*[19] were always described as using *beng*, or hemp, and henbane, mixed" (Burman, 1987). There were definitely distinguishing factors between unadulterated hemp products and preparations made with henbane, as the use of cannabis could be associated "with fits of rage... especially if there is an admixture of any preparation of henbane" (Houtsma, et al., 1936/1993). In reference to the use of hashish in early 20th century Islam it has been noted that "sometimes to increase its intoxicating

---

19   A branch of the Zoroastrian influenced Islamic sect the Isma'ili, also known as the "Assassins."

effect it is mixed with the seeds of the henbane (*hyocyamus muti-cus*, *sekaran*) or *stramonium* (datura)" (Houtsma, et al., 1936/1993). Likewise in India, "Datura… seeds are sometimes mixed with Sidhi (Bhang)…to induce delirous intoxication, and with other narcotics to intensify their actions" (Gerloczy, 1897). In regard to cannabis in India "the question of adulterants, especially datura must always be borne in mind" (Smith & Taylor, 1920).

Conceivably, the name Henbane itself, may have originated as a means of distinguishing this supplemental use from the true '*bang*' cannabis, via '*hen-bang*', becoming "henbane," 'hen- here meaning "death" [20], which would be a distinguishing factor indeed! (although in this linguistical interpretation we would clearly be going against the accepted etymology of '-bane' in this regard). In the Indian world this differentiation is recorded as *Kohi-bhang*:

> *Kohi* (or *Jabali*) *Bhang*; a kind of henbane, smoked and drunk, after being prepared like bhang. It is usually taken by Fakirs and religious mendicants, as it is supposed to produce aberration of intellect. Novices find the contractions of the nerves of the throat caused by it peculiarly painful. (Burton, 1851)

The use of *bhang* to designate intoxicating plants in general seems to be much more identifiable in the Persian language than the Indian, and as the term in both languages is now generally assumed as designating cannabis, it seems unlikely that *bhang* originated as a generic term, and this use of the word developed in later times, otherwise these multiple meanings would have carried over into the Indian language. This linguistic situation has never been adequately explained by any of the researchers who see the term as originating as a generic name for psychoactive plants in general.

Proponents of the 'henbane' theory offer no reasonable examples opposing the more generally accepted view that *mang*, *bang* were references to cannabis, nor do they adequately explain why if this were the case in the ancient world, how the designation of cannabis as *bhanga* came about in both the ancient Persian and Indian dialects. On the other hand a reasonable explanation has been given on how the designation of the Persian term *bang*, meaning 'hemp,' came to be borrowed and corrupted as banj, meaning '*henbane*.'

---

20   "The first element of the plant name henbane seems to go back to the root *hen- 'death,' preserved in the names of places,people and gods."(Liberman & Mitchell, 2008).

"Bhang" as "cannabis" has clearly been the long-standing view; As James Samuelson noted in the 19th century in *The History of Drink*: "A... very deleterious drink called *"banga"* is mentioned in the *Zend-Avesta...* Like the modern *bang*, referred to... in India, it is believed to have been extracted from the hemp plant (*Cannabis sativa*)" (Samuelson,1880). In the *Avesta*, Bleek and von Spiegel recorded, *"Bana* is the *Cannabis sativa*, Skr. *Bhanga"* (Bleek & Spiegel, 1864). As Darmesteter also noted in his translation of the *Zend-Avesta*; *"Banga*, is *bang* or *mang*, a narcotic made from hemp seed" (Darmesteter, 1880).

This designation of *mang, bhang* as identifying cannabis has also been accepted by a variety of Zoroastrian scholars, such as Dr. Jahanian Daryoush, who refers to *bhang* in his essay "Medicine" in *Avesta and Ancient Iran*: "Bangha (Avesta: bhangh, Sanskrit: bhanga, Persian: Bang, hashish) – It is extracted from the seeds of Canabis Indica (hempseed or Per: shahdaneh) has hallucinating effects. In ancient Iran it was mixed with wine to deliver anesthesia" (Daryoush, 2005). As Parvaneh Pourshariati has also noted more recently in the *Decline and Fall of the Sassanian Empire*, "mang – a mixture of hemp and wine, with intoxicating properties" (Pourshariati, 2008). Referring to the variation of the 'b-' in the Avestan, to the 'm-' in the Pahlavian, the authors of the *Annual of Armenian Linguistics* used the following examples, which also identify hemp with the terms in question, "Zoroastrian Pahl. *mang, bang* 'hemp.' Old Indian *bhanga-*; *mag-, bag-* 'to intoxicate'" (Cleveland State University, 1987). As also noted by other Zoroastrian scholars; *"Bhanga...* or *mang*, a narcotic made from hempseed... the dried leaves and small stalks of *Cannabis indica"* (Dubash, 1903); "hemp (Av *ba gha-* Phl. *mang*)" (De Jong, 1997).

E.J. Brill's First Encyclopaedia of Islam 1913-1936, records; BENG, (Sanskr. *bhanga*, Avest. *Banha*, Pahl. *bang, mang*, hemp), strictly the name of various kinds of hemp" (Houtsma, et al., 1987).[21] In reference to Zoroastrian expeditions into the world of the afterlife, Shaul Shaked noted that "The preparation of this journey was done... by administering to the officiant a dose of *mang* (hemp), mixed with wine" (Shaked, 1999). "Zoroaster is commonly said to have spiked the haoma with mang, which was probably hashish. It

---

21   Although, it should be noted this particular reference is not exactly clear cut, as the authors list "hemp (*Hysoscyamus niger*)," so here there may be a case of mistaking the term 'hemp' for henbane! This shows just how confusing the situation has become.

would have prolonged the intoxication and further stimulated the imagination of the drugged man. Of such are the wonders of Heaven" (Oliver, 1994). In the Zoroastrian tale *"...the Artak Viraz Namak...* Hell, Purgatory, and Heaven, the rewards bestowed on the good, and the punishment awaiting the sinner are here described in a vision induced by hashish" (Campbell, 2000). Referring to this same account, van Baaren and Hartman also noted the hero "imbibes an intoxicant composed of wine and hashish and after this his body sleeps for seven days and nights while his soul undertakes the journey" (van Baaren & Hartman,1980). 19th century author James Francis Katherinus also refers to the "enlightening prophet drug Bangha (Cannabis Indica), the Hashish by which the Zoroastrian priests were inspired" (Hewitt, 1901) This was also the view of Nyberg (1938), whose work we have discussed, and the German Iranist, Geo Widengren (1965), as well as more recent researchers:

> The *Zend-Avesta*, the holy book of Zoroastrianism, which survives in fragments, dating from around 600 BCE in Persia, alludes to the use of *Banga* in a medical context, identified as hemp.[22] (Russo, 2005)

As well, in regard to the claim there was no awareness of hemp's intoxicating properties till the 11th century, this is discounted by the works of the 5th century north Armenian monk Eznik, who lived amongst the Zoroastrians (and preached against their religion). Eznik was clearly familiar with cannabis, referring to its medicinal value, as well as a treatment for "wantonless" (Eznik , Book I. 68).[23]

Possibly, having followed up on Henning's research regarding *mang*, Flattery and Schwartz saw that the references Henning cited didn't really take the identification of banj as henbane any earlier than the Islamic period. Thus in order to make their case, the coauthors decided to take it a step further, and included ancient India, with a claim that the intoxicating properties of hemp were unknown until the early medieval period there as well!: "With regards to 'hemp' called bhanga and sana in Sanskrit, there is no evidence for its use as an intoxicant in either India or Persia before well within the Islamic era" (Flattery & Schwartz, 1989).

In the case of the term *'sana',* Flattery and Schwartz were either unaware of, or decided not to refer to, the *Satapatha Brahmana*

---

22   (Darmester, 1895)
23   (Blanchard, et al., 1998)

(3.4.3.13; 4.2.5.15-17) references, which refers to the "plant Usana, [prefix 'u-' – '-sana' (hemp)]'... they fetch it hither and press it; and by means of the consecration... they make it into Soma." [24]

In the case of the Indian references to *bhang*, Flattery and Schwartz decided against identifying this with henbane, as there seems to be no evidence for the use of henbane in ancient India:

> Henbane, though a native of the Himalayas, was probably unknown as a medicine to the ancient Hindu physicians. "Parasika-yamani" and "khorasam-yamani," the names which it bears in some recent Hindu books, indicate its foreign source. Mahometan writers call it "banj," an Arabic corruption of the Persian "bang." (Dymock, 1881)

Instead, in regard to the Indian references, Flattery and Schwartz claim all early Indian mentions of the term only refer to the fiber of the cannabis plant. The Duo even take this view regarding the *Atharvaveda*, reference to *bhang* as being amongst herbs that release one from anxiety and under the dominion of the God Soma,[25] stating that this identifies the hemp plant's fibrous qualities and are "due to its use as a traditional means of binding... it is also a means of fastening amulets,"[26] which would seem to have little reference to the plant's use as a medicine against anxiety as described in the *Atharvaveda*. Indeed the authors offer little in way of evidence for their novel interpretation that the passage makes reference to fiber.

> The dismissal of hemp, as being purely used for fiber or "binding" and not burning, would seem to contradict the meticulous research of Flattery.... That a culture obsessed with psychoactive plants and fire rituals would be ignorant of *Cannabis* as either a fuel or entheogen would seem patently absurd, especially as it is mentioned explicitly in the Atharva-Veda in the context of Soma, and has an ancient use in the region... (Dannaway, 2009)

Flattery and Schwartz then refer to a Vedic passage that makes direct reference to *bhang* as an epithet of Soma, with the correct etymology that *bhang* originally meant "smashing, breaking

---

24   Translated from the Sanskrit by Julius Eggeling (1885).

25   "We tell of the five kingdoms of herbs headed by Soma: may it and the Kusha grass, and bhanga and barley, and the herb Saha release us from anxiety" (*Atharvaveda*).

26   Flattery and Schwartz fail to note that the stalks of the Homa were woven together and worn as a ritual amulet.

through,"[27] but then continue with the statement that this "numinous epithet with its victorious resonances, could have been another factor in the naming of the hemp *'bhanga*,' although the fact that *bhanga* occurs with regard to soma only in a single, contextually conditioned passage makes a connection questionable. In any event, it can be concluded that bhanga, as either as a name of hemp or an epithet of soma, is independent of psychotropic reference"[28] (Flattery & Schwartz, 1989). As already discussed in Chapter 4, the references to *bhang* as 'smashing, breaking' came about through the preparation of cannabis as the Soma, and the method of banging the stalks of the Soma plant with rocks in order to break it apart in preparation of the sacred beverage, as described in the *Vedas*.

Flattery and Schwartz claim that in the Indian literature, "there is no evidence for its [cannabis'] use as an intoxicant… before well within the Islamic era" (Flattery & Schwartz, 1989). But, as other researchers have noted: "Historically, the consumption of… hemp drugs is reported to be in use up to the 8th or 9th century A.D., i.e., prior to the advent of Muslims in the country" (Hasan, 1975). Moreover, if the use of cannabis were unknown prior to the advent of Islamic influences, there would have been considerable Indian historical material from the time period detailing the discovery of this 'new use' of cannabis, and there are certainly no historical accounts that can be pointed to in Indian literature from the Islamic period detailing what would have been the discovery of a new and phenomenal healing and medical plant, as occurred in Europe with the medieval and 19th century re-introduction of cannabis. In fact the term just carried on as it had always been used, as a designation of cannabis. To suggest that there was no knowledge of its medical or narcotic properties goes against the collected knowledge on the matter, and the views of numerous historians.

> The *Atharva Veda* of India dates to between 1400 and 2000 BCE and mentions a sacred grass, *bhang*, which remains a modern term of usage for cannabis. Medical references to cannabis date to Susruta in the 6th to 7th centuries BCE. (Weiner, 2002)

---

27   English *'bang'* comes from the same Indo-European root-word.
28   But there are different views on this designation "In the Rigveda (IX.61.13) (bhanga) is an epithet of Soma, presumably in the sense of 'intoxicating' which then came to designate hemp" (MacDonell & Kieth, 1958). [As quoted in (Merlin, 1972)]

As noted by other researchers: "In India and Iran, it [cannabis] was used as an intoxicant known as bhang as early as 1000 BC."(Goldfrank, 2002); "The narcotic properties of *C. Sativa* were recognized in India by 1000 BC." (Zohary & Hopf, 2000); "The narcotic and euphoric properties of cannabis were known to the Aryans who migrated to India thousands of years ago and there is little doubt they made use of these properties" (Chopra & Chopra, 1965); Cannabis' "narcotic properties were known in India by (1000 BCE)" (Southworth, 2005)[29]; "The use of hemp for medicinal purposes has been known in India from ancient times when it is highly probable that it was also used in a restrictive way, as an intoxicating drug" (Hassan, 1922). Dr. Ethan Russo, an expert on all things cannabis, including ancient world references, notes:

> The earliest written reference to cannabis in India may occur in the *Atharvaveda*, dating to about 1500 BCE... Grierson [(1894)] suggested this to be part of an offering, and ingestion or burning would both be typical of ancient practices for this purpose. In the *Sushruta Samhita*... dating from the third to the eighth centuries BCE, cannabis was recommended for phlegm, catarrh and diarrhea[30]... Similarly, Dwarakanath has maintained that cannabis was employed in Indian folk medicine in aphrodisiacs and treatments for pain in the same era,[31] while Sanyal observed that "They also used the fumes of burning Indian Hemp (*Canabis Indica*) [sic] as an anaesthetic from ancient times...[32]" (Russo, 2005)

And finally, as Dr. R.J. Bouquet explained of the role of cannabis in ancient India and Persia:

> The... *Zend Avesta*, composed in Northern Iran some six centuries before the Christian era, is the first to mention hemp (*Cadaneh*) and its inebriating resin. The Fourth Book of the *Vedas* refers to it sometimes under the name of *Vijahia* (source of happiness) and sometimes under that of *Ananda* (laughter-provoker). It was not, therefore, for its textile properties that hemp was used in India to start with; at the beginning of the Christian era the use of its fibre was still unknown there.

---

29   Citing Simmonds, NW (ed.) (1976) *Evolution of Crop Plants*, London
30   Ibid.
31   (Dwarakanath, 1965)
32   (Sanyal, 1964)

> It is solely to its inebriating properties that hemp owes the signal honour of being sung in the *Vedas*, and it was probably the peoples of Northern Iran who discovered those properties, for they were already using the leaves (*Cheng*) and the resin (*Cers*) as inebriants and narcotics before the Hindus.
>
> It was thus through the Iranian tribes that the priestly class in India - the only educated class at that time – learned of the properties of Cannabis, at a period which we cannot, at present, determine exactly. (Bouquet, 1950)

Despite some excellent etymological and historical research, at best Schwartz's explanation in regards to *bhanga*/Soma/Homa/cannabis/harmaline only adds to the linguistical confusion on the matter, and few scholars agree with his assessment on the subject. As Schwartz tries to explain away the reality of the ancient connection between cannabis, *mang*, *bhanga* and Haoma, he only digs a deeper hole.

Considering my own knowledge of the data collected in the composition of this book and other projects as well (Bennett, et al., 1995; Bennett & McQueen, 2001), to suggest that cannabis was unknown in this area of the world is a curious statement indeed. These authors are suggesting that both in Persia and India, cultures which had extensive herbal knowledge, which were making hempen ropes and clothes, and which came into contact with other cultures who used cannabis as an intoxicant, had somehow let the resinous properties of its flowers escape them![33]

Zoroaster and *Bhanga*

As it has been noted that that Zoroaster took both the Mazdean religion and the Haoma sacrifice itself through a number of reforms which indicated the extraction of cannabis from the Haoma recipe, and as the terms *mang* and *bhanga* start to play a role around this same time period, it seems probable that there is a relationship. Perhaps Zoroaster, who, according to Eliade was unhappy with the "immoderate absorption of *haoma*" amongst the masses who used it in nocturnal "orgiastic" rituals, decided to weaken the punch, so to speak? The coup in this case being the removal of cannabis from

---

[33]   Understandably Flattery and Schwartz make no reference to the extensive medical knowledge of cannabis in both ancient Persian and Indian literature, as this alone would be enough to break their case.

the Haoma recipe, and the reinstitution of a non-psychoactive placebo drink as a substitution, while the use of cannabis continued to
be used secretly by Zoroaster and his selected elite.

The surviving tradition clearly indicates that Zoroaster continued to utilize cannabis for his own Shamanic purposes and for initiation of a chosen few, under the name *mang*. This situation accounts for both the appearance of *bhanga/mang* in the Zoroastrian
tradition as well as the survival of the tradition which currently recognizes Ephedra as the *Hom*. As well, this scenario also substanti-
ates the view that for a time "Haoma was under the ban of the great
reformer [Zoroaster]" (Griswwold, 1923).

Harri Nyberg[34] in "The Problem of the Aryans and the Soma: the
botanical evidence"[35] makes some interesting comments on the connection between bhang with Haoma/Soma which must be addressed:

> In R.V. [*Rig Veda*] 9.16.13, the word [*bhang*] is used an ephitet of
> soma... In Iran, modern Persians have the name *bang*, which cor-
> responds to the Avestan *bhanga*, and Pahlavi *mang*. In the Artai Vi-
> raz Namak, [Ardu Viraz] *mang* is mentioned several times (*mang,
> mang-i-Vistap, mang-i-Zaratuxst*), often translated as 'a narcotic.'
> 'Medical mang' (*mang besaz*) is mentioned in the Bundahisin 4:20,
> and it also states that *mang-I Vistaspan* was mixed with *Hom* (Den-
> kard 7.4.85)... Thus, in the Avesta or the Pahlavi texts *banja, mang*
> or *bang* are not considered to be identical with *haoma*. We have to
> conclude that hemp is certainly not identical with *soma/haoma*,
> although it might have been an ingredient in some preparations
> derived from the original soma/haoma. (Nyberg, 1995)

Nyberg discounted cannabis as an ingredient in the original Haoma, based upon the appearance in Zoroastrian literature as something separate. This reasoning was shared by Yves Bonnefoy and
Wendy Doniger (returning to the subject more than two decades
after her work with Wasson) who also noted in reference to the
identity of Haoma: "Hashish has been considered (*bhanga* in Iranian, *bhang* in Sanskrit), but a passage from the Denkart seems to
contradict this suggestion, for we read that Zarathustra's patron,
King Vishtaspa, drank one day a cup of *haoma* mixed with hash-

34   This is a different person than Henrik S. Nyberg, whose 1938 *Die Religionen des
alten Irans*, we have been referring to in reference to bhanga/mang.
35   Which appeared in *The Indo-Aryans of Ancient South Asia: Language, Material
Culture and Ethnicity* (1995).

ish... so the two ingredients can not have been the same" (Bonnefoy & Doniger, 1993).

But this view would be hard to maintain in light of the fact that the shamanic use of *bhanga/mang* in the Zoroastrian tradition coincides with massive changes in the Haoma ritual which changed the formula, which removed the cannabis and made the Haoma into a placebo sacrament with only the mildly stimulating effects produced by Ephedra remaining. Zoroaster prohibited the mass use of cannabis in the Haoma, in a revolt against the nocturnal orgiastic rites that accompanied its consumption, but then continued to use extracts of cannabis in potent preparations for shamanic trance amongst his inner circle. Clearly, as with the Indian tradition of Soma, the distinction that made any preparation Haoma in Zoroastrian times was the act of consecration, and as such the Zoroastrian sacrament maintained the name even without the plant with which its use originated.

This brings about a number of important points. Psychoactive preparations of Haoma, from the earlier Avestan accounts, seem much milder and different in effect than those associated with the shamanic trance induced by *bhanga/mang*. Haoma, being a preparation of cannabis mixed with the stimulant Ephedra, was used in nocturnal rituals, where there was singing, dancing, animal sacrifices and in some cases orgiastic activities. In this scenario, the Haoma was not particularly directed at inducing a psychonaut into a shamanic trance, but rather a collective, awake, and involved shared experience.

Bhanga/mang, on the other hand, was, from the ancient accounts, used in a potent shamanic preparation that would quite literally send the devotee into a death-like coma that was filled with vivid dream-like visions. Because of these descriptions, few researchers have considered cannabis potent enough to have been the substance in question, but this is an assumption based on dosage. Although such a powerful experience would seem unlikely to most western users of cannabis, as Dr. Michael Aldrich explains:

> There is a myth that pot is a mild and minor drug. Usually in context of American useage it is, but it doesn't have to be. The hard part about expressing this, however, is that the anti-marijuana people who pose visions of disaster about 'hashsish' or about 'legalizing the stronger forms of cannabis' are also wrong. In and

of itself there's nothing wrong with cannabis being a potent hallucinogen; this has certainly accounted for its vast popularity
through these many centuries. When one seeks a shaman's drug
one generally wants something more powerful than a 'mild hallucinogen.' Of course, knowing when and where to use cannabis
at a dosage or strength suitable for real visions is also important.
It's obviously not a good idea to try in an unrefined social context,
or when working in the fields or factory. This use of cannabis has
traditionally been confined, by rational custom in ancient societies, to *rituals* which help define and control, measure and mag-
nify, the raw experience. (Aldrich, 1980)[36]

As it stands, in my own research, I have come across numerous references that refer to descriptions from a variety of sources
detailing such experiences induced by cannabis preperations, particularly amongst 19th century occultists. Besides the well-known
vivid voyages into the astral realms recorded by members of the
le Club des Haschichins, which included such figures as Alexander Dumas, Victor Hugo, Theophile Gautier, Gerard de Nerval and
Charles Baudelaire, we also have more than a dozen such accounts
recorded in L.A. Cahagnet's *Sanctuary of Spiritualism* (1848) which
recorded the descriptions of a variety of French psychonauts who
partook of three grams of hashish, and were interpreted by Cahagnet as evidence of communication with the World of the Dead.
Other such examples have been recorded (Bennett, et al., 1995).

Health and consciousness researcher Andrew Weil gives us
a more recent first hand account of an intense case of marijuana
overdose:

In 1968, when I was studying marijuana in Boston, I deliberately
consumed [orally] an overdose (6 grams) of potent hashish in order to experience the reaction.... The effects of the drug were felt
within forty minutes and were pleasant but strong for about a
half-hour. Thereafter, things became quite confusing. I could not
understand what was said to me, felt physically sick, and soon was
unfit to do anything but lie in bed and wait for morning. Auditory
hallucinations were prominent, especially threatening voices that
rose in volume to a crescendo, then faded out. For about twelve
hours I remained in a stage of consciousness between sleeping
and waking, marked by vivid nightmares. Lucid intervals were

36   As quoted in *High Culture*, William Novak.

rare; for much of the time I did not know where I was, even thinking I was six years old and sick from measles. By morning, most
of the worst symptoms had disappeared, but I had a powerful
hangover that left me prostrate for another twenty-four hours. I
would not willingly repeat the experience. (Weil 1972)

Under the proper set and setting, such as the context of religious
initiation, an experienced Shaman leading a new initiate could
channel such effects as described by Weil in a number of directions. Indeed, later evidence indicates that cannabis was used for
just such purposes by the Zoroastrian influenced Islamic heretical
sect the *Hashishin*, aka Assassins, as discussed in Chapter 19.

Nyberg felt that the terms *mang*, and *bhanga* were not only references to hemp, but more specifically a "hemp extract" (1938). From
the descriptions of the potency and the way it was used, added to
wine or "hom," this seems a likely case. Later Islamic accounts refer
to a potent hash oil preparation known as *dūg-e wahdat*, which may
be similar to the Persian *mang*. "Hashish oil is generally consumed by
thoroughly mixing a drop of it with a liter of *dūg* (a drink made from
yogurt), and drinking the resulting mixture. This mixture, which is
extremely potent and dangerous, is called *dūg-e wahdat* (the *dūg* of
annihilation)" (Gnoli 1979). As *Encyclopedia Iranica* describes:

> DŪG-EWAHDAT "beverage of unity," concoction made from
> adding hashish extract (*jowhar-e haīš*) to diluted yogurt (Šahrī,
> VI, pp. 412, 423). The resulting tonic is drunk by certain mystics
> as a hallucinogen during their rites. Alī-Akbar Dehkodā, in his
> compendium of Persian proverbs and dicta (1339 Š./1960, I, p.
> 255), quoted a verse from Kamāl-al-Dīn Kojandī (d. 803/1399)
> in which the use of the narcotic by a Sufi sheikh is mentioned.
> Apparently some less scrupulous Sufis used the drink to attract
> followers (Šahrī, VI, p. 419).[37] (Omidsalar, 1999)

The use of *dūg-e wahdat* has continued through to the modern-
day in Iran, despite considerably harsh penalties surrounding its
consumption and distribution. The preparation is also known as
"*bangaab*" (*bang* = hashish + *aab* = water), but more commonly it
is *dugh* (water + yoghurt, scented with herbs) and powdered hashish. *Dūg-e wahdat* is a favoured libation of the dervishes). Its po-

---

37   J. Šahrī, *Tārīk-e ejtemāh-e Tehrān dar qarn-e sīzdahom*, 6 vols., Tehran, 1368 Š./1989.

tential to make one unconscious has resulted in some rape cases where it was alleged to have been given to women to knock them out. (It was likely a preparation such as this that Henning referred to earlier in the account regarding cannabis non-toxicity even in extreme doses).

In relation to this, it is important to note that one of the effects attributed to *bhanga/mang* in the Zoroastrian accounts is that it "brought about a condition outwardly resembling sleep (i.e. stard) in which targeted visions of what is believed to be a spirit existence were seen" (Flattery & Schwartz, 1989). The literal meaning of the term "stard" or means "spread out, sprawled." From the descriptions given this state could last for days. In an earlier work I discussed 19th century accounts of cannabis to induce such a state of coma. Although it is little known "in extremely high doses, and through powerful extracts... cannabis has been reported... to put its imbibers into a state similar to animal 'hibernation'":

> ...Robert Anton Wilson referred to tests sponsored by the US army in the 1950's, where "THC (tetrahydrocannabinol)[38]... put dogs into 'hibernation' or deep sleep for eight days, after which they were awakened and showed no ill effects"- (Wilson 1973).[39]

Apparently the U.S. army was by no means the first to find out about this little known quality of marijuana, as the following had appeared some years earlier before the American tests, in Emily Murphy's 1920 piece of Canadian anti-marijuana propaganda, *The Black Candle*: "Eminent medical doctors in India, principally Calcutta, have made experiments with Cannabis Indica and have discovered that it induces symptoms of *catalepsy* or even trance. It is also claimed that the fakeers of India who suffer themselves to be buried, and who are later disinterred, do so through the agency of this drug. Some years earlier a Dr. James Braid of Edinburgh wrote a monograph on this subject entitled *Trance and Human Hibernations*."[40] (Murphy 1920)

Some excerpts of Braid's research which discussed hashish and the human hibernation state, appear in the 1855 classic *Plant In-*

---

38   A psycho-active chemical that is found in cannabis

39   The Army felt this would revolutionize Battlefield medicine; injured soldiers could be kept in storage until the proper medical help were made available. According to Wilson's account, a Scientist involved with this study fought the Army in the courts for twenty years to have this information released.(Wilson 1973).

40   The full title was *Observation's on Trance; or Human Hybernation* (London 1850).

toxicants, by Baron Ernst Von Bibra in a chapter on hashish.[41] Braid discussed a number of eye-witness accounts of Indian Fakirs who had allowed themselves to be buried alive, amongst which are the words of one Sir Claude Wade, who was present at the court of Runjeet Singh, when one such Fakir was buried in a specially prepared room that was "completely sealed off from the access of atmospheric air" and then disinterred six weeks later!

Other such cases were reported by reliable eyewitnesses and like Wade's description, when the Fakir's bodies were disinterred they "were found stiff and rigid like a corpse, but on application of the aforesaid [their limbs were massaged with ointments and they were slowly brought back to wakefulness] treatment they were restored to life.... It is possible that some of the *fakirs* possess a hemp preparation that enables them to undergo the described experiments. This is especially supported by the catalepsy that sets in after hemp resin has been taken" (Von Bibra 1855). (Bennett & McQueen, 2001)

Thus, it can clearly be seen that cannabis preparations taken in higher dosages have been known to produce a state identical to those attributed to *bhanga/mang* in the Avestan and Pahlavian accounts. Considering the historical and etymological connections as well, cannabis is by far and wide the most obvious candidate for the ancient Zoroastrian Shamanic preparation, *bhang, mang*.

After the time of Zoroaster's reforms and the installation of the placebo-Haoma, *bhanga/mang* had to be added to the Haoma in order for visionary purposes, and the indications are Zoroaster used this method himself. As the authors of *Apocalypticism in the Mediterranean World and the Near East* explain:

Zoroaster's role as apocalyptic revealer is intimately tied up with the type of religious type he represents. The indication in the Gathas, particularly Yasna 43, suggest that he was an ecstatic visionary who a number of times had an overwhelming experience of the divine, the Ahura Mazda.... How was this ecstasy... brought about?.... There are good reasons to assume that there were in the early Zoroastrian community... means of attaining the ecstatic vision, e.g... the use of a specific beverage. The last one is most clearly attested to with respect to Vistaspa... [who] is visited by a divine messenger who urges him to drink a cup of

---

41   Reprinted in 1995 by Healing Arts Press.

wine or haoma mixed with henbane or cannabis (*mang*). He then falls into a deep sleep during which his soul is taken to heaven... the same procedure was used by Artay Viraz before undertaking his journey to the other world. Now it appears from a passage in Bahman Yast, based upon Avestan traditions, that a similar technique was used by Zoroaster. The beverage mentioned in Bahman Yast only contains water, but there are grounds to believe that the mention of mang has been suppressed by later tradition.[42] A passage from the Pahlavi Videvat, hitherto not adduced in this context, supports the view that the original tradition behind the Bahman Yast knew the narcotic beverage. In IV,14 mention is made of old women bringing henbane [unlikely][43] or hemp to be used for abortion and the text adds that this mang either was that of "Vistaspa or Zoroaster." (Hellholm, et al., 1989)

Although references to the use of *mang* are much more clear cut and straight forward in the other accounts which shall be discussed, the identification of Zoroaster's use seems to be quite veiled. Hellholm and his co-authors make an important point in their statement that "According to the Bahman Yast, Zoroaster receives from Ahura Mazda the 'wisdom of omniscience'" which appears to be closely related to drinking the cup of ecstasy: (Hellholm, et al., 1989) A situation on which a number of Iranists have commented. "The visionary receives the divine quality of omniscience... which is thought to be transmitted in liquid form, as told in Bahman Yasht" (Johnston, 2004).

And he (Ahura Mazda) put the wisdom of omniscience in the form of water in the hand of Zoroaster and said: "Drink." And Zoroaster drank from it and he intermingled the wisdom of omniscience with Zoroaster. Seven days and seven nights Zoroaster was in the wisdom of Ahura Mazda. (*Bahman Yast*, 11.5-6)

As the authors of *The Encyclopedia of Apocalypticism* have noted of this passage, "The expression 'in the form of water' in the Bahman Yast to denote the drink Zoroaster consumed before his vision does not mean that it was water but only that it was liquid"[44] (McGinn, et

---

42   (Widengren, 1965; 1979)
43   Here referring to the assertion that *mang* is a reference to henbane, which as we have show is not a likely case.
44   The authors accepted Henning's assertion of henbane as *mang*: "The Pahlavi texts show that trance preparing the mystical experience is induced by a specific technique performed in a ritual context. The drinking of a cup with sacred juice and henbane

al., 2000). As we shall see, the drinking of the "cup of omniscience" by Zoroaster clearly resulted in a identical shamanic trip as that attributed to the drinkers of *bhanga/mang* in the Zoroastrian tradition:

> After having consumed the "wisdom of omniscience," Zoroaster sees the seven world continents and he is able to distinguish the finest details of humans, cattle, and plants. This is best explained on the assumption of a movement in space. In fact, we find a reference to an otherworldly journey undertaken by Zoroaster in a short citation from the sacred tradition preserved in the Denkard. Ohrmazd and the beneficient immortals address Zoroaster with the following words "You have come to paradise (*garodman*); now you know the actions that are done in the corporeal world and those that will be done, even in secret" (Dk IX,28:2). (McGinn, et al., 2003)

As noted above, Hellholm and his co-authors relate that the respected Iranist Geo Widengren, in his German language edition *Die Religionen Irans* (1965) believed that mention of *mang* was suppressed in the above accounts by later Zoroastrian religious writers, which would explain a lot of the confusion on the matter. A statement which left this researcher with the task of locating a copy of Widengren's German language book *Die Religionen Irans*, and then acquiring translations of the relevant passages, some of which are reproduced below:

> ...[In] the Phalavi-apocalypse Bahman Yast... it is recounted – and we are moving here within a sphere of Avestan traditions – that Zarathustra assimilated the so-called 'rationality of omniscience' by means of drinking water. Moreover it is recounted that, in doing this, the 'rationality of omniscience' was mixed with Zarathustra and this remained for seven days and nights in the reason of Ahura Mazda.
>
> The most important thing about this description is that Zarathustra, in accordance with an established Avestan tradition, adopted an intoxication technique, to put himself in to a trance, during which he lies in deep sleep for seven days and nights. In Pahlavi at this point, the term for this deep sleep is *xvamn*; this is a 'modern' development of the Avestan word *xvafna*. It may therefore be assumed that the original Avestan tradition even used the term *xvafna* here. (Widengren 1965)

seems to have been the usual means of achieving the trance state" (McGinn, et al., 2000).

This state of *xvafna* was the core of both the Haoma and the *mang* experience. As Eliade explained, "...haoma is rich in xverenah, the sacred fluid, at once igneous, luminous and spermatic. Ahura Mazda is preeminently the possessor of xvarenah, but this 'flame' also springs from the forehead of Mithra and like a solar light emanates from the heads of sovereigns." (Eliade, 1978). Referring to Zoroaster's ingestion of the "cup of omniscience" Widengren wrote that in "a trance similar to that of the deep sleep, xvafna> xvamn, Zarathustra experienced his visions and heard the divine words of Ahura Mazda. It was probably also customary in the eldest congregations to induce this trance with a narcotic potion. This technique of intoxication presumably has Indo-Iranian ancestry, because it is documented in India as well." (Widengren, 1965)

> ...[T]he tradition preserved in the Bahman Yt. does not mention the hemp potion as a physical ecstatic substance but it obviously concerns a potion, which Zarathustra partook of. It is possible that the later Pahlavi tradition thus blurred the original character of the potion, that it only states *pat ap-karp... frac xvart* – 'in the form of water... he swallowed it.' Behind this transition from wine and hemp in AVN II 29 ff. to water in the Bahman Yt., one can well assume various tendencies of the Sassanids era...
>
> ...Now this description in Bahman Yast is however consistent in some respects with two other visionary narratives. One account is found in the Pahlavi Rivayats to Datastan i Denik, where it is told, how Zarathustra's guardian, Kavi Vistaspa, obtains wine mixed with a narcotic [*mang*] from the messenger of the gods, Neryosang. Vistaspa immediately becomes unconscious and his soul is escorted to Garodman, the paradise.
>
> This account bases itself meanwhile on an older version which we find in the Denkart. This Denkart text can be proved as an adaptation of a missing Avestan original due to the exegetical glosses, the quotes from the Avesta as well as the precious terminology. This original version shows several discrepancies: firstly the cup, which Vistaspa is passed, contains in this case *hom ut mang*, being haoma and hemp. (Widengren, 1965)

Widengren felt that based on this similar Avestan account of Vistaspa drinking Haoma mixed with hemp, and achieving a similar mystical experience to that of Zoroaster in the Bahaman Yast, the account of Zoroaster drinking water in the Bahman Yast, was based on an earlier Avestan tradition which involved the partaking of *mang* and later accounts were edited during the Sassanian period to hide this fact.

The Avestan and the Pahlavian references to Vistaspa drinking *mang* are pivotal in identifying Zoroaster's own use of hemp as described in the 'censored' account recorded in the Bahman Yast.

> ...[W]e have to realize that the previously quoted Pahlavi text Bahma Yt, where Zarathustra's ecstasy with his visionary experiences is described, bases itself on Avestan material, and in actual fact predominantly on the missing *Stutkar Nask*.[45] It can therefore be subject to no doubt that the Avestan tradition also knew Zarathustra as a genuine ecstatic. (Widengren,1965)

Accounts of Zoroaster's shamanic flights are recorded in: *Bahman Yasht* 4.1-66, 5.1-10, 6.1-13, 7.1-39, 8.1-8, 9.1-8; Bundahishn 34.4-5; Denkard 8.8.22-59, 9.6, 10.11, 14.13. The suggestion that there was a connection between the *mang* and Haoma consumed by Vishtasp and the 'water' by Zoroaster has been noted by a variety of scholars. "Since sauma [mixed with *mang*] was the means by which Ohrmazd brought such vision to Zoroaster's champion, Wishtasp, [Vistaspa] there is no reason to doubt that sauma [and *mang*] would also have been the means whereby Zoroaster (who as a zaotar consumed sauma in Yasna rites) also saw into menog existence [spiritual realm] and drew from it his knowledge of Ohrmazd and his revelation" (Flattery and Schwartz, 1989).

> Ancient texts such as the Avesta provide evidence hemp was used in the Iranian world... to produce ecstatic states of mind. Zarathustra himself used this technique to nourish his mystique. In this he was imitating his protector, King Vishtasp, who received from the gods the cup with narcotic ingredients, "haoma and hemp." Thanks to this "illuminating beverage" the possessed could "open the eye of the soul to obtain knowledge" – in other words, he experienced hallucinations and an intoxication that was certainly real, though considered as magico-religious. The king thought he was in this way escaping his body and sending his soul to travel in paradise. But the descriptions of the place or state of mind in question as being full of "illumination" are typical of the visions experienced by the consumer of hashish, along with a sleep like trance which obliges him to lie down. (Charriere, 1979)

---

45   One of the texts that was lost in the Sasannian period.

Vistaspa, the Shamanic King

The aforementioned King Vistaspa was an instrumental figure in the acceptance of Zoroastrianism as a religion on a wide scale, but this was said to have happened a full decade after Zoroaster's own revelation. Not surprisingly, Zoroaster's initial battle with the age-old ecstatic Haoma cult was unpopular with the locals, and he had to flee the area in order to save his own life. Yasna 46 begins with a sad verse about Zoroaster leaving his homeland after rallying against the Haoma cult.

> To what land should I turn? Where should I turn to go?
> They hold me back from folk and friends.
> Neither the community I follow pleases me,
> nor do the wrongful rulers of the land...
> I know... that I am powerless.
> I have a few cattle and also a few men. (Yasna 46)

The story has it that Zoroaster wondered the countryside for ten years without winning over the people to his new religious concepts. It was not until he met King Vistaspa, who converted to Zoroaster's religion after drinking a cup of *mang* that the Iranian prophet's beliefs began to take hold on a wide scale. "Vishtaspa used hemp (bhang) to obtain ecstasy: while his body lay asleep, his soul traveled to paradise" (Eliade 1978). Vishtaspa's shamanic journey is recorded in *Denkard* 7.4.83-6 and Pahlavi Rivayat 48.27-32. In the ninth century text the *Denkard* derived from a lost Avestan source, when Vishtaspa drank *bhang* "he became *stard* (unconscious) immediately, and they led his soul to paradise and showed him the value of accepting the Religion":

> To enlighten Vishtasp (and teach him)... and that he would attain a high post, permanent power, riches and food, Ohrmazd the Creator sent at the same time to the house of Vishtasp the yazat [a lesser divine being] Neryosang with a message urging... Arthavist to give to drink to Vishtasp the lightened drink that would grant the eye of whomever took it a glimpse at the spiritual world.... And speak to Arthavist: 'Lord Arthavist! Take the nice plate, the nicest of all that have been made... to take, from us, Hom [Haoma] and mang... (*Denkard* 7.4.84-86)

Seeming to agree with Widengren about censorship of references to *bhanga/mang*, Vicente Dobroruka has noted, "In the *Dinkard*

[sic] 7.4.84-86 Vishtapa drinks a mixture of wine or haoma with some narcotic, possibly henbane [or as we have shown, hemp].[46] The same episode in the *Zand-i Vohuman Yasn*, a later redaction, has this potation replaced by water... possible evidence of the practice being rejected in later times" (Dobroruka, 2006).

Gherardo Gnoli recorded: "bang was... an ingredient of the 'illuminating drink' (*rōšngar xwarišn*) that allowed Wištāsp to see the 'great *xwarrah*' and the 'great mystery.' This *mang ī wištāspān* (Pahlavi Vd. 15.14) was mixed with *hōm* (*Dēnkard* 7.4.85) or wine (*Pahlavi Rivayat* 47.27). It was an integral part of the ecstatic practice aimed at opening the 'eye of the soul' (*gyān čašm...*)" (Gnoli, 1979). As Widengren explained:

> Hemp and wine or hemp and haoma were mixed in the cup that was passed to Vistaspa... it is said that Neryosang was sent forth to let Vistaspa drink 'the eye of the soul' with the view up above to the forms of existence of the heavenly beings, the illuminating potion thanks to which Vistaspa saw the great lucky splendour and mystery.' The typical expression *gyan casm*, 'eye of the soul,' causes problems here. One could be tempted to replace this expression with 'source of life,' and this in actual fact is how it was translated, which in a pure formal philological sense is completely possible. However the expression can be explained via two points in the Denkart, where, in regards to the enlightenment, it is stated that it is of two types: on the one hand it consists of a view with the eye of the body, *tan casm*, on the other hand it is a view with the eye of the soul, *gyan casm*, which is defined as 'the opening of the eye of the soul to obtain knowledge.' The eye of the soul' means introspection. The visionary sight is conveyed to Kavi Vistaspa using a haoma potion mixed with hemp. With this his soul can repair to Garodman, [Paradise] to view the heavenly existence. (Widengren, 1965)[47]

A similar reference to the "eye" is found in the Indian *Aitareya Brahmanam*, "When... the Adhvaryu hands over... the Soma cup

---

46   Dobroruka discounted hemp based on the view the ancient seers remembered their visions, "This can be understood as a negative conclusion regarding the use of hemp, whose physiological effects, regardless of other opinions seen above, include partial loss of memory" (Dobroruka, 2006). Although there may be temporary short-term memory loss from cannabis ingestion there is no evidence of long-term memory harm and this is a very unfounded comment, as the considerable memory of this author and copious user of cannabis can well attest to.
47   Translated by Jake Czerpak.

to drink... to the Hotar, he receives it with the... mantra... (By the words): 'This is a good which has knowledge; here is a good which has knowledge; in me is a good which has knowledge; ruler of the eye, protect my eye' the Hotar drinks Soma from the Maitravaruna graha. (Then he repeats): 'The eye with the mind is called hither.'" Martin Haug in his translation of this passage, noted "This formula resembles very much one of the most sacred prayers of the Parsis... which is particularly repeated when the Zotar priest (the Hotar of the Brahmans) is drinking the Homa (Soma) juice..." (Haug, 1863). In relation, in India the drinking of *bhang* by devotees is still believed to open up the "eye" of Shiva, i.e the "third-eye."

As Mary Boyce explains, the drinking of *mang* led to the moment of conversion for Vishtaspa: "Vistasp received... a bowl containing *Hom*-juice mixed with *mang*; when he drank this he lost consciousness and saw in a vision the glories of heaven which awaited him hereafter. On recovering his senses he accordingly accepted wholeheartedly the new teachings" (Boyce, 1982).

> Ormazd sent Nêrôsang: 'Go to Artvahist and tell him: Put *mang* in the wine and give it for Vishtasp to drink.' Artvahist did so. Having drunk it, he evaporated into the field. His soul was taken to Garôtman [Paradise] to show him what he could gain if he accepted the Religion. When he woke up from the sleep, he cried to Hutôs: 'Where is Zoroaster so that I may accept the Religion?' Zoroaster heard his voice, came and Vishtasp accepted the Religion. (*Pahlavi Rivayat* 47.27-32)

In *Haoma and Harmaline*, Flattery and Schwartz make some very important points about the account of Vishtaspa drinking *mang* (they use the blanket term 'sauma,' regarding the Haoma and *mang* references), in order to see into the Spirutal realm (*Menog*):

> Fundamental to ancient Iranian religion was a belief in two existences, the material, tangible, visible existence... and the intangible, invisible, spirit existence.... Middle Persian menog, as was glimped by.... Wishtasp [Vistaspa] by means of sauma [and *mang*].... All material things and creatures exist simultaneously in spirit form. These spirit forms include the double or frawahr (Avestan fravasi-) of each person, living, dead and unborn...
>
> The consumption of sauma [and *mang*] may have been the only means recognized in Iranian religion of seeing into menog existence

before death... and is the means used by Ohrmazd when he wishes to make the menog existence visible to living persons. In ancient Iranian religion there is little evidence of concern with meditative practices which might foster development of alternative, nonpharmacological means to such vision. In Iran, vision into the spirit world was not thought to come about simply by divine grace nor as a reward for saintliness. From the apparent role of sauma in initiation rites, experience of the effects of sauma, which is to say vision of menog existence, must have at one time been required of all priests (or the shamans antecedent to them). (Flattery and Schwartz, 1989)

Besides bringing back an account of the afterlife, the revelations received by Vishtaspa in this psychedelic voyage included divine knowledge about the fate of mankind, and give us the origin of the whole concept of an Apocalypse or Holy Armageddon. Vishtaspa was one of the first to conceive of a cosmic beginning and end of history, placing himself and Zarathustra at the mid-point.

Vishtaspa's Eschatological vision was apparently prohibited literature in ancient Rome, and in the eyes of the Romans with good reason: "In the second and first century B.C. an apocalypse written in Greek was in circulation under the title Oracles of Hystaspes (Hystaspes is the Greek form of Vishtaspa); it was directed against Rome (whose fall was announced) but formed part of the Iranian eschatological literature" (Eliade 1978\1982). Vishtaspa's vision, known as the "Great Renovation," also foretold of a coming Savior and the institution of the White Hom (the celestial counterpart of *Haoma*) a mythos that would directly influence the Judaic and later Christian concepts of the Messiah with his Tree of Life and its healing leaves in the New Testament's Book of Revelation.

Zoroaster also initiated Vishtaspa's son Jamasp, but rather than using a beverage, this account simply describes a "flower":

In the *Jāmāsp Namag*... Jāmāsp receives from Zoroaster the gift of knowledge by means of a flower. This is also the theme of the Pahlavi text *Wizirkard i Denig* 19.... In the *Zardush Nameh*... it is said that Jāmāsp acquired his gift by smelling the flower consecrated by Zoroaster in a ceremony:

He gave to Jāmāsp a bit of the consecrated perfume, and all sciences became understandable to him. He knew about all things to happen and that would happen until the day of resurrection.

....In Mary Boyce's translation[48]... the flower is rendered as "incense." (Dobroruka, 2006)

Apparently, Zoroaster's wife was not satisfied with only a secondary shamanic experience, and after hearing about Zoroaster's visions, she preys to the Supreme Being that Zoroaster "give her his good narcotic, bangha." Darmesteter commented on this in his 19th century translation of the relevant passages from the *Den Yasht*, 16.14-15:[49]

> To whom the holy Hvovi (Zarathustra's wife) did sacrifice with full knowledge, wishing the holy Zarathustra would give her his good narcotic (bangha; so-called Bang of Zoroaster, Vendidad XV, 14, what must have been its virtue may be gathered from legends of Gustap [Vistaspa] and Ardu Viraf, who are said to have been transported in soul to heavens, and to have had the higher mysteries revealed to them, on drinking from a cup prepared by the prophet—Sardust namah - or from a cup of Gustap-bang) that she might think according to the law, speak according to the law, and do according to the law. "For her brightness and glory, I will offer unto her a sacrifice worth being heard...." (Darmesteter, 1883)

Darmesteter mentions the Zoroastrian psychonaut Ardu Viraf (aka Arda Wiraz and other spellings), a figure widely credited with bringing to the world many of the concepts of Heaven and Hell.

The Persian Origins of Heaven and Hell

In the Zoroastrian tale "...the *Artak Viraz Namak*... Hell, Purgatory, and Heaven, the rewards bestowed on the good, and the punishment awaiting the sinner are here described in a vision induced by hashish" (Campbell, 2000). As Herbert Gowen explained in *A History of Religion*, some centuries after the time of Zoroaster, when the people had grown sceptical and began to lose faith it was decided by the "the *dasturs* (an order of priests) to send one of their number, through the use of hashish, to the other world, that he may report on his return as to the realities of future reward and retribution. Ara Viraf, chosen by lot, makes the journey..." (Gowen, 1934)

---

48   "On the antiquity of Zoroastrian apocalyptic" in: *Bulletin of the School of Oriental and African Studies*, 47, 1984. P.60.
49   Found in the larger *Khorda Avesta*

The *Book of Arda Wiraz* is generally thought to have originated sometime around the 3rd century A.D., but existing copies are believed to have not been written down until around the 9th century, and it underwent many redactions before it came into its final form some time after the advent of Islam. If we take into account that the accepted date for the life of Zoroaster is around 600 B.C., or earlier, this later account attests to the ongoing use of *bhanga/mang* for shamanic purposes for a millennia, despite the existing prohibitions on its use in the wider and more public Haoma ceremonies.

> In the Book of Arda Viraf, which describes the dream-journey of a devout Zoroastrian through the next world is bhanga (narcotic) mentioned in Part 1., Chapter 2, 24: "And then those Dasturs of the religion filled three golden cups with wine and narcotic of Vishtasp." Similarly, the ancient Aryans that settled in India used Cannabis, but in their worship of the deity Shiva. In one of the Tantric Scriptures we find this revealing statement: "Intoxicating drink (containing bhang) is consumed in order to liberate oneself, and that those who do so, in dominating their mental faculties and following the law of Shiva (yoga) - are to be likened to immortals on earth." [The *Mahanirvana Tantra* (XI,105–108).] (Hanu , 2008)

The *Book of Arda Wiraz Namag* takes place in a period where the Mazdaean religion was in the state of confusion and people were in doubt of the faith. In reaction to this the religious leaders gathered together in order to find a solution and the decision was that they needed to seek word from spiritual realm, using the time tested technique of ingestion of *mang*. The Priests gathered together seven of the most righteous men in the community, and then through a picking of lots, Arda Wiraz was selected. After enjoying a luxurious last meal and saying goodbye to his seven wives, the *Book of Arda Wiraz* continues with the account:

> And this Viraz washed (his) head and (his) body, and put on a new garment; perfumed (himself) with an agreeable perfume, spread a new, clean blanket on some appropriate boards. At a (given) moment (he) sat down on the clean blanket, and performed the (rite of sacrifice), and remembered (the departed) souls, and ate food. And afterwards the theologians of the Religion filled three golden cups with wine and with the Vishtaspian narcotic [*mang*], and they gave one cup over to Viraz (in conformity) with the

'good thought,' and the second cup (in conformity) with the 'good speech,' and the third cup (in conformity) with the 'good deed.' And he drank that wine and narcotic and consciously said grace and fell asleep on the blanket. (The *Book of Artay Viraz*, 2.25-31)[50]

Arda Viraf drinks "three gold cups with wine and 'vistaspic' hemp (in other words hemp extract)...has some time to thank consciousness, and then falls asleep on the gown. He sleeps for seven days and nights, and during this time his soul visits heaven and hell" (Nyberg, 1938). After partaking of an extremely strong psychedelic dose of *mang* Ardu Viraf lay in what appeared to outsiders as a deathlike coma and had a classic out-of-body-experience, in which the ancient psychonaut believed he traveled on the mythical Cinvat bridge to Heaven where he witnessed: "All dwell among fine carpets and cushions in great pleasure and joy....Viraf, after return-

Fig 15.1: Zoroastrian afterlife.

ing to the bridge, was then taken to hell that he might see the lot of the wicked...He saw the 'greedy jaws of hell, like the most frightful pit.' Everyone in hell is packed in so tight that life is intolerable, yet all believe that they are alone..." (Hinnels, 1973).

Referring to Ardu Viraf's hemp inspired heavenly voyage, Mircea Eliade wrote, "...we must take... into consideration the symbolic value of narcotic intoxication. It was equivalent to a 'death,' the intoxicated person left his body, acquired the conditions of ghosts and spirits. mystical ecstasy being assimilated to a temporary 'death' or leaving the body, all intoxicants that produced the same were given a place amongst the techniques of ecstasy" (Eliade 1964). "The most explicit detailed Iranian account of intoxication for religious purposes is the Arda Wiraz Namag... [it] demonstrates the belief that pharmacologically induced visions were the means to religious knowledge and that they were at the basis of the religion that the Magi claimed to have received from Zoroaster" (Flattery & Schwartz 1989).

As noted earlier, Widengren (1965), Hellholm, et al. (1989), Dobroruka (2006) have all suggested that references to the use of *bhanga/mang* may have been suppressed in the later Sasannina period when many of the accounts first made the transition from oral traditions to the written traditions which have survived. Notably, as Widengren mentions, "The term for 'hemp,' *bangha*, is used in the *Avesta*, however it is missing in the Gathas" (Widengren, 1965). The Gathas, being the book directly attributed to the authorship of Zoroaster, which is also silent on the topic of Haoma.

> If we go in contrast to the late-Zoroastrian 'Vendidad,' hemp is demonized here. From 15 it emerges, that it was used as an abortifacient agent, and in 19 it is linked with the demon Kunda. In 19 it is emphatically stated by Ahura Mazdah that it is '*axafna abanha*,' which means 'without trance and without hemp.'
> ...If a man in the ancient congregations could now be called *Pouru.banha* ['possessing much hemp'] just like that and his 'fravasi' remained nevertheless an object of worship, then without a doubt it can be perceived, in the opinion of the 'Vendidad,' that there is a conscious polemic against the elder rites of the congregation. At this later stage, the old ecstasy was considered as a demonic nuisance; the metamorphosis of the old trance-goddess Busyasta in to the demon of somnolence goes in parallel with the

denunciation of hemp, while in contrast Chwafna, originally the trance, is worshipped further, without a doubt with altered significance. (Nyberg, 1938)

In relation to this demonizations, it is interesting to note that Nyberg noted that a "very interesting list of demons exists...It includes the following female demons: Budhi with the parallel form Budhiza, Kundi with the parallel form Kundiza and finally the old goddess of ecstasy Busyansta, 'things to come,' the demon of somnolence in Zoroastrianism" (Nyberg, 1938). Apparently these deities were important figures in the early use of cannabis, and may give us some insights into the more ancient pre-Zoroastrian cultic use of cannabis amongst the Aryans:

In Budhiza, true Budhiza, and Kundiza, true Kundiza, one can again recognise the word 'iza,' which serves as a synonym for Armaiti, the godly tribe, in oldest Zoroastrianism; Budhiza therefore actually means 'tribe and cult congregation of the goddess Budhi' and Kundiza 'tribe and cult congregation of the goddess Kundi'...

Alongside the goddess Kundi there is also a masculine Kunda, who needless to say is now a demon. Vend. 19,41 deals with him as follows "the Sraosa accompanied by Asi would like to slay the demon Kunda, the one with the hemp, so that he no longer has hemp." Kunda and indeed also Kundi were therefore very closely linked with the old ecstatic substance of hemp, which was used since ancient times by the Aryans in the North and East. Kundiza was a body or guild of ecstatics, who reached the ecstatic state through narcotization with hemp. If, as I believe, the Median town Kunduru, mentioned in the Behistun Inscription and written Kuntarrus = Kundaru in the Elamite version, is linked with this pair of gods, then it must have been an old West Iranian hashish nest...

The goddess Busyansta is probably regarded as the common oracle deity of the West, which views oracle as a divine strength. As she represents the demon of somnolence, then we must assume that she began to function in trance. She [the goddess Busyansta] receives the epithet 'zairina,' that in my opinion should not be translated as 'exhausting, flagging' rather 'golden';[51] that is an epithet in the same style as Zairica. It alludes presumably to the

51   The term "zairi," meaning "yellow, golden, green" is often used to describe Haoma in the Avesta.

ingested ecstasy potion. Maybe it was hemp extract in wine ...
(Nyberg, 1938)

If there were a polemic against hemp, as these passages indicate,
it would explain a lot about the confusion on the matter. As for
the contradictions surrounding the figure of Zoroaster this raises, I
have proposed one possibility regarding the prohibitions of Haoma
and the use of *mang*, indicating that it was the use by the wider
public against which Zoroaster rallied, and this could also be clearly applied to the use of hemp as well, which would also explain any
movement to suppress the use of cannabis such as those noted by
Nyberg above. Still one must remain open to the very real possibility that the term 'Zoroaster' itself, may be less of a personal name
and more of a title, which was apllied to different individuals with
different views on the use of *mang* and Haoma, with some 'Zoro-
asters' approving of its use, and others condemning it.

Any Zoroastrian prohibitions of *bhanga/mang* seem initially to
have been far from successful, as the historical record indicates that
such shamanic practices were continued by the Zoroastrian elite
for some time, at least for the first few centuries AD.

Around the most popular estimated date for the time of Zoroaster, 600 BC, Cyrus the Great was born, and through this king, Persia
came to be one of the greatest empires of the ancient world. The
empire that expanded under his rule included most of Southwest
Asia and much of Central Asia, from Egypt and the Hellespont in
the west to the Indus River in the east, to create the largest state
the world had yet seen. Cyrus died in battle, fighting the Scythians
along the Syr Darya in August 530 BC or 529 BC.

Beyond his nation, Cyrus left a lasting legacy on Jewish religion
(through his Edict of Restoration), and as a result on the Christian
Old Testament. The prophet Isaiah referred to Cyrus the Great of
Persia as 'the anointed of Yahweh,'[52] whom Yahweh himself led, "to
subdue nations before him that gates may not be closed." Yet historically, Cyrus, referred to in the Old Testament as "the King of Kings,"
(the same title applied to Jesus Christ in the New Testament), and
who returned the different peoples that he had conquered to their
homelands and restored each of their gods to their temples, continued to worship the pre-Mazdean Aryan gods of his own ancestors.

---

52   The ancient Hebrew anointing oil contained sacred *keneh-bosm* (Cannabis) as
the pre-eminent psycho active ingredient.

The Bible records that a remnant of the Jewish population returned to the Promised Land from Babylon, following an edict (reproduced in the Book of Ezra) from Cyrus to rebuild the temple. As a result of Cyrus' policies, the Jews honored him as a dignified and righteous king. He is the only Gentile to be designated as a messiah, a divinely-appointed king, in the Tanakh (Isaiah 45:1-6). However, at the time, there was also Jewish criticism of him after he was lied to by the Cuthites, who wanted to halt the building of the Second Temple. They accused the Jews of conspiring to rebel, so Cyrus in turn stopped the construction of the temple, which would not be completed until 516 BC, during the reign of Darius the Great. This as we shall see is in the next Chapter, was a pivotal time in Jewish history.

Darius was Cyrus' son in law, and he was able to take the throne by marriage, as both of Cyrus' own sons had died in battle. Important to our study, according to Zoroastrian tradition, Darius' blood father was Hystaspes, the Greek version of the name Vishtaspa - the aforementiond king who converted to Zoroaster's religion after drinking *mang*! It has been argued that Vishtaspa, the patron of Zarathustra and Hytaspes, father of Darius are distinct persons, but such an argument relies on the validity of an early dating for the life of Zarathustra.

If, we accept that by the name "Hystaspes" (i.e. Vištâspa), the Avestan texts do refer to the father of Darius I, then according to Zoroastrian scripture, Zarathustra lived during the 6th C. B.C.. Other Zoroastrian sources corroborate this. The Bundahishn, a scripture written down around the time of the Islamic conquest of Persia (AD 637), places the birth of Zoroaster at 588 BC. It has also been noted that Cyrus and Cambyses adhered to the Mazdean pantheistic beliefs of their ancestors, leaving no mention of Zarathustra in their inscriptions, while on the other hand it is clear that Darius and his successors were monotheistic Zoroastrian followers of Ahura Mazda. In addition, the very nature of the Zoroastrian reformation, a transformation of an ancient religion from pantheism to monotheism, may be seen as supportive of a 6th C. dating, because such a dating corresponds with the cohabitation of Persia by significant numbers of a monotheistic people – the exiled Jews.

It was at this period in history, as we shall look at in the next Chapter, that the Semitic ancestors of the Jews adopted so many of the Zoroastrian ideas that were pivotal for the later development of Christianity. As shall be discussed, some have even suggested that it was at this late date that Jewish monotheism itself was first born.

> Zoroastrian monotheism was made the state religion through-out the Persian empire, with its one hundred and twenty-seven provinces, by Darius Hystaspis, whose reign extended from India to Ethiopia, B.C. 521.... And this, too, was true of her many provinces until they were wrestled from her by superior force. (Brown, 1890)

From accounts that can be gathered from ancient sources, there is every indication that both before and after the time of Darius the rite of visionary experience induced by *mang* experienced by Darius's father Vishtaspa, had continued as part of the rites of initiation of a new king.

> Among the situations where sauma seems most likely to have been used was at the inauguration of pre-Islamic Iranian rulers. This is indicated by King Wishtasp's consumption of "hom and mang" at his "initiation," which is still commemorated by Zoroastrians at the New Year.... A reflection of the initiation of kings with sauma may be preserved in Plutarch's Life of Artaxerxes III. 1-3: "A little while after the death of Darius [II], the new king made an expedition to Pasargadae that he might receive the royal initiation at the hands of the Persian priests. Here there is a sanctuary to a war-like goddess whom one might conjecture to be Athena. Into this sanctuary the candidate for initiation must pass, and after laying aside his own proper robe must put on that which Cyrus the Elder used to wear before he became king; then he must eat a cake of figs, chew some turpentine-wood, and drink a cup of sour milk. Whatever else is done besides this is unknown to outsiders." Zoroaster also put on a garment when he came up from the hom liquid as, it seems, did his father Porushasp when he approached the hom and as also did Arda Wiraz. This suggests that a change of clothes may have been a regular feature of sauma-drinking in the initiation of Iranian rulers. (Bedrosian, 2006)

Fig 15.2: Sassanian Bowl, the king drinking the Cup of Haoma or wine, mixed with *mang*.

These accounts are consistent with stone inscriptions found in Fars about 300 A.D., by Kirdir, the founder of the Sassanian Zoroastrian ecclesiastical establishment. "Kirdir's inscription asserts in this passage, as a basis of his claim to religious authority, that his spirit double visited the other world and was shown heaven and hell. The account thus parallels the Arda Wiraz Namag in reaffirming the reliance placed on a vision of menog existence as the means to religious truth" (Flattery & Schwartz 1989). As Shaul Shaked noted in *Quests and Visionary Journeys in Sassanian Iran*:

> Visions as done by Kider and Arda Wiraz, was one way of communicating with the gods and obtaining direct knowledge of the things of the next world, a way of verifying the truths of the religion..... [The devotee] would be transported to the other world; when he came back his arrival would be celebrated with a great show of joy and relief. Several of these elements show strong similarity with the complex of practices associated with shamanic cults. Such cults are nowadays typical of the fringes of the Iranian world, [i.e. the continued use of *dūg-e wahdat*] and it makes sense to assume that they formed part of the Iranian civilization itself...
>
> It is striking that Pahlavi literature of the late Sassanian and early Islamic period is practically obsessed with descriptions of the hereafter and of entities that belong to the invisible world. The classic example is the Book of Arda Wiraz, but it is not unique... visions... are alluded to quite frequently in the Pahlavi books, together with the discussion of the possibility of the seeing of menog, the invisible world, by the organ dedicated to this kind of vision, "the eye of the soul."
>
> ....The preparation for this journey was done, as we have seen, by administering to the officiant a dose of *mang* (hemp) mixed with wine. (Shaked, et al., 1999)

רֹאשׁ מָר־דְּרוֹר חֲמֵשׁ מֵאוֹת וְקִנְּמָן־בֶּשֶׂם מַחֲצִיתוֹ חֲמִשִּׁים

24 וּמָאתָיִם (וּקְנֵה־בֶשֶׂם) חֲמִשִּׁים וּמָאתָיִם : וְקִדָּה חֲמֵשׁ

25 מֵאוֹת בְּשֶׁקֶל הַקֹּדֶשׁ וְשֶׁמֶן זַיִת הִין : וְעָשִׂיתָ אֹתוֹ שֶׁמֶן

מִשְׁחַת־קֹדֶשׁ רֹקַח מִרְקַחַת מַעֲשֵׂה רֹקֵחַ שֶׁמֶן מִשְׁחַת־

26 קֹדֶשׁ יִהְיֶה : וּמָשַׁחְתָּ בוֹ אֶת־אֹהֶל מוֹעֵד וְאֵת אֲרוֹן הָעֵדֻת :

27 וְאֶת־הַשֻּׁלְחָן וְאֶת־כָּל־כֵּלָיו וְאֶת־הַמְּנֹרָה וְאֶת־כֵּלֶיהָ וְאֵת

28 מִזְבַּח הַקְּטֹרֶת : וְאֶת־מִזְבַּח הָעֹלָה וְאֶת־כָּל־כֵּלָיו וְאֶת־

29 הַכִּיֹּר וְאֶת־כַּנּוֹ : וְקִדַּשְׁתָּ אֹתָם וְהָיוּ קֹדֶשׁ קָדָשִׁים כָּל־

הַנֹּגֵעַ בָּהֶם יִקְדָּשׁ :

— **fragrant cane.** *Keneh bosem* in Hebrew. Ancient sources identify this with the sweet calamus (Septuagint; Rambam on Kerithoth 1:1; Saadia; Ibn Janach). This is the sweetflag or flag-root, *Acoras calamus* which grows in Europe. It appears that a similar species grew in the Holy Land, in the Hula region in ancient times (Theophrastus, *History of Plants* 9:7). Other sources apparently indicate that it was the Indian plant, *Cympopogon martini*, which has the form of red straw (*Yad, Kley HaMikdash* 1:3). On the basis of cognate pronunciation and Septuagint readings, some identify *Keneh bosem* with the English and Greek *cannabis*, the hemp plant.

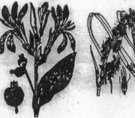

Canna   Cympopogan   Hemp

There are, however, some authorities who identify the "sweet cane" with cinnamon bark (Radak, *Sherashim*). Some say that *kinman* is the wood, and *keneh bosem* is the bark (Abarbanel).

30:24 **cassia** (Radak, *Sherashim*; Peshita; Vulgate). *Kidah* in Hebrew; *ketzia* in Aramaic (*Targum*; Rambam on *Kelayim* 1:8). Cassia is the common name for the bark of the tree *Cinnamomum cassia* or *Cassia lignea* belonging to the laurel family, which grows in China. (*Pachad Yitzchak*, s.v. *Ketoreth*; cf. Pliny 12:43; Theophrastus, *History of Plants* 9:7;

Top: A page from Aryeh Kaplan's The Living Torah (New York, 1981) which discusses the first of 5 Hebrew references that appear in the Old Testament texts which the Polish etymologist Sula Benet identified as cannabis in 1936. Bottom left: Moses and the Burning Bush, illustration from the 1890 Holman Bible. Bottom right: High priest offering incense on the altar, as in Leviticus 16:12; illustration from Henry Davenport Northrop, "Treasures of the Bible," published 1894.

16

KENEH BOSEM: SACRED PLANT OF THE HEBREWS

The identification and role of cannabis in the Bible is a subject that this researcher has pondered and considered for close to two decades, and has been discussed at length in an earlier work, *Sex, Drugs, Violence and the Bible* (Bennett & McQueen, 2001) from which much of this Chapter has been adapted. Readers who wish to understand this subject more fully, are directed to that considerable edition. In the composition of *Sex, Drugs, Violence and the Bible* (*SDVB*) the influence of the Mesopotamian religions and Zoroastrian were both taken into account, but it was not until researching this volume that I realized the full extent of the influence of the Persian religion on the development of the Bible, both the New and Old Testament, and how this was also directly related to the fate of Haoma and *bhang* use amongst the Persians.

Probably seen as even more controversial than the debate about the identification of the Haoma/Soma as cannabis are the ancient Hebrew references to a plant known as *keneh bosem* that a growing number of researches are identifying with cannabis.

Although it is little known to most modern readers, a number of sources have noted that psychoactive plants and inebriants played a very important role in ancient Hebrew culture and originally appeared throughout the books that make up the Bible's Old Testament. The Bible openly discusses the use of mandrake, which is psychoactive, along with intoxication by wine and strong drink (alcoholic solutions that contained a variety of plants) so the Hebrews were more than familiar with altering their consciousness.

What will be surprising to most modern readers is the frequent use of cannabis-sativa, by both the Hebrew Priests and Kings. Indicating, as anthropologist Vera Rubin noted, that cannabis "appears in the Old Testament because of the ritual and sacred aspect of it" (Rubin 1978).

For more than a century various researchers have been trying to bring attention to potential cannabis references within the Old Testament. "Like the ancient Greeks, the Old Testament Israelites were surrounded by marijuana-using peoples. A British physician, Dr. C. Creighton, concluded in 1903 that several references to marijuana can be found in the Old Testament. Examples are the *'honeycomb'* referred to in the Song of Solomon, 5:1, and the *'honeywood'* in I Samuel 14: 25-45" (Consumer Reports 1972). Creighton felt that in "the O.T. there are some half-dozen passages where cryptic references to hachish may be discovered... But that word, which is the key to the meaning, has been knowingly mistranslated in the Vulgate and in the modern version, having been rendered by a variant also by the LXX in one of the passages, and confessed as unintelligible in the other by the use of a marginal Hebrew word in Greek letters" (Creighton 1903).

> Hachish, which is the disreputable intoxicant drug of the East...is of unknown antiquity. It is known that the fiber of hemp-plant, *Cannabis sativa*, was used for cordage in ancient times; and it is therefore probable that the resinous exudation, "honey" or "dew," which is found upon its flowering tops on some soils, or in certain climates (*Cannabis Indica*), was known for its stimulant or intoxicant properties from an equally early date...we may assume it to have been traditional among the Semites from remote antiquity. There are reasons, in the nature of the case, why there should be no clear history. All vices are veiled from view; they are *sub rosa*; and that is true especially of the vices of the East. Where they are alluded to at all, it is in cryptic, subtle...and allegorical terms. Therefore if we are to discover them, we must be prepared to look below the surface of the text. (Creighton 1903)

Dr. Creighton was not alone in this view. A few decades later the German researcher Immanuel Low, in his *Die Flora Der Juden* (1926\1967) identified a number of ancient Hebrew references to cannabis, here as an incense, food source, as well as cloth. In more recent times Professor Stanley Moore, chairman of the philosophy department of the University of Wisconsin-Olatteville, has stated that Biblical references to "*aromatic herbs*" and "*smoke*" could mean psycho-active drugs used in religious observances that Moore said are as old as religion itself. "Western Jews and Christians, who shun psycho-active drugs in their faith practices, are the exception, not the norm."[1]

More recently Raphael Mechoulam and associates at the Hebrew University in Jerusalem have suggested the following etymology for cannabis: Greek *cannabis* < Arabic *kunnab* < Syriac *qunnappa* < Hebrew *pannag* (= *bhanga* in Sanskrit and *bang* in Persian). Mechoulam explains that in Hebrew, only the consonants form the basis of a word and the letters p and b are frequently interchangeable. The authors think it probable that *pannag*, which they saw as indicating a preperation of cannabis rather than whole plant, mentioned in the Bible by the prophet Ezekiel as being an item of trade on an incoming caravan (Ezekiel 27:17) (Mechoulam, et al., 1991).

Mechoulam's suggestion of '*pannag*' may have some support through its similarity to the Egyptian *Ne-penthe*, discussed earlier, which was powdered and mixed with wine. In relation to Burton's suggestion of a connection between *Ne-penthe* and the Sanskrit and Avestan '*bhang*' it is interesting to note that it has been suggested that "Scythians took cannabis into Egypt via Palestine..." (Mathews, 2005). Indeed from what we have seen such etymology could have easily carried over.

A cultural connection between the Scythians and Hebrews, including trade, has long been suggested, and the Polish anthropologist Sula Benet felt that cannabis was an important item of trade between the two cultures.

> Since the history of cannabis has been tied to the history of the Scythians, it is of interest to establish their appearance in the Near East. Again, the Old Testament provides information testifying to their greater antiquity than has been previously assumed. The Scythians participated in both trade and wars alongside the ancient Semites for at least one millennium before Herodotus encountered them in the fifth century B.C. The reason for confusion

---

1   In an article that appeared in the *Dubuque Telegraph Herald*, Friday, March 26, 1993, page 2A, about a court case involving the Israel Zion Coptic Church. Like the Ethiopian Zion Coptic Church, which they grew out of, the Israel Zion Coptics believe hemp is the *true* Biblical Eucharist.

and the relative obscurity of the role played by the Scythians in world history is explained by the fact that they were known to the Greeks as Scythians but to the Semites as Ashkenaz. Identification of the Scythian-Ashkenaz as a single people is convincingly made by Ellis H. Minns (1965) in his definitive work on Scythians and Greeks. The earliest reference to the Ashkenaz people appears in the Bible in Genesis 10: 3, where Ashkenaz, their progenitor, is named as the son of Gomer, the great-grandson of Noah. The Ashkenaz of the Bible were both war-like and extremely mobile. In Jeremiah 51: 27, we read that the kingdoms of Ararat (known later as Armenia), Minni (Medea), and Ashkenaz attacked Babylonia. In 612 B.C. Babylonians with the aid of the Medeans (Medes) and Scythians, coming from the Caucasus, dealt a deadly blow to Assyria (Durant 1954). Referring to the threat of war, Herodotus reports that Scythians attempted to invade Egypt by way of Palestine and they withdrew only after the Pharaoh paid them to retreat.

There is evidence of the presence of the Scythians in Palestine. The city known as Beizan in modern times was originally called Bethshan and later renamed Scythopolis by the Greeks during the Hellenistic period, since many Scythians settled there during the great invasion of Palestine in the seventh-century B.C.

The importance of the geographical position of Palestine cannot be overlooked when considering the trade routes through which caravans moved, laden with goods and precious "spices." Palestine was situated along the two most vital trade routes of the ancient world. One was between Egypt and Asia and the other ran west from Arabia to the coastal plain, from there branching off to Egypt to Syria.[2] (Benet, 1975)

Interestingly, indications of such trade may be seen in the Hebrew adoption of a word for cannabis that is more clearly of Scythian origin, *keneh bosem*. Of the historical material indicating the Hebraic use of cannabis, the strongest and most profound piece of evidence was established by this same researcher Sula Benet (a.k.a. Sara Benetowa), a Polish etymologist from the Institute of Anthropological Sciences in Warsaw. Creating a controversy that has increased ever since, Benet claimed that "In the original He-

---

2   "The Incense Road, like the Silk Road, was a conduit of exchange in the ancient world blending languages, religions, cultures and ideas with its spices and herbs. Linking Egypt and India with a route running right through the Holy Lands…, it is perhaps the oldest continuous trade route in history" (Dannaway, 2009).

brew text of the Old Testament there are references to hemp, both as incense, which was an integral part of religious celebration, and as an intoxicant" (Benet 1975: 1936). Through comparative etymological study, Benet documented that in the Old Testament and in its Aramaic translation, the Targum Onculos, hemp is referred to as *keneh bosem* (variously translated as *kaneh bosem, kaniebosm, q'neh bosm*) and is also rendered in traditional Hebrew as *kannabos* or *kannabus*. The root *"kana"* in this construction means *"cane~reed"* or *"hemp,"* while *"bosm"* means *"aromatic."* This Hebrew word *"kaneh"* occurs many times in the Bible, and in some instances, it can simply mean *"reed," "cane,"* or *"stalk,"*[3] but Benet stated that in certain Biblical passages such as Exodus 30:23, Song of Songs 4:14, Isaiah 43:24, Jeremiah 6:20, Ezekiel 27:19, the word specifically refers to cannabis.

Benet believed that the word *keneh-bosm* was mistranslated as *calamus*, a common marsh plant with little monetary value that does not have the qualities or value ascribed to *kaneh* or *kanehbosm*.[4] The error occurred in the oldest Greek translation of the Hebrew *Torah*, the *Septuagint* in the third century BC, and was repeated in the many translations that followed such as the *Vulgate*. "This conclusion (i.e. *keneh bosem* as cannabis) has since been affirmed by other scholars…" (Ruck et al., 2001). However, it should be noted that calamus itself is said to contain some psycho-active

---

3   Through the use of stiff stalks or "*canes*" for measuring, the Indo European term "*kanna*" came to be adopted into names for measurements, such as "*canon*," and in the sense of long hollow tubes, "*cannon*." In the same way the term originally used to identify "cannabis" in Hebrew, "*kaneh*," likely came to have other connotations. "The history of hemp… teaches us a valuable lesson: the arrival of a word for a particular object or substance does not necessarily coincide with the first introduction of this generic item, but it may be a new variety, style, or function which carries with it a new vocabulary" (Smith & McConvell, 2003).

4   Alternatively, Michael V. Fox, saw the Hebrew references to *kaneh* as *Cymbopogon martini* or *Andropogon nardus*" (Fox 1985). The one other argument against kaneh bosm being hemp that I am aware of appears in Ernest Abel's *Marihuana: the First 12,000 Years*. Abel stated that the *Kanna-bosm* in Exodus 30:23 'suggest sugar rather than cannabis' and stated that the references referred to a 'sweet tasting' plant, rather than a 'sweet smelling' plant (Abel 1980). But, the Hebrew word **bosm**, in this context, clearly refers to fragrance not taste (Strong 1979). Also, as pointed out in an earlier work (Bennett et al., 1995), and as Dale Pendell has expressed in his very entertaining *Pharmako/Poeia*, sugarcane would have no place in an ointment. Sugar cane would cause the whole mixture to become a gummy mass that would also be susceptible to contamination from micro-organisms. Such a sticky mixture would hardly have been suitable for a Holy anointing oil. As the later writer of Ecclesiastes commented "*Dead flies make the ointment of the perfumer fetid and putrid…*" (Ecc. 10:1), such a fate would surely befall any ointment containing sugar cane.

alkaloids, and its use for these purposes has been reported[5] (Ott 1993, Schultes & Hoffman 1979).[6]

Both the *Septuagint* and the later *Vulgate* are known for their mistranslation of Hebrew words into Greek (Gordon, 2006; Henslow, 2009). Most notable is the Septuagint mistranslation of the Hebrew term *"almah"* meaning "young woman," which was translated into the Greek as *"parthenos"* - "virgin." This single example had a monumental effect on later Christian cosmology and theology as it resulted in the later belief that the Messiah must be born of a virgin. Moreover, in relation to our study, the mistranslation of Hebrew botanical names is also believed to have occurred:

> The fast-growing plant referred to in the biblical Book of Jonah is most often translated into English as "gourd." However, this is a mistranslation that dates to the appended Septuagint, the Greek translation of the Hebrew Bible, in which the Hebrew word *qiqayon* (castor, *Ricinus communis*, Euphorbiaceae) was transformed into the somewhat similar-sounding Greek word *kolokynthi* (colocynth, *Citrullus colocynthis*). In translation of the Greek into Latin, kolokynthi became the similar-sounding *cucurbita* (gourd). This is reflected in early iconography, the plant most often depicted being a long-fruited *Lagenaria siceraria* (bottle or calabash gourd), a fast-growing climber. (Janick & Paris, 2006).

As Sula Benet noted in regards to *kaneh*, the arguments for identification with cannabis went far beyond similar cognate pronunciations, and also included textual descriptions of the term. "Another piece of evidence regarding the use of word *kaneh* in the sense of hemp rather than reed [or calamus] is the religious requirement that the dead be buried in *kaneh* shirts. Centuries later linen was substituted for hemp (Klein 1908)[7]" (Benet, 1975). (Calamus is not a fibre plant).

I would suggest that a further potential direct use of the term *kaneh* in reference to cannabis occurs in Genesis 41:22, and this passage, which refers to grains, also disallows an interpretation of calamus, as calamus is not known for edible seeds or grains: "In my dreams I ...saw seven heads of grain, full and good, growing on a single stalk [*kaneh*]." The highly nutritious seeds of cannabis have been referred to as grains, and 7 heads, or large kola buds, on a marijuana plant would be a sign of abundance.[8] The hemp seed's use as a food and oil source can be traced back to the very beginnings of civilization. The German botanist, Immanuel Low, referred to a sixth century BC Persian name for a preparation of cannabis seed, *Sahdanag* – "Royal Grain"; or "King's Grain," which demonstrates the high regard the ancient Persians held for the nutritious oil rich seeds that came from the same plant which provided them also with a means of religious revelation by means of the drink *banga*. *Sahdanag* was generally prepared in the form of a heart shaped cookie, possibly indicating that the ancient Persians

---

7   Referring to Sigfried Klein's Tod und Begrabnis in Palistina. There is also at least one apocryphal story that refers to cannabis fibres, in a tale of Solomon forcing a demon to spin hemp (Testament of Solomon, 4:12). But this work also mentions the hill of Golgotha and the cross of Christ, so most scholars agree that it is not of Hebrew origin or written during the days of Solomon.

8   Indeed the imagery used in Genesis 41:22 brings to mind the Hebrew religious symbol the *menorah*, which itself looks very much like a blossoming hemp plant glistening with resin (Bennett & McQueen). The name *menorah* itself has relationships to the name of a loom, used in weaving; and plough used in farming; the second part of the name, *owrah*, refers not only to brightness, but to a bright-plant. (Strong 1979). The word *owrah* appears in this context in 2 Kings 4:39, when the prophet Elisha orders one of the men to go "out into the field to gather herbs [*owrah*]," from which he makes a strange stew that strikes terror into the hearts of the men who taste it The second appearance is recorded in a more reverenced tone, coming from the eloquent pen of Isaiah: "thy dew is, is as the dew of herbs [*owrah*]"(Isaiah 26:19). Possibly, the biblical instructions for making the elaborate candle holder that were given to Moses, offer us the strongest sense of the vegetative symbolism incorporated into it; "Make a lampstand of pure gold and hammer it out, base and shaft; its flowerlike cups, buds and blossoms shall be one piece with it. Six branches are to extend from the sides of the lampstand--three on one side and three on the other. Three cups shaped like almond flowers with buds and blossoms are to be on one branch...the buds and branches shall all be of one piece with the lampstand...." (Exodus 25:31-36)

recognized the seed's close relationship with health and vitality (Low, 1925; reprinted 1967). Sometime after the Persian Empire took control of the ancient world, the Jews adopted this Persian preparation of hemp seed and retained its name of *Sahdanag*. Immanuel Low also suggests that the formerly unidentified Hebrew word, *tzli'q*, (*Tzaddi, Lamed, Yod, Quoph*), makes reference to a Jewish meal of roasted hemp seeds that was popular into medieval times and was sold by Jews in European markets. (The first part of the name *tzli'q* simply means roasted, the final letter, *Quoph*, an abbreviation of *kaneh*, which begins with that letter – Low's reference to this also indicates independent support for Benet's interpretation of the term *kaneh* as cannabis) (Low, 1925; reprinted 1967).

Considerable academic support has emerged for Benet's theory on the identification of kaneh with cannabis. In 1980 the respected anthropologist Weston La Barre (1980) referred to the Biblical references in an essay on cannabis, concurring with Benet's earlier hypothesis. In that same year respected British Journal *New Scientist* also ran a story that referred to the Hebrew Old Testament references: "Linguistic evidence indicates that in the original Hebrew and Aramaic texts of the Old Testament the 'holy oil' which God directed Moses to make (Exodus 30:23) was composed of myrrh, cinnamon, cannabis and cassia" (Malyon & Henman 1980). A modern counterpart of the word is even listed in Ben Yehudas *Pocket Dictionary* and other Hebrew source books[9]. Further, online, the Internet's informative *Navigating the Bible*, used by countless theological students, also refers to the Exodus 30:23 reference as possibly designating cannabis. This online text is largely based on the very popular *The Living Torah*, by Rabbi Aryeh Kaplan, a popular gift at bar mitzvahs, which correctly notes that "On the basis of cognate pronunciation and a Septuagint reading, some identify *Keneh bosem* with English and Greek cannabis, the hemp plant" (Kaplan, 1981). One can only speculate that before his death in 1983, Kaplan began to suspect that these connections went beyond linguistic theories, as in another work, published just prior to his death, Kaplan described later Jewish Kabbalistic writings that refer to the burning of certain grasses,

9   Hayim Baltsan ~ Webster's *New World Hebrew Dictionary: Hebrew/English English/Hebrew*, 1994, pg. 650; Eliezer ben-Yehuda ~ *Pocket English-Hebrew/ Hebrew-English Dictionary*, 1961, pg. 140; Eliezer ben-Yehuda ~ *A Complete Dictionary of Ancient and Modern Hebrew*, in 8 volumes; NY: Thomas Yoseloff, 1960.

which the learned rabbi stated "were possibly psychedelic drugs" (Kaplan, 1982).

As well, William McKim noted in *Drugs and Behaviour: an introduction to behavioral pharmacology*, "It is likely that the Hebrews used cannabis... In the Old Testament (Exodus 30:23), God tells Moses to make a holy oil of 'myrrh, sweet cinnamon, kaneh bosem and kassia'" (McKim, 1986). *A Minister's Handook of Mental Disorders* also records that "Some scholars believe that God's command to Moses (Exodus 30:23) to make a holy oil included cannabis as one of the chosen ingredients" (Ciarrocchi, 1993). In the essay "Psychoactive Agents and the Self," in *The Lost Self: Pathologies of the Brain and Identity*, (which deals with the biological basis of the human mind) Roy Mathews notes "The holy oil God instructed Moses to make... is believed to have contained cannabis. The previous translation of Kaneh Bosn as 'calamus,' a marsh plant, was found to be erroneous; the Hebrew Kaneh Bosn and Scythian cannabis were probably the same" (Mathews, 2005).

Numerous other researchers have also come to acknowledge that cannabis is in fact the most likely botanical candidate for the Hebrew *keneh bosem*. Most recently, author and Professor of Classical Mythology at Boston University, Carl Ruck,, who is also a linguist, has summarized:

> Cannabis is called *kaneh bosem* in Hebrew.... The translators of the bible translate this usually as 'fragrant cane,' i.e., an aromatic grass. Once the word is correctly translated, the use of cannabis in the bible is clear. Large amounts of it were compounded into the ointment for the ordination of the priest. This ointment was also used to anoint the holy vessels in the Inner Sanctum or Tabernacle ('tent'). It was also used to fumigate the holy enclosed space. The ointment (absorbed through the skin) and the fragrance of the vessels (both absorbed by handling and inhaled as perfume) and the smoke of the incense in the confined space would have been a very effective means of administering the psychoactive properties of the plant. Since it was only the High Priest who entered the Tabernacle, it was an experience reserved for him, although as the chrism of priestly ordination it was probably also something experienced in a different way by the whole priesthood. This same psychoactive chrism was later used for the coronation of the kings. (Ruck, 2009)

Benet's etymological research regarding the Hebrew terms '*keneh bosem*' and '*keneh*' was based upon tracing the modern word 'cannabis' back through history to show the similarities between the cognitive pronunciation of '*cannabis*' and '*keneh bosem*'[10] and as well as comparing the term to the names used for cannabis by contemporary kingdoms, such as the Assyrian and Babylonians terms for the plant '*qunubu*'. Sula Benet believed that the term cannabis "is derived from Semitic languages and both its name and forms of its use were borrowed by the Scythians from the peoples of the Near East" (Benet, 1975).

Independent support for Benet's view of the Semitic origins of the term *kaneh* can be found in *The Word: The Dictionary That Reveals the Hebrew Source of English*, by Isaac E. Mozeson. In reference to Hebrew *kaneh*, Mozeson follows a similar view to Benet's that the "so-called IE root *kanna*... is admitted to be "of Semitic origin."...the IE word *kannabis* (hemp - a late IE word borrowed from an unknown source)" (Mozeson, 1989).

> ...*Kanboos* is an early post biblical term for hemp... The word Hemp is traced to Greek *kannabis* and Persian *kannab*... The ultimate etymon is conceded by *Webster's* to be "a very early borrowing from a non-IE, possibly Semitic language."
>
> In seeking related words... consider Aramaic... *Kenabh*... and [Hebrew] *Kaneh*...[11] (Mozeson, 1989)

This author's view differs in this respect, and I would suggest the term '*keneh bosem*', also rendered *q'neh bosem*' is the Hebrew transliteration of an earlier Indo-European term for the plant '*kanna*' combined with the Hebrew term for fragrance '*bosem*'. The Indo-European term '*kanna*,' was spread around the ancient world by nomadic Scythian tribes, and has left traces through the vernacular '*an*' seen in various modern terms for cannabis in Indo-European family languages, such as the Indian *bhang*, the Persian *bhanga*, the Greek *kannabis*, the French *chanvre*, the Dutch *canvas* and the German *hanf*. This is also the view of Prof. Carl Ruck who has commented that "*kaneh bosem* in Hebrew... is now recognized as the Scythian word that Herodotus wrote as *kannabis* (or cannabis)" (Ruck, 2009). Anthroplogist Weston La Barre noted in regards to this as well:

---

10   As with the Semitic term '*kinamon*' the source of our modern 'cinnamon.'
11   Interestingly Mozeson makes no reference to calamus in the context of the term *kaneh*.

...[T]he word would seem very old in Indo-European, rather than multiply borrowed... [I]f as the anthropologist Sula Benet proposes, the cannabis terms are borrowed from a Semitic language, then there is the problem of a seemingly pan-Indo-European term diffused from ancient northern Eurasia. And cannabis, of course grows wild in north central Eurasia, whence the Indo-Europeans came. That the terms [in IE languages for *cannabis*] are manifest dialectic equivalents would constitute the solidest possible evidence for the antiquity of the word, since the undivided Neolithic Indo-Europeans began to migrate (spreading prehistorically all the way from Ireland to Ceylon) and to break up dialectically in the early Bronze Age. (La Barre, 1980)

This use of an Indo-European word in the Semitic language shows that the ritual use of cannabis came to the Hebrews from foreign sources and, as an item of trade, likely via the Scythians, it retained the core aspects of its original name. Indeed, in both the Jeremiah 6:20 and Ezekiel 27:19 references referred to by Benet, cannabis is identified as coming as an item of trade from a foreign land, and indeed as the additional references noted by Benet tell when put into the context of the Biblical storyline, this foreign association with the plant may in fact have been the cause of its disfavour amongst the ancient Hebrews.[12] Certain researchers, who claim the designation of 'calamus' as *keneh bosem* stands correct, have failed to note that The plant *kaneh* is clearly described as an item of trade in the Ezekiel and Jeremiah and these references disallow the *Septuagint* identification with calamus, as calamus is indigenous to the area in question and can commonly be found throughout the Middle East (Bennett & McQueen, 2001). Further, as has been shown elsewhere (Benet 1975; Bennett & MCQueen, 2001), and shall be further demonstrated here, evidence for this connection goes far beyond a mere linguistic theory.

The Holy Anointing Oil of Exodus

The first of the references to *keneh bosem* occurs in the story of Moses, who, it should be remembered, initially met the

---

12   However, Sula Benet, who, ironically, lived in Poland close to the area that the root word for cannabis likely originated, disagreed with this view and felt that "the ritual use of hemp as well as the name, cannabis, originated in the ancient Near East" (Benet, 1975).

angel of the Lord from "flames of fire within a bush." Exodus 30:23 describes cannabis in a list of ingredients in the "Holy Anointing Oil."

> Then the Lord said to Moses, "Take the following fine spices: 500 shekels of liquid myrrh, half as much of fragrant cinnamon, 250 shekels of fragrant cane [*keneh-bosem*], 500 shekels of cassia—all according to the sanctuary shekel - and a hind of olive oil. Make these into a sacred anointing oil, a fragrant blend, the work of a perfumer.[13] It will be the sacred anointing oil. Then use it to anoint the Tent of the Meeting, the ark of the Testimony, the table and all its articles, the lampstand and its accessories, the altar of incense,[14] the altar of burnt offering and all its utensils, and the basin with its stand. You shall consecrate them so they will be most holy, and whatever touches them will be holy."
>
> Anoint Aaron and his sons and consecrate them so they may serve me as priests. Say to the Israelites, "This is to be my sacred anointing oil for the generations to come. Do not pour it on men's bodies and do not make any oil with the same formula. It is sacred, and you are to consider it sacred. Whoever makes perfume like it and whoever puts it on anyone other than a priest must be cut off from his people." (Exodus 30:22-33)

As one shekel equals approximately 16.37[15] grams, this means that the THC of over 9 pounds of flowering cannabis tops were extracted into a hind, about 6.5 litres of oil. The entheogenic effects of such a solution, even when applied topically, would undoubtedly have been intense. Health Canada has done scientific tests that show transdermal absorption of THC can take place.

---

13   The ointment was mixed in the large cauldrons required for the extensive ingredients, and the sacred craft of making the holy ointment was passed down through a guild of Perfumers (de Waal 1994). Possibly, the Hebrews placed all the ingredients of the Holy Oil into such cauldrons, along with a quantity of water, and then boiled all the ingredients together, later separating the Holy oil which would be imbued with the oil soluble properties of the other ingredients, such as the psycho-active resin of the cannabis that was used. As well double-rimmed earthenware pots used for distillation have been found in the Ancient Near East, dating as far back as 3,000 b.c.. "The raw material would be placed between two rims, and a lid put over the vessel. A solvent (water or oil) would be boiled in the bottom pot: the vapor would condense on the lid, run down over the raw material, extract the ingredient sought, and drip back into the bottom of the pot. The principle was in fact that of the coffee percolator" (Saggs 1969).

14   Where the holy oil would be burned alongside other fragrant incenses.

15   This amount varies according to the version of the Bible. For instance the New International translation lists a temple shekel as equaling 11.5 grams. In any event, the amount weighs in between 7.5 and 9 pounds.

The skin is the biggest organ of the body, so of course consider-ably more cannabis is needed to be effective this way, much more than when ingested or smoked. The people who used the Holy oil literally drenched themselves in it. Based upon a 25mg/g oil Health Canada found skin penetration of THC (33%). "The high concentration of THC outside the skin encourages penetration, which is a function of the difference between outside and inside (where the concentration is essentially zero)" (James Geiwitz, Ph.D, 2001).

Cross cultural references to such topical preparations of can-nabis have been identified (Bennett & McQueen, 2001; Bennett, 2006). Closer to Moses' own time, as noted earlier, ancient Assyr-ian inscriptions indicate that a similar preparation was in use for identical purposes:

> An Assyrian medical tablet from the Louvre collection (AO 7760) (Labat, 1950)(3,10,16) was transliterated as follows…, 'ana min sammastabbariru sama-zal-la samtar-mus.'[16] Translating the French [EBR], we obtain, 'So that god of man and man should be in good rapport: - with hellebore, cannabis and lupine you will rub him.' (Russo 2005)

Only those who had been *"dedicated by the anointing oil of… God"* (Leviticus 21:12) were permitted to act as priests. In the "holy" state produced by the anointing oil the priests were forbidden to leave the sanctuary precincts (Leviticus 21:12), and the above pas-sage from Exodus, makes quite clear the sacredness of this oint-ment, the use of which the priests jealously guarded. These rules were made so that other tribal members would not find out the secret behind Moses and the priesthood's new found shamanistic revelations. Or even worse, take it upon themselves to make a simi-lar preparation. An event that would likely lead to Moses and his fellow Levites losing their authority over their ancient tribal coun-terparts. Those who broke this strong tribal taboo risked the pen-alty of being "cut off from their people," a virtual death-sentence in the savage ancient world. Secrets revealed equals power lost, is a rule of thumb that is common to shamans and magicians world wide, and as shall be seen, the ancient Hebrew shamans guarded their secrets as fiercely as any.

---

16   The term 'sam,' means 'plant.'

> The sacred character of hemp in biblical times is evident from Exodus 30:22-23, where Moses was instructed by God to anoint the meeting tent and all its furnishings with specially prepared oil, containing hemp. Anointing set sacred things apart from secular. The anointment of sacred objects was an ancient tradition in Israel: holy oil was not to be used for secular purposes.... Above all, the anointing oil was used for the installation rites of all Hebrew kings and priests. (Benet 1975)

Moreover, this Holy Oil was to be used specifically in the Tent of the Meeting, where the Lord would "speak" to Moses. From what can be understood by the descriptions in Exodus, Moses and later High Priests, would cover themselves with this ointment and also place some on the altar of incense before helping the incense itself to burn via the olive oil, a common fuel, but here enriched with psychoactive properties. "Besides its role in anointing, the holy oil of the Hebrews was burned as incense, and its use was reserved to the priestly class" (Russo, 2007). The Exodus account describes Moses as seeking the Lord's advice, from a pillar of smoke emanating from the altar of incense, in the enclosed chamber of the tent of the meeting. This is reminiscent of the cannabis burning tents of the Scythians and also Assyrians.

> The burning of specific psychoactive plants in tents may have spread from the Indo-European nomadic cults the prime example of which are the Scythians... [participating] in the enclosed inhalations of *Cannabis* vapors... the enclosure in tents or closed rooms is similar to the common practice in modern *Cannabis* culture referred to as "hot-boxing." (Dannaway, 2009)

In the Torah, the pillar of smoke that arose before Moses in the 'Tent of the Meeting,' is referred to as the 'Shekinah' and is identified as the physical evidence of the Lord's presence. None of the other Hebrews in the Exodus account either see or hear the Lord, they only know that Moses is talking to the Lord when the smoke is pouring forth from the Tent of the Meeting. It is hard not to see all the classical elements of shamanism at play in this description of Moses' encounter with God, and like Zoroaster, Moses can be seen as a ecstatic shamanic figure who used cannabis as a a means of seeking celestial advice.

Samuel and Saul: The Age of Kings

At the time of the prophet Samuel, the use of the shamanic Hebrew anointing oil was extended from the use of just priests, to include Kings as well. Although cannabis is not mentioned directly by name in Samuel, the description of events that take place after Samuel anoints Israel's first king, Saul, make clear the psycho-active nature of the ointment used. Samuel *"took a flask of oil and poured it on Saul's head"* (1 Samuel 10:1). After the anointing Samuel tells Saul: *"The Spirit of the Lord will come upon you in power...and you will be changed into a different person"*(1 Samuel 10:6), a statement indicating that the *magical* (psycho-active) power of the ointment will shortly take effect. Samuel tells Saul that when this happens, he will come across a band of prophets (*Nebiim*) Coming down from a mountaintop, *"with harp, tambourine, flute, and lyre before them prophesying"* (1 Samuel 10:5), and that Saul will join them.

> [After Saul's anointing] As Samuel foretold, the spirit of Yahweh came mightily upon the new king and he 'prophesied among them.' The verb 'to prophecy' in this context [*nebiim*] meant not to foretell the future but to behave ecstatically, to babble incoherently under the influence of the Spirit. This bizarre conduct associated with prophesying is apparent when in a second burst of such activity, Saul stripped off his clothing and lay naked all day and night, causing the people to ask, 'Is Saul among the prophets?' (1 Samuel 19:24). (Cole 1959)[17]

Clearly in the account of Saul's anointing we are dealing with the effects of much more than a mere placebo. The next direct literary reference to cannabis in the Old Testament, here just as *keneh*, occurs in Solomon's Song of Songs 4.14, where it where it grows in an orchard of fragrant and exotic fruits, herbs, and spices:

> Come with me from Lebanon, my bride, come with me from Lebanon.... How much more pleasing is your love than wine, and the fragrance of your ointment than any spice! ... The fragrance of your garments is like that of Lebanon.... Your plants are an orchard of pomegranates with choice fruits, with henna and nard, nard and saffron, keneh [cannabis] and cinnamon, with every kind of incense tree... (Song of Songs 4:8-14) [18]

17   As quoted in (Bennett & McQueen, 2001).
18   It has also been noted that Solomon, the alleged author of the Songs, ordered hemp cords amongst other material for the building of his temple. (Salzberg 1912).

Solomon's Songs

The Song of Songs is without a doubt the most beautiful piece of prose that can be found in the whole Old Testament. Interestingly, rather than being a song in praise of the Monotheistic worship of Yahweh, modern research has convincingly shown it to be the Semitic counter part of the ancient fertility poems dedicated to the sexual relationship of the ancient Near Eastern deities Tammuz and Ishtar (Pope, 1977). A view discussed at length in *SDVB*:

> ... Apparently, Solomon did not limit his use of incense, to the temple of Yahweh, or the Lord's worship. *"Solomon loved Yahweh: he followed the precepts of David his father, except that he offered sacrifice and incense on the high places."* (I Kings 3:3). Here we can see references to Solomon's worship of Astartre\Ishtar[19], who was conventionally worshipped on mountains and hilltops. The Old Testament itself testifies to this fact, telling us that Solomon's *"foreign wives*[20] *led him astray"* and that through them the Hebraic king had began *"following Astarte,*[21] *the goddess of the Sidonians..."*[22] (1 Kings 11:3-5). (Bennett & McQueen, 2001)

These references certainly bring to mind the "aromatic of Ishara," discussed in Chapter 10, which contained cannabis and was used in sacred rites dedicated to the Goddess under her various near eastern names (Reiner, 1995; White, 2008). More pointedly, in the case of the Song of Songs, the hymn is far more likely dedicated to the Hebraic counterpart of the Goddess, Asherah. According to entheobotanist William Emboden, the "shamanistic Ashera priest-

---

19   Further evidence of the connection with the Songs to Ishtar are the Songs' references to 'doves' (2:14); "The dove is the lovebird par excellence and the symbol and attribute of the love goddesses, Ishtar, Atargatis, Aphrodite... At Beth-shan in the older strata of the Astarte Temple were found small shrines with figures of doves" (Pope 1977). The "dove in the cleft of rocks... on the mountainside" (Songs 2:14), particularly brings to mind not only the goddess, but the veneration of natural yonic images in her honor.

20   King Solomon counted many foreign women amongst his 700 wives. It would later become a sin to marry foreign women for the Israelites, who were told they "must not intermarry...because they will surely turn your hearts after other gods" (1 Kings 11:2).

21   Some translations Ashtoreth. "Astarte and Ashtoreth in the Old Testament is plainly the Babylonian Ishtar, the goddess of war and love.... Many other female deities were merged with her, so that the Bible speaks of Astartes in the plural, referring to all goddesses" (Cole 1959).

22   "The Biblical associations of illicit magical incenses and foreign women informed the world-view of religious persecutions into the Early Modern Era in the persistent use of psychoactive plants" (Dannaway, 2009)

Fig 16.1: The Goddess Asherah and her sacred plant (illustration by author).

esses of pre-reformation Jerusalem... anointed their skins with... [a cannabis] mixture as well as burned it" (Emboden 1972).[23]

The onetime marriage of Yahweh with this goddess is well attested. Archaeologists working in Israel have found Hebrew inscriptions at Kirbet el-Qom in the Judaean hills which refer to "Yehouah and his Asherah." Asherah is also linked with Yehouah-Teman and Yehouah-Samaria in blessings inscribed at Kuntilla Ajrud in Sinai.[24]

Ezekiel

As noted, indicating its foriegn source, in Ezekiel 27.19, the term 'keneh' appears on a list of the luxurious arriving on a trade caravan: "Danites and Greeks from Uzal bought your merchandise; they exchanged wrought iron, cassia and *keneh* (cannabis) for your wares."

Although not mentioned elsewhere in Ezekiel by that name, there are indications that hemp, or possibly some other entheogen, was eaten by the prophet for shamanic purposes. Ezekiel 3, describes such a shamanistic scenario perfectly, referring clearly

---

23   I am unsure as to what Emboden based this assumption on, as he sited no ancient text in reference to it. I am assuming he came to the conclusion as I did after studying Benet's references to keneh bosem in the context of the Old Testament storyline.

24   See Rapahel Patai's The Hebrew goddess (1967) for a detailed account of Yahweh's ancient consort and the eventual decline of her role in Semitic worship.

to the ingestion of an unknown entheogen to initiate shamanistic flight. The ancient prophet tells us that the Lord told him:

> "Son of man, eat what is before you, eat this scroll; then go and speak to the house of Israel." So I opened my mouth and he gave me the scroll to eat....So I ate it, and it tasted as sweet as honey in my mouth....Then the Spirit lifted me up, and I heard behind me a loud rumbling sound - May the glory of the Lord be praised in his dwelling-place! - the sound of the wings of the living creatures brushing against each other and the sound of the wheels beside them, a loud rumbling sound. The Spirit then lifted me up and took me away... (Ezekiel 3:4-14)

The account in Ezekiel, is amongst those suggested by Dr.C.Creighton in 1903, as evidence of hashish use in the Old Testament. Creighton believed that cannabis dipped in honey was a "secret vice" of the Hebrew Temple and Palace, and was evidence of a polluting foreign influence:

> ...[I]n the first chapter of Ezekiel a phantasmagoria of composite creatures, of wheels, and of brilliant play of colours, which is strongly suggestive of the subjective visual perceptions of hachish, and is unintelligible from any other point of view, human or divine. This is the chapter of Ezekiel that gave so much trouble to the ancient canonists, and is said to have made them hesitate about including the book. Ezekiel was included in the Canon, but with the instruction that no one in the Synagogue was to attempt to comment upon Chapter I, or, according to another version, that the opening chapter was not to be read by or to persons under a certain age. The subjective sensations stimulated by hachish are those of sight and hearing. It would be easy to quote examples of fantastic composite form, and of wondrous colours, which have been seen by experimenters. (Creighton, 1903)

Referring to Creighton's research, Harvard Medical School Professor, Dr. Lester Grinspoon commented that the account in Ezekiel "does sound like a description of an intense cannabis intoxication – an almost psychedelic experience" (Grinspoon 1971).

Interestingly, the whole scenario of ingesting a scroll for the purpose of prophecy plays out almost identically in the New Testament's Book of Revelation (10:10) as well. Likewise a clear influence on the Book of Revelation's Tree of Life (22;2) can also be noted in Ezekiel:

> And by the edge of the river, on this side and on that, will come up every tree used for food, whose leaves will ever be green and its fruit will not come to an end: it will have new fruit every month, because its waters come out from the holy place: the fruit will be for food and the leaf will make well those who are ill. (Ezekiel 47:12)

Although the above reference refers to a variety of "trees," it seems that in Ezekiel there was also concern for one particular plant as well, as can be seen in this quote often referred to by Rastafarians and other cannabis using Biblical influenced groups: "And I will raise up for them a plant of renown, and they shall be no more consumed with hunger in the land, neither bear the shame of the heathen any more" (Ezekiel 34:29).

Isaiah

In Isaiah, the Lord complains he has been short changed his offering of cannabis, and this is due to the popularity of the herb in the temples of competing deities. Isaiah 43:24 reads: "Thou hast bought me no sweet[25] cane (*keneh*) with money, neither hast thou filled me with the fat of thy sacrifices: but thou hast made me to serve with thy sins, thou hast wearied me with thine iniquities." Here Yahweh condemns the Hebrews for not bringing both cannabis and enough of the lavish animal sacrifices common in the Old Testament, as offerings to him.

Other textual evidence from Isaiah, although not identifying cannabis by name, gives clear indications that at other times the Lord's hunger for it was being appeased and hemp was being used as a shamanic incense inside the precincts of the temple, in elaborate ceremonies such as that indicated in the account of Ezekiel to which we just referred. Clearly Isaiah also received the *keneh bosem* anointing rite insituted by Moses: "The Spirit of the Sovereign Lord is on me, because the Lord has anointed me..." (Isaiah 61:1). Another dramatic episode in Isaiah describes a shamanistic ceremony involving the use of an entheogenic incense;

---

25   In the original Hebrew "sweet" in this context can also refer to scent.

And the posts of the door moved at the voice of him that cried, and the temple was filled with smoke.

Then said I, "Woe is me, for I am undone; because I am a man of unclean lips, and I dwell in the midst of a people of unclean lips; for mine eyes have seen the King, the Lord of hosts."

Then flew one of the seraphims unto me, having a live coal in his hand, which he had taken with the tongs from off the altar, And he laid it upon my mouth and said, "Lo, this hath touched thy lips; and thine iniquity is taken away, and thy sin purged." (Isaiah 6:4-7)

As this passage was explained in *SDVB*:

Those of us who are familiar with hashish know that it burns in a similar way to both incense and coal and it's not hard to imagine an elaborately dressed ancient shaman, or *seraphim*, lifting a burning coal of hashish, or pressed bud, to the lips of the ancient prophet Isaiah. Interestingly, the holder of the tongs is described as a "*seraphim*," which translates as a "fiery-serpent," and has been associated with the Nehushtan that Moses made and Hezekiah later destroyed during his reforms, because the Israelites were burning incense to it [inside the temple]. In the context of this passage it would appear that "*seraphim*" may have been another word for Levite, which... had connotations of "serpent."[26] (Bennett & McQueen, 2001)

Jeremiah

By the time of the prophet Jeremiah, the association between cannabis and its use by other cults, particularly the Goddess, was so strong that its use was finally prohibited. "What do I care about incense from Sheba or good[27] cannabis [*keneh*] from a distant land? Your burnt offerings are not acceptable; your sacrifices do not please me" (Jeremiah 6:20).

Jeremiah's reference tying the sacred incense with Sheba, are likely an allusion to its use in the rites of the Sacred Marriage, dating back to the time of King Solomon, who was believed to have had the famous love affair with the Queen of Sheba. "Sheba was the land-name

---

26   Through the term Leviathan. This serpent holds a important theme throughout the Bible, and this association is fully explored in SDVB.

27   The original Hebrew word used here, towb, is usually translated as sweet, but has nothing to do with flavor. Rather the word has connotations of 'good,' in the widest sense, as well as 'kind,' 'favor,' 'glad,' 'joyful,' 'pleasure,' 'Precious,' and other like meanings (Strong 1979).

and Goddess-name of the Arabian queens in the ancient seat of government, Marib, in southern Arabia (now Yemen)" (Walker 1983). Solomon's own mother was Bath-Sheba, so this analogy can clearly be made, and the involvement with cannabis incense and ointments in such rites has been clearly indicated (Bennett & McQueen, 2001).

Of the five references to *keneh* and *keneh-bosm* (Exodus 30:23, Song of Songs 4:14., Isaiah 43:24, Jeremiah 6:20, Ezekiel 27:19.) the first three have cannabis appear in Yahweh's favour, the fourth definitely in his disfavour, and the fifth on a list from a kingdom that had fallen from grace in the eyes of the Israelite God. One might wonder at the reason for these apparent contradictions, and the answer can be found within the story of the suppression of the cult of Ashera, or Astarte, the ancient Queen of Heaven. In *The Chalice and the Blade*, Riane Eisler explains this as follows:

> There are of course some allusions to this in the Bible itself. The prophets Ezra, Hosea, Nehemiah, and Jeremiah constantly rail against the "abomination" of worshipping other gods. They are particularly outraged at those who still worship the "Queen of Heaven." And their greatest wrath is against the 'unfaithfulness of the daughters of Jerusalem,' who were understandably 'backsliding" to beliefs in which all temporal and spiritual authority was not monopolized by men. But other than such occasional, and always pejorative, passages, there is no hint that there ever was - or could be – a deity that is not male. (Eisler, 1987)

The Queen of Heaven

The ties between cannabis and the Queen of Heaven are probably most apparent in Jeremiah 44, where the ancient patriarch seems to be concerned by the people's continuing worship of the Queen of Heaven, especially by the burning of incense in her honour, and pouring out drink offerings:

> This is what the Lord Almighty, the God of Israel says: "You saw the great disaster I brought on Jerusalem and on all the towns of Judah. Today they lie deserted and in ruins because of the evil they have done. They provoked me to anger by *burning incense* and by worshipping other gods... Again and again I sent my servants the prophets, who said, 'Do not do the detestable things I

hate!' But they did not listen or pay attention; they did not turn from their wickedness or stop *burning incense* to other gods. Therefore my fierce anger was poured out; it raged against the towns of Judah and the streets of Jerusalem and made them the desolate ruins they are today."

....Then all the men which knew that their wives had *burned incense* unto other gods, and all the women that stood by, a great multitude, even all the people that dwelt in the land of Egypt, in Pathros, answered Jeremiah, saying, "As for the word that thou hast spoken unto us in the name of the Lord, we will not hearken unto thee. But we will certainly do whatsoever thing goeth forth out of our own mouth, to *burn incense* unto the queen of heaven, and to pour drink offerings unto her, as we have done, we, and our fathers, our kings, and our princes, in the city of Judah, and in the streets of Jerusalem: for then we had plenty of victuals, and were well, and saw no evil. But since we left off to *burn incense* to the queen of heaven, and *poured out drink offerings* to her, we have wanted all things, and have been consumed by sword and by famine."

The women added "When we *burned incense* to the queen of heaven, and poured out drink offerings unto her, did we make her cakes to worship her, and *pour our drink offerings* to her, without our men?"

Then Jeremiah said unto all the people, to the men, and to the women, and to all the people which had given him that answer saying, The *incense that ye burned* in the cities of Judah, and in the streets of Jerusalem, ye, and your fathers, your kings, and your princes, and the people of the land, did not the Lord remember them, and came it not into his mind? So that the Lord could no longer bear, because of the evil of your doings, and because of the abominations which ye have committed; therefore is your land a desolation, and astonishment, and a curse, without an inhabitant, as at this day. Because ye have *burned incense* and because ye have sinned against the Lord, and have not obeyed the voice of the Lord, not walked in his law, nor in his statutes, not in his testimonies; therefore this evil has happened to you, as at this day. (Jeremiah 44:1-23)

Jeremiah's reference to the previous kings and princes that burned incense and poured out drink offerings to the Queen of Heaven can be seen as referring to King Solomon, and the vast majority of other Biblical kings up to that time, who worshipped the Goddess alongside Jehovah and other deities in a polytheistic pantheon that was the norm for the time and place.

Even from the Biblical account only two kings, Hezekiah and his grandson Josiah, are recognized as champions of the monotheistic Yahweh alone worship which has come down to us as modern Judaism. The Bible reports that the kings before Hezekiah "set up images and groves in every high hill, and under every green tree; And there they burnt incense in all the high places..." (1Kings 17). 2 Kings 18 identifies the key elements of Hezekiah's reforms[28]: "He removed the high places, and brake the pillars, and cut down the Asherah: and he brake in pieces the brazen serpent that Moses had made; for unto those days the children of Israel did burn incense to it; and he called it Nehushtan" (2 Kings 18:4).

This is the first reference to this brazen serpent forged by Moses since the Exodus. Educated speculation would leave one to believe that the incense referred to was likely *keneh-bosem* incense. From the account in 2 Kings the brazen serpent had been worshipped by the Israelites continuously in the interceding centuries. Here in the Temple of Jerusalem itself, which held the image of the serpent, the Ashera, the Cherubim, and the Menorah - representing the Tree of Life, we can clearly see the images of the fabled Garden of Eden that had been so demonized in the Genesis tale, continuing as regular aspects of Hebrew cultic worship! Obviously these figures all played an important role in the ritual dramas practiced in the Hebrew kingdom since the time of Solomon.

The story of the other Monotheistic zealot, Josiah, offers even more fascinating insights into these reforms.

The "Lost" Book of the Law

From *Sex, Drugs, Violence and the Bible*:

Josiah became king when he was all of eight years old, and it was during his reign that one of the greatest frauds in history was perpetrated. The repercussions from what was likely one of the

28   According to other ancient Jewish sources, Hezekiah's pogrom included a ban on herbal medicines: "In ancient Israel, the prophets, who were the masters of spiritual discipline were also masters in herbal arts and healing. The use of herbs and natural healing was widespread in Biblical times. The *Talmud* relates that in the days of King Hezekiah, the *Sefer Refuot*, the Book of Healing had to be concealed because everyone was being healed of everything and no one was dying. The *Zohar* (II, 80B) says, 'The Holy One has purposely hidden this wisdom from men that they should not turn from His way by trusting in that wisdom alone, forgetting Him'" (Tzadok, 1993).

earliest cases of perjury went vastly beyond the scope of those who committed the crime and are still with us today, as it has had a profoundly formative influence on history. The narrative of 2 Kings recalls that in the eighteenth year of his reign, Josiah ordered some renovations to the temple of Yahweh. He tells one Shaphan the scribe to go to Hilkiah the high priest and carry out these repairs. During the course of this work a startling discovery is made: *"Hilkiah the high priest said to Shaphan the secretary, 'I have found the Book of the Law in the temple of the Lord.'"* (2 Kings 22:8). This lost Book of the Law is none other than the book of Deuteronomy,[29] that allegedly had been written by Moses some six hundred years earlier....

That this fifth book of Moses is mysteriously unearthed from the temple is extremely curious, as the temple wasn't constructed until the reign of Solomon and no mention of it had ever been made until this time. To ascribe this book's authorship to Moses raises some problems. It is known that the culture of the Hebrews was an oral tradition not to be committed to the written word until approximately the time of David. In fact by the style of writing in Deuteronomy, Biblical scholars have placed the text at a much later date of composition. "This new literary style, found in the Deuteronomic literature and the prose sections of Jeremiah, seems to have been characteristic of the late seventh and early sixth centuries B.C." Anderson 1975). Anderson suggests that the Book of the Law was written by an anonymous author in the seventh century who put his own words in the mouth of Moses; he also felt that the work was "not a complete literary fiction.... [and] is essentially a revival of Mosaic teachings as it was understood in the seventh century b.c." (Anderson 1975).

Other scholars have been far more hard-hitting in their comments upon this so-called discovery suggesting that it was a forgery created by a Jerusalem lawyer and produced by a priest of the temple. An act committed by the Hebrew priesthood in hope of eradicating the competing cults and their deities, which were getting more sacrifices from the people than the Temple of Yahweh was.

> Sometime about 630... a lawyer in Jerusalem produced a new code as a program for future reforms, including the prohibition of the worship of gods other than Yahweh, and relief of the poor. He drew on older "Yahweh alone" traditions , common usage , and ancient taboos, but his work was organized by his own thought, replete with his own invention, and cast

---

29   Deuteronomy means the second (deutero) giving of the Law (nomas).

with his own style. He represented it as "the law of Yahweh" and – probably – as the work of Moses, and he arranged to have it "found" by the high priest in the Jerusalem temple in 621. It was taken to king Josiah, authenticated by a prophetess, and accepted. Most of it is now preserved, with minor interpolations, in chapters 12-26 and 28 of Deuteronomy. (*Columbia History of the World* 1981)

....As archeological evidence, historical records and the Old Testament writings themselves indicate, up "...until the eighteenth year of the reign of King Josiah of Judah neither kings nor people had paid attention whatsoever to the law of Moses which, indeed, they had not even known. They had been devoted to the normal deities of the nuclear Near east, with all the usual cults..." (Campbell 1964). Until the "discovery" of the Book of the Law, the "Hebrew people worshipped in the old ways, practicing their cult in open places on peaks and hills and mountains, and even caves below" (Gadon 1989). Clearly, monotheistic Judaism was a new event, and an attempt at a combined religious and political movement to consolidate the Hebrew people under one rule, in some ways an understandable political view in light of the encroaching Assyrians.

There are a number of laws in Deuteronomy that testify to its new theology. The most extraordinary of these changes is the centralization of worship: *"you are to seek the place the Lord your God will choose from among all your tribes to put his name there for his dwelling. To that place you must go; there bring your burnt offerings and sacrifices, your tithes and special gifts"* (Deuteronomy 12:5-6). The tribes of Israel are being directed to the temple in Jerusalem for their principle sacrifices. They are no longer to make burnt offerings or sacrifices anywhere in Israel except for the Temple in Jerusalem. All tithes also are to be brought from throughout the kingdom to the Temple. Apparently, this was done "at the insistence of the Jerusalem priesthood, on whom...[Hezekiah] may have depended for support and who no doubt lost prestige – and tithes – when many sacrifices were diverted to the numerous 'high places.' [The priesthood] insisted on... an unwavering affirmation of Yahweh's exclusiveness" (Patai 1990). Prior to the Deuteronomic reforms, the priests of Yahweh's temple, had to angrily and jealously sit by and watch the wealth of the kingdom dispersed throughout the many different temples of numerous deities which were spread throughout the kingdom of Judah. (Bennett & McQueen, 2001)

The most notable effect rendered by the *Book of the Law's* supposed "discovery" were Josiah's murderous purge of the cults of the high places. The book of Deuteronomy is explicit in its instructions of how best to deal with all the religious worship going on in Judah, other than the centralized worship of Yahweh in the temple in Jerusalem:

> Destroy completely all the places on the high mountains and on the hills and under every spreading tree where the nations you are dispossessing worship their gods. Break down their altars, smash their sacred stones and burn their Asherah poles in the fire, cut down the idols of their gods and wipe out their names from those places. (Deuteronomy 12:2-3)

2 Kings 23:4-20 tells the violent story of Josiah's reforms after the discovery of the Book of the Law, and tells how when he was finished destroying the High Places and images of Asherah "Josiah slaughtered all the priests of those high places on the altars and burned human bones on them." And Josiah's reward from Yahweh for his monotheistic Zeal? He his shot dead with an arrow in a battle with the Egyptians, and his kingdom is lost, first to the Egyptians and then later the Assyrians, followed by a host of other Empires to follow.

In the account of Josiah and Hezekiah's reforms, along with the condemnation of prophets like Jeremiah, one is reminded of the similar reforms of Zoroaster, and his own rallying against the Haoma cult and its pantheon of Gods and Goddesses. This similarity brings us to an interesting point about the creation of not only the Book of the Law, but much of the Old Testament itself. As first noted more than 100 years ago by the very astute scholar George W. Brown in his Researches in Oriental History, the true inspiration for much of the Old Testament's final rendition may have been derived from a cup of the Persian Haoma!

Ezra and the Cup of Fire

> It was B.C. 634 years, Bible chronology, that 'Josiah began to manifest great zeal towards the pure worship of God.' Only 47 years thereafter to wit; B.C. 587, the walls of Jerusalem were broken down by the armies of Nebuchadnezzar, the temple was burned,

and the people were led, with hooks in their noses, to Babylon. Seventy years went by, the temple was rebuilt, and some 42,000 persons, according to Ezra 'came again into Jerusalem and Judah, everyone to his own city.' Another long period passed. 'Ezra went up from Babylon,' Ezra 7:6. He was a ready scribe, and Josephus says he was a high priest. This event occurred B.C. 447, 130 years after the destruction of the temple. He took a large party with him, was four months on the way, and bore letters from Artaxerxes, virtually making him governor of Judaea. A year later, to wit; 446 B.C. Nehemiah was sent to 'Judah to build it.'

...In Nehemiah, 8:5, we read, 'Ezra opened the book in the sight of all the people;' verse 9, 'All the people wept, when they heard the words of the law;' and verse 18, 'Day by day, from the first day unto the last,' for seven days, 'he read from the book of the law.' Where did Ezra get 'the book of the law?'

Biblical writers universally concede that between the years B.C. 433, 444 'Ezra prepared and set forth a correct edition of the Scriptures,' – See chronological index to the Holy Bible. And in the "Introductory and Concluding remarks on Each Book," in a Polyglot Bible now before us, we read:

"Ezra appears to have made the sacred scriptures during the captivity his special study.[30] And perhaps assisted by Nehemiah and the great synagogue, he corrected the errors that had crept into the Sacred Writings, through negligence or mistakes of transcribers; he collected all the books of which the Sacred Scriptures then consisted, disposed them in their proper order, and settled the canon scripture for his time. He occasionally added, under the superintendence of the Holy Spirit, whatever appeared necessary for the purpose of illustrating, completing, or correcting them.... Though not styled a prophet, he wrote under the Divine Spirit; and the canonical authority of his book has never been disputed."

In Kitto's *Cyclopedia of Biblical Literature*, article "Ezra," the author says: "Ezra is even said to have rewritten the whole Old Testament from memory, the copies of which had perished by neglect."[31]

---

30   "The captivity closed B.C. 515. Ezra first visited Jerusalem B.C. 445, seventy years after the end of the captivity. How ridiculous the claim that Ezra studied the sacred scriptures 'during the captivity.' But this demonstrates that the ordinary theologian never even regards Bible chronology when it is in the way of elucidating a complex subject" (Brown, 1890).

31   "Jo Smith, with his pretended engraved plates in his hat, and a stone which

We find the Book of the Law in Ezra's possession about 150 years after the beginning of the Jewish captivity, and we find him for seven days reading from the holy book while the people listened and wept. The temple at Jerusalem was burned, and the natural presumption is, the Jewish library was burned with it. Where did Ezra get the Book of the Law from which he read? Nehemiah does not tell. The book of Ezra is silent.

Biblical writers concede that besides writing the book which bears his name, Ezra wrote the two books of Chronicles, probably Esther and Nehemiah, and the first and second book of Esdras.

Kitto says, quoted above, that the first books of the Old Testament *perished by neglect*. Ezra gives us the facts, 2 Esdras 14: 20, 21, 22, addressing himself directly to what is understood as the fountain of inspiration:

> Behold Lord,.... The world is set in darkness, and they that dwell therein are without light, for *thy law is burnt*, therefore no man knoweth the things that are done of thee, or the works that shall begin; but I have found grace before thee, *send the Holy Ghost into me* and *I shall write all that hath been done in the world since the beginning*, which were written in thy law, that men may find thy path, and that they which live in the latter days may live.

From the time the temple was burned, with the sacred books of the Jews, and the people were taken captives to Babylon, B.C. 587, to this period when Ezra was about to 'set forth a correct edition of the Scriptures' between 444 and 433 B.C., about 150 years had intervened, during all of which period there had been no Sacred Scriptures, no Inspired Word of God, no books of the Jewish Law, no national library, because they were burned with the temple. How could Ezra repeat from memory, as Kitto suggests, this voluminous record, which had no existence in his day, or the several generations before him?

Ezra must have been born in Babylon, and there learned the profession of scribe, and there must have been made high priest.

Zoroastrian monotheism was made the state religion throughout the Persian empire, with its one hundred and twenty-seven

---

he claimed possessed miraculous powers, read from undoubtedly previously prepared pages, said to be a sort of Indian romance, the wonderful Book of Mormon, which Sidney Rigdon committed to paper, as an 'Inspired Word,' and as such it is received by near a half million as devout worshippers as any who bow to the knee of God. We hope it will not be considered profane to mention a generally recognized fraud in connection with the writings of the *inspired* Ezra" (Brown, 1890).

provinces, by Darius Hystaspis, [son of Vishataspa] whose reign extended from India to Ethiopia, B.C. 521. That continued the established religion throughout Persia until it was partially succeeded by the monotheism of Mohamet. And this, too, was true of her many provinces until they were wrestled from her by superior force. It was the law of Judea by virtue of Persian authority, when Ezra decided to write the history of the world from the beginning—shall we say, copied the holy books from Assur-banipal's Library, duplicates of some of them, with the story of creation, the fall of man, the general deluge, the tower of Babel, and the confusion of language are now on file in the British Museum, written on earthen plates, in cuneiform characters...under the direction of a Babylonian priest...

But this quotation from Esdras, as regards the burning of the law with the temple, and Ezra's declared purpose to write a history of the world from the beginning, with a quotation to follow, are from one of the apocryphal books, not recognized as canonical by the Protestants. What are the facts? The apocryphal books were placed on an equality with the residue of the *inspired* Scriptures by the Council of Trent, in 1545; therefore they are portions of the infallible 'Word of God' with Catholics; but as this action of a general council occurred after the Reformation under Luther, its action is not binding on Protestants; though the Church of England allows the books to be read for 'edification and instruction,' and they are as *genuine* as any other portion of the holy writ, and of equal authority with the best; but in the honesty and simplicity of the author, Ezra – Esdras, the Latin form of the name – he unwittingly told how the sacred books were made, and under what influence. This has prejudiced their standing.

Again, in the "Library of Universal Knowledge," we are told that the title, apocryphal, was 'sometimes given to *writings whose public use was not thought advisable;*' that is to say, 'God did not exercise good judgment when he inspired his prophets to write, therefore we, the priests, must suppress portions of his Word!' We apprehend in the case of 1st and 2nd Esdras this was the real reason for not making the apocryphal books canonical at the Council of Laodicia, A.D. 360, when the other books were declared the 'Word of God.'

Here is Ezra's own account of the process of making Jewish history. After telling the people not to seek him for forty days, and taking with him five persons whom he names, who could write swiftly, they retired to a field where they remained:

"The next day, behold a voice cried to me saying. Esdras open thy mouth, and drink what I give you thee to drink! Then opened I my mouth, and behold, he reached me a full cup, which is full as it were with water, but the color of it was like fire. I took it, and drank: and when I had drunk of it, my heart uttered understanding, and wisdom grew in my breast, for my spirit strengthened and my memory; and my mouth was opened and shut no more: and they sat forty days, and they wrote in the day, and at night they ate bread. As for me, I spake by the day, and I held not my tongue by the night. In forty days they wrote two hundred and four books" 2 Esdras 14:38 to 44.

A voice bid him open his mouth, he–*the voice*, of course–reached Esdras a full cup. It would be interesting to know whose *voice* it was which possessed such unnatural powers; yet we apprehend the reader is much more anxious to know the contents of the cup, which was fiery red, and which possessed such wondrous ability, probably the same possessed by the 'fruit of the tree' which grew 'in the midst of the garden,' the eating of which opened the eyes of our first parents, and enabled them to see 'as Gods knowing good and evil.' We think we can furnish this desired information, to do which we are compelled to anticipate some facts existing among Zoroastrian worshippers; many centuries before the date religionists ascribe to Abraham, and which was practiced in Persia, Assyria and Babylonia at the very time Ezra was writing Jewish history under the influence of the 'fiery cup.'

Among other duties required on occasional sacrifices of animals to Ahura-Mazda, additional to prayers, praises, thanksgiving, and the recitation of hymns, was the performance from time to time of a curious ceremony known as that of the Haoma or Homa. This consisted of the extraction of the juice of the Homa plant by the priests during the recitation of prayers, the formal presentation of the liquid extracted to the sacrificial fire... the consumption of a small portion of it by one of the officiating ministers, and the division of the remainder among the worshippers. (See Haug's essay, page 2390

Says Clarke in his *Ten Great Religions*, Page 202:

"The whole Sama-Veda is devoted to this moon-plant worship; an important part of the *Avesta* is occupied by Hymns to Homa. This great reverence paid to the plant, *on account of its intoxicating qualities*, carries us back to a region where the vine was unknown, and to a race to whom intoxication was so new an experience as to seem a gift of the gods. Wisdom appeared to come from it, health, increased power of body and soul, long life, victory in battle, brilliant children. What Bachus was to the Greeks, the Divine Haoma, or Soma, was to the primitive Aryans."

What was the Haoma or Homa, the production of the moon-plant, growing in those regions of Asia too far north for the successful growing of the grape, and yet yielding such intoxicating properties? It is known in the medical books as Apocynum Cannabinum, and belongs to the Indian Hemp family, Cannabis Indica being an official preparation from it. It is now known in India as bhang, and is popularly known with us as hashish, the stimulating and intoxicating effects of which are well known to physicians. The extract from its young and tender top has a fragrant odour, and a warm bitterish and acrid taste.

The adoration paid to the prepared juice of this plant, and its use on sacrificial occasions, and the drinking of it by the high priest Ezra, as he was about to 'open his mouth,' while the 'five swift scribes' wrote down his words when he was filled with wisdom and understanding, and was about to dictate history 'from the beginning of the world,' can best be appreciated by members of the medical profession who have personally experienced its exhilarating effects on some fellow student, who was elevated by his own estimation, on a high pedestal and was capable of taking in all that has been, is, and may be in the material universe. Indeed, an acquaintance with this fact explains all those graphic descriptions in that celebrated history of the creation of the world; of the making of man – and of woman in particular; their expulsion from the garden — not forgetting that interesting interview with the snake, the materialized form of Angro-Mainyus, or in our vernacular, the Devil; the account of the deluge; Noah's drunken debauchery; Lot's wife changed into a pillar of salt; and the widower's escapade with his daughters; Jacob wrestling with God, getting a broken thigh and seeing angels ascending and descending a ladder to and from heaven; the terrible plagues on Egypt; the parting of the Red Sea; the law passed down through a cloud to Moses by God himself;[32] the adventures of Samson with the foxes, his contest with the lion, and the loss of his hair; David with his sling; the Hebrew boys in the fiery furnace; not omitting Jonah's wonderful gourd, nor his fishing exploits; Elijah's ride to heaven; and Elisha's children eating bears. No criticisms are required when it is known what kind of drink Ezra was regaled with before 'opening his mouth' to dictate history for his swift scribes to write.

But reader, there is still another fact we may as well state with this connection. The wine in the sacrament of the 'Lord's Supper' is a survival of the adoration and use, with prayers and hymns, of this divine Haoma, a substitution of a more pleasant intoxicant [wine] by the later worshippers of Mithra, who, in after years are known as Christians.

This is a faithful history of the making of the Bible, as detailed by the author himself. He informs us, 2 Edras 14.44 to 46, that of the 204 books thus written he was instructed by the Highest to publish the first openly, 'that the worthy and unworthy may read it; but keep the 70 last that thou mayest deliver them only to such as be wise among the people: for in them is the spring of understanding, the fountain of wisdom, and the stream of knowledge.

From this statement it is very clear we have only that part of the 'Holy Scripture' designed for the worthy and the unworthy. That part containing 'wisdom' and 'understanding' failed to reach our times. (Brown, 1890)

In the account of Ezra drinking from the cup of fire, one is clearly reminded of the tradition of fiery cups amongst the Scythians, but even more so the Zoroastrian accounts of the drinking of *mang* mixed with Haoma or wine. "The image of a blazing cup was apparently related to... Zoroastrism; Zoroastrian texts mention ritual vessels with fire burning inside them" (Kisel, 2007). Interestingly, Immanuel Löw, referred to an ancient Jewish Passover recipe that called for wine to be mixed with ground up saffron and *hasisat surur*, which he saw as a "a kind of deck name for the resin the *Cannabis sativa*" (Low, 1924). Low suggests that this preparation was also made into a burnable and fragrant concoction by being combined with Saffron and Arabic Gum (Low, 1926\1967). Such preparations were also noted by the 19th century Biblical scholar John Kitto, and like the Hebrew references to cannabis, such con-

---

Both Moses and Zoroaster limited the use of their entheogenic preparations to an elite selected group.

coctions went through periods of Hebraic free use and strict prohibition. "Woe to you who make your neighbors drink, who mix in
your venom [i.e. drugs or herbs] even to make them drunk so as to
look on their nakedness!" (*Habakkuk* 2:15).

> The palm wine of the East... is made intoxicating... by an admix-
> ture of stupefying ingredients, of which there was an abundance...
> Such a practice seems to have existed amongst the ancient Jews,
> and to have called down sever prohibition (comp. Prov xxii. 30;
> Isa. i.22; v. 11, 22...)" (Kitto, 1861)

In relation to this it is interesting to note that the 19th century
scholar John Kitto also put forth two different potential Hebrew
word candidates for the origins of the term "hashish" in *A Cyclopaedia of Biblical Literature*. Kitto pointed to the Hebrew terms
Shesh, which originates in reference to some sort of "fibre plant,"[33]
and the possibly related word, *Eshishah* (E-shesh-ah?) which holds
a wide variety of somewhat contradictory translations such as
"flagon" "sweet cakes," "syrup," and also interestingly for our study
"unguent." According to Kitto, this *Eshishah* was mixed with wine.
"Hebrew *eshishah*... is by others called *hashish*.... this substance,
in course of time, was converted into a medium of intoxication by
means of drugs"[34] (Kitto 1845: 1856). With the cognate pronunciation similarities found between the Hebrew *Shesh* and *Eshishah*
one can only speculate on the possibility of two ancient Hebrew
references to one plant that held both fibrous and intoxicating
properties.

In light of this it is interesting to note that "Some high biblical commentaries maintain that the gall and vinegar or myrrhed
wine... was a preparation, in all probability, of hemp, which was...
occasionally given to criminals before punishment or execution...
it is possibly spoken of... by the prophet Amos as the 'wine of the
condemned'" (Simpson, et al. 1856).

Another possibility for Ezra's infusion might also be found in
Biblical descriptions of "strong drink" (*shekar*): "An inebriating Potion described in the Old Testament; but distinct from Wine; probably a Soporific or visionary vinous infusion, analogous to ancient
Greek Wines, of one or many Psychoactive plants" (Ott, 1995).

---

33   See Appendix E for a fuller account of Kitto's etymology.
34   Ibid.

> ... Like the ancient Greeks, the ancient Israelites did not know distillation technology, but possessed an inebriant other than wine, which apparently was more potent. Was the Biblical *shekar*, 'strong drink', not an inebriating potion analogous to the ancient Greek wines, some of which were entheogenic potions? Down through history there are innumerable instances of the addition of psychoactive plants to wines and other alcoholic beverages. (Ott, 1993)

As well, the idea that Ezra's fiery cup contained some sort of preparation analogous to those used by Zoroastrian figures, and that this tradition was carried on by certain Jewish figures, has garnered some interesting independent support.

> It could be that after the Exile some Hebrews had adopted the name of cannabis, which was used by their former Persian overlords, as could be indicated by the references to the suama plant, similar in pronunciation, and possibly identical to the Iranian *haoma*, (and Indian *soma*). In a 1967 article, Melvin Clay referred to recipes for the suama plant found around Tell Abu Matar, appearing on urns and cups, of high quality workmanship. Clay wrote that the recipes, which he placed around the third century b.c.e., originated with a hermit named Zin, who had been banned from the Temple in Jerusalem. This may indicate that he was practicing the older pre-exilic forms of Hebraic worship. Apparently, as cannabis had been, the plant was used at religious feasts, the roots boiled and drunk or the leaves smoked. Clay wrote that the suama plant was originally found in region of Kadesh-barnea, northeastern Sinai. An area near where Moses first heard the Word of the Lord in a fiery bush.

> Dr. W.F. Cartwell of Oriental Institute has no recollection of recipe but speaks of leaves smoked and inhaled at a Palestine synagogue during the writing of the Hasteric Scrolls (Books of Joy). He adds that "The suama plant is known to us from the time of the Pentateuch. Some very early discoveries have been made concerning the suama plant. We find it coming up again and again under different names. Smoking its leaves or using its roots as a herbal drink always produces states of flashing colors and euphoric bliss." (Clay 1967)[35]

---

35   As quoted in (Andrews & Vinkenoog, 1967).

Unfortunately, we have been unable, as of yet, to find out more about the research from Melvin Clay, or Dr.W.F. Cartwell, so we are unable to prove this point to the extent of the other ancient cannabis references to which we have referred to. In his 1925 German edition, *Flora der Juden* (Reprinted in 1967, as *Die Flora Der Juden*). Immanuel Low, made a brief reference to the name "Sumna," which is likely identical with the "suama plant" described above, being applied to cannabis by Jewish sources, but unfortunately Low also fails to go into detail. (Bennett & McQueen, 2001)

In the article "Preparation for Visions in Second Temple Jewish Apocalyptic Literature," Vicente Dobroruka also noted a comparison between the Persian technique of shamanic ecstasy and that of Ezra:

> ...4 Ezra 14:38-42 - "And on the next day, behold, a voice called me, saying, 'Ezra, open your mouth and drink what I give you to drink.' Then I opened my mouth, and behold, a full cup was offered to me; it was full of something like water, but it's color was like fire. And I took it and drank [...]." Similar drinks appear in Persian literature, e.g. *Bhaman Yasht* 3:7-8, when Zoroaster "drinks" the water he acquires the wisdom of Ahura Mazda. Similarly, Vishtapa has an experience quite equivalent in the *Dinkard* 7:4.84-86 where mention is made to a mixture of wine (or *haoma*) and hemp with henbane... opposition to those practices may have generated their replacement in the later BY [*Bahman Yast*]. The *Book of Artay Viraz* also mentions visions obtained from wine mixed with hemp, and for the preparations of the seer cf. ch. 2.25-28. (Dobroruka, 2002)

Dobroruka revisited this theme in more detail in his later 2006 article, "Chemically-induced visions in the Fourth Book of Ezra in light of comparative Persian material," and again draws direct comparisons between Ezra's cup of fire, and the *mang* mixed infused beverages of the Zoroastrian psychonauts. Dobroruka expanded on this connection by noting the similar accounts of the flowers eaten by Ezra in 4 Ezra 9, and those used for similar revelation by the Zoroastrian figure Jamasp:

> *But if you will let seven days more pass – do not fast during them, however; but go into a field of flowers where no house has been*

built, and eat only of the flowers of the field, and taste no meat and drink no wine, but eat only flowers, and pray to the Most High continually – then I will come and talk with you. (4 Ezra 9:23-25).

In the *Jāmāsp Namag* (also a pseudepigraphic text, written in the name of an old sage), Jāmāsp receives from Zoroaster the gift of knowledge by means of a flower. This is also the theme of the Pahlavi text *Wizirkard i Denig* 19... indeed, the tradition that described the acquisition of mystical knowledge by Jāmāsp resembles very much that of Ezra regarding the flowers, as the drinking of the blessed wine looks like the experience of 4Ezra 14 – the main difference in the passage being the fact that here we have two different seers [i.e. Jamasp & Vishtaspa]. (Dobroruka, 2006)

Dobroruka also compared Ezra's chemically induced inspiration to other Biblical accounts, "The episode has parallels in the scroll eaten by Ezekiel (Ez 2:8-3:3) and thus to the author of the Book of Revelation (Ap 10:9-10), who also claims to have had sensory experiences related to ingestion" (Dobroruka, 2006).

As noted in Chapters 14 and 15, the oldest existing copies of many of the Zoroastrian texts referred to are dated much later than the period in question (although they are thought to be adapted from older accounts) and for this reason, some might argue against a Persian influence on the accounts of Ezra, but as Dobroruka notes, this is not necessarily the case:

...[T]he figure of Vishtaspa... is much older than the earliest Jewish apocalypses themselves (i.e. earlier than III century BCE) and... at least assures that the figure of Vishtasp cannot be later than that of Ezra... [also there are the] fourth century BCE... fragments collectively known as the *Oracle of Hystaspes* [Greek Vishtaspa]). This is indirect evidence that late Persian texts contain cores that can be of earlier date... The theme of the cup that gives wisdom, being already present in the Yasna 10.17... [which] deals with the theme of the wisdom cup, in this case related to haoma:

Thereupon spake Zarathushtra: Praise to Haoma, Mazda-made. Good is Haoma, Mazda-made. All the plants of Haoma praise I, on the heights of lofty mountains, in the gorges of the valleys, in the clefts (of sundered hill-sides) cut for the bundles bound by women. From the silver cup I pour Thee to the golden chalice over. Let me not thy (sacred) liquor spill to earth, of precious cost.

The dating of the *Yasna* depends on the dating attributed to Zoroaster, but even supposing the prophet to be a figure living as late as the sixth century BCE... the *Yasna* is much earlier than 4Ezra.... All this tends to support the idea that the two mythical themes examined that find way in 4Ezra (namely, that of the cup and that of the flower, both of which bestow wisdom) were, both by their antiquity and their frequency, primarily Persian ecstatic practices that found themselves echoed in a Jewish apocalypse. (Dobroruka, 2006)

Not surprisingly a profound Zoroastrian influence on Biblical theology has also long been noted:

Zoroastrianism is the oldest of the revealed credal religions, and it has probably had more influence on mankind, directly and indirectly, than any other single faith. In its own right it was the state religion of three great Iranian empires... Iran's power and wealth lent it immense prestige, and some of its leading doctrines were adopted by Judaism... (Boyce, 1983)

Zoroastrian-Canaanites?

The idea that Jewish monotheism finds its origins in the Persian tradition likewise has modern support. In *Persia & Creation of Judaism*, Dr M.D. Magee gives a detailed explanation of how Judaism was created by the Persians in 500 BC. "Historical Israel, the actual flesh and blood people who dwelt in the central mountains during the Iron Ages, didn't come from Egypt. They were descendents of earlier, Bronze Age inhabitants of the places where they lived. Their culture and religion was a slightly evolved form of the earlier, Bronze Age Canaanite ones" (Magee, 1998; 2008).

...Israel and Judah remained Canaanite until the Persians came at the end of the sixth century BC. Only in the following century were books about Jewish history written down.... Some events of the Bible are confirmed by external investigation. Some of the kings of Israel and Judah appear in Assyrian records and therefore can be dated. However, given that the history of Israel was only first written in the Persian period, and the Persians had conquered Assyria and Babylonia, and had access to their archives covering hundreds of years, it is more than likely that the scriptural stories of the monarchical period were simply written from the official king lists, inscriptions and diplomatic correspondence of those formerly mighty powers. In short, it is largely historical fiction but set in a realistic historical framework. (Magee, 1998; 2008)

As Dr. Magee explains, part of the Persian return, included bringing in a monotheistic element of worship, directed at unifying worship into a single manageable source, through which the people could be more easily governed, as well as taxed.

The Jewish scriptures make up a constitution for the Jewish people to whom they were given. The earliest time that rules like reading the Torah publicly and observing its charges faithfully, abstention from work and commerce on the sabbath, avoiding intermarriage, tithing, maintaining temple sacrifice through a self-imposed tax (Neh 10:30-40) could appear is when Ezra and Nehemiah were sent by the Persian king during the fifth century BC to determine civil and religious policy in Yehud [Israel]. (Magee, 1998; 2008)

Magee puts forth that part of the Persian policy of restoration of people back to their homelands, included having the main male deity from each existing pantheon elevated to the same state as that of their own monotheist god Ahura Mazda, at the sacrifice of the powers of the gods and goddesses of the earlier pantheons. In each place that such a god was placed upon this lone throne, he took with him the title, "king of heaven."

As Magee explains it, for reasons of political consolidation the rulers wanted the people to worship one sole god, the concept being that everyone would worship a "king of heaven" with the same broad characteristics but with different regional names. "The Great King of the empire could then be shown to have the same role on earth as the universal king of heaven, and the various kings of heaven could be shown to be different versions of Ahuramazda, unifying everyone" (Magee, 1998: 2008). The outcome of this universal mixing of peoples was:

Aramaic became the language of the whole area.

"Jews" accepted that they had "returned" but they never accepted the natives of the hill country as being Jews.

The "Jews" that had "returned" used some Samarian legends but rejected the rest of the cult and devised a new religious "tradition." The people that had remained in Judah never accepted those who returned.

The people who had remained in Judah did not accept the "restored" religion.

Whoever the mixture of peoples were that returned to the city of Jerusalem after 500 BC, they were led to believe—and came to believe—that they were the remnant of ancient Israel returning to their rightful land to create a new Israel. ... Much of the Old Testament saga is Persian propaganda. The ancestor of the Jews is from Mesopotamia, so, in the myth of Abraham, the Jews are shown to have an ethnic affinity with that region. The anachronism of calling it the Chaldees betrays its late composition. Immediately, the descendants of Abraham are enslaved by the Egyptians and have to undergo countless tribulations before they escape and set up in Israel. The propaganda purpose is plain—to dissociate the inhabitants of the Palestinian hill country from Egypt and paint the Egyptians as their enemies. (Magee, 1998; 2008)

Magee puts forth that proof close to the time can be found in the works of the Egyptian Jew Philo of Alexandria (20 B.C.-50 A.D., who wrote in *Vita Moysis* of the Jewish texts "Originally the laws were written in the Chaldaean language."

The Chaldaean language was the language of Babylonia (Ezra 5:12) at the time of the project of Ezra to set up a new religion in Jerusalem. Why then would Moses, a Hebrew brought up in Egypt under some Pharaoh like Rameses, write in a language of a distant country 800 years later? Philo, an Egyptian Jew, effectively admits the Torah was written by Ezra, a Persian from Babylonia.

Israelite religion must therefore have been a variant of the religions practised by Canaanites in general. The main difference which arose between this religion and other neighbouring ones was that the Persians selected Jerusalem as the centre of a pseudo-Zoroastrian cult based on the local god Yehouah. There was no particular slow variation from other Canaanite religions, but there was a sudden imposition of a foreign cult on to the local religion of Jerusalem. The imposition was resisted by locals for

many decades but ultimately it triumphed, albeit in a highly frag-
mentated state. (Magee, 1998; 2008)

Complicating things, shortly after this monotheistic coup, Persia
itself fell to the Greeks, then the Greeks to the Romans. This roll
call of empires which held rule over the Jews separated them further
from their past, and created a void which the new history provided
by Ezra and his cohorts quickly filled. The confusion created by these
religious reforms and succession of empires led to different fractions
in Judaism, such as the Sadducees, Pharisees, Rabbis, Essennes and
Jewish Gnostic sects all of whom began to interpret things slightly
differently and in some cases vied for power over the people.

Most notably, it seems after the period of Persian conquest either the ears of the prophets grew deaf, or the voice of Yahweh
silent. Any evidence of shamanic practice soon faded shortly after
the sphere of Persian influence receded to other imperial forces.
At the time of the Persian return the "mere idea that Ezra was 'dic-
tating' sacred books (not yet canonical) implies that the Sinaitic
revelation still had room to be enlarged, an idea that may reinforce
the presence of the Holy Spirit in Ezra as he drank from the cup"
(Dobroruka, 2006). After the Law had been given, there seemed to
be little room for new revelation, and the rule of the religion of the
day was simply "obey and pay."

This turning point is most marked by the aforementioned
prophet Jeremiah, whom we noted earlier in relation to his role in
the eventual prohibition of *keneh-bosem*. Jeremiah is the least shamanic of all Biblical prophets, and save for Job and Jonah the works
attributed to him come across as the most self-concerned and pa-
thetic of the whole Old Testament.[36] In relation to his campaign
against cannabis, it is interesting to note that Vicente Dobroruka
saw Jeremiah as condemning practices such as those alluded to in
the story of Ezra and the Persian accounts. "There seems to be a
parallel, if in different settings and intentions, between the cup that
maddens the nations in Jeremiah 25:15-16" (Dobroruka, 2002);
"The cup may also have a negative connotation as the means for
God to madden peoples or nations [(Jeremiah 25:15-16)]" (Dobroruka, 2006). The Zoroastrian-Babylonian ordeal-cup is handed
back to Babylon as poison in the words of Jeremiah:

---

36   For a more thorough analysis of the reforms of Jeremiah see (Bennett & Mc-
Queen, 2001).

Babylon [claimed to be] a cup of gold in the hand of Yahu, That made all lands to reel. Of her wine the nations drank So that the peoples went mad. Suddenly Babylon falls and is convulsion-rent! Wail over her – get balsam for her wounds – perhaps she can be cured? We would like to cure Babylon, But she cannot be cured! Leave her there, and let us all go home! For her doom rises to heaven, And touches the very skies. (Jeremiah 51:6)

Clearly Jeremiah condemned the "cup of fire" for the same reasons as he did the incense burning and drink offerings of former priests and kings; like the modern religious elite, his only interest was in the stated law, there was no room for new revelation:

One reason for the war of the Hebrew prophets upon the incense rituals of their time would be clearer to any person who would study the methods of modern seance-rooms. Much incense is a tradition of the profession, especially with those who make a business of "developing' mediumistic or clairvoyant powers in their disciples. A "trance gift" or power of "spirit vision' is sure to be discovered in those sensitive to a little narcotic stimulation. The mutterings of a half-stupefied disciple in a "pipe dream" are explained to others as "trance manifestation" or "spirit control." All alienists know that even mild odors may stimulate neurotic subjects to imaginative visions, as in the case of Mohammed. A whole roomful – a "school of the prophets" of today - may thus be set gibbering. Some mediums, making a business of furnishing spirits upon demand, willy-nilly, have been known to make themselves complete "dope wrecks." Such practices are known in all lands; observers report them from almost every savage tribe; they figure in a host of orgies and religious frenzies. The reader of the Arabian Nights may recall that in some tales spirits of jann arise in the smoke of powders thrown on the fire. Lane (I, 61), in his discussion of Arab magic, says that "illusions or hallucinations are still produced by such devices." From ancient Babylonia to the present they are a favorite resort of those who pretend to summon the spirits of the dead. Isa. 57:9 declares: "You have gone (so you say) to the King with ointments; You have greatly multiplied your odors. You have sent your messengers to Far-Land. You have descended even to Sheol!" (Godbey, 1930)

As Dobroruka noted, these practices were demonized as a foreign influence: "Chemical induction related to the visionary present the most 'paganizing' reference to the means for inspiration found among the apocalypticists (i.e. the passages that most resemble pagan practices of artificial ecstatic practices); this may be so for the same reason that 'classical prophets' have a 'calmer' ecstasy than their pagan counterparts, i.e. for editorial reasons" (Dobroruka, 2006).

This situation left its most obvious mark on one of the last stories composed in the Old Testament, the tale of the fabled and prohibited trees in Eden. Both the Tree of Life and the Tree of knowledge have long been associated with the Iranian Haoma and its Vedic counterpart the Soma. As scholar E.K. Bunsen pointed out as long ago as 1867:

> The records about the "Tree of Life" are the sublimest proofs of the unity and continuity of tradition, and of its Eastern tradition. The earliest records of the most ancient Oriental tradition refer to a "Tree of Life," which was guarded by spirits. The juice of the sacred tree, like the tree itself, was called Soma in Sanskrit, and Haoma in Zend; it was revered as the life preserving essence. (Bunsen 1867)[37]

As also noted in *The Legends of the Old Testament* by Thomas Lumisden Strange:

> The tree of life is traceable to the Persian Paradise. "The haoma is the first of the trees planted by Ahura Mazda in the fountain of life. He who drinks its juice never dies" (Muir, *Sansk. Texts*,II...).... The original is the Soma of the Hindus, early deified by them, the sap of which was the beverage of the gods, and when drank by mortals made them act like gods immortal.... The Hebrews have exactly adopted the idea: "And Jahveh Elohim said, 'Behold the man has become one of us to know good and evil; and now, lest he put forth his hand, and take also of the tree of life, and eat, and live forever: therefore Javeh Elohim sent him forth from the garden of Eden... and he placed at the east of the garden of Eden cherubim, and a flaming sword which turned every way, to keep the way of the tree of life"... (Strange, 1874)

Joseph Campbell's description of the mythical white Hom certainly brings to mind the tree of Life as well: "the...White Haoma Tree arose, which counteracts old age, revives the dead, and be-

37   *The Keys to Saint Peter* As quoted in (Doane 1882).

stows immortality. At its roots Angra Mainyu [the Persian Devil] formed a lizard" (Campbell 1964). One can only speculate that the lizard lost his legs in this mythical transition and became the Biblical serpent. "The concept of the tree of life is found among many ancient people.... In the Zoroastrian religion of the Persians the sacred tree was called haoma, which grew in a garden from which all the waters of the earth flowed (cf. Gen. 2:10)" (Gray, 1969).

Interestingly, F. Max Muller indicated that the cherubim and seraphim of the Old Testament further the connections between the mythical trees of Eden and the traditions surrounding Haoma and Soma:

> We... consider the comparison of the Cherubim who keep the way of the tree of life and the guardians of the Soma in the Veda and Avesta, as deserving attention, and we should like to see the etymological derivation of "Cherubim" from... Greifen, and of Seraphim" from the Sanskrit "sarpa," serpents, either confirmed or refuted. (Muller, 1873)

Numerous scholars have since discussed the similarities between the Old Testament's forbidden Trees and the Soma/Haoma, but one startlingly profound difference stands out between the two myths: the Haoma and Soma were give freely to humanity, delivered willingly by the Garuda bird, the Biblical trees are instead forbidden, and instead of offering the sacred fruit of the tree to humanity, the Cherubim now holds a flaming sword, preventing all from obtaining the mythical sacraments of life and knowledge.[38]

---

38   In relation to the Zoroastrian influence on the Bible, and the use of cannabis in the Holy Oil, it is curious to note references to topical preparations by the Zoroastrians:

"It is a part of Magian lore that plants are the part of the good creation of Ahura Mazda to fight the counter order of evil. As Pliny says, "The Magi are crazy about this plant verbenaca. Smeared with it they gain whatever they want in prayer, they drive out fear, they cement friendship, and there is not an illness they do not cure. It has to be gathered at the rising of the Dog (constellation of Sirius) when neither sun nor moon can see it...it must be dried in the shade with its leaves, stalk and roots separate." (Bagli, 2005).

Verbenaca is usually identified as *Salvia verbenaca*, also known as Wild Clary or Wild Sage, a tall perennial herb with hairy stems and branches, and blue flower. *Salvia verbenaca* has no known psychoactive properties or particularly noted medical qualities beyond the use of its essential oils as an anti-bacterial agent. The intoxicating and medical effects evident from Pliny's description, as well as the practice of drying in the shade, all have indications of cannabis. If one considers a Persian word may have been at the root, and breaks the word used by Pliny into components *ver-bena-ca*, one finds, *bena*, which is easily identifiable with the Avestan *banha* (hemp) opening up the possibility that both the Jews and Zoroastrians were aware of topical preparations of the plant. Interestingly,

It is hard not to see in this final redaction of the Eden myth as it comes down to us in the Book of Genesis, as a symbolic rendering of the rejection of entheogenic substances,[39] by the closing editors of the Old Testament texts. Shortly after this period, through translations of the Jewish texts into Greek, evidence of cannabis all but disappeared from the Old Testament.

> It was during the radical changes instituted by Greek rule that cannabis disappeared from the Old Testament text. "The error occurred in the oldest Greek translation of the Hebrew Bible, Septuagint in the third century B.C.,[40] where the terms *kaneh, kaneh bosm* were incorrectly translated as 'calamus.' And in the many translations that followed, including Martin Luther's, the same error was repeated" (Benet 1975). Although this mistake did not happen in either surviving Aramaic or Hebrew scriptures, where "the two words *kaneh* and *bosm* were fused into one, *kanbos* or *kannabus*, known to us from [the later] Mishna [200 c.e.], the body of traditional Hebrew law" (Benet 1975). (Bennett & McQueen, 2001)

The cultic use of cannabis amongst the Hebrews was not easily suppressed, and it seems likely that certain mystically inclined sects of Judaism retained the method of shamanic ecstasy used by their predecessors. Rabbi Aryeh Kaplan has noted of early Kabalistic magical schools who used magic and other means of communion for mystic exploration, that "some practices include the use of 'grasses,' which were possibly psychedelic drugs" (Kaplan, 1982). As mentioned earlier, Kaplan's *The Living Torah* includes cannabis as a possible candidate for the Hebrew *keneh bosem*, "due to cognate pronunciation" (Kaplan, 1981). The Kabalistic text the *Zohar* records:

> "There is no grass or herb that grows in which G-d's wisdom is not greatly manifested and which cannot exert great influence in heaven" and "If men but knew the wisdom of all the Holy One,

---

as discussed in Chapter 3, Christian Ratsch reports of an ancient European plant under the similar name of verbena, which with good reason he suggested was likely a reference to hemp (Ratsch, 2001).

39   Such as indicated by the wrath of Jeremiah against burning incense, and his final condemnation of cannabis (Jeremiah 6:20).

40   "The translation of the Hebrew scriptures into Greek was undertaken in Alexandria under Ptolemy Philadelphus (284-246 B.C.), and completed somewhere around 150 B.C. The work is of very unequal merit, and the translators manifest a freedom which is variously traceable to prejudice, insight, or ignorance" (Alexander 1902\1980).

blessed be He, has planted in the earth, and the power of all that is to be found in the world, they would proclaim the power of their L-rd in His great wisdom." (*Zohar*.2,80B)

Like the Zoroastrian royalty and priesthood, there are indications that early Kabbalists enjoyed the use of the herb, but prevented its consumption by the common people. In the *P'sachim*, "Rav Yehudah says it is good to eat... the essence of hemp seed in Babylonian broth; but it is not lawful to mention this in the presence of an illiterate man, because he might derive a benefit from the knowledge not meant for him – *Nedarim*, fol. 49, col. 1" (Harris, et al., 2004). Other sources have noted a Kabbalistic comparison to the effects of cannabis with divine perception, noting an "intriguing reference to cannabis in the context of a fleeting knowledge of God: *Zohar Hadash, Bereshit*, 16a (*Midrash ha-Ne'elam*)" (Gross, et al., 1983).

Clearly, a strong Persian influence on the texts of the Old Testament is undeniable. That this foreign influence included cannabis can now be seen to be equally obvious, from both the way that the two cultures utilized the plant for religious inspiration, and also the Hebrew adoption of the cognate Indo-European word for the plant in the form of *keneh bosem*. It should also be noted that the marriage of the traditions of the Persians with those of the Semites bore fruit, and the child of this union has become one of the leading religions of the modern world... Christianity. A religion whose connection with cannabis and the traditions of Soma/Haoma we shall explore in the next Chapter.

In every Mithraeum the centrepiece was a representation of Mithras killing a sacred bull; the so-called tauroctony.

The image may be a relief, or free-standing, and side details may be present or omitted. The centre-piece is Mithras clothed in Anatolian costume and wearing a Phrygian cap; who is kneeling on the exhausted bull, holding it by the nostrils with his left hand, and stabbing it with his right. As he does so, he looks over his shoulder towards the figure of Sol. A dog and a snake reach up towards the blood. A scorpion seizes the bull's genitals. The two torch-bearers are on either side, dressed like Mithras, Cautes with his torch pointing up and Cautopates with his torch pointing down.

The event takes place in a cavern, into which Mithras has carried bull, after having hunted it, ridden it and overwhelmed its strength . Sometimes the cavern is surrounded by a circle, on which the twelve signs of the zodiac appear. Outside the cavern, top left, is Sol the sun, with his flaming crown, often driving a quadriga. A ray of light often reaches down to touch Mithras. Top right is Luna, with her crescent moon, who may be depicted driving a biga. (chariot)

In some depictions, the central tauroctony is framed by a series of subsiduary scenes to the left, top and right, illustrating events in the Mithras narrative; Mithras being born from the rock, the water miracle, the hunting and riding of the bull, meeting Sol who kneels to him, shaking hands with Sol and sharing a meal of bull-parts with him, and ascending to the heavens in a chariot.

From Wikipaedia

17

MITHRISTIANITY

C hristianity has been instrumental in the development of Western culture's "morality;" its breadth and influence in the realms of myth and religious beliefs are felt the world over. Christianity's acceptance as a national religion by the Roman Empire in the third century A.D., required the suppression of all other faiths and competing philosophies, sending European humanity into a Dark Ages that lasted more than a millennia, and from which our society is in many ways still recovering. How intertwined this situation with the history of haoma and the prohibition of cannabis, as we shall discuss shortly, is indeed a fascinating tale.

Christianity, in its barest origins, before taking on the mantle of Persian prophecy and mythology, was in fact a political movement as much as a religious one. Despite having played subservient host to a number of empires since the fall of Israel in the 6th century BC, along with going through a variety of political and cosmological changes, the Israelites never gave up their aspirations for independence, which could only be restored by a Messianic (Anointed) King in the line of David. Thus Israel's political situation, as much as any theological influence, contributed greatly to the development of Christianity.

The Jews, who had suffered under a number of kings appointed by the empires which controlled the area, continually hoped for an "anointed" King in the line of David, as they had in the supposed glory days of the Kingdom period, who would unite the people and restore Israel's former glory and independence.

> In reaction to continuous subjugation and defeat, the Hebrews consoled themselves with dreams that continually magnified the

role of the prophesied Davidic king, taking him to cosmic pro-
portions as the judge of all humanity at the end of time, selecting
the righteous from the wicked and inaugurating the 'kingdom of
heaven.' This is the Apocalyptic Messiah that, like most aspects
of the Hebrew religion, only came into existence through foreign
influences.

> "It is too small a thing for you to be my servant to restore the
> tribes of Jacob and bring back those of Israel I have kept. I will
> also make you a light for the Gentiles, That you may bring my
> salvation to the end of the earth."(Isaiah 49:6)

> Here, in the words of... Isaiah, we can see the influence of the
> traditionally Zoroastrian concept of the cosmic savior, or Sasyo-
> shant, being superimposed on the Messianic expectations of the
> wishful Hebrews. The Savior of humankind would herald the end
> of time and after the resurrection of all humanity they would be
> judged good from evil and each will go to their eternal reward or
> punishment. The syncretistic Hebrew religion adopted this Per-
> sian image of the coming savior easily as it fit into their own na-
> tional aspirations perfectly. (Bennett & McQueen, 2001)

As we shall see, the full extent of this Zoroastrian influence on
the development of Christianity, including everything from Christmas to the resurrection, themes which would not be fully developed till sometime after the life of Jesus, has proved to be quite
considerable.

For the first four hundred years after Jesus' birth, the term "Christian" was used to describe a wide variety of sects and a large volume
of different documents. Through the acceptance of one of the more
ascetic branches of Christianity by the Roman ruling class, Christianity eventually became the state religion of its former persecutors.

In an effort to unify the faith into a controllable mass, the newly
formed Roman Catholic Church held a number of councils. These
councils prohibited not only pagans, but also differing Christian
sects, and edited a wealth of Christian documents down to the few
meager samples which have survived as the modern New Testament.[1] A subject discussed in all its gory detail in *Sex, Drugs, Violence and the Bible.*

---

1   The New Testament in its present form was composed and edited between 367-
397AD, about twelve generations after the events in question.

In an attempt to save their manuscripts from the editorial flames of the Roman Catholic Church, certain Christians, now considered Gnostic heretics, hid copies of their scrolls in caves. One of these ancient hiding places was rediscovered in 1945, and the large collection of early Christian documents was named the *Nag Hammadi Library*, after the Egyptian area where it was found. Prior to this discovery, what little was known of the Gnostics came from a few fragmentary texts, and the many polemics written against them by the founders of the Roman Catholic Church.

There is no reason to consider these ancient Gnostic documents as less accurate portrayals of the life and teachings of Jesus than the New Testament accounts, unless the meter of judgment be swung in favour of "might being right." In a sense, the rediscovery of the *Nag Hammadi Library* marks the literary resurrection of a more historical Jesus, an ecstatic rebel sage who preached enlightenment through rituals involving magical plants including the use of a Eucharist similar to the Haoma and Soma, and who is more analogous to the Indian Shiva, or the Greek Dionysus, than the pious ascetic that has come down to us through the Bible's New Testament.

The Anointed

Despite the harsh reforms of the Old Testament, and even the apparent final editorial rejection of keneh (cannabis) (Jeremiah,6:20) it seems clear from the New Testament accounts that Jesus and his followers had continued with the tradition of the Holy Oil as described in Exodus 30:23, utilizing it like haoma for both healing and enlightenment. But here with the Christians, the Holy Oil was not to be limited to the use of the select few, but instead was freely distributed amongst the community. A controversial situation that is further explained by surviving Gnostic Christian texts.

Following in the footsteps of Benet's research regarding *keneh-bosem* (1936;1975), which laid out a template for Judaic references, in *Sex, Drugs, Violence and the Bible* we were able to follow the history of the sacred anointing oil into the early Christian period. This use of the cannabis infused oil was particularly found amongst heretical Gnostic Christian sects, which were later brutally banned, along with pagan cults, at the inception of the Dark Ages and the rise of Catholicism.

The term 'Christ' itself is Greek rendering of the Hebrew 'Messiah' and this means the 'anointed one' makes direct reference back to the original anointing oil as described in Exodus 30:23. Contrary to the depiction given in the New Testament gospels of Matthew and Luke, Jesus was likely not born as the Messiah. He received this title through his initiation by John the Baptist, and so it is not surprising that both Mark and John are conspicuously absent of the virgin-birth mythology, and begin their stories of Jesus' short career with his initiation by John. More recently, as Prof. Carl Ruck has summarized:

> Jesus was probably trained as an Essene before the years of his proselytizing. The Essenes were known as healers and had extensive knowledge of drug plants. It is highly likely that Jesus experienced psychoactive sacraments. Since healing medicines were commonly compounded as oils, it is quite probable that the healing performed by Jesus involved administering the traditional Essene herbal pharmaceuticals, which would have, and in fact did on the basis of archaeological remains, included cannabis. One must remember also that the gospel account of his ministry is partly mythologized and certainly reworked from earlier documents. Healings recorded as miracles may well have involved skills of a physician.
>
> Additionally, Jesus was called the 'Christ,' which means that he was 'anointed.' The chrism of his anointment would have been the one described above for the Jewish ordination, which is to say, Jesus would have to have experienced the effect of cannabis. The biblical account of this chrismation is the encounter with John the Baptist at the River Jordan. It is the effective cause of the ensuing vision of the opened heavens, which can only be termed a mystical experience. The bible also seems to state that Jesus did not abide by the traditional reservation of this ointment for the priests and the elite, but that he shared it with the commonality of his followers. (Ruck, 2009)

As anthropologist Prof. Scott Littleton has also noted: "I've long been convinced that cannabis played an important role in many ancient belief systems... That the Hebrews, especially Hebrew mystics & healers, like *Yeshua ben Yosuf* (aka in Latin as "Jesus") also made use of this psychotropic substance is extremely probable. Thus, in effect, Jesus, John the Baptist, and others of that ilk, like the Pythia and the Scythian shamans who used cannabis in their rituals, were all probably 'stoners'!" (Littleton, 2003)

Although the Biblical version of Jesus' baptism by John describes it as involving submersion under water, the term "baptism" has connotations of "initiation," and Gnostic scriptures indicate that the original rite was performed in conjunction with the *keneh-bosm* anointing rite, "the annointing taking place either before or after the baptismal ceremony" (Rudolph, 1987). Some Gnostic texts also specifically state that Jesus received the title Christ "because of the anointing" (*Gospel of Philip*), not because of a water baptism.

Conceivably, the washing off of the oil with water as described in Mark would have been a means to begin the termination of ritual and the oil's effects. The description of the after-effects of the rite clearly indicates that Jesus underwent an intense psychological experience, more than one would receive from a simple submersion in water.

> Jesus came from Nazareth Galilee and was baptized by John in the Jordan. As Jesus was coming up out of the water, he saw heaven being torn open and the Spirit descending upon him like a dove. And a voice came from heaven "You are my Son, whom I love; with you I am well pleased." At once the Spirit sent him out into the desert, and he was in the desert for forty days, being tempted by Satan. He was with wild animals, and angels attended him. (Mark 1: 9-13)

It should be noted that in this account the vision and words described were seen and heard only by Jesus, as it specifically states that "he saw." The role played by John the Baptist, as priest and prophet is very similar to that of the Old Testament prophet Samuel. Just as Samuel's anointing of Saul and David marked them as Messiah-king, so did Jesus' initiation by John make him the Christ.

In the events after Jesus' vision and his overwhelmed recluse into the desert, there are clear parallels with the story of the prophet Samuel's initiation of Saul with the cannabis-rich holy ointment, and Saul's ensuing madness in the form of possession by the Spirit, and wandering off to make nabi (act in a frenzied ecstatic manner) (1 Samuel 10).

It should also be remembered that in the New Testament Jesus does not baptize any of his own disciples, but rather in the oldest of the synoptic Gospels, Mark, Jesus sends out his followers to heal with the anointing oil: "they cast out many devils, and anointed with oil many that were sick, and healed them" (Mark 6:13). Likewise, after Jesus' passing, James suggests that anyone of the Christian community who was sick should call to the elders to anoint him with oil in the name of Jesus (James 5:14). "Is any one of you sick? He should call the elders of the church to pray over him and anoint him with oil in the name of the Lord."

In the ancient world, diseases such as epilepsy were attributed to demonic possession (Alexander 1902) and to cure somebody of such an illness, even with the aid of certain herbs, was the same as exorcism, or miraculously healing them. "Epileptics were often treated with fumigations and aromatic substances. In Islamic medicine, European folk medicine, and in the self-medication of today, hemp smoke is sometimes used to revive a person after a seizure" (Ratsch, 1998). Interestingly, as discussed at length in *Sex, Drugs, Violence and the Bible* with comparative medical documentation, cannabis has been shown to be effective in the treatment of not only epilepsy, but many of the other ailments that Jesus and the disciples healed people, such as skin diseases (Matthew 8, 10, 11; Mark 1; Luke 5, 7, 17), eye problems (John 9:6-15), and menstrual problems (Luke 8:43-48) (Bennett & McQueen, 2001).

According to ancient Christian documents, even the healing of cripples could be attributed to the use of the holy oil. "Thou holy oil given unto us for sanctification... thou art the straightener of the crooked limbs" (*Acts of Thomas*).

One ancient Christian text, *The Acts of Peter and the Twelve Apostles*, which is older than the New Testament, estimated to have been recorded in the second century AD, has Jesus giving the disciples an "unguent box" and a "pouch full of medicine" with instructions for them to go into the city and heal the sick. Jesus explains that you must heal "the bodies first" before you can "heal the heart."

The New Testament makes it clear that the Holy Oil contained more than mere medical properties, and like the Soma-Haoma it was a means of revealing divine knowledge as well: "The anointing you received from him remains in you, and you do not need anyone to teach you. But as his anointing teaches you about all things and as that anointing is real, not counterfeit—just as it has taught you, remain in him" (1 John 2:27).

The Christians, the "smeared or anointed ones," received 'knowledge of all things" by this "anointing from the Holy One" (1 John

2:20). Thereafter, they needed no other teacher, and were endowed with their own spiritual knowledge. As Jesus and his followers began to spread the healing knowledge of cannabis around the ancient world, the singular Christ became the plural term "Christians," that is, those who had been smeared or anointed with the holy oil.

In the first few centuries AD, Christian Gnostic groups such as the Archontics, Valentians and Sethians rejected water baptism as superfluous, referring to it as an "incomplete baptism" ("The Paraphrase of Shem").

Fig. 17.1 "Cannabis and the Christ," for article in *Cannabis Culture*, January 1998, by author.

In the tractate, the *Testimony of Truth*, water baptism is rejected with a reference to the fact that Jesus baptized none of his disciples (Rudolph, 1987). Being "anointed with unutterable anointing," the so-called "sealings" recorded in the Gnostic texts, can be seen as a very literal event. "There is water in water, there is fire in chrism" (*Gospel of Philip*). "The anointing with oil was the introduction of the candidate into unfading bliss, thus becoming a Christ" (Mead, 1900). "The oil as a sign of the gift of the Spirit was quite natural within a Semitic framework, and therefore the ceremony is probably very early. . . . In time the biblical meaning became obscured" (Chadwick, 1967).

The surviving Gnostic descriptions of the effects of the anointing rite make it very clear that the holy oil had intense psycho-active properties, which prepared the recipient for entrance into "unfading bliss." In some Gnostic texts like the *Pistis Sophia* and the *Books of Jeu*, the "spiritual ointment" is a prerequisite for entry into the highest mystery (Mead, 1900).

In later time, as Christianity fragmented into different sects, one of the main points of contention between those collectively known as Gnostic Christians, and those of the Church of Rome which

formed around the teachings of Paul, was initiation by this ointment, seen as heretical by the Catholic Church, versus what the
Gnostics saw as the Catholic's placebo rite of baptism. In the Gnostic view, as described in the *Gospel of Philip*, those who "go down
into the water and come up without having received anything":

> The anointing (*chrisma*) is superior to baptism. For from the
> anointing we were called 'anointed ones' (Christians), not be-
> cause of the baptism. And Christ also was [so] named because
> of the anointing, for the Father anointed the son, and the son
> anointed the apostles, and the apostles anointed us. [Therefore]
> he who has been anointed has the All. He has the resurrection,
> the ligh... the Holy Spirit... [If] one receives this unction, this
> person is no longer a Christian but a Christ.

Similarly, the *Gospel of Truth* records that Jesus specifically came
into their midst so that he, "might anoint them with the ointment.
The ointment is the mercy of the Father. . . those whom he has
anointed are the ones who have become perfect."

The apocryphal book, the *Acts of Thomas*, refers to the ointment's
entheogenic effects as being specifically derived from a certain plant:

> Holy oil, given us for sanctification, hidden mystery... you are
> the unfolder of the hidden parts. You are the humiliator of stub-
> born deeds. You are the one who shows the hidden treasures. You
> are the *plant of kindness*. Let your power come by this [unction].
> [emphasis added]

Descriptions of the Holy Oil give clear evidence that like Soma and
Haoma, it had both healing and spiritual properties, and these effects
in all cases were associated with the plant from which it was derived,
and the 'divine' power inherent within it.[2] In reference to the "plant of
kindness" referred to in the *Acts of Thomas*, it is important to note that
the account where the above reference occurs, takes place in India!

2   Referring to the Jewish and Christian cannabis based anointing oil theory, and
the earlier work of both this author and Professor Carl Ruck, in *Where God and Science
Meet: how brain and evolutionary studies alter our understanding of religion*, author Patrick
McNamara writes that "Reenactments of these possible historical events under laboratory conditions or in religious settings or clinical laboratories via chrismation experiments
could test these claims supporting or weakening the credibility of this alleged religious
history. Institutional review boards may need some convincing.... Would existing Eucharistic services gain profundity and real (rather than symbolic) meaning with entheogens?"
(McNamara, 2006) Patrick McNamara is Director of the Evolutionary Neurobehavior Laboratory in the Department of Neurology at the Boston University School of Medicine.

The *Acts of Thomas* also includes a hymn, "The Ode to Sophia," that is connected with the 'Bridal Chamber' ceremony, a Gnostic sex rite[3] analogous to the rite of *mathuna* (sexual union) in Tantrism, where "a man and woman come together for the mingling of their bodies, the exchange of their fluids, and the mutual recharging of their energy" (Walker 1982). As cannabis has been commonly used since ancient times in such Indian rites (see Chapter 18), it is important to to note that the room prepared for this Gnostic counterpart of Tantric rituals was rich with the scent of "Indian Leaf":

> Her chamber is bright with light and breatheth forth the odor of balsam and all spices, and giveth out a sweet smell of myrrh and *Indian leaf*, and within are myrtles strown on the floor, and of all manner of odorous flowers... ("Ode to Sophia")[4] [emphasis added]

Accounts from early Catholic sources attacking these practices, such as Irenaeus' condemnations of the Gnostic figure Marcus below, make it abundantly clear that the use of drugs in such sex rites was an integral part of the ritual:

> Moreover, that this Marcus compounds philters and love-potions, in order to insult the persons of some of these women, if not of all, those of them who have returned to the Church of God – a thing which frequently occurs – have acknowledged, confessing, too, that they have been defiled by him, and that they were filled with a burning passion towards him. A sad example of this occurred in the case of a certain Asiatic, one of our deacons, who had received him (Marcus) into his house. His wife, a woman of remarkable beauty, fell a victim both in mind and body to this magician, and, for a long time, travelled about with him. At last, when, with no small difficulty, the brethren had converted her, she spent her whole time in the exercise of public confession, weeping over and lamenting the defilement which she had received from this magician. (Irenaeus of Lyons, *Adversus haereses*, Book I, Chapter 13:5, 178 A.D.)

Gnostic texts indicate that besides topical use, entheogenic preparations of cannabis were also burnt and inhaled as well as drank and ingested, and through these the Zoroastrian influence is further identified. Indeed, the Gnostic tractate, *The Apocryphon of*

---

3   Gnostic sacramental-sexual practices are discussed in detail in my earlier work, *Sex, Drugs, Violence and the Bible*.

4   From the translation in (James 1924).

Fig. 17.2: Keneh bosem, the fragrant cane (Illustration by author).

John,[5] has Jesus make mention of Zoroaster's teachings himself, de-
claring to John the son of Zebedee: "if you wish to know them, it is
written in the book of Zoroaster." A tractate that was popular with
early Gnostics had the title of *Zostrianos*, and the author has been
identified as a person in "the lineage of the famous Persian magus
Zoroaster" (Sieber 1988),[6] and by others the Persian shaman Zoroaster himself; "[I]n the Nag Hammadi document Zostrianos,...
the ancient Iranian prophet is [Zoroaster] portrayed, in accordance
with the ideas of late antiquity, as the proclaimer of secret doctrines. His wisdom he obtains in the course of a heavenly journey
which he experiences in the desert" (Rudolph 1987).

As shown in Chapter 15 Zoroastrian texts indicate that Zoroaster used a preparation of hemp to achieve the type of shamanistic

5   The main teachings of the tractate are believed to have historically existed since
185 c.e., and was still in use up until the eighth century by the Audians of Mesopotamia
(Wisse, 1988)-Nag Hammadi. By comparison, the New Testament in its present form was
compiled between 367-397.
6   *The Nag Hammadi Library*, Robinson Ed., (John N.Sieber 1988) Intro.

flight that is described in the Gnostic tractate *Zostrianos*, and that the ancient Persian sage initiated others into its use. Interestingly, and pointedly, the sadly fragmented Gnostic tractate *Zostrianos* has some obvious references to a drink which acted as a catalyst for the author's voyage: "After I parted from the somatic darkness in me and the psychic chaos in mind...I did not use it again..." And again later, tying in the effects of the drink with references to "baptism"; "And I said, I have asked about the mixture [....] it is perfect and gives [...] there is power which [has...those] in which we receive baptism..."

> The experiences of the ancient Gnostic psychonaut recorded in *Zostrianos*, with its Baptism to the different levels or realms of heaven, closely parallels the experiences had by the Zoroastrian hero Ardu Viraf, who was transported in soul to heaven after drinking a preparation of bangha (hemp, *bhang*). The similarities between Viraf's ascent and those attributed to the later Gnostic groups have been noted (Hinnells, 1973). In fact it is from the Zoroastrian tradition that the supposedly Christian concept of Heaven and Hell originated. How sadly few modern Christians are aware that historically their belief in these Fantastic Realms have their origins in visions from the hemp induced shamanistic ecstasy of a non-Judaic pre-Christian tradition! (Bennett & McQueen, 2001)

Clearly in the 2nd century account of Zostrianos we find further corroboration of a Zoroastrian influence and origin of Ezra's fiery cup, discussed in the previous Chapter, and this later Gnostic text attests not only to the popularity of this method through the intervening centuries, but also of its considerable antiquity, a fact that has until now remained in question due to the later age of the existing Zoroastrian texts (although they are believed to have been derived from an older oral tradition).

One of the more significant and widespread Gnostic sects, the Manicheans, which survived into the twelfth century in parts of Europe and China, worshipped Jesus right alongside Zoroaster,[7] and performed ceremonies similar to the one that Jesus is described as presiding over. As noted in Chapter 9, Tocharian speaking people

---

7   As well as Buddha, Mithras and other deities. "When a Manichean Christian came over to the orthodox Christians, he was required to curse his former friends in the following terms:'I curse Zarades (Zoroaster ?) who, Manes said, had appeared as a god before his time among the Indians and Persians, *and whom they call the Sun*. I curse those who say *Christ is the Sun*, and who make prayers to the *Sun*. ... *I curse those persons who say that Zarades and Budas and Christ and the Sun are all one and the same*'" (Doane 1882) In relation to this it is also important to note that the church fathers traced the origins of Manicheans

are thought to have brought the Manichean religion into China, and there the "general opinion of their religion was that it involved drug-induced ecstasy, for their leaders had titles like 'spirit-king' and 'spirit-father' and 'spirit-mother,' but the common folk deliberately mispronounced the word for 'spirit' (mo) as 'ma,' meaning 'cannabis sativa' (as if 'Pater' were changed phonetically to 'pot-head')" (Ruck et al. 2001).

The Treasure of Light and the Mystery of the Five Trees

In the Gnostic text the *Second Book of Ieou* Jesus takes on the role of shamanic initiator, and in this text we find of evidence of an incense akin to that which had been dedicated to the Queen of Heaven, causing Jeremiah to burn with anger, and Yahweh to reject future offerings of *keneh bosem* (Jeremiah 6:20)

At the turn of the present century Professor G.R.S. Mead summarized a German translation of a surviving Gnostic text, the *Second Book of Ieou*.[8] The text describes Jesus bidding both male and female disciples to join him so that he can reveal to them the great mystery of the Treasure of Light.

In order to accomplish this, the candidates have to be initiated by three Baptisms: The Baptism of Water, the Baptism of Fire, and the Baptism of the Holy Spirit, "and thereafter the Mystery of the Spiritual Chrism [anointing]." Jesus tells his followers that the master-mysteries of the Treasure of Light are involved with the mystery of the Five Trees, which may mean having knowledge of the magical plants that were used in the ceremony.

> All of these mysteries Jesus promises to give to His disciples, that they may be called "Children of the Fullness (Pleroma) perfected in all mysteries." The Master then gathers His disciples, and sets forth a place of offering, placing one wine-jar on the right and on the left, and strews certain berries and spices round the vessels; He then puts a certain plant in their mouths, and another plant in their hands, and ranges them in order round the sacrifice. (Mead, 1900)

Continuing with the ritual, Jesus gives the disciples cups, along with other articles, and seals their foreheads with a magical dia-

---

8   One of the few that managed to survive the Catholic Church's editorial flames, without being hidden with the Nag Hammadi codices, and instead passed down secretly through a number of generations of heretics to survive into the modern day.

gram. Then, like shamanistic and magical ceremonies the world over, he turns his disciples to the four corners of the world, with their feet together in an attitude of prayer, and then offers a prayer which is prefixed with an invocation, and continues with a number of purifications and into the Baptism of Fire.

> In this rite vine-branches are used; they are strewn with various materials of incense. The Eucharist is prepared...
>
> The prayer [this time, is to] the Virgin of Light... the judge; she it is who gives the Water of the Baptism of Fire. A wonder is asked for in "the fire of this fragrant incense," and it is brought about by the agency of Zorokothora. What the nature of the wonder was, is not stated. Jesus baptizes the disciples, gives them of the eucharistic sacrifice, and seals their foreheads with the seal of the Virgin of Light.
>
> Next follows the Baptism of the Holy Spirit. In this rite both the wine-jars and vine-branches are used. A wonder again takes place, but is not further specified. After this we have the Mystery of Withdrawing the Evil of the Rulers, which consists of an elaborate incense-offering. (Mead, 1900)

The "wonder" in the incense which so perplexed Mead was presumably a reference to its psychoactive effects, as does the other undefined "wonder" likely indicate the magical properties of the different plants used in the ceremony. As well, the references to "wine-jars and vine-branches" opens up the possibility that the Gnostics were practicing the age old method of infusing cannabis into wine.

It would seem to follow that the identity of the different plants, vines, and berries described in the excerpts were identified to the participants as the Mystery of the Five Trees.

At this time we can only speculate what other plants were used in the ceremony. The account of mandrake in Genesis 30: 14-16 and in the Song of Songs 7: 13 (which seems to indicate its addition to the holy anointing oil) clearly document the long term interest the Hebrews had with these seemingly magical plant angels.

That the use and knowledge of such plants could have been passed down by Zoroastrian and Jewish sources to certain "heretical" branches of the faith like the Gnostics seems self evident. The addition of such a powerful hallucinatory drug such as mandrake (or belladonna, datura, henbane, all of which were also popular in the Middle East at that time) would help to explain some of the extreme experiences related to the holy anointings and baptisms described in the Gnostic literature. Recipes for medieval witches' "flying ointments" contain cannabis, mandrake, belladonna and other entheogens, and the out-of-body experiences attributed to the Gnostics have many parallels with the Witches Sabat, as do aspects of their cosmology.

Although there is clear evidence of the use of a variety of psychoactive substance amongst the ancient Jews, in the case of the Gnostic's "five trees," it is likely that a marked Persian influence can be found. The surviving Mithraic iconography indicates that as with the Gnostic's Five Trees, a number of psychoactive plants may have come into use among Mithra's cult by Roman times. Interestingly, the pscilocybin containing mushroom popularly known as the "Liberty Cap" mushroom, gets its name from Mithra's cap (which was also worn by the medieval alchemists and gained popularity during the French Revolution). but as the hat is red, it is more likely symbolic of the *Amanita muscaria* mushroom.[9] In favor of this is Mithra's connection with the Greek hero Perseus (whose name is derived from Persia), who wore a magic hat that was simi-

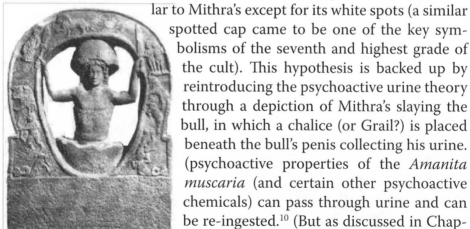

lar to Mithra's except for its white spots (a similar spotted cap came to be one of the key symbolisms of the seventh and highest grade of the cult). This hypothesis is backed up by reintroducing the psychoactive urine theory through a depiction of Mithra's slaying the bull, in which a chalice (or Grail?) is placed beneath the bull's penis collecting his urine. (psychoactive properties of the *Amanita muscaria* (and certain other psychoactive chemicals) can pass through urine and can be re-ingested.[10] (But as discussed in Chapters 2 and 14, this may also be a carryover from the Persian practice of drinking Bull's urine for ritual purification).

Fig. 17.3:, Mithra being born from the Earth, looking like the mushroom personified.

---

9   Mithra's hat can also be seen in the phallic imagery of the uncircumcised penis, as Mithra can be seen to be a Solar Phalic deity.

10   See (Ruck, et al. 2008) For more details on the potential role of the *Amanita Muscaria* in the Mithraic religion..

Fig. 17.4: Mithra's slaying the sacred bull, note chalice placed beneath bull's genitals for collecting urine.

Franz Cumont in *The Mysteries of Mithra* put forth that by the Roman period "Grapes... in the West replaced the Haoma of the Persians.... Haoma, a plant unknown in the Occident, was substituted for the juice of the vine," (Cumont, 1956). A similar suggestion was put forth by Nyberg in 1938, who felt that with the reemergence of the Mithraic Haoma cult in Zoroaster's day, "the clean alcoholic intoxication" eventually beat out "holy intoxication of the magus, which was possibly supported by the much deeper acting hemp intoxication.... The drinking of Haoma caused a more ordinary/standard inebriation than ecstasy" (Nyberg, 1938). Although this case seems unlikely when set against the background of Iran, as there is no record of the Iranian Haoma as an alcoholic beverage and the reforms there likely resulted in the Ephedra concoction still used. However, considering the Mediterranean love of wine, and that Roman depiction of Mithra holding a bunch of grapes are known, it is clearly plausible that such may be the case in this later defused foreign situation for the cult. If this is the case it would explain much about the later Roman Catholic sacraments of bread and wine, as the Catholics borrowed so much from the Roman period cult of Mithras for the mythology of their own Messianic savior, Jesus Christ.

Considering the Perisan origins of Mithraic worship, the age-old practice of mixing mang (hemp) with wine, can not be easily dismissed in regards to the Roman rituals of Mithra. Regardless of what substances were used in the Mithraic rites, and as it has been demonstrated that intoxicants were used in the Gnostic initiation ceremonies, it is interesting to note that even the use of wine in these rites has been connected with the planetary ascension, and stages of initiation. Originally, the ritual consumption of wine, was "unquestionably due to its power to stimulate the mystical faculties of human nature, usually crushed to earth by the cold facts and dry criticisms of the sober hour" (James 1929).

Fig. 17.5: Mithras, Zoroastrian Haoma God, emerging from the earth, with grapes in hand. From (Cumont, 1956).

Franz Cumont believed that it was only the Mithraic devotees being initiated to the level of Lion, that were given the sacramental wine, and the ritual commemorated the banquet Mithra celebrated with the Sun before his ascension.

From this mystical banquet, and especially from the imbibing of the sacred wine, supernatural effects were expected. "All religions in which mysticism and contact with the supernatural play an important part attribute a sacred character to an intoxicating drink or other intoxicant. The tradition of sacred drinks and ritual libations is found in all ancient civilizations. Wine is still today a part of the Christian ritual" (Danielou 1992).

> The intoxicating liquor gave not only vigor of body and material prosperity, but wisdom of mind; it communicated to the neophyte the power to combat the malignant spirits, and what is more, conferred upon him as upon his god a glorious immortality.... The fermented beverage which he imbibed excited his senses and disturbed his reason to the utmost pitch; he murmured his mystic formulas, and they evoked before his distracted imagination divine apparitions. In his ecstasy, he believed himself transported beyond the limits of the world, and having issued from his trance

he repeated... "I have transcended the boundaries of death, I have trodden the threshold of Proserpine, and having traversed all the elements I am returned to earth. In the middle of the night I have seen the Sun scintillating with a pure light; I have approached the gods below and the gods above, and have worshipped them face to face." (Cumont 1956)

As Dannaway has noted, the "cult of Mithras, which may have been one of the main cults that retained and preserved... [ancient] mysteries for later generations of mystics, had strange incense rites as well" (Dannaway, 2009). In "Did the Mithraists Inhale?" Prof. Radcliffe Edmonds describes Mithraic fumigation rites in relation to sha-

manic-flight, indicating that this rite may have eclipsed the drinking of Haoma in its importance: "The magician in the Mithras Liturgy raises himself to the world of the gods through the inhaling of pneuma[11]... and the sun rays are the path by which the pneuma from the divine realm comes down to the magician. Although the references to this ritual practice are brief in the Mithras Liturgy, they are clearly the primary means of [shamanic] ascent, since no other mode of ascent is ever

Fig. 17.6: Illustration of a Mithraic Lion-Headed deity and altar of incense, from a Roman period relief (artist unknown).

mentioned" (Radcliffe, 2000). Radcliffe refers to the "incense burning lions" as seen in Fig. 5 as indications of this practice.[12]

The entheogenic effects of the Mithraic sacraments were focused and magnified by the clever manipulation of light on divine statues, the movement of costumed participants, chanting, and animal noises such as wings flapping and lions roaring.[13] As discussed in *Sex, Drugs, Violence and the Bible* in some detail, the Gnostics used entheogenic sacraments for their almost identical planetary ascension. In Mithraism, seven different sacraments were given

---

11   Pneuma is an ancient Greek word for "breath," and in a religious context for "spirit" or "soul."

12   From http://www.ceisiwrserith.com/mith/whatismith.htm

13   Similar to the rites described by Ezekiel, Isaiah, and other Babylonian influenced Jewish prophets.

to the initiate as he passed through the seven grades of the cult. This Mithraic rite itself was an adoption of the Babylonian and Semitic initiatory shamanistic ascension through the seven planetary spheres and elements of this earlier mythology also carried over into the Gnostic counterpart of the ritual.

Like the numerous animal-headed deities depicted in Mithraic art, and enacted by costumed participants in Mithraic rites,[14] Celsus, who pits Mithraism against Christianity in his *True Discourses*, ridiculed the Christian Gnostics[15] of the second century for what he saw as their make-believe ascents through the planetary spheres, accomplished through "the demonic words addressed to the lion, the animal with double forms and the one shaped like an ass, and the other illustrious doorkeepers, whose names you hapless folk have wretchedly learnt by heart." Celsus description of the Gnostic text *The Ophite Diagrams* describes the seven archontic demons, all of which but the amphibian appear in Mithraic depictions: "the first is lion-shaped; the second is a bull; the third is amphibious and hisses horribly; the fourth is in the form of an eagle; the fifth has the appearance of a bear, the sixth, that of a dog; and the seventh, that of an ass named Thaphabaoth or Onoel. Some persons return to the archontic forms so they become lions or bulls or serpents or eagles or bears or dogs."

Such similarities were obviously more than the product of mere accident, and indicate that at some early point in Christian development the two faiths had come into contact.[16] It can safely be concluded that the profound similarities in the rites of the Gnostic and Mithraic rites included the use of entheogenic potions and plants, such as those Jesus is depicted as giving his disciples in the *Second Book of Ieou*, and elsewhere.

Significantly, in the case of the *Second Book of Ieou*, the "fragrant-incense" is offered to the Virgin of Light, and this would seem to be reminiscent of the offering of *keneh-bosm* incense to the Queen of Heaven that we have discussed so fully in Chapter 16.[17] Also of

---

14   Costumes in such rituals are as old as shamanism itself, and likely go back to a time when the disguised participants represented different animal totems.

15   Celsus made no distinction between the Christians and Gnostics and regarded them as the same.

16   A fact exemplified by the adoption of aspects of Mithraic mythology by the orthodox Church. From its very beginnings, Christianity was influenced by its Mithraic predecessor, and their early Persian counterparts.

17   Another Gnostic tractate, *The Gospel of the Egyptians*, possibly written by the

interest concerning the incense, and further evidence of syncretism, is that the wonder of the incense is brought about by a figure known as Zorokothora, a name which Mead records is interpreted as Melchizedek, who was an ancient Canaanite king. On the other hand, indicating further cultural syncretism, Zorokothora does have strong indications of the name Zoroaster, the Persian sage who played psychopomp initiator to his disciples, in a similar way to that attributed to Jesus in the *Second Book of Ieou.*

The suggestion that cannabis was in use in this area of the world in the first few centuries A.D. is not left to pure textual interpretations, but rather solid archeological evidence indicating its use as both a topical preparation and medicinal fumigant has been documented. "Residues of cannabis, moreover, have been detected in vessels from Judea and Egypt in a context indicating its medicinal, as well as visionary, use" (Ruck 2003).

A 1992 archeological dig in Bet Shemesh near Jerusalem has confirmed that cannabis medicine was in use in the area up until the fourth century. Thus it would seem to stand to reason that it was used for these purposes throughout the intervening Christian period. In the case of the Bet Shemesh dig, the cannabis had been used as an aid in child bearing, both as a healing balm and an inhalant. This find garnered some attention, as can be seen from the Associated Press article, "Hashish evidence is 1,600 years old," that appeared in Vancouver newspaper the *Province*, on June 2, 1992:

> Archaeologists have found hard evidence that hashish was used as a medicine 1,600 years ago, the Israel Antiquities Authority said yesterday. Archaeologists uncovered organic remains of a substance containing hashish, grasses and fruit on the abdominal area of a teenage female's skeleton that dates back to the fourth century, the antiquities authority said in a statement. Anthropologist Joel Zias said that although researchers knew hashish had been used as a medicine, this is the first archeological evidence. (AP 1992)

individual who hid the Nag Hammadi texts, wrote that he had been inspired to do so, after inhaling certain fumes, "the incense of life is in me... in order that I may live with thee in the peace of the saints." This is reminiscent of the "incense... with the prayers of the saints" from Revelation 5:8; 8:3 (Bennett & McQueen, 2001). In the article "Strange Fires," which deals with hallucinogenic smoke, Frederick Dannaway suggests that such "visionary rites are present in the New Testament book of Luke I:11 'And there appeared to him an angel of the Lord, standing on the right side of the altar of incense.' Likewise, the hallucinatory book of Revelations VIII: 3 finds an angel holding a censer in the midst of the four horned altar 'and there was given to him much incense'" (Dannaway, 2009).

As Zias and his colleagues explained: "We assume that the ashes found in the tomb were cannabis, burned in a vessel and administered to the young girl as an inhalant to facilitate the birth process" (Zias, et al., 1993). This find of cannabis in a Judean cave was further supported by the later analysis of glass vessels from the site which also contained evidence of cannabinoid residues (Zias, 1995).

Although the idea that Jesus and his disciples used a healing cannabis ointment may seem far-fetched at first, when weighed against the popular alternative (one that is held by millions of believers) that Jesus performed his healing miracles magically, through the power invested in him by the omnipotent Lord of the Universe, the case for ancient accounts of medicinal cannabis seems a far more likely explanation. When one considers that Jesus himself may have healed and initiated disciples with such topical cannabis preparations, the modern reintroduction of cannabis based medicines becomes, if not a miracle, at least a profound revelation.

Mithristianity

Superimposed over the story of this shamanic initiator and the obvious political inspiration of independence which surrounded his short ministry are mythical elements associated with the Persian god Mithra, a Zoroastrian deity referred to earlier, who inherited the Haoma rite from Indra, albeit, possibly in a denatured form, at least in most quarters.

After the time of Zoroaster the figure of the world-saviour or Soshyant merged with one of the older pre-Zoroastrian Vedic gods, known originally as Mitra-Varuna, but later and more popularly as Mithra, "The Unconquered Sun." The *Mihr Yast* has Ahura Mazda declare; "When I created Mithra of the broad pastures I made him as worthy of veneration as myself." The god-plant *Haoma* was then consecrated as the priest of Mithra and all further Haoma sacrifices were made in Mithra's honor.

The worship of this Persian God, and its seven stage system of initiation, became so popular in the ancient world, that up until around 350 ad, it rivaled Christianity for the attention of the masses. Mithra's cult is said to have been spread throughout the ancient world and particularly to Rome, by a group of Cilician pirates, who adopted the god and extended his worship to the West.

...The Roman Mithras is very different from the Persian Mithra of the Zend-Avesta, and seems to have represented a type of Persian paganism condemned by the pure Zoroastrians of that country... the god collected in his travels a selection of "magical" beliefs. From the Chaldean Magi astrology was borrowed, and from the remnants of Greek philosophy a whole theology was devised to unite the different elements in Mithra's cult. The Emperor Comodus (A.D. 180-92) was initiated into the Mysteries; and from that period onwards, continuing favour was shown to the cult from the Imperial house. Mithras made many converts, but principally in the army, for his religion was that of a soldier. (Webb, 1974)

Mithra's followers were very secretive and left little written records regarding their beliefs and activities. Most of what is now known of the cult has come to us through interpretations of pieces of monuments which survived the destructive hammers of Christian monks upon the commencement of the Roman Catholic Empire, an event which marked the beginning of the Dark Ages.

The Christian monks were obsessed with destroying any surviving remnant of the cult of Mithra's, because the Persian God particularly threatened the supremacy of their own god in the form of Jesus. In fact, many existing Churches were built right over the top of Mithraims. Thus, in both a very real and symbolic sense, Christianity based its foundation on Mithraism. Historically, the undisputable fact is they had borrowed so much symbolism from the Persian god's mythology that many historians now refer to Mithra as the proto-Christ.

Mithras was born in a cave and watched over by shepherds on December 25th, and it wouldn't be until over three hundred years after the life of Jesus, that this date became Christmas. After his death and resurrection, Mithras celebrated a last supper with his elect before ascending to heaven, telling them in a voice almost indistinguishable from that of the later Jesus: "He who will not eat of my body and drink of my blood, so that he will be made one with me and I with him, the same shall not know salvation" (Goodwin, 1981). The fathers of Christianity, explained the many similarities between Jesus and the earlier Mithras, by suggesting that Satan had found out about God's plans for his divine son, and "had plagiarized their most sacred rites by anticipation"[18] instilling their own

---

18   G.R.S. Mead, *Fragments of a Faith Forgotten* (Theosophical Publishing, 1900) (refering to comments made by early Christian apologist Justyn Matyr.)

candidate and Eucharist rituals before Christ's divine birth. "It is clear that Christianity when making its invasion of Indo-Germanic peoples would find itself not the first interpreter of mystic Sacraments" (Harris, 1927).

> Mithra was a protector and supporter of man in this life; he watched over his soul in the next, defending it against the impure spirits, and transferring it into the realms of eternal bliss. He was represented as all-seeing and all-hearing. Armed with a club — his weapon against Ahriman and the Devas — he unceasingly ran his course between heaven and earth. He was represented as born on the 25th of December, on which an annual festival was held on his behalf. His worship extended into all the countries colonized by the Aryans, or which became subject to Persian power. It found its way to Rome at an early period, and the *Mysteries* of Mithra, which fell on the vernal equinox, was the most famous of the Roman festivals. Baptism and the partaking of a mystical liquid to be drank with utterance of sacred formulas, were among the inaugurate acts.
>
> From Persia the worship of Mithra and the Mysteries, were carried into Syria, Lydia, Judea, Egypt, Greece, Northern, Central and Western Europe. His devotees were not suppressed in Rome until virtually superseded by the teachings of Jesus — really Mithras under a different name, — A.D. 378.
>
> ….a survival of the haoma worship… appearing as the 'Lord's Supper,' the 'body and blood'of the divine master, under another alias."
>
> Mithras was believed by his worshippers to have been put to death, and to have again *risen from the dead*. By his sufferings he was thought to have worked the salvation of those who trusted in him, for which reason he was known as their Savior. His priests watched at his tomb, and at midnight, on the 25th of March, the third day after his death, with loud shouts they proclaimed :
>
> 'Rejoice, O, brothers, your God is risen! His death, his pains, his sufferings, have worked our salvation!'
>
> His sacred flambeau was then lighted, and his image anointed with chrism, ~oil. (Brown, 1890)

Indeed, even the typically thought Catholic rite of baptism seems to have a Mithraic origin. It has long been recognized that the water submersion, as practiced by John the Baptist, was not a Jewish rite, and the Old Testament is void of references to it. As Geo Widengren noted:

...[W]ater rites took up an important place in the ancient Iranian religion. Yt. 10: 121 f. thus dictates that... one should also wash one's body in order to drink the 'the pure affusion offering,' zaovra. So here a kind of baptism emerges together with sacrifice and haoma potion, which we must evidently perceive as a 'repentant baptism.' Given that this baptism is mentioned in the Mithra devoted Yast, it has been coupled together with the water purification that occurs in the much later disseminated Mithra mysteries. The water rites evidently played a role in the Mithra cult... and were then handed down later on in the Mithra mysteries. (Widengren, 1965)

Writing the end of the 19th century George W. Brown, also cited above, felt that the Mithraic cult continued on with the age old practice of drinking the hemp infused form of haoma:

Mithra is presented in the Zoroastrian system as an intermediate between Ormazd and Ahriman, and was known as a mediator. He taught mankind to make vows and offerings, and introduced animal sacrifices. It was he who introduced the Haoma worship. This was an intoxicating beverage, prepared from the green stalks of the moon-plant, otherwise *Cannabis Indica*, or Indian hemp... It was tasted by the priests on sacrificial occasions, whilst hymns were sung in its praise. Its action was that of hashish. It produced intoxication and stimulation of the senses, which were taken for inspiration. (Brown, 1890)

Besides having the same birth date of Jesus, many scholars, such as Brown above, have noted the startlingly strong similarities between the Christian Eucharist and the Mithraic sacraments. "It is in the ancient religion of Persia – the religion of Mithra, the Mediator, the Redeemer, and the Savior – that we find the nearest resemblance to the sacrament of the Christians, and from which it was evidently borrowed" (Doane 1882). Commenting on the essay, "Eucharistic Origins," by Dr. Rendel Harris, a 1928 edition of *The Journal of Education* noted that:

Everything that Dr. Rendel Harris writes is bound to be interesting even if unconvincing.... The main constructive suggestion [of "Eucharistic Origins"] is that the Greek word *soma* in the sentence ascribed to Christ "this is my *soma* (body)" has been misunderstood. It represents the term actually used by Jesus, but not in the Greek sense. In fact, it is the *soma* of the *Rig Veda*, viz. The intoxicating drink which the author describes as "the elixir of immortality"! On these lines Christian origins can be interpreted in a new and original way indeed. (Ministry of Education, 1928)

In his intriguing essay, Dr. Harris discussed the similar Eucharistic elements found in such diverse rites as those of Old World apple tree cults to the New World's peyote religion. Seeing a diffusion of the Aryan Soma cult coming into Christianity slightly altered through the Greek Dionysus,[19] Harris explained:

...[T]he word which we have translated 'body' is the Greek... soma; suppose we write it with a capital letter and do not translate it. Since Soma is the great Aryan Sacrament, and has come down even to our own times, we can, by reading it in the text without the change of a single letter, get rid of the absurdity of the equation between the 'cup' and the 'body' for there is no difficulty in the cup being a Soma cup. This, then, was what Jesus said and did: He took a cup and said 'This is my Soma.'

What He meant was that the end was come and immortality was at hand. It was a mystical expression, an occult saying, if we like to put it so: a figure of speech expressing exactly the situation in which He found Himself, but not expressing it clearly to His companions: He appears to have invited the disciples to drink Soma with Him, i.e. to die with Him, and with Him to enter upon an immortal life. They did drink, but, as in so many other cases, they only understood in part. From that partial misunderstanding sprang, in a little while, the... [Eucharist] and the Mass.

The restoration of the original form shows us clearly... that the doctrine of immortality was involved in the Eucharist from the start, for immortality is the characteristic accompaniment of the draught of the Soma... We can see now why, in the closing eucharistic prayer in the Teaching of the Apostles we have the expres-

19   "Was there any relation between the Christian ritual and the Dionysiac ritual? One remembers that the Syrian domination over Palestine had been signalised in the pre-Maccabean times by the introduction of the Cult of Dionysos, and that, not far off, at Alexandria the worshippers had been branded as well as decorated with the ivy-leaf of the god.... [T]he influence of the Mysteries was natural, and almost inevitable... Dionysos is only the Soma-drink one degree further in evolution. It was natural, then, and as we have said, almost inevitable, that when Christianity moved into the Greek-speaking and Greek-thinking world, it should take on a colour from these mysteries in which immortality was supposed to be conferred." (Harris, 1927)

sions of thanksgiving for 'the knowledge and faith and immortality which thou hast made known to us through Jesus thy Servant . . . to us thou hast given spiritual food and drink and eternal life through thy Servant."[20]

....No doubt there are many points from which our hypothesis furnishes objective to an assailant, and we are far from thinking that a final statement can be made: but it is lawful to suggest that some of the possible objections result from our ignorance rather than from our knowledge. This ignorance is not merely a defect in the knowledge of historic cults, of this religion or of that; it extends to the knowledge of historic persons, and, in particular, it affects the person of the Founder of the Christian Faith. It is assumed that He was so wholly a Jew that He never looked outside the limits of Judaism in religion nor transgressed its limits territorially, except for a few days, perhaps, in which He was eluding capture, which was likely to occur within those limits. Yet it is not universally admitted that we know where He was born, and, if He was brought up in Galilee, whether He spent the whole of His first thirty years within those limits. One does not need to surrender to Dr. Paul Haupt's challenge, when he claims Aryan ancestry for the Lord Jesus, but he has on his side good historical evidence that Galilee was not populated by a purely Semitic race. Tradition said that it had been occupied at one time in history by a deported population from Media, and in that case, the tenacity of religious practices might have planted the Soma ritual in Galilee itself. Apart from this possibility, the fact of the existence of Northern trade-routes makes it reasonably certain that India and Persia both found their way to the Mediterranean, and not necessarily by Antioch or by the Red Sea. The whole question of the points of contact of East and West in the first century of our era needs to be reconsidered.

....But suppose we say that traffic and traders never came this way, or if they came, gave no hint of the religion to which they belonged, there is always the possibility that, if Soma did not come to Jesus, Jesus went to Soma; the possibility, that is to say, of His having been a traveller, a religious pilgrim, an inquisitive visitant to shrines or to peoples. This does not commit Him to a journey to Tibet, nor to intercourse with imaginary Mahatmas; it only means that we have an almost complete blank for the first thirty years of his life; half of this period might belong to history if we could pick up the missing threads and find the missing links. One such Eastern journey would explain the allusion to the Soma.

20   *The Didach* (100-200 AD).

.... It will, perhaps, be said that there is no need to send Jesus to India in search of the Soma draught... in the Syrian Church the Eucharist was known as the 'Sama' or medicine... of life; and... Ignatius of Antioch... described [the Eucharist] in Greek language as medicine of immortality. The coincidence in the terms is so striking, that it is natural to suggest that there is something primitive about it. .... The word Sama is not genuine Semitic ; it has been borrowed from some other language...It is very common in Syriac and Aramaic and might easily have been used by our Lord. It would not, however, call up the Greek word for 'body' [soma] quite as readily as the Indian word would do.

.... Jesus was speaking of the Indian, Avestan, Indo-Germanic Soma, when His disciples thought He was speaking of His body. That single conjecture explains the mystery and shows us how the parallel with the pagan Mysteries was invited from the start. It is not necessary to assume, though it seems probable, that Jesus had travelled Eastward at some time in His early life. The conjecture may find support without the added speculation. Let us leave that for further enquiry. (Harris, 1927)

Problems arise with Harris' theory, when one considers that it requires the 'saviour' to have conversed in Greek, rather than the more accepted idea that he spoke Aramaic, and Harris does try to justify this, although somewhat unsatisfactorily.[21] A more power-

---

21   "If Jesus did not speak Greek at the Last Supper, St. Luke certainly represents him as doing so; our Lord, according to the Lucan account, addresses His disciples in words which, at the first glance, are convincingly Semitic language. He says: 'I should have greatly liked to eat this Passover with you before I suffer.' Here the opening...(commonly, but wrongly rendered as 'with desire I have desired') is a form of speech which is, at first sight, much more like the representation of an Aramaic sentence than of a Greek original. But when we look more closely at the sentence we see that Luke is making a Greek play upon words out of (the Passover festival) and [suffer] ('this Passover before I suffer')....The same popular Greek derivation is implied in Tertullian: 'Moyses oracularly foretold that they were to eat the solemn feature of this day with bitter herbs ; and he added the words 'It is the Pascha of the Lord,' i.e. the Passion of Christ.'...The equation, then, between Passover and Passion is very early. No translator is necessarily involved in the words, ...It is impossible to escape from the play on words: whether it is primitive or not, is another question. At all events St. Luke is in evidence for it: he, at least, was thinking Greek and representing Jesus as talking Greek when he wrote his account of the Last Supper....

We can go a step further than this by the introduction of a second consideration. There has recently come to light the remarkable discovery that the words which Jesus used to Judas at the time of the actual Betrayal (Matt. xxvi. 50): 'Companion, what are you here for?' were a familiar legend on drinking glasses in the first century and in the East. Thus the speech of Jesus to Judas is history and not editorial fiction: the words were taken off the margin of the glass cup out of which they had drunk together. But this implies that Jesus addressed Judas in a Greek formula and not in Aramaic; and it will follow that there is no

ful case is made through his comparisons with the medicinal and immortal aspects associated with both the Eucharist and the Soma from which it was borrowed. As well, although Harris notes the role of similar sacraments in such contemporary cults as those of Dionysus and Isis, and discusses the Vedic Soma at some lengths, he mentions the obviously more prominent Avestan connection only in passing and failed to note clearly the more likely source of Haoma and the Mithraic Mysteries on the development of the Christian Eucharist, and from which so much of Christian mythology is already known to have been taken.

At the Last Supper, Christ communicated his "spirit" to his disciples through the Eucharist or Christian sacrament. Christ said in describing the sacrament, "Take, eat, this is my body, this is my blood. Do this as often as you will in remembrance of me" (I Corinthians 11:24-25). "Before returning to heaven, Mithra celebrated a last supper with his twelve disciples......In memory of this, his worshippers partook of a sacramental meal marked with a cross. This was one of seven Mithraic sacraments,[22] the models for the Christian seven sacraments" (Walker 1983). In a voice almost indistinguishable from that of the later Jesus, Mithras is said to have told his followers: "He who will not eat of my body and drink of my blood, so that he will be made one with me and I with him, the same shall not know salvation" [As quoted in (Goodwin 1981)]. The rites which Christianity and Mithraism "practiced offered numerous analogies";

> The sectaries of the Persian god, like the Christians, purified themselves by baptism; received a species of confirmation, the power necessary to combat the spirits of evil; and expected from a Lord's supper salvation of body and soul. Like the latter, they also held Sunday sacred, and celebrated the birth of the Sun on the 25th of December, the same day on which Christmas has been celebrated, since the fourth century at least. They both preached a categorical system of ethics, regarded asceticism as meritous, and counted among their principal virtues abstinence and continence, renunciation and self-control. Their conception of the world and of the destiny of man were similar. They both admitted the existence of a Heaven inhabited by beatified ones, situate in

---

obligation to believe that they talked in Aramaic at the Last Supper. The obligation, if any, is the other way. The glass cup and the Greek legend are historical." (Harris, 1927)

22   Related to the Mithraic ascension through the seven planetary spheres.

the upper regions, and of a Hell peopled by demons, situate in the bowels of earth. They both placed a Flood at the beginning of history; they both assigned as the source of their traditions a primitive revelation; they both finally, believed in the immortality of the soul, in a last judgment, and in a resurrection of the dead, consequent upon a final conflagration of the universe. (Cumont 1956)

Rather than being a diabolical pre-imitation of the Christian sacraments, as Justin Martyr and other Church fathers tried to suggest, the Mithraic sacraments were a remnant of the even earlier Persian haoma ceremony, an ancient rite tied with the Vedic Soma of the Indian religion. The Haoma, or Soma was considered "a god as well as a plant, just as the wine of the Christian sacrament is considered both the juice of the grape, and the blood of the redeemer" (Doane 1882).

Gnostic scriptures also give evidence that a similar relationship to that of the Eucharist haoma being considered both a god and a plant (attributes which to some extent were passed on to Mithra), and Shiva being *bhang* in India; existed to some extent between the spirit of Christ (whom they saw as distinct from the mortal Jesus, descending on him at his anointing) and the image of the Tree of Life, as can be seen in the *Teachings of Silvanus*. "For the Tree of Life is Christ. He is Wisdom...the Word...the Life, the Power, and the Door. He is the Light, the Angel, and the Good Shepherd." As was mentioned, the Ophite Christians referred to being anointed from the Tree of Life, in an obvious reference to an entheogenic anointing oil analogous to the one used by the ancient Hebrews. And another Gnostic initiate, the Seth of *The Gospel of the Egyptians*, refers to receiving inspiration from "the incense of life," which again brings to mind the image of the Tree of Life being utilized as an entheogen.

The *Teachings of Silvanus* may give indications (as does the *Zostrianos* tractate) that the Gnostics made a drinkable potion from the plant as well: "Give yourself gladness from the true vine of Christ. Satisfy yourself with the true wine in which there is no drunkenness nor error. For it (the true wine) marks the end of drinking since there is usually in it what gives joy to the soul and mind through the Spirit of God. But first, nurture your reasoning powers before you drink of it (the true wine)." i.e. - as opposed to the 'false wine' and 'false vine.' Perhaps like many proponents of the modern entheogenic revival, some Gnostic sects opposed the drinking of alcohol? The *Acts of Thomas*, which makes reference to the 'plant of kindness,' also refers to the 'true vine,' and in connection with what is likely another entheogenic preparation as well; "...we speak of the world which is above, of God and angels, of watchers and holy ones of the immortal (ambrosial) food and the drink of the true vine."

In relation to Jesus' use of cannabis-based haoma like sacraments, it should also be noted that the use of such a substance may account for what can be seen as the most fundamental element of the Christian mythos, the Resurrection. "...[T]he Persians say ... the Haoma plant,... is the first of the trees, planted by Ahura Mazda in the fountain of life. He who drinks of its juice never dies....Haoma... gives health and generative power, and imparts life at the resurrection" (Windischmann, 1846).[23]

Death On The Cross?

Three decades ago Dr. Hugh Schonfield shocked the theological world with his sensational book *The Passover Plot*, which suggested that Jesus may have feigned death on the cross through a soporific potion - a hypothesis which if suggested only a few centuries earlier, would have seen the author burned at the stake, or worse. Suggesting that Jesus' cry from the cross, 'I am thirsty,' could have been a signal to receive a specially prepared potion, Schonfield speculated that the "plan may... have been suggested to Jesus by the prophetic words, 'They gave me also gall for my meat; and in my thirst they gave me vinegar to drink.'" With precision scholarship, Dr. Schonfield noted that if what Jesus "received had been the normal wine diluted with water the effect would have been stimulating. In this case it was exactly the opposite. Jesus lapsed quickly into complete unconsciousness. His body sagged. His head lolled on his breast, and to all intents and purposes he was a dead man.... Directly it was seen that the drug had worked..." (Schonfield 1965).

Deeply influenced by Schonfield's research, the authors of the sensational international best-seller, *The Holy Blood and the Holy Grail*, expanded more fully on this theme in the early 1980s.

23   Quoted in (Muir, 1860)

In the Fourth Gospel Jesus, hanging on the cross, declares that he
thirsts. In reply to this complaint he is proffered a sponge allegedly soaked in vinegar - an incident that also occurs in the other
Gospels. This sponge is generally interpreted as another act of
sadistic derision. But was it really? Vinegar – or soured wine – is a
temporary stimulant, with effects not unlike smelling salts. It was
often used at the time to resuscitate flagging slaves on galleys. For
a wounded and exhausted man, a sniff or taste of vinegar would
induce a restorative effect, a momentary surge of energy. And yet
in Jesus' case the effect is just the contrary. No sooner does he
inhale or taste the sponge then he pronounces his final words and
'gives up the ghost.' Such a reaction to vinegar is physiologically
inexplicable. On the other hand such a reaction would be perfectly compatible with a sponge soaked not in vinegar, but in some
type of soporific drug – a compound of opium and or belladonna,
for instance, commonly employed in the Middle East at the time.
But why proffer a soporific drug? Unless the act of doing so, along
with all the other components of the Crucifixion, were elements
of a complex and ingenious stratagem – a stratagem designed to
produce a semblance of death when the victim, in fact, was still
alive. Such a stratagem would not only have saved Jesus' life, but
also have realized the Old Testament prophecies of a Messiah.
(Baigent, Leigh & Lincoln, 1982)

Besides opium and belladonna, a preparation of mandrake,
which was in use during this time period, may have helped to induce the deathlike stupor needed to fool the Roman soldiers and
Jewish populace. Thomas Cisteriensis (d. 1190 A.D.) wrote of the
mandrake "The mandragora is a plant which effects such a deep
sleep that one can cut a person and he feels not the pain. For the
mandragora symbolizes striving in contemplation. Its reverie allows a person to fall into a sleep of such delicious sweetness that he
no longer feels any of the cutting which his earthly enemies inflict
upon him, and he no longer cares about any earthly thing. For his
soul has now closed off its senses from all that is external – it lies in
the benevolent sleep of the eternal."
More recently, Dana Beal and Paul De Rienzo have hypothesized
that the substance which put Jesus into his deathlike stupor on the
cross was a preparation of the drug plant *Peganum harmala*, or
Syrian rue, which they also suggest was a Gnostic sacrament, referring to its continued use by the Gnostic Mandeans, as well as

joining the speculations of Flattery and Schwartz (1989), that Syrian rue was the main ingredient in the Persian Haoma (Beal & De Rienzo 1997). As Dana Beal explains his line of reasoning (which does not exclude cannabis):

> ...the key ingredient of the lost soma of the Vedas was the very same "vinegar and gall" administered to Jesus on a sponge at the moment of his crucifixion, according to the Book of John. We know this because of the telltale action of harmaline at the antistroke (NMDA) receptor, and because the body's own version of harmaline is implicated in the mechanism of a kind of naturally occurring *deathlike suspended animation*, discovered at the coronary unit of Henry Ford Hospital in Detroit. This is big news for the Jesus Seminar. Not only does it go a long way in explaining the takeover of Mithras, the orthodox religions of late Roman times, by the Christ cult (whence comes the wine and wafer), it explains the actual relationship of cannabis to the Zaotar cup (Grail), since the preparation of an active soma mixture involved cannabis in virtually every recipe, according to [German researcher] Hans-Georg Behr. (Beal 1997)

Clearly some of the above substances, considered magical sacraments in the ancient world, are so powerful that they can put the people who ingest them in requisite amounts into a deathlike coma that could conceivably have made other ancient onlookers think that they had actually died.

As well, as discussed in Chapter 15 in relation to the death-like coma state known as "*stard*" induced by *mang* in Zoroastrian accounts, in extremely high doses, and through powerful extracts, cannabis has been reported also to put its imbibers into a state similar to animal "hibernation" which is combined with a rigor-mortis like physical condition of catalepsy. "Catalepsy is a mysterious condition, characterized by immobility of the muscles which can sometimes be mistaken for death. The limbs have a 'waxy flexibility' and can be molded into bizarre positions where they remain indefinitely" (Wilkins 1992).

As noted in Chapter 15, the 19th century researcher Dr. James Braid wrote a monograph entitled "Trance and Human Hibernations," which suggested that in India cannabis was used by fakir's in order to induce just such a state.

Some excerpts of Braid's research appeared in the 1855 classic *Plant Intoxicants*, by Baron Ernst Von Bibra in a chapter on hashish. Braid discussed a number of eye-witness accounts of Indian Fakirs who had allowed themselves to be buried alive, and were later disinterred and found still alive. Amongst these accounts are recorded the words of Sir Claude Wade who was present at the court of Runjeet Singh when one such Fakir was buried in a specially prepared room that was "completely sealed off from the access of atmospheric air" and then disinterred weeks later! Wade described the end of the allotted time period when he joined Runjeet Singh and the fakir's servant and broke the seal of the specially prepared room:

> Provided with light, we descended about three feet below the floor of the room, into a sort of cell. This cell too, was locked and sealed, and it contained a wooden box, about four feet long by three feet broad, with a sloping cover, placed upright.
>
> Opening the box we saw a figure enclosed in a white bag. The Fakeer's servant took this figure out of the box and placed it upright against the door. When he took off the bag, the legs and arms of the body were shrivelled and stiff, and the head reclined, corpse-like, on the shoulders. No pulse in the heart, the temples, or the arms could be discovered.
>
> The servant then sprinkled warm water on the body, while we forcefully rubbed its arms and legs. During this time the servant placed a hot wheat cake on the head, a process which he twice or thrice renewed. He then pulled out of the nostrils and ears the cotton and wax contained in them; and after great exertion opened the Fakeer's mouth by inserting the point of a knife between his teeth and drew his tongue forward, which, however, flew back several times to its former position. He then rubbed the Fakeer's eyelid with ghee, or clarified butter, for some seconds, until he succeeded in opening them, when the eyes appeared quite motionless and glazed. After he applied the cake for a third time to the head, the body was violently convulsed, the nostrils became inflated, and the limbs became pliable and began to assume a natural fullness. The servant then put some of the ghee on the Fakeer's tongue and made him swallow it. A few minutes later, the pupils became dilated and the eyes recovered their natural appearance, and the Fakeer said, in a low, sepulchral tone, scarcely audible, "Do you believe me now?" From the opening of the box to the recovery of the Fakeer's voice, not more than half

an hour could have elapsed, and in another half hour the Fakeer talked with us, although with a feeble voice. (Sir Claude Wade)[24]

Other such cases were reported by reliable eyewitnesses and like Wade's description, when the Fakir's bodies were disinterred they "were found stiff and rigid like a corpse, but on application of the aforesaid treatment they were restored to life.... It is possible that some of the *fakirs* possess a hemp preparation that enables them to undergo the described experiments.[25] This is especially support-ed by the catalepsy that sets in after hemp resin has been taken" (Von Bibra 1855). In reference to "catalepsy," Von Bibra is referring to the research on the effects of hashish that had been conduct-ed in India during the first half of the 19th century by a Dr. W.B. O'Shaughnessy, who reported the following account of a patient that had been given "one grain of the resin of hemp... administered in a solution." Worried by the effects the drug was apparently hav-ing on the patient some hours after it had been administered, a nurse summoned Dr. O'Shaughnessy to the hospital, where he was alarmed to find the patient "lying on his cot quite insensible";

> ...I chanced to lift up the patient's arm. The professional reader will judge of my astonishment, when I found that it remained in the posture in which I placed it. It required but a very brief ex-amination of the limbs to find that the patient had, by the influ-ence of this narcotic, been thrown into that strange and most ex-traordinary of all nervous conditions, into that state what so few have seen and the existence of which so many still discredit - the genuine *catalepsy* of the nosologist.... We raised [the patient]... to a sitting position, and placed his arms and limbs in every imag-inable attitude. A waxen figure could not be more pliant, or more stationery in each position, no matter how contrary to the natural influence of gravity on the part. (O'Shaughnessy 1839)[26]

---

24   Originally quoted in Baird's 1850 work, and then requoted by Von Bibra in 1855, and then later in the 1995 reprint of Von Bibra's *Plant Intoxicants*.

25   It has also been reported that Indian Fakirs use cannabis to induce the concen-tration and mystical states needed for the performance of the self inflicted extreme physi-cal stress and pain that they perform as part of their yogic training. In an article entitled "Sham Asceticism" (*The Theosophist*, Vol. IV, No.6, March,1883), H.P Blavatsky comments on a Hindu ascetic, who was said to have arrived in Surat. "He does not receive alms, but only accepts drugs like ganja and sooka. He does not require any food. On the wooden shoes that he wears, and on the bench and on the planks of the cot he sleeps upon, are fixed some hundreds of thousands of pointed nails."

26   *On the Preparation of the Indian Hemp* (1839) - reprinted in (Mikuriya 1973)

Although it doesn't happen often, there have been accounts of people being presumed dead, while in just such a state of extreme cannabis intoxication.

A well known example of a medicinally induced cataleptic state, is that of Shakespeare's *Romeo and Juliet,* where the Christian monk, Father Laurence gives Juliet a philtre that put her into a death-like state for almost two days. Interestingly, emerging evidence indicates Shakespeare was aware of the narcotic effects of cannabis, possibly even using it himself (Thackeray & Van Der Merwe, 2001):

"Take thou this vial, being then in bed,
And this distilled liquor drink thou off;
When presently through all thy veins shall run
A cold and drowsy humour, for no pulse
Shall keep his native progress, but surcease:
No warmth, no breath, shall testify thou livest;
The roses in thy lips and cheeks shall fade
To paly ashes, thy eyes' windows fall,
Like death, when he shuts up the day of life;
Each part, deprived of supple government,
Shall, stiff and stark and cold, appear like death:

And in this borrow'd likeness of shrunk death
Thou shalt continue two and forty hours,
And then awake as from a pleasant sleep."
                                    Romeo and Juliet: Act 4 Scene 1

Referring to the tale of Romeo and Juliet, as well as a medieval Arabic account, the mid 19th century author W. Ley, Esq., discussed these potentially powerful soporific effects of cannabis, and also reported on accounts contemporary to his own time.

In the "Arabian Nights' Entertainment" frequent mention is made of the drug... under the name of benj. In one tale, the heroine, Koot-el-Kuloob, is represented to be thrown into a profound sleep by the medicine given her, and buried alive; on being dug up again, the fresh air revives her; she is still under the influence of the dose, but the only manifest effects of it are her strong appetite for love and food. This tale was published in Egypt about the year 1450 or 1500. The story of Romeo and Juliet was published at Venice in 1549, as an occurrence of real life at Verona. We have

the authority of Lord Byron for the faith still placed in the truth of this story by the inhabitants of that part of Italy. He visited the tomb of the lovers, and mentions the ruins of the castle at Montecchi.... These are curious points rather than satisfactory evidence that the account of the sleeping draught was possible. It is on the possibility of any draught of such potency being without danger to life that the probability of the story principally depends.... I can fearlessly say that, of all known soporifics, I should push to the extremity with most confidence. Having given it for relief of titanic spasm, my patient felt that she had taken too much; she was overpowered; the spasms were relieved, and she fell into a stupor that lasted ten hours. The face was relaxed, the eye closed, the jaw fallen, the breathing scarcely perceptible. She showed no sensibility; there was no motion; she was in the calmest sleep; her skin was warm and her pulse maintained its strength. These assured me that it was not the sleep of death. She awoke without any disagreeable feeling from the powerful dose, but with relief beyond expression. Had this influence been produced in a climate where coldness is not an accompaniment of death, and where the funeral takes place before the body has time to cool, a premature burial might have been a prospect. Dr. O'Shaughnessy will tell you that a Persian physician of high character, seeing him doubtful and alarmed at the stupor produced by one grain, bade him give thirty without fear, adding "You will think him dead, but it is of no consequence; he will recover again"... Mr. O'Brien, who has been familiar with the remedy at Calcutta, has also seen person whom he believed dead, but recovered after twelve hours' stupor, without any unpleasant effects remaining.
...Although experiments on dogs are not conclusive as to the effects and remedies on the human subject, they afford evidence that is not to be disregarded. On the human adult, one-sixth of a grain of fresh extract of hemp prepared at Calcutta produced decided effects. Dr. O'Shaughnessy, gave to a moderate sized dog half an ounce of the same preparation; the result that he slept, in a state of stupor, with the limbs stiff, as from catalepsy, for two days. It then recovered and ate voraciously. (Ley, 1843).

The turn of the century author L. W. De Laurence reported the following tragic case of a cannabis overdose:

A case of living internment which came under this author's notice in India was that of a young Hindu of low caste, about thirty years of age, who took an Indian drug called Cannabis Indica or Indian Cannabis (made from the plant Cannabis Sativa), with suicidal intent. He was to all appearances dead when found by relatives. An English physician was called and after making the usual examination and tests in such cases, pronounced the young man dead. His funeral services were held three days later; the coffin containing the supposed corpse being placed in a receiving cave. At the expiration of the ten days, the time set for burial, the coffin was opened by the attendant in order that the relatives might have a look at their dead. A horrible site met their gaze—a sight that filled their hearts with horror and unutterable grief. The young man had turned half over on his left side, while in his right hand, clenched in death's agony, was found fragments of hair which had been torn from his head. The cloth around his neck also showed evidence of his attempt to tear it during the struggle he had made against death. (De Laurence, 1905)

In the 19th century, James Simpson and co-authors, likely referring to the work of Dr. Braid and other sources regarding the Fakirs apparent ability for extended periods of "hibernation," noted that the "wonderful power of endurance of the Hindu Suttee appears to have been sometimes procured by the influence of this powerful drug [i.e. cannabis]":

> Some high Biblical commentaries maintain that the gall and vinegar or myrrhed wine offered to our Saviour immediately before his crucifixion was a preparation, in all probability, of hemp, which was in these, as well as in later times, occasionally given to criminals before punishment or execution—while 700 years previously it is possibly spoken of, according to the same authorities, by the prophet Amos as the "wine of the condemned." (Simpson, et al., 1856)

Shortly after the above was written in an 1860 meeting between the Ohio State Medical Society and a group of Biblical Scholars, the group concurred that "the gall and vinegar or myrrhed wine... was a preparation of Indian Hemp."[27] Talmudic reference indicate this use as well: "The one on his way to execution was given a piece of incense in a cup of wine, to help him fall asleep" (Sanh. 43a).[28] As Jesus'

27   (From the transactions of the 15th annual meeting of the Ohio Medical Society at White Sulphur Springs, June 12th through 14th, 1860, pp. 75-100).
28   As quoted in (Kersten 1986).

crucifixion is said to have taken place during the Passover, it is interesting to note that such a hemp preparation may have been widely
available at this time. According to Immanuel Low in his German
ethno-botanical text, *Die Flora Der Juden* the Passover incense contained cannabis resins (Low 1926\1967).[29] Closer to our own time
and independently, the German researcher Holger Kersten has also
suggested that cannabis may have been amongst the ingredients in
the drink which put Jesus into a deathlike stupor, here connecting it
with the traditions of Soma and Haoma (Kertsen 1986).

> How did Jesus come (apparently) to die immediately after he had
> taken the bitter drink? Was it really vinegar that he was given?....
> Perhaps the supposed drink of vinegar instead contained the ac-
> tive ingredients of the sacred drink of the Indians and Persians,
> Soma and Haoma (respectively) ...
>
> Soma, the sacred drink of India, enabled an adept to enter a
> deathlike state for several days, and to awaken afterwards in an
> elated state that lasted a few days more. In this state of ecstasy,
> a 'higher consciousness' spoke through the adept and he had vi-
> sionary powers. In addition to Asclepias acida, the Soma might
> also have contained Indian hemp (Cannabis indica) – tradition
> has it that it featured in the drink of Zarathustra. (Kersten 1986)

Although Kersten seems to be confusing Zoroastrian accounts
of the effects of mang, with those of the Vedic Soma (as we have
commented there are some marked differences between the two)
it is still of interest that an independent researcher has commented on this identical effect of a cannabis extract. As well, in later
Persian Islamic times hashish preparations were used for similar
effects by the Gnostic influenced Hashishin for their own roman-
ticized near death experience initiations, as shall be discussed in
Chapter 19. In relation to the other Biblical resurrection, that of
Lazarus, it is important to note that Professor Morton Smith has
suggested that Lazarus did not suffer death, but went through an
intense initiation into the "mystery of the kingdom of God" (Mark
4:11) (Smith, 1978). Indications of such shamanic initiations can
be found throughout the ancient Gnostic texts, as well as in the

29   Low referred to a recipe that had marijuana resin, *hasisat surur* (*surur* being an
undercover reference to the resin of cannabis), ground into powder and mixed with wine,
then made burnable and more fragrant by combining it with Arabic gum and saffron (Low
1926\1967).

Catholic Church's condemnations of the Gnostics (Bennett & Mc-
Queen, 2001). Thus the idea that the Jesus and his early followers
may have had access to powerful cannabis extracts used in death
and rebirth ceremonies, such as those used by the earlier Zoroastrians and later Hashishins, is not at all farfetched.

If Christ arranged to receive such a cannabis extract on the day
of the Crucifixion, the resulting cataleptic state of hibernation induced by cannabis taken in its most condensed and powerful form
could easily have been mistaken for death by the Romans who stood
guard over him, and the Jewish crowd who had come out to watch
another claimant to the title of "Messiah" meet their typical fate. As
the powerful preparation took effect, the limbs would begin stiffen-
ing, the heartbeat slowing down to an occasional thud, the breath
dropping off to a faint whisper of a still body that more and more
resembled a corpse.... John 19 tells of the night of the crucifiction
in detail that fits in completely with this hypothesis:

> Later, knowing that all was now completed, and so that the Scrip-
> tures would be fulfilled, Jesus said "I am thirsty." A Jar of wine
> vinegar was there, so they soaked a sponge in it, put the sponge
> on a stalk of the hyssop plant, and lifted it to Jesus' lips. When he
> had received the drink, Jesus said, "It is finished." With that, he
> bowed his head and gave up his spirit.
>
> Now... the next day was to be a special Sabbath. Because the
> Jews did not want the bodies left on the crosses during the Sab-
> bath, they asked Pilate to have the legs broken and the bodies
> taken down. The soldiers therefore came and broke the legs of
> the first man that was crucified with Jesus, and then those of the
> other. But when they came to Jesus and found that he was already
> dead, they did not break his legs. (John19:33)

Death, in the case of a crucifixion, came through suffocation; as
the arms and legs gave out from exhaustion and stress, the lung cav-
ity contracted, and in some cases this took days.[30] By lessening these

---

30   There were cases of crucifixion victims of some days on the cross surviving after
their removal. The historian Flavius Josephus (37-95? ad) recorded such an event in his ancient autobiography. Returning from a mission he was sent on by Titus Caesar, Josephus
recorded seeing three of his former companions amongst the prisoners who were crucified. Much affected, Josephus went to Titus and with tears in his eyes, requested for their
appeal. Titus apparently, "at once gave the orders that they should be taken down and
given the best treatment so they might recover. But two of them died while being treated
by the doctor; the third did get better." [From an excerpt in (Kersten 1986)].

supports considerably, the breaking of the legs hastened this process. John has it that because Jesus was already dead, the soldiers do not break his legs, but instead pierce Christ's side with a spear. There is even a witness to this, one unnamed bystander: "The man who saw it has given testimony, and his testimony is true. He knows that he tells the truth, and he testifies so that you also may believe" (John 19:35). (The man doth protest too much!) Schonefield suggested that the story of the spear thrust into Jesus' side "may have been introduced to historicise certain Old Testament testimonies" (Schonfield 1965).[31]

This brings us to the pivotal point of the Biblical narrative, where, to all outsiders, including Jesus' own apostles, all seems to be over for the charismatic leader that they had believed was going to lead them into a new age of glory.

> It is the moment before sundown in Jerusalem. On the hill of Golgotha three bodies are suspended on crosses. Two – the thieves - are dead. The third appears so. This is the drugged body of Jesus of Nazareth, the man who planned his own crucifixion, who contrived to be given a soporific potion to put him into a deathlike trance. Now Joseph of Arimathea, bearing clean linen and spices, approaches and recovers the still form of Jesus. All seems to be proceeding according to plan. (Schonfield 1965)

The aloes and spices brought by Nicodemus and Joseph of Arimathea to Jesus's tomb to supposedly embalm their now dead leader pose a particularly curious question, as embalming was not a practice of the Jews of the time. Perhaps these lotions served some other purpose? The account in John regarding Jesus removal from the cross, and the role of Joseph of Arimathea and also Nicodemus, bears an uncanny resemblance to the tale which was discussed earlier of the Fakir and the assistant who helped to revive him after his deathlike entombment. "[I]n reality there were efforts behind the scenes to 'bring Jesus back to life' in the privacy of the tomb cavern, under the direction of Joseph and Nicodemus" (Kersten 1986).

> Later, Joseph of Arimathea asked Pilate for the body of Jesus. Now Joseph was a disciple of Jesus, but secretly because he feared the Jews. With Pilate's permission, he came and took the body away.

---

31   John (19:36), refers to the non-breaking of Jesus' leg and the piercing of his side as fulfilling Exodus 12:46; Numbers 9:12; Psalm 34:20 and Zechariah 12:10.

He was accompanied by Nicodemus, the man who had earlier
visited Jesus at night. Nicodemus brought a mixture of myrrh and
aloes, about seventy-five pounds. Taking Jesus' body, the two of
them wrapped it, with the spices, in strips of linen. This was in
accordance with the Jewish burial customs.[32] At the place where
Jesus was crucified, there was a garden, and in the garden a new
tomb in which no-one had ever been laid. (John 19:38-41)

It does not take an overly active imagination to picture Joseph
and Nicodemus rubbing the stiffened joints of Jesus' bodies with
large quantities of healing herbs and spices which they had brought
in preparation, and slowly waking their master from his death-like
cataleptic state which had been induced by the substance delivered to him on the cross. A scenario that is reminiscent of the role
played by the fakir's helper in the account discussed earlier. Such a
scenario, although sounding somewhat fanciful, is far more believable than that of the alternative, held to be true by literally millions
of Christians – That a man died, decomposed for three days and
three nights, then arose from the Dead!

The subject of the crucifixion and resurrection of Jesus would
later become one of the main points of contention between Gnostic Christians and the Roman Catholic Church. The Gnostic text,
The Second Treatise of the Great Seth, has Jesus himself disclaim
the doctrine of the literal resurrection. Referring to the increasingly popular concept of the resurrection, Jesus speaks of those
who "think that they are advancing the name of Christ," but are
instead "unknowingly empty, not knowing who they are, like dumb
animals. They persecuted those who have been liberated by me,
since they hate them." He describes their theology as "ludicrous...
an imitation... a doctrine of a dead man." A theme that the figure of
Jesus clearly returns to in other Gnostic tractates;

They will cleave to the name of a dead man, thinking that they
will become pure. But they will become greatly defiled and they
will fall into the name of error and into the hand of an evil, cun-
ning man and a manifold dogma... there shall be others of those
who are outside our number who name themselves bishop and
also deacons, as if they have received their authority from God.
They bend themselves under the judgment of the leaders. These
people are dry canals. (*The Apocalypse of Peter*)

32   Or rather up until the third century, they used, *keneh*, hemp (Klien,1908)

Jesus' reference to "bishop and also deacons," who didn't exist in the early Christian period and came into existence some time later, shows that the Gnostic tractate was the work of an eager, later writer, who like the New Testament and Old Testament editors and compilers, was given to adding to existing traditions and putting new words into the mouths of long dead figures. But clearly amongst the Gnostics, since earliest Christian times, there was a long tradition in which could be found a repudiation of the physical resurrection of the dead Jesus, which they termed the "faith of the fools."

The Persian Apocalypse

In Chapter 15, we discussed the Zoroastrian apocalyptic literature in relation to its Jewish counterparts, noting the tradition's origins in the cannabis-induced revelations of one of Zoroaster's first converts, King Vishtaspa. Once again we return to the account of the ancient Persian king, for its profound influence on the later Chrisitian Book of Revelation. After the time of Alexander the Great, many Holy texts of the Near East were translated into Greek, this not only included the Old Testament texts, but many Persian works as well, including the story of Vishtaspa, whose name in Greek became Hystaspes, or Hystaspes. "In the second and first century b.c. an apocalypse written in Greek was in circulation under the title Oracles of Hystaspes: it was directed against Rome (whose fall was announced) but formed part of the Iranian eschatological literature" (Eliade, 1982). Because of its seditious content, much like the radical elements of the early Christian tradition, the Oracle of Hystaspes was outlawed by Rome, but its secret circulation continued well into Christian times: "The... Oracle of Hystaspes mentioned by Christian writers has been identified as a Mithraic oracle foretelling the god's coming at the end of the world to destroy the wicked with fire and to save the righteous," (Parrinder, 1971). A scenario that undeniably describes the mythic plot that has generally been attributed to the later Book of Revelation.

As Werner Sundermann explains, the Oracle of Hystaspes is "a collection of prophecies ascribed to Vištāspa, the patron and follower of Zarathustra, whom the Middle Iranian and part of the ancient tradition also identified with Darius's father. The text of the work is not extant, except for resumés in Greek and Latin, attributable to the Oracles if they mention the name Hystaspes and contain prophetic material" (Sundermann, 2004). Sundermann refers to the following ancient documents that make reference to Hystaspes and which can be quoted with confidence as excerpts from the Oracle of Hystaspes:

> ...Justin Martyr (ca. 150 C.E.), *Apology* I, 20, 1... : "And both the Sibyl and Hystaspes have said that the extermination of the corrupt will happen by fire."
>
> ...Clement of Alexandria (ca. 190 C.E.), *Stromata* VI, 5, 1... quoting an apocryphal speech by Paul: "Grasp also the Hellenic books, recognize the Sibyl more perfectly . . . , and grasp and read Hystaspes, and you will find the Son of God described much more distinctly and clearly, and how against Christ many kings will fight, hating him and those who bear his name, and his followers, and the suffering [of Christ] and his coming."
>
> ...Lactantius, *Divinae Institutiones* (written between 305 and 310 C.E.) VII, 15, 19...: "Hystaspes, too, who was a very old king of the Medes (after whom a river was named, which is now called Hydaspes), has handed down to the memory of his successors a wonderful dream interpreted by a prophesying lad: the Roman empire and its name will be removed from the face of the earth. Long before that Trojan race came into being, this was foreseen."
>
> ... Lactantius, *Divinae Institutiones* VII, 18, 2...: "For Hystaspes, whom I mentioned above, maintains, after having described the injustice of this last century, that the pious and faithful, once they are separated from the wrongdoers, will raise their hands to the sky with tears and lamentations and beseech the fidelity of Jupiter (*fidem Jovis*). And Jupiter will look upon the earth and hear the voices of the people and exterminate the godless ones."
>
> ... Excerpt from the *Theosophy*... a work anonymously handed down from the late 5th century...: "In the fourth (or eleventh) [chapter] he mentions the oracles of a certain Hystaspes (*Khrēseis Hystaspou*), who, as he said, was an extremely pious king of the Persians or Chaldeans and therefore received the revelation of the divine mysteries about the incarnation of the Savior."

As Sundermann explains, a clear picture of the Oracle of Hystaspes would be hard to make from this surviving data. But what is obvious is the combination of explicitly Christian and Zoroastrian cosmological elements. "Ernst Kuhn... [has] given unequivocal support

to a Christian origin of the oracles...: 'I assume that these prophecies of Hystaspes go back to a rather early period and serve the obvious purpose of recruiting followers for rising Christianity among
the Mazda worshippers influenced by Hellenistic culture.') All other
investigations lead to the assumption of a Christian rearrangement
of a non-Christian collection of oracles, in which the precise 'heathen' proportion is problematic...." (Sundermann, 2004).

> ...[T]he history and object of the Hystaspes oracles can be summed
> up as follows: the work was written in the Hellenistic Near East, in
> Asia Minor or a neighboring country (in any case not in Alexandria
> or anywhere in Egypt), in the 2nd or 1st century B.C.E. Perhaps it
> was a sign of the anti-Roman atmosphere which prevailed during
> the war of Mithridates VI Eupator of Pontus (ca. 132–63 B.C.E.)
> against Rome.... As an apocalypse with political relevance and as
> a polemic claiming the priority of the most ancient wisdom, it was
> attributed to the Zoroastrian King Hystaspes and availed itself of
> Iranian apocalyptic motives... the work must have been written
> in Greek. Precisely because the oracles were a product of the Hel-
> lenistic mind, they succeeded in achieving what the Zoroastrian
> apocalypses failed to do: they were able to feel at home in the tradi-
> tions of various nations suffering under Roman sovereignty. A Jew-
> ish and a Jewish-Christian version may be assumed, and a Chris-
> tian adaptation is certain. (Sundermann, 2004)

Thus the coming of the Jewish Messiah was hailed by a Persian
king who drank *mang* (cannabis) mixed with Haoma in order to
open the "eye of the soul" and foretell the future of the world! Little
wonder so many Zoroastrian motifs would find their way into the
Christian book of Revelation.

The Zoroastrian idea of the Day of Judgment finds its full expression in John's Revelation, documenting that as early as the end of
the first century the emerging Christians had, through their assimi-
lation of foreign mythological motifs, made the Persian apocalypse
their own. The Zoroastrian Bundahish gives the following account
of the end times:

> And when a great meteor then falls[33] the distressing of the earth
> will become as of a sheep fallen upon by a wolf. Fire and the an-

33   Compare with Revelation 8:10, "a great star, blazing like a torch, fell from the
sky..."

gel of Fire will melt the metals in the hills and mountains, which
then will flow upon the earth as a river. All men then pass into the
metal and become pure…

   And in the end, with the greatest affection, all come together,
father and son, brother and friend, and they ask each other thus:
"Where have you been these many years and what was the judgment of your soul? Where you righteous, or were you wicked?"
(Bundahish 30)[34]

Comparatively, in Revelation's Day of Judgment, all of humanity
is to be physically resurrected in the flesh and aligned before the
"Great White Throne" to be judged for the actions of their lives:
"I saw the dead, great and small, standing before the throne; and
books were opened. Then another book was opened, the book of
life; and the dead were judged by their deeds according to what
was written in the books. The sea gave up its dead, and death and
Hades gave up their dead; and they were judged, each by his own
deeds" (Rev. 20:12-13). John also goes on to describe briefly the
punishments that are destined for those unfortunates[35] that are to
be damned: "Then Death and Hades were thrown into the lake of
fire. This lake of fire is the second death; and into it anyone is flung
if his name is not found in the book of life" (Rev. 20:14-15).[36]

   As with the Day of Judgment the role of "Satan" as he appears in
Revelation is one of the strongest influences from the Zoroastrian
eschatological literature on the Christian apocalyptic text. Originally in Israelite folklore "Satan" was one of the heavenly host, an
angel of the Lord. The actual term "satan" in Hebrew means 'adver-
sary," or "accuser." It "can be used of a man who brings an accusation
against another in a lawcourt" (Caird 1966). Even in the later Jewish

---

34   From an excerpt in (Campbell 1964). An example of this mythos being adopted
by the pre-Christian Jews can be seen in the writings of Malachi who lived in the post
exilic Persian period: "'Surely the day is coming; it will burn like a furnace. All the arrogant, every evildoer will be stubble, and that day that is coming will set them on fire,' says
the Lord almighty. 'Not a root or a branch will be left to them. But for you who revere my
name, the sun of righteousness will rise with healing in its wings….Then you will trample
down the wicked; they will be ashes under the soles of your feet on the day when I do
these things'" (Malachi 4:1-3). Interestingly, the "sun of righteousness" is a title of the Persian world savior, Mithras.

35   The damned include "cowards, the faithless and polluted, murderers, fornica-
tors, sorcerers, idolaters, and liars of every kind, their lot is the lake that burns with sulfu-
rous flames, which is the second death" (Rev. 21;8).

36   Here the Zoroastrian and Christian traditions differ a little, for in the Zoroastrian account, even the most horrendous criminal is eventually purified in the River of Fire,
whereas in the Christian tradition, the damnation of Hellfire was believed to be eternal.

tradition of the Book of Job, Satan's role is that of an "accuser" and all that he does is in accordance with the will of God. However, in Revelation, Satan appears as the wicked one, the "deceiver of the world," cast down from heaven above and then left to wreak havoc on the earth: "Then war broke out in heaven. Michael and his angels were to wage war on the dragon. The dragon and his angels fought, but they were overpowered, and left not a trace to be found in heaven. So the great dragon was overthrown, that old serpent whose name is the Devil, or Satan, the deceiver of the whole world, thrown down to the earth, and his angels with him," (Rev. 12:7-11). Clearly, the depiction of Satan here in this cosmic battle with the Hosts of Heaven, is far removed from that of the Jewish "accuser" in the heavenly court and brings this figure much closer to the Zoroastrian Ahriman (a.ka. Angra Mainyu), the "Evil One" and his role as the opponent of Ahura Mazda, the Wise Lord and God of Light.

In the Zoroastrian apocalyptic mythos we find a variety of interesting concepts which have become very familiar to us through Christianity, particularly the way that the concept of the duality of good and evil is very delineated. Ahura Mazda is all goodness, truth and light while Ahriman is all darkness deceit and evil. They are separate entities who do battle with each other on the battle field of earthly creation. Likewise, in both the Zoroastrian and Christian cosmologies we come across the concept of a final battle at the end of time in which the righteous and the evil are sorted out once and for all, ending with the establishment of the kingdom of the good.

Joseph Campbell described how in the Persian tradition, with the return of the messiah-like Saoshyant,[37] "there will take place a final battle and cosmic conflagration, through which the principle of darkness and the lie will be undone" (Campbell 1962). Similarly, according to the Revelation of John, with the return of the Messiah, Satan "that old serpent," will be "flung into the lake of fire, to join the monster and the false prophet, there to be tormented day and night for ever and ever" (Rev. 20:10). Likewise, similar to the

37   Another aspect of Zoroastrianism here described which should be very familiar to all of us of Judeo-Christian culture is the notion of a savior who will come at the end of history to establish this kingdom of the good. It's not just that this savior will come, but that he will come again! The Persian Saoshyant, like Mithras, with whose mythology he is so entwined, and the later Jesus, is also of a virginal birth. A maid, Eredad-ereta while bathing in the lake Kansava is to conceive from the seed that Gayomart, the first man, bestowed to the earth. From this virgin is to be born the Savior Saoshyant who is to come at the end of time.

formation of a "New Jerusalem," and the dawning of the Heavenly Age, after the vanquishing of evil in the Persian Apocalypse, "all will be light, there will be no further history, and the kingdom of God (Ahura Mazda) will have been established in its pristine form forever" (Campbell 1962).

Much like the prophecies of the Tree of Life that appear at the end of the Bible, it is said in the Zoroastrian prophecies, that the final savior, the Saoshyant, or in some traditions the god Mithra, would return at the end times to initiate the faithful with a powerful sacrament known as the White Haoma. Zoroastrians believed that the Haoma ritual itself was a foretaste of this more powerful entheogen. As noted the haoma and the White Hom have long been compared to the Tree of Knowledge and the Tree of Life of the Christian and Judaic traditions, and as shown earlier, the indications are that all originated from the same earlier mythology.

Like the Tree of Life in the Biblical tradition, the White Haoma appears at the beginning and end of the Persian cosmological history. The ancient Persians believed that the identity of the White Hom would be revealed at the Great Renovation, when the Saoshyant, *Final Savior*, sacrifices the final sacred ox, and mixes it's fat with the White Hom to prepare the elixir of immortality. In light of the slaying of the ox symbolism, it is interesting to note that in the Zoroastrian creation myth, Ahura-Mazda (God) gave the first created ox "cannabis to ease her discomforts in the throes of death"[38] after she was afflicted with disease and hunger by Ahriman. If this is the case, then cannabis is more than a fitting plant to pour forth beneficially from the sacred animal's wound as the White Hom, and the sacred ox to heal mankind at the consummation of the age with the same plant that eased it's own pain at the beginning. (Especially when we consider that the plant played the role of entheogen with the ancient authors who recorded these inspired texts). As Payam Nabarz, author of *The Mysteries of Mithras: The Pagan Belief That Shaped the Christian World*, notes;

> Some, basing their theories on the Zoroastrian creation story of the white bull being slain by Ahriman, have suggested that the Bull Homa and perhaps the later slaying of the Bull by Mithras is a sym-

---

38   (Hinnels 1973). The *Iranian Bundahisn* clearly records that the drug which alleviates the death throes of the primordial ox, is "the medicinal/healing, *mang*, which is (also) called *bang*."

bol of the pressing of the Homa juice! This is a controversial but interesting view, as Ahura Mazda feeds the white Bull hemp to sedate
him so when Ahriman kills him, the Bull wouldn't feel the pain.
From the Bull comes all life – animal and plant. (Nabaiz, 2005)

The central mythology of the cult concerns Mithra's sacrifice of
the sacred bull, or ox, an act he commits reluctantly, but for the
benefit of humanity. Grabbing the bull by the nostrils, the Persian
Christ plunges his knife into the animal's side; from the sacrificial
body of the bull are born all health giving plants and "from its spi-
nal marrow, bread bestowing wheat; from it's blood the vine which
produces the sacred drink of the mysteries" (Eliade 1982). Prof.
Dan Merkur, in reference to the Christian Eucharist, Jewish Taboos
about the consumption of blood, and Mithra's sacrifice of the sacred Bull, recently commented that:

> ...[T]he historical Jesus never said "this is my blood," that's a Gen-
> tile insert into the legend. ... in several Gospel controversy stories,
> where Jesus argues with Pharisees about the law, he regularly cites
> as precedent for himself what the Mishnah presents as the rare
> lawful exception to a generalization. So these tales show Jesus
> as more learned in the law than his opponents, because he both
> knows the conventional lore and the rare exceptions, making the
> latter work for him. Which means that either the historical Jesus
> or, if the tales are fictions, the author(s) of the tales, was *exception-
> ally* learned in fine details of law. No way would a gross error in
> knowledge of Judaism, such as "this is my blood," date back to the
> original stratum of storytelling about Jesus. But like John's "the
> true vine" (implicitly, as Morton Smith argued, a counter-claim
> aimed to rival an unnamed vine god's claim), we have to think of
> the Gospel phrasing as aimed against another, unmentioned cult
> where blood figured prominently--perhaps the blood gushing out
> of the bull's throat as Mithras plunges his knife? And what was
> that? Syrian rue? Amanita muscaria? Holy moly!" (Merkur, 2010)

Of course, as has been amply shown in this study, cannabis
should be at the front of that last list. The Saoshyant's distribution
of the long-lost White Hom, is undeniably paralleled by the access
to the formerly prohibited Tree of Life at the end of Revelation. "To
him who overcomes, I will give the right to eat from the tree of life,
which is in the paradise of God" (Rev. 2:7)

Paul the Revisionist

As discussed in *Sex, Drugs, Violence and the Bible*, it was likely through Paul, who never met Jesus, and the church in Rome which was based around his teachings, that much of the adoption of the Mithraic symbolism came about. For it was clearly through Paul, a citizen of Rome, who was initially persecuting Christians, that a leader of the Israeli independence movement came to be adapted to suit the theological tastes of the same empire against which he and his followers had been rallying.

It was likely also through Paul, who seems to have been overwhelmed by his own samplings of the Gnostic sacraments (Acts 9:8-9; 2 Corinthians 12:2) and the church which formed around his interpretation of Jesus' teachings, that the later prohibition of the entheogens came about as well:

> Likely, the rejection of the Gnostic sacraments by the newly forming "orthodox" Christian church, was done for similar reasons to that which caused them to fall out of favor in the Old Testament period. As the use of kaneh-bosm, [cannabis], became associated with pagan aspects of the Judaic faith, which patriarchal Yahwehist reformers like Hezekiah, Josiah, and Jeremiah so fiercely tried to excise, its use had to be prohibited. Likewise the Christians' use of psychoactive substances became intertwined and associated with the ecstatic worship of the Gnostic branches [and influential cults like Mithras] and so, too, had to be prohibited. In both cases, the continued utilization of the entheogens, as in the faith's beginnings, would mean continuing revelations from the ingesters.
>
> The Roman church was more interested in creating an unchanging dogmatic code founded on Pauline theology than dealing with the ongoing realizations of Gnostic psychonauts who had traveled deep into the hidden realms of consciousness. As early as Irenaeus (130-200 ce), accusations concerning "secret sacraments" began being leveled at Gnostic branches from the Roman church, and this would seem to be one of the main points of contention.[39] It is possibly here with Irenaeus, that we first see the entheogens condemned by members of the Roman congregation. In hindsight, it can be seen that the Pauline Church's sepa-

---

39   Clementine, an early Christian writer refers to "the frenzy of the lying soothsayer," as a "mere intoxication produced by the reeking fumes of sacrifice" (Homilies); Tertullian refers to "...those persons who are supposed to be god-possessed, who by sniffing at altars inhale a divine power in the smell..." (Apologticus), [From a quote in (Thorne, 1998)].

ration from the entheogenic induced ecstasies of the religious movement's originators, accounts for the Church's separation from the Holy Spirit itself. Throughout the Old Testament the recipient of the anointing oil interpreted its psychoactive effects as the Lord's blessing in form of possession by the Holy Spirit. As Jesus himself is recorded to have stated[40] on claiming his messianic mantle: "The Spirit of Yahweh God is upon me, because Yahweh has anointed me." (Bennett & McQueen, 2001)

With the later adoption of Christianity as the religion of the Roman Empire, this situation was compounded and expanded to include the prohibition of all competing religions, an end result of which was the inception of the Dark Ages. The words of the early church father Ignatius show distinctly the substitution of the placebo sacraments of the Catholic Church, in place of the Gnostic entheogens, setting the stage for drug war hysteria that has lasted into our present day. "At these meetings you should heed the bishop and presbytery attentively, and break one loaf, which is the medicine of immortality and the antidote which wards off death but yields continuous life in union with Jesus Christ.... Thus no *devil's weed* will be found among you."[41]

Finalizing the Dark Ages prohibition of the entheogenic sacraments, the Christian Emperor Theodosius decreed that all sacrifice to idols, meaning libations of wine and burning of incense, were declared treasonous-crimes against the state punishable by death. "Many of these rites were hardly connected with the pagan cult...." (Seligmann 1968). Indeed, as much as for ridding the land of all pagan deities and their various Mystery Cults, Theodosius' prohibitions were directed at ridding the

Fig. 17.7: Emperor Theodosius.

empire of the entheogenic sacraments and the shamanistic revelations they provided...

The Christian enmity [of the entheogens] is easy to explain. Since the Christians were promulgating a religion in which the core mystery, the holy sacrament itself, was conspicuous by its

---

40   Quoting (Isaiah 61:1)
41   As quoted in (Russell 1998).

absence, later transmogrified by the smoke and mirrors of the Doctrine of Transubstantiation into a specious symbol, an inert placebo entheogen, the imposture would be all-too-evident to anyone who had known the blessing of ecstasy, who had access to personal religious experience... Thus a concerted attack on the use of sacred inebriants was mounted, and the supreme heresy was to presume to have any direct experience of the divine, not mediated by an increasingly corrupt and politicized priesthood. The pharmacratic Inquisition was the answer of the Catholic Church to the embarrassing fact that it had taken all the religion out of religion, leaving an empty and hollow shell with no intrinsic value or attraction to humankind, which could only be maintained by hectoring, guilt-mongering and plain brute force. (Ott 1995)

Om Shiva Shankara Hari Hari Ganja! Boom Somnath! Lord of Soma, the Herb of Vitality!

18

INDIA, LAND OF *BHANG*

I n India we are dealing with a sacramental role for cannabis ranging from ancient times to the present day. This continued use of cannabis through the millennia offers many insights into the beliefs and role of cannabis likely held in the ancient world. Writing in the 19th century, William Dymock recorded in his *The Vegetable Materia Medica of Western India*, "*Cannabis* has been in use as an intoxicating agent in the East from a very early period; whether its properties were first Known in Persia or in India is difficult to decide..." (Dymock, 1885). However, over a century later the general consensus seems to be that cannabis came to India, via the Indo-Europeans. "By *ca.* 3000 BP, *Cannabis* had most likely migrated west and south over the Himalayas and into India, probably coming with nomads and traders over the trade routes that crossed the region" (Clarke & Fleming, 1998).

> The original Aryan tribes probably introduced the hemp plant into India sometime in the second millennium B.C. These migrating invaders most likely entered the Indian subcontinent via accessible passes in the high mountainous regions bordering the area... Thus, in the early phases of Indian history, hemp probably was a relatively obscure plant for the mass of population centered on the lowland *doabs* (interfluves) and in the riverine valleys. (Merlin, 1973)

Indeed, the Sanskrit word for cannabis comes from an earlier Indo-European root for the word. As Alphonse de Candolle noted in *Origin of Cultivated Plants*, "It has Sanskrit names, *bhanga* and *gangika*. The root of the word *ang* or *an*, recurs in all the Indo-European and modern Semitic languages: *bang* in Hindu and Persian, *ganga* in Bengali, *hanf* in German, *hemp* in English, *chanvre* in French, *kanas* in Keltic and modern Breton, *cannabis* in Greek and Latin, *cannab* in Arabic" (de Candolle, 1886).

In light of the generally accepted antiquity of cannabis in Indian culture, it is curious to note that no remains of the plant have been found at archeological sites in the area. "Although archaeological and historical data provide a foundation for our understanding of *Cannabis* dispersal in Asia, there remains a severe lack of palynological and archeological references with which to correlate these data" (Clarke & Fleming, 1998).

> We were not able to find many references dealing with analytic evidence of *Cannabis* pollen for the entire Asian region and no archeological finds of *Cannabis* remains at all from southern India. Certainly, archeological sites have been investigated, but translations of foreign studies appear to be rare. This may simply be the result of researchers focusing their investigations on other topics besides *Cannabis* remains. Many early excavations overlooked botanical evidence in their search for cultural objects. Long core samples dating further back in time may reveal *Cannabis* pollen grains giving us a much earlier time scale for the origin, evolution and migration of *Cannabis*. This is an area worth pursuing and will help broaden our biological and historical knowledge of this important crop plant. (Clarke & Fleming, 1998)

As we shall show in this Chapter, the use of cannabis in India, as both a medicine and spiritual intoxicant, clearly goes back to ancient times, although as has been discussed there has been some debate about this. As the late pioneer of medical Marijuana Dr. Todd Mikuriya noted "There seems to be some disagreement on the nature of the earliest medical applications of cannabis in India. It was used as medicine before 1000 B.C." (Mikuriya, 1973). "Medical and sacred use in India... predates written records (*Atharva Veda*, 1400 B.C....)" (La Barre, 1980). "For millennia in India, *Cannabis* has been cited as a medicine for almost any ailment: to ameliorate catarrh, to relieve haemorrhoids, gonorrhoea, asthma, 'stitches on the side,' and diarrhea. It was cited as aphrodisiac..." (Nahas, et al., 1999).

The ancient Ayurvedic system of Indian medicine contains a number of references regarding cannabis. The *Ayurveda* traces its mythological roots back to gathering of sages in the Himalayas that took place about 5000 years ago. The Sages, who arrived from all areas of the country, exchanged their knowledge of healing, and this was passed down verbally for some generations until finally being committed to writing sometime around the first century AD.

> Ayurvedic physicians of India use bhang to treat dozens of diseases and medical problems including diarrhea, epilepsy, delirium and insanity, colic, rheumatism, gastritis, anorexia, consumption, fistula, nausea, fever, jaundice, bronchitis, leprosy, spleen disorders, diabetes, cold, anemia, menstrual pain, tuberculosis, elephantiasis, asthma, gout, constipation, and malaria... (Robinson 1996)

There is also considerable agreement that cannabis in India was not regulated to only the use of it for medicinal and fibre purposes, and that hemp was also revered for its intoxicating properties as well:

> The Fourth Book of the *Vedas* refers to it sometimes under the name of *Vijahia* (source of happiness) and sometimes under that of *Ananda* (laughter-provoker). It was not, therefore, for its textile properties that hemp was used in India to start with; at the beginning of the Christian era the use of its fibre was still unknown there.... It is solely to its inebriating properties that hemp owes the signal honour of being sung in the *Vedas*... (Bouquet, 1950)

As others have also noted: "In India and Iran, it [cannabis] was used as an intoxicant known as bhang as early as 1000 BC." (Goldfrank, 2002); "The narcotic properties of *C. Sativa* were recognized in India by 1000 BC." (Zohary & Hopf, 2000);"The narcotic and euphoric properties of cannabis were known to the Aryans who migrated to India thousands of years ago and there is little doubt they made use of these properties" (Chopra & Chopra, 1965); Cannabis' "narcotic properties were known in India by (1000 BCE)" (Southworth, 2005);[1] "The ancient sacred book of the Aryans, the Artharva Veda, [1400 B.C.,] called it [cannabis] a 'liberator from sin' and 'heavenly guide'" (La Barre, 1980); "The *Atharva Veda* of India dates to between 1400 and 2000 BCE and mentions a sacred

1   Citing Simmonds, NW (ed.) (1976) *Evolution of Crop Plants*, London.

grass, *bhang*, which remains a modern term of usage for cannabis. Medical references to cannabis date to Susruta I the 6th to 7 th centuries BCE" (Weiner, 2002).

> In the Indian scripture of the *Atharva Veda*, the fourth book of the Vedas, the ancient scriptures of the Brahman religion (ca 2,000–1,400 BC), bhang (hemp) was identified as one of the five sacred plants of India. Bhang is "a sacred grass" and its use is considered to "preserve one from disease . . . and prolong the years we have to live." [both qualities of Soma] In the Book II, Hymn IV, 5, we can read "May the hemp and may gangida protect me against vishkandha [hostile demon]! The one (gangida) is brought hither from the forest, the other (hemp) from the sap of the furrow." (Hanus, 2008)

Writing at the end of the 19th century, G. A. Grierson also noted the following early references to cannabis, in his well researched essay "On References to the Hemp Plant Occurring in Sanskrit and Hindi Literature":

> The name *Bhanga* occurs in the *Atharvaveda* (say, B.C. 1400). The hemp plant is there mentioned simply as a sacred grass. Panini (say, B.C. 300) mentions the pollen of the hemp flower (*bhanga*). In the commencement of the sixth century we find the first mention of *vijaya* which I have noted. It is a sacred grass, and probably means here the hemp plant....

Cir. B.C. 1400.
In the *Atharvaveda* (cir. 1400 B.C.) the bhang plant is mentioned (11, 6, 15) once:
    "We tell of the five kingdoms of herbs headed by Soma; may it and *kuca* grass, and *bhanga* and barley, and the herb *saha* release us from anxiety."
    Here reference is evidently made to the offering of these herbs in oblations.
    The grammarian Panini (5, 2, 29) mentions *bhangukata*, the pollen of the hemp flower, as one of his examples.

Cir. B. C. 300.
The fact that the pollen of this special flower was quoted is worth noting. (Grierson, 1893)

Evidence of cannabis near the area is not limited to literary evidence. "It should also be noted here that recent archeobotanical evidence for cannabis dating between 400 B.C. - 100 A.D. has been found in the Kali Gandaki Valley of Nepal which connects the Tibetan plateau with the plains of India" (Merlin, 2003). "In Nepal, ascetics, shamans, and magicians have been consuming small amounts of this agent [cannabis] since ancient times in order to induce trance states" (Gruber,1991).[2] Thus, cannabis has clearly played a pivotal part in ancient India, as a medicine, a mild social intoxicant, and a religious sacrament.

The renowned anthropologist Weston La Barre believed that use of cannabis in India even predated written accounts:

> In India, the use of cannabis as a narcotic has been continuous since prehistoric times.... One is tempted to suggest that even if cannabis were indeed not as early as Mohenjodaran[3]-Harappan India (suspiciously adjacent geographically to Mesopotamia Sumeria and/or to Scythian southwest Asia), whence the shamanic Pasupati "master of animals" prototype of pot-loving Shiva emerged, then cannabis might just as well have been brought by the first Aryan invaders, given the pan-Indo-European extent of the hemp-word. In such an event, despite the incalculably great influence of the *Rig Veda* (earliest literate recording of any Indo-European tongue), soma-ambrosia was lost to the Brahmanic man-god, while cannabis remained the soma of the poor. (La Barre, 1980)

Moreover, in relation to this study, through ritual consecration performed by a Brahmin priest, cannabis was made into the sacred beverage of the *Vedas*, the Soma. As discussed, in Chapter 4 the 5th century BC text the *Satapatha Brahmana* clearly identifies that it was the "consecration" of cannabis (*usana*, prefix u-, -*sana*, 'hemp') which "make it into Soma" (*Satapatha Brahmana*, 3.4.3.13). As we shall show, it was this Brahmanic ritual relationship alone that disappeared, not the Soma-plant itself.

Unlike the other cultures we have examined, in India we have a culture that has continued with a somewhat open relationship with cannabis into the present day. In relation to this study, the fact that

---

2   As quoted in (Ratsch, 2005)
3   Interestingly, a variation of this name has also been interpreted as a name of cannabis. "In the name of Mohenjo Daro... the Vedic equivalent of cannabis, munja grass is preserved" (Richter-Ushanas, 1997).

cannabis has continued in its role as a medicine and ceremonial intoxicant raises some interesting issues – If cannabis were the Vedic Soma, and its use originates back to the Vedic period, and the use of cannabis has continued to this day, how could the identity of Soma come to have long been lost and forgotten in this same period, while the use of cannabis itself continued?

From what can be gathered from the historical record, there is an explanation for this situation – nothing disappeared, what happened is that cannabis stopped being consecrated as Soma by the Brahmins. Likely, as shall be discussed, this happened at first through the gentle influence and reforms of Buddhism, and then more fully by the harshest of prohibitions listed in the *Laws of Manu*. The prohibition of the Soma rite, coincided with and was related to, the prohibition of alcohol and intoxication in general in Indian society.

Another complicating factor in the disappearance of the Soma was likely a growing public resentment over the increasing prices of Soma, which in the early Vedic period, was largely imported. Evidence indicates it took some time for indigenous agriculture of the cannabis to take hold. Like the booming illicit cannabis market of today, Soma was big business in the ancient world as well. For the Vedic Indians, "Cattle was their standard value and medium of exchange. Some taxes were levied on some imports, particularly on Soma (*Cannabis Sativa*). Some traffickers (*Soma Vikrayin*) became unpopular, for they charged a high price for their commodity..." (Chakraberty, 1944). "...[T]he sacrificer pays the price of a cow in money to the Brahman who brings him the Soma. To sell soma is regarded as very disreputable. The seller is not admitted to the sacrificial compound nor invited to the great dinner which the sacrificer must give to Brahmans at the end of the sacrifice" (Haug, 1863).

As noted above, cannabis had to be consecrated in a rite performed by a Brahmin, in order to become Soma. As Mark Merlin noted; "...[O]riginally knowledge of the pristine Aryan hymns and, consequently, the psychoactive sacrament *soma* were restricted to the Aryan invaders themselves":

Eventually the indigenous priestly elite usurped much of the religious authority held by the writers of the Aryan hymnal and gained control of theological interpretation and ritual. "Vedism in its formal sense was not a religion of the masses."[4] Apparently for some time members of the priestly clique limited the knowledge and use of *Soma* to their own esoteric activities. Thus a small influential segment of ancient Indian society controlled religion and the distribution of the Soma plant. The ordinary Soma sacrifice was clearly a sacrifice of rich patrons."[5] (Merlin, 1972)

In his 1995 booklet, *The RgVedic Soma*, the Vedic scholar Dr. N. R. Warhadpande, who as noted earlier, identified cannabis with Soma, suggested that the loss of the knowledge of Soma's identity was through the decline of the Vedic ritual, the Yajna, which came about under the influence and development of Buddhism. Sacrifice continued in the Vedic mode, but this was far different from the Yajna being in common practice (Warhadpande, 1995). Apparently, in India during Buddhist times, there was a wide spread prohibition of intoxicants, as Khwaja Hasan notes in "Social Aspects of the use of Cannabis in India":

> The Buddhist Age in India began in the sixth century before Christ, and Buddhism gradually supplanted Brahmanism as a national religion. Buddhism prohibited the use of intoxicants to its followers... However, Brahmanism was revived in the tenth century of our era. Modern day Hinduism, therefore, is the result of cumulative influence of post-Vedic times... Historically, the consumption of alcoholic drinks and hemp drugs is reported to be in use up to the 8th or 9th century A.D., i.e., prior to the advent of Muslims in the country. (Hasan, 1975)

Buddhist Sobriety

Buddhist prohibitions, and the suppression of the Soma cult was also noted by Badrul Hassan, some decades earlier, in his 1922 edition of *The Drink and Drug Evil in India*. Hassan, mistakenly considered Soma to be an alcoholic beverage, and indeed, as noted, the prohibition of cannabis as Soma is intertwined with the prohibition of alcohol, but this is rather due to the intoxicating properties of both, rather than any similarities in preparation. As Hassan explains of the prohibitions of the Buddha:

---

4   (Drekmeier, 1962).
5   (Macdonell & Kieth, 1958).

In the sixth century before the Christian era... the Brahmin oligarchy had reached an ascendency so supreme that every one from the king and the court down to the peasant and the outcast bowed low before them in abject awe. The commonest act of daily life was performed only on the advice of the Brahmins. Not only did they exercise full control in political affairs; but in ministering to the religious needs of Aryan India, they had by this time developed an intricate and costly ritual, and had assumed control over the social and private life of the people. It was the age of *Mantras*. "A *Mantram* could bring victory or defeat in wars, assure the prosperity of the State or the destruction of its enemies; it could be used to win votes in the popular assembly or to silence the arguments of an opponent, and either by itself or in conjunction with medicinal prescriptions it could stop a cough or promote the growth of hair. In short the *Mantram* embodied in itself the dynamic principle of the universe; there was no concern of daily life, great or small, which could not be affected by it for better or worse."[6]

The divine power of sacrifice was another instrument that helped the Brahmin ascendency. In the course of many centuries, an involved and expensive ritual had been evolved to a fine art. The mere reciting of a *Mantram* entailed a sacrifice, and has been explained above, a *Mantram* had become a necessity for the commonest act of daily life. The performance of domestic sacrificial rites was incumbent on the king and the householder alike. In the former case, legions of Brahmins were employed and fortunes spent in their performance. The ordinary household dispensed with the services of a Brahmin for his daily rites; but there were innumerable occasions when the presence of a Brahmin was indispensable. There were ceremonies connected with the donning of the sacred thread and the piercing of ears; ceremonies of feeding and naming; ceremonies of birth to be repeated every month; ceremonies of marriage and death; ceremonies galore. These ceremonies entailed "the indiscriminate slaughter of animals and the *free indulgence of the intoxicating juice of the soma plant*"[7].

Against these corrupt practices which had by now grown into institutions, Buddha had rightly rebelled.... The Buddha started a crusade against the evils found in Hinduism, with an ascendant Brahmin oligarchy, with intricate rituals that made it difficult for the people to even worship the Supreme Being; with its approval of drinking and slaughtering of animals; with its innumerable corruptions.

6   Havell's *Aryan Rule in India*, p.46.
7   Emphasis added.

Buddhism was essentially a social revolution. It taught no new philosophy; it laid down no dogma; it neither appealed to the credulity of the people, nor excited their cupidity with the blessings of Paradise in lives to come. Instead the Buddha taught the truest truth that has ever been spoken by lips of man, and as an earnest faith, he himself set the example. He purified the whole life of Aryavarta, and his simplicity, his earnestness, have to this day exerted their influence on us. If to-day it is abhorrent to a Hindu to eat flesh, let him remember that it was the result of the Buddha's teaching; if it is obnoxious for him to drink wine, let him again remember that Buddha still exerts his purifying influence.

...Not only was abstinence compulsory in the order of monks he founded, but it forms one of the five Buddhist commandments ['*ye shall drink no maddening drink*'].... [I]n the Kutadanata Sutta... a Brahmin... questions the Buddha as to the different values of forms of sacrifice. He is told that.... "When a man with a trusting heart takes on... abstinence from strong, intoxicating, maddening drinks, the root of carelessness—that is a sacrifice than open largesse, better than perpetual alms, better than the gifts of dwelling places, better than accepting guidance." (Hassan, 1922)

Buddha's influence of sobriety took in some quarters, but not in all, and despite this frowning on the use of intoxicants and the complicated rituals of the Brahmins, cannabis continued to be used and consecrated as Soma, and enjoyed by both the common people and the aristocrats for at least a few centuries, until much harsher reforms, contained in the *Laws of Manu*, seem to have effectively driven it away from the ceremonial life of the Brahmins.

No ancient references to Buddha's use of the popular intoxicants of his culture exist, but it is hard to believe that in his time as a prince he did not partake of the Soma at some point.

In respect to Buddha's culture, it should also be note that many have suggested that Buddha was of Scythian heritage, a culture known to have burned cannabis and consumed it in beverages as well. As discussed in chapter 7, the Persian Scythians, referred to as the *Saka*, were known as the *Haomavarga* (Haoma-gatherers). Some have seen the term *Sakya*, as in the 7th century Chinese Buddhist text the *Memorial of Sakya Buddha Tagathata*, as being derived for the Persian name for the Scythians, and this title identifying Buddha as a Scythian prince. As the 19th century author Sir William Wilson Hunter noted "...[It] is certain with the advent of Buddhism,

Scythic influences made themselves felt in India. Indeed, it has been attempted to establish a Scythic origin for Buddha himself. One of his earliest appearances in the literature of the Christian Church is as Buddha the Scythian. It is argued by no mere accident did the Fathers trace the Manichean doctrine to Scythanius, whose disciple, Terebinthus, took the name of Buddha... a Scythic origin would be congenial to the Northern school of Buddhism: to the school which consolidated by the Scythic monarch Kanishka, and which supplied a religion during more than ten centuries of Scythic tribes of Central Asia.... The sacred books of Tibet constantly speak of Buddha the Sakya. In them, Buddha is the heir apparent of the Sakyas; his doctrine is accepted by the Sakya race... But the exact meaning of Sakya, although generally taken to be the Indian representative of Scythian, as the Persian Sakae was the equivalent of Scythae, has yet to be determined" (Hunter, 1886). Over a century later the debate is still going on regarding the identification of the meaning of Sakya as Scythian, "Gautama, was a prince born to a Sakya- or Scythian-tribe on the border of present-day Nepal and India... (hence his later name, Sakyamuni – sage among the Sakyas)" (Whitfield, 2001)

Fig 18.1: Left: The Book The Scythian Period (1949) details the Scythian influence on Northern Indian art and culture, particularly in regards to Buddhism, which took place from about 100 B.C. to about 300 A.D. Right: The Indo-Scythian (Kushan) Buddhist monk Lokaksema, who is the first known translator of Buddhist Mahayana scriptures into Chinese, around 170 A.D.

The evidence I could find of Buddha's relationship with cannabis, generally relate to the ingestion of hemp seeds, although an account occurring in the medieval Buddhist text the *Tārātantra* indicates a later use of cannabis to produce "ecstasy" amongst some Buddhist of that time.

In the 19th century account, *The Gospel of Buddha* (1897) Paul Carus, PhD (1852-1919), recorded the following passage:

> So the Bodhisattva continued for six years
> Patiently torturing himself and suppressing the wants of nature.
> In the modes of a rigorous ascetic life.
> At last he ate each day one hemp grain only,
> Seeking to cross the ocean of birth and death
> And arrive at the shore of deliverance

Unfortunately Carus, like many 19th century researchers, failed to identify a particular reference for this quote, but this tradition can be traced back to much earlier accounts. In the "Text and Commentary of the Memorial of Sakya Buddha Tathagata," by Wong Puh (Translated from the Chinese by the Rev. S. Beal.) which appeared in the *Journal of the Royal Asiatic Society of Great Britain and Ireland*, Volume 20 (1863), a parallel is drawn between the 7th century AD Chinese Buddhist text the *Memorial of Sakya* [Saka, Scythian} *Buddha Tathagata*, which is a story of the life of Buddha, and the 3rd century AD Indian biography of Buddha, *Lalita Vistara* (Sanskrit), by Dharmarakcha, (308 AD). The *Memorial of Sakya Buddha Tathagata*, contains the passage, "He ate grain and hemp seed, subduing pain, subduing pleasure." In reference to this text, Rev. Spence Hardy noted that:

> There is no life of Gotama Buddha, by any native author, yet discovered, that is free from the extravagant pretensions with which his history has been so largely invested; from which we may infer that the records now in existence were all prepared long after his appearance in this world. The Chinese work, of which the following is a translation, was written about the middle of the seventh century after Christ. We learn from "The History of the Sung Dynasty" that there was constant intercourse between China and Ceylon at this time, as well as in much earlier periods. The pilgrims from China were accustomed to take from the island relics, extracts from the

sacred books, and models of the most celebrated images of Buddha. We are, therefore, prepared to discover a similarity between
the mythical records of India and China. (Hardy, 1863)

In relation to the hemp-seed reference in the Chinese work, the
following earlier verse from 3rd century AD Indian text, the *Lalita
Vistara* was cited as a likely source:

> The prince coming to the Ka-ye (Gaya) mountain, to the Ni-h'n
> (Nairanjana) river, reflected, considering that, as he intended to
> penetrate to the secret influences which actuate the conduct of
> men, he might, after six years, be in a position to save them. Thus he
> addressed himself to the practice of austerities (Dushkaracharya),
> each day eating one grain of hemp, one grain of rice; by this means
> reducing himself to a condition of overcoming all pleasure. After-
> wards, perceiving that this was not the true way, he pursued the
> contrary method, using indulgencies, bathing, perfuming himself,
> and so on; by these means he subdued sorrow (as the text says).[8]

The *Lalita Vistara* does mention "indulgencies" to subdue sorrow, which opens up some possibilities of intoxication, but a vague
reference from a text thought to be composed some eight centuries
after the life of Buddha, is unfortunately a weak piece of evidence
to make any case. However, in the much later Buddhist text the
Tārātantra, cannabis is described as being essential to spiritual
"ecstasy." The author of the medieval text, *Taranatha* records the
Buddha saying that drinking wine without also having consumed
cannabis "cannot produce real ecstasy," which was seen as a pivotal
step in attaining enlightenment (Maitra, 1983; White, 1996). Of
course though, it should be noted that the *Tārātantra* is a relatively
minor text, composed two millennia after the life of Buddha, (1600)
and it has not exerted much influence on the Buddhist religion.

Other medieval Buddhist references have also been noted. "Over
the last few decades, university religious studies departments have
produced translations of Buddhist tantric texts of unprecedented
quality, providing ample material for an examination of psychoactive plant use by Buddhists in Asia" (Parker & Lux, 2008).

There are several reasons to look to tantra for psychoactive substance
use in pre-modern Buddhist Asia. The first and most important is

8   As quoted by (Beal, 1863)

Fig 18.2: Cannabis is used as a rasayana (with literal meaning: ayana, 'Path' rasa, 'of the Juice' or Elixir vitae), preparation in a Tibetan Taratantra a text dedicated to the Buddhist goddess Tara, (Vedantatirtha 1914; Arya, 1998) "…In the Buddhist Tara Tantra, cannabis is 'essential to ecstasy.' In that tantra, Buddha says that drinking wine without having consumed cannabis 'cannot produce real ecstasy'" (Parker & Lux, 2008).

that non-tantric monastic Buddhism is far less tolerant of violations of scriptural precepts than tantric Buddhism. Buddha's injunction against consuming intoxicants precludes the open use of psychoactive substances by members of the Buddhist monastic establishment. In contrast, tantric Buddhism can allow for, and even applaud, shocking transgressions as a sign that the yogi has transcended ordinary patterns of valuation and behaviour. (Parker & Lux, 2008)

In there well researched essay, "Psychoactive Plants in Tantric Buddhism; Cannabis and Datura Use in Indo-Tibetan Esoteric

Fig 18.3: Left – During the period preceding his enlightenment, the fasting Buddha is said to have nourished himself with just two hemp seeds per day.
Right – In the Himalayas, the Medicine Buddha is venerated as the god of healing plants. One of the sacred herbs is hemp. (Ratsch, 2001)

Buddhism," researchers Parker and Lux identify references to cannabis, datura and other psychoactive plants in medieval Buddhist
Tantric texts such as the *Mahākāla Tantra*, where the "plants are
employed to attain health, wealth, wisdom, and supernatural powers such as seeing underground and flying" (Parker & Lux, 2008).

> These formulas include cannabis in several different forms, in-
> cluding leaves, resin, and other plant material. Given that these
> cannabis products are included in the "perfect medicine' formu-
> las of the *Mahākāla Tantra*, cannabis may perhaps be considered
> a significant part of this tantric lineage. (Parker & Lux, 2008).

The *Cakrasamvara Tantra* also identifies a magico-medical role for
cannabis and datura, recording that a mixture of compounds including cannabis will help one "become a yogin who does what he pleases
and stays anywhere whatsoever." Although, like the *Tārātantra*, the
Mahākāla Tantra and the *Cakrasamvara Tantra*, can by no means
be considered mainstream Buddhist texts, and have had limited im-

Fig 18.4: Left – Tantric Buddhist kapala, (skull bowl) with image of Mahakala, (author's collection). Right – Tibetan thanga with image of Mahakala, note third eye, skulls, Trident or Khatvanga, Kapala in left hand, Shiva's hour glass shaped drum the damaru and tiger's skin, all symbolic items of Shiva.

pact on modern Buddhist traditions. Even at its peak, from about 700-900 AD, well over a millennia after the life of Buddha, medieval Tantric Buddhism was a fringe tradition, practiced by laypersons and not ordained Buddhist monks or nuns (Parker & Lux, 2008).

In regards to the Buddhist use of cannabis, it is interesting to note that a form of Shiva, (known for his strong cultic connections with hemp), holds a pivotal role in the Tantric Buddhist pantheon. Mahakala, is a Sanskrit title meaning 'Great Time', this deity is a Dharmapala ("protector of dharma") in Vajrayana Buddhism (Tibetan Buddhism and Japanese Shingon Buddhism), and is an adoption of the more ancient God, Shiva, whose cultic traditions directly influenced the development of Tantric Buddhism. "Bhairava and Mahakala are two of the most popular epithets of Siva [sic] to denote his angry manifestation. Hindus and Buddhists worship this form of Shiva and virtually use the same image. While Hindus use both names, Bhairava is the more common. Buddhists generally prefer Mahakala" (Pal, 1988).

Interestingly, along with considerable symbolism, the use of cannabis seems to be one of the key aspects the Tantric Buddhist cult of Mahakala has retained from earlier Shaivism. "A number of the 'major' tantras within the Vajrayana tradition specifically mention entheogens (datura and/or cannabis) and their use. These include the...Mahakala-tantra" (Parker, 2007; 2008)[9] In the Mahakalatantra cannabis is included in a long list of medicinal recipes and described as the "perfect medicine".

> "...We beseech, kindle the perfected ambrosia; The supreme nectar of sacred knowledge, the sacramental substance, here for all the assembled yogis." (The Mahakalatantra).[10]

George Stablein, in his commentary and translation of the texts of The Mahakalatantra, discusses the role of cannabis and other substances as elixirs to transform the body and mind in the service of liberation. As Stablein notes, "Tantric medicine includes pharmacologically induced experiences that could indeed be called religious. This may indicate a unique transmission of Buddhist Tantra that is not unlike the psychedelic phenomenon in the New World shamanism and the Vedic rites" (Stablein, 1976).

> ...[T]he Mahalakalatantra gives substances a special emphasis... it is clear that the Tantra has a rather full blown pharmacopeia which includes psychotropic substances... In the Mahakalatantra we are presented with a theory of power that is reminiscent of... the Vedic use of Soma... The Mahakalatantra shows without a doubt that psychotropics used in a ritual context produced altered states of consciousness. (Stablein, 1976)

In relation to Stablein's comments regarding the Mahalakalatantra, and Soma, it is worth repeating that in Tibet, where Mahalakala is a popularly worshipped deity, cannabis has retained such names as so ma, so ma rtsa, so ma ra rtsa, so ma rwa dza, and as noted in chapter 4, these have been suggested to have been derived from the Sanskrit soma-raja, 'King Soma', (Crowley, 1996).

Thus, these medieval Tantric Buddhist references to cannabis, likely give indications of later influences on Buddhism from the religious and cultural milieu that was medieval India, such as devotees of Shiva, who used hemp in an identical way to achieve "ecstasy," rather than being regarded as actual edicts from Buddha.

9   See Parker for an excellent Bibliography pertaining to the use of cannabis and datura in Tantric Buddhist rites and texts.
10   From a translation in (Stablein, 1976).

The Laws of Manu

Although early researchers dated the *Book of Manu* (aka, the *Laws of Manu*; the *Code of Manu*) as far back as 1200 BC, the more current view is that it was created sometime between 200 BC and 200 AD, although some scholars see the *Book of Manu* as a modern versified rendition of a 500 BC *Dharma-Sutra*, which no longer exists.

In the first half of the 19th century, Dr. William O'Shaughnessy, who was largely responsible for the introduction of cannabis medicine into the Western pharmacopeia, noted that "The learned Kamalakantha Vidyalanka has traced notice of Hemp in the 5th chapter of Menu, where Brahmins are prohibited to use the following substances, *plandoo* or onions; *gunjara* or *gunjah*; and such condiments as have strong and pungent scents" (O'Shaughnessy, 1839). In 1970, *The Eastern Anthropologist*, also reported that "The Laws of Manu... provided very severe penalties for indulging in intoxicating drinks and drugs." One of the more known 20th century proponents of cannabis prohibition, Dr. Gabriel Nahas referred to this as well: "In the fifth chapter of *Menu*, a prohibition appears that suggests sociological implications; Brahmins are prohibited from using *Cannabis*"[11] (Nahas, et al., 1999).

In relation it is important to note, that similar prohibitions were extended towards the use and distribution of Soma. A list of items a Brahman is forbidden from selling includes: "cloth made of hemp... (medical) herbs... soma... Kusa-grass... [and] spirituous liquor" (Manu, 10:86-88). In Manu 3,158, the "seller of soma" is listed amongst those who are forbidden entrance to the Sraddha (a important Vedic era ceremony for dead ancestors). The disdain for the Soma seller is given even more explicitly, Manu says "food given to a soma seller becomes excrement" (Manu 3,180). Thus in the *Book of Manu*, anyone who freely partakes of Soma, formerly the source of Vedic ritual, risks not only being excluded from Vedic rites but also being made an outcaste of his society.[12] As Badrul

---

11   Some sources have suggested that this is a misinterpretation and that prohibition in Book 5 of Manu, was for garlic and not 'gunjah.'

12   Some of the origins for these Vedic era prohibitions may be found in the earlier *The Sacred Laws of the Aryas* (450 B.C) [As translated in (Buhler, 1882)] which recorded that "a minor offence causing loss of caste (...is committed by him) who... forsakes the sacred fires,... offends a guru, ...by an atheist, by him who takes his livelihood from atheists, and by him who sells the Soma (plant)" (*Vasitha* 1: 23). A Brahmana and a Kshatirya who have been demoted to the lower caste of the Vaisya (who traditionally worked as traders and

Hassan, recorded of the role of Soma in the *Book of Manu* in his own *The Drink and Drug Evil in India*:

> The cult of Soma, probably imported from ancient Eran [Iran] where Haoma (Aryan Soma) worship flourished... [and] had at this time attained in India equal, if not larger, proportions than the Haoma worship of neighbouring Eran. Passages after passages in the Rig-Veda are given to the praise of Soma, the liquor, which was afterwards incorporated with the worship of Soma – the Moon God. Whatever the parallelism between the God and the liquor may be, and however they came to be so closely identified in one symbol, the facts remain that not only did this liquor play an important part of the worship of this and other deities, but it was regarded with an affection, and endowed with such virtues, and gifted with such properties, that even the God may have envied... which show the hold the liquor had on the Brahmins — if not the people.
>
> ....It must be reiterated... that at the beginning of our history, the Aryan peoples indulged in spirituous liquors, perhaps to excess, but the evil consequences and baneful results demonstrated to the thoughtful the necessity of repressing this growing habit, and brought about a revulsion of feeling, so that the later Vedas prohibited the use of spirits for gratification of the senses saying, "wine is unfit to be drunk, unfit to be given, unfit to be accepted." A step in the right direction was thus taken, and though the use of spirits could not entirely be done away with, they were employed solely at religious ceremonies...
>
> ...[Thus] in the later Vedic period a compromise was effected by sanctioning the use of liquors at ceremonial and sacrificial functions only, whilst condemning its common usage, so that in the age of Manu, that thoughtful sage, knowing full well that, for an evil to be resisted, it must be abolished, and not confined... turned his attention to rooting out the evil.

---

businessmen, or peasant farmers) is forbidden to sell "hempen (cloth)... flowers,... the juice extracted from plants; nor soma." (*Vasitha* 2: 22-26). Food given by "a prisoner, a sick person, a seller of the Soma-plant" and a "dealer in spirituous liquor" is not to be eaten (*Vasitha* 14: 3). Although use of Soma itself was apparently permitted; "He (who possesses wealth) sufficient for (the expenses of) a Soma-sacrifice shall not abstain from offering it" (*Vasitha* 8: 10; see also 11:46). As well it is recorded that 'To live on milk alone, as if one were fasting, to eat fruit only, (to live on) barley gruel prepared of a handful of grain, to eat gold, to drink Soma (are modes of subsistence which purify)" (*Vasitha* 22: 11). Further, benefits are promised to the partaker of Soma; "If he worships the sages through the study of the Veda, Indra with Soma sacrifices, and the manes of his ancestors through (the procreation of) children, he will rejoice in heaven, free from debt" (*Prasna* II, *Adhyaya* 9, *Kandika* 16:5).

He laid down strict rules for prevention of drinking. He held that drinking was the most pernicious of the king's vices. He counseled the king instantly to banish sellers of spirituous liquors and to brand the drinker on the forehead with the sign of the tavern (i.e., wine-cup). For a twice-born, drinking was a mortal sin. If he did not perform the prescribed penances, he was "excluded from all fellowship at meals, excluded from all sacrifices, excluded from instruction and from matrimonial alliances; excluded from all religious duties." A terrible punishment, but not enough, from Manu. He was forthwith to be cast off by his "paternal and maternal relations, and receive neither compassion nor salvation; that is the teaching of Manu" [(Manu, IX, 239)]. Nor were the penances less rigorous as only death could put an end to them... even a seller of Soma – the sacred liquor – was to be avoided at sacrifices offered to the Gods and the *manes*, [(Manu, III, 158)] and food given to the seller of Soma became ordure, [(Manu, III, 180)].

It would seem, therefore, that, whilst previous moralist had allowed the use of liquor for religious purposes, Manu was opposed even to this indulgence and was determined to put it down. He therefore, put restrictions in the way of selling Soma by regarding a seller as a low person, and in the way of drinking by laying it down that "he who may possess (a supply of) food sufficient to maintain those dependent on him during three years or more than that, is worthy to drink Soma juice" [(Manu, XI,7)]; but a twice-born who had less "did not derive any benefit from drinking the soma juice though he may have formerly drunk it" [(Manu, XI, 8)].... This... is conclusive proof that a section of the people, who were entitled to respect, and of weight, were opposed to the use of intoxicant. (Hassan, 1922)

The *Laws of Manu* created a situation where the Brahmin were virtually forbidden to use, trade or possess soma-cannabis, and as it was the Brahmins who led the complicated rites which consecrated cannabis as the soma, the rite itself had to be modified to include a non-intoxicating replacement, such as the currently used, *Sarcostemma acidum*, and the ritual use of cannabis as soma came to a close.

Shubhra Sharma noted that the "Aitareya Brahmana even suggests a substitute" for the soma (Sharma, 1985). This soma replacement in the *Aitareya Brahmana* is also referred to by Parmeshwaranand:

Divine origin has been attributed to it [*nyagrodha*, the banyan tree] for making this tree a substitute of the Soma plant which did

not grow in the plains of Northern India... It has been enjoined
in the *Aitareya Brahmana* that a Ksatriya should not drink the
juice prepared of the Soma plant. He may, however, take the same
extracted from the airy descending roots of the nyagrodha tree....
(Parmeshwaranand, 2001)

The Ksatriya, referred to, were one of the four Varnas (social orders) in Hinduism. It constituted the military and ruling order of
the traditional Vedic-Hindu social system as outlined by the *Vedas*
and the *Laws of Manu*. Lord Rama, Lord Krishna, Lord Mahavira
and most notably Lord Buddha all belonged to this social order.
The identity of Buddha within this group, brings to mind the *nyagrodha*, or banyan tree, for it was under the branches of this placebo replacement of the soma, that Buddha had his allegedly sober
revelation. "Guatma Buddha received his salvation under the Banyan tree at Bodh Gaya" (Chaterjee, 1995). Considering the prohibition of intoxicants alleged to have begun in India with the Buddha,
one is left speculating on some sort of connection in this switch.

In regard to the prohibition of soma to the Ksatriya, in Martin
Haug's 1863 translation of the *Aitareya Brahmanam*, we find that
this sacramental restriction is related to a similar celestial one which
forbade the god Indra from the soma sacrifice! Durring a priestly
battle over who holds the administration of the soma rites, a Rama
Murgaveya (distinct from the God Rama) relates the following:

*Why Indra was excluded from his share in the Soma. The Kshat-
trlya race became also excluded.*

(Rama said) "I know it from the fact, that Indra had been excluded by the gods (from having any share in the sacrifices). For
he had scorned Vis'varupa, the son of Tvashtar, cast down Vritra
(and killed him), thrown pious men (*yatis*) before the jackals (or
wolves) and killed the *Arurmuyhas*, and rebuked (his teacher)
Brihaspati. On account of these faults Indra was forthwith excluded from participation in the Soma beverage. And after 1ndra
had been excluded in this way from the Soma, all the Kshattriyas (at whose head he is) were likewise excluded from it. But
he was allowed a share in it afterwards, having stolen the Soma
from Tvashtar. But the Kshattriya race remains excluded from the
Soma beverage to this day." (*Aitareya Brahmanam*)[13]

---

13   Translated by (Haug, 1863)

Haug explains of the crime which caused Indra to fall out of favour with the other Gods and be prohibited from the celestial soma sacrifice:

> ... Indra is said to have cut the three heads of Vis'varupa, which were *somapanam* (drinking of Soma), *surapanam* (drinking of spititous liquor), and *anuddnnam* (eating of food). The reason alleged for Indra's killing him, is that he, as a relation of the Asuras, informed them about the secret portions of the sacrificial food, Soma, &c., whilst he told the Devas, whose associate he was, only the real and visible ones. Indra holding that he who knows the secret portions of Soma, &c. will come to know the real ones also, become afraid lest the Asuras might, strengthened by Soma, overthrow his rule, and killed the perpetrator of such a treason by cutting off his three heads, each of which was transformed into a particular kind of bird. Vairupa being a Brahman, Indra thus became guilty of the horrible crime of Brahman murder (*brahmatiat-ya*).[14] All beings called him "murderer of a Brahman," so that he could not find rest anywhere... Tvashtar, the father of Vairftpa, excluded Indra from any share in the Soma sacrifice; but he took his share with force. The remaining portion of Indra's share was thrown into the sacrificial fire by Tvashtar with the words, "grow (*etudiiateo*) into an enemy of Indra." This became the terrible foe of Indra, known in the legends by the name of *Vritra*. (Haug, 1863)

Thus as a result of this prohibition of soma, the Ksatriya are directed to a substitution in the *Aitareya Brahmanam*:

> ... the following is his own portion [of the Soma rite], which he is to enjoy. He must squeeze the airy descending root of the *Nyagrohda* tree, together with the fruits of *Udambara A'svaltha*, and *Plaksha* trees, and drink the juice of them. This is his own portion.
>
> ....he thus obtains the soma beverage by means of a substitute; for the *Nyagrohda* is just this substitute of the Soma. (*Aitareya Brahmanam*)

---

14   Shiva carries the kapala, or skull bowl for a similar act of Brahmacide. In a moment of anger Shiva severed the fifth head of Brahma which resulted in the skull getting stuck to his palm and Shiva getting the penalty of Brahmahatyadosham (becoming an outcast for killing a Brahmin). One is also reminded of the Scythian practice of making a skull cup from the heads of the enemies they have slaughtered in battle.

The *Aitareya Brahmanam*, explains that with the roots of the *Nyagrohda*, the priest "perform for the king several ceremonies... just in the same way as the real soma is treated":

> Then the priest gives into his hands a goblet filled with spirituous liquor, repeating... [a] mantra,.... He then should drink the... [Soma replacement] when repeating the following two mantras: "Of what juicy well prepared beverage Indra drank with his associates, just the same, *viz.* the king Soma, I drink here with my mind being devoted to him (Soma)." The second mantra (Rigveda, 8,45, 22), "To thee who growest like a bullock (Indra), by drinking Soma, I send off (the Soma juice) which was squeezed to drink it; may it satiate thee and make thee well drunk."
>
> The Soma beverage which is (in a mystical way) contained in the spirituous liquor, is thus drunk by the king, who is inaugurated by means of Indra's great inauguration ceremony (the ceremony just described), and not the spirituous liquor. (After having drunk this mystical Soma) he should repeat the following mantras, *apama Somam*... i.e. we have drunk Soma, and... Be it propitious to us! (*Aitareya Brahmanam*, Haug, 1863)

Haug, in his commentary on this chapter notes "The spirituous liquor is here a substitute for the soma, which the Kshattriyas were not allowed to drink.... By means of mantras the liquor was transformed into real soma. We have here a sample of a supposed miraculous transformation of one matter into another" (Haug, 1863). But even the ancient text clearly acknowledges this "is a substitute for the soma sacrifice. Some spirituous liquor is taken instead of soma, and milk. Both liquids are filled in the soma vessels" (*Aitareya Brahmanam*, Haug, 1863). In this new relationship, one is clearly reminded of the similar placebo Catholic transubstantiation (which, as discussed, was another haoma substitution).

Another account in the *Aitareya Brahmanam* refers to the altering of the celestial soma rites in order to prevent intoxication of the Gods as well, symbolically also accomplishing in Heaven, what was first set out on Earth:

> The King (Soma) made the gods drunk. They then said, "A poisonous serpent (asivishn) looks at our King! Well, let us tie a band round his eyes." They then tied a band round his eyes. Therefore they recite the spells over the Soma squeezing stones, when having

tied (round the eyes) a band in imitation (of what the gods did). The King (Soma) made them drunk. They said, "He (the Serpent Rishi) repeats his own mantra over the Soma squeezing stones. Well, let us mix with his mantra other verses." They then mixed with his mantra other verses, *in consequence of which he (Soma) did not make them drunk.* By mixing his mantra with other verses for effecting propitiation, they succeeded in destroying the consequences of guilt. (*Aitareya Brahmanam*, Haug, 1863) [Emphasis added]

As with the *Laws of Manu*, in the *Aitareya Brahmanam* the seller of soma is depicted as ritually unclean, and a destroyer of the senses:

...[A] seller of the Soma is... found unfit (for intercourse). For such a man is a defaulter. When the Soma after having been bought was brought to men (the sacrificers), his powers and his faculty of making the senses sharp moved from their place and scattered everywhere. (*Aitareya Brahmanam*, Haug, 1863)

Thus in later Indian accounts, Indra, who was so fond of soma in the *Vedas*, and was the main recipient of the soma sacrifice, transferred his love to unconsecrated cannabis. In the late 19th century G.A. Grierson mentions hemp under the name of "Indra's food," and indicates that this name had likely been in use since ancient times.

The *Rajavallabha*, a *materia medica*, by Narayanadasa kaviraja, the date of which I do not know, but which is quoted in the *Cabdakalpadruma*, and is believed to be ancient, has the following:

Indra's food (i.e. ganja) is acid, produces infatuation, and destroys leprosy. It creates vital energy, the mental powers, and internal heat, corrects irregularities of the phlegmatic humour, and is an elixir vitae... To those who regularly use it it begets joy and destroys every anxiety. (Grierson, 1893)

Tenth century references to hemp, which coincided with a return of the Vedic religion as the 'National religion,' refer to cannabis under the name Indracana, also Indrasana (Indra's food, Indra's hemp). Thus at the time of a return to Vedic traditon it is duly noted that Indra's favorite drink is prepared from hemp (Watt 1889). "*Indrasana* as a name for hemp (perhaps by confusion with *Indra-sana*, which would mean the hemp of Indra) is mentioned in the *Sabdamalan* (quoted in the *Sadakalapadruma*) and appears in its prakit form – *Indrasana* – in *Dhurtasamagama*" (Doniger-O'Flaherty, 1970). As discussed earlier (see Chapter 4) the term *Indrasana* is likely derived from the the *Satapatha Brahmana*, written in the first half of the 1st millennium, which refer to the plant called 'usana' (prefix *u-*, Sk. *-sana*, hemp) from which soma is made and which was dedicated to Indra (*Satapatha Brahmana*, 4.2.5.15). When the consecration of cannabis as the soma came to be virtually prohibited to Brahaman through the *Laws of Manu*, and the *Aitareya Brahmana*, Indra's soma, became the unconsecrated Indrasana, i.e. Indra's hemp.

> According to shamanic tradition, Indra... discovered cannabis and sowed it in the Himalayas so that it would always be available to the people, who could then attain joy, courage, and stronger sexual desires by using the plant... hashish is also called indra-cense, 'incense of Indra.' (Ratsch, 2001)

The Decline of Indra

The prohibition of the consecration of cannabis as soma, inevitably resulted in a decline in popularity of the god Indra, and also the transference of many of his attributes to the increasingly popular indigenous Indian god Shiva, including the use of cannabis. "...[I]t is not clearly known why Hindus associate hemp drugs with *Shiva*... the plant *soma* was identified with the moon and so was *Shiva*" (Hasan, 1975).

In later mythology recorded after the reforms of Buddha and the *Laws of Manu* Indra was supplanted from his position as "King of the Gods" by the Hindu trinity of gods known as Vishnu, Shiva and Brahma. Indra's role in mythology began to change as well. As George Williams explains in the *Handbook of Hindu Mythology*:

> In the *Epics* and *Puranas* Indra was reduced to the mere leader of the demigods who were still called *devas* but had little power or energy. *Indra* was pictured as always being afraid of losing his position as Indra, the office of king of the *devas* that he did in fact keep losing... Worst of all, Indra's character had changed. He was no longer a proud and powerful warrior... Drunk and disorderly, he had become a mere clown with the honorary title of king of the gods.

...There were further degradations in his decline: his castration in an episode with Ahalya and Guatama, being cursed with a thousand yonis later made into eyes.... He was turned into a killer priest, castrated, beheaded, and cursed to have no temple to worship him. In no other mythology has an orthodox priesthood so treated one of their most sacred deities. (Williams, 2003)

Dr. Koenraad Elst has convincingly suggested that Shiva of Puranic Hinduism is in fact the continuation of the Vedic Indra. Indra has a variety of epithets and attributes which later seem to have been inherited by Shiva. But, in relation to his study, it is important to note that Shiva and Indra are both associated with intoxication, Indra is praised as having a tremendous appetite for the soma juice, Shiva drinks copiously of *bhang*, he is the Lord of *Bhang*, and Shiva seems to have taken this mantle on in the same period that there was prohibitions regarding soma and a decline in Indra worship.

As Dr. Elst explains, the basic view has been that, being seen as the supreme god of the Aryan invaders, Indra fell into disfavor with indigenous elements of Indian culture and as a result an "antagonism was elaborated between the Aryan sky-god Indra and the pre-Aryan fertility god Shiva:"

Indra being the winner of the initial military confrontation, but Shiva having the last laugh by gradually winning over the conquerors to the cult of the subdued natives. As I heard a Catholic priest from Kerala claim, Shiva is not a Hindu god, because he is the god of the pre-Aryans.

That Shiva was the god of the Harappans, is based on a single Harappan finding, the so-called *Pashupati* seal. It depicts a man with a strange headwear sitting in lotus posture and surrounded by animals... The common speculation is that this is Shiva in his *Pashupati* (lord of beasts) aspect. Ever since the discovery of the Gundestrup cauldron in Central Europe, which depicts the Celtic[15] horned god Cernunnos similarly seated between animals, this Pashupati seal is actually an argument in favour of the IE [Indo-European] character of Harappan culture.

Let us, nevertheless, go with the common opinion: Shiva for the Harappans, Indra for the Aryans. Those who see it this way have never explained why the dominant Aryans have, over the centuries, abandoned their victorious god (Indra is practically not worshipped

---

15   Celtic use of cannabis has been identified, see Chapter 3.

in any of the temples manned by Brahminical priests) in favour of
the god of their defeated enemies. At any rate, when we study these
two divine characters, we find that they are not all that antagonistic.

Shiva is usually identified with the Vedic god Rudra. It so happens that Indra's and Rudra's domains are more or less the same:
both are thundering sky gods. In mythology, Indra is, like Shiva, a
bit of an outsider, who is in conflict with the other gods, shunned
by them (and even by his mother), left alone by them to fight the
Dragon, doing things that disrupt the world order. Christians who
picture Jesus as the friend of the outcasts, may like to know that
the despised Aryan racist god Indra is in fact on the side of the
outcasts: Indra, you lifted up the outcast who was oppressed, you
glorified the blind and the lame. (Rg-Veda 2:13:12) As David Frawley has shown, Indra has many epithets and attributes which were
later associated with Shiva: the dispeller of fear, the lord of *mAyA*
(enchantment), the bull, the dancer, the destroyer of cities (Indra
purandara, Shiva *tripurahara*). Both are associated with mountains, rivers, male fertility, fierceness, fearlessness, warfare, transgression of established mores, the *Aum* sound, the Supreme Self.

Shiva and Indra are both associated with intoxication. Indra is
praised as having a tremendous appetite for the psychedelic *soma*
juice. Shiva has *Soma-Shiva* as one of his aspects, a name containing one of those Brahminical etymology games: Soma is the Vedic
intoxicant, and also the moon (as in *SomwAr*, Monday), which is
part of Shivas iconography (hence his, epithet *SomanAtha*).

....The outsider role of Shiva in the Puranic pantheon is the
continuation of Indra's role in the Vedic pantheon, which in turn
is only the Indian version of a role which exists in the other IE
pantheons as well, e.g. the Germanic fire god Loki or the Greco-
Roman warrior-god Ares/Mars. Shiva also continues Indra's role
of warrior-god. Till today, many Shiva sadhus are proficient in
the martial arts. The Shaiva war-cry *Hara Hara Mahadev* is still
used by some regiments of the Indian army as well as by Hindu
demonstrators during communal confrontations.

Finally, shiva, "the auspicious one," is an epithet of not only Rudra but of Vedic gods in general. Indra himself is called *shiva* several times (Rg-Veda 2:20:3, 6:45:17, 8:93:3). Shiva is by no means a
non-Vedic god, and Indra never really disappeared from popular
Hinduism but lives on under another name. (Elst, 1999)

Elst's connection with Indo-European culture and the God
Shiva are particularly interesting considering the continued ritual
use of bhang in the worship of Shiva and the role the Indo-Euro-

Fig 18.5: Left, Pashupati seal, Proto-Shiva, Lord of Beasts and Right, Celtic Cernunos.

pean Scythians have had with the use and spread of cannabis, as well as evidence of the ancient Celtic ritual use of hemp, as discussed in Chapter 3.

Shiva worship was particularly popular with a Scythian cultural offshoot known as the Indo-Scythians, or Kushans, who took that name from the Hind Kush Mountains where they had dominated for some centuries, and which have been known for millennia for the powerful Cannabis indica strains of hemp which they produces. The Indo-Scythians are a branch of Sakas (Scythians), who migrated from southern Siberia into Bactria, Sogdiana, Arachosia, Gandhara, Kashmir, Punjab, Gujarat, Maharashtra and Rajasthan, from the middle of the 2nd century BCE to the 4th century CE. Indo-Scythian Kushan kings of the first few centuries AD, such as Kadphises, Kanishka, Vasudeva were known to have been worshippers of Shiva, and they issued coins with Shiva's image on them (Handa, 2001).

The Kushan rulers seemed to have alternated between periods of orgiastic Shaivite influences and more ascetic Buddhist worship, and as noted, Buddha himself has been considered by a number of researchers to have been a Scythian, or Saka Prince who renounced his royal role.

Coin [Fig. 18.6] from period of the Indo-Scythian Kushan King Huvishka (ruled 160-190 AD), depicting Shiva, under the name Oisho, with 3 faces, as in the Pashupati seal, and identifying items such as the trident, drug jar, club and some sort of offering of stalks, possibly cannabis, in the upper right hand, which appears to be destined for the altar just below it. In regards to this last item,

Fig 18.6

one is reminded of ancient Zoroastrian depictions of the offering of barsom, (see Chapter 5), and it should be noted in this context, that the Kushites worshipped a number of Zoroastrian deities, as well as their Greek counterparts, i.e. Zeus as Ahura Mazda.

Gold coin of Kushan/Bactrian emperor, Vasudeva I, 191 to 225 CE. His name, Vasudeva, is that of the father of Krishna, the popular Hindu god, and he was the first Kushan king to be named after an Indian god. He converted to Hinduism during his reign as king. Front: [Fig. 18.7a] Vasudeva in Scythian garments with tall helmet, holding a scepter in one hand, and trident in the other and making an offering over an altar, possibly indicating

Fig 18.7a

the classic Scythian method of burning cannabis on hot stones. Legend in Kushan language and Greek script (with the Kushan letter þ "sh"): þAONANOþAO BAZOΔHO KOþANO ("Shaonanoshao Bazodeo Koshano"): "King of kings, Vasudeva the Kushan." Backside: [Fig. 18.7b] OHþO (oesho), a conflation of Zoroastrian Vayu and Hindu Shiva, with 3 faces and four arms, holding a trident, with the bull Nandi behind him.

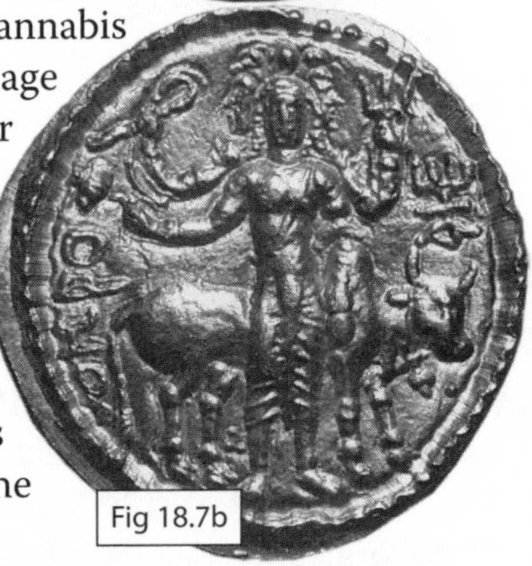

Fig 18.7b

Indo-Scythian gold coin [Fig. 18.8] from the

Fig 18.8

Kushan period of India issued during the reign of Kanishka II, 225-240 AD. Front, showing a figure dressed in typical Scythian clothes, pointed hat, pants, likely representing Kanishka II but with Shiva attributes of dreadlocked hair, serpent around the neck, and trident. Backside of the coin representing Shiva, holding trident with his bull Nandi behind him. (From the author's personal collection).

Thus, there are a number of indications that Shiva may in fact be a Indo-European god in his origins, and that Indo-European culture penetrated the area much earlier than previously thought. This would account for the similarities between Shiva and Dionysus/Bacchus that has been alluded to by a number of other researchers, as noted in chapter 12. And regardless of this, if Shiva was an indigenous god of the Harappans, he was clearly adopted by the Indo-Scythians and the Indo-European descendants of the authors of the Vedas, very early on, and incorporated many attributes from these cultures.

Many indigenous tribal myths have... converged and been appropriated into the mainstream of the Shiva cult. The cult of Rudra-Shiva shows distinct influences of the great Shamanic traditions of Siberia and Central Asia.... The use of the skull and skeleton in mystical ceremony and much Tantric approach shares common antecedents with these traditions.... (Gokhale, 2001)

In this connection one is also reminded of the use of skull cups, the *kalapa*,[16] by both the Scythians and Shaivites (devotees of Shiva), as well as Shiva's association with bhang, alongside the Scythian ritual use of the herb and spread of its cultic influences. It has also

Fig 18.9: A kalapa, (skull cup)

been suggested that it was during the Scythian period of India, that "Tantra... found roots in the Western Himalaya region... when it was introduced... by the Magi priests of the Scythians..." (Handa, 1994).

Indra's Soma becomes Shiva's *bhang*

Mahadev (Siva) and Gaurja (Parabati) [Parvati] are straining *bhang*.
He is always drunk, but can do no wrong.
With matted hair and top-knot, a snake on his neck, and red

16   Siva wears a necklace of bones and skulls, and carries a skull in his hand. The Saiva Puranas give the following explanation of them. At the end of a Kalpa, [aeon] Siva destroys Brahma and Vishnu with the rest of the creation, but he wears their bones and skulls as a garland. The skull which he holds in his hand is from the central head of Brahma which he cut off. He is therefore called Kapali. The ashes with which Siva smears himself were produced as follows: At the end of one of the early Kalpas, Siva reduced Brahma and Vishnu to ashes by a spark out of his central eye; after which he rubbed their ashes upon his body as an ornament. Hence the saying of the Saivas, 'Without beauty is the forehead destitute of sacred ashes.'" (Murdoch, 1887)

loin-cloth on his body,
He sits and strains bhang and his bull sits in the yard.
In the summer-house he sits and talks on all kinds of subjects
with Parbati.
Who would be drunk, can come and drink *bhang.*
                          –Northern folk song, (from Temple, 1884)

Clearly, the decline of Indra worship completely coincided with the
timing for the prohibition of the consecration of cannabis as soma.
Likewise, in this same time period, we see the beginnings of Shiva's relationship with *bhang* more fully cemented in a mythology that clearly
takes the plant out of the realm of Brahmanic control. In the *Rudraya-
mal Danakand* and *Karmakand* Shiva tells his consort: "Oh Goddess,
Parvati, hear the benefits derived from bhang. The worship of bhang
raises one to my position."[17] As the 19th century *Indian Hemp Drugs
Commission Report* recorded of Shiva's cultic connection to cannabis:

> It is chiefly in connection with the worship of Siva, the… great god
> of the Hindu trinity, that the hemp plant, and more especially per-
> haps ganja, is associated. The hemp plant is popularly believed to
> have been a great favourite of Siva, and… the drug in some form or
> other is… extensively used in the exercise of the religious practices
> connected with this form of worship… [R]eligious ascetics, who
> are regarded with great veneration by the people at large, believe
> that the hemp plant is a special attribute of the god Siva, and this
> belief is largely shared by the people… There is evidence to show
> that on almost all occasions of the worship of this god, the hemp
> drugs in some form or other are used… these customs are so inti-
> mately connected with their worship that they may be considered
> to form in some sense an integral part of it. (IHDCR, 1894)

The Churning of the Ocean of Milk

In Hinduism, *Samudra manthan* or "The Churning of the Ocean
of Milk" is one of the most famous episodes in the *Puranas* (500-
300 BC) and the story is still celebrated in the popular festivals
known as the Kumbha Mela. Interestingly, this ancient myth, composed within about two centuries after the initial pogrom against
soma, seemingly takes sacramental hemp use out of the cult of Indra, and instills it with the devotees of Shiva.

17   (IHDC, 1894).

"The Churning of the Ocean of Milk" tells the story of the search for the elixir of immortality, *"amrita"* by both the gods in order to restore their waning strength. The myth relates that long ago, Indra, king of the gods and all of the three worlds, had grown rude and arrogant. As a result of this insolence, when the great rishi Duravas, a portion of Shiva, placed a garland as an offering before Indra, who rode upon an elephant, Indra placed the offering on the trunk of the elephant, who grew irritated at its smell, throwing it off and stomping on the garland in front of the insulted Duravas, who called down a curse on Indra for his arrogance.

Due to Duravas' curse, Indra and all his domain of the three worlds, including the other Gods, were weakened and sent into ruin and this allowed the demons the opportunity to exert their strength against the weakened gods. The Gods turned to Brahman, who advised them to seek Vishnu, the tamer of demons. Brahama led the gods along the edge of the Ocean of Milk to Vishnu's seat, where they prayed for his aid.

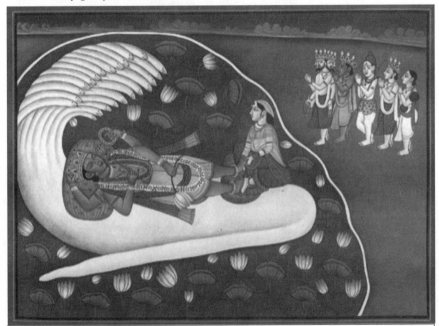

Fig 18.10: Contemporary painting of Vishnu seated in the Ocean of Milk, as Brahma, Shiva and other deities approach from the shore, (by Kailash Raj).

Vishnu promised to restore their strength by ordering them to prepare the *amrita*, a sacred substance that bestows immortality and vigor, telling them "Do now as I command: cast into the Milky

Sea potent herbs, then take Mount Mandara for churning-stick, the serpent Vasuki for rope, and churn the Ocean for the dew of life [*amrita*]" (Coomaraswamy & Nivedita, 1914). Thus wrapping the huge serpent around the mountain, together they could use it as a giant pestle in order the churn the "potent herbs" they cast into the Ocean of milk and make amrita! Here we see a cosmic account that clearly parallels the use of the mortar and pestle to grind milk and cannabis in order to make the earthly *bhang*.

Vishnu tells the Gods that the job before them will be far too large for them to complete on their own, and they will need the help of the *daityas* (demons) to accomplish the task. Vishnu then tells the Gods to promise a share of the *amrita* to the demons, and to tell them it will bestow immortality upon them. But this was a trick, as Vishnu explained "I shall see to it they shall have no share of the water of life, their share will be of the labor only" (Coomaraswamy & Nivedita, 1914).

As the Gods and demons joined together in churning the Ocean of Milk, various things began to rise out of as a result, first the wish-giving cow, Surabhi, rose out, delighting gods and demons alike, then Varuni, with rolling eyes, the divinity of wine, followed by the *Parijata*, the fragrant tree of Paradise, then the graceful troops of *apsaras*. These were followed by the moon, which was grasped by Shiva and placed upon his brow, and then a draught of deadly poison, also taken by Shiva who drank of it, lest it should destroy the world, a selfless act that is said to have turned the God blue when the poison became

Fig 18.11: 19th century painting depicting the gods and demons using a mountain as a pestle to churn "potent herbs" into the Ocean of Milk in order to produce the sacred amrita, i.e making the cosmic bhang.

stuck in his throat. Then appeared Dhanwant-
ari holding in his hand the vessel of *amrita*,
the dew of life, lighting up the eyes of both
the Gods and demons with desire.

The story has it that after the *amrita* appeared in the *Kumbha* (urn) the demons attempted to gain control of it and as a result
a twelve day battle, equal to twelve earthly
years , took place between the Gods and the
demons in the heavens. During the battle,
the celestial bird, the Garuda, (known for
his association with Soma) flew away with
the *Kumbha* of *amrita* to protect it from the
hands of the demons.

Fig 18.12: Vishnu Riding
Garuda (10th century A.D)
Changu Narayan, Nepal.

To insure that the precious *amrita* did not
fall into the hands of the demons, the *Kumbha*
(vessel) of nectar was temporarily hidden at four places on the
earth - Prayag (Allahabad), Haridwar, Ujjain and Nasik. At each of
these places, a drop of the nectar was said to have spilled from the
pot and from these drops of this precious water of immortality it
is believed that these places acquired mystical power. A *Kumbha
Mela* is celebrated at the four places every twelve years for this reason. Ancient tradition has it that one of the miracles that resulted
from the spilling of the amrita was the creation of Hemp.

> [Cannabis]... was originally produced, like nectar from the ocean by
> the churning with Mount Mandara, and inasmuch as it gives victory in
> the three worlds, it, the delight of the king of the gods, is called *vijaya*,
> the victorious. This desire-fulfilling drug was obtained by men on the
> earth, through desire for the welfare of all people. (Grierson, 1893)

> In Hindu mythology the plant is said to have been produced while
> the gods were churning the ocean with Mount Mandara. It is called
> in Sanskrit Vijaya (giving success), and the favorite drink of Indra
> is said to be prepared from it. On festive occasions large quantities
> are consumed by almost all classes of Hindus. The Brahmins sell
> sherbet prepared with bhang at the temples; religious mendicants
> collect together and smoke ganja. Shops for the sale of preparations
> of hemp are to be found in every town, and are much resorted to by
> the idle and vicious. (Dymock, 1885)

With the aid of Vishnu, the Gods finally overcame the demons and eventually gained control of the pot of *amrita*. Invigorated by the sacred elixir, the Gods were able to drive the demons down to hell and order and prosperity was restored to the three worlds. In honour of their success against the demons the Gods gave cannabis the name *Vijaya* ("Victory") to commemorate the event.

The God most closely associated with the collecting of the *amrita*, was Shiva, and his devotees still partake of cannabis in commemoration of this event to this day. "The votaries of Eudra-Siva are addicted to Cannabis sativa" (Chakbraberty, 1944). "According to the old Hindu poems, God Shiva brought down the hemp plant from the Himalayas and gave it to mankind" (Chopra, 1939).[18] This close association clearly goes back back to the myth of "The Churning of the Ocean of Milk": "Shiva on fire with the poison churned from the ocean was cooled by bhang." (Campbell, 1894)

Fig 18.13

According to one account, when nectar was produced from the churning of the ocean, something was wanted to purify the nectar. The deity supplied the want of a nectar-cleanser by creating bhang. This bhang Mahadev [Shiva] made from his own body, and so it is called *angaj* or body-born. According to another account some nectar dropped to the ground and from the ground the bhang plant sprang. It was because they used this child of nectar or of Mahadev in agreement of religious forms that the seers or Rishis became Siddha or one with the deity. He who despite the example of the Rishis, uses no bhang shall lose his happiness in this life and in the life to come. In the end he shall be cast into hell. The mere sight of bhang, cleanses from as much sin as a thousand horse-sacrifices or a thousand pilgrimages. He who scandalizes the user of bhang shall suffer the torments of hell so long as the sun endures. He who drinks bhang foolishly or for pleasure without religious rites is as guilty as the sinner... of sins. He who drinks wisely and according to rule, be he ever so low, even though his body is smeared with human ordure and urine, is Shiva. No god or man is as good as the religious drinker of bhang. The students of the scriptures at Benares are given

18   As quoted in (Merlin, 1973).

bhang before they sit to study. At Benares, Ujjain, the other holy places, the yogis, bairagis, and sanyasis take deep draughts of bhang that they may center there thoughts on the Eternal.

The Hindu poet of Shiva, the Great Spirit that living in bhang passes into the drinker, sings of bhang as the clearer of ignorance, the giver of knowledge. No gem or jewel can touch in value bhang taken truly and reverently. He who drinks bhang drinks Shiva. The soul in whom the spirit of bhang finds a home glides into the ocean of Being freed from the weary round of matter-blinded self.

.... So the right user of bhang or of ganja, before beginning to drink or smoke, offers the drug to Mahadev saying, lena Shankar, lena Babulnath: [19] be pleased to take Shankar, take it Babulnath. According to the Shiva Parann, from the dark fourteenth of Magh (January-February) to the light fourteenth of Asbadh (June-July), that is, during the three months of the hot weather, bhang should be daily poured over the Ling [sacred phallic image] of Shiva every day, bhang should be poured at least during the first and last days of this period. According to the Meru Tantra on any Monday, especially on Shravan (July-August) Mondays, on all twelfths *pradoshs*, and on all dark fourteenths or *shivratris* still more on the Mahashivratri or Shiva's Great Night on dark fourteenth of Magh (January-February.), and at all eclipses of the sun or moon, persons wistful either for this world or for the world to come should offer bhang to Shiva and pour it over the Ling. (Campbell, 1894)

Contemporary depiction [Fig 14] of Shiva partaking of *bhang*, which is being offered by his wife Parvati while his elephant headed son Ga-

–Hymn of Praise

From his matted hair and knot the Ganges flows,
While Shankar (Siva) strains the bhang.
Parabati (Parvti) has taken the straining-cloth
And Ganpat (Ganesh) sits and looks on.
Beneath (the cloth) is the wooden bowl and the brass cup near:
Taking the bhang into his hand he strains.
Wearing his necklace of skulls and sacred earrings,
He talks what his mind desires.
A follower fans him behind,
With a rosary in his hand.
His bull sits in the yard,
Placing his hoof in front of him.

(from Temple, 1884)

Fig 18.14

19   Mahadev , Shankar, Babulnath are all epithets of Shiva.

nesh[20] prepares more of the sacred elixir with a mortar and pestle in the foreground, (by Kailash Raj). Considering this image of family bliss and the making of *bhang*, it is interesting to note that in one myth about the discovery of cannabis, Shiva "enraged with family worries...withdrew to the fields. The cool shade of a plant soothed him. He crushed and partook of the leaves, and the *bhang* refreshed him.... So the right user of *bhang* or of *ganja*, before beginning to drink or smoke, offers the drug to Mahadev saying, lena Shankar, lena Babulnath: be pleased to take Shankar, take it Babulnath."(Campbell, 1894)

"The Churning of the Ocean of Milk" is not only particularly important in understanding the relationship between cannabis and *amrita*, but also the clear association of the *amrita* with soma. The *Satapatha Brahmana*, which we have discussed for its identification of soma with cannabis (Chapter 4) also clearly records of the amrita that this "same nectar of immortality is soma."[21] "In some Puranic texts soma, the moon god, was seen as the receptacle of the *amrita. Amrita* and soma are often conflated. Like *amrita*, soma is also compared in the *Rig Veda* to rain or the milk from the heavenly cows, which are the clouds" (Duncan, 1990). "In the *Vedas*, the name *Amrita* is used to signify various items that are sacrificed, but it is particularly applied to soma juice" (Coulter & Turner, 2000). "*Amrita*: ... 'Immortality.' Literally 'without death (*mrita*).'. This word is apparently related to Greek *ambrotos*, 'immortal,' hence ambrosia the food or drink of the Gods, which has its Vedic equivalent in the legendary elixir called soma, a central element in Vedic rites...." (Subramuniyaswami, et al., 2007)

> Literal meaning [of *amrita*]: 'non-dead.' The water of life in Hindu mythology. It was recovered by the Churning of the Ocean....
> Probably identical with soma, the favorite beverage of Indra, amrita is an echo of practices that must antedate the Aryan in-

---

20   Ganesh's acquisition of an elephant's head is also another story that accounts the degradation of the former king of the Gods Indra. Ancient Puranic myths relate that at bathing time, the Goddess Parvati, wife of Shiva, created Ganesh as a Suddha, or pure white being, out of the essence of her body, and placed Him at the entrance of the house. Parvati commanded her son not to allow anybody inside and then went for a bath. After a long sojourn away, Shiva returned home to Parvati, and Ganesh blocked Shiva's way. In the ensuing battle Shiva took Ganesh to be an outsider and cut off the head of Ganesh. Shortly after, as Parvati emerged from their home and he witnessed her sorrow and grief upon seeing the body of her beheaded son, he realized the grievous mistake he had made. Vishnu, seeing the tragedy that had befallen this holy family, went to bring the head of any creature that might be sleeping with its head northwards and thus, the head of the Iravat (The elephant of Indra) was cut off and Vishnu joined the head of the elephant to the beheaded body of Ganesh.
21   *Fifth Adhyaya First Brahmana*: 8

vasion…. "We have drunk Soma," the Vedas recall, "we have become immortal, we have entered into the light, we have known the gods." Its exhilarating qualities serve to remind us of the role of drugs in ancient religions. (Cotterell, 1979)

Thus the *amrita* of the *Puranas* can be seen as the "Heavenly soma" which was drunk by the gods from the receptacle of the moon, and when the nectar spilled from the khumba (vessel) which held it fell upon the earth, the earth produced cannabis, the worldly portion of amrita, an identification clearly marking hemp as the earthly counterpart of the heavenly soma/*amrita*.

Drinking of cannabis in the form of *bhang* can be traced considerably back in time. The current form follows the tradition of ritual use prescribed for *soma*, such as washing, grinding, mixing with milk and spiritual invocation…. The use of *bhang* by Brahmans and householders at festivals has a form and style that may be traced to *soma*… (Morningstar, 1985)

In reference to how cannabis was used in a similar way to the ritual libations of Soma in the Tantric tradition as it stood in the 19th century, Arthur Avalon, (Sir John Woodroffe), wrote that "… bhang being very largely used under the name of Vijaya and Amrita" (Avalon, 1918). More than a century later the German entheobotanist Christian Ratsch noted that:

In Tibetan and Tantric medicine, elixirs of life (nectar, amrita, soma) based upon secret recipes are still being manufactured. Many of these recipes include hemp. This Tantric scepter (kathvanga), [Fig 15] an attribute of Padmasambhava, is one of the

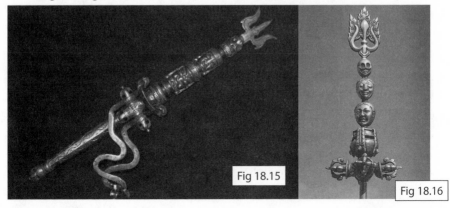

Fig 18.15

Fig 18.16

magical weapons related to the spirit dagger (phurba). The ritual device depicts the vessel of amrita as well as the three stages of aging. The vessel rests upon a double thunderbolt. Symbol of the Tantric path, and is crowned by Shiva's trident. In worldly rituals, the inebriating and vision-producing soma drink is seen as the counterpart of the divine amrita. (Ratsh, 2001)

A similar *kathvanga* [Fig 16] on eBay, with the description "This exquisite solid khatvanga wand has skull, human and Mahakhala head represent past, present and future...The Khatvanga (Skt.) could be called a magic wand or magicians' stick and represents the 'magic powers' or siddhis (Skt.) of an accomplished tantric practitioner." "Tantriks call cannabis... 'siddhi,' energy, and frequently use it in their ceremonies" (Walker, 1982). Interestingly, the items on these *kathvanga* have at their base, the symbol of Indra, the *vajra*, the four sided thunderbolt, (or *dorje*, as it has become popularly known through its Tibetan adoption); followed by the *Khumba mela* or pot of *amrita/soma*; next three heads representing the past, present and future, i.e a cycle of time; and finally topped with Shiva's trident – a totem-pole like display rife with occult symbolism regarding the transference of Indra's Soma to Shiva's *bhang*.

As Alain Danielou explains of the connected dual nature of both Shiva and the amrita in The Gods of India: Hindu Polytheism:

> The lord-of-sleep (Siva), who is the principle of disintegration (tamas), the source of an ever-expanding (disintegrating universe, is the principle of time, the destroyer, and at the same time the embodiment of experience, of enjoyment, whose symbol is the fount of life, the source of pleasure, the phallus (linga). Thus enjoyment that is life and time that is death are shown as the two aspects of one entity. The source of life and immortality (a-mrta) is the same as that of death (mrta), a symbol that expresses itself in all traditions are the oneness of life and death (a-mor and mor-tis). (Danielou, 1985)

To this day, Hindu Holy men, *sadhus*, and other worshippers, celebrate their most important festival, the Kumbha Mela, smoking chillums of hashish, and drinking draughts of *bhang* in honour of Lord Shiva every three years at one of the four sacred spots that the *amrita* is believed to have been spilled, returning to each of the four holy sites in a twelve years cycle. Over 60 million worshippers are said to have attended the 2001 Kumbha Mela, making it the largest human gathering ever.

Fig 18.17: 1842 illustration by W. Taylor, 'The Sunyasees', depicting two sadhus, one smoking a ritual chillum, also with a traditional 'nargila', coconut water-pipe at his feet.

A 19th century edition of the *Gazetteer of the Bombay Presidency* recorded of such figures: "They do not drink liquor, but are fond of smoking tobacco, drinking hemp or *bhang*, and eating opium. They rub their bodies with ashes and dishevel their hair. Their clothes are a loincloth and a long reddish-brown gown. They shave neither the head nor face and generally have their long matted hair rolled in a great coil at the back of their heads. They are very lazy, irritable, and given to hemp-smoking. They practice such austerities as sitting in the sun surrounded by fire, exposing themselves to pinching cold, standing for a long period on one leg, and holding one or both their hands over their heads. They live on charity, especially rations distributed in temples... They rank next to Bráhmans. They go to beg in the mornings and evenings passing the rest of their time in cooking, smoking *gánja*, and sleeping.... They have no social organization, but they often travel and live in bands, one of them being head and keeping the rest in order. Some can read and write and some are well acquainted with the doctrines of their religion" Campbell, 1883).

The Sacred Smoke

Fig 18.18: Lord Shiva, with half closed eyes, perpetually stoned, smoking a chillum, and with the crescent moon in his hair symbolizing the drained cup of celestial Soma.

Shiva, epithet's include Somasundara: beautiful as the moon; Somnath: lord of Soma, the herb of vitality. As Namita Gokhale notes of these relationships: "The crescent moon rests like a diadem on Shiva's long matted hair. According to myth, Soma, the moon, was discredited by an assembly of the gods for some indiscretion and so cast into the ocean. Later, during the samudra manthan, the churning of the ocean, Shiva resurrected Soma by placing the moon on his brow, thereby restoring the intuitive faculties to their rightful position" (Gokhale, 2001). Soma. (illustration by author).

The smoking of cannabis and hashish in chillums or hookahs is believed to be a relatively new development, a method thought to be introduced after the New World discovery of smoking tobacco, and may have spread in popularity due to attempts to control the ritual use of *bhang*:

> In Hindustan, in distant ages when the secret of the priests was revealed or stolen, hemp was used solely for the preparation of potions. The Brahmins appear to have attempted to control its use. They authorized it only on the occasion of certain important religious celebrations (Kali festivals, Druga-Puja etc.). We cannot know whether the people readily accepted the restriction of their consumption of Cannabis potions to the permitted dates; nor can we say whether it was not precisely in order to gratify the passion for the intoxicating drug, while at the same time respecting the law promulgated by the ministers of the divinity, that the custom of smoking hemp arose. This practice, more attractive, quicker in its effects, and less dangerous [?], spread with great rapidity, and at the present time smokers form the great majority of the hashish addicts of India. (Bouquet, 1950)

In *Sadhus—India's Mystic Holy Men*, Dolf Hartsuiker explains more about Shiva's special relationship with cannabis and the development of smoking it:

> ...the smoking of *charas* [cannabis] is... regarded as a sacred act.... Intoxication as a 'respected'... method of self-realization is related to *soma* the nectar of the gods, which is recommended in the *Vedas* as a sure means of attaining divine wisdom.
>
> Mythologically, *charas*, is intimately connected with Shiva: he smokes it, he is perpetually intoxicated by it, he is the Lord of Charas.... Babas offer the smoke to him; they want to take part in his ecstasy, his higher vision of reality. (Hartsuiker, 1993)

Fig 18.19: Right, 1898, depiction of a group of sadhus, clothed man second from left holding a chillum.

As one 19th century Christian missionary noted of these mendicants: "Some of the worst men in India are the professed devotees of Siva, who wander about the country as beggars. They stupefy themselves with bhang, and are so dissolute that they dare not remain long in one place. They frequently extort alms from ignorant people, who foolishly dread their curses, though these only harm their utterers." (Murdoch, 1875)

In reference to the inhalation of cannabis smoke it is interesting to note the comments of the *Indian Hemp Drugs Commission Report* that in "the funeral ceremony amongst the Gonds of these [central India] provinces, *kalli* or flat ganja is placed over the chest of the dead body of the Gond, and when the funeral party returns home, a little of the ganja is burnt in the house of the dead person, the smoke of which is supposed to reach the spirit of the dead"

(IHDCR, 1894). No indication of a pipe or chillum is given in this account, and if burned in an open censer, this may be evidence of a continued Indo-European tradition, as it is clearly reminiscent of Scythian funerary rites where cannabis was burnt and inhaled in honour of the dead.

As with the development of smoking cannabis in chillums and pipes, the transference of Indra's soma to Shiva's *bhang*, did not happen quickly, but rather over more than a dozen centuries, as is indicated by 10th to 14th century Indian references to Indrasana, or Indra's hemp. With the time frames involved there is little wonder that much of the awareness of the switch faded beyond memory.

Sex, Drugs and Shiva

Shiva's symbolism is loaded with erotic elements. The god's main cultic image, is the lingam, a cosmic phallus; he rides the vehicle of Nandi the Bull, and the testicles of statues depicting Nandi are grasped for good fortune; His sons are Skanda, the jet of sperm, and the serpent, symbolic of the sexually invoked kundalini energy. Like Shiva's dual nature of god of creation and destruction, the incorporation of this phallic element in his worship ranged from extreme acts of asceticism to the orgiastic libertine rites of Tantrism.

From existing Hindu myths and poems regarding the adoption of Shiva into the Vedic pantheon, through his marriage to Parvati, we can see that even in the myths and poems, the blue skinned god came with a strong element of controversy.

The Marriage of Mahadeva

Oh, heavens ! such a fool for a husband brought!
The father looks and looks, in wonder lost;—A lout who cannot even ride a horse
Who's boon in all his paces broken in; Stretched on a bullock is a lion's skin,
A snake strapped round to serve for girth ;
He rattling keeps a pebble in a box, Crack, crack, [his bones all in] his body go ;
Gobble, gobble, lumps of bhang go down, Flop, flop, chuck, chuck, his [swollen] chops

both go, Decked out with painted streaks of sandalwood, Be-
grimed with ashes o'er his body all,
Arrayed a cloud of demons various, see;
 The [river] Ganges flowing from his head;
'Tis Bidyapati sings, listen Manain.
Patience, [it is the god] "digambar [sky-clad, naked] bhang."[22]

Fig 18.20: contemporary image of Shiva "Concocting Bhang" by churning hemp with a
pestle into a bowl of milk.

---

22   From (Fallon, 1875)

As the 19th century Christian missionary and author John Murdoch recorded in his *Religious Reform of Shiva*:

Fig 18.21: Parvati

> Siva's wife, Parvati, is said often to have rebuked him for his evil habits and associating with prostitutes. She was almost ruined by his habits of intoxication, in which he indulged to such a degree as to redden his eyes. He danced naked before Atri, and from the curse of that Rishi was punished in a way which is too shameful to be mentioned. He was ready to part with all the merit he had acquired by his austerities in order to gratify his evil desires but once with Mohini. Daksha gave in marriage the youngest of his daughters to Siva; but he became enraged when he saw the habits of his son-in-law—a beggar, smearing his body with ashes, living where the dead are burned, and wearing a necklace of skulls. When Daksha made a great sacrifice, his daughter came; but he abased her greatly on account of her dirty and beggarly appearance, on which account she threw herself into the fire and was reduced to ashes. Upon this Siva, it is said, produced an enormous giant with three eyes, called Virabhadra, who destroyed the sacrifice of Daksha and cut off his head. Brahma and Vishnu then came bending at the feet of Siva, and at their request he put a goat's head on Daksha's body... A feeling of modesty, found in all men except the lowest savages, requires certain parts of the body to be covered. Among the Saivas, on the other hand, they are the favourite forms of worship [i.e. lingam (phallus) worship]. What must be the moral influence of the contemplation of such objects?

The Saiva ascetics, who profess to copy the example of their lord, are some of the worst men in India. The Hindus are cleanly in their habits; but, strange to say, they appear in certain cases, to regard filth as a proof of sanctity. The Saiva beggars are dirty and disgusting. Some of them wander about quite naked. Though strong and able to work, they live in idleness, preying upon the industrious. If any refuse them alms, they threaten them with most awful curses. They stupify themselves with bhang, and are guilty of the vilest immoralities. That such men should be regarded as holy, is a sad proof of the debasing influence of Hinduism. (Murdoch, 1887)

Worshipping Shiva's lingam, "The wish of him who with pure mind pours bhang with due reverence over the Ling of Mahadev will be fulfilled.... If the fever-sticken performs the Vijaya abhishek, or bhang-pouring on the Ling of Shankar, the god is pleased, his breath cools, and the portion of his breath in the body of the fever-stricken pleased to inflame. The bhang offered to Mahadev is without pepper or other spice. It is mixed with water, water and milk, or milk and sugar. It is poured over the Ling. According to some authorities the offerer should not touch the offered bhang. Temple ministrants Atits, Tapodhans, Bhojaks, Bhopis, Bharadis, Gutaras alone should drink it. If there are no ministrants the remains of the offering should be poured into a well or given to cows to drink. Other authorities encourage the offerer to the bhang, since by sipping the bhang reaches and soothes the Shiva-Shakti or Shiva-spirit in the sipper. On certain social occasions during failures of rain, during eclipses, and also in times of war libations of bhang are poured ever the Ling." (Campbell, 1894)

Another mid 19th century Christian tract by Murdoch took direct aim at the sacraments of the cult of Shiva:

Concerning the Drunkenness of Shiva.

O Reader, as Shiva was lustful, so also was he a drunkard. He spent all his time in attending to (Ganja) hemp buds, (Sidhi) hemp leaves, (Bhang) hemp pills; this you know very well. And Shiva in his frequent fits of intoxication, wandered about in cemeteries, in places for burning the dead, wearing a necklace of skulls and smearing his body with ashes, and being joined to a serpent, in the world of spirits, associating with Asurs or Demons as his attendants, evil spirits and such like; and as a drunkard he wandered about naked, this also is known to you.

Now, O Reader, I ask you, can the wise and blessed God be a madman and a drunkard? Certainly, even a child will acknowledge that God is perfectly pure, and without any stain of sin, and that he punishes lustful persons and drunkards. If it be so, then,

O Hindu gentlemen, why do you consider the drunken Shiva to be God? and continue to look for salvation from him? This is what I cannot understand.

Alas, if Shiva were existing at the present time, then by taking many kinds of intoxicating articles, as (Ganja) hemp buds, (Charas) a decoction of hemp buds, opium, opium pills, spirituous liquors, (Bhang) hemp pills, (Sidhi) a preparation of hemp, native spirituous liquors, &c., like his servants, he would make himself like a beast. Alas! how astonishing! "As the teacher, so the learner," this saying which is current among women, is fulfilled. For his servants, the Sannyasis, &c., even more than Shiva, spend their time like beasts, always taking intoxicating articles.

0 Reader, by the pure Christian religion it is said, that no lustful or drunken person will obtain a place in the kingdom of God. Alas, what will be the condition of Shiva and of his disciples! O Reader, do you decide this. And if you are desirous of salvation, then abstain from the vain service of Shiva, and cleave to the service of the true God, otherwise, after death, there will be no time for repentance. Relinquish falsehood to-day and search for and rely upon the truth, whereby you will be happy for ever. (Murdoch, 1861)

One can only speculate that such cultural prejudices as those evident in the writing of Murdoch and other Christian authors, has much to do with the basis of the prejudices of their modern counterparts. Cannabis prohibition, in its roots, has always been "Christians vs. Devil's weed"! As for how the Shaivite saddhus viewed such comments from Christian missionaries, it was likely with the greatest amusement.

According to the sutras... followers of Shiva are instructed to behave in ways whereby they actively seek the insults and censure of those around them, for it is a part of their esoteric discipline to earn the active contempt of the uninitiated populace. They can thus deviously pass on their bad karmas to their unsuspecting revilers. These are all standard proto-shamanistic and cultic ideologies, devices for achieving isolation and worldly detachment. These devices for subjugation of troublesome ego help subdue the desire patterns that lead to the need for sexual and material gratifications. These stratagems for detachment do not deny the daily realities of life, they simply despise them. Yet, unlike many other streams of ascetic denial, the Tantric way accepts and even confronts material existence. The five mystic tenets of madira, matsya, mamsa, maithuna and mudra, or wine, fish, flesh, sexual activity and parched grain use the stimulus of intense experience as a catalyst for entering other mind-realities. It is in these schools of tantric thought and ritual that the contrarieties of Shiva's ascetic and erotic impulses are most corporeally united and reconciled. (Gokhale, 2001)

Considering the view of Shiva and his devotees held by Murdoch and other Christian missionaries to the East, it is not without divine irony, that a century or so later, when other Westerners made that fabled journey to the East, in search of the forbidden fruit of their own culture, they ended up at the gates of the Serpent Lord of bhang, and the Eden Hashish Centre in Nepal!

Fig 18.22: Calendars from the Eden Hashish Centre in Kathmandu, Nepal, which legally sold cannabis products up until 1974, when under pressure from the Nixon Whitehouse, the king of Nepal prohibited all sales.

Kali Weed

As Indra was not the sole recipient of soma rites in the Vedic pantheon, it is also important to note that the same held true of *bhang* in later Hinduism. Although Shiva is the Lord of *Bhang*, cannabis appears in offering to a number of other deities such as those dedicated to Shiva's consort Kali, Goddess of Life and Death. Kali's cannabis mantra is, "*Om, Hrim Ambrosia, that springeth forth from ambrosia, Thou shalt showerest ambrosia, draw ambrosia for me again and again. Bring Kalika within my control. Give success; Svaha*" (Avalon, 1913). In Tantric rites, cannabis retained its ancient Vedic epithet of 'Vijaya' (Victory). As Arthur Avalon (aka, Sir John Woodroffe) explained: "Vijaya, (victory) used in ceremonies to Kali: That is the narcotic *Bhang* (hemp)... used in all ceremonies" (Avalon, 1913).

Fig 18.23: Wood engraved print from 1892 of Kali dancing over the 'corpse' of Shiva, who holds a chillum for smoking gunja in his left hand.

In medieval India and Tibet, sorcerers in search of magic powers glorified the use of a marijuana drink (bhang)... in Tantric sex ceremonies derived from the ancient *soma* cult. A circle of naked men and women is conducting an experiment of the central nervous system. They consecrate a bowl of bhang to Kali, goddess of terror and delight. As the bhang begins to take effect, the worshippers mentally arouse the serpent at the base of the spine, sending waves of energy up to the cortex. (Aldrich, 1978)

Cannabis also played an important role in the *Durga Puja*, the annual Hindu six day festival that celebrates worship of the Hindu goddess Durga. Up until the 19th century, at the close of the *Durga Puja*, it was customary to drink bowls of *bhang* and to offer them to others. As the *Indian Hemp Drugs Commission Report* recorded:

The custom of offering an infusion of the leaves of the hemp plant to every guest and member of the family on the... last day of the Durga Puja, is common in Bengal, and may almost be said to be universal. It is alluded to by many of the witnesses who refer to its use on this occasion as well as on other days of the Durga Puja festival. But, while there can be no doubt as to the existence of the custom, there is considerable divergence of opinion as to the true nature of it. The custom itself is a simple one. On the last day of this great festival the male members of the family go forth to consign the image to the waters and on their return the whole family with their guests exchange greetings and embrace one another. During this rejoicing a cup containing an infusion of the leaves of the hemp plant is handed round, and all are expected to partake thereof, or at least to place it to the lips in token of acceptance. Sweetmeats containing hemp are also distributed. Opinion is almost equally divided as to whether the custom is a mere social observance, or whether it is an essential part of the religious ceremonial of the festival. There is difference whether there is any injunction in the opinion among the witnesses as to *Shastras* rendering obligatory the consumption of hemp; but Tantric religious works sanction the use, and the custom whatever be its origin may now be said from immemorial usage to be regarded by many people as part of their religious observances. From the evidence of the witnesses it would appear that there is no specific direction in the *Shastras* of the manner in which the drug should be used but from the references quoted it would appear that the use alluded to is authority that of bhang in the form of an infusion. (IHDCR, 1894)

Vishnu's Party Plant

Cannabis was consecrated to the Vedic God Vishnu as well, which is not really surprising considering the important role Vishnu played in the Puranic myth "The Churning of the Ocean of Milk." This relationship likely goes back to the earlier days when cannabis was consecrated as soma, as Vishnu's love of soma, was duly noted in the *Vedas* "Drink of this meath... Vishnu; drink ye your fill of soma... The sweet exhilarating juice hath reached you" (RV.6.69). In the late 19th century Campbell recorded: "Vaishnavas [Vishnu worshippers]... make offerings of bhang. The form of Vishnu Or, the Guardian to whom bhang is a welcome offering is Baladev... in the worship of Baladev all present, worshipper and, ministrant alike, join in drinking" (Campbell, 1894). Kaempfer recorded an ecstatic celebration involving *bhang* taken in honor of Vishnu in this 300 year old account:

> In Malabar, at the time of the sacrifices in honour of Vishnu, virgins pleasant to behold and richly adorned were brought from the temple of the Brahmins. They came out in public to appease the god who rules over plenty and fine weather. To impress the spectators, these young women were previously given a preparation with a basis of hemp and datura, and when the priest saw, by certain symptoms, that the action of the drugs was about to

Fig 18.24: 1926 Photagravure of the Jagganath Temple in Puri.

show itself, he began his invocations. The Devadassy (servants of the gods) then danced, leapt about yelling, contorted their limbs, and, foaming at the mouth, their eyes ecstatic, committed all sorts of eccentricities. Finally the priests carried the exhausted virgins into the sanctuary, gave them a potion to destroy the effect of the previous one, and then showed them again to the people in their right mind, so that the crowd of spectators might believe that the demons had fled and the idol was appeased.[23] (Kaempfer, 1712)

Cannabis is also ritually consumed by the Jagannath cult in Puri, particularly in their famous "Festival of Chariots," a traditional remnant of the char-iot riding Aryans and which is of pre-Vedic origins. Jagannath, "the Lord of the Universe" is a form of the God Vish-nu. The Temple of Lord Jagannath is one of the major temples in India. The worship of Lord Jagannath is so ancient that there is no accu-rate record of how long it has been going on. It is strictly forbidden for non-Hindus to enter the Jaganath temple.

Fig 18.25: Old circa 19th century postcard depicting one of the Giant chariots used in the Jagganath festival. Devotees of the cult have been known to be crippled or even killed at the ecstatic celebration due to being crushed through throwing themselves in front of the wheels of these massive contraptions, as offering themselves to the God.

As the *Indian Hemp Drugs Commission Report* recorded, "bhang is largely used by the attendants and worshippers at the temple of Jagannath at Puri" (IHDCR, 1894). In this ancient, and still partially performed rite, massive elaborately decorated

23   As quoted in (Bouquet, 1950).

chariots[24] (representing the world in motion) are drawn carrying the veiled figures of Jaganath and his bride.

> The Jagannath Mandir was the last temple to maintain classical [Indian] dance, up until the mid-1950s - now it is strictly a theatrical art... The British... suppressed this aspect of liturgy as rude, calling the *devadasis* or *maharis* (the ritual wives of the god) *nuatch-girls* or prostitutes (they performed naked, judging by the sculpture on the *natamandapas* or *natamandiras*, 'dance platforms or temples', for the public, and among their duties was *maithuna*-type ritual sex with the Brahmins in the temple, with which *Cannabis* use seems to be associated, to please Indra and bring on the monsoon). As a result the practice, once widespread throughout India... all but disappeared, except in Puri, and the other styles were preserved only in villages by *gotipuas*, boys dressed as girls, only to be revived as classical art in our time... (Ott 1996)[25]

The Bauls

Fig 18.26: Leftt Baul musicians; Right, Miniature painting of Baul musician smoking chillum.

The Baul musicians of Bengal, who practice worship through song and poetry, originated amongst the worshippers of Vishnu, but Krishna,[26] the eighth incarnation of Vishnu, is the one

---

24   The English word Juggernaut, comes from "Jaganath," and its 'colossal' meaning is derived from the gargantuan size of the chariots used in the cultic ceremony.
25   Personal correspondence.
26   In the Bhagavad Gita Krishna declares "it is I who am the ritual, I the sacrifice, the offering to the ancestors, the healing herb, the spiritual chant" (9.16).

whom the Bauls love and worship above all others. The Baul spiritual view has mixed elements of Vaishnavism Tantra, Sufi Islam, and Buddhism. The origins of the name Baul is debated, some see it as being derived from the Sanskrit vatula, meaning "divinely inspired' and others vyakula, "impatiently eager."

Bauls are known for both their musical parties, and the copious amounts of ganja consumed at them. In The Path of the Mystic Lover: Baul Songs of Passion and Ecstasy, Bhaskar Bhattacharyya and his coauthors describe how such gatherings can have an element of musical one-upmanship in them, as ganja inspiration and improvised song, often turns into melodious debates:

Preparations are made after sunset. Lamps are lit, and the Bauls sit together in a large circle, smoking ganja, talking, tuning their instruments. The first strains of invocatory song start, gently at first, then slowly growing more impassioned as the rhythms accelerate and voices wail....

To begin the debate, a Baul from one group rises and taunts the members of the rival group who are still sitting and smoking chillums (clay pipes) of ganja:

> *Know also*
> *That thousands of "mad ones"*
> *Smoking ganja endlessly*
> *Do not get anywhere!*
>   song 7

A glazy-eyed Baul from the rival group draws on his chillum and then stands to deliver his reply:

> *Come, come, O brothers!*
> *All who want to smoke*
> *The Ganja of Love!...*
> *"can one who smokes the ganja of Love*
> *Really get high on anything else?"*
>   song 11
>   –(Bhattacharyya, et. al. 1993)

And thus the exchange of song continues on until the early hours of morning, when voices raspy from the smoke of the chillum, can no longer sing...

India's Festival Intoxicant

In his exquisite essay on the importance of cannabis in Indian spirituality, "On the Religion of Hemp," J.M. Campbell noted that "So holy a plant must play a leading part in temple rights" (Campbell, 1894). Clearly with celebrations like the *Kumbha Mela* and other holidays where hemp products have been commonly consumed in India for centuries if not millennia, the same can be said of Indian festivals as well. It should also be noted that the "use of *bhang* by Brahmans and householders at festivals has a form and style that may be traced to *soma...*" (Morningstar, 1985)

It has been suggested that the Holi festival of India, in which thousands of participants drink *bhanga* and playfully throw colored paint on each other in a celebration of life and joy, is a remnant of the Soma cult. The Holi festival "the Saturnalia of India... terminates with feasting, drunkenness, obscenity and a bonfire..." (Boleton, et al., 2000).

The whole festival is one of sex and fertility worship and presents in India the pictures of bands of noisy and excited revellers

Fig 18.27: Revellers intoxicated on bhang, being prepared in the tub at the right, alongside edible 'bhang balls' on plates, throw coloured paint on each other during the Holi Festival in this 19th century image.

parading the streets, unrestrained in demeanour, gesture and speech... their dress dip wet and bespattered with daubs of red powder and yellow water.... the red powder... and yellow... water... with which the Holi revellers bespatter one another... appear to have their origins in Hinduism and the *soma* tradition of Mount Meru.... the intoxicating juice of the soma plant when mixed with milk represents the nectar of the gods (Indra): the wine of immortality among men; the elixir of life: the heavenly water....In seeking an explanation of the red powder and yellow water used in the Holi... we are reminded that Vedic ritualists recognized *two elements* in the immortal properties of Soma, the one food, the other a beverage... it may be possible that the red powder... and the yellow water... used in... the Holi... may represent these elements. (Bolton, et al., 2000)

As the 19th century *Indian Hemp Drugs Commission Report* noted of this and other festivities, "at the Holi festival... bhang is commonly consumed; and, according to many witnesses, at such festivals as the Diwali, Chait Sankranti, Pous Sankranti, Sripanchami, Sivachaturdasi, Ramnavami, and indeed on occasions of weddings and many other family festivities" (IHDCR, 1894).

The Warriors Herb

Just as soma was the drink of the warrior God Indra, cannabis continued with this role on the earthly plain, as Grierson noted at the close of the 19th century:

In folk-songs, ganja or bhang (with or without opium) is the invariable drink of heroes before performing any great feat. At the village of Bauri in Gaya there is a huge hollow stone, which is said to be the bowl in which the famous hero Lorik mixed his ganja. Lorik was a very valiant general, and is the hero of numerous folk-songs. The epic poem of Alha and Rudal, of uncertain date, but undoubtedly based on very old materials (the heroes lived in the twelfth century A.D.), contains numerous references to ganja as a drink of warriors. For instance, the commencement of the canto dealing with Alha's marriage, describes the pestle and mortar with which the ganja was prepared, the amount of the intoxicating drink prepared from it (it is called *sabzi*) and the amount of opium (an absurdly exaggerated quantity) given to each warrior in his court. (Grierson, 1893)

As also noted by J.M. Campbell in his essay "On the Religion of Hemp":

> Another great spirit time during which bhang plays an important part is the time of war. Before the outbreak of a war and during its progress the Ling of Mahadev should be bathed with bhang. Its power of driving panic influences from near the god has gained for bhang the name of Vijaya, the unbeaten. So a drink of bhang drives from the fighting Hindu the haunting spirits of fear and weariness. So the beleaguered Rajput, when nothing is left but to die, after loosing his hair that the bhang spirit may have free entrance, drinks the sacramental bhang and rushing on the enemy completes his *juhar* or self-sacrifice. It is this quality of panic-scaring that makes bhang, the Vijaya or Victorious, specially dear to Mahadev in his character of Tripur, the slayer of the demon Tripurasur. (Campbell, 1894)

This association between cannabis and the courage needed for battle, is one of the key reasons why the plant has played such an important role in the Sikh religion for centuries.

Fig 18.28: 19th century illustration by Armitage of 'The Battle of Meeanee (Sind) – Pakistan,' which was fought on the 17th of February, 1843, and was an account of British Imperialistic forces encountering fierce resistance from Sikh warriors said to be under the influence of bhang. According to British sources hemp provided the Sikhs with a furious excitement under which their assaults against the British were made, so much so that the usually steady front of the 22nd regiment, armed with rifles against the Sikh's swords and spears, lost many soldiers to the Sikh's cannabis inspired courage.

The Sikhs and Sukhnidhaan

Besides its prominent role in Hinduism, cannabis has also played an important part in the later Sikh religion of the Punjab region. Sikhism grew out of Hinduism and began in the 16th century AD, but is now one of the world's five major religions. The name Sikh itself comes from a Sanskrit root śisya meaning "disciple" or "learner," or śiksa meaning "instruction." In a chapter on "Social and Religious Customs" the *Indian Hemp Drugs Commission Report* reported on the 19th century Sikh relationship with cannabis:

> Among the Sikhs the use of bhang as a beverage appears to be common, and to be associated with their religious practices. The witnesses who refer to this use by the Sikhs appear to regard it as an essential part of their religious rites having the authority of the Granth or Sikh scripture. Witness Sodhi Iswar Singh, Extra Assistant Commissioner, says: "As far as I know, bhang is pounded by the Sikhs on the Dasehra day, and it is ordinarily binding upon every Sikh to drink it as a sacred draught by mixing water with it." *Legend* – Guru Gobind Singh, the tenth guru, the founder of the Sikh religion, was on the gaddi of Baba Nanak in the time of Emperor Aurangzeb. When the guru was at Anandpur, tahsil Una, Hoshiarpur district, engaged in battle with the Hill Rajas of the Simla, Kangra, and the Hoshiarpur districts, the Rains sent an elephant, who was trained in attacking and slaying the forces of the enemy with a sword in his trunk and in breaking open the gates of forts, to attack and capture the Lohgarh fort near Anandpur. The guru gave one of his followers, Bachittar Singh, some bhang and a little of opium to eat, and directed him to face the said elephant. This brave man obeyed the word of command of his leader and attacked the elephant, who was intoxicated and had achieved victories in several battles before, with the result that the animal was overpowered and the Hill Rajas defeated. The use of bhang, therefore, on the Dasehra day is necessary as a sacred draught. It is customary among the Sikhs generally to drink bhang, so that Guru Gobind Singh has himself said the following poems in praise of bhang: "Give me, O Saki (butler), a cup of green colour (bhang), as it is required by me at the time of battle (vide 'Suraj Parkash,' the Sikh religious book)." Bhang is also used on the Chandas day, which is a festival of the god Sheoji Mahadeva. The Sikhs consider it binding to use it on the Dasehra day-The quantity then taken is too small to prove injurious." As Sikhs are absolutely prohibited

> by their religion from smoking, the use of ganja and charas in this
> form is not practised by them. Of old Sikh times, is annually per-
> mitted to collect without interference a boat load of bhang, which
> is afterwards distributed throughout the year to the sadhus and
> beggars who are supported by the dharamsala. (IHDCR, 1894)

In the 19th century, one of the twelve confederacies of the Sikhs
was identified by the name "Bhangi, called from their fondness for
Bhang, extract of hemp" (Eastwick & Murray, 1883). However, for
the most part, it seems the use of cannabis preparations have fallen
out of favor with the devotees of the Sikh religion. "The Nihang of
Punjab, who are the defenders of Sikh shrines, are an exception.
They take cannabis to help in meditation" (Beck & Worden, 2002).

> The Akali Nihang claim direct lineage from the founding Gurus of
> Sikhism. Their itinerant lifestyle, rites and rituals have been sanc-
> tioned from the time of the sixth Sikh Guru - Hargobind Singh.
> Yet as Sikhism has grown and spread around the globe, the Nihang
> have been outcaste by their own people. Once seen as heroes and demi
> gods, they are now vilified as thieves and drug addicts. (Kandola, 2009)

The Nihang also referred to as the Akalis, are a largely nomadic Sikh
military order known for their military prowess, and historical victories
in battle even when they were greatly outnumbered. Nihang are easily
identifiable by their steel iron bracelets, weaponry and particularly by
their "electric blue" attire and tall turbans. The Nihang's defence of Sikh
sacred sites has earned them the title of "Knights of God." With their
cannabis use, prowess in battle, excellent horsemanship, and nomadic
lifestyle, it is hard not to see this sect in parallel with the ancient Scythians who are known to have left a cultural imprint in Northern India.

Up until 2001, cannabis use was a condoned part of Nihang ritual and spiritual practice and this use was identified by them a "time-
respected tradition' bestowed upon the order by the tenth Guru of
Sikhism, Gobind Singh (1666-1708). The Nihang used the name of
Suhka, meaning 'Peace-Giver' for the preparer of their ritual cannabis preparations which they used in the form of baked cookies
and a bhang like beverage referred to as *sukhnidhaan*. As described
in Nav Kandola's fascinating film *The Nihang – A Secret History
of the Sikhs*, cannabis is clearly viewed as a "sacred herb," that is
used to "help meditation, reciting mantras and is cooling internal-

ly," other names for cannabis used by the Nihang include *Shaeedy Degh*, meaning the "Martyr's Sacrament" and also "the Guru's herb" (Kandola, 2009).Nihang use of cannabis has been particularly associated with the Sikh holiday *Hola Mohalla*, a sort of military celebration where it is consumed *en mass* in a large rowdy celebration.

Fig 18:29 19th century miniature painting depicting the tenth Guru of Sikhism, Gobind Singh, who is said to have made the following poem in praise of bhang: "Give me, O Saki (butler), a cup of green colour (bhang), as it is required by me at the time of battle (vide 'Suraj Parkash,' the Sikh religious book)."

Singh Sahib Bhai Joginder Singh Ji offered the following references in support of the Nihang's use of Sukhnidhaan:

1. According to the 'Janamsakhi Bhai Bala', Mogul King Babur offered 'Bhang' to Sri Guru Nanak Dev Ji. Delighted on this, Sri Guru Nanak Dev Ji granted him the boon to have the kingdom for seven generations. Guru Ji recited a '*Shabd*' also on this occasion, in which he did not condemn 'Bhang'. On the other hand, when Yogi Jhangar Nath offered a cup of wine to Guru Nanak Dev Ji, Guru Ji recited a '*Shabd*', in which drinking wine was condemned.

2. The 'Mahant' (abbot) of 'Gurusar Satlaani' got license for '*Sukhnidhaan*' from the British government.

3. The '*Sukhnidhaan*' is being offered at Sri Amritsar Sahib, Taran-taaran, and Sri Anandpur Sahib Ji.

4. '*Nihangs*' of the 'Budhha Dal' offer '*Sukhnidhaan*'.

5. There is description of 'Sukhnidhaan' on many pages of book 'Sooraj Prakash'.

6. At 'Shaheedi Baag' in the city of Sri Anandpur Sahib, a small room, which was constructed during Guru's time, has been excavated, in which there were big 'Suneharas' (a kind of big vessel). It proves that '*Sukhnidhaan*' was prepared and offered during the time of Guru Sahib.

7. According to the book 'Khalsa Dharam Shaastar', Guru Gobind Singh ordered to take intoxicants to remove sadness. The quantity of 'Chhatar-dhara' (opium) and '*Sukhnidhaan*' was fixed.

Fig 18.30: Left, Nihang soldiers; Right, Nihang mystic.

8. All the 'Rahats' can be known only from Guru history and 'Rahat-namas.' We cannot know 'Rahats' from Sri Guru Granth Sahib Ji.[27]

Ninteenth century Europeans certainly held a disdain for the Nihangs, who themselves in return considered the British as a foreign power with clear imperialistic desires to rule over their native homeland. As a Colonel Stienbach recorded of the sect in 1846 after encountering them in the Punjab: "They are without exception the most insolent and worthless race of people under the sun. They move about constantly armed to the teeth and intoxicated on cannabis. Insulting everybody they meet, particularly Europeans. They are quite uncontrollable and the only way to deal with them is to exterminate them."[28] As we shall see at the conclusion of the next chapter, similar condemnations of hashish ingesting Islamic *faqirs*, sufis and mendicants

Fig 18.31: Sikh Nihangs preparing *Sukhnidhaan*, a *bhang* preparation, with their traditional large pestle and mortar

for their similar unruly behaviour, was also expressed by the British raj.

It was probably from over a century of such European influence that in 2001 the apex Sikh clergy instituted a prohibition of cannabis products as part of their "campaign against drug addiction." This prohibition of their sacred cannabis beverage *sukhnidhaan* was vehemently rejected by the Nihang leader Baba Santa Singh, along with 20 other chiefs of the sect. As the Indian paper the *Tribune* recorded "Baba Santa Singh pointed out that the consumption of 'bhang' among the Nihangs was not a new phenomenon. He said it had been going on ever since the Nihangs came into existence and fought battles against Mughal and Afghan invaders" (Tribune, 2001) As a result of his refusal to accept of the prohibition

27   As quoted by (Singh, 2008)
28   As quoted in (Kandola, 2009).

Fig 18.32: Shiv saroop of Nihang Singh, the piece of loose cloth, or 'farla' at the top of the Nihang turban represents the Ganges river flowing out, as does the stream flowing from the top of Shiva's hair, in the accompanying contemporary image of the God (Right). The keeping of uncut hair and tying it up in a jura, bundle, at the top of the head, is traced to Shaivite yogic Nath sampradya. Nihang Sikhs have traditions such as *Sukhnidhaan* where cannabis is taken in a similar act of devotion to charas in the Shaivite chillum and particularly the older ritual consumption of *bhang* by devotees of Shiva. It is clear that some Shavaite Nath Yogi influence has existed within Sikhism since its beginnings. Guru Nanak Dev said that for Sikhs: "The Guru is Shiva, the Guru is Vishnu and Brahma; the Guru is Paarvati and Lakhshmi. Shiva, Brahma and the Goddess of Beauty, ever adorned, sing." Besides the Nihangs, the Shaivite influence is particularly found in Sikh groups such as the Shri Chand Yogi and the Udasi Panth Orders.

of cannabis products, Baba Santa Singh was excommunicated and replaced by Baba Balbir Singh who complied with the apex Sikh clergy's ban on the use of hemp, and although many Nihang still reject this prohibition, in orthodox circles this controversial ban has been maintained until the present.

The People's Medicine

While soma was attributed with the power to bestow divine vision, it was also a healing agent. Considerably more recent than the Rig-Veda is the Atharva Veda, a collection of medicinal texts and incantations from the seventh century B.C.E. Soma is also mentioned in these texts, as is medicinal hemp, which is referred to as vijaya, the "victor." Although the botanical identity of the soma plant remains uncertain, more recent Indian medical litera- ture often equates it with hemp. What we do know for certain is that hemp was being used as a medicine during Vedic times. The name victor is indicative of its great power in overcoming the demons of illness. Both soma and vijaya are regarded as rasayana, elixirs with the greatest healing power.... According to the Athar- va Veda hemp is a sacred plant because "a guardian angel [deva] lives in its leaves." (Ratsch, 2001)[29]

L ike its other aspects, the medicinal qualities of soma continued on as cannabis medicines in India. Later Indian texts such as the *Tajni Guntu*, the *Rajbulubha* and the *Susruta* list cannabis as a treatment for clearing phlegm, expelling flatulence, inducing cos- tiveness, sharpening memory, increasing eloquence, as an appetite stimulant, for gonorrhea, and as a general tonic.

> The *Bhavaprakaca*... [a] medical work written by Bhavadevami- cra (cir. A.D. 1600), has as follows:
> "Bhanga is also called *ganja, matulani, madini* (the intoxicat- ing), *vijaya* (the victorious), and jaya (the victorious). It is anti- phlegmatic, pungent, astringent, digestive, easy of digestion, acid, bile-affecting; and increases infatuation, intoxication, the power of the voice, and the digestive faculty." (Grierson, 1893)

Much of cannabis' medicinal attributes were combined with the magical and ritualistic beliefs from the Vedic period and this influ- ence lasted well into the 20th century:

> Bhang the cooler is a febrifuge. Bhang acts on the fever not directly or physically as an ordinary medicine, but indirectly or spiritually by soothing the angry influences to whom the heats of fever are due. According to one account in the Ayurveda, fever is posses- sion by the hot angry breath of the great gods Brahma, Vishnu, and Shiva. According to another passage in the Ayurveda, Shan-

---

29   The Atharvaveda is "the apocryphal last Veda...which many believe is non-Aryan" (Mathews, 2005). The Atharvaveda records cannabis being governed by the god Soma, and may have been indicative of other plants used in the sacred drink at later times, leading to substitutions: "We tell of the five kingdoms of herbs headed by Soma: may it and the Kusha grass, and bhanga and barley, and the herb Saha release us from anxiety" (Atharvaveda).

kar or Shiva, enraged by a slight from his father-in-law Daksha, breathed from his nostrils the eight fevers that wither mankind. If the fever-stricken performs the Vijaya abhishek, or bhang-pouring on the Ling of Shankar, the god is pleased, his breath cools, and the portion of his breath in the body of the fever-stricken pleased to inflame. The Kashikhanda Purana tells how at Benares, a Brahman, sore-smitten with fever, dreamed that he had poured bhang over the self-sprung Ling and was well. On waking he went to the Ling, worshipped, poured bhang this cure brings to Benares sufferers from fever which no ordinary medicine can cure. The sufferers are laid in the temple pour bhang over the Ling whose virtue has gained it the name Jvareshwar, the Fever-Lord. In Bombay many people sick of fever vow on recovery to pour bhang over a Ling. Besides cure for fever bhang has many medicinal virtues. It cools the heated blood, soothes the over-wakeful to sleep, gives beauty, and secures length of days. It cures dysentery and sunstroke, clears phlegm, quickens digestion, sharpens appetite, makes the tongue of the lisper plain, freshens the intellect, and gives alertness to the body and gaiety to the mind. Such are the useful and needful ends for which in his goodness the Almighty made bhang.

 ... Shitaladevi, the Cooler, the dread goddess of small-pox, whose nature, like the nature of bhang, is cooling, takes pleasure in offerings of bhang. During epidemics of small-pox the burning and fever of the disease are soothed by pouring bhang over the image of Shitaladevi. So for the feverishness caused by the heats especially to the old no cure equals the drinking of bhang. (Campbell, 1894)

From most ancient times, to the near present, cannabis "remained one of the important drugs in the *Indian Materia Medica...* until 1945. *Cannabis* was widely used in the rural areas for asthma and bronchitis" Nahas, et al., 1999). Not surprisingly, current research into medical marijuana has reawakened practitioners of Ayurvedic medicine to the use of the ancient healing plant of their ancestors, as Ancient Wisdom has become modern scientific fact.

 As well, numerous Indian texts indicate Soma's reputation for ensuring longevity continued on with cannabis, The *Mahanirvana Tantra* (XI,105-8) recorded: "Intoxicating drink (containing bhang) is consumed in order to liberate oneself, and that those who do so, in dominating their mental faculties and following the law of Shiva (yoga) – are to be likened to immortals on earth."[30] The *Ru-*

30 As quoted in (Danielou, 1992). This same text contains a prayer or mantra to be used before one consumes the sacred herb: "*Bhava na sana hridayam,*" which means: "may

drayamal Tantra, from the eighth century relates that a drink made from cannabis and other herbs, makes humans "equal to the gods and immortal" (Ratsch, 2001). Again, "the well-documented Indian treatise, Anandakanda, ca. 1200 c.e., suggested strong neuroprotective effects of cannabis as part of a rigorous medical, religious, and ritualistic regimen of celibacy... 'it is claimed that the man lives 300 years free from any disease and sign of old age'" (Russo, 2007). "...[T]he *Root of Bliss* (̄*Anandakanda*).... has been called 'the most encyclopaedic work of the entire Hindu alchemical canon'..and although much of the work is derivative of earlier authors, one innovates a long and detailed chapter on cannabis (*vijay ̄akalpa*: i.15.313–499)" (Wujastyk, 2001).

> [T]he Anandakanda describes rejuvenation treatment based on cannabis. This involves treatment over a long period in a specially constructed hut (kut.i). This procedure is strongly reminiscent of a similar rejuvenation procedure described in the earliest Sanskrit medical literature, one that requires not cannabis but the unknown plant Soma. And that procedure itself echoes a rite of ritual rebirth that dates from the mid-first millennium BC. (Wujastyk, 2001)

The Religion of Hemp

Clearly, it was in the continued medicinal and religious use of cannabis in India, that soma has left its greatest historical echo. The role of cannabis as a religious sacrament in India was most eloquently captured in J.M. Campbell's report for the British Raj, who were trying to decide whether to tax or prohibit the popular intoxicant of the Indian people at the close of the 19th century. Not before or since the *Vedas* sang the religious praise of the Soma, has cannabis been the subject of such sanctifying words as in Campbell's 1894 essay, "On the Religion of Hemp" from which we have already freely quoted, and now quote again in closing this chapter:

> To the Hindu the hemp plant is holy. A guardian lives in the bhang leaf... the bhang leaf is the home of the great Yogi or brooding ascetic Mahadev [Shiva].
> So holy a plant should have special rearing. Shiva explains to his wife, Parvati, how, in sowing hemp seed, you should keep re-

this *sana* (Sanskrit for cannabis) be a blessing to my heart."

peating the spell 'Bhangi,' 'Bhangi,' apparently that the sound of
that guardian name may scare the evil tare-sowing influences.
Again, when the seedlings are planted the same holy name must
be repeated, and also at the watering which, for the space of a year,
the young plants must daily receive. When the flowers appear the
flowers and leaves should be stripped from the plant and kept for
a day in warm water. Next day, with one hundred repetitions of
the holy name Bhangi, the leaves and flowers should be washed
in a river and dried in an open shed. When they are dry some of
the leaves should be burnt with due repeating of the holy name
as a *jap* or muttered charm. Then, bearing in mind Vagdevata,
or the goddess of speech, and offering a prayer, the dried leaves
should be laid in a pure and sanctified place. Bhang so prepared,
especially If prayers are said over it, will gratify the wishes and desires of its owner. Taken in the early morning such bhang cleanses
the user from sin, frees him from the punishment... of sins, and
entitles him to reap the fruits of a thousand horse-sacrifices. Such
sanctified bhang taken at day break or noon destroys disease....

Such holiness and such evil-scaring powers must give bhang
a high place among lucky objects. That a day may be fortunate
the careful man should on waking look into liquid bhang. So any
nightmares or evil spirits that may have entered into him during
the ghost-haunted hours of night will flee from him at the sight
of the bhang and free him from their blinding influences during
the day. So too when a journey has to be begun or a fresh duty
or business undertaken it is well to look at bhang. To meet some
one carrying bhang is a sure omen of success. To see in a dream
the leaves, plant, or water of bhang is lucky; it brings the goddess
of wealth into the dreamer's power. To see his parents worship
the bhang-plant and pour bhang over Shiva's Ling will cure the
dreamer of fever. A longing for bhang foretells happiness: to see
bhang drunk increases riches. No good thing can come to the
man who treads under foot the holy bhang leaf.

....[T]oo its devotee bhang is no ordinary plant... [it] became,
holy from its guardian and healing qualities.... [T]o the worshippers of the influences that, raising man out of himself and above
mean individual worries, make him one with the divine force
of nature, it is inevitable that temperaments should be found to
whom the quickening spirit of bhang is the spirit of freedom and
knowledge. In the ecstasy of bhang the spark of the Eternal in
man turns into light the murkiness of matter or illusion and self
is lost in the central soul-fire..... To the meaner man, still under

the glamour of matter or maya, bhang taken religiously is kindly thwarting the wiles of his foes and giving the drinker wealth and promptness of mind.

....To forbid or even seriously to restrict the use of so holy and gracious a herb as the hemp would cause widespread suffering and annoyance and to the large bands of worshipped ascetics deep-seated anger. It would rob the people of a solace in discomfort, of a cure in sickness, of a guardian whose gracious protection saves them from the attacks of evil influences, and whose mighty power makes the devotee of the Victorious, overcoming the demons of hunger and thirst, of panic fear, of the glamour of Maya or matter, and of madness, able in rest to brood on the Eternal, till the Eternal, possessing him body and soul, frees him from the having of self and receives him into the ocean of Being... "We drank bhang and the mystery I am He grew plain. So grand a result, so tiny a sin." (Campbell, 1894)

The Kali Yuga and the Return of Shiva

It is also important to note, that the Hinduism has its own counterpart to the end of time myths of the Zoroastrians and Christians, known as the Kali Yuga. (This name has nothing to do with the Goddess Kali, but here refers to "conflict"). The Kali Yuga, is the finale of the Hindu declining cycle of ages, which began at a high point with the golden age of Hindu mythology, the Satya Yuga, where man was a sage and close to the divine; followed by the silver age, the Treta Yuga, where humanity only knows the gods through ritual worship; then, continuing with this pattern of decline, the Davapara Yuga, the bronze age, a time of worldly indecision; and finally the last age, the age which we are said to be living in now, the age of dense materiality, the iron age of the Kali Yuga, the time of conflicts in which man becomes the engineer of his own destruction.

During the Kali Yuga, the disruption of the balance of nature, as well as society and its basic values, occurs at an ever-increasing pace. These disruptions announce the end of the cycle and the near destruction of mankind, and end which can no longer be far away. Man's supremacy over the terrestrial world and his gradual destruction of other living species provokes the god's vengeance which is revealed in the folly he inspires in those who oppose

him. This folly is very evident of mankind today, formed of ignorant masses led by irresponsible leaders. (Danielou, 1992)

As Danielou explains, like the Christian and Zoroastrian myths,
it's not all doom and gloom, as the Kali Yuga is also, in a sense "a
privileged era. The first men, those of the Satya Yuga, were sages
still close to the divine. But the last men, those of the Kali Yuga,
in drawing near to death, also draw near to the principle to which
all things return at the end. In the middle of the moral decadence,
injustice, wars and social conflicts which are characteristic of the
end of the Kali Yuga, contact with the divine by means of the descending, Tamasic way is more easily accomplished" (Danielou,
1992). "The end of the Kali Yuga is a particularly favorable period
to pursue true knowledge: 'Some will attain wisdom in a short time,
for the merits acquired in one year during the Treta Yuga can be
obtained in one day in the age of Kali' [Shiva Purana 5.1.40]" (Danielou, 1987)[31]

> According to the doctrine of the Tantras, the cult of Shiva-Di-
> onysus[32] and the practices of Tantrism are the only ways open
> to mankind in the Age of Conflicts – in which we are at present
> – to approach the divine. Without a return to the respect of na-
> ture and to the practice of erotico-magic rites allowing the self-
> realization of man in harmony with the other forms of being, the
> overall destruction of the human species cannot be long delayed.
> Only the followers of the god will survive to give birth to a new
> human race.
> All religions which oppose Shivaism, Dionysism and the mys-
> tical sects, have accentuated those tendencies which lead to the
> destruction of world harmony. Each return to Shivaite concepts,

31   In his book *While the Gods Play: Shiva oracles and predictions on the Cycles of History and destiny of Mankind*, Alain Danielou explores this apocalyptic Indian theme fully.
32   In his *Gods of Love and Ecstacy; The Traditions of Shiva and Dionysus*, Danielou offered considerable research connecting the origins of the two Gods, and amongst things
noted, was a comparison between the Hindu Yugas and the Greek Ages of Man, which
began with the Golden Age, and descended through the Silver, bronze and Iron. "According to Orphic and Pythagorean texts, the supremacy of Dionysus will reappear during
the second part of the Age of Iron, or the Kali Yuga, and his cult will be the only form of
religion. This is also the affirmation of Shivaism. Only Tantric Yoga methods are efficacious
in this age in which values are lost; the rites, asceticism and virtues of other ages are inef-
fective. It may be observed that the recent discoveries of psychology, ecology and natural
science, suggest the same approach to universal and human problems as those which
Shivaism has always recommended." (Danieleou, 1992)

even if only a trend in that direction, is equivalent to a new era of equilibrium and creativity. The great periods of art and culture are always connected with an erotic-mystical renewal. Danielou, 1992)

Like the return of Mithra and Jesus in the Zoroastrian and Christian traditions, "At the end of the Kali Yuga, the god Shiva will appear to reestablish the right path in a secret and hidden form"(Danielou, 1987)

> During the Age of Kali, the Great God, Shiva, the peacemaker, dark blue and red, will reveal himself in a disguised form in order to restore justice. Those who come to him shall be saved" (Linga Purana 1.40.12)[33]

As noted in Chapter 4, Alain Danielou, whose work we have been citing in relation to the return of Shiva and the Kali Yuga, was amongst those who believed that Soma was a hemp preparation. "The description of the way soma was prepared and its immediate use without fermentation, can only apply to bhang and is identical to the method employed today" (Danielou 1992). Further, Danielou clearly states that the use of bhang is an integral part of Shivaite worship, and compared it directly to the traditions of Soma: "Every Shivaite has to consume bhang at least once a year. The drink, which intensifies perceptivity, induces visions and above all leads to extreme mental concentration" (Danielou, 1992).

As the return of Mithra was accompanied the white Hom, and Jesus by the Tree of Life and its healing leaves, is it too much to put forth that the return of Shiva is marked by the widespread use of his sacred hemp? Is the "body-born" (angaj) bhang, which is said to have been made from Shiva's own flesh the "secret and hidden form" through which this most ancient of Gods is now revealing himself? Are the dread-locked, eco-conscious, ganja smoking, hemp preaching youth of today the beginnings of the return of the perennial cult of Shiva, the matted haired Lord of bhang?[34] Thoughts to ponder the next time you partake of the blue god's most favored plant. "Om Shiva Shankara Hari Hari Ganja! Boom Somnath! Lord of Soma, the Herb of Vitality!"

---

33   As quoted in (Danielou, 1992)

34   Even the dreadlocks of the Rastafarians, like their use of the terms "ganja" and "Kali weed" is likely evidence of the influence of Indian migrant workers on the syncretic Jamaican religion.

In many ways Shiva has served humanity as the God whose cult has delivered the holy Soma tradition back to humanity almost intact after its hidden sojourn through time. Thus in India despite the attempted reforms of Buddha, and the harshest of penalties of the *Laws of Manu*, although the identity of soma became lost and confused over time, the sacramental role of cannabis continued into the modern day, albeit, under its unconsecrated name of *bhang*, and various other epithets. As for its role as soma, the *Laws of Manu* seem to have succeeded where the gentler reforms of Buddha failed, and the strict prohibitions against selling and using soma placed on Brahmins led to an end to the act of consecration of cannabis as soma, as described in the *Satapatha Brahmana*, and its replacement with non-intoxicating placebos, as described in the *Aitareya Brahmanam*. As a result of the prohibition and reforms of the Vedic soma rite, cannabis, popular with the people, was taken for a time outside of Vedic ritual, and over the centuries through this, the worship of Indra, having lost the entheogneic sacrament which ensured the success of his cult, slowly declined. As Indra's attributes and sacrament became more and more associated with Shiva, so too did this god's popularity rise, bringing him into the present day as the 'Lord of *Bhang*.' Clearly, in India, nothing was lost, just a former name forgotten and misplaced. A completely conceivable hypothesis, as in India we are dealing with not just centuries, but millennia.

HASHISH AND ISLAM

Seese thou this little berry, this green pill?
It is made of dreams; yet, so sustaining it,
Thirty fat birds all cooking on a spit
Would not thy belly half so subtly fill.

It is this berry the Sufis eat
When they would fall into an ecstasy,
And tell their precious lies to you and me,
A little hasheesh is the whole big cheat.

Thirty birds, said I? Yea! In one small grain
A hundred times that number cook for thee;
Eat thou—it will harm thee not—and thine shall be
Houris outnumbered ere thou wakest again.

Hafez (1315-1390 ad)[1]

The popular and widely used Arabic term "hashish" is itself a nickname believed to have been derived from a more general word meaning "herb," and was applied to hemp resin products in the same way the generic "grass" came to refer to cannabis in the 20th century. "Most likely, it may may be simply '*the* herb' as distinguished from all other (medicinal) herbs" (Rosenthal, 1971).[2] Translations of other Medieval Islamic names for cannabis

---

1 Khwāja Šamsu d-Dīn Muhammad Hāfez-e Šīrāzī known more commonly by his pen name Hafiz, or Hafez, was Persia's most celebrated lyric poet. Hafiz's life and poems have been the subject of volumes of analysis, commentary, and interpretation and he influenced the course of post-fourteenth century Persian poetry more than any other figure from that time. "We may well suspect that nearly every poet and productive amateur of verse, from the thirteenth to the sixteenth centuries, wrote at least some playful poems on hashish, although these poems might at times have been excluded from published collections of his work" (Rosenthal, 1971).

2 Alternatively, in *A Cyclopedia of Biblical Literature*, the 19th century scholar

products include "the one that cheers," "little morsel," "shrub of emo-
tion," "shrub of understanding," "peace of mind," "girlfriend," "the
one that facilitates digestion," "the pleasing one," "visit of the green
Khidr," "the one that connects the heart," "provisions," "branches of
bliss," "thought morsel," "the one that lightens the load," "medicine,"
"holy Jerusalem," "sugary," "pill," "the pretty one," "medicinal powder," "theriac" (heal-all), "peacocks tail," "consolation," "the one that
causes good appetite," "the one that softens the temperaments,"
"the one that brings the party together," "the little agent," "amber
scented" "from Zion," "emerald mine" (Rosenthal, 1971).

This rich variety of epithets bears evidence of the long and magical history of hemp products in the Arab world, and this widespread
popularity is due to the fact that cannabis is not explicitly prohibited like alcohol in the Koran. Early Islamic commentators "never
failed to remark on the fact that hashish is not mentioned in the
Qur'an or the old Prophetic traditions, nor were they able to find
any express reference to it in the name of the four legal schools"
(Rosenthal, 1971).

> While there are a number of local differences, the use of can-
> nabis with a varying intensity has had a time-honoured role in
> many Muslim countries. This is in contrast to the use of alcohol
> which, from the religious point of view, became the prime for-
> bidden intoxicant.... There are many reports... that hashish was
> also used in medical preparations... [It has been] suggested that
> the interpretation of the Quranic law on intoxicants might have
> been more tolerant towards the use of drugs such as opium and
> hashish because of the paucity of means of relieving pain in the
> medieval Muslim world.[3] (Palgi, 1975)

John Kitto put forth two different potential candidates for the Origins of the term 'hashish' through the Hebrew terms *Shesh*, which originates in reference to some sort of 'fibre
plant,' and the possibly related word, *Eshishah* (*E-shesh*—ah?) which holds connotations
such as 'syrup,' or 'unguent,' and was mixed with wine (Kitto 1845: 1856). See Appendix E
for a fuller account of Kitto's etymology.

3   "Arab scientists were various centuries ahead of our current knowledge of the
curative powers of hemp (*Cannabis sativa* L.). Modern scientific literature ignores their
contribution on the subject... [I]n Arabic medicine between the 8th and the 18th century... Arab physicians knew and used its diuretic, anti-emetic, anti-epileptic, anti-inflammatory, pain-killing and antipyretic properties among others." (Lozano, 1997) "...Moslems
excelled in surgery... they induced anaesthesia by the use of hemp fumes" (Dietz & Lehozky, 1963). "Many well known Arabic doctors described medical uses of cannabis, especially
Avicenna... He mentions the plant in his work, *Canon of Medicine*, (ca. 1000 A.D.). This
medicinal oeuvre is often considered as the leading and most comprehensive medicinal

As a result of this lack of clarity about the morality of its use, cannabis has been surrounded in controversy and thus a matter of debate in Islamic society since very early times, with devotees of the plant in some areas and periods enjoying the widest freedoms, and other times the severest of penalties for its use. In *The Herb: Hashish versus Medieval Muslim Society*, Franz Rosenthal discusses a number of medieval Islamic poems and stories regarding Islam and cannabis, some accounts arguing that unlike alcohol its use was condoned[4] by Quranic law and by others, that along with all intoxicants Mohammed condemned it,[5] (Rosenthal, 1971).

> Once hashish consumption had become a widespread and debated custom, there was much discussion among Muslim scholars and other interested parties about its history... The theories put forward range from the fanciful to the strong semblance of fact... The samples preserved in literature make us suspect that there was once much more which went unrecorded and that the legal and political struggle over the drug was accompanied by arguments derived from history favouring one side or the other. (Rosenthal, 1971)

As Rosenthal explained, it "is even possible that some authorities who denounce the use of drugs in the strongest terms were secret addicts or at least had some actual drug experience that informed their judgement" (Rosenthal, 1971).

At times of the strictest prohibition the user was criminally culpable but not condemned with death, as were those "heretics' who tried "declared the use of hashish lawful and permissible." Such figures were to be refused funeral prayers and Muslim burials. "When the government decided to proceed energetically against the use of drugs, severe penalties were demanded and apparently imposed. This included the death penalty. In the thirteenth century, Baybars

treatise well into the fifteenth century."(Frankhauser, 2002).

4   Rosenthal quotes the following anonymous medieval verse with comments attributed to the Almighty himself: "When God created this plant and called it to appear before Him, it went to Him, and He said to it: By my might, majesty, splendour, and perfection! I have not created a plant nobler and finer than you are. Nowhere else have I let you dwell but in clean minds and the clean stomachs of my servants" (Rosenthal, 1971).

5   Hudhayfah b. Al-Yaman: "I went together with the prophet into the countryside. He saw a tree and shook his head. I asked him why he was shaking his head, and he replied: a time will come upon my nation when they will eat from the leaves of this tree and get intoxicated. They are the worst of the worst.... as god has nothing to do with them."[As quoted in (Rosenthal, 1971)].

prohibited the consumption of wine and hashish and invoked the sword as punishment... for it. In the latter part of the fourteenth century, Sudun ash-Shaykhuni punished people accused of making hashish with the extraction of their molars, and many suffered this fate..." (Rosenthal, 1971).

Despite these harsh attempts at prohibition, by later medieval times hashish use was surprisingly widespread. Rosenthal, citing Fuzuli (1483-1556) wrote that in the late medieval period, "Hashish can claim to be the friend of dervishes and to be available in the corner of every mosque and among all kinds of scholars" (Rosenthal, 1971). In regard to the medieval Islamic attitude to cannabis, it is important to note, in relation to this study, that numerous scholars have suggested a Zoroastrian influence on the development of Islam, and conceivably such a Persian influence created a predisposed cultural acceptance of hemp use in Islamic esoteric circles. As Joseph Campbell explained: "It is obvious that in every syllable Islam is a continuation of the Zoroastrian-Jewish-Christian heritage..." (Campbell, 1964). This influence is particularly apparent in Persian Islamic groups such as the Sufis, Ismailis and Assassins, who were all largely influenced by the Zoroastrian tradition, and their use of hashish, and *dūg-e wahdat* (the dūg of annihilation), as discussed in Chapter 15, is clearly a carry-over of the Persian *mang*/Haoma tradition.

The respected cannabis historian Jack Herer puts forth that "Moslem 'mystical' priests... have taught, used and extolled cannabis for divine revelation, insight and oneness with Allah, for at least the last 1,000 years. Many Moslem and world scholars believe the mysticism of the Sufi Priests was actually that of the Zoroastrians who survived Moslem conquests of the 7th and 8th Centuries A.D. and subsequent conversion (change your religion... or be beheaded)" (Herer, 1990). Other evidence indicates that both the Zoroastrian influence and the use of cannabis may be even earlier than the 1000 years suggested by Herer, and in fact extends back to the origins of Islam.

> Muhammad knew of the *Zoroastrians*, and they had a psychedelic *Haoma* drink concocted with unknown ingredients. "Allusions to the twigs and branches of *Haoma*... suggest... perhaps, hemp."[6] (Natan, 2006)

6   Citing *Encyclopaedia Britannica*. In relation to the role of the moon in the soma/haoma cults, it is interesting to note that Yoel Natan's *Moon-o-theism*, which identifies cannabis use in the Islamic tradition, is also a study of moon worship in the development of Islam.

A Zoroastrian influence has been suggested in the account of Mohammed's ascent to the heavens as described in the Koran and discussed in detail in the *Hadith* literature. A number of researchers have suggested that this event, as well as the details in it, had been borrowed from the Persian story of *Arda Wiraz Namag*, and his *mang* induced journey into the after-world (Gray, 1902; Jackson, 1928). The Cinvat Bridge mentioned in the *Arda Wiraz Namag* was particularly compared with the bridge over hell as mentioned in the *Hadith* literature.

In 1905, thinking that in some way it discredited Islam, the Rev. W. St. Clair Tisdall gleefully claimed that the *Arda Wiraz Namag* was the source of the Prophet's ascent to the heavens and his witnessing of the denizens of heaven and hell. And this view has been echoed by other researchers: "This ascent to heaven (or *Miraj* in Arabic) can be compared to the account in the Pahlavi text called *Arta* (or *Artay*) Viraf written several hundred years before the Muslim era" (Warraq, 1995). "…[T]he ascent of Muhammad to heaven and the passing visit to hell and paradise may be found in Zoroastrian tales dating some four hundred years before the time of Muhammad"[7] (Masood, 2001).

In the essay, "Celestial Botany Entheogenic Traces in Islamic Mysticism," Frederick Dannaway also suggested that Muhammad's shamanic flight was "reminiscent of the ascent of Arda Viraf who takes a narcotic and takes a visionary flight through heaven and hell… This… may indicate that regional cults viewed the Islamic revelation through their own shamanic traditions or that Islam retained the ritual heritages of the ancient world. These traditions would be enshrouded in the mysteries of Shia gnosis, alchemy and Sufism…" (Danaway, 2007).

Muhammad was a merchant from an early age and worked the ancient trade routes between the Mediterranean Sea and Indian Ocean. Undoubtedly as a result of this he would have come under much foreign influence and into contact with the rare commodities traded by other travelers, which we can be sure included cannabis

---

7   In *Arda Wiraz Namag* (Iranian *'Divina Commedia"*) *And The Prophet's Night Journey*, M. S. M. Saifullah disputes this influence, noting that the Persian manuscripts in question, although believed to be based on older material, are themselves younger than Islam (Saifullah, 2002; 2005). However, the Gnostic tractate *Zostrianos*, discussed in Chapter 17, which records this same technique of shamanic ecstasy and with a document composed in the 2nd century AD, shows that this method and tradition long predate the life of Mohammed and advent of Islam.

products, as well as the myths of magic which surrounded its consumption.

Mohammed's potential relationship with cannabis has been
more fully explored recently in Yoel Natan's *Moon-O-Theism*. Natan is amongst those who have seen the origins of Islamic cannabis
use with the Zoroastrian haoma tradition. He also believes that Koran references to Mohammed rubbing devotees may be evidence
that the Prophet was using the cannabis-based ointments of the
Hebrews and Christians discussed earlier (Chapters 16 & 17) and
moreover, that the Islamic sacred site of the Kaaba was nothing
more than a medieval Hashish den!

> *Muhammad* may have applied marijuana or Hashish-laced oint-
> ment since there are records of *Muhammad* rubbing other men.
> A *Hashish*-laced ointment would have been more potent than an
> ointment laced with marijuana.
>
> ....Those coming to the *Kaaba* may not have thought it unusu-
> al to be anointed, or to smoke various plants. During this period,
> priests were pharmacists and *Shamanistic* healers, and they dis-
> pensed drugs and ointments.... Worshippers at the *Kaaba* may
> have been drugged involuntarily just by being in a smoky room.
>
> ....After either smoking marijuana with *Muhammad*, or after
> *Muhammad* applied the ointment, the person affected felt an
> abnormal peace come over him, saw a hallucination or dreamt
> psychedelic dreams....
>
> The drug-induced psychedelic experience then convinced the
> person of the truth of *Islam*... Marijuana use can easily explain
> most of what passes for *Muhammad's* religious experience and
> that of some of his followers too. (Natan 2006)

As evidence of Islamic cannabis use, Natan sites Koran events
like the Prophet's Night flight from Mecca to Jerusalem, visions of
Jinn and Spirits, and the tale of *72 Hour's in Heaven* (which as shall
be discussed shortly was carried on by the 'Assassins' in their own
hashish based initiations). That such otherworldly ascents as Muhammad's flight to Mecca could be produced by the effects of cannabis preparations was clearly known in the Islamic world. As the
poet Al-Is'irdi (1222-1258) noted of hashish: "It is the secret. In it
the spirit ascends to the highest spots on a heavenly ascent of disembodied understanding."[8] More pointedly, hashish was reputedly

---

8   Translated in (Rosenthal, 1971)

used for an almost identical purpose as that attributed to Zoroastrian psychonauts amongst the Persian Islamic heretics known as the Assassins, a branch of the still existing Isma'ilis who are known for their ties to mystical Sufi sects that used hashish as well.

Muhammad is described as meditating in a desert cave in order to receive his initial visions, and from Zoroastrian descriptions of the use of *mang*, a cave would serve as the ideal sort of sensory deprivation chamber that would be suited for such an experience. Interestingly there is a cave where the Old Testament's Elijah is said to have taught his disciples and after the advent of Islam this site became venerated as a mosque known as "Al Khidr" (Comay & Pearlman, 1964). "Al Khidr" is an Islamic name for a figure who is not only identified with Elijah, but who has since very early in the Islamic period also been considered the patron saint of cannabis and mystical initiation (Campbell, 1894; Rosenthal, 1971; Bennett et al., 1995; Wilson, 1988, 1993). We shall return to this figure later in the chapter, as there are also ties with the early haoma cult, and his worship was particularly venerated by certain Islamic sects which claimed a tradition of hereditary descent from Muhammad that included secret knowledge about the faith and the use of hashish in initiation ceremonies, including the consecration of cannabis as "Homa."

As Natan also notes, the Indian text, the *Dabistan*, thought to have been composed in the 17th century, records a fascinating account of Muhammad's alleged introduction to cannabis, and the association of its use with his hereditary clan, the *Hashim*:

> There is a class among the *Hindus* who give themselves the term of *Musslman-Sofis* [Muslim-Sufis] and really agree in several tenets and opinions with the *Sufis*... they relate that one day the Prophet was taking a pleasure-walk under the guidance of *Jabril* [The Muslim angel *Gabriel*] and came to a place where a great tumult was heard. Jabril said 'This is the threshold of pleasure; enter into the house.' The Prophet consented to go in and there he saw sitting forty persons naked as they came from their mother and a band busy serving; but whatever service the Prophet requested them... to do, they did not comply, until the moment to grind *bhang* arrived. When they had ground it, they had no cloth through which they could strain and purify it; then the Prophet, having taken his turban from his hand, purified through it the

juice of bhang, the color [green] of which [the *bhang*] remained on the turban; whence the garment [heraldry] of the *Bini Hashem* [Muhammad's sub-tribe] is green. When the Prophet rendered them this service, they were glad and said among themselves, 'Let us give to this messenger of God, who is always running to the door of the ignorant, a little of the *bhang*, that he may obtain the secrets of the Almighty power.' So they gave the remains of the juice to the Prophet. When he had drunk it he became possessed of the secrets of the Angel of Destiny, and whatever men heard from him came through the means of this bounty. (*Dabistan*, 1655)[9]

Browne, writing in the 19th century noted that in his time one of the secret names of cannabis was "'Master Seyyid'.. from a fancied resemblance between its green color and the green turbans worn by reputed descendants of the Prophet" (Browne, 1897), so this was clearly a lasting traditon. Although the *Dabistan* is clearly a late addition to the Muslim tradition, earlier accounts of cannabis use, such as that of the Assassins, Isma'ilis and Sufi groups, gives clear indications that such practices were known very early in the Islamic world and, as the research in this volume has clearly shown, pre-dated Islam by millennia. Moreover, these "heretical" Islamic sects, considered themselves part of an authentic tradition, passed down by the Prophet through his descendants and their closest devotees, in much the same way as heretical Gnostic sects thought of themselves as the authentic "Christians" through association with Mary and other apostalistic figures.

Considering the story of the *Dabistan* and the association between of *bhang* with the green colour of Muhammad's sub-tribe the *Bini Hashem*, it is interesting to note that the hashish ingesting Isma'ili believed their own esoteric wisdom and some of their leaders came from the hereditary lineage of Muhammad. The Isma'ili are an offshoot of one of the two main factions of Islam, the Shi'a, and the importance of hereditary descent from Muhammad is pivotal in the schism between this group and the other main faction, the Sunnis. Early after Muhammad's demise, Islam split into two main factions, the Sunnis and the Shi'a, the Shi'a being mostly Persian while the Sunnis are the predominant force throughout most of the rest of the Islamic world. These two groups hold a major

9   (Fani, 1937; 1979), As quoted in (Natan, 2006)

point of contention about who the successor of the prophet was. As the 19th century Persian scholar Edward G. Browne explained of the situation:

> To the Persians, habituated from ancient time to [Zoroastrian] monarchical institutions, and accustomed to regard their kings as beings of another order, almost as divine, the idea of popular election in a matter so important as the choice of the Supreme Pontiff of the faith was revolting in the highest degree. They therefore refused to recognize the *Khalifas*, caliphs, or vice-regents of the Prophet elected by the Sunnis, whom I will venture to term the democratic party, but instead transferred their allegiance to Imams belonging exclusively to the Prophetic family... The caliph was a mere a defender of the faith chosen by the Mohammedan church for its guidance, the Imam was immaculate, of the seed of the Prophet, divinely appointed, divinely inspired, the accredited interpreter of the holy writ... (Browne, 1897)

Overtime, the Shi'ites themselves broke into "a number of sects, of which the most important were the 'Sect of the Seven,' with which we are concerned, and the 'Sect of the Twelve,' which is at present the national religion of Persia. The manner in which the former broke away from the latter was as follows. The sixth Imam... named his son Iama'il to succeed him":

> Unfortunately, Isma'il was – unless otherwise he has been calumniated – partial to the wine cup, and was one day detected by his father indulging in the forbidden drink. His nomination as Imam-designate was consequently rescinded, and his younger brother Musa was chosen in his stead, and recognized by most of the Shi'ites. There remained, nevertheless, a faction who continued to be loyal to Isma'il. "The first nomination was best," said they, "and irrevocable. The Imam is immaculate, and cannot do wrong. If he drank wine, it was because he wished to teach us that the precepts and prohibitions of the Qur'an are not to be taken literally but metaphorically..." Thus arose the germ of that method of allegorical or symbolical interpretation of the sacred text which... played so great a part in the development of the sect of Isma'il, the seventh Imam... (Browne, 1897)

Notably, Isma'il's alleged indiscretion led to the use of the forbidden wine amongst some Sufi sects, well others were known for their use of hashish. The preference for the use of hashish versus that of wine led to much poetic debate between Sufi sects. In *Scandal: Essays in Islamic Heresy*, Peter Lamborn Wilson refers to the Turkish Sufi poet Fuzuli (1483-1556) who "wrote a treatise on *Bang* and Wine in which he claimed that wine is merely 'an eager disciple setting the world afire', but hashish is the Sufi master himself. Wine shows the way to the hermitage of the Shaykh of Love... but hashish is the refuge itself. Once a certain Sufi of Basra began to consume hashish regularly, his shaykh realized this meant he had reached the ultimate degree of perfection, and no longer stood in need of guidance. This (says Fuzuli) 'proves that hashish is the perfect being, sought after by mankind with great eagerness. It may not be the perfect being for everybody, but it most certainly is for the seeker of mystical experience'" (Wilson, 1988). As the 12th century Sufi poet Ibn al-A'ma wrote in a poem praising hashish over wine (which makes reference to Haydar an 11th century Persian Isma'ili Sufi Sheik, accredited by some sources with introducing the herb to the Sufis):

> Give up wine and drink from the wine of Haydar,
> Amber scented, green the color of emerald.
> It is presented to you by a Turkish gazelle, slender,
> Swaying like a willow bough, delicate.
> In his hand, you would think, as he turns it
> It is like the traces of down on a rosy cheek.
> The slightest breeze makes it reel,
> And it flutters toward the coolness of the continuing breeze.
> The grayish pigeons coo upon its branches in the morning.
> And the cadences of the warbling doves cause it emotion.
> It has many meanings the like of which are unknown to wine.
> Therefore do not listen with respect to it to the words of the old censor.
> It is virginal, not deflowered by rain,
> Nor has it ever been squeezed by feet or hands,
> No Christian priest has ever played around with a cup containing it,
> Nor have they ever communion from its cask to any heretic's soul...
> Nothing has been said expressly from Malik to declare it unlawful,
> Nor is the hadd penalty for its use... prescribed...
> Thus take it with the sharp edge of steel.
> Stay the hands of worry with kyff and achieve joyful repose.
> Do not lightly postpone the day of joy till tomorrow.
> 'The days will show you what you were ignorant of,

And someone for who you did not provide (to serve as your messenger) will bring you the news.'[10]

Rosenthal notes that in the medieval Islamic literature it is "constantly stressed that wine causes quarrelsomeness, and hashish a kind of languid placidity. It is noteworthy... that no truly violent actions directed against other persons under the influence of hashish are mentioned in any of our stories" (Rosenthal, 1971). As a more recent proponent of this view explained "actual wine, while enjoyable and even spiritually refreshing in moderation, seems only rarely to produce in humans... the true dionysan ecstasis... but cannabis inspires some of its devotees with precisely the sort of 'state' which the Koran appears to associate with paradisal wine, which 'causes no headaches,' and enhances the play of houris and cup boys" (Wilson, 1988).

Interestingly, hashish use was thought to be particularly prominent in the main sect that formed around the teachings of the 'heretic' Imam Isma'il, who themselves came to be known as the aforementioned Isma'ili.

There can be no doubt that the use of hemp as an intoxicant was encour-

HASCHISCH   Alfred Zimmermann (München)

Fig 19.1: A 1910 illustration by Alfred Zimmerman, depicting a kief smokers vision of a houri.

10   From a translation in (Rosenthal, 1971)

aged by the Ismailians in the 8th century, as its effects tended to assist their followers in realizing the tenets of the sect:

"We've quaffed the emerald cup, the mystery we know,
Who'd dream so weak a plant such mighty power could show!"(Dymock, 1893)

The above reference, which I was unable to trace beyond Dymock, seems to indicate a drink of some sort. As the Isma'ili and related sects were accused of drinking wine and consuming hashish, and the Isma'ili initially arose in Persia – the home of Zoroastrianism, alongside Muhammad's own Zoroastrian-like shamanic flight, one is left with the reasonable speculation that perhaps the hidden "7th" Imam, Isma'il, had taken it upon himself to sample of the mang (cannabis) laced wine that had been the prize of the priesthood and royalty in that area for more than a millennia. Such a situation would account for the use of hashish in initiation ceremonies by the branch of the Isma'ili that came to be known as the Assassins and also certain Sufi sects that were known to have been influenced by them. An 'out of turn' sampling of such a holy sacrament, could also be a reason for the controversy surrounding the persona of Isma'il, for as we have seen from the Zoroastrian period, the use of cannabis was restricted to a select few and the king.

In relation to this, it is interesting to note that both the Persian Sufi Sheikh Haydar and his followers, and the Isma'ili Assassins, are believed by some sources to have consumed their hashish by mixing it with wine. The 19th century pioneer of cannabis medicines, Dr. William Brooke O'Shaughnessy, suggested: "A tincture of the hemp leaf in wine or spirit seems to have been the favorite formula in which Sheikh Haider [sic.] indulged himself. An Arab poet sings of Haider's emerald cup, an evident allusion to the rich green color of the tincture" (O'Shaughnessy, 1843). Peter Wiley, in his book on Ismaili castles, published in association with Institute of Ismaili Studies, wrote that the original stories indicate "the assassins were... given wine laced with hashish" (Willey, 2005).

Although seen as particularly heretical, in the medieval Islamic world, the "combination of wine and hashish was quite often attempted...":

A respectable scholar found nothing wrong in using both wine and hashish on the same occasion. The combination was praised as engendering at the same time "the laziness of hashish and energy of wine." Similarly, Ibrahim al m'mar (d. 749/1348), called in this connection "master of the craft"... might wonder about the extraordinary effects of wine plus hashish:

> He mixed hashish with wine
> And died of intoxication and became confused on the spot,
> And I asked: what is this unexpected occurrence?
> When he was sober (again), he answered me saying;
> Be kind to your brother when he mixes.

However, the combination was considered as particularly sinful... (Rosenthal, 1971)

As noted in Chapter 15, the pre-Islamic use of cannabis laced wines in Persia is well established. The 19th century work, *The History of Ancient and Modern Wines* by Dr. Henderson, indicates that such combinations continued in the Islamic world for some centuries: "The Jews and Armenians prepare wine on purpose for the Mahomedans, by adding lime, hemp, and other ingredients, to increase its pungency and strength; for the wine that soonest intoxicates is accounted best, and the lighter and delicate kinds are held in no estimation among the adherents of the Prophet" (Henderson, 1824). As Charles Dickens also noted:

The best vineyards of Persia are situated in the mountainous districts that stretch from the Persian Gulf to the Caspian Sea. Sixty-five kinds of grape are grown there, its cultivation being abandoned to the Ghebers, the Armenians, and the Jews; for, though the Mohammedan part of the population drink wine without scruple, they assert that the infringement of the law of Islam consists in making the wine, not in drinking it—a convenient conclusion, which satisfies their consciences, and enables them to gratify their inclinations. Pure wine, however, is not for the topers of Ispahan and Teheran, the Jewish and Armenian dealers ministering to that fondness for narcotics which tend so greatly to enervate the East, by mixing myrrh, incense, and the juice of the Indian hemp with the finest growths. (Dickens, 1862)

The Hashish-Takers

The Nizari "Assassins" represent yet another schism in a chain of Islamic sects that spring from pre-existing cults while still managing to maintain certain Islamic and even pre-Islamic tenets and beliefs. The Nizari Assassins first appeared in the late eleventh century as an offshoot of the Isma'ili, a split which was again the result of a hereditary dispute over claim to the title of Imam, with the sect this time forming around the 11th century heir designate Nizar. They called themselves "Nizaris" or "Fida'i," meaning the "faithful ones." But, to other Muslims they were known as the "hashishiyyum," a derogatory term meaning 'hashish taker', which linguistically developed into "Assassin' as legends of the cult spread to Europe,.

> ...Muslim historians, mainly from the thirteenth century, ...use the term *hashishiyya* in reference to the Nizaris of Syria (al-Sham); while the Nizaris of Persia are called *hashishis* in some Caspian Zaydi texts. Evidently the term has only been used once in any known Isma ili source; namely in the second half of the highly polemical epistle issued in the 1120s, by the Fatimid caliph al-Amir against his Nizari adversaries who eventually assassinated him." (Daftary, 1992)

The origins of the term 'Hashishin' has been a matter of much debate. "The etymology of the word 'Assassin' is said to come from Hashishin, i.e. hashish-taker.[11] It was transmitted through the Romance language by the Crusaders who in the 12th century, fearful of this sect, associated their daring killings with the power of the drug" (Palgi, 1975). Although some authorities see an origin for the name through "Hashish" an Arabic word thought to mean "grass" or "herbage" others claim the name "Hashashin" is derived from the Persian 'hassasin', which holds connotations of "healer" or "herb seller." Still others see the origins of the name coming though "followers of Hassan" in reference to a prominent figure in the cult, Hassan-i Sabbah, the notorious childhood friend of the famous Islamic poet Omar Khayyam, who was known variously as the "Old Man of the Mountain," "Shiek of Alamut" and "Keeper of Hashish." Adding to this, as we are dealing with a hereditary cult, one could

---

11   Some sources say the term also means "producer of hashish."

also speculate that an etymological connection might be found in the name of the tribe Muhammad came from, "*Hashim.*"

> ...[T]he nickname, and with it, the drug's extended use, appear to have surfaced during the late eleventh century, and both may have been promoted by the real or alleged use of cannabis by sectarians who were engaged in spreading a vast network of open and secret influence over the Muslim world... (Rosenthal, 1971)

The Hashishin clearly considered themselves the guardians of sacred knowledge and tradition, and this is evident in some of the other names the sect has been known under such as "Batiniyya," meaning the "esoterics" and from their detractors, "Malahida," "the heretics." Usually based in mountain fortresses, such as the famous Alamut, between the 11th and 13th centuries the Hashishin spread from Persia into Syria, central Asia and India, using assassination as only one of a number of methods of achieving their aims.

The Assassins stronghold at Alamut fell to the Mongrols around 1256. The Mongrols slaughtered the inhabitants, destroyed the castles and burnt the libraries, leaving little in the way of historical material regarding the sect's beliefs. Survivors and supporters made a number of attempts to regain control of the Alamut and other fortifications, but were continually defeated. In following years, like accusations of witchcraft in Europe, the punishment for anyone suspected of being a hashsishin was death, and it was common for political and social rivals to claim that their enemies were secret members of the sect. For several centuries after this period, both the Isma'ili Imam and their closest devotees traveled in disguise, taking the garb of a tailor, or Sufi mystic master and followers, and it is was through this covert period of the Isma'ilism that Iranian Sufism received its greatest influence of Isma'ili philosophy.

As the legendary and sensationalized 13th century account of the Assassins by Marco Polo recorded, prior to their fall, novices being initiated into the sect were alleged to have been tricked through the use of hashish and a hidden garden within the mountain top castle of the Assassins in Alamut, into believing they had received a foretaste of the afterlife paradise described in the Koran:

The Grand Master of the Assassins, whenever he discovers a young man resolute enough to belong to his murderous legions . . . invites the youth to his table and intoxicates him with the plant "hashish." Having been secretly transported to the pleasure gardens the young man imagines that he has entered the Paradise of Mahomet.

The girls, lovely as Houris, contribute to the illusion. After he has enjoyed to satiety all the joys promised by the Prophet to his elect, he falls back to the presence of the Grand Master. Here he is informed that he can enjoy perpetually the delights he has just tasted If he will take part in the war of the Infidel as commanded by the Prophet. (Marco Polo, 12th century)[12]

It should be remembered that Marco Polo's and other European accounts were based on myths and half-truths that grew around the Assassins, who were considered heretics by orthodox Islam and Crusaders alike. The ruins of the Assassins' castle still exist, and no evidence of a hidden garden as described have been found. Thus Antoine Sylvestre de Sacy in early 19th century account was likely a little closer to the mark:

...[T]here might be some exaggeration in the Venetian travelers account,... rather than believe in the existence of enchanted gardens..., we should reduce all the wonders of that magnificent place to a phantom produced by the exalted imagination of young men intoxicated with hashish, who, from their infancy, had been nursed with this idea of happiness, it would be no less true that we find here the idea of a liquor to deaden the senses, and we cannot forget that its use or abuse is spread throughout a great part of Asia and Africa. At the time of Ismaili power these intoxicating preparations were not yet known in Moslem countries. It was only later that knowledge of them was brought from the eastern regions, perhaps from India, into the Persian provinces. From there it was communicated to the Moslems of Asia Minor, Mesopotamia, Syria, and Egypt. No doubt the Ismailis, whose doctrine had several points of resemblance with those of the Indian, had acquired this knowledge earlier and preserved it as a precious secret, one of the main sources of their power.... (de Sacy, 1809)[13]

As we have shown in this study, cannabis has a long and ancient history in many of the places de Sacy refers to as not knowing it;

12   As translated in (Geller & Boas, 1969).
13   From an excerpt in (Kimmens, 1977)

however the 19th century scholar was correct in noting that cultural influences likely resulted in the Islamic paradise-themed visions of the Assassins, in the same way the mythology of the Zoroastrian religion effected the partakers of *mang*. As well, de Sacy also correctly pointed to the inherent similarities between the cosmologies of the Persian Isma'ili and Indian influences.

The fida'i were few in number compared to their enemies, so all-out war was not a viable option. As the story has it, the Islamic devotees who had been through this form of initiation willingly assassinated enemies of the cult. Like the terrorists of today, it was believed that the Assassins "were especially threatening because they had no fear of death. If they were to die in the execution of their mission they were hailed as martyrs and promised eternal life in a secret garden of paradise. Indeed, most of the assassinations they carried out were suicide missions, usually committed in public in broad daylight and with little opportunity for the Assassin to escape" (Sutton, 2002). Such assassinations were said to take place after the devotee had placed himself beyond suspicion, months or even years prior, as a servant or friend of a selected enemy of the cult, eventually unsuspectedly striking at the ideal time. This was seen as an alternative way of striking a specific enemy, rather than going to war and being outnumbered by an army and losing the lives of many as a result.

As well, secret drugging of potential devotees with hashish as claimed by Marco Polo is discounted by the fact that the "use and effects of *hashish* were known at the time, as best witnessed by the existence of the name *hashishiyya*. Therefore the drug could not have been the secret property of the Nizari chiefs... (Daftary, 1992). It should also be noted that the hashish was used as an initiatory substance directed at invoking a mystical experience rather than inducing a frenzied state of murderous rage for assassination as has been suggested.;

> The drug employed for initiation into the cult was used to obtain a vision of paradise. It did not nerve them up for slaughter, was not used during their missions and did not make them crazy. Quite the contrary, it... gave them at least a fleeting glimpse of an altogether higher order of existence. If anything, political and religious intrigue, not hashish, caused assassination. (Aldrich, 1978)

In his medieval dissertation on Hashish, al-Badri referred to an elaborate hashish eating ritual attributed to a Shaykh Qalandar, which gives us some idea as to the piety and intent of the medieval mystics that were using the drug:

> You must know that it behoves the intelligent, educated, virtuous, and sophisticated individual, who wishes to use this drug which has the advantage over wine of being lawful, to cleanse his body of impurity and his garments of stains and adorn himself with the acquisition of the virtues and to discard the commission of the vices. He must ask for it someone who knows its secret and disapproves of keeping it concealed, and eat it in his place and not partake of it in the company of non-users. He must hold it in his right, not in his left, and say:
>
> "In the name of God, the Lord of the last world and the first, who brought forth the pasturage (qur'an 87: 4/4), created and then formed (87: 2/2), provided and gave, destined and guided (87: 3/3), and taught the secret and disclosed (it). May God pray for Muhammad, the prophet of right guidance, and his companions, the leader in piety! (I know) that you have deposited wisdom in Your creatures and created usefulness in the things You have made. You have shown their specific properties to those with whom You are pleased, and revealed their secrets to those whom You have chosen. You have managed this plant with Your wisdom, brought it forth with Your power, and made it a nourishment for many of Your creatures by Your decision, volition, power, and will. Thus I am asking you by Your generosity that encompasses the elite and the common people, to let me succeed in using it in obedience to You and with avoidance of any disobedience to You, that you remove from me desires with their hindrances, the doubts with their consequences, and the troubles with their disturbances, that You let me see the existent things that really are, and that you provide me with the benefits and ward off from me its harmful results, You who has the power over everything and sees every situation!"
>
> He then puts it into his mouth, grinds... it very strongly (with his teeth), drinks (something to go) with it, moves his jaws, and sends it down into his guts. Then he praises God for his kindness. He cleanses his mouth of its remnants, washes his face, and raises his voice in song... for the Creator of beauty, for (beauty) provokes hashish intoxication... and rest. He rubs antimony on his teeth so that coarser souls... will not notice

what is the matter with him, and he braids the hair of his beard. Cheerfulness (?) does not leave his mind, and he is restful (?) in the way he walks and in his commands and prohibitions. He uses the most delicate food and the noblest of sweet speech. He gazes at beautiful faces and sits in the most pleasant of places. He stays near where water is murmuring, and keeps company with experienced friends. He turns to reflecting about the cause and the thing caused, about doer and thing done, about event and result, about speaker and thing spoken, and about agent in sweetness (?) and the thing caused by action. In this condition, (enough) of the eternal knowledge of God and His universal grace emanates upon him to let him perceive the views and their meanings and to show him the things with their contents. He notices the heart with the eyes and controls the eyes with the hearts. He separates from his idea of humanity and joins with the idea of divinity. The name of which the poor are known... becomes lawful for him in reality, and he reaches the degree of divine success... (al-Badri, 1463)[14]

Shayk Qalandar warned against the improper use of cannabis and also against revealing its secrets to the common people, "dissimulation was considered necessary to throw the uninitiated off the users scent..." (Rosenthal, 1971).

...[T]here can be little doubt that hashish was rather widely employed by... [Sufis] as a... aid for achieving enlargement of the individual's... spiritual perceptions. By tasting the "secret" and the "meaning" of hashish, Sufis... hoped to gain... mystic experience... they made... the use of the drug "an act of worship"... (Rosenthal, 1971)

According to legend, hashish was first introduced to the Sufis by the Persian Isma'ili Shayk Haydar (1155-1221) and some have even claimed Haydar was also the source of the penetration of cannabis in the Islamic world (Houtsma, et al., 1936/1993).

The story has it that after years of silent recluse, Haydar one day decided to leave his monastery. While walking in the desert, he noticed a plant that seemed to sparkle and shiver as it basked in the still desert heat. Wondering what this mysterious plant was, he felt compelled to taste of its leaves and flowers

---

14   As translated in (Rosenthal, 1971).

Usually a reserved and silent man, when he returned to his monastery afterwards his disciples were amazed at how talkative and animated he seemed. Cajoling Haydar into telling them what he had done to make himself so happy, his disciples ran off into the desert to try the magical plant for themselves.

Upon the return of the plant's new devotees, Haydar made them take an oath to refrain from revealing the mystery of the herb, telling them "God has granted you the privilege of knowing the secret of these leaves. Thus when you eat it, your dense worries may disappear and your exalted minds may become polished."

After living another ten years as the Sufi's psychedelic shaykh, subsisting mainly on cannabis preparations, Haydar passed on, leaving the request that seeds of his holy plant be sown around his tomb, so that even in death he might enjoy the shade of its leaves and scent of its flowers. (Bennett, 2001)

In relation to the use of cannabis-infused wine in Persia noted in Chapter 15, it is worth noting that it has been reported: "A tincture of hemp leaves in wine or spirit seems to have been the favorite formula in which Sheikh Haidar indulged himself" (Pharmacal Advance, 1930).

As Ahmet Karamustufa notes in his excellent *God's Unruly Friends: Dervish Groups in the Islamic Later Middle Period, 1200-1550*, Sufi groups like that formed around the teachings of Shayk Qalandar and Shayk Haydar were criticized for their traditional pre-Islamic Persian influences, and as noted Haydar is believed to have preferred the Persian method of ingesting cannabis (mang) infused wine for his own use. In 761/1359-60 a decree was issued which "forbade the Qalandars to shave and dress in the manner of Iranians and magi" (Karamustafa, 2006).

In the Syrian and Egyptian cultural spheres, the Qalandariyah appears to have continued throughout the seventh-eighth/thirteenth-fourteenth centuries mostly as an Iranian group... also the Haydariyah... were viewed as foreign, predominantly Iranian, phenomena. (Karamustafa, 2006)

Fig 19.2: Qalander (Green, 2009)

Other sects, however, regarded their traditional use of cannabis, as part of the typically Biblical and Islamic tradition. There is a huge Islamic cannabis tradition based around the prophet Elijah, under the name Khidr, to be discussed shortly, but the fascinating medieval band of musical dervishes known as the Abdals

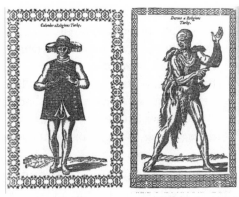

Fig 19.3: Left Abdal of Rum, Right Haydari, (Karamustafa, 2006)

of Rum, believed their own copious use of hashish could be traced back to the earliest of Biblical figures.

> ...Abdals maintained that the Prophet Adam was their model for many of their practices. When he was expelled from Paradise, Abdals explained, Adam was completely naked except for a fig-leaf that he used to cover his private parts and had to survive on "green leaves" only. Similarly, Abdals wandered around naked except for a tennure symbolizing Adam's fig-leaf and consumed hashish ("green leaves") in considerable quantities. Their nudity was a symbol of "tearing the garment of the body" and the nothingness of this world. Hashish was a means to find respite from the unreal phenomena of time and space and to attain the hidden nature of reality.
>
> ....They were very fond of food (a long list of dishes is provided). The meals were followed by hashish-taking and musical sessions... They normally slept on the ground and were awakened with the sound of a horn, a symbol of the trumpets of archangel Israfil: thus every morning was likened to resurrection. Abdals were free from all prescribed religious observances since they were not really in this world at all. (Karamustafa, 2006)

The Abdals were also particularly devoted to Mohammed's son-in-law Ali, who we discussed for his influence over Isma'ili sects like the Hashishin. "A picture of 'Ali's sword was drawn or his name was written on their chests.... Their true guide was Ali" (Karamustafa, 2006). That the Abdals use of hashish was done with true Islamic religious intent is amply demonstrated by the contemporary account of the sect by the 16th century writer Giovanni Antonio Menavino:

....After the meal, the chief rises to his feet and the rest do likewise. They say a prayer to God and then all cry out in a loud voice *Ala-cabu Eilege*, that is, may God accept this our prayer. Also among them are certain youths called *cuccegler*, who carry in certain hand-trays a pulverized herb called *asseral*,[15] which, when eaten, makes one merry just as if one had drunk wine. First the chief then all the others in order take this into their hands and eat, and this done, read of the book of the new story. (Menavino, 16th century)[16]

After the story, music and dancing ensued in an ecstatic hashish intoxicated form of medieval worship. The Abduls "were very fond of consuming hashish and wine. They... claim to have completely subdued the animal soul and to have attained the state of 'death before death'" (Karamustafa, 2006).

In *The Dervishes, Or, Oriental Spiritualism*, John Porter offers some enlightening insights about the use of hashish in the Islamic world:

The first intention of Hasheesh was evidently not as a stimulant. It was intended as a "spiritual" soporific, producing that quiescence of soul so dear to Orientals, and known throughout all the regions under Arabian influence by the name of "Kaif."[17] But this stolid annihilation of ideas was not sufficient for the more exalted natures; these found a higher power in the drug — that of raising the imagination until it attained to a beatified realization of the joys of a future world. (Brown, 1868)

Another 19th century Persian scholar, Edward G. Browne noted in "A Chapter from the History of Cannabis Indica,"[18] that use of hemp preparations in the area extended from Zoroastrian times to the 19th century, where its use was still deeply cloaked in the Isma'ilian mystical beliefs about the plant:

...Cannabis Indica... appears to have been known in Persia in very early times, as students of the ancient Zoroastrian scriptures as-

---

15   This name is probably related to the term '*esrar*', meaning 'secret'. "As much was made of addicts of the ability of hashish to show them 'secret meanings', or, as we might say, to open up for them new levels of mental perception, it is not surprising to find 'secrets' (*esrar*) as a commonly employed nickname for hashish among the Turks." (Rosenthal, 1971).
16   As translated in (Karamustafa, 2006).
17   As noted in Chapter 11, occultist Oliver Bland suggested that the term "*kaif*" originated with the name of the Egyptian "*kyphi*" perfume and incense, which was believed by some sources to contain cannabis (Bland, 1920).
18   Reprinted in (Bey & Zug, 2004)

sert, allusion is made to it in the Avesta... At the present day it is extensively used here... as the inspirer of the wildest pantheistic speculations, the most disordered metaphysical phantasies, and the most incredible visions and ecstasies. It is known generally as *hashish* – an Arabic word meaning cut grass or dried herbs, - or by its Persian name, *bang*. Besides these there are special preparations known by special names, such as *chars*, *barsh*, [related to *barsom*?] and *hub-i-nishat*, or "pills of delight," of which preparations the first is smoked, the last two eaten... At present as I am informed by one of my Persian friends, the method most fashionable amongst the dervishes of Tehran is to employ the *bug-i-wahadat*, or "trumpet of unity." A small piece of paper or cardboard is rolled up into the shape of a funnel, of which the smaller end of the funnel is placed in the mouth. A piece of *chars*, laid on the lighted end of a cigarette, is then held under the larger end of the funnel, and the smoke of the burning hemp is then inhaled. The effects of the drug are produced much more rapidly when it is smoked than when it is eaten. Subjectively it produces an extraordinary dislocation of the ideas of times, space and personality...it seems that all those present in the assembly are in reality animated by one spirit and that the barricades of personality and individuality are, in some inexplicable way, broken down. It is this sensation or illusion which is specially craved after by the dervishes, who find therein a foretaste of Nirvana, or Absorption into the Universal Spirit, which is the aim of their pantheistic mysticism to attain; and this is the "unity" alluded to in the name of the bug-i-wahadat of which I have spoken. (Browne, 1897)

The sense of ego-obliteration, or what one medieval hashish using poet saw as the "removal from existence in existence,"[19] possible with cannabis preperations, as in the case of the *bug-i-wahadatin* in the description above, was likened to a mortal death in medieval literature. This was also true of the use of hashish itself, which had to be sacrificed, i.e. eaten, to have an effect, "puns on the term 'to kill' [were] used in connection with the preparation and use of hashish... {A] play upon the 'killing' of hashish... is apparently the case in a verse stating that 'the green one' is 'a *hashishah* that makes every man a *hashishi* (assassin) unbeknown to himself' " (Rosenthal, 1971).

Such future-worldly and "pantheistic" associations with cannabis amongst the Persian *Hashishin* and Sufis as those cited above, have clear parallels in the preceding Zoroastrian religion. As the

---

19   Cf. al-Badri in (Rosenthal, 1971)

'Assassins' grew out of the Islamic Persian sect the Isma'ilis, the use of cannabis can well be seen as a remnant of the earlier Zoroastrian tradition. Some medieval sources recorded that the intoxicating properties of cannabis were known in pre-Muhammadan times under the Sassanian King Khusraw Parwez,[20] (590-628 A.D.), which seems a likely source considering the similar shamanic use of cannabis and the evidence that the consumption of *mang* (hemp) laced haoma or wine was likely carried on by the Sassanian priesthood and royalty right up until the fall of their Empire to Islam.

Others have suggested that the introduction of hashish into Islam may have come via Zoroastrians secretly hiding as Sufis during periods where conversion to Islam was made mandatory with a death penalty for those that refused (Herer, 1990; Bennett, et al., 1995). "The Gathas, or hymns of Zoroaster... particularly the Haoma Yasht... might supply a source of the 'spiritual wine' of the Sufis, and of the hasheesh... of the Assassins..." (Carus, 1918). A Zoroastrian influence on the Assassins was noted early on by Islamic author al-Busti (1029 A.D.), who traced Isma'ilian beliefs to "Iranian dualistic and Zoroastrian origins" (Daftary, 2004).

Referring to the Ismaili's syncretic connections between Islam and Zoroastrianism, Claude Reignier Conder commented that up until his time "The... Ism'ailiyeh preserve the grades of initiation, allegorical interpretation of the Koran, beliefs in transmigration, and a sacred libation (the haoma). The lower orders believe in the worship of sun, moon, and stars, and celebrate (it is said) annual orgies of a phallic character" (Conder, 1886). As Littel & Littel's 1883 edition of *The Living Age* similarly recorded of the sect:

> The Ismalleh sect.... are the most degraded and poverty-stricken of all the inhabitants of Syria. They are a medieval remnant of the medieval assassins or "hemp smokers"[21] (Hashishisn).... The old Haoma ritual still survives among these heretics, together with a veneration of the sun, moon and planets, and stars, which is most probably of Persian derivation. (Littel & Littel, 1883)

Another interesting factor regarding the Islamic use of hashish and the Persian tradition of haoma, is that at least until the late 19th cen-

---

20   (Houtsma, et al, 1936/1993).
21   This seems an unlikely translation, as smoking of cannabis and/or hashish in pipes in the Old World is generally thought to only have occurred after the New World introduction of smoked tobacco products, although the possibility of hashish or cannabis based incense does remain. (Bennett, 2005)

tury, there is an account of a cannabis beverage under the name of 'homa' was being taken in Syria by the Nosairiyeh tribesmen, a group often confused with the Isma'ilis by historians due to some similarities in belief (although the two sects have feuded for a thousand years[22]). Indeed, the above 19th century references of Littel & Littel and Conder may be evidence of this confusion between the two related sects. " [M]odern schoarlship... has come to see the Nusa'iri... as offshoots of twelfth-century... Isma'ilism..." (Deveney, 1997).

Orthodox Muslims of the 11th and 12th centuries saw the name Nosairiyeh as being derived from "Nasarini," meaning "little Christians" and considered them a remnant of the heretical ancient Christian Gnostic sects. The Nosairiyeh, or Ansayree (minus the elision of 'N') can still be found in isolated mountainous areas of Syria, as well as in areas of Palestine, Kurdistan, Egypt and Iran. "What has mainly set the Nusa'iris apart and made them the object of persecution and massacre by more orthodox Muslims... and Crusaders alike is the belief that they practiced the pagan and Gnostic sexual rites of antiquity" (Deveney, 1997). Writing in the mid 19th century Habeeb Risk Allah Effendi commented:

> By some... the Nosairiyeh are considered to be an aboriginal tribe, which has survived the many changes that have swept over the country, and have preserved such peculiar traits as distinguish them from all other inhabitants... I am inclined to believe that this is the case; and I am also disposed to regard them as probably a sect of heretical Christians, who having originally retired among the mountains to secure the free exercise of their opinions, thus became isolated... (Effendi, 1854)

Referring to "The Nusiereh," Littel & Littel noted that some "have identified them with the Manichean Gnostics, but the points of resemblance are more probably due to the Persian origins of many of the tenets of Manes... [T]hey themselves connect their mystic Eucharist with the Christian rite, as well as with the 'veiling of the Lord in light that is in the eye of the Sun'" (Littel & Littel, 1887). Conder also commented the Nosairiyeh's mixing of the Zoroastrian and Christian traditions, noting that sect still preserves "this curious syncretic system with a Eucharistic supper, and a ceremony of

---

22   Like many of the battles found amongst faiths of identical origins, this has been described "a struggle over theological niceties that has masked the fundamental areas of agreement amongst them" (Deveny, 1996).

'consecrating the Fragrant Herb,' probably originating in the haoma worship of the Persians" (Conder, 1886). From the Zoroastrian influenced Christian Gnostic texts of the *Nag Hammadi Library* discussed in Chapter 17 we can see this mixing of traditions went back very far indeed.

Haoma in the 19th century

Not much is known of the Nosairiyeh cosmology, as they were highly secretive. "The Nusseiriyeh conceal their religion from the outer world with the greatest care, and do not even initiate their own sons into its mysteries until they have arrived at years of discretion; the women are never initiated at all" (Besant and Palmer, 1871).

The following description of a Nosairiyeh Haoma ritual from just over a century ago, may give us some insights into the 'orgiastic' activities which accompanied the ritual consumption of Haoma in the Ancient Near East, and also for Zoroaster's reforms. As the sensational 1895, *New York Herald* story "Orgies of the Hemp Eaters"[23] describes (with original illustrations included):

ORGIES OF THE HEMP EATERS.

Hashish Dreamers' Festival in North-western Syria Occurs at the Time of the Full Moon.

WOMEN JOIN THE CEREMONY.

Scenes at the Sacred Dance That Surpass the Wildest Ecstasy of Any Opium Dream.

Fig 19.4

THE DRUG AND ITS EFFECTS.

Standing in the outskirts of the little town of Latakieh, in North-western Syria, famous everywhere for the excellent tobacco which takes its name from the otherwise obscure and insignificant place - and turning his back on the ramshackle houses the flea infested caravansary, the malodorous bazaar and garbage strewn streets, where the scavenger dogs lie stretched out [in the] noonday sun - the traveller sees in the distance, beyond a wide stretch of green slope and alternate level, a low range of hills, on which a soft purple haze[24] seems always to linger. These hills

---

23   Reprinted in *The Dope Chronicles* (1979).
24   Shades of Jimi Hendrix!

lie between the Lebanon, where the fierce Druses dwell in their highland fastnesses, and the Nahr-el-kebir, "The Mighty River." They are known nowadays as the Nosairie Mountains, the home of the so-called Nosairiyeh tribesmen, the modern "Assassins," or "Hemp Eaters," as they should be designated from their ceremonial use of hemp, in Arabic "hashish."

The festival or gathering of the hemp eaters is celebrated monthly, at the time of the full moon, the moon being then supposed to exert a specific influence upon human beings.[25] The sectaries meet under a sacred oak tree growing upon a hill....

Fig 19.5

There is an enormous drum, some three feet in diameter, standing at the entrance to the village... and as soon as it begins to darken... a deafening boom comes from the instrument and rolls over the mountain tops like the rumble of thunder, rousing the tribesmen to activity, and in a moment they are on the alert. Lamps are quickly lit and suspended to the branches of the sacred oak among the dangling rags and buttons and feathers and metal scraps that decorate it. A square heap of wood is built up in front of the tree.... A sheep is brought forward by one of the men, and the rest of the tribesmen then gather around... The Sheikh puts his hand gently on the head of the bleating animal, it is thrown down, its throat cut... the carcass is divided and placed on the wood heap, to which fire is applied and kept up till all flesh as well as timber is utterly consumed. Now the Nosarriyeh seat themselves in a circle upon the earth, the Shiekh in the centre, with an attendant on either hand, one holding a large earth-

25   The full moon is also a special time for the Soma sacrifice.

enware bowl containing a liquid, the other a bundle of stems to which leaves are attached[26] – the leaves of the sacred hemp plant. The chief takes the stems in his left and the bowl in his right hand and slowly walks around the circle, stopping in front of each man present, who takes from him, first the greenery, at which he sniffs gently, then the bowl, the contents of which he sips. The vessel contains a sweetened infusion of hemp, strong and subtle in its action.

WHAT THE DECOCTION IS LIKE

The taste of the decoction is sweet, nauseously so... and its first effects are anything but pleasant, for it produces a distinct tendency to vomit... As soon as all have in succession partaken of the drink, which is termed "*homa*," big horns are produced containing spirits, for the Nosarriyeh are great dram drinkers. The horns of liquor are passed about and in a few moments the effects are apparent, following upon the hemp. The eyes brighten, the pulse quickens, the blood seems to bound more actively in the veins, and a restlessness takes possession of the whole body. At this moment the booming of a giant drum is heard again, giving the signal for the sacred dance which is the next item in the ceremonial of the evening. From each of the dozen parties or so into which the clansmen are divided one steps out, and the dozen individuals so designated form up against a gentle declivity in rear of them. Two of the tribe with a "reba," one string fiddle, and a tambourine, seat themselves and start a peculiar air in a minor key, which all those around take up, clapping their hands the while rhythmically, and to this rhythm the dancers, joining hands as they stand, begin to move gently to and fro.

The moonlight is full on them, showing up their white nether garments, but leaving the dusky faces and dark upper garments in a semi-shadow. First the dancers move slowly, a few steps to the right and further to the left they go each time, till the movement becomes a positive allegro. Faster goes the music, faster the dancers, until with a finale furioso the men stop, panting and out of breath, at the signal of the Sheikh. He claps his hands and twelve others step out, and the figure begins as before. When these are exhausted a fresh set take their place, and this is continued until each of the clansmen has taken part in the dance. In conclusion all join hands and go seven times round the sacred oak in the direction left to right.

26   Is this a surviving tradition of the barsom? I.e. bundle of haoma, see Chapter 5.

A CRAZY FESTIVAL

The solemn supper is now ready, and is served by the wives of the tribesmen, who have been busy preparing it in huge earthern-ware dishes placed upon the ground in the middle of each group. And the moonlight meal in the shade of the sacred oak is none the less striking by reason of its being dished up by women who wear in their sash-bands a sharp yataghan, of which the handle shows clearly, and a brace of pistols in the girdle. The plates are peculiar... Each person has a wooden spoon to eat with, and the etiquette of the table requires one to eat much and eat quickly, and to drink as much as one eats. The appetites of the Nosairiyeh are proverbial in Syria, the usual allowance of meat being a sheep or two. I can vouch for their tippling powers. Scores of them finish their pint horn of arrack in a couple of draughts, taking a couple of quarts in the course of their supper. The meal is really a match against time, and, with such good trencher men as the hemp eaters, is quickly finished.

The real business of the evening now begins. The hemp, pow-dered and mixed with sirup[27] [sic], is brought round in bowls, together with the decoction of the leaves well sweetened. Each of the tribesmen secures a vessel of arrack -- for it quickens and heightens the action of the drugs -- and disposes himself in the most comfortable attitude he can think of. Then, taking a good spoonful of the hemp, and washing it down with an equally good

---

27   "Soma was a non-alcoholic *syrup* like thing prepared out of the juice of Soma-plant" (Regmi, 1940).

drink from the liquor receptable [sic], he lies or leans back to allow it to operate. I take a reasonable allowance of the compound (it tastes very much like raw tea leaves flavoured [sic] with sugar water), and then lie back to note the action on my own person, and watch, so far as I can, its effects upon the modern assassins whose systems are seasoned and more accustomed to the drug. Five, ten minutes pass, and there is no sensation; the men around me, with closed eyes, look like waxwork figures. Another ten minutes, and the pulse begins to beat rapidly, the heart commences to thump against the sides of the chest, the blood seems to rush to the head, and there is a sensation of fullness, as if the skull would be burst asunder at the base. There is a roaring in the ears, and strange lights, blurred and indistinct, pass before the eyes. In a moment and quite suddenly all of this passes off, leaving a feeling of delicious languor, and an idea that one is rising from the ground and floating in space. Little things assume an enormous size, and things seem far off.

Fig 19.7

EFFECTS OF THE DRUG.
The oak tree close by appears to be a mile off, and the cup of drink looks a yard across, the size of a big barrel. One's hands and feet feel heavy and cumbersome, and then feel as if they were dropping off, leaving one free to soar away from the earth skyward, where the clouds seem to open to receive one, and one long perspective of light shines before the eyes. The feeling is one of estatic [sic] restfulness, contented unconsciousness, suggesting the "ninirvana" [sic] of the Buddhist. This marks always the end of the first stage of hemp eating. The aphrodisiac effects, the visions of fair faces and beauteous forms, the voluptuous dreams

and languishing fancies which the Easterns experience -- these are the results of larger and oft repeated doses of the drug.

Already the larger quantities of the compound, repeated many times in the meantime and stimulated by frequent draughts of arrack, are beginning to show their results upon the hitherto immobile figures of the Nosiariyeh round the sacred oak. Again and again they seize the spoon and convey it to their mouths, until the hemp craze is fully upon them. One or two stir uneasily; then another screams for "Ali, Ali!" (their founder Ali), who is identical, they say with Allah. A half a dozen respond lustily, "Ali hu Allah!" then empty the arrack cups beside them. A few move about with outstretched arms as though they were in the clouds trying to clutch the houris, whose imaginary forms they see, and disappointed, sink back, after a fresh supply of the drug has been swallowed. From the extremity beyond, where the women are located, come the sound of singing and of laugher and the rhythmic patter of feet upon the ground. The ladies have been indulging on their own account, and the noise they make rouses the men from their dreams. Three or four jump up from the floor at a single bound, and, seized by the dance mania, begin capering away as for very life. They jig here and there, they twine and twist, and writhe and wriggle and distort themselves, awakening [...fragment missing...] blows off his matchlock as he capers merrily round, while his neighbor [sic] stretches out his fingers for the arrack.

END OF THE HASHISH DEBAUCH

In the distance we hear the sound of the women's voices as they scream and sing and dance in a noisy whirl under the influence also of the intoxicating hemp. Again and yet again the tribesmen quaff from the hashish bowl, and the riot grows wilder and madder than before. It becomes a veritable saturnalia. Flushed and inflamed, they fly from side to side, tear to and fro, whirl round on the heels, skipping in the air and jumping feet high above the ground, to the banging of the great drum in the village; the shouting of those unable to move, the screeching of the "Reba," or fiddle, which still plays on, and the crackling of the guns as they go off. Scimitars are drawn, yataghans flourished, half a dozen engage in mimic combat, slashing and cutting at each other with an all too earnest resolve to draw blood – a result speedily obtained – while yet another batch dance round and round on their heels spinning like tops in play. Faster and furious grows the corybantic rout, and in their mad excitement the men tear the garments from their bodies, throw away their weapons, fling the turbans from their heads and, naked to the waist, with dishevelled hair and eyes ablaze and extended arms, they continue their mad antics, until foaming at the mouth and bleeding from the nostrils, they sink to the earth and lie huddled in heaps, hopelessly and helplessly intoxicated with the hemp.

With its full moon date, ritualistic connotations and animal sacrifice, along with the use of a hemp infused beverage, there are strong indications that this 19th century celebration is in fact a debased form of the ancient haoma ritual,[28] passed down by uncultured and illiterate tribesmen from generation to generation, confused by the advent and influence of Christianity and Islam, causing it to slowly shed the pomp and glory of ancient times, along with the meaning of its forgotten past and origins.....

Hakim Bey[29] notes that the most fascinating aspect of the "Orgies of the Hemp Eaters"[30] is the use of the word "Homa" noting the possibility that a "Zoroastrian influence – or even more intriguing, the possible survival of an ancient Indo-European word in its original meaning... in India Cannabis has in some sense become a kind of soma, prepared by modern-day saddhus and nagas according to a method already ancient in the time of the Rig Veda" (Bey, et al., 2004).

And in the Veda, the pressed-out juices of the Soma plant are sometimes described as green-tinted. 'Orgies of the Hemp Eaters', therefore, may offer some evidence for the continual existence of a Cannabis/haoma cult beginning perhaps 7000 years ago and continuing into the Islamic period and even today — thus making it one of the oldest unbroken spiritual traditions of humankind. (Bey, et al., 2004)

It seems unlikely that one could travel to Syria today and still find this version of the hemp-haoma rite being practiced. Besant and Palmer's 19th century similar but more subdued account of the rite, under the name of the "consecrating of the Fragrant Herb,"

---

28   In relation to the wild and ecstatic celebration of these 'Homa" drinking Syrian tribesmen, it is interesting to note the Prophet Zoroaster condemned the Haoma sacrifice for its excessive consumption of Haoma, orgiastic activity and animal sacrifices.

29   AKA Peter Lamborn Wilson.

30   Bey liked the title of the article so much, he took it for the title of his book on cannabis in the Indian and Arabic traditions.

Fig 19.8: 19th century Hemp Haoma Drinkers.

(here performed with more of a Christian influence), alludes to the substitution of olive branches for the "fragrant herb":

> The officiating priest takes his seat in the middle of the assembly, and a white cloth, containing a kind of spice, called Mahlab, camphor, and some sprigs of olive, or fragrant herb, is then placed before him. Two attendants then bring a vessel filled with wine, and the master of the house in which the ceremony takes place, after appointing a third person to minister to them, kisses their feet and hands all round, and humbly requests permission to provide the materials necessary for the feast. The high priest having prostrated himself on the ground, and uttered a short invocation to certain mystic personages, distributes the sprigs of olive among the congregation, who rub them on their hands, and place them solemnly to their nose to inhale their fragrance. (Besant and Palmer, 1871)

As Conder, who connected the Nosairiyeh rite with the haoma ceremony, also noted of this same passage: "It is difficult to understand smelling olive-sprigs, which are not fragrant; there is perhaps some misconception. The sprigs seem, however, to answer to the Barsom of Persia" (Conder, 1886).

Considering the Biblical import of the olive tree, one is clearly reminded of the Buddhist influences in the replacement of cannabis in the soma beverage with the Banyan tree, as in both accounts the entheogenic properties of hemp are substituted with a non-psychoactive placebo whose power lays solely in its mythical relationship with the religion, as also with the Catholic Eucharists of bread and wine, which as we have shown derives from the exact same origin of the haoma ceremony. Likely, due to cultural influences of orthodox Islam and the West, both of which frowned on the use of cannabis, and the combined confounding factor of the known secrecy of the Nosairiyeh themselves, the true identification of the "Fragrant Herb" originally used in the rite was lost in an almost identical way as the identity of soma in India, and haoma in Persia came to be. But the possibility that the secret has been retained by some of the older and more isolated branches of the sect does remain open.

Luckily the 19th century account recorded in "Orgies of the Hemp Eaters," leaves little doubt to the identity of the plant used in the "consecrating of the Fragrant Herb," and as with its origins in the tradition of the haoma ritual, we can safely conclude that it was cannabis.

Reminiscent of the mang (cannabis) infused wine used by Zoroastrian heroes, and related to the forbidden wine Mohammed's son in law, 'Ali, was said to have partaken of, the Nusayri still perform a rite known as the "ritual of the cup" involving the "wine of the angelic world" (malakut). This angelic world is analogous to the menog (spiritual realm) discussed in chapter 15 which Zoroastrian figures accessed with the aid of hemp infused wine or haoma. This ritual is directed at putting the partakers into contact with their ancestors and providing a means of connectivity to their shared heritage. Indicating the fusion between Islamic, Biblical and Zoroastrian influences at its core, in the invocations of the ritual "an entire cycle of Iranian history… is introduced alongside the cycles of Adam, Noah, Abraham, and Moses. Together, all heroes Mazdean and Abrahmic living in different cycles of history are each imagined in the shape of a dome. Time… is imagined spatially. All inhabitants of these seven domes have already taken part in the Ritual" (Babayan, 2002)

And when the drink has passed to all, then by this cup you hold in your hand, your bodies shall be filled for all periods and cycles to come. For you belong to the holy of holies, and you were of the Bahmanians [Iranians]. (Corbin 1998)[31]

As Kathryn Babayan explains in "Nusayri circles as the disciple drinks from the cup, he is aware of his Iranian past, remembering that in every cycle of history brothers not only partook in this same act but were made of the same substance. Through this imitative process, the novice experiences reincarnation through the seven cycles of history" (Babayan, 2002). As the liturgy from the right describes:

Behold this cup has circulated through the temple of the non-Arabs, throughout all the seven periods of the world. All of them are our brothers in faith and in gnosis... through the drink you have tasted the knowledge of the Malakut [angelic world], the knowledge of that which was in the first of the centuries and is throughout all the ages and cycles of the world. (Corbin, 1998)[32]

As Babayan notes, there 'is a sense of alchemical correspondence between homologous individuals who lived in different cycles of time. Such beliefs enabled Shah Isma'il to claim the reincarnation of... Kay Khusraw,[33] Alexander, Jesus, Muhammad and Ali" (Babayan, 2002). Although no explicit reference to cannabis occurs in these more current references to the Nusayri's "ritual of the cup," based upon what we know about the sects past, its known use of cannabis in earlier similar rituals, as well as the known Zoroastrian influence, it is hard not to see some connection in the spirit of the rites origins at the very least.

The Green One

As haoma was both a plant and a god in the Zoroastrian tradition, it is interesting to note that in medieval Islam a magical saint came to be the personification of hashish. As Franz Rosenthal explains cannabis' "green color enabled hashish to claim the fa-

---

31   As quoted in (Babyan, 2002)
32   Ibid
33   A Zoroastrian figure.

mous al-Khidr 'the green one' as its patron saint" (Rosenthal, 1971). As recorded by the medieval poet Fuzuli, both hashish and Khizr shared the epithet of the "Green One,"[34] and Sufi Mystics referred to the use of hashish as the "visit of the green Khidr," (Rosenthal, 1971). As J.M. Campbell recorded of Khizr's relationship with cannabis in his classic 1894 essay, "On the Religion of Hemp":

> In his devotion to bhang, with reverence, not with the worship, which is due to Allah alone, the North Indian Mussulman joins hymning to the praise of bhang. To the follower of the later religion of Islam the holy spirit in bhang is not the spirit of the Almighty, it is the spirit of the great prophet Khizr, or Elijah. That bhang should be sacred to Khizr is natural, Khizr is the patron saint of water. Still more Khizr means green, the revered color of the cooling water of bhang;. So the Urdu poet sings "When I quaff fresh bhang I liken its color to the fresh light down of thy youthful beard." The prophet Khizr or the green prophet cries "May the drink be pleasing to thee." (Campbell, 1894)

As noted, somewhat sensationally, by the Hope Evangelical Lutheran Church, Khidr is regarded in Islam as a key Biblical figure, Elijah, and the focus of his reverence likely originated with the Assassins and related sects.

> When Mohammed, the great Prophet of Islam, began relating his visions in Arabia he was, and remained, a teller of an oral tradition. He was familiar with the history of the Bible from the numerous Jews and Christians with whom he came into contact in his trading business, but oral tales are seldom related accurately, or completely, or in context. It cannot be known what Mohammed heard from other tellers, only what he related to his listeners.
> What is sure is that Muslims held and continue to hold the prophet Elijah in high esteem. To them he is Elyas, Khizr, or Khidr, the "Green Prophet," the "Verdant One" whose footsteps leave a green print. He is in effect a spirit of nature. On the Golan Heights, the Druze associate Elijah's brook of Cherith with the abundant springs of Banias, a location once sacred to the Hellen-

---

34   In medieval Islam, one "of the most common designations of hashish was *al-khadra*... 'the green one' alluding to its derivation from a highly ornamental green plant... Poets were particularly taken by the expression 'green one'..." (Rosenthal, 1971). Mythologicaly, Khidr is said to have taken the title after his body and clothing turned green after a dip in the Well of Life, which also bestowed him with immortality.

ic nature spirit Pan, whose temple is now buried in the collapsed caves from which the springs surge forth. A Druze oath sworn on the name of Elyas is considered unbreakable.

To certain Sufis, Elijah, as Khizr, became the patron saint of cannabis, an herb not forbidden to Muslims and whose properties were considered by some to be sacred. It is perhaps through this route that Elijah became the unwitting original of the Old Man of the Mountain whose Hashashin (Assassin) followers descended from their wilderness strongholds to wreak death upon the apostate and the enemies of Islam. This is not much of a stretch for it was from the wilderness that Elijah emerged to curse Israel for Ahab's apostasy. It was to the wilderness that he returned to escape the wrath of Ahab and Jezebel, and it was in the wilderness that he was sustained by food brought to him by the ravens or, as some translators argue, the Arabs. It is no surprise that Qal'at al-Subeiba (Qal'at Namrud or Nimrod's Castle) on the slopes of the Golan Heights, above the springs of Banias, was one of the great strongholds of the Hashashin. (Hope Evangelical Lutheran Church, 2006)

As noted earlier, there is a cave regarded as a Mosque, referred to as "Al Khidr" (Comay & Pearlman, 1964). As well, Muhammad received many of his mystical visions and advice while spending days meditating in a cave, an act very reminiscent of earlier Persian figures such as Ardu Wiraf and Vishtaspa who spent days in unconscious trance under the effects of *mang*. Considering the culture milieu in which Muhammad lived, and the evidence presented earlier regarding this, is it too much to put forth that a connection to these earlier Zoroastrian accounts, along with their use of cannabis extracts, may be indicated? The possibility that Muhammad was "visiting with Khidr" (i.e. eating hashish) during his sessions of mystical trance in caves cannot be easily discounted, and it could also conceivably be from this that the traditional connections between Khidr and cannabis in the Islamic world are themselves derived.

The fact that the cultic use of cannabis and the worship of Khidr seems to be focussed around groups which claim a hereditary tie to the Prophet strengthens this connection immensely. Although the knowledge of the assassin philosophy is limited, and for the most part what we do know comes to us through the records of their detractors, we can still identify elements of their philosophical beliefs through looking at the different offshoots of the sect. Of particular note is the focus of Khidr worship amongst the closely related sect of the Druzes. "...Khidr, a prophet of pre-Mosaic times, is greatly honoured by the Druzes" (Louisa & Blomfield, 1940).

Interestingly, the Druze, whose beliefs are said to be similar to both the Assassins and the Nosairiyeh, are a fringe Islamic community found in Syria, Lebanon, Jordan, Israel, and in the Palestinian territories. The Druze religion is said to have begun as an offshoot of Islam, but their incorporation of Gnostic, neo-Platonic, and other philosophies, identify their origins as older and more specifically with the Isma'ili. Because of such incorporation, they are sometimes considered as an independent religion, even though the Druze are officially classified as Muslims. "Their faith makes them in many ways the closest of breakaway sects of Isma'ilism to the Assassins" (Burman, 1987).

Like the Gnostics, Assassins, Noasaireyeh and other occult orders, it was permitted for the Druzes to lie about their faith for their protection, and this has likely been an obfuscating factor in understanding their true origins. "...[T]he Ismaileh and the Druzes are... allowed to publicly abjure in words their real creed in order to avoid persecution... It is to this sect that Lord Baconsfield... rightly attributes... the preservation of many pagan beliefs" (Littel & Littel, 1887).

> Druzes...are... known to venerate El Khidr, known mostly as a figure worshipped by Sufis (quasi-Gnostic Moslems), but who is widely honoured in Turkey, North Africa, and throughout the Middle East. In many Islamic and Arabic traditions, El Khidr is another name for the prophet Elijah. As in Jewish tradition, Elijah/El Khidr is an eternal being who watches over mankind, bringing help and comfort to the righteous in times of need. Belief in reincarnation and the transmigration of the soul is a Druze tenet, and Druze believe that El Khidr and John the Baptist are one and the same. (Gibbs, 2008)

The mythology of Khizr is thought to go back even further than the time of John the Baptist or Elijah. It is generally believed that Islam inherited traits of Khizr from many earlier Near Eastern myths, as can be seen from stories that associate Khizr with such luminary figures as Moses and Alexander the Great.

By medieval times Khizr came to represent the type of esoteric knowledge which breaks the trance of everyday existence through shock, usually in the form of outrage, laughter, or both at once. Wilson explains that Khizr was seen as "the initiator of Sufis who have no human master":

> When you say the name of Khezr [sic] in company you should always add the greeting Salaam aliekum! since he may be there... immortal and anonymous, engaged on some karmic errand. Perhaps he'll hint of his identity by wearing green, or by revealing knowledge of the occult and hidden. But he's something of a spy, and if you have no need to know he's unlikely to tell you. Still, one of his functions is to convince sceptics of the existence of the Marvellous, to rescue those who are lost in deserts of doubt and dryness. So he's needed now more than ever, and surely still moves among us playing his great game. (Wilson, 1993)

In *The Green Man*, William Anderson described Khizr as "the voice of inspiration to the true aspirant and committed artist. He can come as a white light or the gleam of a blade of grass, but more often as an inner mood. The sign of his presence is the ability to work or experience with tireless enthusiasm beyond one's normal capacities" (Anderson, 1990).

Originally a sort of vegetation spirit in whose footprints plants and flowers were said magically to sprout, Wilson explains that "nowadays Khezr might well be induced to reappear as the patron of modern militant eco-environmentalism... Khadirian Environmentalism would rejoice simultaneously both in [Nature's] utter wildness and its 'meaningfulness.' Nature as tajalli (the 'shining through' of the divine into creation; the manifestation of each thing as divine light), Nature as an aesthetic of realization" (Wilson, 1993).

Interestingly, there are legends of Khizr, that like the vegetation gods of the ancient world he was dismembered and reborn. As well, certain prophecies connect him with the end of time and the revealing of esoteric truths. With Khizr's association with Fertility, Immortality, Inspiration, and cannabis, it is hard not to see Khizr as the Islamic counterpart of the spirit of haoma-soma. This is a connection that a number of researchers have noted, including the Islamic Culture Board, who put forth that Khizr is "reminiscent of Soma... from Vedic mythology who corresponds to the two prominent functions of Khidr as 'guardian and genius of vegetation and of the water of life'" (Islamic Culture Board, 2000). The Islamic Culture Board, also suggested that, Khizr "is the centre of many fertility and agricultural cultic rites" (Islamic Culture Board, 2000).

In relation to fertility rites, such as those alleged to have been carried on from ancient times by the cannabis consuming No-sairiyeh tribesmen in Syria, it is interesting to note that Khizr has also been compared to the Syrian "Tammuz, well known as the 'Dying God' of vegetation; comparable in many respects with Soma" (Coomaraswammy, 1989). In the essay "Sir Gawain and the Green Night: Indra and Namuci", Ananda Kentish Coomaraswamy, besides bringing in an often commented on Arthurian connection, pointed out that "As a plant or tree Soma must have been green. In SA. xi Brahma is as it were 'a great green tree' (the Tree of Life)" a fact he equates with Khidr (the Green One), who "is green himself, The earth grows green under his feet at every step" (Coomaraswamy, 1944). Coomaraswamy returned to this theme in later writings:

> Khizr is at home in both worlds, the dark and the light, but above all the master of the flowing River of Life in the Land of Darkness: he is at once the guardian of genius and vegetation and of the Water of Life, and corresponds to Soma... in Vedic mythology....
>
> In the Quran... occurs the legend of Musa's search for the *Ma'jma 'al-Bahrain*, which is probably to be understood as a 'place' in the far west at the meeting of the two oceans; Musa is guided by a 'servant of God,' whom the commentators identify with al-Khidr, whose island is said to be upon an island or a green carpet in the midst of the sea. This story can be traced back to... older sources... In the Gilgamesh epic the hero sets out in search of his immortal ancestor' Utanpishtim who dwells at the mouth of the rivers... his object being to be informed with respect to the 'plant of life,' prototype of the Avestan *haoma*, Vedic *soma*, whereby man can be saved from death. (Coomaraswamy, 1989)

Peter Lamborn Wilson also noted a connection between Khizr and soma, suggesting that there was an Arthurian connection, a view shared by Coomarasamy, and that the mythologies of both Khizr and soma, inspired European legends of the grail:

> The Fountain of Youth in the legend of Khizr and Alexander is guarded by an Angel. Khizr inadvertently "steals" the water and

becomes immortal. In the *Satapatha-Brahamana* IV,1,5,5, Soma is associated with a pool that restores youth. The text (B IV,3,2,5) refers to "undecaying and immortal vital energy" that is drawn into the bowl as Soma. The Grail is guarded by a maimed king, who is thus structurally related to all the deformed Soma-demons ("...If the King (Soma) becomes *exhausted*, they extend him from out of [the *bowl*]" - B IV,2,2,5 - italics mine), and must be stolen by the Grail-knight, who is therefore the same as Indra or Hercules. Indeed, if the Grail mythos can be traced to Persian sources, to the "Cup of Jamshid,"[35] in which distant events appear by a sort of televisual magic, then the Grail may be considered not only structurally but also historically related to Iranian Haoma, or rather to its ritual cup or basin. (Wilson, 1999)

The connections between cannabis, haoma, the assassins and the grail have been explored in some detail (Bennett, et al., 1995) and it is a subject I plan on returning to in a future work; suffice to say there is considerable documentation for this relationship. Clearly, in regard to Islam's own relationship with cannabis, from both the use and mythology surrounding hashish, we can be sure that the spiritual use of hemp was something the Moslem world inherited from the Persian Zoroastrians and their traditional use of *bhang-haoma*. Moreover, this exchange took place at the earliest stages of the Islamic religion, and has left a lasting impression, that still survives in a much smaller to the present day.

The Decline of Islamic Hashish Culture

In no small way, European influences on Islamic culture in the 19th century saw considerable decline of the hashish ingesting *faqirs, sufis* and mendicants that had always played some part in the Islamic community, albeit often as an antinomian force on the fringes of society.

Although, through vows of renunciation and chastity *faqirs* often owned no more than a few rags, a pipe for hashish and a begging bowl, they were viewed by much of Islamic culture as holy men, "intoxicated" by their closeness to God, who were in a perpetual state of 'not-of-this earth', and thus above the religious the laws of

35   The 'cup of divination' held by the rulers of ancient Persian, and identical with the *mang* preparations described in Chapter 15. Jamshid is identified with Yima, a figure credited with the spread of the Haoma cult, see Chapter 15.

the common worshipper. "Such figures were regarded as *majzubs*, persons whose state of permanent and enraptured 'closeness' (*qurbat*) or attraction (*jazb*) to God rendered them the ideal intercessors and workers of wonders. As such, their every transgression was permissible, since it was necessarily committed through divine dispensation" (Green, 2009). Cannabis played a clear and prominent role in producing this state of divine intoxications. "Like his Hindu brother the Musalman fakir reveres bhang as the lengthener of life, the freer from the bonds of self. Bhang brings union with the Divine Spirit" Campbell, 1894).

Despite their abject poverty, many *faqirs* and *sufis* were made rich daily in generous food donations by members of the community, These donations of food given to these *faqirs* were often delicately prepared and shared in large open gatherings that extolled a party like atmosphere. Such dervish figures at the center of this were a remnant of the ecstatic worship of much more ancient times, and their music filled banquets, with dancing and copious

Fig 19.9: *Assembly of fakirs preparing bhang and ganja,* from the Large Clive Album, Mughal School (18th century), note water-pipe for smoking lower left, men grinding cannabis in bowls upper left, man cutting off leaves and flowers from a cannabis stalk lower right, and strainer for pouring *bhang* through in center of picture.

use of hashish, offered a sort of sacred carnival like form of worship as an alternative to the more ascetic and dour practices of the majority of Islamic culture.

When the English and other European countries sought to establish their dominance in the Mid-East and India, they were distressed to find these unruly, half-naked and cannabis intoxicated rebels that were a common and even popular site in many Islamic communities. The British had "culturally protestant notions of what constituted true religion as opposed to superstition and charlantry... the religious forms associated with the *faqir* ...raised the greatest contempt..."(Green, 2009).

> ....While many senior officials expressed a diplomatic ambivalence towards drug-use (sometimes framed in terms of *ganja's* beneficial effects on productivity), in matters of religion the issue was more clear: intoxication played no part in 'true religion,' whether Muslim or Christian. The drug using *faqir* was by definition a 'charlatan'... who clothed his degeneracy in the robes of religion. When combined with the rise of a new class of bourgeois Muslim reformers, this critique was to have tremendous implications in Hyderabad and beyond for the disciplining effects of 'religion' reconceived as modern discourse. So successful has this notion of 'true religion' been in commercial academic culture that the qualifier ('true') is typically implicit in the broader category ('religion'). This is especially the case with regard to Islam, whose inclusive realm was reduced by the course of colonial history. (Green, 2009)

Further, the envoys of the British and other European countries with imperialistic ideals were shocked when such intoxicated half naked *faqirs* publicly cheered and ridiculed them, acting with all the audacity and authority of beggar kings. As George Orwell, who for a time served as a Burmese police officer, wrote, "Every white man's life in the East was one long struggle not to be laughed at" (Orwell, 1971).[36] It did not take long for shock to grow into boiling anger, as the 'disrespectful' antics of these holy clowns, or 'wise-guys' resulted in the laugher and amusement of the common people the Europeans desired to dominate, and such perceived 'disrespect' could not long be tolerated. "The *faqir*, whose religious status and time-honored freedoms lent him a considerable degree of free

---

36   As quoted in (Green, 2009)

expression, was emerging as quite literally the voice of the Muslim 'street'" (Green, 2009).

> We can easily imagine the impression made by the drugged and dirty *faqirs* on the British. In the... 1893 colonial *Report on the Cultivation and Use of Ganja*, we read how "by means of considerable doses of *bhang* frequently repeated, [mendicants] induce a condition of frenzy which is supposed to indicate supernatural 'possession'"... Order needed to be maintained: whatever 'superstitions' the locals might attach to these figures, the streets where sahibs walked had to be free from the haranguing of intoxicated beggars. (Green, 2009)

British and European anger over the antics and the blatant disrespect of these *faqirs*, was thus clearly combined with "legal and moral confoundment at this new mode of intoxication, so far detached from the beer and whiskey-soda of the European clubs and barracks in India" (Green, 2009).

The 'unruly' political influence of these hashish ingesting faqirs on the common people was but one aspect of European concerns. In *Islam and the Army in Colonial India: Sepoy Religion in the Service of Empire*, Nile Green discusses the influence of hashish ingesting *faqirs* and mendicants on Islamic soldiers in service of the British Raj. "In imputing a substitute for the authority of the officer's rank and the agency of the soldier's effort, the alternative authority of the miraculous holy man had the potential to undermine the organizational basis of the modern army" (Green, 2009). Many Islamic soldiers were attending the hashish and music fueled banquets held by the *faqirs*, and as a result being influenced by their *faqirs* disrespect and jeering of the European military commanders who ruled over them. But the issues of concern here went far beyond the mere disruption of the military hierarchy, and the *faqirs* were viewed by the British as rabble-rousing resistors to the takeover by the British Raj in India. Further, such 'political' resistance of *faqirs* against Europeans was in no way confined to India.

> ...[T]he 'dervish' army of millenarian Mahdi of Sudan and the Sufi militia of Naqshhbandi initiates led by Imam Shamil that held at bay Russia's march into the Caucasus are merely the two most famous examples of organized Muslim ascetic resistance to European empire-building... nineteenth-century travelers to

Iran... frequently met with hostility from the *faqirs* they encountered in the streets, public spaces that the *faqirs* in a sense owned as permanent residents of the urban outdoors... *faqirs*... clown's freedom served as a role of increasing political importance as both Iranian and Indian elites entered alliances with the European powers.... In James Fairweathers' memoirs of fighting the rebels of 1857, he recalled a skirmish... with a group of around 200 mujahadin, noting that 'many of them were so drugged with bhang that they did not know whether they were striking with the flat or the edge of their swords.' (Green, 2009)

Such rabble-rousing and unruly aspects of Islamic culture, who would not be swayed by the European's promises of power and riches as were the upper class ruling Islamic elite, were not to go unchallenged, particularly by the British Raj.

....Unable to intervene in religious matters by explicit dint of colonial policy, the British in India... faced the perplexing dilemma in the insulting antics of such figures... taunting them... as they passed in the streets... [I]t was here the new laws on insanity and vagrancy proved useful. For if the *faqir's* activities could not be prohibited so long as they were regarded as part of the autonomous sphere of 'religion' – which the British were compelled to at least make a show of respect for... the problem of silencing the *faqirs*... disappeared if his deeds could instead be classified as those of a madman. (Green, 2009)

Thus, in order to rid these streets of these unruly hashish intoxicated "madmen" new British legislation was drawn up in Colonial India "including legislation on drug use and the incarceration of mendicants in India's insane asylums" (Green, 2009).

The import of the *faqirs* reckless jeers, his nakedness and his open drug-use were for these reasons reinterpreted in official policy as signs of his insanity and his 'anti-social' character. Given the widespread role of *faqirs*..., the expanded role of the asylum was therefore one of several ways in which these unruly agitators were controlled. By these means, the social meaning of the *faqir* was reversed: his activities were no longer evidence of *jazb*, of sweet intoxication in God's presence, but proof instead of insanity. (Green, 2009)

This British agenda in India, fit in well with contemporary medical views about what constituted insanity. In *Madness, Cannabis
and Colonialism: The 'Native Only' Lunatic Asylums of British India, 1857-1900*, James Mills explains.

> The constant reference to the lunatic asylum in British India in dis-
> cussions of cannabis and cannabis users is the first clue in traces
> origins of those discussions. Mark Stewart... specifically referred
> to the asylums in his question to Parliament... 'The Commissioner
> has always looked on a ganja-smoker and a bad character as syn-
> onymous, and has, in his connection with lunatic asylums in dif-
> ferent parts of Bengal, observed that in large numbers of cases
> insanity has been induced by excessive ganja-smoking'...
> The asylum was important as it was the site of... the categori-
> zation and the enumeration of cannabis use as a social problem...
> ....Through this process at the asylum the use of cannabis sub-
> stances among the Indian population became crystallized as a
> category of social problem by the colonial authorities through the
> invention of the hemp user as a dangerous human type.
> ....cannabis use by 1871/3 was associated by colonial officials
> with... immorality, suicide, the murder of Christians, and even
> the revolt against British authority of 1857. The cannabis user
> was identified as a human type, seen as unpredictable, [and] vio-
> lent... (Mills, 2000)

As Nile Green explains: "The genealogy of mental pathology in
Victorian British through the ideas of social reform and the earlier
Enlightenment ideology of reason lent colonial medicine a complex
politico-cultural agenda based on an ingrained bourgeois association
between work and morality on the one hand and notions of self-con-
trol based on the characteristically British formulation of 'common
sense' on the other" (Green, 2009). These ideas also fit in well with
emerging ideas about external "stimulants" as the source of insanity.

> Throughout the nineteenth century medical men in Europe were
> struggling to assert their authority over the psyche... doctors
> needed to prove that the brain and its working were properly
> their concern and not the concern of other professional groups
> like the clergy who could claim specialists knowledge of the
> routes to psychological well-being.... Indeed the emphasis on
> an external stimulant as a cause of insanity corresponded neatly
> with contemporary medical theories that 'the brain, as a material

organ was liable to irritation and inflammation and it was this which produced insanity,' theories which insisted upon the physiological basis of mental illness in order to assert the jurisdiction of medical men over insanity. Blaming hemp was a simple and plausible way of ascribing the aetiology of mental disease in India which thereby reinforced the medical officer's claim that he knew what he was talking about. (Mills, 2000)

The European view of "madness" was in clear conflict with long standing and more inclusive Islamic cultural traditions where "madness possessed a wider range of meaning... drawing on a specifically Islamic notion of the soul's innate 'attraction' (*jazb*) towards the creator, certain expressions of madness could... be interpreted... as... [a]... special intimacy with God" (Green, 2009). The same could also be said for the consumption of hemp preparations and their effects, as both held a millennia long association with spiritual states in the area as well.

There were two stages by which cannabis use and users became categorized as a social problem in the asylums of colonial India. First, medical officers at the asylum came to believe that cannabis use was linked to insanity and violence in Indians. Second the officers used the asylum as a site where they could observe cannabis users and establish the distinguishing signs which marked them as a distinct human type to be watched over because of their dangerous potential....

The British superintendents of the asylums came to believe that cannabis was linked to insanity and violence as they were told by the policemen who had picked the inmates up that many of the people that they brought to the asylum were there because of excessive use of hemp. Perhaps more importantly, the doctors who received this police information had reasons not to dismiss this information and to note it in their records. (Mills, 2000)

As James Mills explains, "Medical officers... became convinced that they were observing many hemp users at asylums. In fact what they observed were individuals who had only come to their attention in the first place as their behaviour was so visibly disordered or disruptive that the police had felt it necessary to intervene and send them to an asylum. This person's behaviour had been ascribed to use of cannabis preparations, often by Indian policemen who had very little evidence that this was indeed the case" (Mills, 2000).

Views of what constituted madness between colonial and Indo-Islamic medicine not only held considerable differences in its identification and qualification, but also, more importantly, treatment, or the perceived need thereof. "By the second half of the nineteenth century, this conflict of interpretations acquired institutional ramifications. The Indian 'insane' were no longer to be left to their own (or their kinsmen's) devices but could now be forcibly incarcerated in the new institution of the asylum" (Green, 2009). As Green also notes: "Combined with the introduction of the workhouse for the undeserving (or 'self-abusing') and the poor, the threat that the authorities *could* incarcerate the mad or unruly had a literally sobering effect on public morality. In large part, the days of the raving and intoxicated *faqir*... were numbered" (Green, 2009).

> ....among the Indians listed in the 'native only' asylums of... Bombay... up to 1900, the predominant occupation recorded was that of "beggar, mendicant, fakir, etc." ....What these data demonstrates is the use of the asylum in a colonial anti-vagrant policy of clearing the streets of 'insane' mendicants.... Caught in the midst of this unofficial policy of clearing the streets were considerable numbers of *faqirs*. What were too many Indians wandering holy men, begging and openly smoking cannabis in accordance with long-established custom, were in the gaze of colonial officialdom seen instead as a public nuisance that needed to be controlled. (Green, 2009)

As Nile Gren has clearly documented "the use of cannabis was central to this process" as identified in the "importance lent to *ganja* and *bhang* as a purported cause of insanity in asylum reports" (Green, 2009).

> .....[C]olonial debates about morality and madness... were... characterized by arguments over the social and psychological effects of cannabis [which was] ...suspected for its connection to the moral disintegration through which insanity was widely understood and thence described in asylum reports. Indeed, one of the central preoccupations and connected the asylum policy to debates in parliament in London, was the specific relationship between cannabis and insanity. This was not unique to India. The re-establishment of the Cairo asylum under British supervision in 1894 was accompanied by similar investigations of the effects of cannabis use on the inmates, research which was explicitly framed with regard to

A FAKIR AT DELHI.   T J T 3509.

Fig 19.10: A 19th century postcard, depicting a hashish smoking faqir, holding a chillum in his right hand, whose left arm has become atrophied by the act of will of being constantly raised in honour of the Almighty.

the more extensive data drawn from India. The annual reports
compiled in India's native asylum during the last decades of the
nineteenth century by the directors of numerous native asylums
delineated in fine detail the newly found 'scientific' connection between cannabis and madness, drawing conclusions which pointed
beyond purely mechanical causality towards the notions of moral
corruption that would prove so amenable to political rhetoric...
with the rise of the cannabis question over the following decades,
the figures recorded [for incarceration in asylums] for the use of
charas, *bhang* and *ganja* became increasingly detailed. By 1891,
some fifty-six of the 162 people confined to... [one British run
Indian] asylum were classified as being insane due to use of one
or other of these preparations of cannabis... some 203 of the 961
persons detained in the native asylums in 1891 were registered as
insane through the abuse of drugs or spirits. (Green, 2009)

Further, "the statistics of the asylums were directly responsible
for governmental decisions about cannabis use and cannabis users" (Mills, 2000), and this would have a lasting effect on Indian
and Arabic cannabis policies to the present. In regards to India's
faqirs and mendicants, as Nile Green concludes, despite "an official
policy of religious toleration, through colonial discourse of insanity
and its institutional expression in the asylum,... the *faqir's* lifestyle
was gradually criminalized by stealth":

Coupled with wider colonial attitudes towards disparaging the
'idle' naked mendicant, such policies carried a clear moral message of self-restraint and sobriety that would also find echo in the
new bourgeois religious movements that flourished under colonial
rule. While the *faqir's* métier would certainly outlive the raj, new
limitations on his public role were now established" (Green, 2009).

Although for the most part, but a shadow of its former self, despite these exhaustive attempts at prohibition, the use of hashish
with the same spiritual intent as that of the *faqirs, sufis, Hashishins*
and other Islamic groups, has survived into the modern day. Such
hashish ingesting devotees in places like Afghanistan and Pakistan,
who use cannabis products, are practicing a spiritual technique that
predates Islam and goes back at least four millennia in those areas.
Chris Turner's 2007 film *A Life in Hashistan* clearly documents the
continuation of these practices with decades worth of fascinating
footage. Also showing that the traditions of music-filled hashish

Fig 19.11: c1915 postcard "Hashish Smoker," holding a traditional coconut water-pipe, called a nargila.

Fig 19.1: Turn of the century postcard depicting Egyptian Hashish smokers.

parties, like those held by the naked faqirs, are still in vogue in some regions, more recently, the UK newspaper, *Guardian*, ran a story on Pakistan's 'heretical' Muslims, that details such activity:

> *Pakistan's 'heretical' Muslims Increasingly threatened by religious extremists, Sufis are the inheritors of a tradition that predates Islam in south Asia*
>
> Recently, the shrines of locally revered Sufi mystic saints – where music and dancing are common occurrences – have come under threat following a series of attacks on places used for spiritual practices not tolerated by orthodox sects....
>
> Earlier this summer, a weekly ritual that has taken place for several hundred years at the shrine of a Sufi saint in Lahore was abruptly discontinued due to bomb threats. In an unprecedented move, the police clamped down on the procession, causing a scuffle to break out as the saint's adherents resisted. The shrine, dedicated to the highly revered Baba Shah Jamal, who lived in the city in the 16th-17th century, is famous for this ritual, which is usually attended by thousands of people. Over the years, the procession, centered on the hypnotic drum-beat of a dhol and dancing mystics and dervishes, has developed a reputation as a den of hashish-smoking and debauchery.
>
> Though it was widely known that hashish and bhang (a cannabis drink) were consumed openly during the ritual, all this was done under the eye of the police, who would respect certain cultural norms. However, the threat from militants made the authorities err on the side of caution by putting an end to the festivities in order to avoid an attack in the crowded area.

...Imagine a suicide bomber amid the thousands of attendees, rubbing shoulders in a haze of smoke across the courtyard and adjacent graveyard of Shah Jamal. Though the would-be bomber and the dervish dancing in intoxication seem diametrically opposed, both are vying for some sort of union with the divine. Their expressions of this desire are vastly different, however. While one is a brutally violent explosion of hatred, the other is an introspective and spiritual dance of love.

Dance is a popular spiritual expression at shrines such as Shah Jamal. Many aspiring fakirs, aided by the hypnotic beats, dance to find a centre within their bodies and an opportunity to connect with the centre of the universe. The symbol of the lover dancing ecstatically in the presence of the beloved expresses musical and bodily harmony.

Physical or emotional intoxication goes hand in hand with the idea of drowning in music, recalling the relation between spiritual ecstasy and intoxication in Sufi culture and poetry. With regard to the culture of smoking hashish in Sufi shrines, Noman ul-Haq, professor of social sciences at the Lahore University of Management Sciences, says that while intoxicants like hashish have always featured in the rituals in some way, it has always been "a hush-hush affair." Social anthropologist Lukas Werth recalls one of the adherents claiming that "charas [cannabis] is a bus driver to God." In this sense, Lukas suggests, the intoxicant is seen as a "method to open the mind for the divine".... intoxication has been a part of the Sufi discourse for more than 1,000 years...

The culture of shrine visitation predates Islam in south Asia. The Sufi saints who have inspired cult followings were radical poets, social critics, and reformers who travelled to areas such as the Punjab through Persia, often on foot. Their message was simply one of peace, love, tolerance, and of introspection dedicated to exploring the divine within the boundaries of human experience. (Akhtar, 2009).

Indeed, perhaps it was the loss of the *faqirs* message of religious ecstasy and spiritual intoxication, a remnant of the more ancient use of *haoma* and *mang*, that has caused so much of that area to become the source of so much fundamentalism, fanaticism and religious intolerance. Salah.

Dan and Mary Quaintance received jail sentences for using cannabis as a haoma.

Dr. Ali Jafarey, whose paper "HAOMA, Its Original and Later Identity," (2001), is referred to in this book, and in the Quaintances' court case.

Zoroastrian expert witness Dr. Ervad Jehan Bagli, testified against the Quaintances.

HAOMA IN THE COURT

Zoroaster's Reforms Reach into the 21st Century!

The history of the identity of haoma has become such a controversial topic for modern day members of the Zoroastrian religion that the periodical *Hamazor: Publication of the world Zoroastrian Organization* has taken up a campaign against a couple, Dan and Mary Quaintance, who are the founders of a group called the "Church of Cognizance," based in Pima, Arizona,[1] who "claimed that they were following 'neo-Zoroastrian practices' by smoking marijuana (using it under the name haoma) in their homes, which they called 'individual orthodox member monasteries'" (Kevala, 2007).

FEZANA[2] and the North American Mobeds Council (NAMC) cooperated with the US Attorney's office to testify against the defendants in a hearing on August 22, 2006....[and] offered to provide an expert witness to the US Attorney's office to testify that haoma is not marijuana and explain the significance of the actual Haom Yasht liturgy. The attorney's office wanted a witness with credentials to speak for North American Zoroastrians. After reviewing our options, the NAMC and FEZANA arranged for Er-

---

1   Wonderful Folks! Very knowledgeable about the history of Haoma. The Church of Cognizance, is a revealed Neo-Zoroastrian faith & experience based ethno-socio-religious organization. On August 12, 1994 the foundation of the COC was concretized a FREE Church, to be legally recognized as a Religious Institute, through recording a Declaration Of Religious Sentiment at the Graham County Recorder's Office, in the State of Arizona. (www.danmary.org)

2   The Federation of Zoroastrian Associations of North America

vad Dr Jehan Bagli, President of NAMC, [as well as WZOs[3] Board Member] to appear as an expert witness at the hearing

Er Bagli prepared and made a statement of the correct Zoroastrian liturgical practices and ritual use of *Haoma*. He testified that *haoma* as used in the present day ritual is not cannabis. Zarathushtra rejected the use of intoxicants or hallucinogens in Zoroastrian rituals. Bagli testified that Zoroastrians believe that Mind is a priceless Divine gift to mankind; and any mind altering substances that abuse that gift are not acceptable. *Haoma* was worshipped as a deity and used as a plant in religious practices in the pre-Zoroastrian Indo-Iranian era. Archaeological evidence shows that different plants were used at different times based on availability.[4] That *haoma* was a plant with hallucinogenic properties remains a speculation rather than fact. (Kevala, 2007)

Well, if it remains speculation, it is speculation that Bagli himself has taken part in as he noted of the haoma that the "original identity of the plant has [been] obliterated through the antiquity" in his 2005 essay "The Significance of Plant Life in Zarathushti Liturgy." In court proceedings Bagli stated that "I know Dr. Jafarey very well" (Bagli, 2008). This is the same Dr. Jafarey whose essay, "Haoma, Its Original and Later Identity" (2001), was discussed at some lengths in chapters 4 and 14 in relation to its identification of the original Haoma with cannabis. Jafarey came to Zoroastrianism as a convert, not by birth as a Parsee (This has been one of the core issues in the attacks against Jafarey)[5] and Bagli played an instrumental role in having him accepted. Thus it seems very unlikely that Bagli, from his comments on the haoma, and close acquaintance with Jafarey, would be unaware of the historical connections noted by Jafarey between haoma and cannabis, although from his testimony he clearly does all that he can to hide this fact, if it is the case.

A closer look at Dr. Bagli and his testimony against the use of cannabis as haoma reveals a divine irony in the story of this modern Zoroastrian priest who was asked by the orthodox Zoroastrian community to take it upon himself to continue the reforms Zoroaster initiated millennia ago.

In court testimony in his role as a state witness against the Quaintances, Bagli, when asked about his dual role as Zoroastrian priest and scientist, explained that his professional specialty was "medicinal chemistry, synthesizing new chemical entities for medical purposes."[6]

> Prosecution: Q: Does this include Plants?
> Bagli: A: Plants; isolation and characterterization of active principles from biological natural products.

This comment indeed brings us to a rather curious situation, as here we see a Zoroastrian priest and scientist, rallying against a natural plant, and the highlight of his own career, as it turns out, has been the extraction of medical isolates from urine! A rather divine irony considering the role of urine in the Parsi religion which we have already had reason to discuss.

Unfortunately the urine with which Bagli has been experimenting seems to have been *muthra* (i.e., evil, dirty), like that of Y.48.10, very bad urine, as it has been associated with cancer and other serious health risks. The highlight of Bagli's medical career was the isolation of Equilin an estrogen from horse urine that is present in the mixture of estrogens isolated from pregnant mares' urine and marketed as Premarin (PREgnant MARes' urINe). Premarin became the most commonly used form of estrogen for hormone replacement therapy in the United States of America. Used by millions of women in America, it is considered by many too dangerous for use as it has an unacceptable risk for breast cancer,[7] heart disease, strokes, and blood clots. After the publication of a National Institutes of Health study that identified some of the risks involved in the drug's use, sales of Premarin hormone replacement drugs, extracted from the urine of pregnant mares, abruptly dropped about 35 percent (Guthrie, 2002; Moody, 2003).

Considering the Zoroastrian concerns with the right treatment of cattle, horses and other livestock, it should be noted that the production of Premarin is of great concern to animal rights activists, who believe that the collection of mares' urine, from horses

---

6   All court testimony cited is from *Evidentiary Hearing On Motion To Dismiss, USA v Quaintance*, August 21-23, 2006, Albuquerque, New Mexico, at the U.S. District Court for the District of New Mexico. Paul Baca (official court reporter)

7   Google 'Premarin cancer' for more information.

that are continually impregnated, causes the animals undue stress. This also produces an overabundance of poorly bred foals which are generally doomed for slaughter. Because of the quantities of urine involved there are about 700 farms with 80,000 horses penned in small stalls, unable to turn around or properly lie down, repeatedly impregnated and continuously drained of urine. When they are considered beyond use, the horses are summarily slaughtered. It is estimated that in total this has been the fate of millions of horses.

Hopefully Dr. Bagli remembers to say the following prayer from the Petet Erani (Kordah-Avesta), daily!

> of all kinds of sins which have committed... against the cattle and the various kinds of cattle, If I have beaten it, tortured it, slain it wrongfully, if I have not given it fodder and water at the right time, if I have castrated it... If I have not protected it from extreme heat or cold, if I have killed cattle of useful strength, working cattle, war-horses... so that alike these good things and their protector Brahman have been injured by me and not contended by me I repent.[8]

If only Bagli knew that "[t]he mere sight of bhang, cleanses from as much sin as a thousand horse-sacrifices..." (Campbell, 1894). Bagli's role in a trial against a plant is also curious for a man, who wrote in his essay, "The Significance of Plant Life in Zarathushti Liturgy," that "It is a part of Magian lore that plants are the part of the good creation of Ahura Mazda to fight the counter order of evil" (Bagli, 2005). A detailed look at Bagli's testimony in the Church of Cognizance case provides some interesting insights into the controversy which the haoma holds for the Zoroastrian faith, and the extreme lengths they will go to avoid discussion of its original identity.

The Quaintance's defense tried to argue that Dr. Bagli's testimony had no relevance to the case, as the beliefs of the Church of Cognizance was a modern synchronistic religion, neo-Zoroastrian, not the orthodox Zoroastrianism that Bagli represented. The prosecution, in an effort at qualifying their witness established Dr. Bagli's scientific credential, his 35 years of studying the Zoroastrian religion, Bagli's role as a hereditary Zoroastrian priest for the over a decade and put forth that Bagli's testimony was relevant because "the defendants, having spoken for many hours about the benefits

8   As quoted in (Kapadia, 1998)

of marijuana and how it is essential to their religion, how it is haoma, how its supposed to be soma, and they've equated it with this Zoroastrian concept and how it is a deity to them":

> Prosecution - And I am going to attempt to show that haoma is not the deity of the Zoroastrian faith, and it is dangerous to the human body, potentially dangerous. And in those ways we attempt to rebut their, their religion of the defendants to show that, that it is not a religion and it's really a lifestyle and philosophy that advocates the legalization, the use of marijuana... but more importantly that haoma and marijuana are not equated, they are not one and the same, as studied by Dr. Bagli, and how... haoma... does not have a central role in the Zoroastrian faith that the defendants claim it does...

The clearly biased Judge, Judith Herrar, allowed Bagli's testimony not only as an expert witness on the Zoroastrian religion, for which he was solicited by the prosecution, but also in regard to his supposed expertise in the field of medicinal chemistry, on which he was not requested to testify by the prosecution. The Judge based her decision on testimony given on the history of Zoroastrianism already by the defendant and other witnesses, and "medicinal chemistry... keeping in mind the government's burden of proving a compelling governmental interest."

This brings us back to the testimony of our good Dr. Bagli, which alternative to what the prosecution wished to demonstrate, showed instead that haoma was a deity and also played a central role in the Zoroastrian faith;

> Prosecution, Q: ... tell us about haoma, what is... haoma?
> Bagli, A: ... well in order to discuss the haoma we have to really take it in the phases and periods over which we are talking about
> Haoma, in the pre-Zoroastrian era before Zarathustra, because it came from north, and moved southward from North Central Asia, some then went to Iran recognize haoma as their, one of their gods, because they worship many gods at that time... Haoma was perceived by the Iranians as... one of the gods they worshipped. The Indians called the same deity Soma.
> Prosecution, Q: And what was it, do we know today what that was that they worshipped, the, these individual, these people, do we know what haoma was? Can we identify it?

Bagli, A:- Well at the time haoma was a deity as well as a plant. And we have no knowledge of what that plant was at the time. Scholars have speculated that it may have had hallucinogenic properties. And historical records and archeological findings indicate that several different plants, may have been used at different parts and areas of the world, and at different times. So we have no knowledge of what the plant was at that time.

As Bagli is a close associate of Jafarey, it is hard not to believe he has seen Jafarey's essay "Haoma, Its Original and Later Identification." As well, having read much of the literature available on the subject myself, it would also seem that references to "archaeological findings indicate… several different plants" likely means that Bagli was likewise familiar with Sarianidi`s discovery of evidence of cannabis, ephedra, and poppies in the BMAC haoma temple. If this is the case, then Bagli`s testimony at his trial was at the very least disingenuous, if not downright contemptible and false.

Q: And what about today, is there a haoma ceremony today amongst Zoroastrians?
A: Today, haoma ceremony is a central sacrament of the higher liturgical ceremony in the Zoroastrian faith.
Q: Are there religious important writings in the Zoroastrian faith?
A… Yes of course there are. *Yesna*… and we have several other-scriptural writings. But the writings, unfortunately many, much of it was destroyed at the time of Alexander's invasion to Iran, and they were rewritten in the language of the time later on in Sassanian times.

Bagli was questioned by the prosecution about the modern performance of the Haoma ceremony:

Bagli, A: …at the present time three small twigs of the plant are pounded in a metal bowl, together with one twig of pomegranate bean, a little bit of consecrated water, and a little bit of milk. And they are pounded in there during the ceremony with utterances of the sacred mantras, and the officiating priest just symbolically sips them, just as a sacramental wine in a Christian ceremony, and as a symbol of good, blessings of the good health and immortality.

Interestingly, Bagli leaves out that the "three small twigs" are of the plant ephedra, which through his field of study Bagli should know was the source of ephedrine, one of the base chemicals in the production of methamphetamine. Likely because of this, Bagli emphasizes that the haoma is only symbolically sipped, and is a purely symbolic sacrament as with the Catholic Eucharist.

The prosecution asked if this modern ritual use of haoma results in any intoxication:

> Bagli, A: No, not that I know of, absolutely not.
> Prosecution, Q: And what does intoxication mean in the Zoroastrian faith?
> Bagli, A: Zoroastrian faith of mind is a crucial core of existence... Any mind altering substances used are defiling and abusing that gift of God, and that is not acceptable in Zoroastrianism and, in fact, prophet Zarathustra opposed the use of these kinds of substances that were used in the preexisting religions of his time.

The prosecution questioned if haoma is still recognized as a god by the Zoroastrian faith, as it was in the pre-Zoroastrian religion:

> Bagli, A: Haoma is not a god, no. At Zarathustra's time haoma was not worshipped, there was no plant in the religious practice of his era.
> Prosecution, Q:... if someone were to smoke a cigarette, is that a violation of the Zoroastrian faith?
> Bagli, A: Right, well fire is, again, a central symbol of the Zoroastrian rituals, and it is actually interpreted by prophet Zarathustra as the representation of truth and what is right. And it is, in fact, in Zoroastrian religion an embodiment of God in the corporeal existence. So... a practicing Zoroastrian is not supposed to smoke because it is a desecration of that sacred element of fire.
> Prosecution, Q: And what if one smokes a narcotic, or marijuana for instance?
> Bagli, A: Well smoking marijuana or any hallucinogenic substance is a desecration, not only of fire, but also the desecration of the good mind that Zarathustra taught is crucial to the living of life of truth and right.
> Prosecution,Q:... are you familiar with Yasna 911?
> Bagli, A: Yasna 911 is a liturgy that was composed to venerate haoma centuries after the time of Zarathustra... after his death,

centuries after his death several of the pre-Zoroastrian deities were brought back into the Zoroastrian religion. And we do not know anything about what plant was used for those ceremonies at that time.

Prosecution, Q: Now does the Zoroastrian faith teach a reality that transcends the here and now, or transcends the physical?

Bagli, A: Afterlife; yes of course. Yes the soul is an immortal entity... after death... it is believed to leave this earthly precinct and proceed towards the spiritual domain.

Ironically, as we have shown, these ideas of an afterlife came to the Zoroastrian religion through psychonauts who drank powerful draughts of *mang* laced haoma! These references are key in defining the continued use of psychoactive substances in the Zoroastrian religion after and during the time of Zoroaster. Unfortunately both sides of this case fail to mention the references to *mang* and *bhanga*.

After establishing their evidence in regards to Zoroastrianism, the prosecution draws the courts attention to Dr. Bagli's supposed expertise on marijuana:

Prosecution, Q:... have you studied the properties of cannabis sativa?

Bagli, A: I have studied the properties of cannabis sativa and cannabis indica, yes.... Cannabis has been used in small dosages for relieving pain, sometimes you know [as with Ahura Mazda's treatment of the first created Ox! (Y.4.20)]. I know of no beneficial effect that cannabis would have on the individual.

Prosecution, Q: Can there be psychological or physical addiction?

Bagli, A: Oh, that certainly, it has hallucinogenic property and psychoactive properties that could endanger the disorders in the mind. And this is the reason that Zoroastrians would not permit such a thing, because the mind is a precious and priceless gift of God.

Curious that Bagli, a chemist whose specialty deals with natural substances, living in a Canada, where there is a Canadian Federal Government medical marijuana program, where cannabis itself is grown on behalf of the government and doctor's prescribe it for a variety of ailments, would have no knowledge whatsoever of cannabis' medical use. Bagli's cross examination by the defense opened with a line of questioning in this regard:

Defense, Q: you haven't heard that cannabis has clearly shown a beneficial impact in connection with the treatment of Glaucoma?

Bagli, A: No

Defense, Q: you haven't heard that it had been shown to have a clearly beneficial impact on the people with multiple sclerosis?

Bagli, A: There have been literature, I have read it, and I am not personally involved in that work so I have not seen the details of that, no" [he read it but he's not familiar with it?]

Defense, Q: So when you say you know nothing that supports the notion that cannabis has a beneficial impact, you don't really know what you are saying, do you?

Bagli, A: Well, the research continues, and I am retired now and I'm not keeping up with research so I cannot answer that.

Defense, Q: That's fine... I just want to make sure we're not making claims for which we don't have support... Lets talk a little about, well, shoot, lets talk about haoma. The first thing you said this morning was we have no knowledge of what haoma was...

Bagli, A: Yes, that is correct.

Defense, Q; So you can really say that a person like Mr. Quaintance, who has concluded on the basis of his research that it's cannabis, you can't really say that that's wrong?

Bagli, A: No, I said that scholars have speculated that it may have had hallucinogenic properties, the plant that was used, and that's all I know.

Defense, Q: Okay. And so certainly you would classify cannabis sativa as a plant that has psychoactive properties?

Bagli, A: Cannabis sativa is a plant that has psychoactive properties; that is correct.

Defense, Q: And so to the extent that scholars have speculated that haoma is a plant that had psychoactive properties, it is possible that haoma was, in ancient times, cannabis?

Bagli, A: In ancient times, before the times of Zarathustra, it may have been.

Defense, Q: Okay. And a person whose religious precepts are based on things that may have existed prior to the existence of Zarathustra might find that haoma is cannabis and incorporate that into their faith?

Bagli, A: The haoma plant that is used in haoma ceremony today was, in fact, harvested in, yes Iran in 1964 by professor Mary Boyce, and it was identified by the royal botanical gardens in Kew, England as Ephedra pachytarda or Ephedra intermedia.

Defense, Q: And that's one theory; right?

Bagli, A: No, that is a fact

Defense, Q: Well, no, but you said we don't know for sure.
Bagli, Q: Well, no, I'm talking about haoma plant used at present time.

The defense tries to establish that there are a variety of sects considered Zoroastrian with varying beliefs, which Bagli was reluctant to accept (but eventually does) and this brings about a very telling exchange:

Defense, Q:Are you a member of the Zarathustrian Assembly?
Bagli, A: No
Defense, Q: why not?
A: I know Dr. Joffrey [sic, Jafarey] very well

Bagli explains he has never had a reason to join the Zarathustrian assembly, but sees where the line of questioning by the defense is going and acknowledges Dr. Jafarey as a member of the Zoroastrian community. This brings about a change in questioning and Bagli is then addressed directly about Dr. Jafarey and his research into haoma and its links with cannabis:

Defense, Q: ... And you're aware that he [Dr. Jafarey] believes that haoma and barestma [barsom] were most likely cannabis?
Bagli, A; No.
Defense, Q: You disagree with that?
Bagli, A: No, I have seen his paper and he talks about that in the pre-Zarathustrian era, not during the time of Zarathustra.
Defense, Q: so what you're suggesting, then, is that what haoma is, changed from pre Zarathustra times to now?
Bagli, A: We do not know what the plant was, it's a speculation.
Defense, Q: Okay. So the plant that you use in your haoma ceremonies is, in effect, a speculation?
Bagli, A: No, the plant we use in our ceremony has been identified as Ephedra.
Defense, Q: Okay. But Ephedra may or may not have been the original haoma?
Bagli, A: we don't know that.
Defense, Q: But Dr. Joffery [sic] feels it might well have been cannabis right?
Bagli, A: No, I don't know that. [earlier he said he read Jafarey's paper on the subject.]

Defense, Q: Okay. But I'm not asking you if you know that, but do you know if he has said that, written that?
Bagli, A: No, no, I don't know. [note previously Bagli clearly says "I have seen this paper"]
Defense,Q: All right. Were you born in India?
Bagli, A : yes, sir.... I spent my first 26 years growing up in India?
Defense, Q: And you are very familiar, not only with Zoroastranism, but also of other religions of the Indian and Iranian traditions in which cannabis is a sacrament; is that not correct?
Bagli, A: No
Defense, Q: There are no religions in that region in which cannabis is a sacrament?
A: I don't know of any.
Q:You don't know of any?
Bagli, A: No.
Defense, Q: All right. So you can't say that the cannabis or hemp plant has a long history of spiritual involvement in India or Iran?
Bagli, A: No

It is hard to imagine that Dr. Bagli having lived in India, and, through his interests in both religious history and natural medicines, would never have come across the clear role of cannabis for spiritual uses in India. Combined with his contradictory statements regarding his knowledge, or lack thereof, of his colleague Dr. Jafarey's research into the identification of haoma, Bagli's seemingly motivated forgetfulness is made more than clear. Moreover, this same view seems to be the prevailing attitude amongst the current Zoroastrian spiritual elite.

As Hamazor: Publication of the world Zoroastrian Organization explains to its Zoroastrian readership of the trial's conclusion, which resulted in the imprisonment of Dan and Mary Quaintance,[9] and the need of further vigilance against such claims about the haoma:

The United States District Court for the District of New Mexico, in a written Memorandum Opinion handed down on December 22, 2006, denied the Church of Cognizance's Motion to Dismiss the Indictment and Incorporated Memorandum. The Memorandum Opinion considered the evidence presented at the hearing on August 21, 2006, which included the arguments of the counsel, written briefs, and applicable law.... By denying the Motion to

9   Dan Quaintance received a five year sentence, his wife Mary, two to three years.

Dismiss, the judge has opened the door to a full trial for violations of the Controlled Substances Act. It is important to understand that this case has no bearing on the laws and conditions in any country except the United States, and it is no longer a RFRA case. Nevertheless, FEZANA is reviewing the legal ramifications of the matter. We want to ensure that no teachings, rituals or beliefs of our religion are used by anyone for illegal or self-serving purposes. FEZANA and NAMC seek everyone's cooperation, vigilance and above all, patience. The Internet is full of misinformation and is open to mischief by anyone.[10] The only way to win is to adhere to our religious principles and continually seek the guidance of Ahura Mazda in all we do. (Kevala, 2007)

Unfortunately the truth has already become a victim in that quest, as it has in so many other quests of "orthodox" religions through history. So, here, in this New Mexico case, we see that certain leading individuals in the Zoroastrian religion recognize the archeological and historical background connecting cannabis with the haoma, and it would seem that they are taking an active part in ensuring that Zoroaster's prohibition of the original form of Haoma continues into the 21st century, more than two and a half millennia after Zoroaster first tried to institute them.

The current issue regarding the identification of haoma is further confounded by the role of many historians of religion who refuse to see a role for psychoactive plants in the development of religious ideas, despite the most obvious evidence. When I approached Harvard University Professor James Russell, who has written a number of books and articles on the Iranian religion, with questions regarding the connections between cannabis and haoma, he flat-out rejected any entertainment of the idea. "There is no reason to think cannabis had anything to do with haoma. See Flattery & Schwartz, 'Haoma and Harmaline'. In modern Persian dialects, 'hom' means Ephedra"...All I really know about cannabis is from Rosenthal's "The Herb," [about Hashish in the medieval Moslem world]... I'm sorry I can't be of more assistance" (Russell, 2008).

On Sarianidi's work in Margiana, Russell responded: "I read it in Russian. And I met Sarianidi. It's unconvincing, and any serious Iranist would tell you he's gone way out on a limb.... There is no basis for Sarianidi's assertion that the building he identified as a temple

10   I wonder if they mean me? http://www.cannabisculture.com/articles/3155. html; http://www.pot-tv.net/archive/shows/pottvshowse-2041.html

was Zoroastrian, proto- or otherwise (whatever 'proto- might mean in this context); and it is most unlikely Zoroastrians, if they lived so long ago (and it is certain they didn't), had temples" (Russell, 2008). Clearly, from the number of researchers that have been referenced here in relation to it, it is pretty obvious that many take Sarianidi's work very seriously. I responded to Russell, that the 'proto' referred to in Sarianidi's title, clearly made reference to the pre-Zoroastrian cult, as does Sarianidi's book (which somehow seems to have escaped Russell - perhaps he should read the English translation!)

Considering the clear-cut role of cannabis in the ancient world, one wonders why an expert on Zoroastrianism and the Indo-European studies would not be more familiar with it. Russell then proceeded to give me a "warning against accepting unfounded assertions" which he felt "maybe more important than adding to the confusion." Russell showed absolutely no interest in looking at what I had collected on the matter, and I responded that the good professor might heed his own advice and warnings. Russell then went on to a virile attack on Jafarey (parelleling that of Birdy's mentioned earlier), to whose work regarding the identification of haoma I had referred him. "I have met Ali Jafarey. These are my impressions. He is an abusive demagogue and is deeply disliked by authentic, orthodox Zoroastrians. He... has managed to distort the content of the texts and mislead a great many people" (Russell, 2008).

Professor Russell's comments are somewhat curious, considering that The World Zoroastrian News Network reported that on Feb 08, 2009, Dr. Ali A. Jafarey was honoured for all of his work regarding Zoroastrian history and heritage, in a ceremony that was organized by the Zarathushtrian Assembly, California Zoroastrian Center, World Zoroastrian Council, Iranian Culture Center of Orange County and Claremont Graduate University.

As I have yet to meet Dr. Jafarey, and my attempts to open up a discussion with him via email went unanswered, I cannot comment on the personality of the man; I will say however, that his paper "Haoma, Its Original and Later Identification," has shown itself to be considerably accurate, and if there are any misleading sources on the matter, it would seem to be on the part of pigeon-holed academia, and an inherent Zoroastrian orthodox prohibitionists' agenda.

Shiva Somanath, Lord of Bhang, grinding bhang with mortar and pestle, drinking bhang, and smoking chillum, with bowl of golis (bhang balls), and bowl with cloth for straining bhang.   Author's collection, (Pravesh Bedi & Sons-Delhi,India)

CONCLUSION

We have followed the story of soma-haoma from their origins in the firey braziers of the proto-Indo-Europeans, and explained how this developed into a drink amongst the Corded Ware Culture. These cannabis drinking, horse-riding figures spread their cult throughout the ancient world, into Western Europe, China, Mesopotamia, and most notable for our study, into Persia and India, where their influence can still be felt in certain spiritual practices through to the modern day. The Indo-European adoption of the Chinese name *hu-ma* for cannabis, and its linguistic development into the Avestan Haoma and Vedic Soma is backed up by etymology, comparative study of ancient texts, as well as the archeological discoveries of cannabis at China's Yanghai Tombs, burial sites of the Scythian *Haomavarga*, and the ancient Soma temple of the Bactria Margiana Archeological Complex (BMAC). As well, as detailed, the eventual prohibition of the cannabis based soma-haoma preparations and their replacement by placebo sacraments has been explained in detail, in both the Persian and Indian traditions. Truly, what was lost, has been found.

Although largely lost in the mists of time, as has been noted, there are a number of historical remnants of the soma-haoma cult. Nineteenth century Western explorers noted that the Ossetes of the Caucus, an Indo-European people believed to be descended directly from the Scythian *Haomavarga*, were still practicing the technique of burning cannabis in tents to hold the smoke, close to 2500 years after Herodotus recorded the technique amongst their ancestors. The continuation of the sacramental role of bhang in India, under the dominion of Shiva, is clearly derived from the Vedic Soma tradition, and thus the *sukhnidhaan* of the Sikhs which derived from the Hindu tradition, as is the use of hashish in Islamic sects a clear carryover of the early use of haoma in Persia.

In light of the profound history, some might see the use of cannabis as a freedom of religion issue. But after close to two decades of researching the cross-cultural history of cannabis, and following its use from the Stone Age to present, I have come to see that the right to cannabis is even more fundamental than religious freedoms; humanity created religion, but no matter what god you believe in, you had better believe that god created cannabis. Even from an atheistic standpoint, from a cross cultural perspective, as possibly our oldest cultivated crop, humanity has had an evolutionary partnership with this plant that likely stretches back more than 25,000 years. Indeed humanity has a natural indigenous right to all the plants of the earth – all people and all plants – any law that stands in the way of that natural relationship is an abomination to both God and nature.[1] It is my sincerest hope that this book helps to establish that relationship on a wider scale and thus play a role in helping to reinstitute humanity's natural right to cannabis, the most useful of all plants.

Having stated that, certain religious symbolism does come into play. In the case of cannabis as the soma-haoma, we are discussing a spiritual tradition that dates back, at the most conservative estimate, at least 5500 years, beginning with the ritual use of cannabis by the Seredeni Stog, and from there we can see cannabis's use leading to the still existing religions of Taoist tradition, Zoroastrianism, Hinduism, Sikhism, Judaism, Christianity, Islam and thus, too, the many off-shoots of these faiths as well. Although some traditional use of cannabis has survived to the present, in India and the Mideast, for the most part this ancient relationship was successfully buried and forgotten to a point that the institutions that initiated its repression have, through the generations, forgotten about it themselves. Interestingly, this situation fits in well with certain mythological aspects of the Persian tradition.

In the Avestan mythology the haoma was a foretaste of the mythical White Hom, the celestial counterpart of the earthly plant and drink. Like the prophesized Tree of Life that grows along the Riv-

---

1   Preservation is an issue that must be addressed, as extinction of a species threatens our collective inheritance, endangered species must be protected for the benefit of all.

er of Life in the Christian account (Rev. 22), the legendary 'White Hom' grows at the junction of the "great gathering place of the waters" and a mighty river. According to the Zadspram, the Soshyant (later identified with Mithra) would come at the end of the ages, and press the White Hom for the benefit of the righteous. Like the Biblical Tree of Life, the great reward at the end of Revelation, the ancient Persians believed that the identity of the White Hom would be revealed at the great renovation, when the Soshyant, *Final Saviour*, sacrifices the final sacred ox, and mixes its fat with the White Hom to prepare the elixir of immortality.[2] A symbolism, in this case, made even more apt, considering that it was with *mang*, hemp, that Ahura Mazda eased the pains of death of the first created ox, when the devil Ahriman, had poisoned him.

In many ways, the haoma has become the mythical White Hom. Through the identity of haoma-soma becoming lost to history, it has become as much a thing of myth as the celestial White Hom, the drink of the gods. Moreover, as we have seen that the mythology surrounding the original soma-haoma is the source of so much of today's religious cosmology (Judaism, Christianity, Islam, Hinduism, and Zoroastrianism – the religions of billions) it can also be seen that the sacred plant has in a sense become trapped in the proverbial 'sacred cow' that those religions represent to their followers.

Indeed, the identification of cannabis with soma-haoma is as much of a threat to the religions of today as it was to those con trolling priesthoods of millennia ago who first soug its use. In my own study of religion, I have come original civilizing elements that organized religic have long ago served their purpose. The outdate contain are as much a burden on humanity world on the shoulders of Atlas – organized greatest stumbling block. Moreover, far fr fundamentalist religion is a source of diff ten, brutal war.

When this scenario is looked at sy analogies can be drawn. In the mag forget that the word magic has its o represents the power of the intell penetrate into the matter of thin

---

2 Bundahish, 30:4-33

ern terms, the sacred cow has come to represent one's religious and philosophical beliefs. Perhaps symbolically by taking the study of the history of entheogens into the realm of study of the origins of the world's religions, we are in a sense plunging the sword of Mithras into the "sacred cow," and, as we do so, the sacred plant of our ancestors pour forth once again, as the soma of the *Rig Veda*, the haoma of the *Avesta*, Shiva's *bhang*, the *sukhnidhaan* of the Sikh Guru Gobind Singh, the *keneh bosem* of the Torah, the "Tree of Life" of the early Christians,[3] "The Plant of Immortality of the Taoists," and the inspirational "visit of the Green Khidr" of the Moslems?

Like the threat that Darwin's revolutionary theory of evolution represented to Biblical creation myths over a century ago, the study of cannabis, other entheogens, and their role in ancient world shamanism poses an identical threat to the world's oldest religions themselves, offering a revolutionary insight into their very origins. In a very real sense Cannabis is the potential alpha and omega of these fundamentalist ancient world faiths. Thus, not surprisingly, much of organized religion has an inherent disdain and fear of the entheogenic experience, and this has always been the source of orthodox religion's war against the 'devil's weed,' whether they are conscious of it or not.

Despite the best efforts of prohibition, including imprisonment and even murder, just as the mythical Adam and Eve reached for the forbidden fruit, in this, the dawn of a new millennium, more and more people are waking up and shedding the fossilized fundamental religions of their ancestors, and instead having new re- ious experiences of their own through the rediscovery of the sacraments. Clearly cannabis, even without people having wledge of its ancient history, can be seen to have played ntal leading role in this entheogenic renaissance of our

book the human-entheogen relationship more widespread the role of cannwith cannabis-soma-haoma. Indeed, its fibres cloth, its seeds a valuable early food source, r first medicine and sacrament. Moreover dern return of cannabis are loaded with when reading the account of the Tree of Life in the bis, that this author was first "inspired" to study ix F Revelation.

potential possibilities. Cannabis medicines are being studied for Alzheimer, cancer, glaucoma, pain and numerous other diseases with very promising results. Industrial hemp for fuel, paper, paints, cloth, plastics and other commodities is just what is needed for a planet feeling the effects of close to a century of toxic petroleum products, healing our planet just as it heals our bodies. Truly, the global circle of people who share cannabis exceeds race, nation, and religion, and many are beginning to recognize it for the holy sacrament that it once was and can be again.

Still, despite its widespread use, its potential benefits and its profound role as a plant species in the web of life, a war has been waged upon cannabis-soma-haoma. The world over, cannabis is destroyed on site; millions of people have been incarcerated for its use, in some countries even executed for its distribution, and countless lies told about its effects and the acts of its adherents. The root of this war, when studied to its core, like so many wars that have plagued the world, has its origins in organized religion. Clearly, the prohibitions of Zoroaster, Manu, Jeremiah, Paul, and the like, have their reforming counterparts in the religions of today, their controlling egos reincarnated in aspects of the cults that formed around them.

It is with that view in mind, aware of the repercussions that may be invoked, bid on by the seductive whispers of the Immortal Green One, that I have dared to pick up the blade of Mithras (not as any prophesized savior but simply as a world weary modern man) and plunge it into the Sacred Cow of the world's oldest religions, with a prayer that the life blood of soma-haoma, which was their original source, might once again more freely flow, and that the earth be made once again all the greener from its open cultivation. May this book mark a turning point in the return of the perennial religion. Praise Soma, long live Haoma, the pressing time has come again........

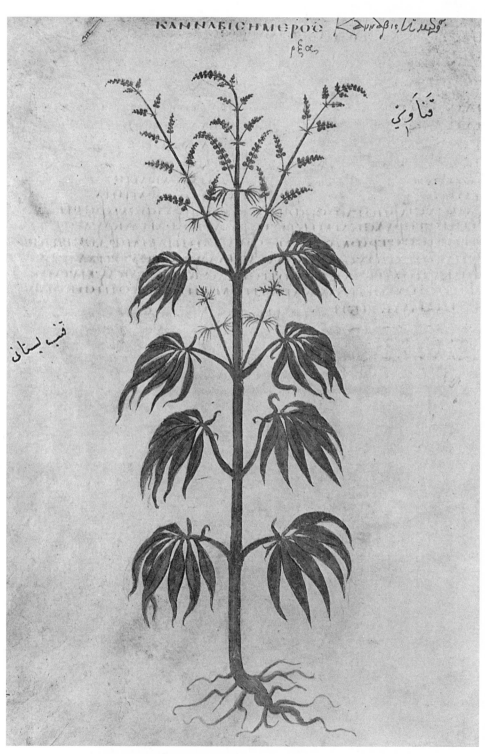

Cannabis sativa: Pedanius Dioscorides – *Vienna Dioscorides*, 512 A.D.

APPENDIX A

Braja Lal Mukherjee, "The Soma Plant," *Journal of the Royal Asiatic Society*, (1921), [footnotes have been added and are not Mukherjee's].

The Soma Plant

I have read with interest Mr. Havell's short paper on "What is Soma?" published in the July number of this valuable Journal. His identification of Soma with *Eleusing coracana* or *ragi* is based, I am afraid, on grounds which may be supplemented by others of a more important character. Mr Havell's impression is that Soma (the plant) resembled cow's udders, but I have not been able to find out the text to which he may have referred. It may be that he refers to R.V. 8, 9, 19, which has been noted by Professor Macdonell as authority for his statement that the shoots swelling give milk, like cows with their udders. This clearly refers to the shape taken by the strainer when the shoots are placed inside it and the juice is strained out. This, therefore, does not help us to identify the plant itself.[1]

Mr. Havell states that the plant itself had a likeness to the fingers of a man's hand[2]. In order to prove this, the original text, if any,

1   Wasson, making the same error, referred to this same passage as identifying the Fly Agaric. Wasson tried to identify the bulbous cap of the mushroom as the udder, milked for its juice, and the stalk (stipe) as the teat!

2   Medieval Moselm authors noted the same similarity in regards to cannabis leaves, and a play on the words 'kif' (cannabis) and 'kaf' (hand) appears in medieval verses dedicated to the plant, (Rosenthal, 1971). "In botany, *kaff*… was used to designate quite a variety of plants, all on the basis of their presumed similarity with the human or animal palm or hand. The hemp plant is described by az-Zarkashi as having the size of the fingers of the hand, and Dawud al-Antaki expressly employs the word kaff and fingers of the hand

on which this statement is based ought to be fully discussed. At the same time, we must remember that even if any text proves this statement to be correct, it will not be of any importance in identifying the plant. If Mr. Havell is referring to the fact that Soma is described as having *parvas*; even then this fact alone does not lead to identification of the plant, but taken with other facts this might be utilized for the purpose of an identification. The colour of Soma has been variously described, and the internal evidence of the texts is that the different terms refer to the colour of the plant, or the drink itself at different stages of preparation. The word harih probably means a pleasant colour, although the word has been generally translates as "tawny." The exact translation requires discussion, but in any case its colour is not such that it will lead to an identification of the plant. The facts therefore on which Mr. Havell relies are that Soma has *parvas*, it is tawny in colour, and that it grows on mountains. These three elements are very general, and are by no means enough to identify the plant.

Mr. Havell seems to believe that the substitutes for Soma given in the Satapatha Brahmana are plants akin to Soma, and he refers to *dub* and *syenahrita*. I believe that in order to ascertain the propriety of substitution we must refer to the Yagnaparibhasa Sutra, and on the basis of the rules prescribed in that work we may be in a position to appreciate the reasons for adoption of particular plants as substitutes. It will be obvious to scholars that simply on the basis of elements utilized by Mr. Havell, it would indeed be difficult to arrive at the identification of Soma with *ragi*.

I propose that the following facts may be taken into consideration in connation with the subject under discussion:-

(1) Svetaketu Auddalaki says that the name of the plant is Usana (or Asana) (Sat, Br., V. 1, 1, 12).

(2) The name Soma was given to the plant after the Vaidik people came to know Asana or usana.

(3) Soma originally was amongst the Kiratas.

(4) Amongst the Kiratas *u* and *a* were particular prefixes.

(5) Therefore Usana or Asana resolves itself into Sana.

(6) According to the Satapatha Brahmana, Uma means the inner portion of the plant Sana. "Inside there is a layer of hemp, for the

to describe the size and shape of the hemp leaves" (Rosenthal, 1971).

purpose that it may blaze up. And as to its being a layer of hemp, the inner membrane (Amnion) of the womb from which Prajapati was born consists of Uma, and the outer membrane (Chorion) of hemp" (Sat. Br.)

(7) The Tanguts call hemp by the name Dschoma.

(8) In Dahuria, the Mughals call hemp by the name Schema.

(9) The Tibetan for hemp is Somaratsa.

(10) In Chinese Si-ma and Tsu-ma are the names of the male and female hemp plants.

(11) Dr. Sir George Watt says that the narcotic is really the female tsu-ma

(12) Hemp = A.S. *han-p* = Old Norse *hanp-r*, Lat. *Cannabis* = Low German (also High German) *hanaf*; Greek *Kavva* = Sk *Sana*.

(13) Soma has a dark skin (R.V., 7, 42, 9, 107, 5; Nirukta, 1, 7, 20).

(14) The prepared liquid is Arunah, Arushah, Sonah, etc.

(15) Soma is called Amsu (a ray) or that which is full of rays or soft hairs or having soft sprays or twigs. CF. Sumerian en-zu = Moon = Soma.

(16) It is called Varaha (Nirukta V., 1, 4).

(17) It is food for cows, it is a medicinal plant, the plant has a very strong and nauseating smell (*vajagandhyam*).

(18) Its habitat is Mujavan.

(19) Soma has the same habitat as that of Kushtha (Ath. V., 19, 39, 5). The north of the Himalayas is the habitat of Kushtha (Ath. V., V, 4, 8); Kushtha is Saussurea. Therefore, Soma's habitat is north of the Himalayas.

(20) Mujavan is one of the hills to the north of the Himalayas, south of the Kailas ranges, and is very probably the same as Memnam-nyim-re, south of Gurla Mandhata.

(21) The use of the drink results in the protrusion of the stomach.

(22) The preparation of Soma is similar to that of Bhang.

(23) The deity Mahadeva is a lover of Bhang.

(24) Bhang is used by the modern representatives of the Vaidik people in the celebration of the worship of the goddess Durga, which is a Soma sacrifice.

(25) Bhang is sacred to Hindus by tradition.

(26) The medicinal and other properties of Bhang should be discussed in connection with the present question and must be compared with those of soma if any can be gleaned from Vaidik sources.

(27) An attempt may also be made to ascertain if Ayurvedic texts give us any clue to the identification. I am myself not very sanguine about success in this direction, as great scholars have been mis-led by the following Ayurvedic text: "Shyamalamla cha nishpatra kheerinee twachi mangshala. Sleshmala vamanee ballee Somakhya chhagabhojanam" and further, because Ayurvedic works give fanciful descriptions of various kinds of Soma.

From what has been stated above, may we not conclude that the weight of evidence is in favour of the identification of Soma with Cannabis (Bhang).

I beg to draw the attention of the readers of this paper to my paper on the Soma plant, which has been very kindly published by the editors of the *Bulletin of the Indian Rationalistic Society of Calcutta.*[3]

Braja Lal Mukherjee, (1921)

---

3   Mukherjee failed to list an issue or date for his other article; thus I was unable to track it down.

Appendix B

On the etymology of *Haomavarga*, from Rüdiger Schmitt, The Old Persian Inscriptions of Naqsh-i Rustam and Persepolis, Corp. Inscr. Iran I/1, texts 2, (London, 2000):

As to the etymology of the name (and its potential translation), there is almost complete certainty only with the first element, OPers. *hauma-* (Av. *haoma-*, Mid. Pers., New Pers. *hōm*, Ved. *sóma-*), which in the Indo-Iranian languages is the name of a plant, as well as of the intoxicating beverage produced from it by pressing (Indo-Ir. **sau-*) and of its deified representation (see HAUMA). Scholars have not succeeded, however, in identifying this plant. The second element of the compound, *-varga-*, is still rather enigmatic (see Holzer... [1988]). Aside from unsubstantiated possibilities (requiring further assumptions) or mere constructions such as the association with Ir. **varg-* 'to drink' (from IE. **uelg-* 'to be damp, moist,' cf. Schmid, p. 21, thus "drinking *hauma*"), or Ir. **barg-* 'to honor, praise' (from IE. **bhergh-*, comparing Khot. *aurggā-*, *orgā-* 'reverence,' thus 'praising *Hauma*'; cf. Gershevitch, 1969... improving on Duchesne-Guillemin... [1974] or Ir. **varg-* 'to treat solemnly, celebrate' (in Av. *var-exeδra-*, supposedly 'ritual utterance,' thus 'revering *Hauma*'; cf. Bailey, 1971, p. 15), or even Ir. **hvar-* (here enlarged by *−g-*) 'to consume, to eat or drink' (cf. Gershevitch, 1974... who gave up his former suggestion for this and thought of a 'nickname' **Hauma-hvarga-* '*hauma*-swiller'), there is only one interpretation worth considering, that of Karl Hoffmann...[1976] compared *−varga-* with Av. *varj*, Ved. *varj*, *vrnákti* 'to turn (over, away), to lay (around something),' especially with Ved. *vrnktá-*

barhis- 'having laid the sacrificial grass around (the fire).' He thus interpreted and translated the entire compound as 'laying *hauma*-plants (instead of the usual grass) around (the fire).' Bruno Jacobs (...[1982]) changed this interpretation to refer to the Scythian custom of laying cannabis seeds on the blaz- ing hot stones of their steam

Representation of Scythian Hamoavarga inhaling cannabis fumes.

baths, by which they produced clouds of vapor having an intoxicating effect (see Herodotus 4.75.1).

All former proposals which had started from the reading *-varka-* (common until 1911) have to be abandoned, i.e., the connections with Ir. **varka-* (Av. *vareka*) 'leaf' (Justi...[1904]: '[boiling] the *hauma*-leaves') or Ir. **vr´kta-* (Av. *vehrka-*) 'wolf" (AirWb., col. 1735: '*hauma*-wolves,' specified by Wikander...[1938] as '[people] who change into werewolves while drunk with hauma')." (Schmitt, 2000).

APPENDIX C

Fitz Hugh Ludlow on Pythagoras and Hashish, from *The Hasheesh Eater*, (1856)

I t would be no hard task to prove, to a strong probability at least, that the initiation to the Pythagorean mysteries, and the progressive instructions which preceded it, to a considerable extent consisted in the employment, judiciously, if we may use the word, of hasheesh as giving a critical and analytical power

Fitz Hugh Ludlow
SOURCE: Wilson, James Grant and John Fiske.
*Appletons' Cyclopaedia of American Biography,
Volume IV*. New York: D. Appleton & Co., 1888.

to the mind, which enabled the neophyte to roll up the murk and mist from beclouded truths till they stood distinctly seen in the splendour of their own harmonious beauty as an intuition.

One thing related of Pythagoras and his friends has seemed very striking to me. There is a legend that, as he was passing over a river, its waters called up to him, in the presence of his followers, "Hail! Pythagoras." Frequently, while in the power of the hasheesh delirium, have I heard inanimate things sonorous with such voices. On every side they have saluted me, from rocks, and trees, and waters, and sky; in my happiness filling me with intense exultation as I heard them welcoming their master; in my agony heaping nameless curses on my head as I went away into an eternal exile from all sympathy. Of this tradition of Iamblichus I feel an appreciation which almost convinces me that the voice of the river was indeed heard, though only by the quickened mind of some hasheesh-glorified esoterie. Again, it may be that the doctrine of the metempsychosis was first communicated to Pythagoras by Theban[1] priests; but the astonishing illustration which hasheesh would contribute to this tenet should not be overlooked in our attempt to assign its first suggestion and succeeding spread to their proper causes.

A modern critic, in defending the hypothesis that Pythagoras was an imposter, has triumphantly asked, "Why did he assume the character of Apollo at the Olympic games? Why did he boast that his soul had lived in former bodies, and that he had first been Æthalides, the son of Mercury, then Euphorbus, then Pyrrhus of Delos, and at last Pythagoras, but that he might more easily impose upon the credulity of an ignorant and superstitious people?" To us these facts seem rather an evidence of his sincerity. Had he made these assertions without proof, it is difficult to see how they would not have had a precisely contrary effect from that of paving the way to a more complete imposition upon popular credulity. Upon our hypothesis it may be easily shown, not only how he could fully have believed these assertions himself, but also have given them a deep significance to the minds of his disciples.

Pythagoras

Let us see. We will consider, for example, his assumption of the character of Phoebus at the Olympic games. Let us suppose that Pythagoras, animated with a desire of alluring to the study of his philosophy a choice and enthusiastic number out of that host who, along all the radii of the civilized world, had come up to the solemn festival at Elis, had, by the talisman of hasheesh, called to his aid the magic of a preternatural eloquence; that while he addressed the throng, whom he had chained into breathless attention by the weird brilliancy of his eye, the unearthly imagery of his style, and the oracular insight of his thought, the

1   The home of the alleged cannabis beverage *Nepenthe*.

grand impression flashed upon him from the very honor he was receiving, that he was the incarnation of some sublime deity. What wonder that he burst into the acknowledgment of his godship as a secret too majestic to be hoarded up; what wonder that this sudden revelation of himself, darting forth in burning words and amid such colossal surroundings, went down with the accessories of time and place along the stream of perpetual tradition?

If I may illustrate great things by small, I well remember many hallucinations of my own which would be exactly parallel to such a fancy in the mind of Pythagoras. There is no impression more deeply stamped upon my past life than one of a walk along the brook which had so often witnessed my wrestlings with the hasheesh-afreet, and which now beheld me, the immortal Zeus, descended among men to grant them the sublime benediction of renovated life. For this cause I had abandoned the serene seats of Olympus, the convocation of the gods, and the glory of an immortal kingship, while by my side Hermes trod the earth with radiant feet, the companion and dispenser of the beneficence of Deity. Across lakes and seas, from continent to continent we strode; the snows of Hæmus and the Himmalehs crunched beneath our sandals; our foreheads were bathed with the upper light, our breasts glowed with the exultant inspiration of the golden ether. Now resting on Chimborzao, I poured forth a majestic blessing upon all my creatures, and in an instant, with one omniscient glance, I beheld every human dwelling-place on the whole sphere irradiated with an unspeakable joy.

I saw the king rule more wisely; the laborer return from his toil to a happier home; the park grow green with an intenser culture; the harvest-field groan under the sheaves of a more prudent and prosperous husbandry. Adown blue slopes came new and more populous flocks, led by unvexed and gladsome shepherds; a thousand healthy vineyards sprang up above their new-raised sunny terraces; every smallest heart glowed with an added thrill of exultation, and the universal rebound of joy came pouring up into my own spirit with an intensity which lit my deity with rapture.

And this was but a lay hasheesh-eater, mysteriously clothed in no Pallas-woven, philosophic stole, who, with his friend, walked out into the fields to enjoy his delirium among the beauties of a clear summer afternoon. What, then, of Pythagoras? (Ludlow, 1856)

PROF. DR. OTTO WILHELM THOMÉ, *FLORA VON DEUTSCHLAND*, 1885

APPENDIX D

Henrik S. Nyberg on the identity of Haoma

Pentti Aalto has noted that "The renowned Swedish Orientalist and historian of religion, H. S. Nyberg, supported the opinion that the plant in question [Soma] was *Cannabis sativa*, or hemp. The Swedish school of Iranist has in general accepted this interpretation of the *haoma* ~ *soma*" (Aalto, 1998). I am not convinced this is a wholly correct interpretation of Nyberg's work. I have a copy of Nyberg's *Die Religionen Des Alten Iran* (1938) and had portions translated for the chapter in Zoroaster, and from what I understand, Nyberg identifies mang with cannabis, but essentially different from haoma, which he describes as unidentified: "Haoma, the *Soma* of the Indians, is the ancient Arian potion of immortality, an intoxicating juice that was extracted from a no longer identifiable plant (the plant that is used nowadays in Haoma offerings is at a guess an alternative)" (Nyberg, 1938).[1] [Translated by Jake Czerpak].

In *Irans forntida religioner*, Nyberg saw the re-emergence of the Haoma cult in Zoroastrian times as "Zarathustra's great spiritual crisis", which Henning's, in disdain for Nyberg's research, felt could be "summed up in four words: alcohol prevailed over hemp" (Henning, 1951).

---

1   Although Aalto's view on Nyberg's research has been put forth by others: "L. Mukherjee proposed hemp, Cannabis sativa/indica, as sauma. Henrik Samuel Nyberg [1938] independently gave support for this, but Walter Bruno Henning (1951...), rejecting his theory of Zoroaster's use of hemp, voiced a modern Western aversion towards psychotropic substances as leading to 'physical, mental, and moral deterioration.' This, however, ignored the importance of dosage" (Taillieu, 2002).

Zarathustra's great spiritual crisis was thus brought about due to the fact that the old Haoma cult disrupted the effect of the magus and destroyed his movement. He was not able to avoid this disruptive effect, as he himself introduced the Haoma cult in his congregation. The magus thereby suffered a 'fatal blow'. It didn't happen at once or through a conscious act of volition, but in the long run and it made the inherent basic forces of the two colliding religious forms possible. The same opposition appeared between the old Mithra religion and the Gatha religion as between the Apollonian and Dionysian religions, which Fr. Nietzsche had discovered in Greece and that E. Rohde wonderfully developed in his monumental work, 'Psyche'. All signs suggest that the Mithra religion is the Apollonian religion of Iran. It has a sober, juristic and formalistic character. It was a religion for warriors and chiefs. Even if its 'Ordal' as with all 'Ordals', was connected to certain primitive ecstatic practices, these did not have a lot to do with holy intoxication, with senseless [Greek word]. Mithra "is awake and doesn't sleep": the sober, ecstasy-free, normal psyche is the spiritual air of the Mithra religion. It had its Haoma intoxication, but that was a clean alcoholic intoxication, and Zarathustra surely had a point that this was incompatible with the ecstasy of the magus. The drinking of Haoma caused a more ordinary/standard inebriation than ecstasy. The Gatha religion, on the other hand, can justifiably be called the Dionysian religion of Iran. In this religion the deity completely satisfies the holy. There is rapture, holy song, trance, the journey of the soul in to the spirit world and its return with the secrets of heaven. Here the deity speaks as a friend to friends. That means a high tension of the soul that cannot continue arbitrarily for much longer, and it is no wonder, that the religion of the sober and clear consciousness, the Mithra religion, won out in the end. Zarathustra himself appears in all his ecstasy to have been a man capable of practical dealings with an unemotional judgment and a clear sense of reality – characteristics that are in no way inconsistent with the *Seelenlage* (spiritual condition) of an ecstatic. As the founder of a religion, he had an open view for the basic spiritual value of the Mithra religion and he gave this a rightful place in the Haoma cult. (Nyberg, 1938).

We now know of course, that Haoma was not an alcoholic beverage, as Nyberg apparently believed, but the same theme he suggests above could well be applied to the situation of the mild Ephedra beverage that resulted from Zoroaster's reforms. As well, from surviving Zoroastrian accounts it clearly seems possible that the use of hemp for such shamanic practices as those attributed to Zoroaster, Vishtaspa, and Arda Wiraf, continued close to, and even up until, the dawn of the Islamic period, where its use was driven somewhat underground but still carried on despite the harshest of penalties.

Cannabineae.

Cannabis sativa L.

W. Müller

FROM *MEDICINAL PLANTER*, BY FRANZ EUGEN KÖHLER, 1887.

APPENDIX E

John Kitto on the origins of the word "Hashish"

In different publications of A Cyclopaedia of Biblical Literature, the 19th century scholar John Kitto put forth two, potentially related, etymologies for "hashish", through Hebrew terms *Shesh*, which originates in reference to some sort of "fibre plant", and the possibly related word, *Eshishah*, (*E-shesh-ah*?) which holds connotations of "syrup" or "unguent."

SHESH... also SHESHI, translated *fine linen* in the Authorized Version, occurs twenty eight times in Exodus, once in Genesis, once in Proverbs, and three times in Ezekiel. Considerable doubts have, however, always been entertained respecting the true meaning of the word; some have thought it signified *fine wool*, others *silk*; the Arabs have translated it by words referring to colours in the passages of Ezekiel and of Proverbs. Some of the Rabbins state that it is the same word as that which denotes the number six, and that it refers to the number of threads of which the yarn was composed. ... This interpretation, however, has satisfied but few....

Shesh... must... be taken into consideration. In several passages where we find the word used, we do not obtain any information respecting the plant; but it is clear it was spun by women (Exod. xxx. 25), was used as an article of clothing, also for hangings, and even for the sails of ships, as in Ezekiel xxvii. 7. It is evident from these facts that it must have been a plant known as cultivated in Egypt at the earliest period, and which, or its fibre, the Israelites were able to obtain even when in the desert. As cotton does not appear to have been known at this very early period, we must seek for *shesh* among the other fibre yielding plants, such as flax and hemp. Both these are suited to the purpose, and were procurable in those countries at the times specified. Lexicographers do not give us much assistance in determining the point, from the little certainty in their inferences. The word *shesh*, however, appears to us to have a very great resemblance, with the exception of the aspirate, to the Arabic name of a plant, which, it is curious, was also one of those earliest cultivated for its fibre, namely *hemp*. Of this plant, one of the Arabic names is… *husheesh*, or the herb *par excellence*, the term being sometimes applied to the powdered leaves only, with which an intoxicating electuary is prepared. This name has long been known, and is thought by some to have given origin to our word assassin, or hassasin. Makrizi treats of the hemp in his account of the ancient pleasure grounds in the vicinity of Cairo, "famous above all for the sale of the hasheesha,, which is still greedily consumed by the dregs of the people, and from the consumption of which sprung the excesses, which led to the name of 'assassin' being given to the Saracens in the holy wars."

"Hemp is a plant which in the present day is extensively distributed, being cultivated in Europe, and extending through Persia to the southernmost parts of India. There is no doubt, therefore, that 'it might easily have been cultivated in Egypt. We are, indeed, unable at present to prove that it was cultivated in Egypt at an early period, and used for making garments, but there is nothing improbable in its having been so. Indeed, as it was known to various Asiatic nations, it could hardly have been unknown to the Egyptians. Hemp might thus have been used at an early period, along with flax and wool, for making cloth for garments and for hangings, and would be much valued until cotton and the finer kinds of linen came to be known.... There is no doubt... that it might easily have been cultivated in Egypt."

"...Indeed, as it was known to various Asiatic nations, it could hardly have been unknown to the Egyptians, and the similarity of the word *hasheesh* to the Arabic *shesh* would lead to a belief that they were acquainted with it..." (Kitto, 1856)

ESHISHAH, *eshishah*, once translated 'flagon' only: in three passages 'flagon of *wine*' and once 'flagon' with grapes joined to it in the original, as noticed in the margin (Hosea iii. 1). The Sept. renders it in four different ways, viz. ... 'a cake from the frying-pan' (2 Sam. vi. 19); in another part, which narrates the same fact..., 'a sweet cake of fine flour and honey' (1 Chron. xvi. 3)... a cake made with raisins (Hos. iii. 1), *raisins here corresponding to 'grapes' in the Hebrew ; and by one copy..., 'sweet cakes' (Cant. ii. 5) ; but in others '*unguents*' [!-emphasis added]. In the Targum to the Hebrew... tzappikhith. in Exod. xvi. 31, the Chaldee term is... [Hebrew] *ethiilian*, 'a cake,' rendered in our version by 'wafers.' Eshishah has been supposed to be connected with [Hebrew]... ash, 'fire' and to denote some sort of 'sweet cake' prepared with fire; but the second part of the word has not been hitherto explained."

"Perhaps the following extract from Olearius (1637) may throw light on the kind of preparations denoted by shemarin [preserves or jellies] and *eshishah*: 'The Persians are permitted to make a sir-rup of sweet wine, which they boyl till it be reduc'd to a sixth part, and be grown as thick as oyl. They call this drug *duschab* [deb-hash], and when they would take, of it, they dissolve it with water.' 'Sometimes they boyl the *duschab* so long that they reduce it into a paste, for the convenience of travellers, who cut it with a knife, and dissolve it in water.' At Tabris they make a certain conserve of it, which they call *halva*... mixing therewith beaten almonds, flour, &c. They put this mixture into a long and narrow bag, and having set it under the press, they make of it a paste, which grows so hard that a man must have a hatchet to cut it. They make also a kind of conserve of it, much like a pudding, which they call *zutzuch*, thrusting through the middle of it a small cotton thread to keep the paste together... Amongst the presents received by the ambassadors there is enumerated 'a bottle of *scherab* [syrup]

The Old Man of the Mountain administers hashish laced wine to neophyte Hashishins

or Persian wine'... This *zutzuch* is but a harsh corruption of the Hebrew *eshishah*, and is by others called *hashish* and *achicha*. Even this substance, in course of time, was converted into a medium of intoxication by means of drugs. Hemp *is* cultivated and used as a narcotic over all Arabia. The flowers, when mixed with tobacco, are called *hashish*. The higher classes eat it (hemp) in a jelly or paste called *majoon* mixed with honey, or other sweet drugs' ... De Sacy and Lane derive the name of the Eastern sect of 'Assassins' (*Hashshusheen*). 'hemp- eaters', from their practice of using shahdanaj [Persian – cannabis] to fit them for their dreadful work. El-ldreesee, indeed, applies the term *Hasheesheeyeh* to the 'Assassins'. (Kitto, 1845/1854)

Appendix F

Revelation

Generally, I try to keep myself out of my historical writings, but I so often get asked about how I came to have such an interest in the role of cannabis in religion, that some explanation may be due.

In 1990, I experienced a synchronization of events that led to a religious experience that is undeniably at the core of my own research interests. At that time, I was a surfer on the West Coast of British Columbia's Vancouver Island. I was living a hedonistic life of many surfers, working 3 nights a week at a union job as a night watchman in a local fish plant, cutting back on living expenses with a hobby cannabis garden in my back shed, and ripping up the cold and un-crowded Canadian Pacific waves. It should also be noted that at that point in my life, I had no background in either writing or religious studies, (in fact I still don't have a high school diploma.)

The first of these synchronistic events occurred with the exposing of the rampant pedophilia problem within the Catholic Church that was coming to light via the testimony of adults who had spent time as children in Newfoundland's Mount Cashel Orphanage. Although I was not brought up within a religious family, these events drew my interests and in an effort to try to understand the problem at its roots, I decided to try and read the Bible, and having a job as a night watchman in a west Coast fish plant, I had plenty of time to do so, so I went out and picked one up. I tried reading it, but found it very hard to read and extremely boring and did not make it far, so it got put away in the night watchman's room and forgot about it for some months.

Another factor was that I had also first learned of the many uses of cannabis besides smoking it, such as fiber for clothes, seed for food, oils for paints and fuels and the like. Up until the 90's term "Hemp" had fallen into such disuse that few even knew this was a reference to cannabis, and when a friend first told me about the industrial uses of Hemp, I was extremely skeptical. As well, it was a hard subject to research, as all literature that was pro cannabis had been virtually banned at that time in Canada, but upon looking through some encyclopedias at the library I began to learn that my friend's claims had a basis of fact behind them. This was of particular interest to me at that time, as the area where I lived was caught up in a battle between loggers and environmentalist and I could see that cannabis (in the form of industrial hemp) may hold the answer in the equation of jobs vs. the environment. Fifty percent of trees harvested go to the pulp mill to become paper products and all of this could be replaced by renewable cannabis crops, which are thought to vastly out produce trees for paper when grown and harvested for those purposes.

Simultaneous with these events, the first Gulf War in Iraq began to unfold which initiated a fear in myself and many others that this war could escalate to a global scale. Accordingly, I came to the belief that not only did cannabis for paper offer the solution to the over-logging of Canada's old growth forests, but that it could also provide a viable bio-diesel alternative to the oil deposits that the first Gulf War seemed to really be about.

One night, or rather in the very early morning hours, while working as a night watchman, I was sitting at the empty lunchroom table by myself, smoking a thumb sized joint of the potent *Cannabis indica* that I had grown in my shed and reading the newspaper. That newspaper contained an advertisement from a well known American Evangelist, about an upcoming stadium service. In the advertisement, the Preacher was positioned at the pulpit, and behind him were military tanks and jests and the theme of the sermon tied the then-ongoing Gulf War with Revelations 18 (The Fall of Babylon).

Babylon once sat in the place of modern Iraq, and having followed the developing story, I knew that people in the Mid-East and

America, due to Saddam Hussein's firing of a scud missile into Israel, were drawing analogies between Saddam and Nebuchadnezzar, the last king of Babylon, who conquered ancient Israel. Thus, I became caught up in the apocalyptic ardor of the moment. Having seen apocalyptic movies like The Omen as a child, along with talking with the occasional Jehovah's Witness, as well as being of the generation that approached the close of the millennia, I was already deeply influenced by societal imprinting that holds the scenario of Revelations as a deep core belief. I immediately retrieved the Bible I had left in the night watchman's office and excitedly read through the Book of Revelations. I noted with interest how the Prophet John was given a scroll to eat before prophesying (Revelation 10:10). The scroll tasted sweet in his mouth and turned bitter in his stomach, which I understood as a descriptive of the ingestion of a psychoactive substance in order to produce a visionary state. After drawing this analogy in my own mind, the references to the incense with the prayers of the Saint and their billowing clouds of smokes (Revelation 5:8, 8:3) along with accounts of God's "witness's" dressed in "sack cloth" (Revelation 11:3) caught my interest, and, finally, I reached the end revelation and read the account of the Tree of Life.

> On either side of the River of Life stood the Tree of Life, bearing twelve manner of fruits, and yielded her fruit every month, and the leaves of the tree were for the healing of the nations.(Revelation 22:2).

At this point, I had an epiphany. It was like a divine information-filled light entered my being leaving me with the strong intuitive knowledge that cannabis was that Tree of Life described at the end of the Book of Revelation. This was the pivotal moment of my entire life and the deciding factor in the path I would follow from then on.

Cannabis has well known, numerous and historical industrial uses (i.e. fruits). Its' leaves have historically been used for healing, it was a major medicine prior to being prohibited for everything from corns and bunions to coughs and consumption (and today Canadian residents are able to obtain legal authority to use cannabis for its healing potential pursuant to the MMAR). The fruits of the tree of life are the cannabis plants many uses, these also aid in

the restoration of the environment and offer eco-friendly alternatives to environmentally damaging cotton production and the use
of petroleum based products. The seed of the cannabis plant, and
oil expressed from that seed, have many nutritional benefits. Cannabis fibers are made into cloth, paper made from hemp offer an
alternative source to the harvesting of trees, and the whole plant
can be used in the production of bio-mass fuels which could help
to solve the world's dependency on fossil fuels. Cannabis is also
harvested every month of the year. Knowing these facts and deeply
under the influence of cannabis and the religious experience it provoked in me in the circumstances, I found it impossible to ignore
these analogies with the Biblical Tree of Life.

When I awoke my then wife with an early morning phone call
relating this revelation, she became extremely upset, crying on the
phone and telling me I was having a mental break down and the
next day, no longer under the immediacy of the cannabis-induced
religious experience, my analytical mind began to feel the stirrings
of doubt about this intuitive experience. I resolved to research
my newfound understanding of cannabis' place in my theology
to determine whether there existed support for my revelation or
whether it was simply the product of a "stoned" mind As I pondered my experience, and looked out of my front window at clear
cut mountain tops, I would think that one thing I did know was
that hemp paper could save those trees and my conscience drove
me to discuss and advocate for the use of cannabis to solve these
environmental issues to all who would hear. As well, I figured that
if cannabis is the Tree of Life, then someone else somewhere will be
aware of that fact, and I soon found there were historical references
to the medicinal and spiritual use of cannabis in diverse cultures
going back millennia which helped identify the "leaves for the healing of the nations", a phrase often quoted in reference to cannabis
by Rastafarians. I began to collect and compile this information.

Shortly after this initial experience I noted that others had independently accepted and come to this same belief in cannabis being the Tree of Life. For example, references appear throughout
Rastafarian texts and music. One day, on a business visit with a
Chinese businessman who was importing hemp cloth into Canada,
I noticed a picture on his wall of an old hippy gentle man poking
his head out between cannabis plants, and the slogan on the im-

age stated "Church of the Universe, Tree of Life Sacrament". The Church of the Universe formed in 1969, when a group of hippies began noticing that whenever they smoked cannabis at their gathering the conversations often took on a tone of the philosophical and spiritual. I joined this Church in 1991 and have remained a member to this day and I am proud to say that I have been instrumental to the Church in documenting the religious connotations and connections of cannabis by providing evidence that has gained notable and increasing academic support, and helping to bring this knowledge to wider public.

In the early 90's I also became friends with members of a Jamaican group known as the Ethiopian Zion Coptic Church which accepted cannabis as the Tree of Life, and one of their members, Jeff Brown, had also been come over with this drive to collect and document the historical role of cannabis in religion. The foundation provided by Jeff in his booklet Marijuana and the Bible was a very real affirmation to me that I was following the right path. Currently there are now dozens of international Churches that use cannabis, and the fight for their rights to this most sacred of plants has taken place in numerous court rooms and continues on.

It has been said that the method of telling a genuine theophany from mere delusion is either by a sudden physical healing or if one is transmitted information which turns out to be true, and which you had no way of knowing in advance. Over twenty years later, after being part of, and witnessing the legalization and advancement of industrial hemp and medical marijuana in Canada and other places, as well as researching and writing dozens of articles and three large books documenting the historical role of cannabis in religion, I find myself believing in the veracity of my original religious experience and the revelations produced in the wake of it more today than I did when it originally occurred, and affirmation has been found.

ILLUSTRATIONS

Cover painting – Bob Nightingale

Fig 3.1, 3.2 - Rudgley, Richard; Essential Substances, (Kodansha International 1993).

Fig 4.6, 18.20, 18.10, 18.14 – www.exoticindiaart.com

Fig 6.1, 6.2, 6.6, 6.7, 7.17 - Sarianidi, Victor I. Margiana and Soma-Haoma, ‚ELEC-TRONIC JOURNAL OF VEDIC STUDIES, VOL. 9 (2003), ISSUE 1 (May)

Fig 6.3 - Fleming, Michael P. and Clarke, Robert C., Physical evidence for the antiquity of Cannabis in Cannabis: The Genus Cannabis By David T. Brown, (CRC Press, 1998)

Fig 6.4, 9.4 - Jiang et. al., The discovery of Capparis spinosa L. (Capparidaceae) in the Yanghai Tombs (2800 years b.p.) NW China, and its medicinal implications, Journal of Ethnopharmacology 113 (2007)

Fig 7.4, 7.5, 7.11, 7.12, 7.13, 7.21, 7.23, 9.14 - Charriere, Georges, Scythian Art: Crafts of the Early Eurasian Nomads, (New York,1979).

Fig 7.7, 7.9 - Rjabchikov, Sergei V., Remarks on the Scythian, Sarmatian and Meotian Beliefs, (2004)

Fig. 7.14 - Rudenko, Sergei I.. Frozen Tombs of Siberia – the Pazyryk burials of Iron Age horsemen, (University of California Press, 1970)

Fig 7.15 - Kisel, V.A., Herodotus' Scythian logos and ritual vessels of the early nomads, Archaeology, Ethnology and Anthropology of Eurasia, Volume 31, Number 3 (October, 2007)

Page 154, 18.3, 18.15 - Ratsch, Christian, Marijuana Medicine, (Inner Traditions, 1998, 2001)

Fig 9.2 - Russo, et. al., Phytochemical and genetic analyses of ancient cannabis from Central Asia, Journal of Experimental Botany, (Oxford, 2008)

Fig 9.3 - Jiang, et. al., A new insight into Cannabis sativa (Cannabaceae) utilization from 2500-year-old Yanghai Tombs, Xinjiang, China,by Jiang Hong-En, Xiao Li, Zhao You-Xing, Ferguson David K., Heuber, Francis, Bera Subir, Wang Yu-Fei, Zhao Liang-Cheng, Liu Chang-Jiang, Li Cheng-Sen, (2006)

Fig. 9.12 - Barber, EW., The Mummies of Urumchi, (New York: Norton, 1999)

Fig 10.2 - Wooley, Sir Leonard, Ur of the Chaldees, (1929)

Fig12.1 - Rudolph, Kurt Gnosis: The Nature and History of Gnosticism. Harper, San Francisco, 1987

Fig 19.2 - Green, Nile, Islam and the Army in Colonial India: Sepoy Religion in the Service of Empire (Cambridge Studies in Indian History and Society, 2009)

Fig 19.3 - Karamustafa, Ahmet T., God's Unruly Friends: Dervish Groups in the Islamic Later Middle Period, 1200-1550 (1994) (B Publications, Oxford, United Kingdom, 2006)

BIBLIOGRAPHY

Aalto, Pentti, Finnish olut and humala, once again, in *Oekeeta Asijoo: Commentationes Fenno-Ugricae in honorem Seppo Suhonen* (1998).

Aanova, Monday 7th October 2002, "Scientists recreate the perfume of the pharaoh"

Abaev, Vasilii Ivanovich, "Contribution aà l'histoire des mots: 1. Vieil-iranien hauma- et le nom eurasien du houblon," tr. Jacques Veyrenc, in Me,langes linguistiques offerts à Émile Benveniste, Collection Linguistique publice,e par la Socie,te, de Linguistique de Paris 70, (Paris, 1975)

Abel, Ernest; 1980, *Marihuana, The First Twelve Thousand Years*, Phenum Press

Akhtar, Asif, Pakistan's 'heretical' Muslims Increasingly threatened by religious extremists, Sufis are the inheritors of a tradition that predates Islam in south Asia, Guardian. co.uk, Friday 23 October 2009 http://www.guardian.co.uk/commentisfree/belief/2009/oct/23/pakistan-sufis-terrorism-shrines

Alakbarov, Farid U. PhD, ScD, *Medicinal Properties of Cannabis According to Medieval Manuscripts of Azerbaijan*, (Institute of Manuscripts of the Azerbaijan Academy, Baku, Azerbaijan, 2001)

Aldrich, Michael, "Cannabis and its Derivatives," *High Times Encyclopaedia of Recreational Drugs*, (Trans High Corp, NY, 1978)

Aleff, Peter, "Maat soul-mate Seshat convicted for possessing pot and undeclared math," http://www.recoveredscience.com/const201seshathempmath.htm#_edn4, (1982)

Alexander; William Menzies;, *Demonic Possession in the New Testament: Its Historical, Medical, and Theological Asepcts*, (Baker Book House, Michigan, 1980 org. 1902)

Allsen, Thomas T., *Commodity and Exchange in the Mongol Empire: A Cultural History of Islamic Textiles*, (Cambridge University Press, 1997)

American Society for Clinical Investigation, "The: Inhibition of skin tumour growth and angiogenesis in vivo by activation of cannabinoid receptors," *Journal of Clinical Investigation*, Authors: M. Llanos Casanova, Cristina Blázquez, Jesús Martínez-Palacio, Concepción Villanueva, M. Jesús Fernández-Aceñero, John W. Huffman, José L. Jorcano and Manuel Guzmán, J. Clin. Invest. 111:43-50 (2003).

Andreas, G. Nerlich, Franz Parsche, Irmgard Wiest, Peter Schramel, Udo Löhrs: "Extensive pulmonary haemorrhage in an Egyptian mummy," *Virchows Arch* (1995) 427:423-429, Springer-Verlag

Anderson, William, *Green Man: The Archetype of Our Oneness with the Earth*, (Harper Collins 1990)

Andrews, George, *Drugs and Magic*, (1975: Illuminet, 1997)

Angus, S., *The Mystery-Religions*, (Dover,1975)

Annual of Armenian Linguistics, (Cleveland State University, 1987)

Anthony, David W., *The Horse, the Wheel, and Language: How Bronze-Age Riders from the Eurasian Steppes Shaped the Modern World*, (Princeton University Press, 2008)

Arata , Luigi, "Nepenthes and Cannabis in Ancient Greece," *Janus Head*, (Summer 2004).

Arya, Dr. Pasang Yonten, *Dictionary of Tibetan Materia Medica* (Motilal Banarsidass Publishers, 1998).

Associated Press, "Hashish Evidence is 1,600 years Old, in *The Province*," Vancouver, British Columbia, (June 2nd, 1992)

Avalon, Arthur, *The Great Liberation, (Ganesh* Publishing, 1913)

Avalon, Arthur , *Shakti and Shackta*, (1918/2008 – BiblioBazaar)

Babayan, Kathryn, *Mystics, monarchs, and messiahs: cultural landscapes of early modern Iran* (Harvard University. Center for Middle Eastern Studies, 2002)

Bacon,Edward, *Archeology Discoveries in the 1960s*, (Praeger, 1971) [as quoted in (Frazier, 1991)]

Bagli, Dr. Jehan, "The Significance of Plant Life in Zarathushti Liturgy," *FEZANA journal*, (Summer 2005)

Bailey, Harold W., "Trends in Iranian Studies, Memoirs of the Research Department of the Toyo Bunko 29," (1971) Idem, *Indo-Scythian Studies Being Khotanese Texts* VII, Cambridge, etc., (1985).

Bakels, C.C., "Report concerning the contents of a ceramic vessel found in the "white room" of the Gonur Temenos," Merv Oasis, Turkmenistan. *Electronic Journal of Vedic Studies*, Vol. 9 (2003), ISSUE 1 (May)

Baigent, Michael, Richard Leigh & Henry Lincoln; *The Holy Blood and the Holy Grail*, (Corgi Books, 1982)

Balabanova, S., F. Parsche and W. Pirsig, "First identification of drugs in Egyptian mummies," *Naturwissenschaften*, (1992)

Barber, E. J. W., *Prehistoric Textiles: The Development of Cloth in the Neolithic and Bronze Ages with Special Reference to the Aegean*, (Princeton University Press, 1991)

Barber, E.W., *Pre-historic Textiles*, Princeton University Press, (1989)

Barber, E.W., *The Mummies of Urumchi*, (New York: Norton, 1999)

Basham, A.L., *The Wonder That Was India. A Survey of the Culture of the Indian Sub-Continent before the coming of the Muslims*,(1954)

Bhattacharyya, Bhaskar with Nik Douglas and Penny Slinger, *The Path of the Mystic Lover: Baul Songs of Passion and Ecstasy* (Destiny Books, 1993)

Beal, Rev. S., "Text and Commentary of the Memorial of Sakya Buddha Tathagata." By Wong Pch. (Translated from the Chinese by the Rev. S. Beal.) *Journal of the Royal Asiatic Society of Great Britain and Ireland*, Volume 20, prefatory remarks by the Rev. Spence Hardy, (Royal Asiatic Society of Great Britain and Ireland, 1863)

Bedrosian, Robert, *Soma Among the Armenians*, (2006) http://rbedrosian.com/soma.htm

Beck, Richard & Worden, David, *GCSE Religious Studies for AQA: Truth, Spirituality and Contemporary Issues*, (Heinemann Educational Publishers, 2001)

Belardi, B., *The Pahlavi Book of the Righteous Viraz*, (Rome: University Department of Linguistics and Italo-Iranian Cultural Centre, 1979)

Benet, Sula; "Early Diffusions and Folk Uses of Hemp," in *Cannabis and Culture*, Vera Rubin Editor, (The Hague: Moutan 1975).

Benetowa, Sara, [Sula Benet]; "Tracing One Word Through Different Languages," (1936), Republished in *The Book of Grass* (1967)

Benjamin, Samuel Greene Wheeler, *Troy: Its Legend, History and Literature*, (1880).

Bennett, Chris and McQueen, Neil, *Sex Drugs, Violence and the Bible*, (Forbidden Fruit Publishing, 2001)

Bennett, Chris and Osburn, Lynn and Judy, *Green Gold the Tree of Life; Marijuana in Magic and Religion*, (Access Unlimited, 1995).

Bennett, Chris, "A History of the Royal Grain," *Cannabis Culture*, (01 Jan, 1999).

Bennett, Chris, Cannabis, "A Healing and Magical Balm," *Cannabis Culture*, (2006).

Bennett, Chris, 'Smoke of the Ages', *Cannabis Culture*, #53, (May, 2005)

Bercovici Konrad, *The Crusades*, (Cosmopolitan Book Corporation, New York, 1929).

Bernardus, Franciscus and Kuiper, Jacobus, "Was the Putīka A Mushroom?" in Shivram Dattatray Joshi, ed., *Amrátadhârá: Professor R. N. Dandekar Felicitation Volume*, Delhi, (1984).

Besant, Walter, and Palmer, E. H., *Jerusalem, the city of Herod and Saladin*, (1871).

Bey, Hakim and Zug, Abel, *Orgies of the Hemp Eaters*, (Autonomedia, 2004).

Birdy, Ervad Jal President of the North American Mobeds Council and the Vice-President of the Traditional Mazdayasni Zoroastrian Anjuman, "Jal bBirdy's response on Jafarey's 'haoma'" (2000). http://www.factnfalse.com/Jal%20Birdy's%20Response%20on%20Haoma.htm

Bleeck, Arthur Henry and von Spiegel, Friedrich *Avesta*, (1864).

Bolton, et. al., Triad Societies: *Western Accounts of the History, Sociology and Linguistics of Chinese Secret Societies*. By Kingsley Bolton, Christopher Hutton, James K. Chin, (Taylor & Francis, 2000).

Bonnefoy, Yves, and Doniger, Wendy, *Asian mythologies*, Translated by Wendy Doniger, Gerald Honigsblum, Edition: 2, (University of Chicago Press, 1993).

Bourke, John G., *Scatalogic Rites of All Nations*, (1891).

Bouquet, R.J., *Cannabis*, Bull Narc (1950).

Bowles, Gordon T., *The People of Asia*, (1977).

Boyce, Mary and Grenet, Frantz, *A History of Zoroastrianism*, (Brill, 1982).

Boyce, Mary, *A History of Zoroastrianism*, Contributor Frantz Grenet, Roger Beck, (Brill, 1982).

Boyce, Mary, "Haoma Ritual," *Iranian Religions: Zoroastrianism*, (1990). http://www.cais-soas.com/CAIS/Religions/iranian/Zarathushtrian/haoma_ritual.htm

Boyce, Mary, *Zoroastrians: Their Religious Beliefs and Practices*, (Routledge, 1979).

Boyce, Zoroastrians. *Their Religious belief and Practice*, (RKP, 2001).

Bremmer, Jan N., *The Rise and Fall of the Afterlife: The 1995 Read-Tuckwell Lectures at the University of Bristol*, (Routledge, 2002).

Brough, J. "Soma and Amanita Muscaria," in *Bulletin of the School of Oriental and African Studies*, (1971).

Brown, George W., "Researches" in *Oriental History* (1890).

Brown, John Porter, *The Dervishes: Or Oriental Spiritualism*, (1868).

Browne, Edward G., "A Chapter from the History of Cannabis Indica," reprinted in (Bey & Zug, 2004).

Budge, Ernest Alfred Wallis, *Babylonian Life and History*, (Barnes & Noble Publishing, 1925, 2005).

Budge, Ernest Alfred Wallis, *Osiris and the Egyptian Resurrection*, (1911).

Buhler, George, *The Sacred Laws of the Aryas*, (1882).

Burkeert, Walter, *Greek Religion*, (1985).

Burman, Edward, *The Assassins: The Holy Killers*, (Crucible, 1987).

Burton, Richard F., *Sindh and the Races That Inhabit the Valley of the Indus,* (1851)

Burton, Richard Francis *A Plain and Literal Translation of the Arabian Nights,* (Kama Shastra society, Benares – 1885).

Cahagnet, Louis Alphonse, *Sanctuary of Spiriualism,* (1848).

Campbell, J. M., "On the Religion of Hemp," *Indian Hemp Drugs Commission Report 1893-94,* Young, M., et.al, (Government Central printing office, 1894).

Campany, Robert Ford, *To Live As Long As Heaven and Earth: Ge Hong's Traditions of Divine Transcendents,* (University of California Press. 2002).

Campbell, George L., *Compendium of the World's Languages: Ladakhi to Zuni,* Edition: 2, revised, (Taylor & Francis, 2000)

Campbell, James, *Gazetteer of the Bombay Presidency,* Volume 15, Part 1 (Government central press, Bombay,1883)

Campbell, Joseph; *Occidental Mythology,* (Viking Penguin 1964)

Camphausen, Rufus C.; *The Encyclopedia of Erotic Wisdom,* (Inner Traditions 1991).

Carus, Paul, *The Open Court: Devoted to the Science of Religion, the Religion of Science, and the Extension of the Religious Parliament Idea,* Harry Houdini Collection (Library of Congress), Published by The Open Court Pub. Co., (1918).

Carus, Paul, *The Gospel of Buddha* (1897).

Chadwick, Henry; 1967, *The Early Church,* Pelican Books.

Chakraberty, *Chandra Sex Life in Ancient India: An Explanatory & Comparative Study,* (Firma K. L. Mukhopadhyay, 1963).

Chakraberty, Chandra, *Literary History of Ancient India in Relation to Its Racial and Linguistic Affiliations,* (Vijaya Krishna Bros., 1952).

Chakraberty, Chandra, *Our Cultural Heritage,* (Firma K. L. Mukhopadhyay, 1967)

Chakraberty, Chandra, *The Racial History of India,* (1944)

Charriere, Georges, *Scythian Art: Crafts of the Early Eurasian Nomads,* (New York,1979).

Chatterjee, Ramananda, *The Modern Review,* (Prabasi Press Private, Ltd., 1943)

Chatterjee, Suhas Mizo *Chiefs and the Chiefdom: Role of Laldenga,* (M.D. Publications Pvt. Ltd., 1995)

Chopra, R.N. and Chopra, G.S., *The Present Position of Hemp-Drug Addiciton,* Indian Medical Research Memoirs, (Calcutta, 1939).

Chopra, Ram Nath and Chopra, Ishwar Chander, *Drug Addiction, with Special Reference to India,* (Council of Scientific & Industrial Research, 1965)

Christen, "On the Nature of Opium," *The Quarterly Journal of Foreign and British Medicine and Surgery,* (1822)

Church of Cognizance Case: August 21-23, 2006, Albuquerque, New Mexico, at the U.S. District Court for the District of New Mexico. Paul Baca (official court reporter)

Ciarrocchi, Joseph W., *A Minister's Handbook of Mental Disorders* (1993)

Clark, Houston, "Drug Cult," *Encyclopedia Brittanica,* 5th edition, (1978)

Clarke, James Freeman, *Ten Great Religions,* (Houghton, Mifflin, 1883)

Clarke, Robert Connell, *Marijuana Botany: An Advanced Study, the Propagation and Breeding of Distinctive Cannabis,* (And/Or Press, 1981)

Clarke, Robert, C., *Hashish,* (Red Eye Press, LA, 1998).

Clermont-Ganneau, Charles; Deutsch, Emanuel & Fennell, Charles Augustus Maude, *La stèle de Mesa: roi de Moab,* 896 av. J.C., (1870)

Clisson, I. et al. "Genetic analysis of human remains from a double inhumation in a frozen kurgan in Kazakhstan" (Berel site, Early 3rd Century BC). *International Journal of Legal Medicine.* (2002.)

CNN, "Ancient cannabis stash unearthed in China" (11/12/2008)

Comay, Joan & Pearlman, Moshe. Israel, (1964)

Conder, Claude Reignier, *Syria Stone-Lore*, (London, 1886)

Conner, Randy P.; *Blossom of Bone*, (Harper-Collins 1993)

Contenau, G., *La divination chez les Assyriens et les Babyloniens*. Avec 13 figures, 1 carte et 8 gravures hors texte. Payot, Paris, (1940)

Coomaraswamy, Ananda K & Sister Nivedita, *Myths of the Hindus & Buddhists* (Harrap, 1914)

Coomaraswamy, Ananda Kentish, *Sir Gaiwan and the Green Night: Indra and Namuci*, Speculum By Mediaeval Academy of America, JSTOR (Organization), (Mediaeval Academy of America., 1944).

Coomaraswamy, Ananda Kentish, *What is Civilisation?, and Other Essays*, (Golgonooza Press, 1989)

Coonan, Clifford, *A Meeting of Civilisations: The Mystery of China's Celtic Mummies*, The Independent, UK, 28 August 2006

Copeland, Mel, *Banquet of the God*, (2007)

Corbin, Henry, *A Shi'ite Liturgy of the Grail, The Voyage and the Messenger: Iran and Philosophy*, trans. Joseph H. Rowe (Berkley, California, North Atalantic Books, 1998)

Corcos, Alain "Beliefs About Aging and Longevity in Ancient China," *Michigan Academician: Papers of the Michigan Academy of Science*, Arts & Letters, By Michigan Academy of Science, Arts and Letters, (Michigan Academy of Science, Arts and Letters, 1981)

Cotterell, Arthur, *World Mythology*, (1979)

Coulter, Russell & Turner, Patricia, *Dictionary of Ancient Deities*, (Oxford U. Press, Oxford, 2000)

Creighton, Dr.C.; "On Indications of the Hachish-Vice in the Old Testament," *Janus*, Archives Internationales pours l'Histoire de la Medecine et la Geogrphie Mediacale, (Huiteme Anee 1903), p.297-303.

Crowley, Mike, "When the Gods Drank Urine, A Tibetan myth may help solve the riddle of soma, sacred drug of ancient India," (*Fortean Studies*, vol. III, 1996)

Cumont, Franz; *The Mysteries of Mithra*, (Dover 1956).

Cumont, Franz; *Oriental religions in Roman Paganism*, (Dover 1956) (As quoted in Walker 1983.)

Cunliffe, Barry, *The Oxford Illustrated History of Prehistoric Europe*, (Oxford University Press, 2001)

Daftary, Farhad, *Ismaili Literature: A Bibliography of Sources and Studies*

Dandekar ,Ramchandra Narayan, *Vedic Bibliography: An Up-to-date, Comprehensive, and Analytically Arranged Register of All Important Work Done Since 1930 in the Field of the Veda and Allied Antiquities Including Indus Valley Civilization*, (Karnatak Publishing House, 1946

Dandekar, N., *Felicitation Volume*, Delhi, (1984).

Danielou, A., *Le Polytheisme Hinduo*, (Paris, 1960)

Danielou, Alain, *Gods of Love and Ecstacy; The Traditions of Shiva and Dionysus*, (Inner Traditions, 1992)

Danielou, Alain, *The Gods of India: Hindu Polytheism*, (Inner traditions International, 1985)

Danielou, Alain, *While the Gods Play: Shiva oracles and predictions on the Cycles of History and destiny of Mankind*, (Inner tradition, 1987).

Dannaway, Frederick, "Celestial Botany Entheogenic Traces in Islamic Mysticism," (2007) http://www.scribd.com/doc/15744793/Celestial-Botany-Entheogenic-Traces-in-Islamic-Mysticism

Dannaway, Frederick R., "Strange Fire," Deleware Tea Society, (2009),

Darmesteter J., *Zend-Avesta, Part I, The Vendidad*, (Oxford University, London, 1895)

Darmesteter, James, *Etudes Iraniennes*, 2 vols., Paris, 1883

Darmesteter, James, *The Zend Avesta*, (Oxford, 1883)

Das, Rahul Peter, "On the Identification of a Vedic Plant," in G. Jan Meulenbeld and Dominik Wujastyk, eds., *Studies on Indian Medical History: Papers Presented at the International Workshop on the Study of Indian Medicine Held at the Wellcome Institute for the History of Medicine, 2-4 Sept. 1985, Groningen Oriental Studies 2*, Groningen, 1987

Dasturji, Dr. Maneckji N. Dhalla, *History of Zoroastrianism*, (New York, 1938)

David, Rosalie *Equinox: The Mystery of the Cocaine Mummies*, TVF, (1996)

Davis-Kimball, J., and Behan, Mona (2002) *Warrior Women: An Archeologist's Search for History's Hidden Heroines* (Warner Brooks, 2002)

Davis-Kimball, Jeannine, "The Kangjiashimenzi Petroglyphs in Xinjiang, Western China," *Indo-European Studies Bulletin*, Volume 7, Issue 2 (May/June, 1998)

de Candolle, Alphonse, *Origin of Cultivated Plants* (D. Appleton, 1886)

de Jong, Albert, *Traditions of the Magi: Zoroastrianism in Greek and Latin Literature*, (Brill, 1997)

de Laurence, L. W., *Sacred Book of Death Hindu Spiritism Soul Transition and Soul Reincarnation* (1905)

De Rienzo, Paul; Beal, Dana & Members of the Project, *The Ibogaine Story: Report on the Staten Island Project*, (Autonomedia 1997)

de Vartavan, Christian & Amoros, Victoria Asensi, *Codex of Ancient Egyptian Plant Remains*. London: Triade, 1997

Deva, Indra and Shrirama *Society and Culture in India: Their Dynamics Through the Ages*, (1999)

Dhalla, Maneckji Nusserwanji, *History of Zoroastrianism*, (New York, 1938)

Dickens, Charles, *All The Year Round*, (1862)

Dietz, Lena Dixon & Lehozky, Aurelia R., *History and Modern Nursing*, (F.A. Davis Co., 1963)

Doane, T.W.; *Bible Myths and their Parallels in Other Religions* (Published in 1882, later republished in 1985 by Health Research).

Dobroruka , V. "Chemically-Induced Visions in the Fourth Book of Ezra in Light of Comparative Persian Material," *Jewish Studies Quarterly*, (2006) - pej-unb.org

Doniger (O'Flaherty), W., "Somatic' memories of R. Gordon Wasson," *The Sacred Mushroom Seeker: Essays on R. Grodon Wasson*. (Riedlinger, Ed.) (Portland, 1990)

Dremeier, Charles, *Kinship and Community in Ancient India*, (California, 1962).

du Toit, B. M. 1975. "Dagga: the history and ethnographic setting of Cannabis sativa in Southern Africa," in *Cannibas and Culture* (Rubin, ed., 1980).

Dubash, Sorabji Edalji, *The Zoroastrian Sanitary Code, with Critical and Explanatory Notes*, (Printed at the Sanj Vartaman Print. Press, 1906)

Dubois, Jean Antoine, *Description of the Character, Manners, and Customs of the People of India*, (1879).

Dubs, *The Beginning of Alchemy*, Isis 38, (1947)

Duchesne-Guillemin, Jacques, "Haoma proscrit et re,admis," in Marie-Madeleine Mactoux and Evelyne Geny, eds., *Me, langes P. Le,vêque I: Religion*, Annales litte,raires de l'Universite, de Besançon 367, Centre de Recherches d'Histoire ancienne 79, (1988)

Duchesne-Guillemin, "Miettes iraniennes," Hommages à Georges Dumézil, Brussels, (1960), in idem, Opera Minora I, Tehran, (1974)

Duncan, James, *The City as Text: The Politics of Landscape Interpretation in the Kandyan Kingdom*, (Cambridge University Press, 1990)

Dwarakanath, C., "Use of opium and cannabis in the traditional systems of medicine in India," Bull Narc. (1965)

Dymock, et. al., *Pharmacographia Indica: A History of the Principal Drugs of Vegetable Origin, Met with in British India*, By William Dymock, David Hooper, Charles James Hislop Warden, Hamdard, (K. Paul, Trench Trubner, 1893)

Dymock, W., "Indian Henbane," *The American Journal of Pharmacy*, Vol. 53, 1881, edited by John M. Maisch

Dymock, William, *The Vegetable Materia Medica of Western India*, (1885)

Eastwick, Edward Backhouse & Murray, John, *Handbook of the Punjab, western Rajputana, Kashmir, and upper Sindh* (1883)

Ebeling, E. (1915): *Keilschrifttexte aus Assur : religiösen Inhalts.* J.C. Hinrichs, Leipzig. (as noted by Russo)

Ebeling, E. (1925): *Liebeszauber im Alten Orient.* Verlag von Eduard Pfeiffer, Leipzig. (as noted by Russo)

Ebeling, E. (1931): *Tod un Leben nach den Vorstellungen der Babylonier.* Walter de Gruyter, Berlin. (as noted by Russo)

Ebeling, E. (1933): *Urkunden des archivs von Assur aus mittelassyrischer zeit.* O. Harrassowitz, Leipzig. (as noted by Russo)

Edmonds , Prof. Radcliffe, "Did the Mithraists Inhale? – A Technique for Theurgic Ascent in the Mithras Liturgy, the Chaldaean Oracles, and some Mithraic Frescoes, in *Ancient World* 32.1 (2000).

Eduljee, K. E. Heritage Institute, 2007 & 2008, "Barsom," http://heritageinstitute.com/zoroastrianism/barsom/index.htm

Eggeling, Julius, Translator, *The Satapatha Brahmana*, (1885)

Eisler, Riane; *The Chalice & the Blade*, (Harper & Row 1987).

Eitel, Ernest J., *Handbook of Chinese Buddhism. Being a Sanskrit-Chinese Dictionary with vocabularies of Buddhist Terms in Pali, Singhalese, Siamese, Burmese, Tibetan, Mongolian and Japanese*, (Trubner & Co, 1888)

Eliade, Mircea; *Shamanism: Archaic techniques of Ecstasy*, (1964)

Eliade, Mircea;"Ancient Scythia and Iran", excerpted from *Shamanism: Archaic techniques of Ecstasy*, (1964), and reprinted in *The Book of Grass*, (1967).

Eliade, Mircea and Adams, Charles J., *The Encyclopedia of Religion*, (Macmillan, 1987)

Eliade, Mircea; *A History of Religious Ideas, Vol.1*; (University of Chicago Press 1978)

Eliade, Mircea; *A History of Religious Ideas, Vol. 2*; (University of Chicago Press 1982)

Eliade, Mircea; *A History of Religious Ideas, Vol. 3*; (University of Chicago Press 1985)

Eliade, Mircea; *Myth and Reality*, (Harper & Row 1963).

Eliade, Mircea; *Myths, Rites, Symbols,Vol.2*,(Harper Colophon Books,,1975).

Eliade, Mircea; *The Myth of the Eternal Return*, (Bollingen Foundation Inc., 1954) Eliade, Mircea; *Mephistopheles et l'Androgynee*, (Paris 1962). As quoted and translated in (Danielou 1992).

Ellis, et., al., *Progress in Medicinal Chemistry*, By G.P. Ellis, Albert Ellis, Geoffrey Buckle West, Contributor G.P. Ellis, Geoffrey Buckle West, (Elsevier, 1987)

Elst, Koenraad, *Update on the Aryan Invasion Debate*, (New Delhi Aditya Prakashan, 1999)

Emboden, William, 'Cannabis in Ostasien-Ursrung, Wanderung und Gebrauch. In *Rausch und Realitat*, Volume 1, edited by G. Volger, (1981)

Emboden, William A. Jr., "Ritual Use of Cannabis Sativa L.: A Historic-Ethnographic Survey," in *Flesh of the Gods*, P.T.Furst, Ed. (Praeger, New York, 1972)

Emboden, William, Jr., "Art and Artefacts as Ethnobotanical Tools in the Ancient Near East with Emphasis on Psychoactive Plants," in Schultes, Richard Evans and Reis, Siri Von, *Ethnobotany: Evolution of a Discipline*, (Timber Press, 1995)

Erbt, Wilhelm; "Die Hebraer: Kanaan im Zietalter der herbraischer Wanderung und hebraischer Staatengrundungen," (1906), as quoted in (Pope 1977).

Erdosy, George, *The Indo-Aryans of Ancient South Asia: Language, Material Culture and Ethnicity*, (Walter de Gruyter, 1995)

Eznik, *A Treatise on God Written in Armenian* by Eznik of Kołb (floruit C.430-c.450), Translated by Monica J. Blanchard, Robin Darling Young, (Peeters Publishers, 1998)

Falk, Harry, "Soma I and II," *Bulletin of the School of Oriental and African Studies* (BSOAS) 52/1, (1989).

Fallon, S.W., 'Specimens of the Mailthili or Tirhuti Dialect of Tirhut', *Indian Antiquary*, Volume 4, (1875)

Fani, Mosham, *The Religion of the Sufis*, (Octagon Press, 1979)

Fani, Mosham, *Oriental Literature*, (Tudor press, 1937)

Farber, W. (1981): "Drogen im Alten Mesopotamien – Sumerer und Akkader." In *Rausch und Realitat: Drogen im Kulturvergleich* edited by G. Volger. pp. 270-291, Rautenstrauch-Joest-Museum, Cologne. (as noted by Russo)

Faulkner, R., *The Ancient Egyptian Pyramid Texts*, (Oxford, 1969)

Fernandez, Lawrence, *The Medical Reporter: A Record of Medicine, Surgery, Public Health and of General Medical Intelligence*, (Medical Publishing Press, 1894)

Ferro-Luzzi, G. Eichinger, 'Food Avoidances During the Puerperium and Lactation in Tamilnad' in Robson, John R. K., Food, *Ecology and Culture; Readings in the Anthropology of Dietary Practices* (Gordon and Breach, 1980)

Filliozat, Jean, *The Classical Doctrine of Indian Medicine: Its Origins and Its Greek Parallels*, (1964)

Fisher, et. al., *The Cambridge History of Iran: The land of Iran*/edited by W. B. Fisher *Vol. 2: The Median and Achaemenian periods*/edited by Ilya Gershevitch *Vol. 3: The Seleucid, Parthian, and Sasanian periods*/edited by Ehsan Yarshater (2 pts.) *Vol. 4: The period from the Arab invasion to the Saljuqs...*, By University of Cambridge, William Bayne Fisher, Ilya Gershevitch, Ehsan Yarshster, R. N. Frye, J. A. Boyle, Peter Jackson, Laurence Lockhart, Peter Avery, Gavin Hambly, Charles Melville, (Cambridge University Press, 1993)

Flattery, David Stophlet and Schwartz, Martin, *Haoma, and Harmaline: The Botanical Identity of the Indo-Iranian Sacred Hallucinogen "Soma" and Its Legacy in Religion, Language, and Middle Eastern Folklore*, (Berkeley, Los Angeles, and London, 1989)

Fleming, Michael P. and Clarke, Robert C., "Physical evidence for the antiquity of Cannabis" in *Cannabis: The Genus Cannabis* By David T. Brown, (CRC Press, 1998)

Frankhauser, Manfred, "History of cannabis in Western Medicine," *Cannabis and cannabinoids: pharmacology, toxicology, and therapeutic potential*, By Franjo Grotenhermen, Ethan Russo, (Haworth Press, 2002)

Frawley, David, *Gods, Sages and Kings: Vedic Secrets of Ancient Civilization*, (Lotus Press, 2000)

Frazier, Jack, *The Great American Hemp Industry*, (Solar Age Press, 1991)

Gait, Edward Albert, *Census of India, (1901 – 1902)*

Geiwitz, James, Ph.D., and the Ad Hoc Committee on Hemp Risks, *THC in Hemp Foods and Cosmetics: The Appropriate Risk Assessment*, January 15, 2001

Geller, A. and Boas, M.: *The Drug Beat*, New York: Cowles Book Company, Inc. (1969).

Gernot L. Windfuhr, "Haoma/Soma, the Plant," in *Papers in Honour of Professor Mary Boyce*, 2 vols., *Acta Iranica 24-25*, (Leiden, 1985).

Gershevitch, Ilya, "Iranian Nouns and Names in Elamite Garb," TPS, 1969 (1970); "An Iranianist's View of the Soma Controversy," in Philippe Gignoux and Ahmad Tafazzoli, eds., *Mémorial Jean de Menasce*, Louvain, (1974)

Ghalioungui, Paul, *Magic and Medical Science in Ancient Egypt*, (Hodder and Stoughton, 1963)

Gibbs, Mark, *The Virgin and The Priest*, (Lulu.com, 2008)

Ginzburg, Carlo, *Ecstasies: Deciphering the Witches' Sabbath*, Translated by Raymond Rosenthal, (University of Chicago Press, 2004)

Gnoli, G. 1979. "Bang." Accessed at http://www.iranica.com/newsite

Gnoli, Gherardo, *East and West 39*, 1989, pp. 320-24, and by K. Mylius, in IIJ 35, (1992)

Gnoli, Gherardo, Lichtsymbolik in "Alt-Iran: Haoma-Ritus und Erlöser-Mythos," Antaios 8, (1967). Idem, "On the Iranian Soma and Pers. sepand 'Wild Rue'," *East and West 43*, (1993).

Godbey, Allen H., "Incense and Poison Ordeals in the Ancient Orient," *The American Journal of Semitic Languages and Literatures*, Vol. 46, No. 4, (The University of Chicago Press, July, 1930)

Godwin, H., *Ancient Cultivation of Hemp*, (Antiquity, March, 1967).

Gokhale, Namita. *The Book of Shiva*, (Penguin/Viking: 2001)

Goldfrank, et. al., Goldfrank's *Toxicologic Emergencies*, By Lewis R. Goldfrank, Neal Flomenbaum, Robert S. Hoffman, Mary Ann Howland, Neal A. Lewin, Lewis S. Nelson, (McGraw-Hill Professional, 2002)

Goodwin, J., *Mystery Religions and the Ancient World* (Thames and Hudson, 1981)

Gordon, R. P., *Hebrew Bible and ancient versions: selected essays of Robert P. Gordon* (Ashgate Publishing Company, 2006)

Gowen, Herbert Henry, *A History of Religion*, (Society for Promoting Christian Knowledge, 1934)

Graindorge, Catherine, "The Onions of Sokar," *Revue d'Egyptologie*, 43, (1992)

Graves, Robert, T*he Greek Myths*, (2 Vol.), (Penguin Books, 1955)

Gray, John, *Near Eastern Mythology; Mesopotamia, Syria, Palestine*, (The Hamlyn, 1969).

Gray, L. H., "Zoroastrian Elements In Muhammadan Eschatology", *Le Muséon*, Volume III, (1902)

Green, Nile, *Islam and the Army in Colonial India: Sepoy Religion in the Service of Empire* (Cambridge Studies in Indian History and Society, 2009)

Grierson, G.A., "The hemp plant in Sanskrit and Hindi literature," *Indian Antiquary* (September, 1894)

Griffith, Ralph Thomas Hotchkin & Abhimanyu , M.L., *Hymns of the Atharva-veda*, (1962)

Griswold, H.D., *The Religion of the Rigveda*, Oxford University Press, 1923)

Grof, Stanislav, *Ancient Wisdom Modern Science*, Stanislav Grof Ed., (State University of New York Press,1984).

Gross, Chaim, et.al., *Rabbinic Fantasy*, By Chaim Gross, Mark Mirsky, David Stern, Ivan G. Marcus, Raymond P. Scheindlin, (City College of New York, Dept. of English, 1983)

Grousset, Rene. *The Empire of the Steppes*, Rutgers University Press, (1989)

Gruber, Ulrich, *Nepal*, Munich, (1991)

Guenon, Rene and Fohr, S. D., *The King of the World*, (Le Roi du Monde, 1927), Translated by Henry Fohr, Published by Sophia Perennis, 2004.

Guthrie, Kenneth, compiler and translator, *The Pythagorean Sourcebook and Library*, (Phanes Press, 1987).

Guthrie, Patricia, "Health risk to women halts hormone study" *Atlanta Journal-Constitution*, (GA) (July 9, 2002)

Hackman, George Gotlob, *Temple Documents of the Third Dynasty of Ur From Umma*, (Yale University, 1937).

Hallet, Jean, Pierre, and Pelle, Alex, *Pygmy Kitabu*, (Fawcett Crest, 1975).

Halman, Hugh Talat; Yamani, Muhammad 'Abduh & Lipton, Abdallah, *Al-Khidr, the Green One: At the Place Where the Two Seas Meet and the Hidden Treasure of the Mercy of Allah*, (International Education Foundation, 2002)

Handa, O.C., *Buddhist Art & Antiquities of Himachal Pradesh: Up to 8th Century A.D.* (New Delhi, 1994)

Handa, O.C., *Buddhist Western Himalaya: A politico-religious history*, Indus Publishing Company, India, 2001)

Hanu, Lumír Ondej, "Pharmacological and therapeutic secrets of plant and brain (Endo) cannabinoids" - Published Online: 5 Sep 2008, Copyright © 2008 Wiley Periodicals, Inc., A Wiley Company

Harris, Maurice Henry, Ed., The Project Gutenberg eBook: *Hebraic Literature; Translations from the Talmud, Midrashim and Kabbala*, by Various, (December 16, 2004)

Harris, Rendel, *Eucharistic Origins*, Cambridge W. Heffer & Sons, Ltd., (1927)

Hartsuiker, Dolf, *Sadhus—India's Mystic Holy Men*, (Inner Traditions, 1993).

Hasan, Khwaja, "Social Aspects of the use of Cannabis in India," in *Cannabis and Culture*, Rubin, ed., (1975).

Hassan, Hadrul, *The drink and drug Evil in India*, (Ganesh& Co., 1922).

Hauer, Jakob Wilhelm, *Die Anfanger der Yogapraxisim Alten Indien*, (Berlin, 1922)

Haug, Martin, *Aitereya Brahamana of the Rigveda*, Translated and Explained, (Bombay, 1863)

Hehn, V. *Cultivated Plants and Domesticated Animals in their Migration from Asia to Europe* (Amsterdam, 1976; originally published in 1885),

Hellholm, et. al., *Apocalypticism in the Mediterranean World and the Near East: Proceedings of the International Colloquium on Apocalypticism*, Uppsala, August 12-17, 1979, By David Hellholm, Kungl. Vitterhets, historie och antikvitets akademien, Uppsala universitet Teologiska fakulteten, (Mohr Siebeck, 1989)

Henderson, Dr., *The History of Ancient and Modern Wines*, (London, 1824)

Henning, Walter Bruno, "Zoroaster: Politician or Witch-Doctor?," *Ratanbai Katrak Lectures 3*, (1949), (Oxford, 1951)

Henslow, G., *The Vulgate the Source of False Doctrines*, (BiblioLife, 2009)

Heras, H. T*he Anu in India and in Egypt*, (V Ind. Hist. Congress, Hyderabad, 1943).

Herer, Jack, *The Emperor Wears No Clothes*, (1990)

Herodotus, *On the War for Greek Freedom: Selections from the Histories By Herodotus*, Translated by Samuel Shirley, Contributor James S. Romm, (Hackett Publishing, 2003)

Herodotus, *The Histories*, (Penguin Books,1972)

Hewitt, James Francis Katherinus, *History and Chronology of the Myth-making Age*, (1901)

Hillman, D. C. A., *The Chemical Muse: Drug Use and the Roots of Western Civilization*, (New York: St. Martin's Press. Thomas Dunne Books 2008)

Hinnells, John R., *Persian Mythology*, (The Hamlyn Publishing Group,1973).

Hinze, Almut ed., and tr. with commentaries, *Zâmyâd Yašt/Der Zam-yad-Yašt*, Wiesbaden, 1994.

Hoffmann, Karl, *Aufsätze zur Indoiranistik II*, (Wiesbaden, 1976)

Hoiberg, Dale and Ramchandani, Indu, *Students' Britannica India: India* (Set of 7 Vols.) 39, (Popular Prakashan, 2000)

Holzer, Georg, "Namen skythischer und sarmatischer Stämme," *Anzeiger der philosophisch-historischen Klassse der Österreichischen Akademie der Wissenschaften 125*, (1988)

Hornsey, Ian Spencer, *A History of Beer and Brewing*, Royal Society of Chemistry (Great Britain),(2003)

Hope Evangelical Lutheran Church, "Elijah in Islam," http://www.hope.evangelical-lutheran.ca/elias.htm, (2006, accessed, March 19th, 2009).

Hopkins, Edward Washburn, *The Religions of India*, BiblioBazaar, (2007)

Houben, Jan E. M., "Report of the Workshop," *Electronic Journal of Vedic Studies*, 9/1b, (May 4, 2003).

Houben, Jan E. M., "The Soma-Haoma problem," *Electronic Journal of Vedic Studies*, 9/1a, (May 4, 2003).

Houck, C. M., *The Celestial Scriptures: Keys to the Suppressed Wisdom of the Ancients*, (iUniverse, 2002)

Houtsma, et. al., *E.J. Brill's First Encyclopaedia of Islam, 1913-1936: 1913-1936* , By Martijn Theodoor Houtsma, M. Th. Houtsma, T. W. Arnold, A. J. Wensinck, (1993)

Houtsma, M. Th., *E.J. Brill's First Encyclopaedia of Islam*, 1913-1936, (Brill, 1987)

Hsü, KJ, "Did the Xinjiang Indo-Europeans leave their home because of global cooling?" In: *The Bronze Age and Early Iron Age peoples of Eastern Central Asia*—Mair VH, ed. (1998) Vol. II. Washington, DC: Institute for the Study of Man. 683–696.

Huard, Pierre, and Wong, Ming, *Chinese Medicine*, (McGraw-Hill, 1959, 1968)

Hunter, Sir William Wilson, *The imperial Gazetteer of India*, Volume 6,(1886)

Hunter, William Wilson *A brief history of the Indian people*, (1884)

Huseynov, I.A., A.S. Sumbatzadeh, A.N. Guliyev, and E.A. Tokarzhevski. *History of Azerbaijan*. vol. 1. Baku: (Academy of Sciences Press, 1958).

Hutter, M., "Weltliche und geistliche Berauschung: die Bedeutung von Haoma im Zoroastrismus," *Mitteilungen für Anthropologie und Religionsgeschichte 11*, 1996 (pub. 1997)

Indian Hemp Drugs Commission Report 1893-94, Young, M., et.al, (Government Central printing office, 1894)

Ingalls, D.H.H., "Soma," [Book review] *New York Times Book Review* (September, 1971)

Institute of Ismaili Studies, (I.B.Tauris, 2004)

Islamic Culture Board, *Islamic Culture*, (Islamic Culture Board, 2000)

Irvin, Jan, Personal Correspondence, May 14, 2009

Ito, G,. "An Interpretation of Yasna 32:14," *Orient 25*, (1989)

Jackson, A. V. Williams, *Zoroastrian Studies: The Iranian Religion And Various Monographs*, (Colombia University Press, 1928).

Jacobs, Bruno, *Persepolisdelegationen und Satrapienordnung, Acta Praehistorica et Archaeologica 13/14*, (1982)

Jacobs, Joseph, *Folklore*,by Joseph Jacobs, Folklore Society (London)., Alfred Trübner Nutt, Arthur Robinson Wright, William Crooke, Folklore Society (Great Britain), MetaPress, JSTOR (Organization), (1895)

Jafarey, Ali A., "Haoma, Its Original and Later Identity," (2001)

Jafarey, Ali A., *The Plain Reality Behind The Intricate Falsity: Avesta: Woman In The Gathas And The Later Avesta: The Zoroastrian Priest In The Avesta: Rituals In The Gathas*, (2007)

Jahanian, Dr. Daryoush, "Medicine in Avesta and Ancient Iran," Vohuman.org, Fezana journal, (Spring 2005

James, M.R.;-"Translation and Notes, Acts Of Thomas;" from *The Apocryphal New Testament*, Oxford: Clarendon Press, 1924

James, William; *The Varieties of Religious Experience*, (New York: Modern Library 1929)

Janick J., Paris HS., "Jonah and the 'gourd' at Nineveh: consequences of a classic mistranslation." In: *Proceedings of Cucurbitaceae 2006*—Holmes GJ, ed. (Raleigh, NC: Universal Press. 2006).

Jaynes, Julian, *The Origins of Consciousness in the Breakdown of the Bicamerial Mind*; (Houghton Mifflin Company, Boston, 1976)

Jiang et. al., "The discovery of Capparis spinosa L. (Capparidaceae) in the Yanghai Tombs (2800 years b.p.) NW China, and its medicinal implications," *Journal of Ethnopharmacology* 113 (2007), Hong-En Jiang, Xiao Li, David K. Ferguson, Yu-Fei Wang, et. al.

Jiang, et. al., '*A new insight into Cannabis sativa (Cannabaceae) utilization from 2500-year-old Yanghai Tombs*, Xinjiang, China,by Jiang Hong-En, Xiao Li, Zhao You-Xing, Ferguson David K., Heuber, Francis, Bera Subir, Wang Yu-Fei, Zhao Liang-Cheng, Liu Chang-Jiang, Li Cheng-Sen, (2006)

Johnson, Buffie; *Lady of the Beasts* (Harper & Row,1981).

Johnston, Sarah Iles, *Religions of the Ancient World: A Guide*, (Harvard University Press, 2004)

Jones, Kenneth, *Nutritional And Medicinal Guide To Hemp Seed*, (Rainforest Botanical Laboratory 1995).

Justi, Ferdinand, "Geschichte Irans von den ältesten Zeiten bis zum Ausgang der Sāsāniden," in Wilhem Geiger and Ernst Kuhn, eds., *Grundriss der Iranischen Phililologie II*, (Strassburg, 1904)

Kandola, Nav, *The Nihang – A secret History of the Sikhs*, film, (2009)

Kane, Rob, "A Joint a Day Keeps the Doctor Away," *New Age* (July 2nd, 2009)

Kevala, Rustom, Update on the Church of Cognizance Case, HAMAZOR - ISSUE 1 2007

Ka´ thia M. Hono´rio Æ Albe´rico B. F. da Silva, *A study on the influence of molecular properties in the psychoactivity of cannabinoid compounds*, Received: 18 March 2004 / Accepted: 27 January 2005 / Published online: 3 May 2005, Springer-Verlag 2005

Kabelik, Prof. Jan, "Hemp As A Medicament- History of the medicinal use of hemp," (1955)

Kane, J.P., *Greece, in Mythology; An Illustrated Encyclopedia*, Richard Cavendish, ed., (Black Cat, 1987).

Kanga, M. F., *Encyclopedia Iranica*, http://www.iranica.com/newsite/

Kapadia, S. A., *Teachings of Zoroaster and the Philosophy of the Parsi Religion* (1905)

Kaplan, Aryeh, *Meditation and the Kabbalah*, (Samuel Weiser, 1982).

Kaplan, Aryeh. *The Living Torah* (New York, 1981)

Karamustafa, Ahmet T., *God's Unruly Friends: Dervish Groups in the Islamic Later Middle Period, 1200-1550* (1994) (B Publications, Oxford, United Kingdom, 2006)

Kawami, Trudy S. Ph. D., *Haoma-Barsom*, Keiser (1921): Letters and contracts, no. 162. *Revue d'Assyriologie et d'Archéologie Orientale*. 18: 97-.(as noted by Russo) https://listhost. uchicago.edu/pipermail/ane/2002-October/004235.html, (2007)

Kelly, Walter Keating, *Curiosities of Indo-European tradition and folk-lore*, (Chapman & Hall, 1863)

Kersten, Holger; *Jesus lived in India, His unknown Life Before & After the Crucifixion*, (Element, Dorset England, 1986).

Khlopin, Igore Nikolaevich, "Mandragora turcomanica in der Geschichte der Orientalvölker," *Orientalia Lovaniensia Periodica 11*, (1980)

Kieth, A.B., *Religion and Philosophy of the Veda and Upanishads*, (Harvard, 1925)

Kitto, John, *A cyclopaedia of Biblical literature*, (New York, 1846-1876)

Kisel, V.A., Herodotus' "Scythian logos and ritual vessels of the early nomads," *Archaeology, Ethnology and Anthropology of Eurasia*, Volume 31, Number 3 (October, 2007)

Klein, Sigfried, *Tod und Begrabnis in Palistina* (1908)

Kohn, Livia, *The Taoist Experience: An Anthology*, (SUNY Press, 1993)

Kotwal, Firoze M. and Kreyenbroek, Philip G. (with contributions by James Russell), eds. and trs., *The Hêrbedestân and Nêrangestân* II, Stud. Ir., Cahier 16, Paris, 1995.

Kotwal,D.F.M. and Boyd, J.W., *A Persian Offering. The Yasna: a Zoroastrian High Liturgy*, (1991)

La Barre, Weston, *Culture in Context; Selected Writings of Weston La Barre*, (Duke University Press 1980)

Lahanas, Michael, *Examples of Ancient Greek Medical Knowledge*, (2006), http://www.mlahanas.de/Greeks/Med.htm

Lal Sircar, Amrita, *The Calcutta Journal of Medicine: A Monthly Record of the Medical Auxiliary Sciences*, (1906)

Langenheim, Jean H., *Plant Resins: Chemistry, Evolution, Ecology, and Ethnobotany*, (Timber Press, 2003)

Laufer, B., *Sino-Iranica*, Chicago, IL Field Museum of Natural History, (1919)

Lenormant, et. al., *The Beginnings of History According to the Bible and the Traditions of Oriental Peoples: From the Creation of Man to the Deluge*, By François Lenormant, Mary Smith Lockwood, Mary Lockwood, (C. Scribner's sons, 1881)

Lenormant, Francois, *Le Magie chez les Chaldeans*, Maisonneuve et Cie., Paris, 1874. As translated and quoted in (Andrews 1997).

Lewin, Louis, *Phantastica* From the 1931 translation by P.H.A. Wirth

Ley, W., Esq., 'Observations on the Cannabis Indica, or Indian Hemp', *Provincial Medical Journal*, Vol. 5, (Henry Renshaw, London, 1843).

Li, Hu-Lin, "The Origin and Use of Cannabis in Eastern Asia: Thier Linguistic-Cultural Implications," in *Cannabis and Culture*, Vera Rubin Ed., (Mouton, 1975).

Liberman, Anatoly and Mitchell, J. Lawrence, *An Analytic Dictionary of English Etymology: An Introduction*, Contributor J. Lawrence Mitchell, (U of Minnesota Press, 2008)

Linssen, Marc J. H., *The Cults of Uruk and Babylon: The Temple Ritual Texts As Evidence for Hellenistic Cult Practises*, (Brill, 2004)

Littell, Eliakim and Littlell, Robert S., *Littell's Living Age*, Volume 158, (1883)

Littleton, Scott, "The Pneuma Enthusiastikon: On the Possibility of Hallucinogenic 'Vapors' at Delphi and Dodona," *Ethos*, (1986)

Littleton, C. Scott and Malcor, Linda, *From Scythia to Camelot*, (NY, 1994/2000)

Littleton, Scott, post, http://health.groups.yahoo.com/group/mmmworld/message/35 (2003)

Littleton, Scott, Personal Correspondence, (2008)

Littleton, Scott, Personal Correspondence, (2009)

Littleton, Scott, affidavit in Bennett vs The Attorney General for Canada and the Minister of Health for Canada, (2009)

Lloyd, John Uri, *Origin and History of All the Pharmacopeial Vegetable Drugs, Chemicals and Preperation*, (American Drug Manufacturers Association, 1921)

Louisa, Sara & Blomfield, Ryan, *The Chosen Highway*, (Bahá'i Pub. Trust, 1940)

Low, Immanuel; *Die Flora Der Juden*, (Georg Olms Verlagsbuchhandlung Hildesheim 1967; originally published as *Flora der Juden* in 1924). (The English interpretation of Low's work concerning cannabis was provided to the authors by Sabina Hotz)

Lozano, Indalecio, "Therapeutic Use of Cannabis sativa L." in *Arab Medicine*, (1997), reprinted in (Bey & Zug, 2004

Ludlow, Fitz, Hugh, *The Hasheesh Eater*, (1856)

MacDonell,Arthur & Kieth, Arthur, *Vedic Index*, (Delhi, 1958)

MacGregor, et. al., *Arktouros: Hellenic Studies Presented to Bernard M. W. Knox on the Occasion of His 65th Birthday*, By Bernard MacGregor Walker Knox, Glen Warren Bowersock, Walter Burkert, Michael C. J. Putnam, (Gruyter, 1979)

MacKenzie, Donald Alexander, *Myths of Babylonia and Assyria*, (1915)

MacKenzie, Donald A., *Myths of China and Japan*, (1923)

Magee, Dr M. D., "Persia & Creation of Judaism," (1998, 2008)

Mahadevan, Iravatham, "The Sacred Filter Stand Facing the Unicorn," in *South Asian Archelogy*, I. Helsinki, (1994)

Mahdihasan, S., "Soma, in Light of Comparative Pharmacology, Etymology and Archaeology," *Janus* 60, (1973). Idem, "A Persian Painting Illustrating Ephedra, Leading to Its Identity as Soma," *Journal of Central Asia* 8, (1985). Idem, *The History and Natural History of Ephedra as Soma*, Islamabad, (1987)

Mahdihassan, S., "Etymology of names – ephedra and cannabis," *Studies in the History of Medicine*, (1982)

Mahdihassan, S, "Ephedra as Soma Meaning Hemp Fibres with Soma Later Misidentified with the Hemp Plant Itself," *Indian Journal of History of Science*, (1986)

Mair, V.H., *Prehistoric Caucasoid corpses of the Tarim Basin*, J Indo Eur Stud, (1995)

Mair, V.H., T*he Bronze Age and early Iron Age peoples of eastern Central Asia, Volume 1.* Philadelphia: University of Pennsylvania Museum Publications.(1998)

Maitra A.K (ed.), *Tārātantra*, author Taranatha (1600) (Varendra Res. Soc. 1983)

Mallory, J. P. and Adams, Douglas Q., *Encyclopedia of Indo-European Culture*, (Taylor & Francis, 1997)

Mallory, J.P., *In Search of the Indo-Europeans: Language Archeology and Myth*, (Thames and Hudson, 1989)

Mallory, J.P, Mair, VH., *The Tarim mummies*, (Thames and Hudson. 2000)

Malyon & Henman, "New scientist," Published by IPC Magazines, (1980)

Mandihassan, S., "Etymology of Names-Cannabsi and Ephedra," *Journal: Studies in the History of Medicine*, Vol.6, 1982

Manniche, Lise, *An Ancient Egyptian Herbal*, (University of Texas Press, 1989)

Markale, Jean. 1989. *Die Druiden: Gesellschaft und Gotter der Kelten*. Munich: Goldmann. 1988, Heidnische Naturreligion. Bergen, Germany [as quoted in Ratsch, 2001)

Martius, George, *Pharakologisch-medicinische Studien uber den Hanf,* 1855/1996, reprint, Berlin, VWB. [from a quote in (Ratsch, 2005)]

Masood, S., *The Bible And The Qur'an: A Question Of Integrity*, (OM Publication: Carlisle, UK, 2001).

Matas, Enric Aguilar I, *Rigvedic Society*, (Brill, 1991)

Mathre, Mary Lynn, *Cannabis in Medical Practice: A Legal, Historical and Pharmacological Overview of the Therapeutic Use of Marijuana*, (McFarland, 1997)

Maurice, Thomas; *History of Hindostan,*(1798) as quoted in (reprinted in Doane 1882)

Mathews, Roy J., "Psychoactive Agents and the Self," Editors, Feinberg, Todd E.; Keenan, Julian Paul, *The Lost Self: Pathologies of the Brain and Identity*, (Oxford Univ Pr, Cary, North Carolina, U.S.A., 2005)

Matt, Daniel Chanan, *Zohar, the book of enlightenment*, (1983)

McConvel, Patrick & Smith, Michael, "Millers and mullers. The archeo-linguistic stratigraphy of technological change in Holocene Australia," *Language Contacts in Prehistory: Studies in Stratigraphy*, Andersen, Henning, Ed., (John Benjamins Publishing Company, 2003)

McEno, John, *Cannabis, Radical Agriculture, and Epistomology of Plant Pathology Cannabis Ecology: A Compendium of Diseases and Pests*, (AMRITA Press, 1978)

McGinn, et. al., *The Encyclopedia of Apocalypticism*, Contributor Bernard McGinn, John Joseph Collins, Stephen J. Stein, (International Publishing Group, 2000)

McGovern, Patrick E., *Ancient Wine: The Search for the Origins of Viniculture*, (Princeton University Press, 2003)

McKenna, Terence, *Food of the Gods*, (Bantam Books,1992)

McKim, William A., *Drugs and behavior: an introduction to behavioral pharmacology*, (Prentice-Hall, 1986)

McNamara, Patrick, *Where God and Science Meet: how brain and evolutionary studies alter our understanding of religion*, (Praeger Publishers, 2006)

Mead, GRS, *Fragments of a Faith Forgotten: Some Short Sketches Among the Gnostics of the First Two Centuries*, (Theosophical Publishing Society, London and Benares, 1900)

Mechoulam, R., W. A. Devane, A. Breuer, and J. Zahalka. "A random walk through a Cannabis field." *Pharmacology Biochemistry and Behavior* (1991)

Mechoulam, Raphael and Ben-Shabat, Shimon, "From gan-zi-gun-nu to anandamide and 2-arachidonoylglycerol: the ongoing story of cannabis," Department of Natural Products, Medical Faculty, Hebrew University, Jerusalem 91120, Israel, (September 1998)

Meißner, Bruno und Wissenschaft, Bildung, 1925, *Die Kultur Babyloniens und Assyriens*. 207 Leipzig : Quelle & Meyer, quoted B.Meissner's 1925 book, *Babylonien und Assyrian*

Merkur, Dan, Personal Correspondence, (May 31, 2010)

Merlin, M., "Archaeological Record for Ancient Old World Use of Psychoactive Plants," *Economic Botany*, 57(3): (20030.

Merlin, Mark, *Man and Marijuana*, (Barnes and Co, 1972)

Messadié, Gérald and Romano, Marc, *A History of the Devil*, Translated by Marc Romano, (Kodansha International, 1996)

Meyer-Melikyan, N. R and Avetov, N.A., *Analysis of Floral Remains in the Ceramic Vessel from the Gonur Temenos*, 1998, appendix to (Sarianidi, 1998)

Mikuriya, Todd H. M.D.,Ed.; *Marijuana Medical Papers*, (Medi-Comp Press 1973)

Mikuriya, Tod H. "International Classification of Diseases 9 - CM 1996 Chronic Conditions Treated With Cannabis Encountered Between 1990-2005" (July 13, 2005) http://www.ca-norml.org/prop/Mikuriya_ICD-9list.pdf

Miller, Jonathan Pett, Unraveling "The Mystery Of The Tien Shan Pai," Inside *Kung Fu Magazine*, (May, 2004)

Mills, James, *Madness, Cannabis and Colonialism: The 'Native Only' Lunatic Asylums of British India, 1857-1900* (Palgrave Macmillan, 2000)

Mills, Lawrence Heyworth (trans.). *Yasna 9-11* (Hom Yasht), In Müller, Friedrich Max (ed.) (1887). SBE. Oxford: OUP.

Minford, John, *Favorite Folktales of China*, (Beijing: New World Press, 1983),

Mirfendereski, Guive, "Homavarka: The potheads of ancient Iran," www.iranian.com (May, 17, 2005)

Mirfendereski, Guive, *The Saka Nomenclature, A Persian appraisal*, (2006)

Modi, J.J., *The Religious Ceremonies and Customs of the Parsees*, (Bombay, 1922)

Moody, Robin J., "Women looking at options for hormone replacement," *Portland Bussiness Journal*, (January 17, 2003),

Morneau, Daniel, "The Punic Warship," *Saudi, Aramco World*, (November/December, 1986)

Morningstar, Patricia J., Thandai and Chilam, "Traditional Hindu Beliefs About the Proper Use of Cannabis," in (Bey and Zug, 2004).

Morris, Edwin T. Fragrance: The Story of Perfume from Cleopatra to Chanel, (Scribner, 1984)

Mozeson, Isaac E., *The Word: The Dictionary That Reveals the Hebrew Source of English* (Shapolsky Publishers, 1989)

Muir, John, *Original Sanskrit Texts on the Origin and History of the People of India*, (1860)

Mukherjee, B. L., "The Soma Plant," JRAS, (1921), Idem, "The Soma Plant," Calcutta, (1922), *The Journal of the Royal Asiatic Society of Great Britain & Ireland* (Royal Asiatic Society of Great Britain and Ireland, 1921)

Muller, F. Max, *Chips from a German Workshop Part One*, (Kessinger Publishing, 2004, 1873)

Muller, Max and Oldenberg, H., *Vedic Hymns*, (1892, 2001)

Murdoch, John, *The Indian Students Manual: Hints on Studies, Moral Conduct, Religious Duties, and Success in Life*, (The Christian Vernacular Education Society, 1875)

Murdoch, John, English *Translations Of Select Tracts*, Published In India, (Madras, Graves and Co, 1861)

Murdoch, John, *Religious reform*, (Christian Literature Society for India 1887)

Murphy, Emily; *The Black Candle*, (1920).

Musaios, *The Lion Path*, 1985

Muses, Charles, "The Sacred Plant Of Ancient Egypt," In *Gateways To Inner Space*, Christian Rätch, ed.(1989)

Nabarz, Payam, *The Mysteries of Mithras: The Pagan Belief That Shaped the Christian World*, (Inner Traditions / Bear & Company, 2005

Nahas, et. al., *Marihuana and Medicine*, By Gabriel G. Nahas, Kenneth M. Sutin, Stig Agurell, Contributor Gabriel G. Nahas, (Humana Press, 1999)

Needham, et. al., *Science and Civilisation in China*, By Joseph Needham, Francesca Bray, Christoph Harbsmeier, (Cambridge University Press, 1954)

Natan, Yoel, *Moon-o-theism*, (2006)

Needham, J. L., and Gwei-Djen, "Science and civilisation in China." *Chemistry and Chemical Technology*, (Cambridge University Press, Cambridge, 1974)

Needham, Joseph, *Science and Civilization*, (Cambridge University Press, 1976)

Newham, Sara, "Expert Testifies Cannabis Helps Slow Aging," May 2 2008 *Nelson Daily News*

"Nihangs 'not to accept' ban on bhang," *The Tribune* (Chandigarh, India; March 26, 2001)

Novak, William; *High Culture*, (New York 1980).

Nunn, John F., *Ancient Egyptian Medicine*, (University of Oklahoma Press, 2002)

Nyberg, Harri, "The Problem of the Aryans and the Soma: the botanical evidence," in *Erdosy*, (1995)

Nyberg, Henrik Samuel, *Irans forntida religioner*, tr. Hans Heinrich Schaeder as *Die Religionen des Alten Iran*, Mitteilungen der Vorderasiatisch-aegyptischen Gesellschaft 43, (Leipzig, 1938)

O'Flaherty, W. D., "The Post-Vedic History of the Soma Plant," in Robert Gordon Wasson, *Soma: Divine Mushroom of Immortality*, (New York, 1968)

Oisteanu, Andrei, "Mythos and Logos." *Studies and Essays of Cultural Anthropology*, (Nemira" Publishing House, Bucuresti, Romania, 1997)

Oliver, Prof. Revilo P., *The Origins of Christianity* , (Urbana 1994)

Omidsalar, Mahmoud "Dūg-Ewahdat, Beverage of Unity," *Encyclopaedia Iranica*, (1999)

"Orgies of the hemp eaters," *New York Herald*, (March 15, 1895)

Orwell, George, *"Shooting an Elephant," Inside the Whale and other Essays*, (Penguin, 1971)

O'Shaughnessy, William Brooke, 'On the preparation of Indian Hemp or Gunjah,' *Provincial Medical Journal*, (London 1843

Ott, Jonathan, personal correspondence, 1996

Ott, Jonathan; *Pharmacotheon; Entheogenic Drugs Their Plant Sources and History*, (Natural Products, Co., 1993).

Ott, Jonathon, *The Age of Entheogens and Angels Dictionary*, (Natural Products, Co.,1995)

Oursler, Will, *Marijuana, the facts, the Truth*, (Paul S.Erikson, Inc. ,1968).

Owen ,Richard, "Lost Punic warships may rise in TV museum; Ancient wrecks found off the Sicilian coast date from the battle of the Egadi Islands in 241BC," *The Times*, (London; August 7, 2004)

Pal, Pratapaditya, *Indian Sculpture, Volume 2*, (University of California Press, 1988).

Parker, R.C., The Use of Entheogens in the Vajrayana Tradition: a brief summary of preliminary findings together with a partial bibliography, (2007; updated 2008)

Parker R.C, & Lux, "Psychoactive Plants in Tantric Buddhism; Cannabis and Datura Use in Indo-Tibetan Esoteric Buddhism," *Erowid Extracts*, (June, 2008)

Parmeshwaranand, *Encyclopaedic Dictionary of Puranas*, (2001)

Parpola, Asko, "The problem of Aryans and the Soma: Textual-linguistic and archeological evidence," (1995) in *Erdosy*, (1995)

Parrinder, Geoffery; Ed., *World Religions; From Ancient History to the Present*, (Facts On File Publications, New York,1971)

Parsche, F., S. Balabanova and W. Pirsig 1993, "Drugs in ancient populations" (letter). *Lancet* 341: 503.

Parsche, Franz and Nerlich, Andreas, "Presence of drugs in different tissues of an Egyptian mummy," (1994) Published in Fresenius' *Journal of Analytical Chemistry*, (1995)

Parsche, Franz, "Reply to 'Responding to 'First identification of drugs in Egyptian mummies,'" Naturwissenschaften (1993)

Patai, Raphael, *The Hebrew goddess*, originally published in 1967, (Wayne State University Press 1990)

Paz, Octavio and Lane, Helen, *Alternating Current*, Translated by Helen Lane, (Arcade Publishing, 1991)

Pendell, Dale, *Pharmako/poeia; Plant Powers Poisons and Herbcraft*, (Mercury House,1995).

Peters, et. al., *The Biomarker Guide: Biomarkers and Isotopes in the Environment and Human History*, By Kenneth E. Peters, Clifford C. Walters, J. Michael Moldowan

Philpot, J.H., *The Sacred Tree, or The Tree in Religion and Myth*, (The MacMillian Company, NY, 1897)

"Pharmacal Advance," *Hashish*, Vol. IX – No. 105, (New York, 1930)

Piankoff, A., "The Pyramid of Unas," *Bollingen Series 40*, (1968)

Pinkham, Mark Amaru, *John The Baptist, And The Water Of Life*, (Adventures Unlimited Press, 2004)

Piper, Alan, "The Milk of the Goat Heidrun An Investigation into the Sacramental Use of Psychoactive Milk and Meat," (2004)

Pliny the Elder, *Natural History, a Selection*, J. F. Healy trans. (New York, 1991)

Pooja, *Economic Botany*, (Discovery Publishing House, 2005)

Pourshariati, Parvaneh, *Decline and Fall of the Sasanian Empire: The Sasanian-Parthian Confederacy and the Arab Conquest of Iran*, (I. B. Tauris, 2008)

Prioreschi, P., and D. Babin, "Ancient use of Cannabis," *Nature* (1993)

Professor V. I. Sarianidi: "The First World Religion - Zoroastrianism - Emerged In Turkmenistan," *Turkmenistan International Magaine*, June, 2006,

Quaintance, Dan and Mary. "Nutritional Haoma Sacrament," (2008), http://danmary.org/tiki/tiki-index.php?page=Nutritional+Haoma+Sacrament&bl

Ragozin, Zenaide A., *Vedic India as Embodied Principally in the Rig-Veda*, (Kessinger Publishing, 1895, 2005)

Ramachandran, M. and Mativānan, Irāman, *The Spring of the Indus Civilisation*, (Prasanna Pathippagam, 1991)

Randhawa, Mohindar Singh, *A History of Agriculture in India*, (Indian Council of Agricultural Research, 1980)

Ratsch, Christian, *Marijuana Medicine*, (Inner Traditions, 1998, 2001)

Ratsch, Christian, *Plants of Love: Aphrodisiacs in Myth, History, and the Present*, (Ten Speed Press, 1997)

Rausing, G., Soma, *Orientalia Suecana* 36-37, 1987-88, pp. 125-26. I. M. Steblin-Kamenskij, "Flora iranskoy prarodini (etimologiceskie zametki)," *Etimologiya*, Moscow, (1972), Idem, review of Papers in Honour of Professor Mary Boyce, 2 vols., *Acta Iranica* 24-25, in BSOAS 50, (1987)

Rawlinson, G., *The Five Great Monarchies of the Eastern World*, (1871)

Ray, Jogesh Chandra, *Ancient Indian Life*, (P. R. Sen, 1948)

Ray, Joseph, Chandra, "Soma Plant," *Indian Historical Quarterly*, vol. 15, no. 2, June, 1939, Calcutta

Reddy, Dr. D.V.S. "The History of medicine in India," *The Journal of Oriental Research*,(Kuppuswami Sastri Research Institute., 1936)

Regmi, Delli Roman, *The Control of Liquor in Ancient India*, (NR 12, 1940).

Reiner, E., *The Assyrian Dictionary* (University of Chicago, 1995) (as noted by Russo)

Reiner, Erica, *Astral Magic in Babylonia*, (Diane Publishing, 1995)

Reininger, W., "Remnants From Historic Times," Andrews G. and Vinkenoog, S., (eds.) *The Book of Grass: An Anthology on Indian Hemp*, London: Peter Owen Limited (1967). Also in *Ciba Symposia*, 8 (Augus-September, 1946).

Rice, Edward, *Eastern Definitions: A Short Encyclopedia of Religions of the Orient*, (DoubleDay, 1978)

Richter-Ushanas, Egbert, *The Indus Script and the Rig-Ved*a, (Motilal Banarsidass Publ., 1997)

Riedlinger, Thomas J., "Wasson's Alternative Candidates for Soma," *The Journal of Psychoactive Drugs*, (1993)

Ringgren, Helmer, *Religions of the Ancient Near East*, (Westminster Press 1973).

Reynolds, Barbara, *Dante: The Poet, the Politcal Thinker, the Man*, (first Shoemaker & Hoard edition 2006, First published in the United Kingdom by I.B. Tauris & Co. Ltd.)

Rjabchikov, Sergei V., "Remarks on the Scythian, Sarmatian and Meotian Beliefs," (2004)

Rjabchikov, Sergei V., "The Interpretation of Some Sarmatian Motifs And Inscriptions," (2001)

Robinson, James, Ed. *The Nag Hamadi Library in English*, Harper Collins, 1978, 1988

Robinson, Rowan, *The Great Book of Hemp: The Complete Guide to the Environmental, Commercial, and Medicinal Uses of the World's Most Extraordinary Plant*, (Inner Traditions / Bear & Company, 1995)

Robson, John R. K., *Culture: readings in the anthropology of dietary practices*, (Taylor & Francis,1980)

Rohde, Erwin, *Psyche: The Cult of Souls and the Belief in Immortality Among the Greeks*, (1925 by Routledge and Kegan Paul)

Rosch, Manfred, "Pollen analysis of the contents of excavated vessels—direct archaeobotanical evidence of beverages, 2004, 2005," *Veget Hist Archaeobot* (2005)

Rosenthal, Franz, *The Herb; Hashish Versus Medieval Muslim Society*, (Brill, 1971)

Rowan, Henbane, *The Insane Seed that Breedeth Madness*, (Lughnasa 1998)

Ruck, Carl and Hoffman, Mark, "Freemasonry and the Survival of the Eucharistic Brotherhoods," *Entheos: The Journal of Psychedelic Spirituality*, Vol. 2, Issue 1, Summer, 2002

Ruck, Carl, 2003, "Was there a whiff of cannabis about Jesus?," (*The Sunday Times*; 12 January 2003)

Ruck, et. al., Conniving Wolves: chapter V, pages 87-124, in Carl A.P. Ruck, Blaise Daniel Staples, José Alfredo González Celdrán, and Mark Alwin Hoffman, *The Hidden World: Survival of Pagan Shamanic Themes in European Fairytales* (Durham, NC: Carolina Academic Press, 2007)

Ruck, Carl, affidavit in *Bennett v The Attorney General for Canada and the Minister of Health for Canada*, (2009)

Rudenko, Sergei I.. *Frozen Tombs of Siberia – the Pazyryk burials of Iron Age horsemen*, (University of California Press, 1970)

Rudgley, Richard, *The Encyclopedia of Psychoactive Substances*, (Little, Brown and Company, 1998)

Rudgley, Richard; *Essential Substances*, (Kodansha International 1993).

Rudolph, Kurt Gnosis: *The Nature and History of Gnosticism*. Harper, San Francisco, 1987.

Russell, Dan; *Shamanism and the Drug Propaganda*, (1998).

Russell, James (Personal correspondence, 2008)

Russo, E., "History of Cannabis as a Medicine," *The Medicinal Uses of Cannabis and Cannabinoids*, By Geoffrey William Guy, Brian Anthony Whittle, Philip Robson, (Pharmaceutical Press, 2004)

Russo, et. al., "Phytochemical and genetic analyses of ancient cannabis from Central Asia," *Journal of Experimental Botany*, (Oxford, 2008).

Russo, Ethan M.D., Unpublished paper 2005, "Clinical Cannabis in Ancient Mesopotamia: A Historical Survey with Supporting Scientific Evidence," I wrote Ethan and he said most of that stuff was included in the following: Russo EB. "History of cannabis and its preparations in saga, science and sobriquet. Chemistry & Biodiversity" 2007;4(8):2624-48.

Russo, Ethan, *Cannabis in India: ancient lore and modern Medicine*, GW Pharmaceuticals, 2235 Wylie Avenue, Missoula, MT 59809, USA, Cannabinoids as Therapeutics, Edited by R. Mechoulam, © 2005 Birkhäuser Verlag/Switzerland

Russo, Ethan, "Hemp for Headache: An In-Depth Historical and Scientific Review of Cannabis in Migraine Treatment," *Journal of Cannabis Therapeutics*, (2001)

Rutheford, Ward, *Celtic Lore*, (Thorsons\Aquarian 1993)

Sagan, Carl, *The Dragons of Eden: Speculations on the Evolution of Human Intelligence*, (Random House, NY, 1977)

Saggs, H.W.F.; *The Greatness That Was Babylon; A Survey of the Ancient Civilization of the Tigris-Euphrates Valley.* (Frederick A. Praeger, New York 1962)

Samuelson, James, *The History of Drink*, 1880

Saifullah, M.S.M., "Arda Wiraz Namag (Iranian 'Divina Commedia") And The Prophet's Night Journey," (Islamic Awareness, 2002: 2005).

Sanyal, Shri Amitava *A story of medicine and pharmacy in India: Pharmacy 2000 years ago and After*, (Calcutta,1964)

Sarianidi V., *Temples of Bronze Age Margiana: traditions of ritual architecture.* Antiquity, (1994)

Sarianidi V., *Margiana and protozoroastrism.* Kapon Editions, (Athens, 1998)

Sarianidi, Victor I. "Margiana and Soma-Haoma," *Electronic Journal Of Vedic Studies*, Vol. 9 (2003), Issue 1 (May)

Sarton, George, *Ancient Science Through the Golden Age of Greece*, (Dover, 1993)

Scheil, P. (1921): *Notules Revue d'Assyriologie et d'Archeaeologie Orientale* 18: 95-100. (as noted by Russo)

Schmid, W. P., *Indogermanistische Modelle und osteuropäische Frühgeschichte*, (Mainz and Wiesbaden, 1978)

Schmitt, Rüdiger *The Old Persian Inscriptions of Naqsh-i Rustam and Persepolis*, Corp. Inscr. Iran I/1, texts 2, (London, 2000)

Schonfield, Dr. Hugh J.; *The Passover Plot*, (Bantam Books 1967)

Schultes, R.E., "Man and Marijuana," *Natural History*, 82 (1973)

Schultes, Richard Evans and Albert Hoffman; 1992, *Plants of the Gods-Origins of Hallucinogenic Use* (McGraw-Hill Book Co. Ltd., England,1979). [Reprinted by Healing Arts Press in 1992].

Scott, et. al., *Impact of the Environment on Human Migration in Eurasia: Proceedings of the NATO Advanced Research Workshop, Held in St. Petersburg, 15-18 November 2003*, By E. Marian Scott, Andrey Yu Alekseev, Ganna I. Zaitseva, North Atlantic Treaty Organization Scientific Affairs Division, (Springer, 2004).

Seff, Phillip & Nancy, *Our Fascinating Earth*, (Contemporary Books, 1996)

Shackley, Myra, *Managing Sacred Sites: Service Provision And the Visitor*, (Cengage Learning EMEA, 2001)

Shah, Idries, *The Sufis*, (1964)

Shaked, Shaul, "Quests and Visionary Journeys in Sassanian Iran," *Transformations of the Inner Self in Ancient Religions*, By Jan Assmann, Gedaliahu A. G. Stroumsa, (Brill, 1999)

Sharma, Shubhra, *Life in the Upanishads*, (Abhinav Publications, 1985)

Sherratt, A. G., "Alcohol and its alternatives: symbol and substance in pre-industrial cultures" in J. Goodman, E E. Lovejoy, and A. Sherratt. 1995. *Consuming habits: drugs in history and anthropology*, (Routledge, London and New York,9 1997)

Sherratt, A. G., "Cups that cheered, Bell Beakers of the Western Mediterranean," BAR Int. Ser. 331, vol. 1. *British Archaeological Reports*, (Oxford.1991)

Sherratt, A. G., "Introduction: peculiar substances" in J. Goodman, E E. Lovejoy, and A. Sherratt. 1995. *Consuming habits: drugs in history and anthropology*, (Routledge, London and New York, 1995)

Sherratt, A. G., "Sacred and profane substances: the ritual use of narcotics in later Neolithic Europe" in E Garwood, D. Jennings, R. Skeates, andJ. Toms, eds., *Sacred and profane: proceedings of a conference on archaeology, ritual and religion.* Oxford University Committee for Archaeology Monographs. (1995)

Sherratt, Andrew, "Alcohol and its Alternatives:Symbol and substance in Pre-Industrial cultures," in *Consuming Habits: Drugs in History and Anthropology*, by Jordan Goodman, Paul E. Lovejoy, Andrew Sherratt, Contributor Jordan Goodman, (Routledge, 1995)

Sherratt, Andrew, *Economy and Society in Prehistoric Europe: Changing Perspectives*, (Princeton University, 1997).

Shukla, Hira Lal, *Semiotica Indica: Encyclopaedic Dictionary of Body-language in Indian Art & Culture*, (Aryan Books International, 1994)

Shulgin, Alexander and Ann, *Tihkal: The Continuation*, (Transform Pr, 1997)

Silver, Gary, *Dope Chronicles*, edited by Michael Aldrich, (Harper & Row, 1979)

Simpson, James Young, *The obstetric memoirs and contributions of James Y. Simpson*, Edited by William Overend Priestly, Horatio Robinson Storer, (1856)

Sinclair, May, *Infamous Eve: A History*, (Wheatmark Inc., 2007)

Singh, Amrit Pal, "The 'Sukhnidhaan' or 'Bhang' (cannabis)," (http://www.amritworld.com/main/articles/cannabis/ 2008)

Smith, Frederick John and Taylor, Alfred Swaine, *Taylor's Principles and Practice of Medical Jurisprudence*: Edited, revised, and brought up to date by Fred. J. Smith, (J. & A. Churchill, 1920)

Smith, Homer, *Man and his Gods*, (Boston, 1952)

Smith, Morton; *Jesus the Magician*, (Harper & Row, 1978)

Sneader, Walter, *Drug Discovery: A History*, (John Wiley and Sons, 2005)

Sokoloff, Heather and Wingrove, Josh, "A toke a day keeps memory loss at bay: Small doses of marijuana improve the function of aging brains, scientists find," *Globe and Mail*, (November 20, 2008)

Southworth, Franklin C., *Linguistic Archaeology of South Asia*, (Routledge, 2005)

Spencer, William, *Iraq: Old Land, New Nation in Conflict*, (Twenty-First Century Books, 2000).

Stablein, William George, *The Mahakalatantra: A theory of ritual blessings and tantric medicine*, Doctoral Dissertation, (Columbia University, 1976).

Stanley, Alessandra, "Tattooed Lady, 2,000 Years Old, Blooms Again," Moscow Journal, *New York Times*, (July 13, 1994)

Starks, Michael, *Marijuana Chemistry. Genetics, Processing and Potency*, (Ronin Publishing, 1990)

Stausberg, Michael, *Zoroastrian Rituals in Context*, (Brill, 2004)

Stefanis, C., Ballas, C. and Madianou, D., "Sociocultural and Epidemiological Aspects of Hashish Use in Greece," in (Rubin, 2005)

Stefanis, et. al., *Hashish: Studies of Long-term Use*, By Costas N. Stefanis, Rhea L. Dornbush, Max Fink, (Raven Press, 1977)

Strange, Thomas Lumisden *The Legends of the Old Testament: traced to their apparent primitive sources* (Trübner, 1874)

Strickmann, Michel, et. al., *Chinese Magical Medicine*, Bernard Faure editor and contributor, (Stanford University Press, 2002)

Strickmann, Michel, "Homa in East Asia, in Agni." *The Vedic Ritual of the Fire Altar*, Volume II, Edited by Frits Staal, (Asian Humanities Press, 1983)

Strong's *Exhaustive Concordance of the Bible* (Thomas Nelson Inc. 1979)

Stuart, G.A., *Chinese Marteria Medica Vegetable Kingdom*, (1911)

Stuhrmann, R., *Worum handelt es sich beim Soma?*, IIJ 28, 1985

Subramuniyaswami, Satguru Sivaya Subramuniyaswami and the Editors of *Hinduism Today*, *What Is Hinduism?: Modern Adventures into a Profound Global Faith*, (Himalayan Academy, 2007)

Sundermann, Werner, "Oracle of Hystaspes," www.iranica.com, (2004)

Suzuki, D.T., *Essays in Zen Buddhism*, (Grove Press, NY, 1961).

Swamy, B.G.L., "The Rg Vedic Soma Plant," *Indian Journal of History of Science*

Szemerényi, Oswald "Four old Iranian ethnic names: Scythian - Skudra - Sogdian - Saka" (Sitzungsberichte der Österreichischen Akademie der Wissenschaften 371), Vienna, 1980 = *Scripta minora*, vol. 4, pp. 2051-2093.

Taillieu, Dieter and Boyce, Mary. "Haoma." *Encyclopaedia Iranica*. New York: Mazda Pub, (2002).

Taillieu, Dieter, "Old Iranian haoma-: A Note on Its Pharmacology," *Acta Orientalia Belgica* 9, 1994 (pub. 1995)

Taillieu, Ed., *Devotional Literature in South Asia: Current Research 1997-2000* (New Delhi, 2002)

Taylor, Norman, *Narcotics: Nature's Most Dangerous Gift*, (Dell, 1966).

Taylor, Rogan, *The Death and Resurrection Show*, (Anthony Blond, 1985).

The Rangjung Yeshe Tibetan-English Dictionary of Buddhist Culture, Version 3 on CD ROM, (August 2003)

Taraporewala,, I.J.S., *The religion of Zarathushtra*, (Madras, 1926)

Temple, R.C., 'Folk Songs from Northern India,' *Calcutta Review*, Volume 78⊠, (University of Calcutta, 1884)

The Journal of Education, By Ministry of Education, Item notes: v. 60, (W. Stewart & Co., 1928)

Thompson, C. J. S., *Mysteries and Secrets of Magic*, (Kessinger Publishing, 2003)

Thompson, George, Soma and Ecstasy in the Rgveda, *Electronic Journal Of Vedic Studies* (EJVS) Vol. 9 (2003) Issue 1e (May 6).

Thompson, R. Campbell, *Devils and Evil Spirits of Babylonia: Being Babylonian and Assyrian Incantations Against the Demons, Ghouls, Vampires, Hobglobins, Ghosts, and Kindred Evil Spirits, which Attack Mankind*, (1903)

Thompson, R.C. & Hutchinson, R.W. (1929): *A century of exploration at Nineveh*. Luzac, London. (as noted by Russo)

Thompson, R.C. (1902): *Cuneiform texts from Babylonian tablets in the British Museum*, Part XIV. British Museum, London. (as noted by Russo)

Thompson, R.C. (1923): *Assyrian medical texts from the originals in the British Museum*. Oxford University Press, London. (as noted by Russo)

Thompson, R.C. (1924a): *The Assyrian herbal*. Luzac and Co., London. (as noted by Russo)

Thompson, R.C. (1924b): "A Babylonian explanatory text." *Royal Asiatic Society of Great Britain and Ireland*: 452-457. (as noted by Russo)

Thompson, R.C. (1929a): "Assyrian medical prescriptions for diseases of the stomach." *Revue d'Assyriologie et d'Archéologie Orientale*. 26(2): 47-92. (as noted by Russo)

Thompson, R.C. (1929b): "Assyrian prescriptions for the 'hand of a ghost.'" *Journal of the Royal Asiatic Society of Great Britain and Ireland*. 29: 801-823. (as noted by Russo)

Thompson, R.C. (1930a): "Assyrian medical prescriptions against Simmatu "poison."" *Revue d'Assyriologie et d'Archéologie Orientale*.: 127-135. (as noted by Russo)

Thompson, R.C. (1930b): "Assyrian prescriptions for treating bruises or swellings." *American Journal of Semitic Languages and Literatures* 47(1): 1-25. (as noted by Russo)

Thompson, R.C. (1931): "Assyrain prescriptions for diseases of the ears." *Journal of the Royal Asiatic Society of Great Britain and Ireland*.: 1-23. (as noted by Russo)

Thompson, R.C. (1934a): "An Assyrian chemist's vade-mecum." *Journal of the Royal Asiatic Society of Great Britain and Ireland.*: 771-785. (as noted by Russo)

Thompson, R.C. (1934c): "Assyrian prescriptions for diseases of the chest and lungs." *Revue d'Assyriologie et d'Archéologie Orientale.* 31(1): 1-29. (as noted by Russo)

Thompson, R.C. (1934d): "Assyrian prescriptions for diseases of the urine, etc. Babyloniaca" 14: 57-151. (as noted by Russo)

Thompson, R.C. (1936): *A dictionary of Assyrian chemistry and geology.* Clarendon Press, Oxford.

Thompson, R.C. (1937): "Assyrian prescriptions for diseases of the feet." *Royal Asiatic Society of Great Britain and Ireland*: 265-286, 413-432. (as noted by Russo)

Thompson, R.C. (1949): *A dictionary of Assyrian botany.* British Academy, London. (as noted by Russo)

Thorne, Robert, *Marihuana: the Burning Bush of Moses*, (Clarus Books, 1998).

Thorwald, Jürgen *Science and Secrets of Early Medicine: Egypt, Mesopotamia, India, China, Mexico, Peru*, (Harcourt, Brace & World, 1963)

Tisdall, Rev. W. St. Clair *The Original Sources Of The Qur'an, Society For The Promotion Of Christian Knowledge*: London, (1905)

"Tracking the Scythians," *Time*, (January 17, 1972)

Twyman, Tracy T. and Metzger, Richard, "The Arcadian Mystique," *The Best of Dagobert's Revenge* magazine, (Dragon Key Press, 2005)

Touw, Mia, "The Religious and Medicinal Uses of Cannabis in China, India and Tibet," *Journal of Psychoactive Drugs*, Vol. 13(1) (Jan-Mar, 1981)

Tzadok, Rabbi Ariel Bar "Kabbalistic Insights Into The Dangers of Drug Use," (1993 by Ariel Bar Tzadok).

Van Baaren, Theodorus Petrus & Hartman, Sven S., *Iconography of Religions*, (1980)

Van Lohuizen-De Leeuw, Johanna Engelberta, *The "Scythian" Period*, (Munishiram Manoharlal Publishers Pvt. Ltd., 1949; 1995)

Vandenberg , Phillip *The Mystery of the Oracles*, (New York: Macmillan, 1979)

Vavilov, et. al., *Origin and Geography of Cultivated Plants*, By Nikolaï Ivanovich Vavilov, Vladimir Filimonovich Dorofeev, Doris Love, Translated by Doris Love, Contributor Vladimir Filimonovich Dorofeev, Doris Love,(CUP Archive, 1992)

Vedantatirtha Girish Chandra, ed., *Tara Tantra, Tara-Tantram*, With an Introduction by A. K. Maitra. (1914).

Vetter, George, *Magic and Religion: Their Psychological Nature, Origin and Function*, (Philosophical Library, 1958).

Vikramasinha, *Glimpses of Indian Culture*, (Kitab Mahal, 1967)

Vindheim, Jan Bojer, "The History of Hemp in Norway" in *Journal of Industrial Hemp* Volume 7, Number 1, (2002)

Von Bibra, Baron Ernst, *Plant Intoxicants*, (Healing Arts Press,1995) (Originally published as *Die narkotischen Genußmittel und der Mensch*, by Wilhelm Schmid, Nuremburg,1855).

Walker, Barbara G., *The Woman's Encyclopedia of Myths and Secrets*, (Harper Collins, 1983)

Walker, Barbara, *The Woman's Book of Myths and Secrets* (Harper Collins, 1986)

Walker, Benjamin, *Tantrism: Its Secret Principles and Practices*, (The Aquarian Press 1982).

Wallechinsky, David, Wallace, Irving and Wallace, Amy *The Book of Lists, The People's Almanac*, (Bantam Books,1978).

Walton, R.P., *Licit & Illicit Drugs*, Brecher Edward M. and the Editors of Consumer Reports (Little, Brown & Co., 1972)

Walton, R.P., *Marihuana* (Philadelphia: J. P. Lippincott, 1938),

Wasson, Robert Gordon, ed., *Soma: Divine Mushroom of Immortality, Ethno-Mycological Studies* 1, (New York, 1968); reviewed by Franciscus B. J. Kuiper, in IIJ 12, (1970). Idem, "Soma of the Aryans: An Ancient Hallucinogen?" *Bulletin on Narcotics* 22, (1970). Idem, "Soma: Comments Inspired by Professor Kuiper's Review," IIJ 12, (1970). Idem, "The Soma of the Rig Veda: What Was It?" *JAOS* 91, (1971). Idem, "Soma and the Fly-Agaric. Mr. Wasson's Rejoinder to Professor Brough," Botanical Museum of Harvard University, Cambridge, Mass., (November, 1972). Idem, "Soma Brought Up-to-Date," *JAOS* 99, (1979).

Warraq, Ibn *Why I Am Not A Muslim*, (Prometheus Books, 1995)

Watt, G. 1889. *A Dictionary of the Economic Products of India*. India Dept. of Revenue and Agriculture, India. (1889)

Watt, George, *Commercial Products of India*, (Calcutta, 1908).

Watt, John and Charles, *The Chemist*, (1853)

Weber, Albrecht, ed., *The Çatapatha-Brahmanâa in the Mâdhhyandina-çâkhâ*, (Belin and London, 1855; 3rd ed. 1964)

Weil, Andrew; *The Natural Mind*, (1972, Revised edition, Houghton Mifflin Company Boston 1986).

Weiner, Richard S., *Pain Management: A Practical Guide for Clinicians*, (2002)

Wheeler, James Talboys, *The History of India from the Earliest Ages*, (N. Trübner, 1867)

White D.G. *The Alchemical Body: Siddha Traditions of Medieval India*, (University of Chicago Press, 1996)

White, Gavin, *Babylonian Star-Lore An Illustrated Guide to the Star-lore and Constellations of Ancient Babylonia*, (Lulu.com, 2008)

Widengren, G., "Stand und Aufgaben der iranischen Religionsgeschichte," *Numen 2*, (1955)

Widengren, G., *Die Religionen Irans.* , (Kohlhammer, Stuttgart, 1965)

Wikander, Stig, *Der arische Männerbund: Studien zur indo-iranischen Sprach- und Religionsgeschichte*, (Lund, 1938)

Willey, Peter, *Eagle's Nest: Ismaili castles in Iran and Syria*, (Institute of Ismaili Studies, & I.B. Tauris and Co. Ltd., 2005)

Wilkins, Robert, *Fireside Book of Death*, (Little, Brown Book Group Limited, 1992)

Wilkinson, John Gardner and Birch, Samuel, *The Manners and Customs of the Ancient Egyptians*, (1878)

Williams, George Mason, *Handbook of Hindu Mythology*, (ABC-CLIO, 2003)

Wills, Simon, "Cannabis Use and Abuse by Man: An Historical Perspective" in *Cannabis: The Genus Cannabis*, Edited By David T. Brown, (CRC Press, 1998)

Wilson, Peter Lamborn, *Scandal Essays in Islamic Heresy*, (Autonomedia, Inc. 1988)

Wilson, Peter Lamborn, *Sacred Drift, Essays on the Margins of Islam*, (City Light Books 1993)

Wilson, Peter Lamborn, *Ploughing the Clouds: The Search for Irish Soma*, (City Lights Books, 1999).

Wilson, Peter Lamborn and Zug, Abel, *Orgies of the Hemp Eaters*, (Autonomedia, 2004).

Wilson, Robert Anton; *Sex & Drugs*, (Playboy Press 1973).

Winternitz, Maurice V. and Sarma, Srinivasa, *A History of Indian Literature*, Translated by V. Srinivasa Sarma, (Motilal Banarsidass Publ., 1996)

Witzel, M., "Early sources for South Asian substrate languages," *Mother Tongue* (October, 1999)

Witzel, Michael, *Aryan and non-Aryan Names in Vedic India. Data for the linguistic situation, c. 1900-500 B.C.*, (Harvard University, 1999)

Wohlberg, J., *Haoma-Soma in the world of ancient Greece*, J Psychoactive Drugs, (1990)

Woods, John E., *History and Historiography of Post-Mongol Central Asia and the Middle East*: Studies in Honor of John E. Woods, By John E. Woods, Judith Pfeiffer, Sholeh Alysia Quinn, Ernest Tucker, Contributor Judith Pfeiffer, (Harrassowitz, 2006)

Wooley, Sir Leonard, *Ur of the Chaldees*, (1929)

Wujastyk, Dominik (d.wujastyk@ucl.ac.uk), Welcome Library London, draft of (Wednesday, September 12, 2001).

Wujastyk D., "Cannabis in Traditional Indian Herbal Medicine, in Ana Salema (ed.) Ayurveda at the Crossroads of Care and Cure," *Proceedings of the Indo-European Seminar on Ayurveda held at Arrábida, Portugal, in November 2001.*

Yar-Shater, Ehsan, *The Seleucid, Parthian and Sasanian Periods*, (Cambridge University Press, 1983)

Yule, et. al., *A Glossary of Colloquial Anglo-Indian Words and Phrases*, By Henry Yule, A. C. Burnell, William Crooke, (1903)

Zaehner, R.C., *The Dawn and Twilight of Zoroastrianism*, New York: G.P. Putnam's Sons, 1961

Zias, J., Stark H, Sellgman J, Levy R, Werker E, Breuer A, Mechoulam R. "Early medical use of cannabis." *Nature*, 1993

Zias, J., In: Campbell S, Green A, eds., *The Archaeology of Death in the Ancient Near East*, Oxford, UK: Oxbow Books, (1995)

Zias, Joel, Personal Correspondence, Oct.02, 2005,

Zohary, Daniel and Hopf, Maria, *Domestication of Plants in the Old World: The Origin and Spread of Cultivated Plants in West Asia, Europe, and the Nile Valley*, (Oxford University Press, 2000)

Zoroastrianism: The rediscovery of missing chapters in man's religious history (Teaching aids for the study of Inner Asia). Asian Studies Research Institute: Indiana University Press, (1977)

Index

[Note about italics and spelling: excerpted material is presented as is, so there is an inconsistency with the italicization and spelling of some words in the book. Editor]

Symbols

72 Hour's in Heaven 522

A

Aalto, Peenti 9, 70, 85, 303, 304, 315, 601
Abaris 272
Abraham 258, 378, 387, 550
Acts of Peter and the Twelve Apostles, The 400
Acts of Thomas 400, 402, 423
A dictionary of Assyrian chemistry and geology 202
Ahriman 284
Ahura Mazda 62, 101, 103, 284, 294, 309, 312, 330-333, 345, 383, 386, 390, 391, 414, 423, 439, 440, 441, 574, 578, 582, 587
Aitareya Brahmana/Brahmanam 13, 82, 336, 465-470, 516
al-Badri, 534, 535, 539
Aldrich, Michael 326, 327, 495, 534
Aleff, H. Peter 229, 230
al-Ghafiki, Ahamad 315
Amanita muscaria (fly agaric) vii, 2, 4, 15-18, 24, 26, 28, 29, 30, 33-37, 39, 41, 47, 71, 261, 288, 304, 408, 442
A Meeting of Civilizations: The Mystery of China's Celtic Mummies 176
American Society for Clinical Investigation, The 252
Amrita 477-483
Anandakanda 75, 511

Ananova 233
Ancient Wine 259
Anderson, William 372, 555
Andronovo culture 124, 146, 147, 182, 189
Annual of Armenian Linguistics 319
Antiatticista 257
Anu in India and in Egypt, The 240
Apocalypse of Peter, The 435
Apocalypticism in the Mediterranean World and the Near East 330
Apocryphon of John, The 403
Apollo 137, 265-267, 269, 276, 294, 598
Arata, Luigi 234, 251-253, 264, 280
Archaeology (magazine) 270
Ardu Wiraf 553
Atharvaveda/Atharva Veda 40, 69, 321-323, 448-450
Avalon, Arthur 494, 616
Avesta 9, 11, 12, 18, 20, 41, 42, 45, 62, 86, 88, 92, 97, 101, 104, 108, 109, 119, 195, 196, 260, 281, 286, 291-293, 295-297, 302, 304, 307, 311, 319, 320, 323, 325, 333, 334, 339, 342, 343, 378, 391, 415, 539, 574, 588
Avesta and Ancient Iran 319
Avetov, NA 110, 112, 113, 115, 116, 122, 123
Ayahuasca 44, 306
Ayurveda 449, 509

B

Baba Santa Singh 507, 508
Babayan, Kathryn 551
Bacchus 9
Bactria-Margiana Archaeological Complex (BMAC) 107, 110, 114-119, 122, 124, 131, 146, 171, 173, 180-182, 186, 196, 259, 281, 283, 290, 576
Bagli, Jehan 88, 103, 297, 391, 572-581
Bakels, Corrie 112, 113, 116, 122
Balabanova, Svetla 241-245, 247-249,
Barber, Elizabeth Wayland 49, 86, 110, 119, 120, 175, 178, 181, 182, 188, 189, 192, 193, 207
Barsom 100-103, 105, 550

X

Xiao, Li 167

Y

Yasna 10, 30, 85, 88-90, 97, 98, 102, 103, 119, 283, 284, 286, 290, 296-298, 330, 334, 335, 384, 385, 577

Z

Zaehner, Robert 288, 291, 293
Zarathustra 11, 91, 283- 287, 289-291, 293, 294, 298-300, 302, 325, 332-334, 338, 339, 344, 345, 431, 436, 575, 577, 579, 580, 601, 602
Zeus 137, 142, 234, 261, 294, 598
Zoroaster v, vi, 91, 104, 105, 181, 193, 197, 272, 283-285, 287-296, 298, 300, 301, 303, 308-312, 316, 319, 324, 325, 330-335, 337-348, 362, 374, 379, 380, 383-385, 403-405, 409, 413, 414, 435, 540, 542, 548, 571, 572, 578, 582, 589, 601, 602, 603
Zostrianos 404, 405, 423, 521
Zwinger, Theodore 235

The True Story of the Bilderberg Group

BY DANIEL ESTULIN — *NORTH AMERICAN UNION EDITION*

More than a center of influence, the Bilderberg Group is a shadow world government, hatching plans of domination at annual meetings … and under a cone of media silence.

THE TRUE STORY OF THE BILDERBERG GROUP goes inside the secret meetings and sheds light on why a group of politicians, businessmen, bankers and other mighty individuals formed the world's most powerful society. As Benjamin Disraeli, one of England's greatest Prime Ministers, noted, "The world is governed by very different personages from what is imagined by those who are not behind the scenes."

Included are unpublished and never-before-seen photographs and other documentation of meetings, as this riveting account exposes the past, present and future plans of the Bilderberg elite.

Softcover: **$24.95** (ISBN: 9780979988622) • 432 pages • Size: 6 x 9

ShadowMasters

BY DANIEL ESTULIN

AN INTERNATIONAL NETWORK OF GOVERNMENTS AND SECRET-SERVICE AGENCIES WORKING TOGETHER WITH DRUG DEALERS AND TERRORISTS FOR MUTUAL BENEFIT AND PROFIT

THIS INVESTIGATION EXAMINES HOW behind-the-scenes collaboration between governments, intelligence services and drug traffickers has lined the pockets of big business and Western banks. Beginning with a last-minute request from ex-governor Jesse Ventura, the narrative winds between the author's own story of covering "deep politics" and the facts he has uncovered. The ongoing campaign against Victor Bout, the "Merchant of Death," is revealed as "move/countermove" in a game of geopolitics, set against the background of a crumbling Soviet Union, a nascent Russia, bizarre assassinations, wars and smuggling. DANIEL ESTULIN is an award-winning investigative journalist and author of *The True Story of the Bilderberg Group*.

Softcover: **$24.95** (ISBN: 9780979988615) • 432 pages • Size: 6 x 9

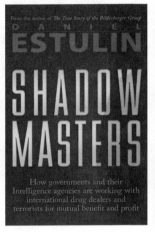

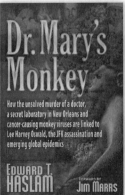

Dr. Mary's Monkey

How the Unsolved Murder of a Doctor, a Secret Laboratory in New Orleans and Cancer-Causing Monkey Viruses are Linked to Lee Harvey Oswald, the JFK Assassination and Emerging Global Epidemics

BY EDWARD T. HASLAM, FOREWORD BY JIM MARRS

Evidence of top-secret medical experiments and cover-ups of clinical blunders

The 1964 murder of a nationally known cancer researcher sets the stage for this gripping exposé of medical professionals enmeshed in covert government operations over the course of three decades. Following a trail of police records, FBI files, cancer statistics, and medical journals, this revealing book presents evidence of a web of medical secret-keeping that began with the handling of evidence in the JFK assassination and continued apace, sweeping doctors into cover-ups of cancer outbreaks, contaminated polio vaccine, the genesis of the AIDS virus, and biological weapon research using infected monkeys.

Softcover: **$19.95** (ISBN: 0977795306) • 320 pages • Size: 5 1/2 x 8 1/2

The Oil Card

Global Economic Warfare in the 21st Century

BY JAMES NORMAN

Challenging the conventional wisdom surrounding high oil prices, this compelling argument sheds an entirely new light on free-market industry fundamentals.

By deciphering past, present, and future geopolitical events, it makes the case that oil pricing and availability have a long history of being employed as economic weapons by the United States. Softcover **$14.95** (ISBN 0977795390) • 288 Pages

THE 9/11 MYSTERY PLANE
AND THE VANISHING OF AMERICA
BY MARK GAFFNEY
FOREWORD BY
DR. DAVID RAY GRIFFIN

Unlike other accounts of the historic attacks on 9/11, this discussion surveys the role of the world's most advanced military command and control plane, the E-4B, in the day's events and proposes that the horrific incidents were the work of a covert operation staged within elements of the U.S. military and the intelligence community. Presenting hard evidence, the account places the world's most advanced electronics platform circling over the White House at approximately the time of the Pentagon attack. The argument offers an analysis of the new evidence within the context of the events and shows that it is irreconcilable with the official 9/11 narrative.

Mark H. Gaffney is an environmentalist, a peace activist, a researcher, and the author of *Dimona, the Third Temple?*; and *Gnostic Secrets of the Naassenes*. He lives in Chiloquin, Oregon. Dr. David Ray Griffin is a professor emeritus at the Claremont School of Theology, and the author of *The 9/11 Commission Report: Omissions and Distortions*, and *The New Pearl Harbor*. He lives in Santa Barbara, California.

Softcoverr • $19.95 • 9780979988608 • 336 Pages

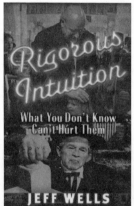

Rigorous Intuition
What You Don'y Know, Can't Hurt Them
BY JEFF WELLS

"In Jeff's hands, tinfoil hats become crowns and helmets of the purest gold. I strongly suggest that you all pay attention to what he has to say."
—Arthur Gilroy, Booman Tribune

A welcome source of analysis and commentary for those prepared to go deeper—and darker—than even most alternative media permit, this collection from one of the most popular conspiracy theory arguments on the internet will assist readers in clarifying their own arguments and recognizing disinformation. Tackling many of the most difficult subjects that define our time—including 9/11, the JonBenet Ramsey case, and "High Weirdness"—these studies, containing the best of the Rigorous Intuition blog as well as original content, make connections that both describe the current, alarming predicament and suggest a strategy for taking back the world. Following the maxim "What you don't know can't hurt them," this assortment of essays and tools, including the updated and expanded "Coincidence Theorists' Guide to 9/11," guides the intellectually curious down further avenues of study and scrutiny and helps readers feel empowered rather than vulnerable.

Jeff Wells is the author of the novel *Anxious Gravity*. He lives in Toronto, Ontario.

Softcover • $19.95 • 978-0-9777953-2-1 • 505 Pages

PERFECTIBILISTS
The 18th Century Bavarian Illuminati
BY TERRY MELANSON

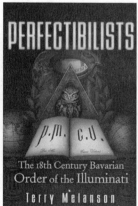

The shadowy Illuminati grace many pages of fiction as the sinister all-powerful group pulling the strings behind the scenes, but very little has been printed in English about the actual Enlightenment-era secret society, its activities, its members, and its legacy ... until now.

First choosing the name Perfectibilists, their enigmatic leader Adam Weishaupt soon thought that sounded too bizarre and changed it to the Order of the Illuminati.

Presenting an authoritative perspective, this definitive study chronicles the rise and fall of the fabled Illuminati, revealing their methods of infiltrating governments and education systems, and their blueprint for a successful cabal, which echoes directly forward through groups like the Order of Skull & Bones to our own era.

Featuring biographies of more than 400 confirmed members and copiously illustrated, this book brings light to a 200-year-old mystery.

Softcover: **$19.95** • 9780977795381 • 530 pages • Size: 6 x 9

The King of Nepal
Life Before the Drug Wars
BY JOSEPH PIETRI

From the halcyon days of easily accessible drugs to years of government intervention and a surging black market, this tale chronicles a former drug smuggler's 50-year career in the drug trade, its evolution into a multibillion-dollar business, and the characters he met along the way. The journey begins with the infamous Hippie Hash trail that led from London and Amsterdam overland to Nepal where, prior to the early1970s, hashish was legal and smoked freely; marijuana and opium were sold openly in Hindu temples in India and much of Asia; and cannabis was widely cultivated for use in food, medicine, and cloth. In documenting the stark contrasts of the ensuing years, the narrative examines the impact of the financial incentives awarded by international institutions such as the U.S. government to outlaw the cultivation of cannabis in Nepal and Afghanistan and to make hashish and opium illegal in Turkey—the demise of the U.S. "good old boy" dope network, the eruption of a violent criminal society, and the birth of a global black market for hard drugs—as well as the schemes smugglers employed to get around customs agents and various regulations.

Softcoverr • $19.95 • 9780979988660 • 240 Pages

Expendable Elite
One Soldier's Journey into Covert Warfare
BY DANIEL MARVIN , FOREWORD BY MARTHA RAYE

A special operations perspective on the Viet Nam War and the truth about a White House concerned with popular opinion

This true story of a special forces officer in Viet Nam in the mid-1960s exposes the unique nature of the elite fighting force and how covert operations are developed and often masked to permit — and even sponsor — assassination, outright purposeful killing of innocents, illegal use of force, and bizarre methods in combat operations. *Expendable Elite* reveals the fear that these warriors share with no other military person: not fear of the enemy they have been trained to fight in battle, but fear of the wrath of the US government should they find themselves classified as "expendable." This book centers on the CIA mission to assassinate Cambodian Crown Prince Nordum Sihanouk, the author's unilateral aborting of the mission, the CIA's dispatch of an ARVN regiment to attack and destroy the camp and kill every person in it as retribution for defying the agency, and the dramatic rescue of eight American Green Berets and hundreds of South Viet Namese.

DANIEL MARVIN is a retired Lieutenant Colonel in the US Army Special Forces and former Green Beret.

Softcover: **$19.95** (ISBN 0977795314) • 420 pages • 150+ photos & maps

Fighting For G.O.D.
(Gold, Oil, Drugs)
BY JEREMY BEGIN, ART BY LAUREEN SALK

This racehorse tour of American history and current affairs scrutinizes key events transcending the commonly accepted liberal/conservative political ideologies — in a large-size comic-book format.

This analysis delves into aspects of the larger framework into which 9/11 fits and scrutinizes the ancestry of the players who transcend commonly accepted liberal/conservative political ideologies. This comic-book format analysis examines the Neo Con agenda and its relationship to "The New World Order. This book discusses key issues confronting America's citizenry and steps the populace can take to not only halt but reverse the march towards totalitarianism.

Jeremy Begin is a long-time activist/organizer currently residing in California's Bay Area. Lauren Salk is an illustrator living in Boston.

Softcover: **$9.95**, (ISBN 0977795330) 64 Pages, 8.5 x 11

The Last Circle
Danny Casalaro's Investigation into The Octopus and The Promis Software Scandal
byCheri Seymour

The Last Circle is an unparalleled investigation into one of the most organized and complex criminal enterprises that American has ever seen.

Investigative reporter Cheri Seymour spent 18 years following the trail of the Octopus, probing the behind-the-scenes dynamics of a labyrinth that encompassed multiple covert operations involving a maze of politicians; NSC, CIA, and DOJ officials; organized crime figures; intelligence agents; arms sales; drug-trafficking; high-tech money laundering; and the death of Washington D.C. journalist Danny Casolaro.

Through law enforcement agencies as far-ranging as the FBI, U.S. Customs, police and sheriff's departments, and even the RCMP national security division, Seymour learned that the official head of the Octopus resided in the U.S. Department of Justice, supported by an out-of-control presidential administration, its tentacles comprised of a cabal of "Old Boy" cronies, true believers, who held that the end justified the means.

They gave corruption a new meaning as they stampeded through the Constitution, cowboyed the intelligence community, blazed new trails into drug cartels and organized crime, while simultaneously growing new tentacles that reached into every facet of criminal enterprise. The theft of high-tech software (PROMIS) for use in money-laundering and espionage; illegal drug and arms trafficking in Latin America; and exploitation of sovereign Indian nations were just a few of these enterprises.

The Last Circle educates and inspires because it proves that an average citizen can make a difference in exposing and bringing to justice high-level criminals. For readers who like mystery and intrigue, it is an interesting first-person account of a female sleuth's journey through the nation's most hidden criminal underworld.

Softcover • $24.95 • ISBN 978-1936296002 • 480 Pages

America's Nazi Secret
An Uncensored History of the US Justice Department's Obstruction of Congressional Investigations into Americans Who Funded Hitler, Postwar Immigration of Eastern European War Criminals to the US, and the Evolution of the Arab Nazi Movement into Modern Middle Eastern Terrorists
by John Loftus

Fully revised and expanded, this stirring account reveals how the U.S. government permitted the illegal entry of Nazis into North America in the years following World War II. This extraordinary investigation exposes the secret section of the State Department that began, starting in 1948 and unbeknownst to Congress and the public until recently, to hire members of the puppet wartime government of Byelorussia—a region of the Soviet Union occupied by Nazi Germany. A former Justice Department investigator uncovered this stunning story in the files of several government agencies, and it is now available with a chapter previously banned from release by authorities and a foreword and afterword with recently declassified materials.

John Loftus is a former U.S. government prosecutor, a former Army intelligence officer, and the author of numerous books, including *The Belarus Secret*, *The Secret War Against the Jews*, *Unholy Trinity: How the Vatican's Nazi Networks Betrayed Western Intelligence to the Soviets*, and *Unholy Trinity: The Vatican, the Nazis, and the Swiss Banks*. He has appeared regularly as a media commentator on ABC National Radio and Fox News. He lives in St. Petersburg, Florida.

Softcover • $24.95 • ISBN 978-1-936296-04-0 • 288 Pages

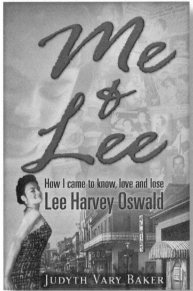

Me & Lee
HOW I CAME TO KNOW, LOVE AND LOSE
LEE HARVEY OSWALD

BY JUDYTH VARY BAKER

FOREWORD BY
EDWARD T. HASLAM

JUDYTH VARY WAS ONCE A PROMISING science student who dreamed of finding a cure for cancer; this exposé is her account of how she strayed from a path of mainstream scholarship at the University of Florida to a life of espionage in New Orleans with Lee Harvey Oswald. In her narrative she offers extensive documentation on how she came to be a cancer expert at such a young age, the personalities who urged her to relocate to New Orleans, and what lead to her involvement in the development of a biological weapon that Oswald was to smuggle into Cuba to eliminate Fidel Castro. Details on what she knew of Kennedy's impending assassination, her conversations with Oswald as late as two days before the killing, and her belief that Oswald was a deep-cover intelligence agent who was framed for an assassination he was actually trying to prevent, are also revealed.

JUDYTH VARY BAKER is a teacher, and artist. Edward T. Haslam is the author of *Dr. Mary's Monkey*. Hardcover • $24.95 • ISBN 9780979988677 • 580 Pages

1-800-556-2012

Mary's Mosaic
MARY PINCHOT MEYER & JOHN F. KENNEDY AND THEIR
VISION FOR WORLD PEACE

BY PETER JANNEY

FOREWORD BY DICK RUSSELL

CHALLENGING THE CONVENTIONAL WISDOM surrounding the murder of Mary Pinchot Meyer, this exposé offers new information and evidence that individuals within the upper echelons of the CIA were not only involved in the assassination of President John F. Kennedy, but her demise as well. Written by the son of a CIA lifer and a college classmate of Mary Pinchot Meyer, this insider's story examines how Mary used events and circumstances in her personal life to become an acolyte for world peace. The most famous convert to her philosophy was reportedly President John F. Kennedy, with whom she was said to have begun a serious love relationship in January 1962. Offering an insightful look into the era and its culture, the narrative sheds light on how in the wake of the Cuban Missile Crisis, she helped the president realize that a Cold War mentality was of no use and that the province of world peace was the only worthwhile calling. Details on her experiences with LSD, its influences on her and Kennedy's thinking, his attempts to negotiate a limited nuclear test ban treaty with Soviet Premier Nikita Khrushchev, and to find lasting peace with Fidel Castro are also included.

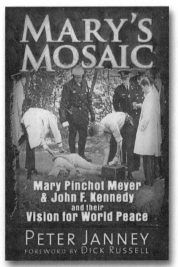

Peter Janney is a former psychologist and naturopathic healer and a cofounder of the American Mental Health Alliance. He was one of the first graduates of the MIT Sloan School of Management's Entrepreneurship Skills Transfer Program. He lives in Beverly, Massachusetts. Dick Russell is the author of *Black Genius: And the American Experience*, *Eye of the Whale*, *The Man Who Knew Too Much*, and *Striper Wars: An American Fish Story*. He is a former staff writer for *TV Guide* magazine, a staff reporter for *Sports Illustrated*, and has contributed numerous articles to publications ranging from *Family Health* to the *Village Voice*. He lives in Boston, Massachusetts and Los Angeles.

Hardcover • $24.95 • ISBN 978-0-9799886-3-9 • 480 Pages

Radical Peace
BY WILLIAM HATHAWAY
REFUSING WAR

THIS SYMPHONY OF VOICES — a loosely united network of war resisters, deserters, and peace activists in Afghanistan, Europe, Iraq, and North America — vividly recounts the actions they have personally taken to end war and create a peaceful society. Frustrated, angered, and even saddened by the juggernaut of aggression that creates more counter-violence at every turn, this assortment of contributors has moved beyond demonstrations and petitions into direct, often radical actions in defiance of the government's laws to impede its capacity to wage war. Among the stories cited are those of a European peace group that assisted a soldier in escaping from military detention and then deserting; a U.S.-educated Iraqi who now works in Iran developing cheaper and smaller heat-seeking missiles to shoot down U.S. aircraft after U.S. soldiers brutalized his family; a granny for peace who found young allies in her struggle against military recruiting; a seminary student who, having been roughed up by U.S. military at a peace demonstration, became a military chaplain and subverts from within; and a man who expresses his resistance through the destruction of government property — most often by burning military vehicles.

WILLIAM T. HATHAWAY is a political journalist and a former Special Forces soldier turned peace activist whose articles have appeared in more than 40 publications, including *Humanist*, the *Los Angeles Times, Midstream Magazine*, and *Synthesis/Regeneration*. He is an adjunct professor of American studies at the University of Oldenburg in Germany, and the author of *A World of Hurt, CD-Ring*, and *Summer Snow*.

Softcover: **$14.95** (ISBN: 9780979988691) •240 pages • Size: 5.5 x 8.5

Fixing America
Breaking the Stranglehold of Corporate Rule, Big Media, and the Religious Right
BY JOHN BUCHANAN, FOREWORD BY JOHN McCONNELL

An explosive analysis of what ails the United States
An award-winning investigative reporter provides a clear, honest diagnosis of corporate rule, big media, and the religious right in this damning analysis. Exposing the darker side of capitalism, this critique raises alarms about the security of democracy in today's society, including the rise of the corporate state, the insidious role of professional lobbyists, the emergence of religion and theocracy as a right-wing political tactic, the failure of the mass media, and the sinister presence of an Orwellian neo-fascism.
Softcover: **$19.95**, (ISBN 0-975290681) 216 Pages, 5.5 x 8.5

PARADISE LOST?
HIGH-SPEED TRAINS GET WAYLAID, SHADY POLITICIANS GET BILLIONS AND TAXPAYERS GET THE SHAFT!
BY RICHARD TRAINOR.

Reminiscent of a detective novel, this political exposé explores the corruption of some of the richest and most powerful political figures in California. From Mayor Willie Brown, Senator Dianne Feinstein, and a 50-billion-dollar insider-trading scandal to whistle blowers, phantom high-speed trains, and unbridled greed, this investigation details the complex history of California's public works projects that were promised and commissioned, but never built. From a Bay Bridge addition that never materialized to the San Francisco airport expansion that disappeared, this hard-hitting look at the Golden State's political shenanigans outlines the slimy details behind massive pump-and-dump schemes that have plagued progress in the state. With direct parallels to the corruption that inspired the films *Chinatown* and *The Two Jakes*, this investigation reveals how money and relationships have played into a slick political game in recent California history.

Richard Trainor is the author of *Sacramento: The Heart of California: A Contemporary Portrait*. He has contributed to *Elle*, the *Los Angeles Times*, the *Sacramento Bee, The Saturday Review, Sight & Sound*, and the *Vancouver Sun*. He is a former capitol bureau correspondent for *California* magazine and a former managing editor of *France Today* magazine.

Softcover • $24.95 • ISBN 978-0-9799886-4-6 • 384 pages

The Franklin Scandal
A Story of Powerbrokers, Child Abuse & Betrayal
BY NICK BRYANT

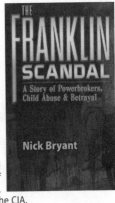

A chilling exposé of corporate corruption and government cover-ups, this account of a nationwide child-trafficking and pedophilia ring tells a sordid tale of corruption in high places. The scandal originally surfaced during an investigation into Omaha, Nebraska's failed Franklin Federal Credit Union and took the author beyond the Midwest and ultimately to Washington, DC. Implicating businessmen, senators, major media corporations, the CIA, and even the venerable Boys Town organization, this extensively researched report includes firsthand interviews with key witnesses and explores a controversy that has received scant media attention.

The Franklin Scandal is the story of a underground ring that pandered children to a cabal of the rich and powerful. The ring's pimps were a pair of Republican powerbrokers who used Boys Town as a pedophiliac reservoir, and had access to the highest levels of our government and connections to the CIA.

Nick Bryant is a journalist whose work largely focuses on the plight of disadvantaged children in the United States. His mainstream and investigative journalism has been featured in Gear, Playboy, The Reader, and on Salon.com. He is the coauthor of America's Children: Triumph of Tragedy. He lives in New York City.

Hardcover: **$24.95** (ISBN: 0977795357) • 480 pages • Size: 6 x 9

Strength of the Pack
The Personalities, Politics and Intrigues that Shaped the DEA
BY DOUG VALENTINE

Through interviews with former narcotics agents, politicians, and bureaucrats, this exposé documents previously unknown aspects of the history of federal drug law enforcement from the formation of the Bureau of Narcotics and Dangerous Drugs and the creation of the Drug Enforcement Administration (DEA) up until the present day. Written in an easily accessible style, the narrative examines how successive administrations expanded federal drug law enforcement operations at home and abroad; investigates how the CIA comprised the war on drugs; analyzes the Reagan, Bush, and Clinton administrations' failed attempts to alter the DEA's course; and traces the agency's evolution into its final and current stage of "narco-terrorism."

Douglas Valentine is a former private investigator and consultant and the author of The Hotel Tacloban, The Phoenix Program, The Strength of the Wolf, and TDY.
Softcover: **$24.95** (ISBN: 9780979988653) • 480 pages • Size: 6 x 9

A TERRIBLE MISTAKE
THE MURDER OF FRANK OLSON AND THE CIA'S SECRET COLD WAR EXPERIMENTS
BY H.P. ALBARELLI JR.

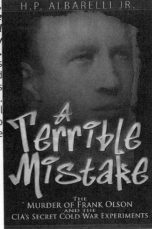

In his nearly 10 years of research into the death of Dr. Frank Olson, writer and investigative journalist H.P. Albarelli Jr. gained unique and unprecedented access to many former CIA, FBI, and Federal Narcotics Bureau officials, including several who actually oversaw the CIA's mind- control programs from the 1950s to the early 1970s.

A Terrible Mistake takes readers into a frequently bizarre and always frightening world, colored and dominated by Cold War concerns and fears. For the past 30 years the death of biochemist Frank Olson has ranked high on the nation's list of unsolved and perplexing mysteries. *A Terrible Mistake* solves the mystery and reveals in shocking detail the identities of Olson's murderers. The book also takes readers into the strange world of government mind-control programs and close collaboration with the Mafia.

H. P. Albarelli Jr. is an investigative journalist whose work has appeared in numerous publications and newspapers across the nation and is the author of the novel The Heap. He lives in Tampa, Florida.

Hardcover, $34.95 ISBN 978-0977795376 • 852 pages

America's Secret Establishment
An Introduction to the Order of Skull & Bones
BY ANTONY C. SUTTON

The book that first exposed the story behind America's most powerful secret society
For 170 years they have met in secret. From out of their initiates come presidents, senators, judges, cabinet secretaries, and plenty of spooks. This intriguing behind-the-scenes look documents Yale's secretive society, the Order of the Skull and Bones, and its prominent members, numbering among them Tafts, Rockefellers, Pillsburys, and Bushes. Far from being a campus fraternity, the society is more concerned with the success of its members in the post-collegiate world.

Softcover: **$19.95** (ISBN 0972020748) 335 pages

Sinister Forces
A Grimoire of American Political Witchcraft
Book One: The Nine
BY PETER LEVENDA, FOREWORD BY JIM HOUGAN

A shocking alternative to the conventional views of American history.
The roots of coincidence and conspiracy in American politics, crime, and culture are examined in this book, exposing new connections between religion, political conspiracy, and occultism. Readers are taken from ancient American civilization and the mysterious mound builder culture to the Salem witch trials, the birth of Mormonism during a ritual of ceremonial magic by Joseph Smith, Jr., and Operations Paperclip and Bluebird. Not a work of speculative history, this exposé is founded on primary source material and historical documents. Fascinating details are revealed, including the bizarre world of "wandering bishops" who appear throughout the Kennedy assassinations; a CIA mind control program run amok in the United States and Canada; a famous American spiritual leader who had ties to Lee Harvey Oswald in the weeks and months leading up to the assassination of President Kennedy; and the "Manson secret.

Hardcover: **$29.95** (ISBN 0975290622) • 396 pages • Size: 6 x 9

Book Two: A Warm Gun
The roots of coincidence and conspiracy in American politics, crime, and culture are investigated in this analysis that exposes new connections between religion, political conspiracy, terrorism, and occultism. Readers are provided with strange parallels between supernatural forces such as shaminism, ritual magic, and cult practices, and contemporary interrogation techniques such as those used by the CIA under the general rubric of MK-ULTRA. Not a work of speculative history, this exposé is founded on primary source material and historical documents. Fascinating details on Nixon and the "Dark Tower," the Assassin cult and more recent Islamic terrorism, and the bizarre themes that run through American history from its discovery by Columbus to the political assassinations of the 1960s are revealed.

Hardcover: **$29.95** (ISBN 0975290630) • 392 pages • Size: 6 x 9

Book Three: The Manson Secret
The Stanislavski Method as mind control and initiation. Filmmaker Kenneth Anger and Aleister Crowley, Marianne Faithfull, Anita Pallenberg, and the Rolling Stones. Filmmaker Donald Cammell (Performance) and his father, CJ Cammell (the first biographer of Aleister Crowley), and his suicide. Jane Fonda and Bluebird. The assassination of Marilyn Monroe. Fidel Castro's Hollywood career. Jim Morrison and witchcraft. David Lynch and spiritual transformation. The technology of sociopaths. How to create an assassin. The CIA, MK-ULTRA and programmed killers.

Softcover **$24.95** (ISBN 9780984185832) • 422 pages • Size: 6 x 9